FASHION
THE WHOLE STORY

General Editor
Marnie Fogg

Foreword by
Valerie Steele

FASHION
THE WHOLE STORY

First published in the United Kingdom in 2013 by
Thames & Hudson Ltd, 181A High Holborn,
London WC1V 7QX

© 2013 Quintessence Editions Ltd.

This book was designed and produced by
Quintessence Editions Ltd.
230 City Road
London EC1V 2TT

Project Editor	Katharina Hahn
Editors	Becky Gee, Fiona Plowman
Designer	Alison Hau
Picture Researcher	Jo Walton
Production Manager	Anna Pauletti
Proofreaders	Lisa Morris, Sarah Yates
Editorial Director	Jane Laing
Publisher	Mark Fletcher

All Rights Reserved. No part of this publication may be reproduced
or transmitted in any form or by any means, electronic or mechanical,
including photocopy, recording or any other information storage
and retrieval system, without prior permission in writing from
the publisher.

British Library Cataloguing-in-Publication Data
A catalogue record for this book is available from
the British Library

ISBN 978-0-500-29110-8

Printed in China

To find out about all our publications, please visit **www.thamesandhudson.com**.
There you can subscribe to our e-newsletter, browse or download our current
catalogue, and buy any titles that are in print.

CONTENTS

FOREWORD *by Valerie Steele*   6

INTRODUCTION   8

1 | 500 BC TO 1599   16

2 | 1600 TO 1799   72

3 | 1800 TO 1899   128

4 | 1900 TO 1945   202

5 | 1946 TO 1989   296

6 | 1990 TO PRESENT   464

GLOSSARY   554

CONTRIBUTORS   558

SOURCES OF QUOTATIONS   560

INDEX   562

PICTURE CREDITS   574

FOREWORD

Is it possible to tell 'the whole story' of fashion? 'Fashion' is such a complicated concept. There are fashions in all kinds of things, not only clothes, but also ideas and even personal names. Indeed, fashion seems to be a kind of general mechanism that applies to many aspects of modern life, especially those involving taste. For example, just as we do not wear the same clothes as our parents and grandparents did, we also do not listen to the same music.

It helps to remember that fashion is also a verb. To fashion something is to make it in a particular way. We fashion our appearance, not only through our choice of clothing, but also with particular hairstyles, body language and behaviour. Changes in the way we make things—such as clothes— are obviously related to wider socio-economic changes, but other causal factors include developments within the field of clothing creation, as well as individual choices.

Even if we define 'fashion' more narrowly, as the prevailing style of clothing, subject to change (ie, fashionable dress), it may still be impossible to tell the whole story, because the subject involves such an enormous (and constantly expanding) body of information, involving new designers, new trends, new collections and new ideas. Moreover, scholars cannot even agree on when fashion began, and how it might be distinguished from other forms of dress and adornment.

Histories of fashion often begin by surveying the clothing styles of ancient Greece and Rome (from about 500 BC), although they might, with equal validity, begin with ancient China, Egypt or India. People in different parts of the world developed different styles of dress and adornment, which usually remained relatively stable over long periods of time. The rise of capitalism in 14th-century Europe helped inaugurate a new emphasis on a regular pattern of sartorial change. This is often identified as the 'beginning' of fashion. In recent years, however, scholars have emphasized that something like fashion also existed in a number of non-European countries. As early as the 7th century, in Tang-dynasty China, for example, there were already factories producing complex silk fabrics, which were made into a variety of elaborate styles of dress that changed significantly over time, and which differed from the styles of previous and subsequent dynasties.

One of the central characteristics of fashion is change over time. But it is unclear how rapidly, regularly and extensively changes in dress must occur before we can call the phenomenon 'fashion'. Perhaps it was only in the 18th century that regularly changing ('fashionable') styles of dress ceased to be the prerogative of small elites and became adopted by the majority of urban people in western Europe. Because of the history of European capitalism, imperialism and colonialism, western fashions were eventually introduced around the globe. But styles also moved in the other direction, and today the fashion system is a global phenomenon.

Fashion touches on many aspects of life, including art, business, consumption, technology, the body, identity, modernity, globalization, social change, politics and the environment. The aesthetic aspects of fashion are extremely important, and much of the literature on modern fashion has focused on individual fashion designers. Whether or not fashion can be considered 'art', designers are typically regarded as the primary creators of fashion. However, designers only propose new styles; ultimately, consumers decide what is 'in' or 'out' of fashion.

Because we wear clothes on our bodies, and the clothes express our personal taste, which develops within a particular cultural context, fashion plays an especially important role in the individual's sense of identity. It is a kind of 'second skin' that conveys to others a sense of who we are—or who we would like to be.

Fashion is also a multi-billion-dollar global industry, employing a vast, international labour force. Indeed, we might better think of it as a network of industries, since the fashion system involves every activity, from the production of raw materials to the manufacture, distribution and marketing of a wide range of fashions—from couture ballgowns to blue jeans. Moreover, fashion exists, not only as objects, but also as image and meaning. In addition to those who create the clothes, many others (such as fashion photographers, journalists and even museum curators) create and disseminate images and ideas that tell us what these particular clothes might signify. Indeed, it is sometimes said that the fashion system is not so much about selling clothes but about selling lifestyles or dreams.

Fashion has often been dismissed as a trivial or frivolous subject, unworthy of serious attention. This could hardly be less true. Far from being a whirligig of meaningless change, fashion is a crucially important part of modern society and culture.

VALERIE STEELE
MUSEUM DIRECTOR, CURATOR AND AUTHOR

INTRODUCTION

With its origins in the Latin *facito*, literally 'making', the term 'fashion' has come to express a series of values that include such diverse notions as conformity and social connections, rebellion and eccentricity, social aspiration and status, seduction and beguilement. The desire to dress up transcends historical, cultural and geographical boundaries, and although form and content may vary, the motivation remains the same: the adornment of the human body as an expression of identity.

Some 11,000 years ago, once humanity had abandoned its hunter-gatherer existence for a more static way of life, fundamental requirements such as shelter, food and clothing were transformed into forms of cultural and artistic expression. Garments constructed from lengths of cloth required a fixed abode and temperate climates for the growing of raw materials, such as flax and cotton. Clothes constructed from animal skins worn through the Ice Ages necessitated a tanning procedure to soften the hide, and the beginning of the tailoring process was defined by the shaping of the hide to fit the body and the subsequent invention of the eyed needle. The phenomenon of fashion emerged from these two diverse sources: cuts based on the development of animal skins and garments dependent on the rectangular form of woven cloth.

The costume of the earlier civilizations of the Assyrians, Egyptians, Greeks and Romans depended on the simple method of draping and wrapping cloth around the body (left), secured in place with a *fibula* (pin brooch). The weaving process was initially a method of tufting, and once this technique was applied to the borders of woven cloth, a shawl-type garment could be created, which was worn initially by Assyrians of both sexes. This was replaced, for the male costume, with a tunic and sleeves with ornate patterning, embroidery and jewelled embellishment, worn with a characteristic headdress known as a Phrygian cap. Silk was used in addition to wool and linen in Assyria, whereas the Egyptians thought wool unclean and confined themselves to linen. Hierarchical dress was already in place at this time: slaves were naked and clothes were worn only by the upper strata of society, of whom only kings and dignitaries wore the linen cloth stiffened and pleated. The chief garment of the Egyptians in the period before 1500 BC, known as the Old Kingdom, was the *schenti*, a length of cloth worn around the waist and secured by a belt. During the era of the New Kingdom, between 1500 and 332 BC, this developed into a semi-transparent, long, fringed tunic called a *kalasiris*, worn over the loincloth. For women, the garment reached to just under the breasts and was secured with shoulder straps. This stylized costume prevailed for 3,000 years until after the Greek conquest.

Fashion: The Whole Story begins with the draped, wrapped and bound clothing of the Hellenic Greeks and the Romans (see p.18) and draws a clear distinction between clothing and fashionable dress. Classical dress, although hierarchical, was not subject to fashionable change; it was rather a form of dress made from a woven rectangular length of cloth, partially sewn into simple tunics. However, throughout the history of dress, garments influenced by classical antiquity have been deemed fashionable, resurfacing in the 19th-century vogue for neoclassicism and again in the evening wear of the 1930s exemplified by the columnar classically draped designs of Parisian couturière Madame Grès (1903–93; see p.250). Likewise, the occupational dress of the English rural farmer—a voluminous smocked overshirt in rough, undyed

▼ A Roman copy dating from c. AD 40–60 of a Greek original marble statue of Dionysus, god of the grape harvest. The statue was reputedly found at Posillipo, Campania, Italy. Unlike most contemporary figurations of Dionysus as a lithe youth, the god is heavily draped in cloth with an ivy wreath and a long archaic-style beard.

linen—was not considered fashion until it was adopted as such by the London emporium Liberty & Co at the beginning of the 20th century in an attempt to recapture the homespun pleasures and virtues of a fantastical Arcadia.

The concept of fashionable dress is often considered to be particular to Western society, and to have its roots in the royal courts of the 14th century, when a shift occurred from peasant dress to the French-inspired emphasis on contour and cut and the implementation of tailoring techniques (above). Reflecting a hierarchical society, various styles of clothing and fabrics were denied to the majority of the populace by the enforcement of sumptuary laws, a dress code that defined and allocated social status across both time and continents, from the regulation of silk wearing during the Japanese Tokugawa period (1600–1868) to the Statutes of Apparel issued in 1574 by Elizabeth I and her Privy Council, which forbade everyone except duchesses, marquises and countesses to wear certain materials including sable on their gowns.

Various historians consider the industrialization of society in the mid 19th century to be the starting point of fashion. It was at this time that fashionable styles came to be dictated by the work of the couturier or fashion designer. US couturière Elizabeth Hawes (1903–71) described this theory in her book *Fashion Is Spinach* (1938) as 'the French legend', that 'all beautiful clothes are made in the houses of the French couturiers and all women want them'. However, contemporary theorists also acknowledge that fashion cycles occur in non-Western dress, alongside national and regional dress. This concept is explored throughout *Fashion: The Whole Story* in a series of essays that examine the costume of various cultures, including those of the American

▲ The Arras tapestry *Offering of the Heart* (c. 1400–10) features a young knight wearing a robe of scarlet cloth. His robe is dyed with the *graine de kermes*, an intense red considered to be the most prestigious colour and a symbol of feudal power. The object of his passion wears blue, a colour associated with fidelity.

Southwest, Africa and Asia. Clothing in other cultures, such as those of China and Japan (opposite), continues to be influenced by and developed alongside contemporary Western fashion. The term 'kimono', meaning 'the thing worn', was first used during the Meiji period (1868–1912)—Japan's first era of modernization—and was introduced in response to the heightened awareness of Japanese clothing in the West following a period of enforced isolation.

The book also offers some complex connections. Conspicuous consumption was the reason for the monochrome severity of the man's top hat in Victorian England—signifying the purposeful quest for money in a newly industrialized Britain—in the same way that the lush court dress of 14th-century Italy represented a desire for magnificent adornment utilizing the luxurious silks on which the wealth of Venice and Florence was founded. Panniered skirts so broad that doorways had to be enlarged—a style that originated in Spain during the 17th century before spreading to France and the rest of Europe—flaunted material wealth and restricted movement to elite activities only. In addition, scientific advances accounted for certain fashions: the invention of starch in the 1560s allowed for the enormous circumference of the ruff during the Renaissance (see p.56); likewise the invention of the steel crinoline (see p.147), first patented in Britain in 1856, was responsible for the distortion of the Victorian silhouette (below). Sir Walter Raleigh could not have turned a shapely calf without the invention of the stocking frame by the Reverend William Lee in 1589, and the invention of tights in the 1960s allowed the mini skirt to be elevated to ever greater heights.

As Western fashion developed as a result of both a creative and an industrial process in the 19th century, the desire for change was accelerated by the dissemination of fashion information and the introduction of widely distributed illustrated magazines (see p.208). Advances in the production and distribution of garments, and the accessibility of new department stores with improved transport, contributed to an increase in consumption. For long periods in history, fashionable dress was women's only route to power, as seen in the court of Louis XV at the Palace of Versailles when the *déshabillé* garments of the boudoir enticed the king, and power was conferred on the mistress through association. With the onset of World War I, the hobble skirt

◀ Generally recognized as the national dress of Japan, the kimono is a simple 'T'-shape garment constructed from rectangular lengths of cloth forming a square-shaped sleeve, with a stitched seam allowing a small slit for the hand. The edges are padded and a sash, or obi, is used to secure the kimono around the body (c. 1900).

▼ The circumference of the cage crinoline underskirt was at its most excessive in the 1860s, when the steel crinoline replaced the earlier volume of weighty petticoats worn to give fullness. The width of the skirt rendered the woman both helpless and isolated, as the upper part of her body proved unreachable.

INTRODUCTION 11

▶ Fashion dedicated to sportswear emerged after World War I, when women celebrated a new-found freedom in an increasingly leisured and consumerist society. This two-piece striped bathing suit by Parisian couturier Jean Patou, dating from c. 1928, is made from knitted woollen jersey, and the hip-length tunic top features the geometric Art Deco patterning then in vogue.

introduced by Paul Poiret (1879–1944) and the tortured silhouette of the 'S'-shape corset were abandoned in favour of the functional easy-to-wear clothes epitomized by French couturière Coco Chanel (1883–1971), with simple cardigan suits, and the sportswear-influenced garments of Jean Patou (1880–1936; above). Elsa Schiaparelli (1890–1973) provided diversion with her Surrealist-inspired designs (see p.262), and the Hollywood film studios during the Great Depression of the 1930s offered escapism with the white satin and fox fur glamour of its stars and the androgynous appeal of Marlene Dietrich (see p.266).

Fashion is a great borrower, both from diverse cultures and from other times. The challenge of constructing a three-dimensional garment from a two-dimensional length of cloth involves a manipulation of material that often references very early ways of cutting and shaping fabric. The methods of attaching a sleeve or a skirt to a bodice, or utilizing the seams that create the bifurcation in a pair of trousers, might vary, but they are not infinite. Paris-based couturier Cristóbal Balenciaga (1895–1972; see p.306) perfected the dolman sleeve in the mid 20th century, at the height of the golden age of couture; cut in such a way that it was integral to the bodice of the dress yet allowed freedom of movement, it owes its provenance to the Hungarian *dolmány* jacket, derived from the Turkish *dolama* robe. Sarah Burton's Ice Queen dress for Alexander McQueen (2011; see p.516) recalls Marcus Gheeraerts the Younger's portrait of Elizabeth I (c. 1592), which depicts the queen in a dress that is strikingly similar in silhouette, fabric manipulation and embellishment. The queen's face was whitened with Venetian ceruse, a poisonous powder derived from lead, whereas the contemporary model had bleached eyebrows to achieve the same effect.

Whether complex or simply constructed, garments arguably become fashion once they are placed within the context of a social, political and economic culture, thereby representing the aesthetic of the time. In Europe and the United States, a cultural revolution occurred in the mid 20th century when youth movements rejected the fashions of their parents and defined their own look. The zoot-suited African American, the 1950s rebel in leather jacket and jeans, the hippie and the preppy each exemplified a distinctive form of fashion for the young. Although there have been times and circumstances when the sexes have appeared virtually indistinguishable, such as during the free-floating era of the counter-culture of the 1960s and early 1970s when both men and women wore jeans and long hair, serious attempts to formalize interchangeable outfits for men and women have failed, as seen in the 'unisex' outfits designed by Rudi Gernreich (1922–85) during the 1960s (see p.378). Despite this, appropriating the clothes of the opposite gender continues to provide designers with inspiration and transgressing dress codes no longer means vilification. With a new wave of feminism in the 1970s, the classic props of the seductress, the bra and the corset, were subverted by designers such as Jean-Paul Gaultier (b.1952) and Vivienne Westwood (b.1941) into items of female empowerment (see p.460). However, the consolidation of the US ready-to-wear industry in the 1970s eschewed such play on gender (see p.398). A new generation of US designers including Roy Halston Frowick (1932–90; below), Donna Karan (b.1948) and Calvin Klein (b.1942) offered pared-down minimalism in the style of the progenitor of modern US fashion Claire McCardell (1905–58), whereas Ralph Lauren (b.1939) built an empire on elegiac images of a golden past (see p.414).

An increasing interest in the 'designed' world, including fashion, marked the conspicuous consumerism of the 1980s, represented by the globalization of luxury fashion houses such as Gucci and Louis Vuitton (see p.453). This was offset only by the promulgation of the avant-garde and the emergence of radical designers such as Issey Miyake (b.1938), Rei Kawakubo (b.1942) of Comme des Garçons and Yohji Yamamoto (b.1943) showing for the first time on the Paris runway (see p.402).

▼ US designer Halston set the paradigm for sophisticated understatement. The simple, knee-length A-line dress in a single block of colour with dropped cap sleeves represents the designer's restrained sporty aesthetic and his emphasis on functional, easy-to-wear dressing (1980). Halston used a new artificial fibre known as 'ultrasuede' or 'liquid jersey' to achieve a fluid silhouette.

▶ Haute couture by Gary Harvey (see p.489) takes sustainability to a high aesthetic level with base materials transformed into luxury. The skirt of the dress on the left is crafted from eighteen recycled Burberry trench coats in the shape of a modern crinoline and the corseted gown on the right is made up of forty-two pairs of Levi's 501 jeans.

▶ Combining innocence with provocation for her spring/summer 2010 collection, Miuccia Prada juxtaposes sheer nude mesh inserts with demure details, such as the bejewelled shirt collar. The silk-chiffon skirt is embellished with holographic paillettes, a single line of which joins the dipped hip line to the appliquéd bra top.

People continue to be judged on their appearance—their status, sexuality and taste are all subject to the discerning eye. As Italian designer Miuccia Prada (b.1949; see p.480), whose Miu Miu line is recognized for its quirky yet ladylike style (opposite), declared: 'Fashion is a dangerous territory, because it talks about yourself, and it's very intimate. It talks about body, the intellect. Flesh. Psychology. It contains so much about what it is to be a human being.' Fashion has always had cultural meaning, implications and associations, but it has permeated the 21st century in unprecedented ways in its pervasive fascination with its mechanisms. British historian Eric Hobsbawm commented on the ability of fashion designers to predict people's future needs in his book *The Age of Extremes: A History of the World 1914–1991* (1994): 'Why brilliant fashion designers, a notoriously non-analytic breed, sometimes succeed in anticipating the shape of things to come better than professional predictors, is one of the most obscure questions in history; and, for the historian of culture, one of the most central. It is certainly crucial to anyone who wants to understand the impact of the age of cataclysms on the world of high culture, the elite arts, and above all, the avant-garde.'

Fashion is often associated with disposability and perceived as whimsical and ephemeral. It is predicated on the need for change; the industry requires it to flourish, and the consumer desires it. The novel and the new are carefully calibrated to render the existing aesthetic obsolete, an attitude that increasingly is causing concern. In response, 21st-century fashion now aspires to be associated with sustainability and the craft of making clothes (above), as well as acknowledging the need for sophisticated marketing strategies.

Fashion: The Whole Story charts the history of global fashion from the first assembled rectangle of cloth to the present-day importance placed on haute couture, once again the apex of modern fashion. Fashion must fit many body types while capturing something desirable about the way we place ourselves in the world. It is engineering for the body with an added extra. People ask a lot of fashion—it marks ideas, defines group allegiances, helps to express individuality, acts as camouflage, celebrates rites of passage and creates an aesthetic that is in keeping with the times.

1 | 500 BC TO 1599

CLASSICAL GREEK AND ROMAN DRESS 18

EARLY NATIVE AMERICAN TEXTILES OF THE SOUTHWEST 22

PRE-COLUMBIAN TEXTILES 26

CHINESE DRESS – TANG DYNASTY 30

JAPANESE DRESS – HEIAN PERIOD 36

MEDIEVAL DRESS 42

RENAISSANCE DRESS 48

OTTOMAN COURT DRESS 58

INDIAN DRESS – MUGHAL PERIOD 64

CLASSICAL GREEK AND ROMAN DRESS

According to the evidence of statuary and fragmentary textual references, the form of both Greek and Roman costume was dictated substantively by the material and the method of cloth production. The vast majority of garments worn in this period were made from woven cloth, which was the outcome of labour-intensive processes. The finished cloth was highly prized and generally considered too precious to waste by cutting and tailoring it to fit. Consequently, the Greeks (left) and Romans (above) generally wore free-flowing and enveloping garments that were constructed by folding, wrapping, pinning, gathering or, less frequently, stitching the cloth around the body.

Any shaped component in the garment that deviated from the rectangular was created primarily on the loom, with warp ends varying according to the width of the piece of cloth required. In the earlier part of the Greco-Roman period, weaving was a skill admired in a wife or household servant. However, by the end of the 1st century AD, with commerce established across the Roman Empire and an increasingly urbanized population, weaving had become a trade, and home-woven clothes were seen as primitive and of the lower classes.

There are many resemblances between Greek and Roman costume: they each evidence an abundance of drapes and folds, for example. Roman dress has two essential garment combinations: for men the *tunica* and toga, and for women the *tunica* and *palla*. The *tunica*, or tunic, constituted the layer that was

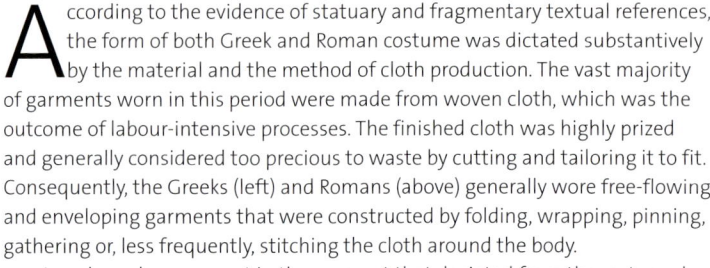

KEY EVENTS

610–560 BC	550–530 BC	480–404 BC	447–438 BC	220–167 BC	c. 200 BC
Early Attic black-figure pottery evolves, with many figurative depictions of long and short chiton tunics showing geometric banded patterning.	A *lekythos* (oil jar) by the Amasis Painter shows women producing woven textiles. They wear chitons with patterning.	The golden age of Athens sees the Greek city-state enjoy a period of economic growth, political supremacy and burgeoning culture.	The Parthenon is constructed in Athens; the sculptures and decorative details depict classical costume.	The Romans bring almost all of the known inhabited world under their rule. Historian Polybius documents the achievement in *The Histories*.	Republican Rome evolves a distinctive civic, administrative and military culture, which is dependent on appropriated Greek models.

18 500 BC–1599

worn closest to the body, classified as *inductus* (put on). The essential tunic shape came in various forms, depending on the class, occupation or sex of the wearer, and in various cloths, according to status. Men wore a version called a chiton (see p.20), later also worn at knee length, whereas women were usually dressed in a longer tunic, sometimes termed a *peplos*. Both of these types of tunic were made from a large rectangle of cloth, which was folded over the body and held in place by clasps. The simpler Doric chiton was usually made from wool, whereas the Ionic chiton was made from a finer material, such as soft linen or even silk. The softness of the cloth meant that there was greater decorative flexibility with the folds, including semi-permanent pleating, attained by starching and pressing in the heat of the sun.

In its simplest form, as worn by slaves and low-born men, the chiton was made from two rectangles sewn together, with holes at the top and bottom for legs, arms and head. Men of higher status wore tunics decorated with vertical stripes, although there were strict sumptuary laws dictating who was permitted to do this. Women wore their tunics loose, but gathered up in one or two places by a girdle: either under the breast, at the waist or around the hips. In each case it was possible to loop the cloth of the tunic over the girdle to conceal it and give the garment ease and shape. More sophisticated tunics incorporated sleeves, either hemmed to the wrist with a stiffer band of cloth, or held in place by one or a series of *fibulae* (pin brooches) or buttons, leaving much of the arm showing.

Both sexes could wear a garment on top of the tunic—for the sake of dignity rather than for protection from the elements—which was known in Greece as a *himation*, and in Rome as a *pallium* or *palla*. This overlayer was classed as *amictus* (wrapped around). It was an outdoor cloak worn by both sexes, but occasionally worn on its own by men without the undertunic. Both garments required an arm to keep the cloth in place (right) and so it was associated with those who did no manual labour. The *chlamys* was a much shorter cloak worn by men and largely associated with soldiers and travellers.

The origin of the toga—the distinguishing male garment of the Roman citizen—lies in Etruscan culture rather than Greek costume. This hypothesis is based on the resemblance of the decorative Etruscan *tebenna* (a long wrapped overgarment) to the later Roman male toga and the female *palla*. This similarity has led to speculation that the toga, like the *tebenna*, was cut to shape as an elongated semi-ellipse, with one straight edge, up to 18 feet (5.5 m) in length. The toga signified not only wealth but also, by its clear impracticality, a leisured supremacy that was available only to the rich and powerful. Free-born sons wore the white *toga praetexta* bordered in a purple stripe, whereas the plain *toga alba* (also *toga virilis* or *pura*) was worn by adult males. The *toga pulla* (dark) was a sign of mourning. The highest distinction of a richly decorated and gold embroidered purple toga—*toga picta*—was reserved for emperors. **EA**

1 Fresco (detail) from the Villa dei Misteri (1st century BC), Pompeii, Italy.

2 Stele with sculpture of a high-born Roman couple from the Temple of Scasato, Italy (c. 2nd century AD).

3 Interior of an Attic red-figure cup (5th century BC) attributed to the Briseis Painter.

149–146 BC	47–43 BC	27 BC–AD 14	AD 66	AD 79	AD 114
With the defeat of the Macedonians, the Achaean League and the Carthaginians, Rome is able to annex Greece and Africa as provinces.	Leading politician, author and orator Cicero consistently uses metaphors and conventions of Roman costume as potent rhetorical weapons.	Augustus, first emperor of the Roman Empire, declares that only those wearing the toga without a cloak might enter the Roman Forum.	After serving Emperor Nero 'as an absolute authority on questions of taste in connection with...luxurious living', Petronius takes his own life.	Vesuvius erupts and buries Pompeii and Herculaneum, leaving an enduring insight into Roman provincial life.	The continuous spiral frieze of Emperor Trajan's column, dedicated to his victory over the Dacians, gives a broad snapshot of Roman military dress.

CLASSICAL GREEK AND ROMAN DRESS 19

Chiton 5th century BC
GREEK DRESS

The Charioteer of Delphi, 470 BC.

NAVIGATOR

This life-size bronze statue, known as Iniohos (he who holds the reins), was discovered in 1896 at the Temple of Apollo in Delphi. It was part of a larger sculpture of horses, chariots and attendants, of which only fragments remain of the other components. Polyzalus, a tyrant in Gela and the owner of the winning chariot and team of horses in the Pythian games, had it installed in Delphi as part of a victory celebration. It was commissioned as a tribute to Apollo, in whose honour the games were held every four years.

The figure depicts the robust charioteer in control and at repose on conclusion of his victory, before an eternally admiring crowd. The horses and chariot are stationary: there is no tension in the exquisitely rendered reins and the robe is static, the figure in equilibrium. There is an idealized clarity in the detailing: the fabric of the long chiton, or this athletic version called *xystis*, is entirely credible in its draped form. Stray fullness around the shoulder is suppressed and made more aerodynamic by a thin strap that passes as a halter around the neck and shoulder blades. A headband of meander-patterned braid or leather, picked out with silver, is knotted simply at the back of the head to keep the clean lines. The cast-bronze sculpture marks a transition, sometimes known as 'Severe style', between the stylized Archaic manner and the idealized realism of the classical style. **EA**

FOCAL POINTS

1 HAIR PATTERN
The close-cropped hair and the youthful traces of incipient beard are rendered in an idealized pattern that not only has sufficient vitality to express the natural energy of the young charioteer but is also decorative.

3 DENSELY PACKED GATHERS
The *xystis* has a detail on the shoulder that shows the broad fabric gathered together. It is likely that the weaver simply pulled a cluster of three or four weft threads to a tighter width, thus creating natural small pleats.

2 HALTER
The 'raglan' line of the strap around the shoulders is achieved by forming a twisted figure of eight that is knotted and pulled over the fullness that hangs below the armhole, with the cross point at the nape of the neck.

4 ANKLE-LENGTH FABRIC
A wide belt contains the excess fabric at the high waist, which results in the perpendicular flow of the fabric to the bare feet, thus providing freedom of movement. The detail of the feet is renowned as true to life.

EARLY NATIVE AMERICAN TEXTILES OF THE SOUTHWEST

Archaeological remains confirm that textiles have been produced in the Southwestern United States for thousands of years. The arid climate of the region, together with the use of dry caves and alcoves by early peoples, has resulted in the preservation of vast quantities of textiles that pre-date contact with the first European settlers in the 16th century. The earliest Southwestern textiles that can be accurately dated are 10,000-year-old yucca sandals: some woven in open twining, others in warp-faced plain weave. These styles of sandals continued to be popular for centuries.

As Southwestern hunters and gatherers became more involved in maize agriculture, they began to experiment with a wider range of plant and animal fibres, finger-weave techniques and mineral pigments for making clothes. Archaeological sites from the northern Southwest, which date to between 500 BC and AD 500, have yielded braided sashes of rabbit, dog or human hair, women's yucca cordage aprons, finely plaited yucca sandals with buckskin fringe, twined yucca bags with self-patterned or painted designs and twined yucca robes. Twined blankets contained wild bird skins, rabbit fur and domesticated turkey feathers, sometimes combined within a single blanket. From 500 to 750, clothing became more complex and ornate. In some parts of the northern Southwest, people wore elaborate twined yucca sandals with colourful geometric designs on the upper surface and raised designs on the sole, which reflected an investment of labour and skill far beyond that required for ordinary footwear.

KEY EVENTS

500 BC	AD 100	600	650	700	725
Yucca aprons, bags and plaited sandals are first made in the northern Southwest.	Finger-woven textiles become more complex and diverse; weaving styles are also more localized.	Highly decorated yucca sandals, women's aprons and burden straps are produced in the Four Corners region of the northern Southwest.	Cotton, introduced from Mexico, is widely cultivated in the major river valleys of the southern Southwest.	The true loom with heddles is established in the southern Southwest; it takes the form of the backstrap loom.	Loom-woven cotton fabrics dominate textile assemblages in areas of the southern Southwest.

Southwestern weaving underwent a major change between 100 and 500 with the introduction of cotton from Mesoamerica. By 700, cotton was being grown in the river valleys of the southern Southwest, and by the 1000s, it was widely farmed in the well-watered regions of the north. Among many historic Southwestern tribes, cotton is linked symbolically to clouds and rain, and it became the fibre of choice for most ceremonial and high-status clothing. Some time before 700, the true loom—a loom that had heddles (parallel cords that separate the warp threads)—was adopted from Mexico. Weavers in the southern Southwest used a backstrap loom and a horizontal staked-down loom, whereas those in the north used the backstrap loom and an upright loom. Men are believed to have been the principal weavers at this time.

A rich variety of weaving techniques and clothing styles exemplified Southwestern dress after the 11th century. Non-loom fabric structures, such as braiding and interlinking, were used to manufacture sashes and shirts. The most common loom-woven fabrics were plain and twill weaves. Balanced plain weave was used to make blankets, breechcloths and kilts, and warp-faced plain weave for belts and bands. Diagonal- and diamond-twill structures were used in blankets and other items. A variation of tapestry weave, known as twill tapestry, was used to decorate men's breechcloths and to create isolated motifs and border designs on larger textiles. Weft-wrap openwork, gauze and supplementary weft weaves—loom techniques introduced from northern Mexico—appeared primarily in the southern Southwest to decorate a variety of textiles.

The major garments of the late pre-contact period (prior to European contact; 1100–1650) were cotton shirts, breechcloths and kilts for men, wraparound blanket dresses for women, and blankets and sash belts for both sexes. Men wore leggings and sandals, and women probably did, too. Sashes were worked in braiding or warp-faced or warp-float plain weave; leggings were made by looping. In the northern Southwest, fancier blankets, dresses, shirts and breechcloths were decorated by twill tapestry, painting or tie-dye (see p.24); the last were imbued with religious iconography. In the southern Southwest, the most elaborate garments were patterned by supplementary weft and openwork weaves, such as weft-wrap openwork, gauze and interlinking (right).

Murals painted between 1350 and 1620 on the walls of Pueblo ceremonial chambers, known as *kivas*, show men and women engaged in ritual activities; their clothes appear to include white braided sashes, shirts and kilts in openwork weaves, and blankets, shirts, kilts, tunics and dresses decorated by painting and tie-dye (opposite). Today most of these types of ceremonial garment are still worn during Pueblo rituals in the Southwest. Although many decorative techniques have changed—for example, knitting and crochet replaced looping and openwork techniques, and embroidery became the most popular way of depicting religious iconography on fabric—most pre-contact styles of dress have been preserved for ceremonies. Pueblo societies have maintained their traditional ceremonies and their textiles remain as relevant to modern ritual practice as they were in the past. **LW**

1 A 17th-century *kiva* mural from Awat'ovi Pueblo in Arizona shows figures wearing tie-dye shoulder blankets, a wraparound dress, kilts decorated with borders and white sashes with tassels.

2 This cotton sleeveless shirt (c. 1300–1450) from Arizona was made from a non-loom technique that creates an interlinked fabric. The design of running triangles and interlocking rectilinear scrolls has also been found on painted pottery.

1050	1100	1150	1400	1540	1600
Cotton begins to be widely cultivated in well-watered areas of the northern Southwest.	The true loom is established in the northern Southwest; it takes the form of the wide upright loom and the backstrap loom.	Loom-woven cotton fabrics are used in everyday and ceremonial clothing throughout the Southwest.	Painted *kiva* murals document the diversity of ceremonial costume in the northern Southwest.	European contact initiates major changes in the production, use and trade of Southwestern textiles.	The Navajo start to learn loom-weaving techniques from Pueblo people.

EARLY NATIVE AMERICAN TEXTILES OF THE SOUTHWEST

Tie-dye Cotton Blanket c. 1250
SHOULDER BLANKET

NAVIGATOR

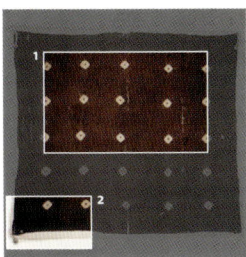

This 800-year-old cotton tie-dye blanket was excavated in 1891–92 from an alcove in Lake Canyon, southeastern Utah. Tie-dye was a popular method of decorating cloth in the Andes, the Maya region, highland Mexico and the American Southwest prior to European contact. Tie-dye probably developed as a way to produce the important dot-in-a-diamond motif on ceremonial cloth. High-status individuals of the Wari Empire (c. 600–1000) wore clothing decorated with circular and diamond-shaped motifs executed in resist-dye techniques. In Mesoamerica, the symbol was used to depict the scaly skin of crocodiles, turtles and snakes, as well as kernels of maize. The clothing of the Maize God, the Feathered Serpent and many other deities was decorated with this powerful maize-reptile iconography. Eventually tie-dye and its associated dot-in-a-diamond imagery spread into the American Southwest. Various examples of tie-dyed fabrics, including this complete blanket, have survived in dry alcoves of the region. Tie-dye is depicted on wall hangings and clothing worn by human figures in ceremonial painted murals from northern Arizona and New Mexico, which suggests the technique persisted for decorating Puebloan ritual fabrics well into the early post-contact period. **LW**

◉ FOCAL POINTS

1 DIAMOND PATTERN
The gridlike pattern has five rows of five white diamonds. To create each diamond, the maker wrapped a small section of the fabric tightly with string. The blanket was immersed in dye and the strings removed to reveal motifs the colour of the original white blanket.

2 REINFORCED SELVEDGES
The four complete selvedges are reinforced with twined cords tied together at the corners. The blanket is made of single-ply, hand-spun cotton yarns worked in balanced plain weave. It was made on a vertical loom with a string heddle and a continuous warp.

▲ This Awat'ovi *kiva* mural shows a figure wearing a tie-dye tunic with a dot-in-a-square motif. Modern Puebloans identify this motif as a metaphor for maize, the source of life for Pueblo people.

PRE-COLUMBIAN TEXTILES

1 This tunic (7th–9th century) utilizes the vibrant hues, skilful tie-dyeing, and discontinuous warp and weft structure often found in Wari textiles.

2 This Moche ceramic vase (2nd–7th century) takes the form of a kneeling warrior wearing a tunic with a spiral motif and a red-dotted breechcloth.

The dynamic visual heritage of South America is conveyed amply in textiles made before the European arrival. The legacy of ancient Andean civilizations extends beyond skills and aesthetics to the underlying beliefs. The garments, accessories and hangings surviving today are only a fraction of those made in ancient times. Although textiles were made throughout the Andean region, the dry Pacific Coast had the best preservation conditions: most surviving textiles come from coastal Peru and Chile, and western Bolivia. Using readily available materials, especially alpaca and cotton, Andean people began producing textiles before ceramics. Textiles were first woven on looms about 2,000 years ago, but knotting, looping, braiding and twining had been used in 3000 BC. At the Huaca Prieta site in Peru, archaeologists found cotton fabrics from about 2500 BC with twined designs such as condors. Cotton remained important, but the fibre of alpacas and other camelids was better suited to dyeing.

Garments generally had simple lines, and non-tailored, wrapped garment types persisted for centuries. Some looms were frames that would yield an exact form; others were upright or backstrap looms that produced rectangles of specific sizes. Rarely was cloth cut after being woven. The arts of hand-spinning fine yarn and creating elaborately patterned cloth in dazzling hues became hallmarks of pre-Columbian indigenous arts. In addition to weft-faced tapestry, warp patterning was also characteristic, especially double cloth, which is identical on both faces, and structures that produce mirror images. Ceramics, metal and stone objects often depict people wearing clothes (opposite). Most

KEY EVENTS

c. 500–300 BC	c. 400 BC–AD 200	c. 100–500	c. 400–550	c. 500–800	c. 1100–1450
Painted cotton textiles are made by artisans of the Chavín culture, which dominates north-central Peru; many are excavated much further south.	In the Paracas culture, which flourished on the south coast of Peru, textile artists produce the most elaborate embroideries made in pre-Columbian times.	The artistic production of the Moche people in northern Peru includes fine woven textiles, ceramics depicting distinct individuals and intricate jewellery.	At Tiwanaku, Bolivia, huge elaborately carved stones dominate the area near Lake Titicaca; textiles with similar iconography are used hundreds of miles away.	The Wari Empire, which develops in central Peru, shares much of the textile technology, and thus possibly the religious beliefs, of the highland Tiwanaku.	The Chimú develop great skill in cotton spinning, weaving and featherwork. The same designs appear on textiles as on adobe walls at Chan Chan.

26 500 BC–1599

garments come from elite burials, featuring elaborate wrapping. Paracas peoples made intricate polychrome embroidery that filled countless garments, found intact in deep shaft tombs two millennia later.

Applied decorative elements included gold, gilded copper and silver beads, and plaques. Tropical bird feathers were woven in and images of feathers and birds also appear. Felines and their features—notably spots, fangs and claws—are often shown. Supernatural beings may combine wings with other animal attributes. Plants depicted include maize, potatoes, squash and coca. Plants also provided dyes, as did minerals and insects. The textile artists, virtuosos of colour use, excelled at tie-dyeing finished cloth and space-dyeing or bound-resist dyeing yarns before weaving.

The textiles of Chavín, in north-central Peru, were often plain-weave cotton, painted with intricate designs, which included complex figures with numerous animals' features, especially fearsome fangs. Plain-weave cloth was also the basis for Paracas embroidery in southern Peru, where a large, high-status stratum of artists and artisans were exclusively clothmakers, producing vast numbers of embroidered, woven and braided textiles.

Skilful dyeing and tapestry weaving overlap in two related cultures: the Wari of Peru and the Tiwanaku of Bolivia. Their fine tapestries, while remarkably similar, differ in materials, spinning and weave structure. Both art styles feature a highly abstracted approach to figural representation: isolated attributes of humans and animals were distorted or grotesquely exaggerated. A sophisticated palette of strong vibrant hues and subtle gradations indicates mastery of the dyer's art. Blue, usually indigo-based, was prized, as were shades of red and violet, especially derived from cochineal. The most vibrant hues appear in Chimú culture, in which an unmistakable brilliant scarlet shows up in large tassels. The same culture also used undyed fibres to great effect. From the native cotton (*Gossypium barbadense*) in natural shades of pale tan, pink and mauve, Chimú weavers forged striking graphic patterns. Use of the pure white of undyed cotton, in bold yet elegant sheers and gauzes, was also perfected.

From Cuzco in highland Peru, the Incas aggressively extended their dominion further than any other Andean society. Inca textiles, although strikingly similar to some earlier works, are readily recognizable. As for the Wari, the sleeveless tapestry tunic was the standard male garment (opposite). Unique Inca designs fused a narrow iconographic repertoire and extreme abstraction, with almost no recognizable figures. Of special interest are complex rectangular motifs (*t'oqapus*) with as-yet-undeciphered meanings (see p.28). Although they are the most recently made pre-Columbian Andean textiles, relatively few Inca stuffs survive. The Inca revered both cloth and their ancestors. The Spanish conquerors burned countless textile-filled storehouses, along with elaborately garbed ancestor mummies. Despite the devastating losses the Andean people never stopped weaving. **BF**

c. 1400–1450	c. 1450–1500	c. 1450–1500	c. 1500	c. 1520s–30s	1532
With their capital in Cuzco, the Incas establish distinctive stonework styles and hard-edged, abstract geometry in their textile design.	As the Incas incorporate other ethnic polities, such as the Chancay, they also absorb their dress styles, and hybrid regional Inca styles are created.	T'oqapu tunics are produced by the Incas (see p.28), with the fabric woven all in one piece.	The Incas extend their territory to its maximum, from today's southern Colombia to northern Chile and Argentina.	European explorers, among them the Spaniard Francisco Pizarro, start to enter the Central Andes.	The Inca emperor Atahuallpa meets with Spanish adventurers led by Pizarro. They capture him, hold him hostage for ransom and execute him.

PRE-COLUMBIAN TEXTILES 27

Inca Tapestry Tunic c. 1450 – 1540
MEN'S CLOTHING

Inca all *t'oqapu* tunic
Late Horizon (1450–1540).

NAVIGATOR

The designs, technique and construction of this tunic reveal that it is Inca. The identities of the man who owned it, that of the designer and of the weaver are all unknown. The very fine weave, excellent craftsmanship and brilliant colours indicate that it belonged to a person of very high status, perhaps the Inca emperor himself. The tunic was the standard basic article of male clothing. Underneath it men wore a breechcloth, and the outer garment was a large, rectangular mantle. Tunics ranged widely in size and proportions, but the general form was a simple rectangle; the diversity and elaboration were in the fabric and embellishments. This spectacular tapestry-woven tunic is almost entirely patterned using woven images; a small amount of embroidered trim graces the seams and edges. The small rectangular design block is called *t'oqapu*; despite numerous attempts at interpretation, there is no consensus about the meaning of *t'oqapus*. This tunic is unique: it is entirely composed, front and back, of these units, except for a black band along the bottom. The fabric was woven all in one piece, then folded at the shoulders and seamed along the sides; the neck slit was also woven in, not cut later. The *t'oqapus* are distributed irregularly; even small numbers of motifs rarely repeat. The overall effect is syncopated and lively. It is a tour de force of design and weaving. **BF**

FOCAL POINTS

1 GRIDS
A narrow border encloses almost every *t'oqapu* block. Further subdivision emphasizes the strong rectilinearity, creating grids within the grid. White borders alternate with white in the motifs, creating an illusion of depth. There is a maximum of ten, always discrete motifs.

3 INCA KEY MOTIF
The most frequent *t'oqapu* block used here is nicknamed the 'Inca key' motif for its perceived similarity to the 'Greek key' motif. It features a diagonal band with bent ends and small blocks in opposite corners; the motif sometimes almost fills a tunic.

2 CHEQUERBOARD MOTIF
The chequerboard with a red 'V'-shape yoke-like area on top is a standard design of Inca tunics. The military wore chequered tunics, but fine tapestry would have been for ceremonial use by officers and nobility. The polychrome edging echoes the embroidered binding.

4 WARM COLOUR PALETTE
Warm colours dominate, with few blues, greens and purples. Sets of contrasts and complements occur in limited combinations. Red with yellow and green with dark blue (the only colourways in the Inca keys) also appear in a wavy stripe motif (centre, bottom row).

CHINESE DRESS — TANG DYNASTY

1 *Spring Outing of Noblemen and Women*, painted by Zhang Xuan in *c.* 750. The women are no longer wearing veils to cover their faces.

2 This figure's hairstyle, shoes and robe with its floral design illustrate the height of dancers' fashion in the 7th-century Tang court.

In the 7th century China was probably the best-clothed nation in the world. The country already had centuries of experience in the rearing of silk worms—sericulture—and the technology to reel and spin silk was considerably advanced. The drawloom in use at this time could produce fabrics with highly complex, multicoloured patterns. Archaeological evidence confirms that in the early 600s drawlooms were capable of incorporating as many as 3,680 weft yarns in one single pattern. By the 9th century, Chinese weavers could produce large patterns with ease. Some of the floral roundels had a diameter of 19 ½ inches (50 cm) and the loom width of the fabric could be as wide as 48 ½ inches (123 cm). In the capital city of Chang'an (present-day Xi'an) there were state-run factories, each with its own specialization. Six factories specialized in dyeing, four in yarn-making, ten in weaving, and five in producing cords and ribbons.

Chinese women enjoyed unprecedented freedom throughout the Tang dynasty (618–907), not only in the clothes that they wore, but also in what they were allowed to do. They danced, went riding (above) and played polo. The custom of binding the feet had not yet made its appearance. It was no coincidence that China's one and only female monarch ruled in this era. Empress Wu Zetian reigned from 684 to 705 in her own right and faced little opposition from the male noblemen and state officials.

The free spirit of Tang women was manifested through their clothing and headwear. Before 618 women wore a long veil when they went outdoors, partly to protect them from dust but also to hide their faces. In about 650 the long

KEY EVENTS

c. 620	c. 630	641	c. 684	691	c. 700
The drawloom with two harnesses is in use. The first harness produces the ground weave and the second produces the pattern.	The imperial treasury stores brocades patterned with paired pheasants, combating goats, flying phoenixes and swimming fish.	Emperor Taizong meets a Turfan envoy wearing an ordinary round-neck robe and a black hat rather than formal costume.	Low-neck garments are commonly worn among women. Outdoors they wear a broad-brimmed hat, leaving their faces uncovered.	During a banquet, Empress Wu gives each of her ministers a tall headdress, which quickly becomes a fashionable item.	Weavers start to form patterns on fabrics using weft yarns. This makes patterning easier and gradually replaces the traditional warp-faced weave.

veil was replaced by a hat. A piece of thin gauze hanging from the broad brim was the only element that shielded the wearer from the gaze of onlookers. In 713 the hat disappeared and, according to the ancient *Tang History*, women 'made no attempt to cover their beautifully made-up faces' (see p.34).

During the reign of Empress Wu it became fashionable for women to wear low-neck garments. Before this fashion became widespread, the standard attire for women consisted of a long-sleeved blouse, a long skirt and a shawl. The blouse had narrow sleeves, no buttons and was closed by overlapping to the right. The skirt rose up to chest level and was tied with a ribbon, with the lower part of the blouse tucked under it. The shawl, which consisted of a slender piece of gauze or thin silk, was about 6 ½ feet (2 m) long. A daring new item was introduced in the late 7th century—a tight-fitting, short-sleeved top that had either a front opening tied with a bow or a wide neck opening to be pulled over the head. The neckline was cut low to reveal a good proportion of the wearer's breasts. The blouse was still worn beneath the short-sleeved top, but it was used in such a way that only the two sleeves were visible.

When the dynasty was at its most prosperous, a spectacular costume was created for female dancers. Dances were not always performed by professional entertainers. The imperial concubine Yang, who was well known for her ample proportions (see p.35), was a consummate dancer despite her voluminous form. The upper garment worn by the dancer had a low neckline, as was popular at the time, but the shoulders flared outwards like small wings. The most eye-catching aspect were the double sleeves, the wide outer sleeves of which flowed or twirled according to the rhythm of the dance. Extra layers of frills were added to the upper sleeves to emphasize the sense of motion, and streamers extending from the lower half of the skirt would have served the same purpose. The costume was finished off by 'cloud-head shoes'—so described because of their large upturned front. The costume became highly fashionable among female dancers of the Tang court (right).

Plumpness in body form was not seen as off-putting, and under the influence of concubine Yang, who was also a great beauty, women's dresses became more voluminous from the 8th century onwards. Pleats were added to skirts and sleeves expanded in width. When fashionable ladies tried to compete with one another by increasing the width of their sleeves, Emperor Wenzong, who reigned from 827 to 840, had to issue a decree limiting the sleeve width to no more than one Chinese foot and three inches—equivalent to approximately 17 inches (40 cm). The decree was met with much complaint and was probably ignored because historical references, both textual and visual, regularly depict women wearing wide-sleeved clothes in the 8th and 9th centuries.

As Tang women's dress became wider, their hairstyles also became correspondingly bigger and taller. Tang women had always been fastidious

c. 700	c. 713	c. 750	756	c. 800	c. 827
The weft-faced weave gives birth to *kesi* (tapestry weave), but the process is too labour-intensive and *kesi* garments only appear centuries later.	The *hufu* (foreigner's clothes) becomes popular with women. Other fashions include the *huadian* (a forehead ornament) and artificial hair.	Tax payments from the populace include 7.4 million bolts of silk fabrics per year. One bolt measures about 39 feet (12 m).	The imperial concubine Yang performs a dance wearing a rainbow skirt and feathered top.	Gauze becomes a speciality of Haozhou in the Anhui province. Two families monopolize its production by keeping the method a secret.	Emperor Wenzong decrees that garment sleeves should not exceed 17 inches (40 cm) in width, but with little success.

CHINESE DRESS — TANG DYNASTY

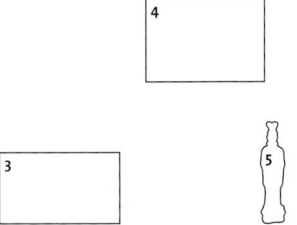

about their hairstyles. They styled their hair into buns of all shapes and sizes, which they piled on top of their heads (opposite above). Wigs and artificial hairpieces were also employed to achieve the elaborate hairstyles desired. The hairstyles were given fanciful names and some of the more descriptive ones, such as 'cloud-style', 'conch-shell', 'rolled-up lotus leaf' and 'double rings', provide clues to their unusual shapes. Ivory or mother-of-pearl combs held the hair in place, and gold and silver hairpins dangled when the wearer moved. Ladies at court wore both real and artificial flowers in their hair.

Tang women valued beauty and paid particular attention to ornamenting their faces with make-up, which was a lengthy process. In order to embellish her face, a Tang woman first applied face powder, which was usually made from lead. The ingredient for rouge came from the juice of red-coloured plants. Eyebrow drawing was an important part of women's facial decoration, too. Legend has it that Emperor Xuanzong, who reigned from 712 to 756, encouraged his palace ladies to draw their eyebrows in innovative ways. He once asked his court artist to paint the ten styles that he liked best, which included eyebrows described as 'small hills', 'pendant pearls' and 'pointed moon'. A dark green mineral called *dai* was used to draw the eyebrows.

Tang women fixed an ornament called a *huadian* onto their foreheads. The ornament was made from a small piece of gold or silver foil that was usually cut into the shape of a plum or flower blossom; other materials, including kingfisher feathers, are also mentioned in historical sources. The foil was stuck to the woman's forehead, between the eyebrows, with a little fish glue. To complete her make-up, a Tang woman applied lipstick, painted two small red dots at the corners of her mouth, then added a red curving line on both temples. These last two features were abandoned after 907.

Tang poets paid so much attention to women's fashion that they wrote very little about their own male clothing. Generally, educated men wore robes, whereas working-class men wore jackets and trousers. This distinction was mainly for practical reasons because trousers afforded greater ease of movement for men working in the fields, for example. The Tang government did not find it necessary to distinguish the various social classes through the dress code, and to a large extent people dressed according to their means.

At court assemblies, state officials wore robes of different colours to indicate their rank: the highest-ranked officials wore purple, moving down through deep red, green and blue. Historical records state that the emperor

3 Emperor Taizong gives an audience to the envoy of Turfan in 641 wearing an ordinary outfit consisting of a round-necked robe and a black hat.

4 Elegant ladies of the Tang imperial court enjoy music at a banquet in a detail from an anonymous 10th-century painting.

5 An 8th-century earthenware figure of a Tang state official wearing a green robe with wide sleeves and a belt.

wore formal attire, but the description is not detailed enough to allow for an accurate reconstruction of the robe and crown. Tang emperors were fairly relaxed about what they wore; when Emperor Taizong, who reigned from 627 to 649, received the envoy of Turfan in 641 he was dressed in an ordinary round-neck robe and a black hat (opposite), similar to those worn by his courtiers. The dragon motif, a strong symbol of the Chinese emperor in later dynasties (see p.84), had not yet acquired its significance.

The cut of men's robes changed very little throughout the Tang period. The robe either had a round neck and narrow sleeves or it had a stand-up collar with wide sleeves (right). These two types of robe were worn by state officials and men of letters alike. If the state official belonged to the military sector, he would wear a simplified form of armour on top of the robe, consisting of a breastplate and a back plate joined by two shoulder straps and tied by a belt at the waist. His shoes had large upturned fronts, very similar to those worn by women. This rather cumbersome footwear would have been replaced by boots when the man went to battle, and his headdress substituted with a helmet.

Traditionally, Chinese men had always worn their hair long, which they tied into a small bun on top of the head. Unlike women, men habitually covered the bun with a black headcloth. As wrapping the hair with a headcloth was a fairly slow process, a rigid headdress, made of rattan strips or stiffened fabric, was introduced as a time-saving alternative. It came in a variety of shapes and heights, depending on the preference of the wearer.

One fashion popular with both men and women was the *hufu*, which literally means 'foreigner's clothes'. The foreigners residing in the capital of Chang'an were mostly Sogdians, who came to China to trade. The traditional Sogdian outfit consisted of a hip-length coat and trousers, worn with a leather belt and boots. The 'foreign' element of the ensemble was the lapels—a feature that was absent from Chinese coats. Coats and trousers were more suitable clothes for horse riding than the loose-fitting Chinese robe. The lifestyle of Chinese women was as active as that of the men, and they embraced the *hufu* with great enthusiasm, turning it into a unisex fashion. In contrast to the sombre colours worn by their male contemporaries, fashionable Tang ladies wore *hufu* made from colourful patterned silks. **MW**

Silk Dress and Surcoat 8th century
WOMEN'S COURT DRESS

Ladies Wearing Flowers in their Hair by Zhou Fang (late 8th century).

Very little Tang dynasty clothing has survived intact, but this handscroll by Zhou Fang is an invaluable source of women's fashion in China. There is general consensus among art historians that it depicts a scene in the imperial gardens. Both ladies wear shoulderless dresses tied at chest level with a sash, on top of which they wear a loose, wide-sleeved surcoat made of thin gauze, open in the front and tied by a bow at knee height. Draped around their upper arms are long shawls made of patterned silk. The lady on the left has a round face and a fairly corpulent body. The transparent surcoat she wears is subtly patterned with a lozenge-shaped design. Although the sleeves measure at least 3 feet (1 m) wide, they would not have been heavy because gauze is a lightweight material. Chinese men loved to see women wearing gauze and wrote enthusiastically that the wearer appears to be 'wrapped in mist and cloud'. The wide sleeves required a considerable amount of fabric to make and proved a drain on the imperial coffers. At the time, a bolt of silk was approximately 39 ½ feet (12 m) long, just enough to make one wide-sleeved surcoat. This extravagant consumption of silk prompted Emperor Wenzong to ban wide sleeves, although it did not stop the practice. Silk fabrics were embellished with either woven or embroidered patterns. By the 8th century the weft-faced twill, a novelty weave that originated from China's western neighbours, had largely replaced the traditional warp-faced tabby weave, allowing more colours to be incorporated into the material. Fabrics with a non-repetitive pattern, such as the phoenix design on the brown shawl worn by the lady on the left, were perfectly produced by skilled embroiderers. **MW**

NAVIGATOR

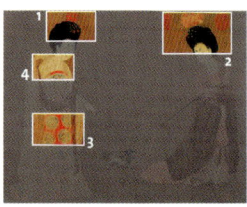

◉ FOCAL POINTS

1 FLORAL HEADDRESS
The floral headdress of the lady on the left is predominantly gold and red. The red colour was obtained by covering flat metal plaques or metal wire with lacquer, which comes from the sap of a tree. When mixed with cinnabar, this creates a brilliant red. The gold hair ornament and hairpins would have glittered in the lady's black hair.

4 TRANSPARENT SURCOAT
The surcoat is made from a transparent gauze and does little to cover the wearer's bare neck and shoulders. The Roman writer Seneca allegedly disapproved of silken clothes, claiming that 'no woman could honestly swear she was not naked'. The Chinese, however, were full of praise for this almost weightless material.

2 OPULENT HAIRSTYLE
The hairstyle of the lady on the right is too opulent to comprise solely natural hair—artificial hair would have been used and further height is given by the large pink peony flower. Her hair is also adorned with small blue kingfisher feathers. The green eyebrows are drawn in the 'cassia leaf' style.

3 ROUNDEL DESIGN
The roundel pattern does not represent a particular botanic species, but is a composite formed by small petals and leaves. A bright pink yarn is used for the ground weave and the roundels are realized in pink, green, light brown and creamy white. Floral roundels were an extremely popular decorative design during the Tang era.

IMPERIAL CONCUBINE YANG

This figurine was modelled after the imperial concubine Yang Guifei, whose beauty was so great that even her substantial waistline was considered part of her charm. She captured the heart of Emperor Xuanzong, a man thirty-four years her senior. The renowned Tang poet Bai Juyi vividly summarized the emperor's infatuation with Yang in a few lines:

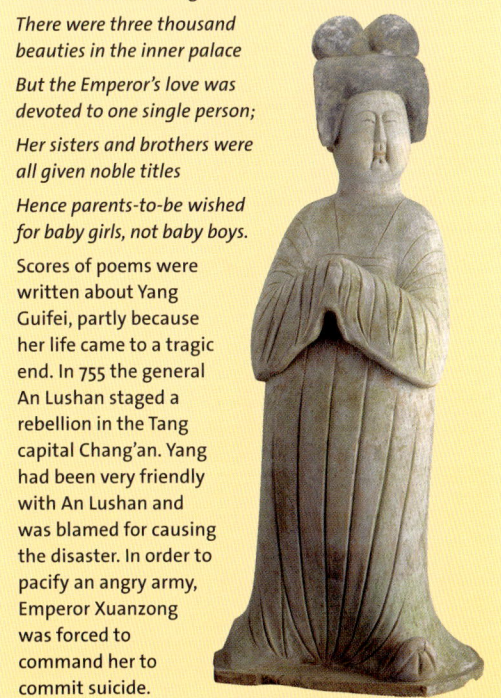

There were three thousand beauties in the inner palace

But the Emperor's love was devoted to one single person;

Her sisters and brothers were all given noble titles

Hence parents-to-be wished for baby girls, not baby boys.

Scores of poems were written about Yang Guifei, partly because her life came to a tragic end. In 755 the general An Lushan staged a rebellion in the Tang capital Chang'an. Yang had been very friendly with An Lushan and was blamed for causing the disaster. In order to pacify an angry army, Emperor Xuanzong was forced to command her to commit suicide.

JAPANESE DRESS — HEIAN PERIOD

There are no known textile artefacts remaining from the Heian era, which began in 794 when Emperor Kammu, who reigned from 781 to 806, moved the Japanese capital from Nara to Heian-kyo (modern-day Kyoto). Our understanding of Heian dress relies almost exclusively on artistic and literary representations from the time, especially the classic works of Japanese literature from the early years of the 11th century. These include *Genji Monogatari* or *The Tale of Genji* (c. 1000)—one of the first novels by Lady Murasaki Shikibu (opposite)—and *The Pillow Book* by Murasaki's rival lady-in-waiting Sei Shonagon. These texts suggest that clothing was the object of an obsessive and agonizing concern for the aristocratic ladies-in-waiting in the capital Heian-kyo—with the main emphasis being on the selection of sartorial colour combinations for the complex layering system known as *irome no kasane* (see p.40). The following passage from Lady Murasaki's diary is one of many examples that indicate a neurotic and fetishistic attention to details of dress in the courts of Heian-kyo in medieval Japan: 'That day all the women had done their utmost to dress well, but, as luck would have it, two of them showed a want of taste when it came to choosing colour combinations

KEY EVENTS

794	794	c. 800	895	c. 1000	c. 1000
The Japanese capital is moved from Nara to Heian-kyo.	The *sokutai* is adopted as official dress for emperors, courtiers and aristocrats for formal occasions. It comprises a yellow outer robe and baggy white trousers.	Buddhism begins to spread throughout Japan, primarily through two major esoteric sects of Tendai and Shingon.	Wealthy Heian people continue to import superior quality fabric from China, even after the cessation of official relations between the two countries.	Sei Shonagon writes *The Pillow Book*. It records her observations as a lady-in-waiting at the Heian court.	Lady Murasaki Shikibu writes *Genji Monogatari*, revealing her love of fashion in the detailed dress descriptions therein.

at their sleeves, and as they served the food they came into full view of the nobles and senior courtiers. Later, it seemed that Lady Saisho and the others had been mortified; but it was not such a terrible mistake—it was just that the combinations were rather uninspiring.'

Taoism and other Chinese influences were at their height during this period, and by the early 9th century Buddhism was also beginning to spread throughout Japan. The court costume was initially copied from the Chinese Tang style (see p.30), and the fabric was imported from China. After imperial communication with China was suspended in 894, a more uniquely Japanese style began to develop among the elite class. The *kosode* (a forerunner to the modern-day kimono) became a staple garment for both men and women during this period. There was a shift away from the Chinese fashion of rich brocaded robes, and the silhouette of Heian court attire became increasingly voluminous and sculptural.

As the Fujiwara clan—a family of courtiers intermarried with the imperial family—rose in power and influence, there was a period of unprecedented wealth and stability during which a new leisure class developed, with an increased demand for luxurious clothing. Silk textile production and dyeing industries flourished in the Heian era with the development of Japanese imperial court culture, and silk became an extremely important national commodity. In the early 10th century thirty-six provinces across Japan were supplying silk to the imperial household, and the period is remembered as a golden age for silk dyeing in the capital.

Faces were whitened with powders and pastes during this era, and both men and women blackened their gums and teeth, a custom that became known as *ohaguro* and was practised exclusively by women in later times. Women shaved off or plucked their eyebrows completely in order to redraw them higher on the forehead, and they also redefined their lips in red, making the mouth appear smaller than its natural shape (opposite). Men cultivated thin moustaches and goatee beards and wore their hair in neat topknots, whereas women aspired to have long, shiny, straight hair, flowing on top of their robes to the floor behind them.

Women's bodies were swallowed into oblivion by their enormous heavy costumes that rendered any individual biological features irrelevant and invisible. In the classic literature of the time, people's physical attributes rarely feature in the lengthy detailed descriptions: it is their clothes that matter. The multiple robes of the *irome no kasane* costume were carefully arranged with an emphasis on the colours formed between the layers. The partial disclosure of the inner structure, so crucial to this dress system, depended not only on the translucency of the fabrics but also on the varying lengths of the robes at their edges, with the hems and sleeves of each layer made successively shorter. The focus was on the most visually accessible peripheries of the enormous sleeves,

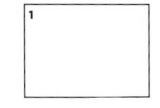

1 A detail from a six-panel folding screen shows the 'Spring in the Palace' scene from *Genji Monogatari*. Court women are dressed in coloured robes appropriate to spring; the white translucent gauzes reference cherry blossoms (c. 1650).

2 In this portrait, Lady Murasaki Shikibu, lady-in-waiting and author of *Genji Monogatari*, is seated at her writing desk surrounded by her myriad robes. The red *hakama* trouser-skirt undergarment can be seen under the desk.

1068	1074	c. 1142	1172	1185	Late 12th century
The Fujiwara clan is overthrown by Emperor Go-Sanjo (r.1068–73).	A sumptuary law is passed limiting ladies' court robes to five layers. Previously the outfit could have weighed up to 40 pounds (15 kg).	Minamoto Masasuke, aide to Empress Fujiwara no Tashi, writes *Colours for a Court Lady's Dress*, a collection of seasonal robe combinations.	Originally an undergarment worn under court dress, the *kosode* becomes acceptable as outerwear for Heian aristocrats.	The Minamoto clan seizes power and establishes the Kamakura shogunate, moving the Japanese capital from Heian-kyo to Kamakura.	The end of the Heian period sees the rise of various military clans, who take power and start the feudal period in Japan.

JAPANESE DRESS – HEIAN PERIOD 37

3 An *emakimono*, or handscroll, shows Prince Genji playing dice and court women seated on the floor behind screens, with their long black hair draped over their trailing robes.

4 This illustration by Hikokuni Tokugawa II shows seated noblewomen glimpsed from behind hanging blinds. Their faces are rendered with standardized features of the *hikime-kagihana* technique (literally 'dashes for eyes, hooks for noses').

which women could push through the gaps of surrounding screens and curtains in order to woo a male suitor (above). The noblewomen spent their time not only covered in myriad wrappings of voluminous robes but also within architectural layers of curtains, folding rice-paper screens, sliding bamboo panels, reed blinds and lattice fences. This complex spacial wrapping shielded them from outside view, and their view of the outdoors. Aristocratic buildings were raised above the ground (opposite) to allow ventilation, and women spent their days sitting on the floor, so men in the surrounding gardens would have the women's partially exposed robes at eye level. Ambient light was filtered through the multilayered partitions, with the dim interiors occasionally lit by a small oil lamp. This caliginous bordered-off world paradoxically vivified the senses: perceptions of colour, touch, scent and sound are exceedingly acute in classic literature.

The only acceptable way for a woman of rank to move about in public was to be carried in a windowless ox cart. With their selected combination of robes considered tantamount to their level of cultivation and sensitivity, the women found that they could publicly display themselves from within these dark sealed enclaves by exposing the layered edges of their sleeves through the gaps under the carriage door. If a potential suitor saw this and thought that the colours of the robes expressed appropriate refinement, he would contact the woman's family (identified by the crest on the cart) and apply to start a relationship with her, beginning with a prolonged period of letter writing in which the chosen colour of the paper would also be subject to painfully intense aesthetic scrutiny. In order to access a noblewoman from outside the layers of dress and built space that distanced her, a male suitor might also embark on *kaimami*, a clandestine courtship custom of 'peeping through a gap' in an obscuring fence, screen or curtain. Depicted in many paintings and literary texts, *kaimami* sees the taboo of furtive peeking absorbed as an aesthetic ritual, in which the coloured robes of the *irome no kasane* become highly eroticized.

The prescribed invisibility of women at court clearly induced anxiety within Lady Murasaki, who wrote in her diary of one night when 'the moon was so bright that I was embarrassed and knew not where to hide'. Even the empress was not exempt from the excruciation of exposure, as Sei Shonagon recalls in *The Pillow Book*: 'When evening came and the lamps were produced, one was lit near where Her Majesty was seated; as the lattice shutters hadn't yet been lowered, she was clearly visible through the open door, so she raised her *biwa* [musical instrument] and held it vertically to shield herself from view. There she sat, in a scarlet robe with quite indescribably lovely gowns and starched robes beneath, in layer upon layer, and it was thrilling too to see how her sleeves fell over the rich glossy black of the *biwa* as she held it, and the sharp contrast of her wonderfully white forehead, clearly visible at the side of the shielding instrument.' This passage evokes the long-standing Japanese aesthetic ideal of *miegakure* (hide and reveal)—the momentary suggestion of something partially obscured.

The vast network of obfuscation that surrounded the women of the Heian courts has been regarded as a tool of patriarchal oppression that kept women immobile and mute, out of sight and unable to see. Although it denied them access to experience, knowledge and power, it also created a separated sphere of inclusion in which they cultivated aesthetic ideals to an extraordinary degree. Highly competitive, these stationary, time-rich and often deeply frustrated women empowered themselves with art, especially the literary arts: all the geniuses in this golden age of literature were women.

The costume and literary arts of Heian-kyo are particularly noteworthy, but there was also remarkable artistic development in many other areas, such as the incense-mixing and tea-tasting ceremonies that were designed to discipline and cultivate the senses. It seems that all elements of quotidian court life in this era were conducted at the level of art, not only court dress but also basic practices such as eating and communicating. Speech was highly stylized and codified, and one was expected to allude to and cite poetry in everyday dialogue. The emphasis was always on the beauty of appropriateness: it did not matter if one had gorgeous robes or could recite rare poems, it was the individual's carefully considered selection from the existing published verses or available coloured robes that won praise. There were hundreds of rules and strict conventions that needed to be followed, but there was always a small crucial arena of nuance, where one could display one's aesthetic refinement in the hope of sexual or political advancement.

The level of sumptuousness in Heian court costume was ultimately unsustainable and the Kamakura period that followed saw aristocratic costume become much less ostentatious, although the legacy of Heian Japan remains strong and the imperial household still dresses in the Heian style for coronations and weddings. Contemporary fashion designers in Japan have often borrowed from their culture's rich aesthetic heritage, and the avant-garde Japanese fashion of the 1980s and 1990s (see p. 402) is also characterized by voluminous layering that disregards the body's physical contours and partially reveals the inner workings of the dress system. **AmG**

Layered Dress 10th century
NOBLEWOMEN'S COSTUME

Portrait of Lady Murasaki Shikibu, wearing the *juni-hitoe* ensemble (10th century).

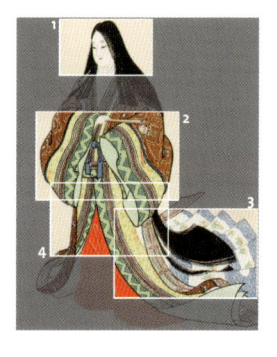

NAVIGATOR

The customary *juni-hitoe* ensemble for women of the Heian court translates literally as 'the twelve layers' but actually consisted of anything between ten and twenty-five separate silk robes. There was occasionally some brocade or embroidery on the outer layers of the dress structure, but the focus was on the selected colour combinations in the *irome no kasane* layering system.

Plain-coloured silk robes of various hues were layered up, usually with the lightest shades on top, gradually deepening in tone towards the innermost robe. Each layer was made from a thin, translucent gauze, known as *usumono*, and the hues were carefully selected according to season, climate and occasion. There were also strict codes that abided by and affirmed rigid social hierarchies, with specific rules for colour combinations relating to the wearer's age, class and imperial rank. The layered structure formed a nuanced interplay of colours in which the inner robes shone through to create new composite tones that referenced ephemeral natural phenomena. For example, red silk showing through translucent white made 'plum blossom', whereas light purple worn under white made 'cherry blossom'. **AmG**

👁 FOCAL POINTS

1 FACIAL BEAUTY
Adhering to Heian standards of beauty, the noblewoman's face is completely whitened. Her teeth would have been blackened, in order not to appear yellow against her white skin. The preference was for a slender nose, narrow eyes and a small mouth painted bright red, and the longer a woman wore her black hair the better.

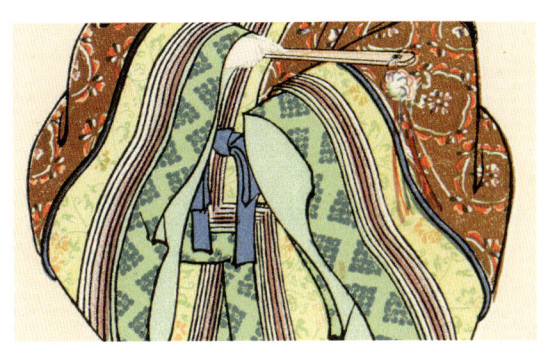

2 GRADATED SLEEVES
In order to display the colours of the robes, the sleeves vary in length, with each layer made successively shorter. The aesthetic focus is on the edges of the sleeves, which the women would push through the gaps of screens or curtains in order to woo a male suitor.

3 PLEATED TRAIN
For formal ceremonies an outer gown, popularly made of crimson beaten silk, was worn over the meticulously selected set of lined robes in various tones, and a long pleated train known as a *mo* fanned out behind. It was considered ideal at the time to drape the woman's straight black hair on top, following the line of the train.

4 VOLUMINOUS LAYERS
The voluminous ensemble starts with a basic white undergarment, on top of which is the red *hakama*, a long and loose trouser-skirt. Over this are as many as twenty-five separate, loose-fitting silk robes, arranged to emphasize the composite colours formed between the many layers.

▲ Empress Kojun wears a *juni-hitoe* ensemble (1926). The sumptuousness of Heian court costume could not be maintained and Kamakura costume was much less ostentatious.

JAPANESE DRESS — HEIAN PERIOD   41

MEDIEVAL DRESS

1. An illuminated manuscript (13th–15th century) shows a crowned figure, surrounded by court musicians, wearing the simple 'T'-shape cotte.

2. An illustration from *Costumes de Paris à travers les siècles* by H. Gourdon de Genouillac depicts a fashionable young man in 1480, wearing shoes with excessive points known as *poulaines*.

3. The liripipe hood evolved into a turban-style hat, seen here worn by Philip I, King of Castile and Duke of Burgundy, in an illustrated manuscript (15th century).

According to some costume historians, the contemporary fashion system originates from the middle of the 14th century. Significant changes occurred in medieval clothing at this time, and a new way of dressing developed that marked a shift from the simple, peasant-style silhouette—based on a 'T'-shape shift, the cotte (above)—to a French-inspired emphasis on contour and cut. At the same time, a newly emerging merchant class replaced the social hierarchy of the feudal manor, where rank, wealth and title depended on the acquisition of land, given by the king in return for military service. The town became a centre for trade, where commercial activities included the fashionable enterprises of drapers, dressmakers, cobblers, hosiers, hat makers, haberdashers and tailors. Before long, desirable clothes became widely accessible to a greater number of people across all social classes.

Textiles were central to the medieval economy, and throughout the Middle Ages wool was the prime fabric for clothing. English farmers exported wool to

KEY EVENTS

1327	1348–49	1350s	1365	1405–33	1419
Edward II creates the Order of the Round Table and introduces the era of chivalry.	The Black Death results in the end of the feudal system as serfs move to towns and cities.	'Points' are introduced to fasten garments. They are threaded through eyelets and often decorated with ornamental aglets.	A sumptuary law forbids grooms, servants and craftsmen to use woollen cloth that costs more than 1s 1d a yard.	Zheng He of China sails through the Indian Ocean to India, Arabia and East Africa to spread China's influence and assure sovereignty.	The Duke of Burgundy, Philip the Good, sets the fashion for wearing black on the death of his father, John the Fearless.

42 500 BC–1599

the major centres of woollen cloth production in Flanders, until the English government enticed the weavers and spinners to England. The mechanization of cloth production introduced specialized guilds of dyers, fullers and shearers. Initially, weavers used vertical looms and worked with the warp and the right side of the fabric facing them, producing the typical diamond and chevron patterns of the era. With the invention of the horizontal loom in the 11th century, it became possible to weave pieces of fabric that were as much as 98 feet (30 m) long and 6 ½ feet (2 m) wide. These longer lengths enabled garments to be cut to shape and, influenced by the French court, clothing began to be fitted to the body, which led to increased differentiation between genders.

Fashionable dress was seen as a male preserve, and most of the pictorial representation of the period—sculptural and architectural sources, panel painting, tapestries and frescoes—records male rather than female dress, a reflection of the social hierarchy of the time. Typically, men wore a close-fitting, button-fronted, padded jacket (gipon), with a belt slung low over the hips, beneath a low-necked tunic (cote-hardie), which was also tight-fitting. The cote-hardie featured a dagged edge, a method of slashing the cloth to form a serrated border; later a collar was added, the length gradually diminished and the sleeves widened. Buttons became increasingly important and were often covered in the same material as the jacket or fashioned from precious metals, embossed with text or animal and plant motifs. A fashion for mi-parti, or parti-coloured, garments made of two contrasting fabrics arose for men mid-century and was popular at the English court. In 1360 a front-opening, loose-bodied, floor-length gown known as the houppelande was introduced (see p.46). A version with a closed front was popular with women later in the century. Men wore the houppelande with the paltok—a hip-length tunic with a padded, rounded bodice—to form a silhouette that remained in fashion until 1420.

The idealized male figure gradually widened at the shoulders and long, slender legs were accentuated by tapering pointed shoes or boots called *poulaines* (above right). The doublet and hose became the staple components of the male wardrobe, with variations only in style and detail. Lacing was introduced across a wide V-neck that allowed the shirt to show through, often richly embellished in silk. The increasing shortness of the doublet required that hose, initially cut on the bias in the 13th century, fastened to the basque with points, or unattached laces. In the 1470s, there was a shift towards the simpler garments of the earlier period. Bulk was rejected in favour of attenuated minimalism, in muted colours and textures. In men's dress, seams were left unfastened on the shoulders or down the front of the robe, giving the impression of undress, with underlinen showing through the joins.

Hats and headgear assumed a great importance during the Middle Ages. Up to 1380, a hood with a long liripipe was worn, which later was wound around the head to form a turban (right). This was followed by the chaperon,

1420s	1434	1453	1480s	1485	1498
Dark furs, such as sable, civet, beaver and particularly astrakhan, become fashionable.	Jan van Eyck paints *The Arnolfini Marriage*, which features the all-purpose garment, the houppelande (see p.46).	The fall of Constantinople marks the end of the Byzantine Empire and the beginning of the growth of the Ottoman Empire.	The points on men's shoes, known as *poulaines*, achieved such impractical lengths that they were restricted by sumptuary law.	Henry Tudor establishes a new dynasty of monarchs, providing stability and emphasis on domestic comfort rather than military service.	Explorer Vasco da Gama and his armada arrive in India from Portugal, thus establishing the first maritime alternative to the Silk Road.

MEDIEVAL DRESS 43

4 *Philosophy Presenting the Seven Liberal Arts to Boethius* (c. 1460–70), attributed to Coetivy, features the voluminous, trailing skirts of a variety of gown styles, including the houppelande and the surcoat.

5 A detail from the Portinari Triptych (1480–83) by Hugo van der Goes shows Maria Portinari wearing a hennin, or steeple headdress.

6 Christine de Pisan presents her book of poems to Isabel of Bavaria, Queen of France. The illustration features two types of headdress: the veil raised from the face by the use of pins, and a cornes, or horned headdress.

a circular padded roll to which was attached a gorget, consisting of folds of material cut in decorative shapes, sometimes worn on the shoulder. Over time this became smaller, and a badge of livery or cockade was added. Fur was now used for its decorative qualities rather than for warmth. Used to edge and line garments, it was a symbol of wealth and power; white ermine with black spots was worn only by royalty.

By 1485 the doublet had acquired a high stand-up collar and had become so short that an accompanying codpiece was required. This was initially created to cover the genital area modestly, but it eventually became a piece of exaggerated decoration. It was formed from a triangular flap or gusset attached to the front of the hose or breeches, with the bottom corner of the triangle sewn to the inseam of the garment and the two top corners attached near the hips with either buttons or laces called 'codpiece points'. The cote-hardie was replaced with a jacket or jerkin, increasingly tight-fitting with padded shoulders and detachable sleeves. Vibrant colours were popular, and they were usually extracted from vegetable dyes. Cloth of scarlet was a smooth-textured and felted fabric, coloured with a red dye extracted from a Mediterranean insect, the kermes. It was the most expensive dye available and replaced the ancient shellfish dye from southern Europe, murex purple, in popularity. Perse, a blue-green dye from woad, instilled from a plant distantly related to the wallflower, was more common and was indigenous to a number of different regions. The outer husks of walnuts provided browns and black, whereas fabrics were whitened by being soaked in buttermilk and exposed to sunlight. Linen was the prerequisite of the rich, and silk was so rare and precious that it was initially reserved for religious ceremonies. The Italian silk trade of Florence, Venice and Genoa developed brocaded velvet and satin for export, but it was worn only by the aristocracy and nobility.

During the 14th century, divergences between male and female clothing became more pronounced. Men's fashions emphasized the width of the shoulders, whereas women's gowns had narrow shoulders and width at the hem of the skirt. Women wore a kirtle, or gown, close-fitting to the waist and flaring out at the hem. Cuffs widened at the wrist or elbow to form trailing pendants. The fabric left over from shaping the sleeves to the arm was used to facilitate movement under the arm or to add width to the hem. The contour of the body was also defined by partial bias cutting, either in the piece or attached to the straight grain of the fabric. From 1380 onwards female dress was cut closer to the body, and laced fastenings down the front of the dress formed an early type of corset. Tight-fitting sleeves extended over the hands. The next layer was the cote-hardie, whose sleeves featured long streamers or tippets that trailed to the ground. A surcoat was worn over the cote-hardie, with openings at the sides. The front formed a stiffened stomacher, known as a plackard, which created the effect of tight lacing. Modesty was relinquished in favour of the décolletage, as the top area of the bodice was cut away to reveal part of the bosom. This fashion was adopted eagerly in Italy, but more reluctantly in northern Europe. Gowns gradually lengthened and broadened until the mid 15th century, when they grew so wide that the extra fabric was caught up in a belt underneath the breasts (opposite). The simple veil was replaced by elaborate, horned, boxed and veiled coronets, constructed from finely wrought ironwork and worn by English noblewomen, with padded heart shapes popular in Flanders and France. Married women adopted the babette, a stiffened circle of white linen, with a broad band passing under the chin.

A series of elaborate headdresses superseded the 13th-century crespine, a type of hairnet that was worn alone or with vertical plaits each side of the face. In the latter part of the 14th century, the veil reappeared, with the nebula headdress made of a half-circle of linen that framed the face. The filet also changed shape, forming two hollow ornamental pillars through which the hair was drawn on each side. The cushion headdress, a padded roll worn over a hairnet, with the hair coiled above each ear in small knobs known as templars, preceded the cornes, or horned headdress (below). This consisted of a wire structure on which the veil was draped. In 1450 the shape of the headdress began to extend upwards rather than sideways; it became more elongated and was worn tilted backwards. The hennin, or steeple headdress (right), was particularly popular in France and could have either a pointed or truncated cone.

During the medieval period, fashionable dress was used increasingly to differentiate between the elite, the merchant class, the artisan and the peasant. This was controlled by the introduction of various sumptuary laws by governments throughout Europe, and particularly Italy, to restrict the wearing of certain items of clothing or to reduce inappropriate excess. **MF**

Houppelande 1360
ALL-PURPOSE MALE AND FEMALE GARMENT

The Arnolfini Marriage
by Jan van Eyck (1434).

NAVIGATOR

In 1360 an all-purpose garment, the houppelande, was introduced, which replaced other sleeved outer garments such as the cotte, surcoat and mantle. The male version was worn over doublet and hose, and finished at mid-thigh or calf. The wide sleeves were gathered on the shoulder, sometimes hung to the ground and exposed the sleeves of the doublet underneath. The houppelande was adopted by women later in the century, although their gowns were invariably closed down the front and worn floor-length, often extending into a train. The folds were caught up in a raised waistline under the bust and the sleeves were very wide. Both hems and sleeves were dagged, scalloped or appliquéd in contrasting colours. So lavish was the use of cloth that moralists derided the style; in *The Parson's Tale*, a treatise on virtuous living during the 1390s, Geoffrey Chaucer describes 'so much pouncing of chisel to make holes, so much dagging of shears, with the superfluity in length of the aforesaid gowns, trailing in the dung and mire, on horse and eke on foot, as well of man as of woman'.

During the first half of the 15th century, the name 'houppelande' was discarded in favour of 'robe' or 'gown'; the cut became less extreme, and decoration was confined to textured or patterned materials. From 1490 the garment became standard academic dress, worn by doctors and magistrates, the hooded cape ornamental rather than practical, with variations in sleeve style and lining. **MF**

FOCAL POINTS

1 MALE HEADGEAR
The width of the houppelande is balanced by the broad brim of the hat, which completely obscures the hair. Sober in hue, the oversized crown balloons out to form a wider circle at the top. Other contemporary styles included hats with flat crowns and narrow brims and hats shaped like a Turkish fez. This is a surprisingly simple hat for the time. It was more usual for a man of this status to wear complex folded headgear called a chaperon, which evolved from a hooded cloak.

2 DECORATED SLEEVES
The sleeves of the woman's houppelande are edged in a narrow strip of fur before extending to the ground with a deep decorative border of self-coloured dagged appliqué. The large opening reveals the contrasting tightly fitting undersleeves in richly figured brocade. The presence of fur and the ankle-length kirtle beneath suggest that this is a winter garment. The heavy, impractical sleeves serve as a reminder that this woman is of the leisured class.

3 COMPLEX FOLDS OF FABRIC
The extravagant and floor-sweeping train of the woman's gown, lined in sheared fur, is an expression of the wealth of this prosperous mercantile couple. The use of Italian-imported bright blue figured silk for the woman's kirtle also confirms their status. Commonly in this period a wedding gown was simply a more intricate and elaborate form of contemporary dress. Green was an extremely popular colour because it symbolized fertility.

4 UNBELTED HOUPPELANDE
The man's houppelande is fastened down the centre with hidden hooks and eyes, and falls free to the hem from the wide shoulder. The fullness across the chest is formed by unpressed pleats. The garment is lined with a dark fur of sable or marten, which was used for its decorative qualities and as a symbol of wealth and power rather than for warmth. Originally, the undergarment would have been more purple, but the pigment of the painting has deteriorated over time.

MEDIEVAL DRESS

RENAISSANCE DRESS

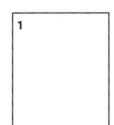

1. In this painting from c. 1520 by Hans Holbein the Younger, the lavish embellishment of the garments, profusion of jewels and abundant use of textiles proclaim Henry VIII as one of the most powerful and splendid figures in Renaissance Europe.

2. In a portrait from 1548 Archduke Ferdinand of Tirol displays a prominent codpiece made from the same fabric as his slashed trunks. His silhouette has the wide, square shoulders typical of the era.

Reviving the aesthetics of the Greco-Roman classical world, the Renaissance was the cultural movement that emerged in Florence during the Late Middle Ages. It encompassed a flowering of literature, science, art, religion and politics, with a concomitant development of a more formal fashion as rigid formality replaced the body-enhancing cut of the clothes of medieval Europe. The invasion of Italy in 1494 by the French king Charles VIII, who reigned from 1483 to 1498, set in motion the infiltration of Renaissance fashion throughout the rest of Europe.

As the 16th century progressed, an increasingly structured silhouette that masked the contours of the body defined the social rank of the wearer. In England, Henry VIII, who reigned from 1509 to 1547, wore garments loaded with precious gems (above) to reinforce his status as the most desirable prince

KEY EVENTS

1501	1509	1520	1536	1555	1556
Catherine of Aragon arrives at the court of Henry VII for her marriage to Prince Arthur. Her entourage introduces the farthingale to England.	On the death of his father Henry VII, Henry VIII succeeds to the throne of England.	Henry VIII and Francis I of France meet at the Field of the Cloth of Gold. Both kings compete in a display of their respective courts' magnificence.	Italian silk weavers settle in Lyons, which becomes the centre for French sericulture.	The Muscovy (or Russian) Company is founded. It holds a monopoly on trade between Britain and Russia until 1698.	Philip II of the Habsburg dynasty ascends the Spanish throne, heading a global empire and extensive New World colonies.

48 500 BC–1599

in Renaissance Europe and set the trend for conspicuous consumption. His redistribution of church lands after the dissolution of the monasteries created newly wealthy families, all ambitious to prove their entitlement to be called noble and eager to appropriate the accoutrements of the fashionable elite, including extravagantly embellished and jewel-encrusted garments. Clothing accounted for a significant proportion of the household expenditure as an affluent bourgeoisie demanded luxurious textiles, including multicoloured silk-satins, figured velvets and brocades from the weaving mills in the Italian cities of Genoa, Lucca, Venice and Florence. At this time Italy monopolized the making of cloth of gold—fabric enriched with expensive metal threads—and fine velvets, a situation that continued over the following centuries. By 1600 the manufacture of silk was vital to the Italian economy.

During this period the etiolated male silhouette of the Gothic north was replaced by an emphasis on the horizontal that reflected the flattened arch prevalent in architecture. The foundations of the cut and craft of tailoring were now in place. The main male garment was the doublet, a close-fitting, buttoned jacket cut from velvet, satin or cloth of gold. The sleeves grew wider and were often paned or slashed (see p.52) and cut to bend at the elbow to facilitate movement, a style that also enabled the wearer to stand hand on hips, as witnessed in many Tudor portraits. The practice of slashing the fabric and pulling through the lining or shirt underneath was applied to both doublet and hose, and reached its most extreme form in Germany.

Over the doublet a jerkin or short sleeveless jacket was worn, closed down the front with laces or buttons. The next layer was the gown, loosely falling in folds from the shoulders to the floor. The nether garments comprised breeches and stockings sewn together, the top edge secured by a row of laces threaded through eyelet holes in both garments and tied in small bows with metal ends known as aglets. The doublet was worn open to display the codpiece (right), which had evolved from a simple triangular piece of cloth to a shaped and padded pouch that exaggerated the genitals in an overt declaration of virility. Named after the contemporary term for testicles, it increased in size until the middle of the 16th century, and was often embellished with jewels and embroidery, and used as a purse. It gradually diminished in size until the end of the century when it vanished altogether.

Men wore flat shoes with a square, 'duck-bill' shaped toe and soles made from leather or cork. Hats were worn indoors and signified the wearer's status, age and affluence. The aristocracy usually wore a soft, low bonnet in dark silk velvet; this was frequently dyed black in an expensive and time-consuming process. A similar style was worn by their social inferiors, but constructed from a felt made from fur or wool. The body of the hat was decorated with metal-thread lace, badges and aglets hooked into place, as well as plumes of coloured feathers. Hats were essential wear and an obligatory accessory

1558	1564	1574	1581	1583	1589
Elizabeth I becomes Queen of England. Costumes are an important status symbol of the Elizabethan court.	Commercial starch is first produced for starching and setting ruffs by Mistress Dinghen van der Plasse in London.	Elizabethan Statutes of Apparel forbid the wearing of 'any cloth of gold, tissue, nor fur of sables: except duchesses, marquises, and countesses'.	The publication of *Habitus Variarum Orbis Gentium* by Jean-Jacques Boissard inspires interest in Middle Eastern dress.	English pamphleteer Philip Stubbes publishes the *Anatomie of Abuses*, a virulent attack on the excesses of fashions of the era.	William Lee invents the knitting frame. Knitted silk or cotton stockings become fashionable; designs known as 'clocks' decorate the finest pairs.

for the non-noble and professional class. Later in the century the *copotain* was worn, a hat made of beaver, leather or felted wool, with a high conical crown.

The use of certain colours and fabrics set apart court dress from that of the mercantile class. An Elizabethan affinity with the natural world and an appreciation of the pastoral ideal resulted in richly textured depictions of flora and fauna, with almost every visible element of the garments decorated with an all-over embroidered pattern featuring birds, insects and flowers. Although fabrics could be woven into a figurative design, these were necessarily repetitive and stylized. Only embroidery could lend an element of realism required by the era's appreciation of flowers and foliage. Well-born women engaged in blackwork embroidery, used extensively on white linen, to strengthen the cloth around areas such as openings, necklines and cuffs. Whitework embroidery was often used for undergarments and ruffs. This could incorporate drawn thread work, cut work and faggoting (an embroidery technique using threads fastened together in bundles). Complex embroidery was the remit of the professional embroiderer, who was usually male, and included pearls, emeralds and rubies as well as gold and silver thread.

The emergence of Spain as a growing global power during the middle of the 16th century saw a move away from bright colours and textures and lavish display towards more sombre hues, usually black, with minimal decoration, as favoured by Philip II (below left), who came to the throne in 1556. Luxury and status were no longer defined by excessive ornamentation, as rigidity of structure and precision of cut took their place. Mary Tudor's marriage to Philip of Spain in 1554 consolidated the trend for austere formality and reflected the etiquette of the Spanish court. In 1570 a change in cut emerged, with the introduction of padding to the doublet, which mimicked the lines of contemporary plate armour and formed a shield-like carapace. The doublet was stuffed with bombast—a mixture of cotton rags, horsehair and flock—to form an overhanging 'peasecod' belly, a style that lasted for the next thirty years. Philip Stubbes complained in his *Anatomie of Abuses* (1583) that the wearers of the peasecod doublet were so 'stuffed, bombasted and sewed, as they can verie hardly eyther stoupe downe'.

Breeches replaced the earlier trunk hose, and the most popular style was the Spanish kettledrum (left), which were padded to reach mid-thigh and were worn from the 1550s to 1570. These were followed by baggy breeches that came to below the knee (Venetians), and extremely baggy breeches known as galligaskins. The introduction of knitting replaced bias-cut fabric and led to well-fitting hose; bright colours were popular and they were held in place with either a ribbon tied below the knee or with a simple form of cross-gartering from 1560. A short cloak was added to the male doublet; designed to be worn indoors as well as out, it was a highly embellished piece with a small standing collar. The mandilion, or mendeville, was a purely decorative garment; a hip-length jacket with faux sleeves, it was worn hung from one shoulder. Leather goods included embroidered and fringed gauntlet gloves and over-the-knee boots with a turned-back cuff; these resulted from developments in leather processing in the Spanish town of Córdoba.

Both men's and women's bodices were décolleté and cut square across the neck with the top of the shirt or chemise showing (opposite). The low necklines of women's gowns were often filled with a partlet, which when constructed from the same rich fabric as the bodice of the gown gave the appearance of a high-necked gown. Sheer or opaque linen partlets were worn over the chemise; towards 1550 this was fastened with a tasselled drawstring. The resulting gathers and small frills eventually expanded to form the ruff (see p.56); this goffered (crimped with irons) linen collar was constructed from *reticella*, a delicate cut-work lace that later evolved into the needle laces of the 17th century.

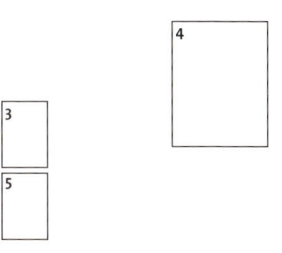

Rigidity of form was also evident in female dress. The principal garment for women was the kirtle, which was originally a full-length, one-piece gown. From 1545 the gown comprised a matching skirt and bodice with the skirt retaining the name of the kirtle. Attached to this was a contrasting, stiffened and decorated triangular piece of cloth tied into place with ribbon or aglets. Corsetry, known as 'a pair of bodies', initially appeared in the second half of the 16th century. Comprised of whalebone or dried reeds known as 'bents' inserted into a stiff, quilted fabric, these compressed the waist and flattened the breasts. The effect was emphasized by the addition of the stomacher; this formed the front of the bodice and was stiffened with buckram or pasteboard and held in place by wooden busks, in effect closing the gap between the two front edges of the bodice. The bodice was made up of two halves, tied into place either side of the torso with sleeves of the same material attached at the shoulders. The wide funnel-shaped outer sleeve, often edged with fur, was turned back at the elbow, revealing a decorated inner sleeve.

During the 1580s the bodice grew narrower and longer. It was shaped by a curved front seam, sloping side seams or a curved back seam rather than darts. The silhouette of opposing triangular forms gave way to a series of circles formed by the starched and goffered linen ruff that framed the head and the circular farthingale (see p.54). Hair was parted in the centre, with fullness at each side; in 1570 it was combed back over a wire support, known as a palisade. **MF**

3 An Italian statesman wears kettledrum breeches in a portrait from 1560. Thickly padded and made from strips of embroidered cloth over a stuffed lining, they resembled a pair of onions at the top of the legs of the wearer.

4 In this portrait from 1545, Eleanora of Toledo wears a silk brocade dress heavily patterned with black arabesques and a pomegranate motif. Her gold lattice-work partlet is studded with pearls. Blackwork embroidery is just visible at the edges of her square-necked chemise.

5 Less lavish cloth and darker hues were common at the end of the 16th century, alleviated by the small goffered ruff in this portrait of King Philip II of Spain.

Slashed Costume 1500s
MEN'S DRESS

Portrait of Charles de Solier, Lord of Morette by Hans Holbein the Younger (1534–35).

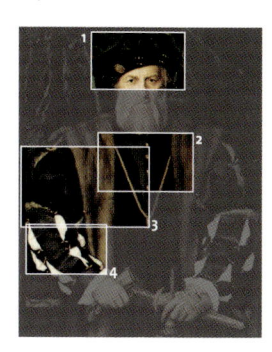

The portrait of Charles de Solier, painted by Holbein the Younger while the French ambassador stayed in London during 1534, shows the sitter wearing a doublet with slashed sleeves. This decorative style is thought to originate from the victory of the Swiss Guard over Charles the Bold, Duke of Burgundy, at the Battle of Grandson in 1476, when the victors patched their torn uniforms with the remnants of the defeated army's rich fabrics. The Swiss troops were copied by German mercenaries known as *Landsknechte*, whose elaborate, conspicuous dress was exempt from sumptuary laws. They in turn were copied by the French court, probably under the influence of the half-German Guise family. The marriage of Henry VIII's sister Mary to Louis XII of France introduced the fashion for slashed clothes to England. Elaborate slashing remained popular, especially in Germany, where a fashion arose for assembling garments in alternating bands of contrasting fabrics. Slashing also appeared in women's clothes, but was not as prevalent. An alternative to slashing was to 'pink' the material of the edges of the cut upper fabric, a technique that limited fraying by cutting across the bias weave of the cloth. This was often performed to a specific shape, more usually a diamond, with the contrasting fabric pulled through to form a raised surface. **MF**

NAVIGATOR

FOCAL POINTS

1 SOFT HAT
Customarily worn both indoors and out, the soft bonnet of black silk velvet is worn slightly to one side. It features a small upturned brim sometimes known as a 'turf'. Badges were worn on the brim to denote affiliation to a particular household or individual.

3 FUR LINING
The jacket is lined with dark fur (sable, wolf or marmot) to match the sombre hues of the doublet. The upper elbow-length sleeves are slashed to reveal the fur lining beneath; the upper fabric is held together with laces threaded through eyelet holes and tied in bows.

2 DOUBLET
Rising to the jawline the padded doublet renders the figure broad across the shoulders and chest. Relatively subdued in both colour and embellishment, the dark doublet is enlivened by metal buttons, probably gold, which would be transferred from garment to garment.

4 SLASHED SLEEVES
The outer sleeve is cut or slashed just above the elbow, with the contrasting white linen undergarment worn beneath pulled through to create decorative puffs. Longer, parallel cuts in the fabric were known as 'panes'.

Spanish Farthingale 1500s
WOMEN'S HOOPED SKIRT

Las Meninas by
Diego Velázquez (1656).

NAVIGATOR

The farthingale was first widely seen in England in 1501 among the entourage of the Spanish Princess Catherine of Aragon on her marriage to Prince Arthur, eldest son of Henry VII. The popularity of the fashion was further consolidated on the marriage of Mary I to Philip of Spain in 1554. The Spanish farthingales seen in the painting *Las Meninas* (The Maids of Honour) consist of an underskirt distended by hoops of wire, wood or twisted willow rushes (whalebone was also used from the 1580s). The farthingale of the young Infanta Margarita grows wider towards the hem and the angle allows the wearer to rest her hands on the ledge-like surface. The young girl is surrounded by her maids of honour in Alcázar, the Madrid palace of her father, King Philip IV of Spain, where the formality of dress was in marked contrast to that of the French court. One of the maids of honour kneels at the Infanta's feet, while the other, Doña Isabel de Velasco, stands behind the princess. Isabel is wearing the cartwheel farthingale, which continued to be worn in Spain long after it had disappeared elsewhere. Flattening the bust, the bodice of her gown extends over the skirt in a circular frill radiating out from the centre, softening the silhouette formed by the rim of the wheel. The upper part of the ballooning, low-set sleeves is obscured by a gauze scarf. **MF**

FOCAL POINTS

1 BODICE
Children wore a miniature version of adult clothing. Here the Infanta's bodice stiffens and lengthens the torso. The high, broad neckline and double sleeves of her gown are identical to that worn by her maid of honour Doña Isabel de Velasco.

2 TILTED HEM
The infrastructure beneath carries the skirt of the farthingale out at right angles from the waist before falling vertically to the ground from the outer rim. The skirt tilts at the waist so that the hem is raised at the back and lowered at the front.

TYPES OF FARTHINGALE

The farthingale was the first device used to extend the width of the female skirt, before the hooped skirt and the crinoline. It was first worn in Spain by Princess Joan of Portugal. The earliest images of Spanish farthingales show hoops displayed on the outer surfaces of skirts; later they only provided shape to the overskirt. The French drum or wheel farthingale (seen below in a painting of Anne Vavasour, *c.* 1615), which followed in 1580, was cylindrical. It was worn chiefly at court until around 1620. Outside court, the most popular style was the roll farthingale, a padded roll of cloth in the shape of a sausage that widened the skirt at hip level.

RENAISSANCE DRESS 55

Dress and Tiered Ruff 1620
WOMEN'S COURT DRESS

Isabel of France by Rodrigo de Villandrando (*c.* 1620).

NAVIGATOR

Isabel of France, the daughter of King Henry IV of France and Marie de Medici, married Philip IV in 1615, before he came to the Spanish throne. In this portrait by court painter Rodrigo de Villandrando, the queen consort of Spain exemplifies the elite dress of the Spanish court, which was one of restrained formality and decorous luxury. Display was limited to gold and gemstone ornamentation, apparent here in the lavish borders of the sleeves and along the lines of the bodice. Although the cartwheel ruff had disappeared in fashionable England by 1613, replaced by the falling collar, it lingered longer in Spanish territories and in Holland long after it had ceased to exist elsewhere. Here the closed cartwheel ruff is attached to a band secured to the high neckline of the elongated bodice. The lace-trimmed edges of the tiered ruff, which is set into elaborate figure-of-eight folds, match the deep cuffs of the long, tight-fitting undersleeves. The goffered effect of the ruff and sleeves was initially created by using unheated setting sticks that fixed pleats into damp, heavily starched ruffs while they dried. Starch began to be commercially produced in Europe in the 1560s and the heated poking stick, similar to a fireplace poker, came into use in *c.* 1570. The farthingale that Isabel is wearing was yet to reach the wide proportions illustrated by court painter Diego Velázquez in *Las Meninas* (1656). **MF**

FOCAL POINTS

1 RIGID BODICE
The stiffened high bodice (*cuerpo alto*) encases the woman's torso from her chin to an extended 'V' point below the natural line of the waist at the front. The bodice takes a triangular form, suppressing the wearer's natural shape. The dense patterning of the skirt of the gown is arranged in a formal ogee repeat—a pattern with a double 'S'-shape curve—woven into the rich black and gold fabric.

2 DOUBLE SLEEVES
The semi-circular outer sleeves of the gown are slit from the elbow, exposing the decorated undersleeves. The sleeves are capped at the shoulder, with an extruding stiffened panel, also lavishly embellished, which exaggerates the triangular silhouette of the bodice. The cuffs at the wrists mirror the elaborate lace ruff at the neckline. Like the ruff, these would have been separate items that could be detached for cleaning or wearing with another dress.

THE HISTORY OF THE RUFF

The ruff evolved during the 1540s from the small frill produced by a tasselled drawstring at the neck of the shirt or chemise. It was usually decorated with either blackwork or whitework embroidery (below). Initially the ruff was a practical way of protecting the neckline of a doublet or bodice from dirt and grease. It eventually became a separate garment that expanded in shape and size until the 1590s, when it developed into a rigid upstanding collar that encircled the head and was sometimes as wide as the wearer's shoulders. These cartwheel ruffs required a wire frame known as a *supportasse*, or underpropper, to hold them in place at the fashionable angle. The discovery of starch in the 1560s enabled ruffs to be made wider without losing their shape. Ruffs could also be coloured during the starching process. At their most extreme, ruffs were a foot (30.5 cm) or more in diameter.

RENAISSANCE DRESS 57

OTTOMAN COURT DRESS

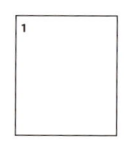

1 This portrait of Süleyman I is from a copy dated September 1589 in the *Descriptions of the Ottoman Sultans* by Seyyid Lokman (1579). It shows the sultan wearing three layers of richly coloured kaftans.

2 This deep red silk velvet is embellished with a design in metal thread (16th century). It was made on a drawloom by a weaver and a drawboy, who helped create the complex pattern.

By the beginning of the 16th century the Ottoman Empire had spread across much of the Middle East. Efficient military and naval campaigns won control of territory in Europe and North Africa, and the empire entered a period of economic prosperity under the rule of a series of sultans. At this time the Ottoman government devoted much effort to the regulation and taxation of the silk industry. Bursa, a centre of silk weaving since the 15th century, continued to produce silk brocades and velvets for the court (opposite) but new workshops were also established in Constantinople (modern-day Istanbul). Ottoman supremacy was centred on Constantinople, which Sultan Süleyman I, who succeeded Sultan Selim I in 1520, transformed into a capital worthy of the vast Ottoman domains. Within the city, the Topkapi Palace was the apex of the Ottoman world order, from which all power and influence emanated.

KEY EVENTS

1513	1517	1520	1526	1534	1536
Piri Reis, captain of the Ottoman navy and renowned cartographer, completes his map of the world for Sultan Selim I in Egypt.	Sultan Selim I captures Damascus and Cairo, confirming the Ottomans as leaders of the Arab territories and guardians of Islam.	The accession of Sultan Süleyman I introduces a period that is remarkable for its economic prosperity, architecture, painting and textile design.	Süleyman's campaign in Hungary results in a catastrophic defeat of the Hungarian army at the Battle of Mohács and the Ottoman occupation of Buda.	Süleyman marries Hürrem, a palace slave of Ukrainian origin. As his legal wife she commands immense power and patronage.	Süleyman and Francis I of France sign a treaty, including trade agreements, that marks the formal entry of the Ottomans into European politics.

Begun by Sultan Mehmet II in 1463, the royal residence became a formidable structure during Süleyman's reign, in effect a walled city within Constantinople. About 5,000 personnel lived and worked there: the sultan, his family and retinue, guards, civil and military officials, specialized servants and skilled craftsmen, all organized into a hierarchy that was subject to strict rules of protocol. In the complex power structure of the Ottoman world, dress was a major visual means of asserting the grandeur and order of the sultanate. The Ottomans well understood the art of dress and realized that clothes had more important functions than merely satisfying the basic needs of warmth, protection and modesty. The shape, fabric and decoration of clothes identified the wearer's official rank, profession, wealth and personal status.

Ottoman court dress impressed all who saw it, especially Ogier Ghiselin de Busbecq, Habsburg ambassador to Constantinople from 1554 to 1562, who was one of many Europeans who recorded their thoughts in letters, memoirs and illustrations: 'Now come with me and cast your eye over the immense crowd of turbaned heads, wrapped in countless folds of the whitest silks, and bright raiment of every kind and hue, and everywhere the brilliance of gold, silver, purple, silk and satin.' The most important source of information, however, is the unique collection of garments of the sultans and their families preserved in the Topkapi Palace Museum in Istanbul. There are about 2,500 pieces, mainly kaftan robes, but also trousers, shirts, caps, sashes and turban lengths. On the death of a sultan, his clothing was stored in bundles, to which labels with the owner's name and other information were sewn. In theory this should have provided an accurate list of Ottoman imperial clothing dating from the late 15th century onwards, but labels have been lost or incorrectly replaced when inventories were taken. Although some garments are dated and attributed to individual sultans, the collection is most significant as evidence of both style and textile design.

In addition to information gathered from garments and archives, a number of portraits of the Ottoman sultans reveal a formal dress code that was dominated by men, because women, however much influence they exerted, did not have a public role. The principles of this code were both classic and versatile, based on long garments of simple shape and cut, worn in layers to display the luxurious textiles essential to the pageantry of court ritual. A stylized portrait of Süleyman (opposite) from an illustrated history of the Ottoman sultans by the court chronicler Seyyid Lokman (produced in various editions from the mid 16th century onwards) depicts the sultan in middle age, a serious, fully bearded figure dressed in richly coloured garments to emphasize the imperial image. The portrait shows him formally clad in three kaftans of contrasting shape, texture and colour. Over a kaftan of plain green atlas silk he wears an *entari*— a garment with wide elbow-length sleeves made of a rich blue *kemha* silk woven in gold with a combination of *cintamani* (stylized double ribbons and Chinese cloud scrolls). His third kaftan is a voluminous garment made of

1538	1557	1558	1566	1571	1581
Sinan is appointed as chief imperial architect. He is responsible for all major buildings in Constantinople and the Ottoman provinces.	After ten years' work, Sinan completes the Süleymaniye, the grandest architectural complex in Constantinople.	The *Süleymanname*, a sumptuously illustrated five-volume chronicle of the history and achievements of the Ottoman dynasty, is completed.	Süleyman dies on campaign in Hungary and is later buried in a splendid tomb in the Süleymaniye complex next to that of his wife, Hürrem.	Don John of Austria defeats the Ottoman navy at the Battle of Lepanto, located on the Gulf of Corinth.	Diplomatic negotiations take place between Queen Elizabeth I and Sultan Murat III. The Levant Company of 'Turkey Merchants' is founded.

OTTOMAN COURT DRESS 59

3 Extravagantly dressed in garments made from the most luxurious fabric, Sultan Selim II is depicted firing an arrow at a target held by the court falconer (16th century).

4 This polychrome silk brocade (*kemha*) kaftan with fur lining (mid to late 16th century) may have formed part of the wardrobe of Sultan Selim II.

orange *kemha* silk and lined with ermine that has floor-length trailing sleeves with slits at the shoulders. Other contemporary Ottoman court paintings from Seyyid Lokman's history, especially the series of portraits of sultans Süleyman, his son Selim II and Ahmet I (see p.62), also indicate how the clothes were worn. Records in the archives of the Topkapi Palace confirm, through inventories of garments, registers of craftsmen, accounts of wages, salaries and allowance, and orders for textiles, the formidable bureaucracy that was necessary to maintain the Ottoman dress system.

The principal garment of Ottoman court dress was the kaftan, an open, ankle-length robe of straight cut. During the daily business of court life and administration, kaftans of plain atlas silk were worn—usually red, green and blue—both by officials and even by the sultan himself. The garment was shaped at the sides and centre front, and this was achieved by adding triangular sections extending from the waist to the hem. Experienced tailors were required to match the motifs of patterned textiles to ensure smooth joins, but standards of tailoring varied considerably and one contemporary note is sharply critical: 'How could you sew the kaftans in such a poor fashion? How could anyone wear such a garment? Who in the world would even put on these black trousers? Have you never heard of fabrics of scarlet or white atlas?'

During the mid 16th century, the new workshops in Constantinople prospered as they strove to meet the Ottoman court's demand for textiles. They were located in the first court of the Topkapi Palace, along with other specialist workshops, and also in the city where they were able to accept private commissions. Three main groups of silk textiles—atlas, *kemha* and *kadife*—were woven for garments in lengths that could be cut and tailored as required. The most versatile was atlas, which was a plain silk in satin-faced weave produced in a range of colours: white, scarlet, green, blue, black and purple. Figured silk brocades, collectively known as *kemha*, of complex weave and rich design were used for formal garments. Kadife was a velvet of dark rich red or green, and sometimes black, often in the form known as catma, in which designs were woven in a combination of cut silk pile and voided areas worked in gold thread. There are also examples of garments made of Italian velvet and silk in the Topkapi Palace because the Ottomans liked these fabrics and local production was not enough to fulfil the court's demands. Eventually, Italian designs influenced those of Turkish velvets so much that it is difficult to distinguish between them.

Seraser, a luxurious brocade of gold and silver threads woven with large bold motifs, was also used for kaftans, particularly those with long trailing sleeves, and for matching trousers. Sultan Selim II had a more flamboyant taste in clothes than his father, who in general favoured simple clothing, and wore a kaftan of gold and a richly patterned silk *entari*. The design of repeated medallions and stems interwoven with tulips and other flowers (opposite), woven in red, blue, yellow and white silk, and lined with fine grey squirrel fur, is comparable to that of a mid-16th-century kaftan in the collections of the Topkapi Palace (right). It is possible that this garment may have belonged to Selim's wardrobe. Essential for the completion of Ottoman official dress was the turban, worn by the sultans and senior ranks of the administration at all public occasions. Lengths of fine white cotton or linen were coiled in towers around tall caps of quilted silk brocade.

Ceremonies required special garments. A sultan's burial was marked by sombre clothes: kaftans of atlas and velvet in black, dark blue, purple and green were worn by his successor and mourners as they followed the funeral procession. Royal tombs were draped with garments and textiles and furnished with a turban, jewellery and other possessions. Multiple burials, including those of women and children, within the tombs of Murat III and Ahmet I contained groups of small kaftan robes of silk velvet and brocades. These tombs were periodically cleared of their contents but some of the artefacts are now in the collections of the Turkish and Islamic Art Museum in Istanbul. After accession ceremonies, in order to acknowledge the new ruler's legitimacy, the sultan participated in a life of public ceremonies and processions, in which he displayed the power of the Ottoman state through his dress. These centred on the regular procession of the sultan to one of Constantinople's great mosques every Friday, to observe the midday prayers, the celebrations of the circumcisions of his sons, the formal receptions of ambassadors and occasionally his triumphant returns from successful campaigns. Despite the general stagnation of the Ottoman Empire from the 17th century onwards, the Ottoman dress code survived remarkably well until the 19th century, when the reformist Sultan Mahmut II replaced it with the European frock coat and trousers—a symbol of modernity and progress. **JS**

Layered Garment 17th century
MEN'S COURT DRESS

Portrait of Ahmet I by
Seyyid Lokman (17th century).

NAVIGATOR

During the late 16th century, biographies of Ottoman sultans were written and illustrated with portraits that, although idealized, offer a reasonable likeness of each ruler. Additionally, from the early 17th century onwards, a taste developed for single-figure studies of fashionably dressed young men and women. The portrait of Ahmet I, who became sultan in 1603, at the age of thirteen, is an example of this relatively informal tradition.

Delicately painted in opaque watercolours on finely polished paper, it presents the sultan as a handsome, dignified, beautifully dressed and cultured young man. Seated within a richly furnished kiosk, Ahmet wears two ankle-length silk kaftan robes of contrasting colour and shape. A green under-robe with long tight sleeves is fastened from neck to waist by a row of closely spaced buttons of plaited gold thread. An orange outer robe, lined with ermine and decorated with bands of gold-frogged braid, is stylishly worn with only the right arm thrust into a sleeve so that both garments are fully displayed. A tall, smoothly coiled white turban with aigrettes of black feathers, jewellery and yellow leather boots complete his court dress. **JS**

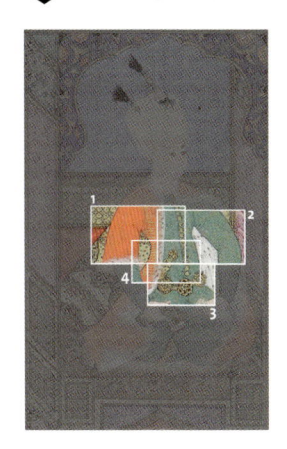

FOCAL POINTS

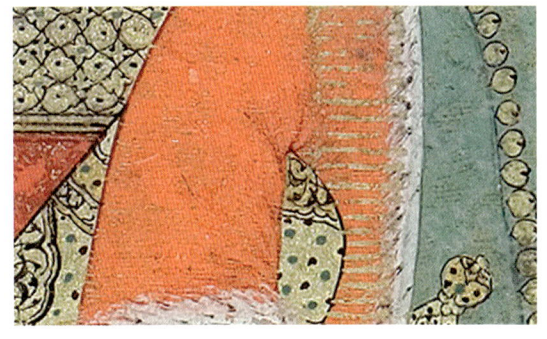

1 ORANGE ROBE
The orange robe is painted with fine gold horizontal hatched lines to imitate the surface sheen of the plain monochrome atlas silk. This was a versatile fabric used equally for garments, linings and facings. Ahmet's garment is additionally lined with ermine.

2 GREEN ROBE
The green robe is painted with a repeated arabesque foliage design of flat leaves. They are filled with horizontal hatched lines in gold, against a continuous network of grey tendrils, to represent *serenk*, a supple brocaded silk.

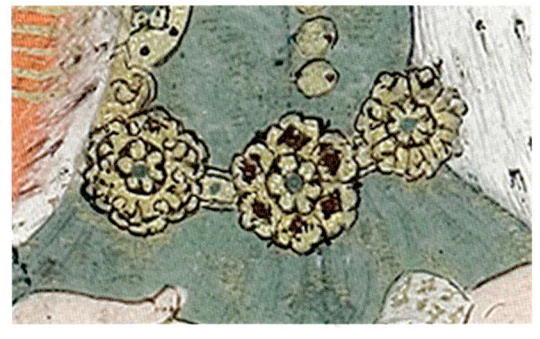

3 LINKED GOLD BELT
The belt is made of linked gold and bejewelled plaques, mounted on leather. Worn over the kaftan, it is a fashionable and tasteful accessory. However, Ottoman court jewellery was relatively austere because the textiles of garments were so richly patterned.

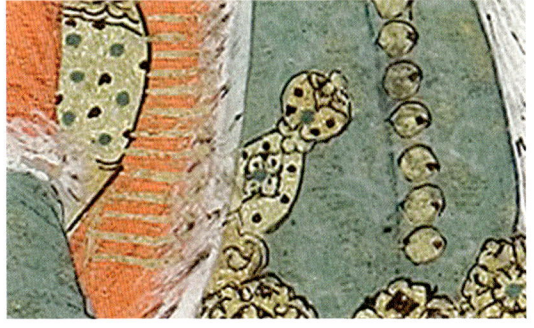

4 BEJEWELLED DAGGER
The dagger is an elegant court accessory whose finely worked steel blade is engraved and inlaid with gold foliage. The hilt may have been carved from semi-precious stones, such as jade and rock crystal, and inscribed with quotations from Ottoman poetry.

INDIAN DRESS — MUGHAL PERIOD

1. An illustration from c. 1650 shows the second Mughal emperor Humayun wearing the elaborate plumed style of turban he is believed to have invented.

2. Emperor Akbar favoured the flat Rajput turban he is seen wearing in this painting from the 16th-century *Book of Akbar*.

3. A 17th-century portrait of the first Mughal emperor Babur depicts him wearing Central Asian-influenced dress.

Fashions throughout the Indian subcontinent during Mughal rule (1526—1858) reflected the mix of Muslim and Hindu subjects living there. The Mughals were Muslims who originated in Central Asia and were descended from the Mongolian ruler Genghis Khan. Initially Mughal dress retained a strong Central Asian influence but as the Mughal Empire grew under Emperor Akbar, who reigned from 1556 to 1605, and his successors from the late 16th century onwards, it incorporated aspects of dress from Hindu Rajput culture. It was not until the 18th century, with the increased Western presence in India, that European styles started to infiltrate Mughal dress.

Dress in the Indian subcontinent has always followed two distinct but sometimes interwoven basic styles: those of the wrapped or draped garment— the sari (see p.70), the *dhoti*, the shawl and the turban—and the tailored or sewn, such as trousers and body-hugging coats and jackets (see p.68). The existence of two contrasting styles is the result of contact with successive

KEY EVENTS

1526	1530	1556	1600	1605	1615
Babur defeats Ibrahim Lodhi at the Battle of Panipat and founds the Mughal Empire in India.	Babur's son, Humayun, becomes the second Mughal emperor.	Akbar ascends the Mughal throne. He encourages art, culture and religious tolerance and is influential in creating new styles in dress.	The East India Company is founded by Royal Charter and begins trading between England and India.	Akbar's son, Jahangir, succeeds to the Mughal throne. The Mughal school of painting reaches a peak during his reign.	The Mughals grant England the right to trade and establish factories in exchange for English naval protection against the Portuguese.

64 500 BC–1599

invaders, traders and other visitors, who entered India from the beginning of the Christian era onwards. All these foreigners, including the Muslim Mughals and the English, favoured fitted coats and trousers in contrast to the draped clothing of the indigenous Indians. Eastern and southern regions of the subcontinent were less penetrated by visitors and tended to retain the traditional styles of simple draped garments more than the north and west, which were closer to the homelands of Central Asian and Muslim invaders and became the centres of the empires they created. In these centres, including the Mughal capitals of Delhi, Agra and Lahore, tailored garments such as shirts (*kurta* and *kameez*) and trousers (*paijama* and *shalwar*) predominated as indeed they do today. Within this broad geographical division between the tailored and the draped garment, other factors such as wealth, religion and occupation, as well as local styles and materials, have always affected regional dress.

Tailored clothing established its influence in the Indian subcontinent with the foundation of the Muslim sultanate of Delhi in the 12th century. Islamic conventions of female modesty had a strong influence on north Indian society and led to the introduction not only of veils to cover the face in public, but also the division of houses into male and female living quarters, a practice widely adopted by both Muslims and Hindus. The predominance of cut and sewn garments continued under the Mughals, whose long rule over much of India developed into one of the world's great empires, which lasted until 1858 — in name at least.

The first Mughal emperor, Babur, who reigned from 1526 to 1530, is always shown in paintings dressed in the Central Asian style (below right), which reflected his birthplace and origins in present-day Uzbekistan and Afghanistan. This style of costume included a round turban and a long, loose decorated coat, sometimes with short sleeves, worn over a thinner robe. For formal gatherings he often wore a Chinese-influenced 'cloud collar' — a four-pointed piece of fabric usually decorated with a woven or embroidered pattern that lay over the shoulders. Babur's son, Humayun, who reigned from 1530 to 1540, continued to favour Central Asian dress, although he modified the turban to create a distinctive headdress known as the *Taj-i 'Izzat* or 'Crown of Glory'. This consisted of a turban folded into points around a tall cap, with a narrow scarf wound around it (opposite). This style derived from his period of exile at the Iranian court, and its use was abandoned by the Mughals after Humayun's reign.

It was during the reign of Humayun's son Akbar, who is generally regarded as the greatest of the Mughal emperors, that a recognizably Mughal style of dress began to evolve. Akbar incorporated the powerful Hindu Rajputs into the empire by marriage and conquest at the end of the 16th century. He adopted several of their fashions, including the flat Rajput turban (above right), which was in contrast to the much rounder, Iranian style favoured by his Muslim predecessors. Akbar is even depicted in some paintings dressed in the Hindu

1615	1628	1632	1757	1857	1858
James I sends Thomas Roe as the first English ambassador to the Mughal court.	Shah Jahan becomes emperor. His reign is a golden age of Mughal architecture.	Shah Jahan begins building the Taj Mahal palace as a memorial to his third wife, Mumtaz Mahal.	The Battle of Plassey marks the beginning of the British East India Company's rule in India.	The Indian Rebellion, also known as India's First War of Independence, takes place.	The Mughal Empire is supplanted by the British Raj and the last Mughal emperor Bahadur Shah II is sent into exile in Burma.

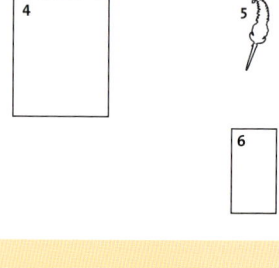

4 This Muslim lady, from a 17th-century Mughal painting, is wearing trousers under a sheer robe, with an additional large head covering. Tailored trousers were particularly popular among Muslim women both at court and in everyday life.

5 A turban ornament made of emeralds, rubies and crystals set in jade. A ring behind the rosette would have held a feather plume. The wearing of plumes in Mughal turbans signified royal status.

6 A 17th-century portrait of the son of the Hindu Rajput ruler of Mewar. He wears a *chakdar jama* tied to the left. The hemline of the diaphanous *jama* is constructed so that the corners hang down like points.

style—bare-chested but for a light muslin shawl around his shoulders, with a sarong-like *lungi* wrapped around his hips and lower body. More commonly, he and his contemporaries are shown wearing the *jama*, a tailored robe tied at the side of the chest. The *jama* was probably an adaptation of the pre-Mughal Indian *angarkha* (literally, 'body-protector'), but the tight-legged trousers (*paijama*) worn with it were a Muslim innovation.

Akbar took a personal interest in fashion and held strong ideas about dress. He is credited with the invention of several Mughal fashions, such as the *chakdar* (or split-sided) *jama*, which had distinctive points around the hem (opposite below), and the practice of wearing two Kashmir shawls together, often of two contrasting colours. He also introduced a rule that Muslims should tie their *jamas* on the right of their chests, and Hindus on the left. Although this does not seem to have been adhered to rigorously, it is often a useful guide when trying to identify courtiers in paintings of the time. Akbar and his courtiers, as well as his successors, are frequently shown wearing a *jama* in plain white cotton, which was most likely made from the fine muslin that came as tribute to the Mughal court from Bengal after its conquest in 1576.

The high point of the Mughal Empire spanned the reigns of Akbar and his successors Jahangir, who reigned from 1605 to 1627, and Shah Jahan, whose reign lasted from 1628 to 1658. Fashion during this period retained the main features of Akbar's reign, with tailored coats and trousers in exquisite materials being the basis of fashionable dress for both men and women. There was an emphasis on fine materials rather than lavish surface textures. Fine, sheer muslin, for example, was prized more highly than heavy velvet for courtly dress. This preference clearly arose from the hot climate in which very thin materials were preferable to thick ones, but it also celebrated the strengths of local textile production. Fine Bengali muslins were renowned both in India and abroad, and the silks of Gujarat were embellished with gold to make a lavish spectacle in dress and furnishings at court.

Although an exquisite Mughal hunting coat from the early 17th century (see p.68) has survived, almost no other items of dress exist from before the 19th century. However, the splendid detailed miniature paintings and manuscript illustrations of the period provide a wealth of information on the dress and furnishings of the courts. These illustrations demonstrate how similar the basic elements of male and female dress were at the Mughal court: diaphanous muslin fabrics were favoured for coats as they allowed the colourfully patterned trousers beneath to be seen. For women, the coat was often replaced by a bodice and the outfit completed by a large, thin, rectangular piece of cloth in a contrasting colour that would be used to envelop the upper body and, when necessary, the face. Rajput women traditionally wore gathered skirts (*ghaghra*) and bodices (*choli*) with a large rectangular veil (*odhni*) covering the upper part of their body rather than the trousers (opposite) and tailored garments favoured by Muslim women. These Hindu fashions are also shown in Mughal paintings and again provide a means of identifying Hindu courtiers. Men accessorized their outfits with decorative turbans adorned with jewels or ornaments (right), ropes of pearls and lavishly decorated sashes (*patka*) with patterned ends. Shoes for both sexes were made of fabric or soft leather in slipper form that could be easily removed when entering a building. These were beautifully embroidered or made of plain red velvet.

Alongside the tailored styles favoured at the Mughal court, the draped tradition continued to dominate in many parts of India during the time of the Mughal Empire, especially in the largely Hindu south and east. Predominant among these draped garments were the sari, the main women's wrapped garment, and the *dhoti* or wrapped waistcloth, the sari's male equivalent. Saris vary in length from about 6 to 29 feet (2 to 9 m). The shortest is just long enough to cover the body and is used by village women, whereas the longest, which lends itself to elaborate pleats and drapes, is worn by wealthy elite groups. Materials ranged from rough cotton to lavish woven and gold-embroidered silks for weddings and formal occasions. Although the style of wrapping a sari has become more standardized through the influence of films and television, traditionally there are dozens of regional variations. Whereas some styles favour the decorative end border (*pallu*) falling down the wearer's back, women in some regions wear the *pallu* in front of the body. Saris used by rural women have to allow active movement and for that reason often have the ends tucked in rather than loose. In a pragmatic solution to this problem, the rural and coastal women of Maharashtra traditionally wear the end of the sari drawn up between the legs and tucked in at the back, very much like a man's *dhoti*, which separates the legs while keeping them covered.

Local weaving, printing and embroidery techniques for sari and *dhoti* fabrics were widespread. While some, such as fine muslin or weaving in gold-wrapped thread (*zari*), were considered appropriate for use by the Mughal or local courts, other techniques remained popular within a localized area. Odisha (formerly Orissa) in eastern India, for example, traditionally produced hand-tied *ikat* textiles, which were, and still are, immensely popular locally but did not find favour at a courtly level. The spotted and zigzag patterned *bandhani* (tie-dye) of Rajasthan, on the other hand, enjoyed a vogue under the Emperor Jahangir because he favoured tie-dyed turbans and sashes, perhaps as a mark of respect for the Rajput origins of both his mother and his wife. **RC**

Mughal Hunting Coat 1620–50
MEN'S COURT DRESS

NAVIGATOR

This exquisitely embroidered coat is a unique surviving example of Mughal court dress. It is made of white silk-satin embroidered in silk chain stitch with images of flowers and animals, including peacocks, lions and deer. The area around the neck has been left free of embroidery because it would have had a separate fur collar attached. Similar short coats are often seen in Mughal miniature paintings of the 17th century. The extremely high quality of the embroidery suggests that it was made for an emperor, either Jahangir or his son Shah Jahan. Jahangir recounts in his memoirs, *The Jahangirnama* or *Tuzuk-i Jahangiri*, that he restricted the wearing of certain garments and fabrics to himself or those to whom he gave them as gifts. These items included a coat that he called a *nadiri* (rarity), which he described as being of thigh length and sleeveless, like this one. He also mentioned that in Iran such coats were called *kurdi* or 'Kurdish'. Patterned sleeveless coats with fur collars are illustrated in the memoirs of Shah Jahan. The magnificent manuscript *The Padshahnama* gives a remarkably accurate picture of life at the Mughal court, including its lavish furnishings and dress. The style of the coat's embroidery, with its naturalistic images of flowers and animals, may have been influenced by English embroidery of the same period. The fine chain-stitch embroidery, however, would have been the work of professional male embroiderers from Gujarat in western India, who had adapted this style of embroidery from leatherworking. **RC**

FOCAL POINTS

1 NATURALISTIC DESIGN
The naturalistic flowers on this coat are partly derived from European books and prints that were brought to the Mughal court from the late 16th century onwards by Western traders, missionaries and diplomats. The design, with its scenes of animals beside water, also shows parallels with English embroideries of the time. It is clear from Jahangir's memoirs that he admired the English embroideries shown to him by the English ambassador to his court, Thomas Roe.

2 CHAIN-STITCH EMBROIDERY
Embroidery in India varies according to the region from which it originates. The chain-stitch embroidery on this coat is typical of the exquisite work done in Gujarat in western India. It first developed as a way of decorating leatherwork using a special hooked tool called an *ari*. Gujarati embroidery was so highly prized that it was commissioned for both the Mughal court and for the export market to England from the 17th century onwards.

▲ An early 17th-century painting of Emperor Shah Jahan shows the Mughal ruler riding a pale grey horse through a landscape. He is wearing a sleeveless embroidered hunting coat.

INDIAN DRESS — MUGHAL PERIOD 69

Sari 18th century
WOMEN'S GARMENT

A barber and his wife (c. 1770).

The sari has been the traditional women's garment of the Indian subcontinent for centuries, although many Muslim women favoured tailored shirts and trousers and certain Hindu groups in western India traditionally wore *ghaghra* (skirts) and *choli* (short blouses). In this painting from Thanjavur in Tamil Nadu, a barber's wife can be seen dressed in the traditional draped sari with her husband wearing the *dhoti*, its male equivalent. The woman wears a short bodice underneath: it has sometimes been suggested that the bodice was introduced by Muslims or Westerners, but tailored bodices have a much longer history in India. Essentially a long piece of cloth wrapped around the body, the sari cloth varied tremendously in length and breadth, with simple saris worn by village women measuring 18 inches (45 cm) by 70 inches (180 cm), while the lavish 'nine-yard saris' of central India measured about 43 inches (110 cm) by 30 feet (9 m). The use of large amounts of cloth to swathe the body was a clear indication of affluence: a sari that merely covered the body marked a person with no money for extra cloth. Materials varied from sumptuous silk and gold-wrapped thread used in the saris of Varanasi and Kanchipuram, to hand-spun, hand-woven cotton in rural examples. A sari could be draped in innumerable ways, with each region of India traditionally having its own style. **RC**

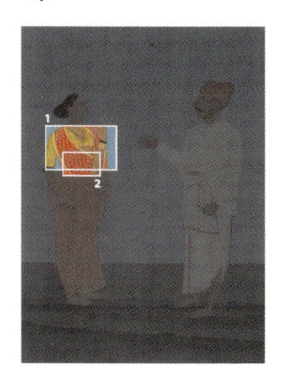

NAVIGATOR

👁 FOCAL POINTS

1 DRAPING
The drape of the sari is typical of south India, with the lower portion pleated and wrapped around the waist and the remainder draped so that it can either be worn pulled across the front or falling down the back.

2 PATTERN
The simple pattern of the fabric is a repeat design of stylized leaf motifs trimmed with plain narrow borders on both edges. Red is a popular colour for saris, especially in south India where it is considered auspicious.

▲ Sari (detail) of woven silk and gold-wrapped thread (c. 1850). The *pallu* (decorative end) of the lavish fabric includes a row of stylized floral motifs called *butas*, derived from Kashmiri shawl patterns.

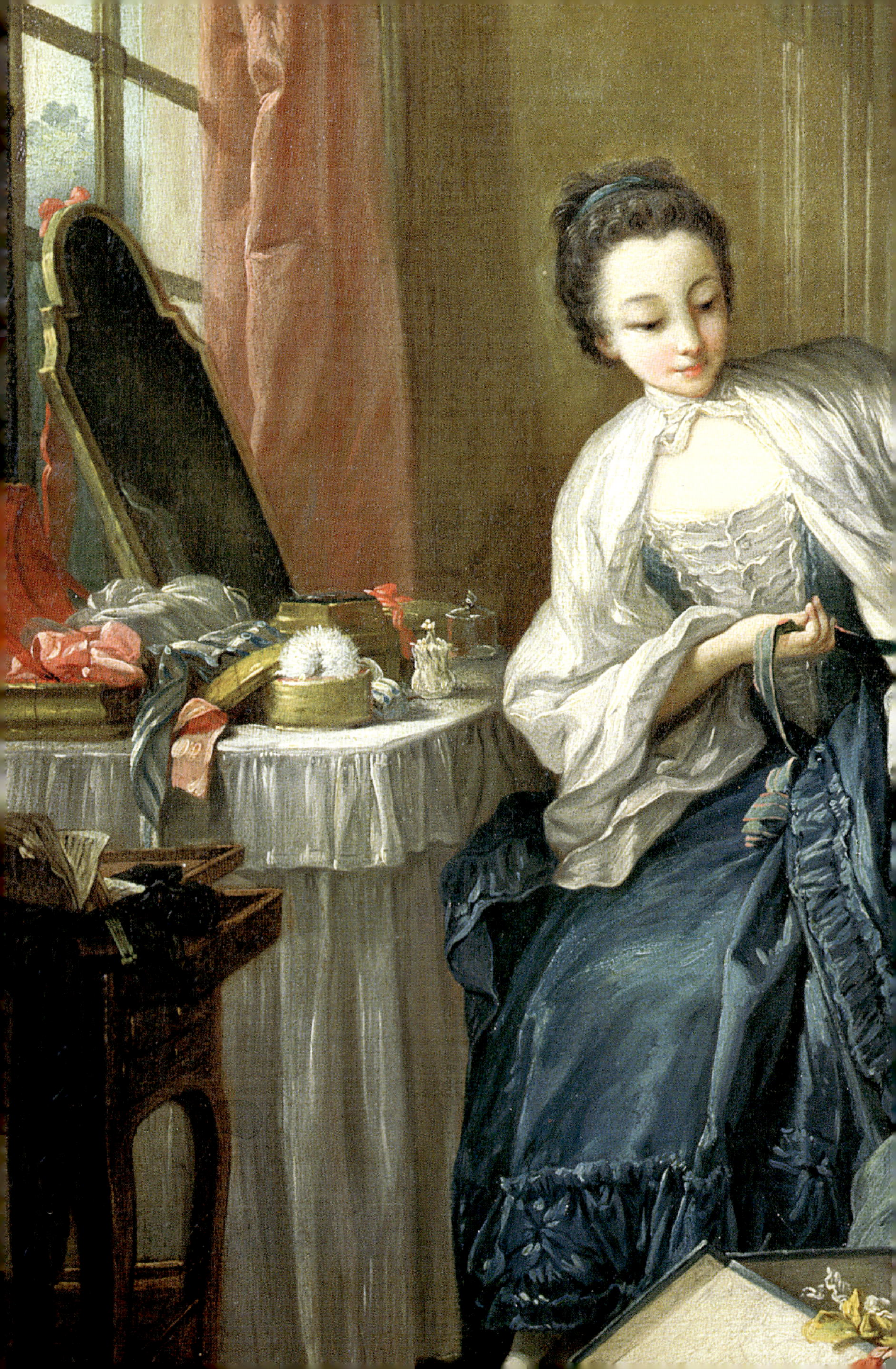

2 | 1600 TO 1799

JAPANESE DRESS – EDO PERIOD 74

CHARLES I AND THE COMMONWEALTH 78

CHINESE DRESS – EARLY QING DYNASTY 82

FRENCH COURT DRESS 86

RESTORATION FASHION 90

THE BIRTH OF MODERN FASHION 94

SCOTTISH TARTAN 102

ROCOCO ELEGANCE 106

THE ENGLISH GENTLEMAN 116

NEOCLASSICAL STYLES 120

JAPANESE DRESS – EDO PERIOD

The Edo period (1603–1867) was an era of unprecedented political stability, economic growth and urban expansion in Japan. Kyoto remained the centre of aristocratic culture and luxury production, whereas Edo (present-day Tokyo) developed into one of the largest cities in the world, a city in which the critical mass of population and wealth led to an extensive fashionable dress culture. The primary consumers of dress were the samurai, who made up about 10 per cent of the population. However, the merchant and artisan classes, who benefited most from peace and prosperity, presented a continuous challenge to the established order. The rigid hierarchy of Tokugawa Japan meant that wealth could not be used to improve status directly. Instead, various other strategies of consumption and display were employed, thereby stimulating an extensive textile industry (above).

As clothing became a key indicator of rising affluence, and as aesthetic sensibilities were used as a challenge to social order, sumptuary laws were introduced that regulated the fabric, techniques and colours used by different classes. Although the laws were not enforced consistently, which led to regular shifts between opulence and restraint, they did create various codes of subtlety. The use of restricted colours and fabrics for undergarments and linings was popular as an understated means of demonstrating wealth and personal style. Such fabrics could only be glimpsed underneath the plainer, rougher outer side of the kimono, a key aesthetic in Japanese clothing.

KEY EVENTS

1603	1633	1635	1639	1641	1657
The emperor appoints Tokugawa Ieyasu as shogun, who moves his government to Edo and founds the Tokugawa dynasty of shoguns.	Tokugawa Iemitsu forbids travelling abroad and reading foreign books.	Tokugawa Iemitsu formalizes the system of mandatory alternate residence (sankin kotai) for feudal lords and their households in Edo.	Edicts establishing national seclusion (sakoku rei) are completed. All Westerners except the Dutch are prohibited from entering Japan.	Tokugawa Iemitsu bans all foreigners, except Chinese and Dutch citizens, from Japan.	The Great Fire of Meireki, allegedly started when a cursed kimono was cremated, destroys most of Edo and kills more than 100,000 people.

One of the principal reasons for the stability and wealth of the Edo period was the highly influential policy of *sankin kotai* (alternate residence), which was in effect from 1635 to 1862. Although its details changed throughout the 260 years of Tokugawa rule, in general it required that all the daimyo landed lords move periodically between their home provinces and Edo. The expenditure necessary to maintain lavish residences in two places and to travel between them discouraged fighting between domains, and also generated an extraordinary amount of economic and cultural activity. The deprovincialization of the backwaters of Japan began at this point as a result of the compulsory stay in Edo, which fuelled a great flow of information and transfer of fashions from the city to the periphery.

The concentration of the ruling classes created ideal conditions for a culture of competition through fashion and displays of wealth and style. However, unlike the situation at Louis XIV's palace in Versailles in France, Japanese value systems would not allow decadence to be taken too far. One reason for this was that the concentration of wealth was never as extreme as it was in France, because the Tokugawa policy on trade was rather free (although Japan was closed to foreign investment). Throughout the Edo period distribution networks developed and the industrial takeover of household crafts and specializations progressed. Currency stability, banking and insurance were all reasonably mature, and trade became a key source of wealth unhindered by excessive tariffs or levies. From comparatively early on, the merchant class flourished economically, while the samurai class was largely inactive during this time of peace. The pleasures of consumption and styling oneself were available in Edo as the distribution of resources slowly shifted among classes. The sumptuary laws were restraints on consumption, but illicit fashions in violation of the laws were common and high-ranking courtesans frequently dressed according to the height of fashion (see p.76).

From the middle of the Edo period, one of the most important developments in the kimono industry, *yuzen* (right), was perfected by Miyazaki Yuzen. It is a method of dyeing cloth in many colours using stencils and rice paste and remains at the heart of kimono high culture. This method allowed for the imitation of more complex brocades and it is thought that once it was introduced, twenty other styles of dyeing fabric became redundant. The superior water resistance and stable colour of *yuzen* meant that the production of clothing was greatly improved, which in turn extended the parameters of Edo fashion. Despite this versatile invention, political factors dominated, or at least placed firm parameters around, the types of clothing that could be worn and which fashions came into existence in Edo period Japan. Most influentially, the *sakoku* (national seclusion) policy, which remained in place until 1854, ensured that there was virtually no influence from the outside world on clothing within Japan. **TS**

1 This woodblock triptych (*c.* 1794) by Kitagawa Utamaro depicts women sorting fabrics and sewing garments.

2 This silk crêpe kimono fabric (*c.* 1850) was resist-dyed using the *yuzen* technique and features stencilling and embroidery. The motifs illustrate the tale of Urashima Taro.

1700	1700	1789	1841	1854	1867
The golden age of Kabuki theatre and *ukiyo-e* woodblock prints begins; the influence of both can be seen in kimono patterns.	*Yuzen* dyeing is perfected by Miyazaki Yuzen in Kyoto.	Unlicensed brothels are banned; many sex workers move to the Edo district Yoshiwara, ending its exclusive reputation and leading to the rise of geisha.	The Tenpo reforms are instituted, including harsh sumptuary edicts banning many forms of luxuries in an attempt to control morality and social order.	The United States forces Japan to sign a trade agreement (Treaty of Kanagawa), which reopens Japan to foreigners after two centuries.	Tokugawa Yoshinobu resigns, the Tokugawa dynasty ends and Emperor Meiji is restored. The capital is relocated to the renamed Tokyo.

Courtesan Dress Late Edo period
WOMEN'S DRESS

Courtesans Strolling Beneath Cherry Trees Before the Daikokuya Teahouse by Kitagawa Utamaro (c. 1789).

Much of the late Edo period was marked by both extravagance and strict sumptuary laws. Being too inventive or showy in fashion was a risky business and many high-profile prosecutions against transgressors of the set order were recorded. One place where fashion was somewhat freer from these concerns was the Yoshiwara pleasure quarter, not only because of its status as a world apart but also because of its patronage by members of the most powerful class.

Top-ranking courtesans defined chic, and books were written about their style and beauty. They could wear extravagant kimonos accessorized with expensive and elaborate hair decorations without offending class sensibilities because social classes were not strictly divided in the Yoshiwara district, where a commoner would be served as equal to a samurai, as long as he could pay. This freedom from the rest of the highly ordered society also meant that many different fashions were seen. Kimonos that featured checked patterns—bold and masculine—contrasted with floral designs were considered sexually ambiguous and therefore erotic. Obi fashion fluctuated greatly: huge knots were sometimes popular and there were alternating trends between tying at the front and at the back. In modern times knots and sizes were greatly standardized. **TS**

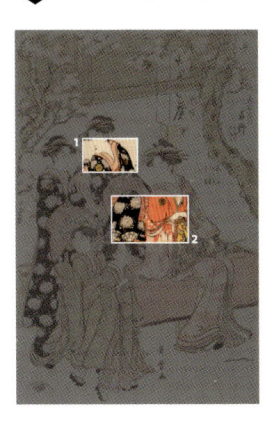

NAVIGATOR

FOCAL POINTS

1 SHOULDERS
An outer robe that was slightly falling off the shoulders was considered alluring. The neck was seen as one of the most sexually charged parts of a woman's body, so to wear one's hair up and have one's robe slightly loose was the equivalent of Regency décolletage.

2 ROBES
Prostitutes traditionally wore plain blue robes but frequently were more experimental in their fashion and wore colourful silk kimonos. For a courtesan, red was considered erotic, especially when used in contrast to the purity of white.

▲ This kimono was worn by a member of the samurai class. The design was created using the *chaya-zome* paste-resist technique, which was reserved for the summer robes of top-ranking samurai.

CHARLES I AND THE COMMONWEALTH

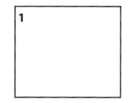

1. This portrait by Sir Anthony van Dyck depicts Charles I and Queen Henrietta Maria with their two eldest children (1632).

2. Queen Henrietta Maria's silver satin bodice is laced with coral ribbon (1632).

3. Robert Walker portrays Oliver Cromwell in fashionable dress (17th century).

The restrained elegance and sombre hues of the court of Charles I relinquished the extravagances and emphasis on male beauty of the Jacobean era, thereby discarding the ruff and eschewing the bombast in doublet and hose to produce a more etiolated silhouette. The apparently simple line of the clothes belied their romanticism, and the less rigid silhouette was embellished with an abundance of ribbons formed into rosettes and used to highlight various parts of the costume: breeches, sleeves and shoes. Although unpatterned, the fabrics were rich, and the starkness of white linen and lace provided a dramatic counterpoint to the preferred colour of black. A discerning patron of the arts, Charles I invited distinguished painters to his London court, such as Sir Anthony van Dyck, who provided enduring images of the Stuart court that depicted the various fashions, including the pointed beard and moustache sported by Charles I himself (above).

The ruff was replaced with a deep soft-falling collar, initially constructed from two or three layers of material, edged in lace and tied with cords. This allowed for the hair to grow to shoulder length, where it was curled into a beribboned lovelock. After 1630 the doublet developed into a short-waisted

KEY EVENTS

1620s	1620s	1625	1626	1630s	1630s
The virago sleeve comes into fashion for women. The style divides a full sleeve into two puffs secured by a ribbon tied above the elbow.	Stiff 'whisk' collars give way to a more relaxed style, known as the 'falling' collar, in soft scallop-edged lace.	Charles I marries the Catholic Princess Henrietta Maria of France, the daughter of Marie de Medici, in Canterbury Cathedral.	Charles I is crowned on 2 February at Westminster Abbey, but without his wife at his side.	Henrietta Maria retains the designer Inigo Jones, the first significant British architect of the modern period, as her surveyor of works.	Womenswear features higher waistlines and lower necklines. Women expose their lower arms with elbow-length sleeves.

jacket with a fairly deep skirt, ending in a point at the front. It was worn left open from the middle of the breast in order to show the shirt bulging out over the breeches; for ease of movement it was also occasionally constructed with a slit in the back. The complicated slashing of the sleeves of earlier days was replaced with one long vertical cut in the front, which was caught once at the elbow, thus allowing the shirt sleeve to show. Sleeves ended in a deep turn-back cuff, sometimes buttoned and with a contrasting lining. The two types of breeches included long breeches decorated at the knee with a bunch of coloured ribbons and breeches of the same width all the way down, loose at the knee and ornamented with a row of points (ribbons tied in bows ending in metal points). The longer breeches were tucked into 'bucket top', or 'funnel', leather boots, which were also worn indoors and lined with silk or leather and trimmed with lace. Boots, cloaks and hats were all worn with a flourish. Large circular cloaks with deep collars were tied at the neck with cords, and hats were positioned on the side of the head, turned up at the front and trimmed with feathers.

Taking the lead from the French-born queen, Henrietta Maria, the farthingale was no longer worn, and the rigidity and extent of the corset were greatly reduced. Women's dress consisted of a bodice, laced with silk ribbon at the front and covered with a plastron, a petticoat and a gown, which was open all the way down the front and gathered up to reveal the skirt beneath. Elaborate lawn collars edged in lace came down well over the shoulders (right). Sleeves were full and, like the men's doublet, were cut in two to display the fabric beneath. Worn with long silk or kid gloves, they were finished with deep falling cuffs of lace or pleated lawn cuffs and extended just below the elbow. Women wore large circular cloaks, similar to those worn by men, or long full coats with loose sleeves. Women's hair was dressed in a coil at the back of the head with the sides curled on each side of the face. A small white lawn cap was worn indoors, and cloak hoods covered the head out of doors.

The escalating conflict and clash of ideologies between Charles I and Parliament were represented by the development of two distinct modes of dress. Cavalier (from the Latin *caballarius*, meaning horseman) was the name used by Parliamentarians for a Royalist supporter of Charles I. Rejecting aristocratic excess and influenced by the dress of the prosperous bourgeoisie of Holland, the Parliamentarians replaced lace collars with plain linen, and silk with woollen stuff; hair was cut short at the front and cropped at the jaw line (below right). Women's clothes also became much plainer: the bodice was increasingly elongated and stiffened, and the décolleté was replaced with a wider, shallower neckline, filled in with a gauze scarf. A white linen apron was worn by all women, not only domestic servants. Furs were imported from the New World and small fur or fabric muffs were carried by both men and women, as depicted in the *Winter* etching by Wenceslaus Hollar (see p.80). **MF**

1639	1640s	1641	1649	1660	1661
A series of civil wars—known as the Wars of the Three Kingdoms—begins, spreading throughout Scotland, Ireland and England.	Large hats, decorated with trailing ostrich plumes, are widely worn among courtiers. The lower classes' hats remain unadorned.	Van Dyck is succeeded by English painter William Dobson as court painter, providing portraits of leading Cavaliers in their luxurious garments.	Styles become more subdued after Charles I is executed and the Commonwealth, led by Oliver Cromwell, is established.	The Commonwealth ends and the monarchy is restored during the Restoration.	French influence leads to the introduction of shorter ribbon-covered 'petticoat breeches', so loose that they resemble a skirt.

Women's Dress 1640s
WINTER WEAR WITH MASK AND MUFF

Winter by Wenceslaus Hollar (1643).

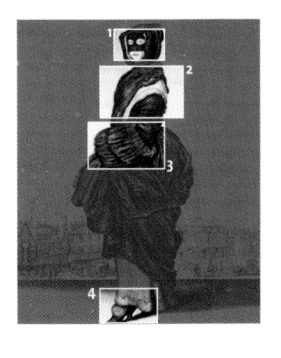

NAVIGATOR

Bohemian-born artist Wenceslaus Hollar produced a series of four etchings of the seasons, each represented by a woman wearing fashionable dress. The expressive quality of the artist's virtuosity as an etcher is apparent from the variety of fabrics and furs that he captures in the woman's garments. During the 17th century furs were plentiful in the New World, and both Britain and France devised ways of obtaining them from their North American colonies. In 1670 the Hudson's Bay Company was established by the Charter of the Governor and Company of Adventurers of England.

The *Winter* etching shows a fashionable young woman wearing a number of skirts, a fur collar, a hood and a half-mask ('loo mask') and carrying a fur muff. Tubular-style muffs became fashionable in Italy during the early 1570s, along with a variety of masks. Hollar's series of etchings provides valuable documentation of 17th-century life. The district of Cornhill in London is shown in the background of this print, with its coal fires burning, and the tower of the first Royal Exchange is visible on the right. The studied eroticism of the image is made explicit by the accompanying verse: 'The cold, not cruelty makes her weare / In winter, furs and wilde beasts haire / For a smoother skin at night / Embraceth her with more delight.' **MF**

👁 FOCAL POINTS

1 HALF-MASK
Masks were made from velvet or silk and covered the whole face except for the eyes. They were worn principally to protect the complexion against the elements, but also provided anonymity. In the *Winter* etching, the half-mask lends the purposeful figure and bold gaze of the woman ambivalent status.

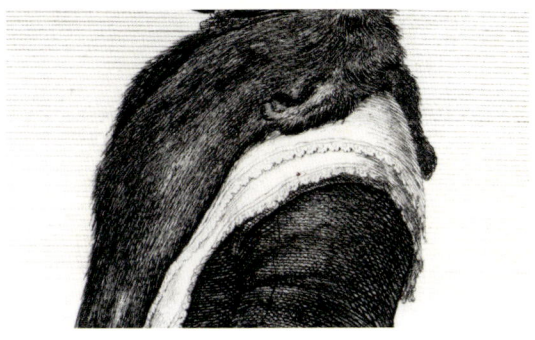

3 TUBULAR MUFF
The padded fur muff was a fashionable accessory among both men and women. It not only kept the hands warm but also had inner compartments to keep daily necessities such as handkerchiefs and money. They were often scented to counteract the odour of the streets.

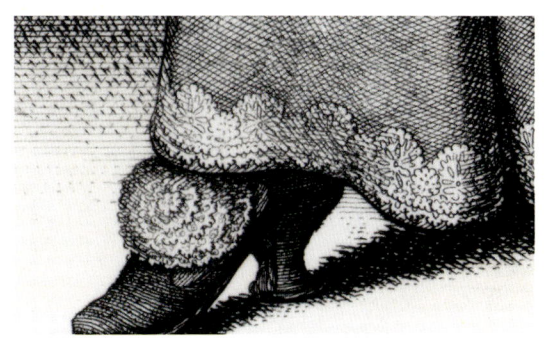

2 SABLE TIPPET
Indicative of her wealthy status, an extensive fur tippet (scarf) is loosely draped around the woman's shoulders, the ends falling together at the centre front. Tippets originated in the Middle Ages, when they were worn predominantly by men. By the 17th century they were part of a fashionable lady's wardrobe.

4 DECORATED SHOE
In order to protect her hem from the mud, the woman gathers up her heavy skirt in a coquettish gesture to reveal a patterned underskirt and a shoe with a curved Louis heel. In the mid 17th century women's shoes became more feminine in appearance and this example is decorated with a ribbon rosette.

THE HISTORY OF THE MASK

Masks were originally worn by courtesans during the 16th century, serving both decorative and practical purposes. The mask protected its wearer from the elements while riding or enjoying other outdoor pursuits, thereby preserving the pale complexion that was in vogue at the time. However, masks were also worn inside. In 1663 diarist Samuel Pepys recorded that 'it has become the fashion for ladies to wear masks to the theatre which hide their whole face'. Full-face masks were made of stiffened black or white cloth, with holes for the eyes and mouth. This enabled the wearer to enjoy theatre performances, which were prohibited for respectable women at the time, while remaining concealed. The masks were held in place by head ties, and a bead or button gripped between the teeth. Fashionable half-masks, by contrast, only covered the eyes and nose, and were frequently worn at masked balls or masquerades. Fastened to a small stick, and held up to the face by the wearer, such masks aided flirtation, which gave rise to a reputation for licentious behaviour.

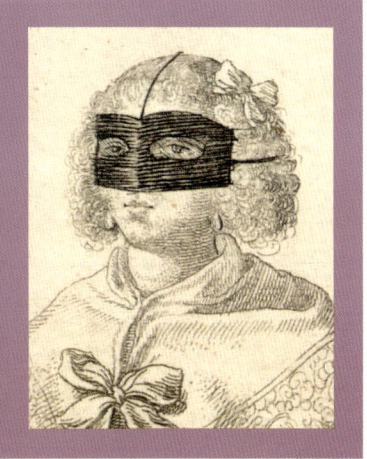

CHINESE DRESS – EARLY QING DYNASTY

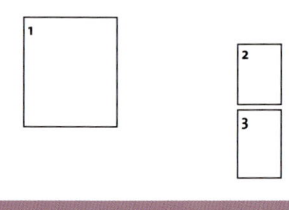

1. This portrait by an anonymous artist shows Emperor Yongzheng wearing a yellow court robe with a pearl necklace.

2. The motifs of the Twelve Symbols appeared exclusively on the court robes of the emperor.

3. Emperor Qianlong inspects a parade wearing a highly decorative suit of ceremonial armour and helmet.

In 1644 the Manchu, a minority people from northeast China, captured Beijing and established the Qing dynasty. In order to assert his authority over the entire Chinese population, the first Qing emperor ordered all male adults to shave their foreheads and wear Manchu-style clothes. At the same time the Manchu rulers were keen to gain the goodwill of the Han Chinese, who made up more than 90 per cent of the populace. They piously followed the centuries-old Han Chinese tradition of offering sacrifices to heaven, earth, the sun and the moon. These rituals, performed in winter, summer, spring and autumn respectively, were the most important tasks of a Chinese emperor. On those occasions he would wear a court robe with the Twelve Symbols. To complete his formal attire he also wore a court hat, necklace, belt and pair of boots (above). For less formal occasions the emperor wore a dragon robe (see p.84).

KEY EVENTS

1644	1645	c. 1646	1661	1715	1722
The Manchus, nomads from northern China, seize Beijing and establish the Qing dynasty, with six-year-old Shunzhi as emperor.	Manchu queue laws require men to shave the front of their heads. State officials must wear robes with cuffs of horse-hoof shape.	The Qing government revives the imperial textile mills in Nanjing, Hangzhou and Suzhou.	At age seven Kangxi succeeds Shunzhi as emperor. He goes on to reign for sixty-one years, making him the longest-reigning Chinese emperor.	Italian artist Giuseppe Castiglione starts work at the Imperial Palace under Emperor Kangxi. He serves as court painter for three successive emperors.	Yongzheng becomes the third Qing emperor, triumphing over his brothers in a disputed succession.

There were strict rules governing the colour of the emperor's court robe. Because the sky is blue he wore blue at the Altar of Heaven. A yellow robe was worn at the Altar of the Earth, red at the Altar of the Sun and moon-white at the Altar of the Moon. The material of his necklace matched the robe, too: lapis lazuli beads were worn to match the blue robe, amber was worn with the yellow robe, coral with the red one and turquoise stones with moon-white. On important festival days, such as Lunar New Year's Day, the emperor wore a necklace made of pearls, and pearl was the jewel that adorned his court hat.

The Twelve Symbols on the emperor's court robe (right) represented his utmost authority and were worn by him alone. According to Chinese texts, kings started wearing the Twelve Symbols in the first millennium BC. The sun, moon and constellation represented heaven, and the mountain, dragon and flowery creature (depicted as a pheasant) things on earth. The axe head, back-to-back 'ji' character and sacrificial vessels were objects for ancestor worship. The waterweed, flame and grain represented three of the five elements: water, fire and earth. The five elements represent direction and natural forces in Chinese philosophy; they are east (wood), south (fire), west (metal), north (water) and centre (earth). By wearing these symbols the emperor showed that he had the blessings of heaven and earth.

The emperor was permitted to have many wives, but only his principal wife, the empress, was entrusted to offer sacrifices at the Altar to the Goddess of Silkworms, as head of the female population. The empress's ceremonial costume was similar to that of her husband, but with more layers. Underneath the court robe she wore a skirt, and on top a sleeveless surcoat. She wore not one necklace but three, and three pairs of earrings. A diadem headband, collar ornament and long silk pendant completed the full costume. With ten items on her body and head, the empress's movement would be extremely slow, giving a great sense of solemnity to the ceremony.

Sacrificial offerings were for the deities, but they were designed to impress humans as well. One secular ceremony was the 'grand military inspection', a spectacular event in which cannons, firearms, weapons, cavalrymen and foot soldiers were placed on parade. At the head of the army was the emperor in his magnificent suit of ceremonial armour (below right). The armour was in fact made of bright yellow satin, with the sleeves and apron sewn with bands of gold thread to resemble shining metal and added copper studs to reinforce the effect. The helmet was made of lacquered leather with protection-invoking Sanskrit letters in gold. The sable strips and jewellery on the helmet, arrows and quiver were also made in strict conformity to regulations.

Emperor Qianlong, who reigned from 1735 to 1796, canonized the dress code in 1766, expecting it to be observed for many generations to come. Little did he realize that a century later a woman from another clan, Empress Dowager Cixi, would throw his grand scheme into disarray. **MW**

1725	1737	1766	1766	1796	1799
Emperor Yongzheng performs ritual ploughing at the Altar of the God of Agriculture, wearing a bright yellow dragon robe.	Qianlong instates Lady Fuca as empress. Empress Xiaoxian, as she becomes known, uses flowers in her hair instead of pearls and jewels.	A book detailing different types of formal dresses, *August Dynasty Ritual Vessels Illustrated*, is completed by imperial command.	Emperor Qianlong enforces a strict dress code for imperial court proceedings. The code demands that women dress according to their husband's rank.	Following his father Qianlong's abdication, Jiaqing ascends the throne as the fifth Qing emperor to rule over China.	Qianlong dies. He effectively retained power until his death, having abdicated only to avoid ruling for a longer period than Emperor Kangxi.

Dragon Robe 1736–95
COURT DRESS

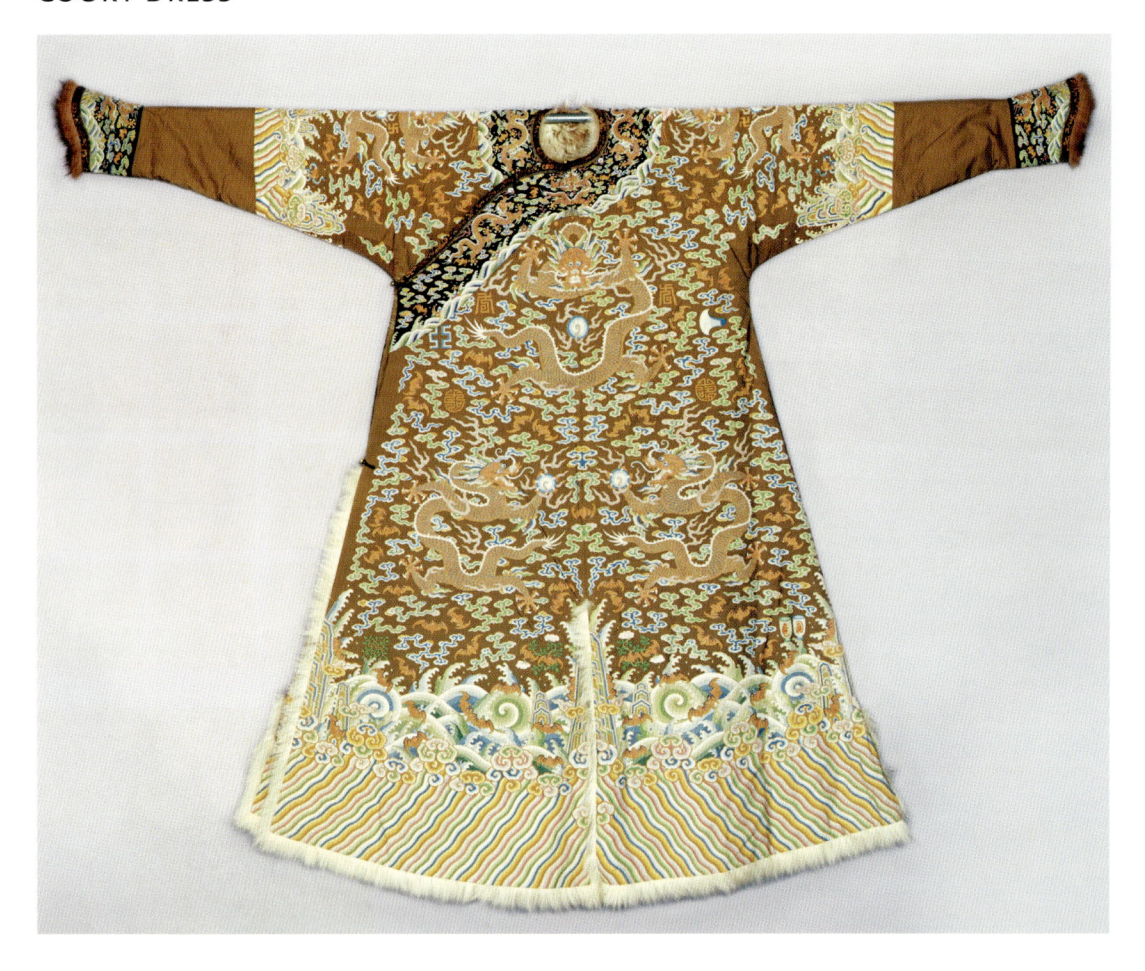

Tapestry weave dragon robe worn by Emperor Qianlong.

The emperor's court robe ranked highest in the Qing dress code, but to people in the West it is the dragon motif that is most representative of China. The emperor wore the dragon robe on celebratory occasions, such as the weddings of princes and princesses, New Year's Eve, the mid-autumn festival and the reception of foreign embassies. When Lord George Macartney, the first British ambassador to China, met Emperor Qianlong in 1793 the latter was clad in a dragon robe.

The robe has a vertical seam running down the middle and flares outwards slightly towards the hem in an 'A' shape. It is invariably patterned with nine dragons: two are positioned on the shoulders, three on the front, three on the back and one on the overlap, which is not visible to the viewer. According to legend the Chinese dragon is a benign and auspicious animal that roamed the land in the second millennium BC. Nine is the highest single-digit number and therefore an appropriate number of dragons for the supreme ruler. The slits in the hem of the dragon robe indicate that the emperor would have worn trousers underneath.

It is widely known that the phoenix motif was reserved for the empress. However, both the empress and the empress dowager wore dragon robes as well. A female dragon robe has slits only at the sides, but not at the front and back. The robe worn by people outside the imperial family is called a mang robe, and the animal displayed on these robes is very similar to a dragon. **MW**

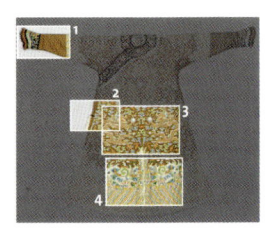

NAVIGATOR

👁 FOCAL POINTS

1 HOOF-SHAPED CUFF
The cuffs on a Manchu robe are shaped like the hoof of a horse, in direct reference to the nomadic origin of the Manchu people, who earned their living from hunting. The horse hoof was also a sign of their military strength; the Qing rulers were said to have 'won the country on horseback'.

4 STANDING WATER
The colourful diagonal stripes at the hem are known as 'standing water'. In Chinese legend the dragon initially lives in water. When it attains full supernatural power it rises up to heaven. The swirling waves above the standing water, with the mountains, form a homophone for 'empire' (*jiangshan*).

2 BUTTON
Buttons were introduced by the Manchu. Before 1644 the Han Chinese fastened their garments by tying bows or knots. The buttons on early Qing robes were invariably spherical—some made of metal, some fabric—and they were fastened with loops. Buttonholes were not used until the 20th century.

EMPRESS ROBE

In this portrait of *c.* 1737, attributed to Italian artist Giuseppe Castiglione, Empress Xiaoxian, Qianlong's principal wife, wears ceremonial winter robes. Court robes were adapted according to the seasons and winter robes were often fur-lined and edged in sable. The extended epaulettes are the most dramatic feature of the costume.

3 DRAGON MOTIF
Three types of dragons feature on this robe: a full-frontal dragon in the middle, two rising dragons in profile on the left and right, and two walking dragons on the dark blue trimming below the collarbone. The rising dragons clutch a flaming pearl in their claws. The background is filled with coloured clouds to represent the sky.

FRENCH COURT DRESS

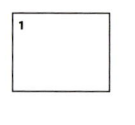

1. In this painting from 1667, Louis XIV wears an embroidered silk *justacorps* and knee-length pantaloons. His clothes reflect the power, grandeur and wealth of the monarchy. Even the king's finance minister, Colbert—dressed in black—wears a lace jabot and cuffs.

2. An early 18th-century silk manteau shows how the overdress was worn on top of an underskirt. It is seen here with a relatively low *fontange*.

In the 17th century France became the undisputed leader of European style. Indeed, the roots of the modern fashion industry belong in Paris of the 1670s, when new fashion journals and boutiques promoted seasons, looks and novelty as drivers of change. This process is synonymous with King Louis XIV, who reigned from 1643 to 1715, but also with the influence of his finance minister, Jean-Baptiste Colbert, who funded state sponsorship of the textile industry, conducted Louis's wars, and created the wealth that the king and his courtiers wore on their backs. Colbert himself was rarely seen out of black and seemed a dour reflection of the glorious king (above). The son of a draper, Colbert understood the allure of luxury products, such as silk, tapestry and lace, and decided that France should have a monopoly on their production and become the centre of fashionable luxury consumption. The Gobelins tapestry workshop in Paris weaved portraits of Louis's feats for the palace at Versailles and created furnishings for chateaux across France. Traders of luxury accessories and jewels were encouraged to establish shops in the newly built royal squares of Paris. Lace workshops were established in Alençon in 1665 and their output included lace jabots (cravats), *fontanges* (headdresses) and cannons (knee ruffles). These high-quality materials became required trimming for all formal court dress. French silks symbolized the utter luxury of the court but when Louis XIV revoked the Edict of Nantes in 1685, many highly skilled Huguenot weavers went into exile in London's Spitalfields, thus breaking the French monopoly.

KEY EVENTS

1660	1665	1672	1675	1678	c. 1678
Louis XIV marries the Spanish princess Maria Teresa. The marriage unites French style with Spanish formality.	Colbert becomes chief finance minister and funds the French luxury industries of lace, perfume, silk and tapestries.	The journal *Le Mercure Galant* is launched. It reports on court and Parisian fashion for a largely provincial audience.	Female seamstresses, or couturières, gain guild status and the right to design and make non-formal court dress. It marks the birth of the boutique.	The manteau—an open coat dress worn over skirts—makes its first noted appearance. It relaxes the formality of aristocratic dress.	'Fashion seasons' are described for the first time in *Le Mercure Galant*.

Court dress achieved an unparalleled level of splendour and from 1661 to 1789 made France the model for other European monarchies. Access to the French court was theoretically open to all subjects, but one had to be properly attired. For occasions such as coronations, marriages and balls, this meant donning the grand habit, an ensemble that could cost more than a modest chateau. The female grand habit (see p.88) was the pinnacle of sumptuary clothing, displaying the wealth and status of both the wearer and the state that produced it. The male grand habit comprised *justacorps* (long overjacket), gilet (waistcoat) and pantaloons, replaced from 1670 by breeches, and in its essential form was the basis of the three-piece suit. Depending on the occasion, these garments featured embroidery, lace swags and jewels, or were cut from plainer fabrics for hunting. The grand habit squeezed women into an inverse cone shape and was the least appropriate design for the plump women of Louis's court. Nevertheless, the conservative and ample Duchess of Orléans adored her dress, preferring it to the more informal manteau (right) that appeared from 1678. This adapted an elaborate front-opening dressing gown into outerwear, worn over a skirt, bodice and stomacher. It revolutionized daywear and softened the female shape.

A royal mistress, Marie-Angélique, Duchess of Fontanges, was apocryphally responsible for revolutionizing hairdressing. In the 1670s, female courtiers began to draw their hair back above their foreheads, pinning it to a wire frame known as a commode. Fontanges ensured its popularity when her hairstyle was dishevelled while out riding and she temporarily tied her hair with a ribbon garter. The king was charmed and overnight a new style was born in which ribbon and hair were looped over a commode. Fontanges gave her name to the wired lace headdress that resulted.

This combination of court and commerce created the modern fashion industry because couturiers could respond more rapidly than court tailors to what women wanted to wear. In 1675 couturières gained guild status and were able to market their goods effectively. Their business was helped in 1672 by the birth of the fashion journal *Le Mercure Galant*. Reporting on who was wearing what, where and how, it sparked fashion trends and the concept of seasons. Female fashion merchants (*marchandes de modes*) also took over accessorizing, a business once monopolized by the male haberdasher, and it was women who cemented the relationship between France and fashion leadership in the 17th century. They consumed French luxury goods, acted as fashion plates, and created the supply and demand for the new and the sartorially fantastic. **PW**

1680	1682	1683	1685	1692	1715
The arrival of the *fontange* headdress elongates the female profile to vertical height.	The French royal court moves from Paris to Versailles, which becomes the official seat of government.	Queen Maria Teresa dies. Louis XIV secretly marries Madame de Maintenon. The fashion mantle passes to the younger generation at court.	The Edict of Nantes is revoked and Protestant Huguenot silk weavers lose legal protection.	In honour of the French victory at the Battle of Steenkerke, women adopt a loose, draped neckscarf and men wear a simpler cravat.	Louis XIV dies. Under the Regency of his nephew, Philippe of Orléans, the court moves back to Paris.

FRENCH COURT DRESS 87

Grand Habit 1660s
WOMEN'S COURT DRESS

Queen Maria Teresa and her son, the Grand Dauphin, in a grand habit by Pierre Mignard (c. 1665).

This grand habit worn by Queen Maria Teresa of France illustrates the magnificent yet restrictive court dress of the early years of Louis XIV's rule that could be made only by court tailors or personal seamstresses, not Parisian couturiers. The grand habit is composed of the *grand corps* or *corps de robe* (bustier), the *jupe* (skirt) and the *bas de robe* or *queue* (train). The bodice is boned with whale cartilage and squashes and exposes the bosom, forcing the shoulders back. All these elements seem to confirm the well-known phrase: 'One must suffer when one is queen.' The silhouette recalls the flat, horizontal extremes of Spanish formal dress at the court of Philip IV, the queen's father. At this point in Louis XIV's reign, sleeves were worn off the shoulder, puffed and to the elbow, festooned with layers of lace and trimming. The skirt is given its shape by panniers, made from whalebone, willow or metal shafts, and padded with stiffened cloth. The dimensions of these panniers would increase with the advent of the 18th century. The train is both a way of indicating status—the queen was entitled to a long train, her ladies less so—and provided another opportunity to display more trimming. Although there was no colour code as such, younger women of the highest status preferred to wear cloth of gold or silver, and older women usually dressed in black. **PW**

NAVIGATOR

FOCAL POINTS

1 MASK
Maria Teresa carries a mask in her right hand to protect her complexion from the sun. The mask also refers to the court opera and ballet, where every performance was an opportunity for the audience to parade their wealth and status through dress.

3 ROYAL COLOURS
The grand habit communicates the wearer's position as queen of France: red, white and black were the traditional royal colours before the Revolution. The colours are continued in the dauphin's clothes, which illustrate the practice of keeping small boys in 'skirts'.

2 JEWELS AND FEATHERS
The queen is festooned with precious natural pearls, but freshwater pearls were also hugely sought after. Ostrich plumes add an exotic touch to her dress. Popular jewellery at the time also included the palatine, a necklace that descended down the back.

4 HEAVY CLOTH
The trimming and rich cloth of the grand habit distinguished the status of the wearer but made the garment extremely heavy; often skirts also had weights inserted. The silks are woven with real silver and gold thread.

RESTORATION FASHION

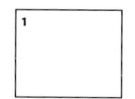

After the austerity of the Commonwealth years Charles II (r. 1660–85; above) was restored to the throne of England and, having spent much of his exile in France, he initially introduced some elements of French court dress. In 1666 the king prompted a dramatic and radical change in men's attire by discarding the doublet, jerkin and hose for a knee-length coat and vest, a form of sleeved waistcoat. This was perceived as a deliberate attempt to differentiate elite dress from the opulent styles that were popular with his French counterpart, Louis XIV, who regarded fashion as a symbol of absolutist power. Following the civil war, the growing wealth and power of the merchant class also meant that there was little differentiation between the styles of the court and the fashions worn by the bourgeoisie. The vest was universally adopted, providing the origins of the male suit and the template for future menswear.

The move towards a new male silhouette was heralded by contemporary diarist Samuel Pepys. On 15 October 1666, he commented: 'This day the King begins to put on his vest, and I did see several persons of the House of Lords and Commons, too, great courtiers, who are in it; being a long cassocke close to the body, of black cloth, and pinked with white silke under it, and the legs

1 This painting attributed to Hendrick Danckerts (c. 1675) depicts Charles II wearing the loose coat, vest and breeches that he introduced to the populace.

2 In this portrait of Sir John Robinson by John Michael Wright (c. 1662), the status and importance of the sitter are conveyed by the adoption of an expensive and voluminous full-bottomed wig.

KEY EVENTS

1660s	1660	1660	1662	1662	1665
Feminine sensuality becomes fashionable in the Restoration period and the style of dress known as *déshabillé* becomes popular (see p.92).	The Commonwealth ends and Charles II is reinstated on the throne.	Samuel Pepys begins his diary, which he continues writing until May 1669.	Charles II marries Catherine of Braganza. She brings many luxury goods from Portugal and sets a trend for drinking tea.	A royal proclamation bans the import and sale of foreign lace. However, Venetian lace continues to be the fashionable choice in London.	The Great Plague of London causes the deaths of 7,000 people in one week. The court moves to Salisbury and Parliament meets in Oxford.

ruffled with black riband like a pigeon's leg.' Diarist John Evelyn, in an entry for 18 October 1666, described the richly patterned vest as being 'after the Persian mode', in reference to a garment made popular by Sir Robert Shirley, the Persian ambassador at the Court of St James's. Worn under a plain coat, the vest initially reached to the knees, with buttons all the way down the centre front, and was elaborately embroidered. Over time it gradually became shorter and was worn over wide petticoat breeches, festooned at the knee with knots of ribbons, which were replaced by buttons in 1680. As the vest became shorter, the coat became longer and the waist became wider. The sleeves developed deeper upturned cuffs, and the earlier falling collar, which had ousted the ruff, now shrank to a *rabat*.

From 1670 to 1730 a cravat of linen or a deep lace collar was worn. The origin of the cravat purports to derive from the neckwear of the Croats in French military service. It consisted of a large square or triangle of either linen, lawn, silk or muslin, often starched, with the ends usually bordered with lace or decorated with tasselled beads, and tied loosely beneath the chin. By the 1680s the cravat was worn falling over a stiffened ornamental cravat-string. As the century progressed the cravat became narrower and longer, was often knotted, and lace was replaced by muslin or cambric. From 1692 the cravat was worn with the ends twisted and pushed through a buttonhole of the coat. This popular style remained in fashion for two decades and was adopted for civilian dress after the Battle of Steenkerke, in which French officers had no time to arrange their cravats when they were summoned to repel a surprise attack. Hats had a moderate crown but wide brim, and were turned up at one point in a practice known as cocking. At the end of the century, the hat began to be turned up in three places, thus forming the 'three-cornered hat'.

In contrast to the simplicity of late 17th-century male garments, men's headwear became the focus of extreme fashion with the adoption of the *perruque à crinière*, or periwig (right), a style that lasted for nearly a century. The full-bottomed wig was worn over a shaved head and was extremely heavy and cumbersome, with stiffened curls framing the face and falling to below the shoulders. For women height was provided by a *fontange*—named after the mistress of a French king—a lace cap with a wire frame that supported vertical tiers of lace frills worn over a row of curls stacked high on the forehead. During the middle years of the 1680s the female wardrobe included the gown or mantua, a length of draped and pleated material that hung from the shoulders to the floor. This eventually evolved into a dress worn looped back, with the skirt divided at the front to reveal the contrasting material of the petticoat beneath. A stomacher, a rigid triangular insert worn pointing down and fastened to the bodice either side, formed a high square neckline. Large lace collars were replaced with a triangular piece of cloth called a palatine, and elbow-length sleeves were finished with tiers of ruffles. **MF**

1666	1669	1670s	1670	1677	1692
The Great Fire of London consumes more than 13,000 buildings, including St Paul's Cathedral.	Sir Christopher Wren is commissioned to design the new St Paul's Cathedral. Work does not begin until 1675.	English theatres, kept closed by the Puritans for religious and ideological reasons from 1649 to 1660, flourish under Charles II.	Actress Nell Gwyn becomes mistress to Charles II. Witty and high-spirited, she is extremely popular after the dour years of the Commonwealth.	The first professional woman playwright, Aphra Behn, produces the comedy *The Rover*.	The Battle of Steenkerke takes place, prompting the fashion for lace cravats looped through a buttonhole.

Nightgown and Undergarment 1660s
FASHIONABLE FORMS OF 'UNDRESS'

Louise de Kerouaille, Duchess of Portsmouth, by Sir Peter Lely (1671–74).

NAVIGATOR

In this portrait by Sir Peter Lely, who was made principal painter to Charles II in 1660, Louise de Keroualle—later the Duchess of Portsmouth and a favourite royal mistress of the king—toys with her hair and looks out at the viewer with a languorous gaze. She is adhering to the new fashion for having one's portrait painted *déshabillé* ('in undress') and is dressed informally in a loosely fastened nightgown: an unstructured one-piece coat of which the draped effect later formed the basis for the mantua. This is worn over a voluminous white chemise.

Although these garments were worn in private for comfort, only the most elevated members of the Stuart court were permitted to wear 'undress' in public. Almost falling off the shoulder and dipping down over one breast before gaping to reveal the undergarment beneath, the bodice of the gown is explicitly erotic. The neckline allows for an unadorned expanse of flesh; the lack of jewellery was in keeping with the faux simplicity of the style in favour with the court at the time. The dark silk-satin folds of the dress contrast with the pale smoothness of the skin and the crisp billowing sleeves. The three-quarter sleeves of the undergarment are loosely turned back to reveal the lower arms, which are also devoid of any jewellery. **MF**

FOCAL POINTS

1 CURLED HAIR
Each side of the centre parting, the front hair is tightly curled and shaped to add width to the head. This was a style that required the nightly addition of curl papers and was often padded out with false hair. The ends are left free and pulled over one shoulder.

3 WHITE CHEMISE
Relinquishing the constricting heavily boned bodice of more formal attire, the chemise—an untailored garment of cotton or lawn not usually on display—is worn without a corset. The state of 'undress' was equated with sexual licence.

2 CLASSICAL DRAPERY
A length of dark-coloured satin is draped over one shoulder of the future duchess. The drapery was not an item of dress but a common device used by painters when referencing the sitter as a classical goddess.

4 LOOSE SLEEVES
The sleeves of the nightgown are loosely secured at the neckline and lower down the arm, with the cuff rolled up to display the pale undergarment beneath. This effect is also seen at the front of the gown.

RESTORATION FASHION

THE BIRTH OF MODERN FASHION

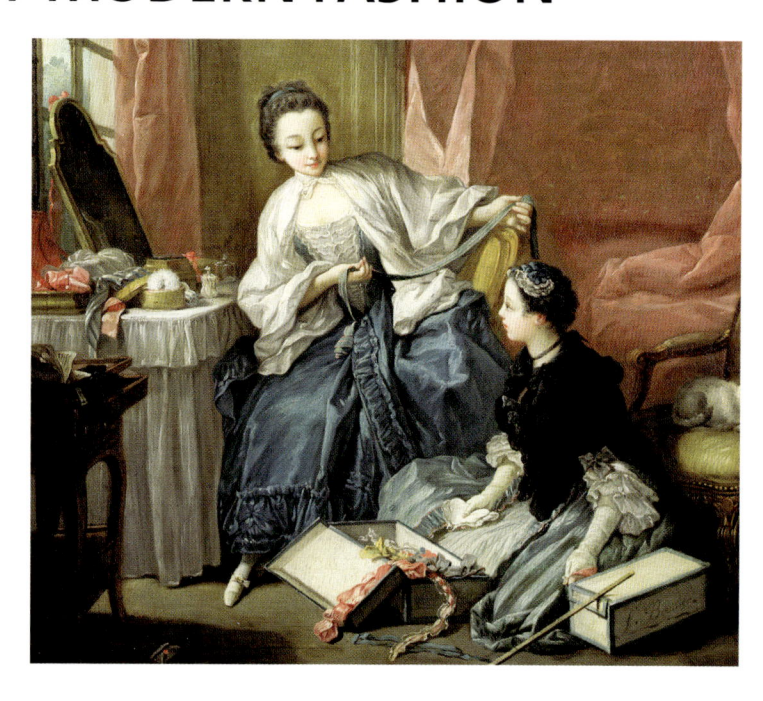

Paris had established its reputation as the centre of luxury goods in the 17th century, but became the epicentre of style in the 18th century when the modern fashion system began to emerge as a result of closer links between the court and the town, the growth in conspicuous consumption among all but the poorest Parisians and the expansion in print media. In 1715 Philippe of Orléans chose to rule as regent from his Paris home, the Palais Royal, where he lived with his mistress, Madame de Parabère. The couple set the cultural tone of the period, in which the elite beau monde mixed shamelessly with the demi-monde at the theatre, in the gardens of the Palais Royal and, most particularly, in the boutiques of the *marchandes de modes* (fashion merchants; above), jewellers and milliners of the rue du Faubourg Saint-Honoré/rue de la Paix axis.

Newspapers, almanacs, fashion magazines and even travel journals lauded the capital's boutiques as cultural destinations. They were loci of rapid cultural change, where one could mingle with the best society, view wonderful collections of curiosities, acquire knowledge of other countries and, importantly, buy fashionable clothes. Indeed, these boutiques set the model for Parisian fashion that survives today. The most expensive establishments occupied commercial ground-floor space in the new aristocratic developments: the remodelled Palais Royal or the Place Vendôme. These businesses were

KEY EVENTS

1715	1720	1745–61	1760	1761	1770
The Regency of Philippe of Orléans is based at the Palais Royal and court life transfers to Paris until Louis XV comes of age in 1722.	The *robe à la française* (see p.98) becomes popular among the aristocracy. Its silhouette characterizes 18th-century fashion.	As the official mistress of Louis XV, Madame de Pompadour adds her flamboyant decorative influence to court costume and culture.	Christophe-Philippe Oberkampf establishes the royal workshop for printed toiles at Jouy-en-Josas.	*Julie, ou la nouvelle Héloïse* is published by Jean-Jacques Rousseau. It extols nature and the pastoral idyll.	Marie-Antoinette of Austria marries the dauphin Louis-Auguste, the future Louis XVI; she slowly becomes the centre of court fashion.

94 1600–1799

shamelessly elitist and the boutiques were named after courtiers. The greatest achievement of all was to be recognized as the official royal supplier of certain items: the king's *marchand ordinaire* or the queen's jeweller, for example. Responding to a wave of anglomania, boutiques were called such names as 'Magasin Anglais' or the unlikely 'Ville de Birmingham' in order to generate an association with luxury that survives to the present day.

Fashion responded to Paris's changing lifestyle. The dominant cultural tone of lax morality encouraged informality in fashionable dress, such as the *robe volante* (see p.96). Furthermore, elaborate prototype dressing gowns, or *robes de chambre*, popularized underwear as outerwear, while visible chemises worn under half-open gourmandine bodices promised much more. A desire for movement, comfort and relative practicality (in contrast to the extremely uncomfortable and impractical grand habit worn at court) fuelled the popularity of the redingote (opposite below). Like its predecessor the manteau, this was a coat dress worn by court ladies for hunting (riding out) and transformed into a tailored day 'suit' for town wear, accessorized with the perfect silk neckerchief. The influence of the Age of Enlightenment was noticeable from the 1740s onwards, when Jean-Jacques Rousseau's 'natural being' was reflected in increasingly destructured clothing and natural motifs and accessories such as English floral chintz, feathers and artificial flowers.

Marie-Jeanne (known as Rose) Bertin (1747–1813) took full advantage of these changing fashion impulses and conditions. As a couturière, she was able to provide a tailored service to every client who competed for her attention: she could extravagantly design and trim a grand habit, complete the perfect wardrobe for life in the aristocratic *hôtels particuliers* or grand bourgeois residences, give a private audience to Russian duchesses, and cater for the increased demand for accessories—feathers, artificial flowers, shawls, fichus, 'poufs' for the hair and fripperies—that marked the reign of Louis XVI during the second half of the century. Although Bertin was a brilliant businesswoman, her popularity was due to her association with one particular client, Marie-Antoinette, who referred to Bertin as 'my minister of fashion'.

In opposition to the perceived extravagance of Marie-Antoinette, the circle of women around the queen set the trend for a more relaxed style of dress, which was provided by Bertin, herself part of the group. Rejecting panniers and boning, the new *robe à l'anglaise* (see p.100) and the *robe chemise* or *batiste* reflected a taste for the natural world. The garments were less structured and more comfortable than previous gowns, and although they still involved corsetry they did not contort the female figure. When Marie-Antoinette was painted by Louise Elisabeth Vigée Le Brun in a muslin white *batiste* tied with a sash (right), Paris was scandalized, and then rushed to Bertin to copy her. Fashion was disseminated more widely by fashion engravings and material sample books sent to Europe's capitals and courts. **PW**

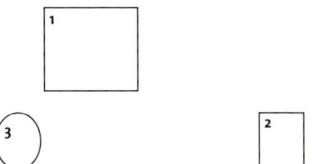

1 In *The Modiste* (c.1746) by François Boucher, a saleswoman for a *marchande de mode* visits a client. Her rich sleeves show that she is fashionably dressed and a good advertisement for the boutique.

2 In a portrait by Louise Elisabeth Vigée Le Brun (1783), Marie-Antoinette wears a *batiste* of almost transparent muslin or silk gauze, displaying the natural waistline and light corsetry of her preferred dress for informal pastimes.

3 Adélaïde Labille-Guiard's portrait (c. 1787) shows Madame Elisabeth of France wearing a redingote. The silk gauze fichu at her neck covers the low bust of the style *à l'anglaise*.

1770	1774	1776	1781	1782–83	1789
Rose Bertin opens her boutique at rue du Faubourg Saint-Honoré, attracting royal patronage across Europe.	Bertin is named *modiste* (dressmaker) to Marie-Antoinette, and designs her court and informal dress.	The community of *marchandes de modes*, plumers and florists is created, organizing the trade in accessories.	Couturières obtain equal rights to male tailors to make the stays and panniers of formal court dress.	Marie-Antoinette's model farm at Versailles is built. She sets up her court of shepherdesses, artists, designers and poets in *robes chemises*.	The storming of the Bastille takes place on 14 July; it fuels the start of the French Revolution.

THE BIRTH OF MODERN FASHION 95

Robe Volante 1705
WOMEN'S DRESS

French emerald green satin *robe volante* with lampas weave (1735).

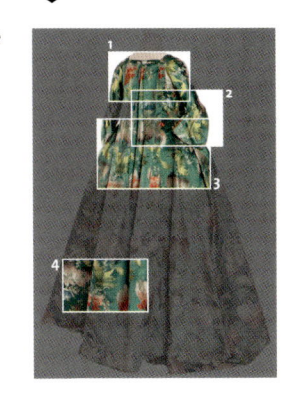

The *robe volante* first appeared in 1705 and represented a more relaxed informal style of female dress, which corresponded to the libertarian emancipated atmosphere of the Regency period. The garment has since become known as the 'Watteau robe', after the painter Antoine Watteau, who depicted many women in early versions of it. However, contemporaries referred to it as a *sacque*, *contouche* or *robe volante*. The *robe volante* developed out of the *robe battante*—a baroque dressing gown—and fastened at the front to show the lacing of the corps and the chemise underneath. The chemise gave the silk robes a grip, and hinted at the derobed female body.

This dress reflects the rich palette of the early reign of Louis XV and an interest in oriental design. At the back neckline, a demi-cape descends to the ground in matching material to the main dress. It is stiffened by wide box pleats, which could themselves be made slightly rigid by whale or willow boning. Although the *robe volante* was too informal for court dress, the cape became a feature of some *robes à la française* and developed into a train or an informal pleated kickback jacket, known as a *pet*. This dress is not lavishly trimmed, but other *robes volantes* are decorated with silk rosettes on the fastenings, or cut with pinked hems. **PW**

NAVIGATOR

FOCAL POINTS

1 PLEATED CAPE
The wide box pleats at the shoulder of the cape show how each ready-made robe could be adjusted for its wearer; slight alterations to the pleats could hint at the figure beneath. This cape was attached to the squared-off neckline with buttons or hooks.

3 ROUNDED PANNIERED SKIRT
The *robe volante* is worn with a gently rounded petticoat pannier, the width of which never reached the extremes of formal court dress. This made the dress relatively practical for everyday wear and it was adopted by women from all ranks of society.

2 RAQUETTE SLEEVES
The tight-fitting raquette sleeves are straight cut to the elbow, where they expand into flat, folded-open cuffs. This cut echoes the straight back and the rounded skirts of the *robe volante*. Cuffs might also be tiered frills made from matching material.

4 PRINTED FABRIC
The fabric indicates the wealth of the wearer. This sumptuous lampas silk, woven in France, incorporates expensive metallic thread into its bold-relief Chinese peony design. The breadth of the robe makes it particularly suitable for the display of large prints.

THE BIRTH OF MODERN FASHION

Robe à la Française 1720
WOMEN'S DRESS

Brocaded silk faille *robe à la française* and petticoat (c. 1760–65).

NAVIGATOR

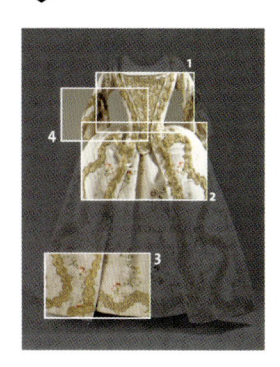

After 1715 the elongated costume of the later reign of Louis XIV was transformed. The emphasis turned to a two-dimensional silhouette—flat-backed and fronted, yet increasingly wide at the hips, up to several feet at each side. Around 1720, the pleated, loose informal robe was combined with rounded pannier or 'basket' petticoats to create a new standard of aristocratic dress—the *robe à la française*. By 1750 it was accepted as an alternative to the grand habit at court. Panniers could create a voluminous rounded skirt, a pedestal shape or, from 1725 when boning was used, a bell skirt. Stiffened petticoats—known as *jansenistes*, after a strict religious group—were also used.

This shimmering *robe à la française* is made of a brocaded silk faille manteau overdress, woven with silver and gold thread, and trimmed with gold metallic bobbin lace. The woven silk displays a broad design of delicate blossom flowers that are linked by irregular serpentine bands. The width of the skirt shows off the lavish quantity of expensive fabric. The manteau fastens to the front of the heavily trimmed corset, which is in turn covered by a stomacher, and exposes a decorated underskirt in matching silk fabric. Held by panniers and stiffened petticoats, the skirts fall in the accentuated bell shape that was popular after 1730. **PW**

👁 FOCAL POINTS

1 WHALEBONE CORSET
A richly embroidered stomacher is attached to either side of the dress. The whalebone corset, which has a low, square neckline, is also decorated. It funnels the body into an inverted cone shape that accentuates the slim waist and extravagant hipline.

3 ORNATE TRIMMING
The ornate trimming displays the wealth of the wearer: metallic lace is used in the serpentine bands on the overskirt and hem. Lace also trims each tier of the *engageantes* at the sleeves. Braid and folded loops of material (*falbalas*) were also used as trim.

2 WIDE PANNIERED SKIRT
The skirt width has been created by a pannier made of three to five tiers of whalebone or willow strips that are tied around the waist with ribbons. Later, the pannier became two separate contraptions, necessary to support the width of the impractical skirts.

4 FLARED SLEEVES
The sleeves are slim to the elbow, pagoda style, and then flare out at the cuff into *engageantes*. Depending on the fashion, one, two or three open frills of lace or muslin trimmed the elbow of each sleeve, which complemented the robe's main fabric.

THE BIRTH OF MODERN FASHION

Robe à l'Anglaise 1780s
WOMEN'S DRESS

Cotton *robe à l'anglaise* embellished with metallic thread (c. 1784–87).

NAVIGATOR

This French *robe à l'anglaise* reflects the late 18th-century propensity for anglomania and the prevalent elite interest in the idealized natural world. Never formal enough to be an official court gown, it was worn in aristocratic salons and upper-class daily life. More comfortable to wear than a *robe à la française*, the *robe à l'anglaise* allowed women greater mobility as skirts could be hitched up while walking.

The single-piece, front-fastening robe worn from 1770 changed the female silhouette completely. Pleats are sewn into the skirt just below the deep 'V'-shape waistline, adding volume to the back of the dress and narrowing the hips. The robe is rendered comfortable by removing excessive boning and panniers, and tight stomachers are replaced by *compères*, made of matching fabric. These two panels are a little less restrictive than a corset, attached by buttons or hooks at the front opening of the dress, and adjustable at the back. Sleeves are simplified, streamlined and less extravagantly trimmed, and narrow to the elbow before widening out from a horizontal seam. A gathering of ecru blonde silk lace is attached to the sleeve, matching the silk of the neckline. The accentuated fullness of the back of the hips did not rely on panniers, but was obtained with the aid of soft bottom padding worn beneath petticoats. **PW**

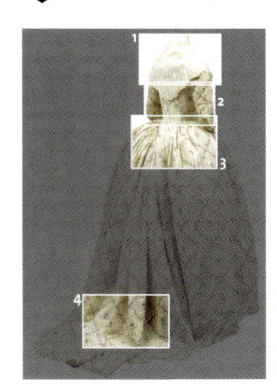

FOCAL POINTS

1 DEEP LACE FICHU
A deep lace fichu—a three-cornered cape worn over the shoulders, with the ends crossed on the chest—is attached to the rounded neckline to protect the skin from the sun. For modesty's sake, the gossamer-light fichu also covers the low neckline of the dress.

2 LONG, FLAT BACK
The cut emphasizes a longer back line, with the skirt pleats falling from the bottom of the spine, where previously the waist had been higher and horizontal. The style references the earlier sack-back dress, where panelled fabric suggested a more vertical silhouette.

3 NEW SILHOUETTE
The accentuated bottom could be further exaggerated by the hems of the dress being pulled back up over the hips to expose a matching underskirt. The rounded back overskirt gives only a slight train in a clear departure from earlier formal trains.

4 FLORAL PATTERNING
This warm chintz is typical of fashionable fabrics worn in the 1770s to 1780s; florals were popular because they reflected the contemporary interest in the beauty of the outdoors. This cotton-silk mix has been embroidered in gold thread, suggesting a high-status wearer.

THE BIRTH OF MODERN FASHION 101

SCOTTISH TARTAN

The evolution of what is generally considered to be traditional Scottish or Highland dress is obscure. In addition to long-standing historical uncertainties, such as the origin of the term 'tartan', the subject has been complicated in recent decades by an 'invention of tradition' thesis, as historians promulgated a belief that the popular image of the Highlander is largely a product of 19th-century romanticism.

The skill of Celtic weavers was acknowledged even in Roman times, and visitors to the Highlands of Scotland in the early 18th century commented on the quality of the fabric that the inhabitants produced. Their woollen cloth had a distinctive checked pattern that, by the 17th century at least, was commonly referred to as tartan. Tartan patterns, or 'setts', are created by using two colours of thread, which results in three colour combinations. All patterns are structured as a series of stripes around a central 'pivot' stripe, which are then repeated as regular blocks of pattern. Typically, early tartans would have been relatively muted in colour and created from natural dyes, but a trend for more colourful patterns emerged as brighter dyes became available.

From 1815 there was a move to register all tartans, and many patterns were created and linked with surnames for the first time. Prior to this, clan tartans

KEY EVENTS

1727	1745–46	1746	1750	1757	1760
Against Jacobite aspirations, George II succeeds his father to the British throne, and the Hanoverian monarchy continues.	The final Jacobite rebellion, led by Charles Edward Stuart (Bonnie Prince Charlie), ends in defeat at the Battle of Culloden.	The Disclothing or Disarming Act becomes law. It bans the wearing of tartan and the shoulder plaid and kilt except by the army.	Poetry and songs express hatred of the Disclothing Act. 'Am Breacan Uallach' (The Heavy Plaid) praises plaid above any English coat.	Highland regiments, dressed in tartan uniforms, start to be formed to support the British army in empire building.	A supposedly ancient collection of Ossian poems is published, popularizing romantic ideas about the origins and dignified nature of Gaelic culture.

may have been a vague notion. It is likely that what started as geographically based patterns (resulting from the local availability of dyes) then became linked with clans in a particular area, and, in turn, with surnames alone. Clansmen may have been expected to wear tartans of similar colours without precise patterns being specified (see p.104).

Originally, the tartan cloth was left untailored as a long rectangular strip of fabric, called a 'plaid', and was worn in the form of a mantle by men, and as a shawl by women. It is not certain when the male style of wearing the plaid transformed into the kilt (known as a 'philabeg' or little plaid) and a separate shoulder plaid (opposite). Records indicate that the kilt was considered a new development in the 18th century and probably arose from a practical need for less cumbersome clothing.

Tartan cloth has been a symbol of Scottish, or at least Highland, identity for many centuries, which has affected how it has been perceived. The 18th century was a tumultuous time in Scottish history and, accordingly, the period witnessed the most significant attack on Highland dress, as well as the start of its greatest surge in popularity. Support for the Jacobite campaign to restore a Stuart monarch grew in Scotland after the Union of Parliaments in 1707, which joined the kingdoms of Scotland and England. Tartan became the uniform of the Jacobite rebels. Although they ultimately failed in their aim, their second major uprising in 1745 was enough of a threat to make the government seek the suppression of Highland culture. The Disclothing Act of 1746 banned the wearing of tartan, kilts and shoulder plaid, but tartan's rebellious associations made it popular among a wider audience. Before the ban, the Highland style had started to spread into lowland areas, as it became a symbol of national loyalty. After the Disclothing Act, the wealthy in Scotland were more inclined to be depicted wearing tartan in their portraits (right). Widespread hatred of the Act was also given voice in popular poems and songs, which frequently claimed the superiority of Highland clothing over English costume.

The second half of the 18th century witnessed a growing concern to protect and promote Scottish traditions and culture. In addition to the impact of the Disclothing Act, traditional Highland ways of life were being radically altered by land clearances and other modernizing influences. A literature was emerging that portrayed early Gaelic culture as virtuous and dignified, as exemplified by the collection of Ossian narrative verse published in 1760. This chimed well with the simultaneous rising reputation of the Highland soldier. The army was exempt from the tartan ban, and the success of Highland regiments in empire-building battles gave their attire great prestige. By 1781, the threat of Jacobite rebels was a distant memory and the Disclothing Act was rescinded. The following decades witnessed a revival, or reinvention, of traditional Scottish culture, and it was from this point that the fashion for tartan and Highland dress began to extend well beyond the borders of Scotland. **IC**

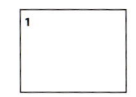

1 *Prince Charles Edward Stuart in Edinburgh in 1745* (19th century) by William Brassey Hole. A retrospective depiction of a victorious moment in the Jacobite campaign. Highland attire was often worn to galvanize support.

2 *Portrait of a Jacobite Lady* (18th century) by Alexander Cosmo, an ardent Jacobite. The sitter's tartan military-style riding jacket, white rose in her hand and rosebuds in her bonnet symbolize support for the Stuart cause.

1771	1778	1781	1788	1799	1815
The poet and novelist Sir Walter Scott is born. He is later credited as being influential in the 19th-century romanticization of Scottish culture.	The Highland Society of London is formed, reflecting rising interest in preserving (and arguably manufacturing) Scottish traditions.	The Disclothing Act is rescinded under pressure from the Highland Society of London. Tartan can be worn legally again.	Charles Edward Stuart dies and with him any last realistic hope for the Jacobite cause.	The Napoleonic Wars start, in which the success of the Highland regiments gives their style of dress new cachet and mass popularity.	Tartan patterns are registered and linked with clan names for the first time.

Shoulder Plaid Late 18th century
MALE SCOTTISH CLAN DRESS

Chief of a Scottish Clan by
Eugène Devéria (19th century).

NAVIGATOR

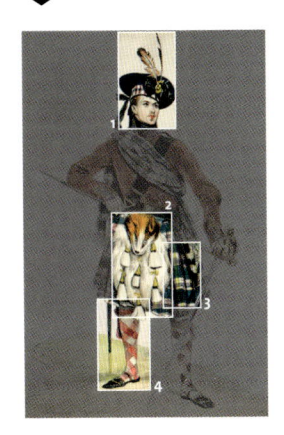

Eugène Devéria's painting epitomizes the romanticized view of the Highlander that had evolved by the 19th century. Clansmen of the past, and particularly their chiefs, had been rehabilitated in the popular mind, from uncouthly dressed savages to noble warriors. The subject in this painting is portrayed in the landscape of his Highland homeland. It is reminiscent of a time when his predecessors would have needed to be self-sufficient hardy individuals, capable of leading their clans in battle and being at one with their beautiful but harsh environment. His costume imitates that of Highland regiment soldiers, and thus appropriates some of their more recent glory.

The chief, or chieftain, has drawn both his dirk and basket-hilted broadsword, weapons associated with Scottish soldiers. The six-tasselled badger sporran was part of the officer uniform for the 93rd (Sutherland Highlanders) Regiment of Foot, and the choice of a red doublet and dicing on the cap is also evocative of Highland military uniform and could indicate a continuing regimental connection. The shoulder plaid harks back to the earlier Highland tradition of wearing a single, untailored piece of cloth or 'big plaid'. For Highland men, this could be used as a blanket at night and arranged into a costume resembling a kilt by day. The fabric was folded into pleats and fixed by a belt to form a skirt; remaining material was used as a cloak or hung over the shoulder. Practical attire for the harsh Highland conditions, the shoulder plaid also had aesthetic appeal. **IC**

FOCAL POINTS

1 BONNET
This style of bonnet was known as a Balmoral in the late 19th century, and had origins in Scotland from at least the 16th century. It is a soft woollen cap, with a large flat crown. It is typically worn tilted to the right, with two securing ribbons hanging from the back. The two eagle feathers, held in the clan crest badge on the bonnet, indicate that the painting may be of a chieftain, the head of a clan branch, rather than a clan chief, who would wear three feathers.

2 SPORRAN
The sporran, like a medieval belt pouch, compensates for a lack of pockets in the kilt. The large hairy sporran was introduced by the military in the mid 18th century and has obvious connotations of male vigour. The association of Highland dress with masculinity appears to have increased from the early 18th century, when women started to wear the plaid less frequently, and the Highland regimental uniform became increasingly well known.

3 TARTAN PATTERN
Clans could have a dress tartan, which was often created by changing one of the background colours in their standard tartan to white. Hunting tartans were another variant, and they were designed with muted colours. From the mid 19th century, the availability of chemical dyes led to a distinction between modern clan tartans and more muted ancient setts. Earlier tartans could be vibrant, and Highlanders were noted for producing dyes from local vegetation.

4 SOCKS
Hose is an important element of Highland dress. The Argyle check hose in this picture would likely have been hand-knitted using the intarsia technique. Before the 19th century, hose would have been made from woven cloth, cut on the bias and sewn so that the pattern wound around the leg. Although not visible in this painting, a single-bladed knife, a *sgian dubh*, would typically be tucked in the hose of the right leg, with only the hilt exposed to view.

SCOTTISH TARTAN 105

ROCOCO ELEGANCE

The essential styles and silhouettes of elegant dress persisted throughout the Rococo period—a name thought to derive from the French words for small rocks (*rocaille*) and shells (*coquilles*)—of the mid 18th century. The grand habit and *robe à la française* remained the model for formal and court dress, while the sack-back dress and mantua provided everyday wear. The male three-piece suit hardly developed from the slim-cut waistcoat, overcoat and breeches worn at the end of Louis XIV's reign. Instead, what changed was the essence of these clothes—the design and colour of their fabrics, their trimming and ornament, and the way in which they were accessorized. The Rococo style is mainly associated with Continental Europe, but it also influenced fashion across the English Channel and Atlantic Ocean. France still led the way in the luxury trade: Lyons was the principal centre of silk weaving and embroidery, and Paris of haberdashery, accessories and innovative drapery. Regular fashion seasons determined preferences for particular colours or prints, and fashion plates disseminated the latest look in the capital to consumers in the provinces.

KEY EVENTS

1735	1745	1753	1756	1759	1761
The reign of Qianlong, emperor of China, begins. He has to negotiate European attempts to control the silk market.	Madame de Pompadour becomes *maîtresse-en-titre* (chief mistress) to Louis XV. She is replaced by Madame du Barry in 1764.	The British Museum is founded to house the many antiquities and curiosities collected from around the globe, largely by the scientist Sir Hans Sloane.	The Seven Years' War begins. It is the first world war, with France and Britain competing for colonial domination in North America, Europe and Asia.	The Royal Botanical Gardens are founded in Kew, in southwest London, to study new plant specimens from around the world.	Jean-Jacques Rousseau publishes *Julie, ou la nouvelle Héloïse*, which later inspires Marie-Antoinette's circle to pursue a 'natural' life.

Although France held the pre-eminent position among weavers, London's Spitalfields had become home to several generations of highly skilled naturalized Huguenot and British weavers. Britain and France were not only commercial rivals, but were also at war for a large part of the 18th century, across the globe. The Seven Years' War settled British control of trade in India and a large part of North America. Until the 1770s, British silk was preferred to French by colonial America. Britain also led the world in industrializing spinning and weaving, which made clothes cheaper for a proliferating market.

In high fashion, the French Bourbon court continued to be influential. Whereas a bold, codified palette had dominated Louis XIV's court, the reign of his great-grandson Louis XV, from 1715 to 1774, is associated with softer, pastel colours and an innovative taste for asymmetry. Fashion was set not by the queen, Marie Leczinska, but by the king's flamboyant mistresses, the cultured Madame de Pompadour and her less refined counterpart, Madame du Barry. Madame de Pompadour's portrait (opposite) shows trimming applied to every surface of her outfit. The silk dress is trimmed with double-headed pink roses, and the stomacher is laden with knotted ribbon bows that are echoed in the choker. The sleeves have multiple tiers of *engageantes* (lace ruffles) at the cuff, and her open-backed Louis heel slippers are trimmed with pearl beads.

The Rococo period is particularly noted for its printed and embroidered silks and chintzes. French and British designers introduced the irregular cartouche to design; this was an asymmetrical or shell-shaped space in which another design, natural or architectural, might appear. Back-to-back 'C' shapes were decorated, whereas a vogue for serpentine garlands or ribbons winding through floral bouquets was popular around 1740. In contrast to French designs that used more decorative ornament, English woven and printed fabrics emphasized naturalistic designs, which reflected popular interest in botany as a result of new plants arriving in Britain from across the globe. Indeed, the English *Gentleman's Magazine* criticized the gaudiness of the designs of the French, 'who have never yet with all the assistance of their Drawing Academy, been able to exhibit true proportion'. Anna Maria Garthwaite (1690–1763) was a prominent supplier of designs to the best weavers in Spitalfields from 1740 to 1760. Producing about eighty designs a year, she specialized in the 'line of beauty', a serpentine scroll garlanded with accurately drawn flowers (right).

There was a revived passion for chinoiserie in this period, stimulated by the activities of the European trading companies in the Far East and India. Whereas French silks tended to produce a fantasy vision of the East, English weavers 'naturalized' elements of the design. English oaks appeared alongside dragons, pagodas and passion flowers. Pattern books of exotic birds and animals were available to designers who were uncertain of their accuracy. This inevitably led to a stylized and uniform appearance; for example, peacocks are usually shown with drooping tails. Although the court of George III was very conservative, his

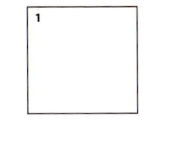

1 This portrait of Madame de Pompadour by François Boucher (c. 1756) illustrates the Rococo taste for trimming and ornament.

2 A naturalistic asymmetrical floral design from 1744 by the leading English silk designer Anna Maria Garthwaite.

1765	1765	1770	1770	1776	1787
Clive of India gains the lordship of Bengal for the East India Company. It strengthens trade links with India's producers and controls Indian fabric markets.	Richard Arkwright constructs his first spinning machine, the water frame, to mechanize cotton weaving.	The *Oxford Magazine* refers to a new phenomenon—the macaroni (see p.112), a precursor to the dandy.	Marie-Antoinette of Austria marries Louis the dauphin of France. The first partition of Poland takes place two years later.	The US Declaration of Independence is made on 4 July; France sends the Marquis of Lafayette to help the colonists against the British.	Construction of the Brighton Pavilion, Prince George's oriental fantasy palace, begins in southeast England.

ROCOCO ELEGANCE 107

son, George, the future Prince Regent, was a slave to fashion, and his Brighton Pavilion reflected the mania for chinoiserie, as did elements of his wardrobe (see p.114). Patterns such as 'Chinese figures', 'Ladies' amusement' and 'Pagoda' were used for dress and haberdashery. In France, the royal embroiderer Louis-Jacques Balzac added peacock plumes, hunting dogs and solar designs in silver and gold thread to the royal outfits.

Fabric designs changed frequently; they would be worn for only a season among high society, then passed on to poorer relations, remodelled or sold. Among less modish consumers, fabric might be kept for decades before being made up into clothing. Trimmings on garments were lavish and included faux flowers—often repeating the design on the fabric—and were worn as corsages or added to hemlines, rosettes and large elaborately trimmed picture hats. Ostrich plumes were favoured for hats and hairstyles. Pearls, cultivated for more than a century, were worn as necklaces, bracelets and trimming on formal dresses. Fringes could add movement to robes, while knotting and bows persisted throughout the period, especially on elaborate stomachers.

Trimming *à la platitude* referred to serpentine or zig-zag pleats on the main robe's trimming, or 'robing' adorning the overskirt's front hems. Trimming *en pouf* added an extra tiered row of frills around the hips. This placing of ruffles added further volume to the skirts. The frills were often held up like garlands with extra rosettes of contrasting fabrics. Pinking remained popular at hems. Oriental influences were seen in corded frog fastenings and appliqué-style embroidered pieces, stitched to silk and chintz. Trimming was also used in shoemaking, a craft that expanded in variety during the 18th century. Shoemakers produced delicate, backless, mule-style slippers for women in every hue of silk. The upper was stiffened by linen and lined with the softest calfskin. The curved Louis heel, made from timber and covered in fabric, was dominant. Buckles were often silver and covered with both real and paste jewels. Shoes for men of high status were also heeled and extravagantly decorated.

The later Rococo period is characterized by its use of drapery. The *robe à la polonaise* (opposite above), an open-fronted mantua gown, was worn over a full skirt, without the enormous panniers of the *robe à la française*. It was gathered at the rear waist into tiny pleats, as with the *robe à l'anglaise*. Its overskirt was looped and bustled onto the hips in three sections—in reference to Poland's partition in 1772—by silk cords and buttons. Brunswicks—three-quarter-length, hooded cape-like jackets—were worn on colder days and for covering fine costumes, and also featured sack-back drapery.

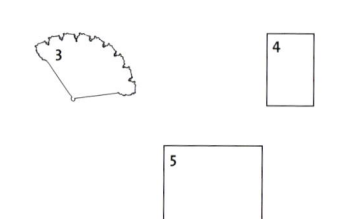

3 A gold and ivory fan from 1730, decorated with one of the painted pastoral scenes popular during the Rococo period.

4 In this *polonaise* printed dress from 1786 the embroidered material is gathered into an extravagant puffball shape.

5 The Duchess of Polignac, depicted here as a well-dressed shepherdess, was a favourite of Marie-Antoinette at court.

Multitudinous accessories were indispensable during the Rococo period. Many of these items were carried in pockets, hung under the main skirt from a waistbelt or accessed through pulled-up loops of drapery known as *retroussée dans les poches*. Fans, in particular, were another way to display exquisite silks—and to aid flirting. The most expensive were made from carved and pierced ivory bones (opposite), and decorated with mother-of-pearl studs. Male accessories, such as canes, eye glasses, smelling salts and decorative swords, also came to signify cultural interests, sexual availability and preferences. The pastoral fantasy featured in the paintings of François Boucher and Jean-Baptiste Greuze was popular throughout the period, with women clamouring to be painted as demure, shy shepherdesses, wearing flat, ribbon-tied straw hats. By 1780, women had adopted a wider, picture-style shepherdess hat, usually made from straw or thin woven strips of 'chip' wood. Such hats were trimmed with long ribbons or festooned with flowers and plumes (below).

The French court started a new fashion for extravagant oversized hairstyles (see p.110) during the 1770s. Although this fashion for wearing one's own hair enraged the city's wig-makers, by contrast hairdressers, jewellers and milliners were delighted, as women began to spend more on their headpieces and headdresses. This fashion was particularly associated with the young Marie-Antoinette, who, as dauphine of France, popularized a bouffant, backcombed hairstyle, with thick lockets at the nape of the neck. This was styled for her by the hairdresser Léonard Hautier, who gained renown in Paris by folding lightweight gauze, horsehair or wool pads into his clients' frizzed and teased hair to give it extraordinary volume. Marie-Antoinette preferred to dress her hair with ribbons and ostrich plumes, a style that became known as *à la reine*, but was referred to as 'horse trappings' by her husband's aunts. **PW**

Fantastical Headdress 1770s
WOMEN'S HAIRSTYLES

Coiffure à l'Indépendance ou le Triomphe de la Liberté, engraving (1778).

In this print a fashionable aristocratic woman is applying the finishing touches to her toilette, perhaps in preparation for a court ball: her hair is extravagantly dressed, with several layers of frizzed poufs, padded out by gauze, and dressed at the neck with lockets *à la reine*. All of the hair and the hidden padding are woven around a metal supporting frame for the crowning model of *La Belle Poule*—a celebrated French warship that gained a rare victory against the British navy in 1778, an event that is regarded as marking France's entry into the American War of Independence.

The model of the ship itself is trimmed with every Rococo accessory—feathers, ribbons and garlands—and there is a pearl-trimmed blazon at its prow, most likely bearing the royal arms. Teardrop pearls hang from the portholes and the rigging is strung with pearls. The woman's *robe à la française* is also lavishly trimmed with serpentine robings, which are just visible on the skirt and at the elbow. The sleeves have two visible layers of *engageantes* at the elbow. The bustline of her gown is woven through with yellow silk ribbon. The dress displays the typical Rococo playfulness with colour palettes, contrasting pink, yellow, green and grey. The woman wears a fashionable pearl parure set of necklace, bracelets and earrings. The choker bracelets have ovaloid cartouches, which often contained cameo portraits. **PW**

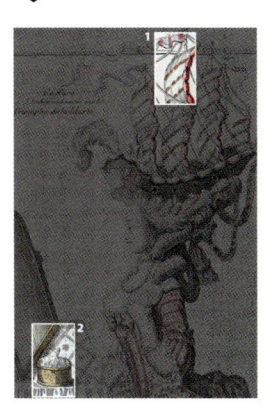

NAVIGATOR

👁 FOCAL POINTS

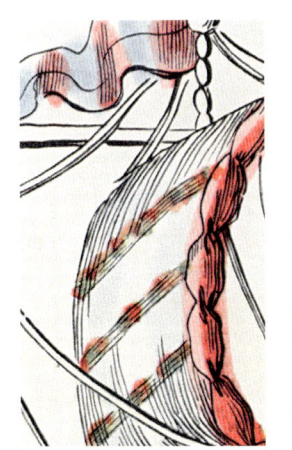

1 PATRIOTIC COLOURS
Although the ship's rigging is in the modern French colours of red, white and blue, in pre-Revolutionary France these colours were linked with the country, rather than the crown. At the time, the royal colours were black and red, or the blue and gold of the fleur-de-lis. The ship featured in the headdress, *La Belle Poule*, was well known for its victory against the British frigate *Arethusa* in 1778, which began French involvement in the American War of Independence.

2 POWDER
The powder puff placed on the table in front of the woman would have been used on her face. Hair was powdered with an atomizer, and the face covered with a mask for protection, an operation that required the help of a servant. Powder was key to giving these hairstyles their volume and malleability. It absorbed the hair's natural oils and prevented the need for restyling. It also disguised differences in tone between the natural hair and any extensions.

ROCOCO HAIRSTYLES

The fashion for outsize hairstyles and headdresses was first set by Marie-Antoinette, but it was taken to extremes by her courtiers. The more outlandish creations, satirized in political journals of the day, were associated with the perceived decadence at court. Critics spoke of such hairstyles as dirty, accusing their wearers of harbouring nests of fleas. Some wove flowers, strings of pearls and other ornaments into their hair (below). The Duchess of Chartres even had tiny figurines of her children and household placed in her coiffure. The *chien couchant* headdress comprised a horizontal cushion in the form of a dog in its basket. Hairstyles could also allude to contemporary events—the 'Montgolfier', a huge silk cap hung with a miniature hot air balloon basket, celebrated the balloon flight at Versailles in 1783.

Macaroni 1770s
EXCESSIVE MEN'S DRESS

'Welladay! Is this my son Tom!', satirical print after Samuel Hieronymus Grimm (1774).

NAVIGATOR

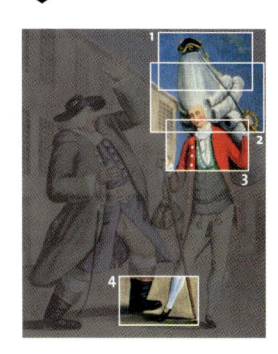

The Grand Tour around Europe was traditionally undertaken by 18th-century English gentlemen in order to complete their education. On their return, the young men were referred to as belonging to the 'Macaroni club', and adhered to the new male mode for excessively detailed formal costumes, affected foppish manners and minute attention to personal appearance. This satirical print captures the moment when the etiolated figure of Tom confronts his hale and hearty English gentleman-farmer father in London. Tom has obviously succumbed to macaroni modishness, and his father finds him an effeminate and ridiculous creature. In contrast to his father's unkempt hair and plain practical clothes in heavy materials, Tom is meticulously dressed. The male three-piece suit, which developed from the late 17th-century breeches, waistcoat and coat, was refined in macaroni style to become a medium of display equivalent to the richest female grand habit. The full range of trimmings and accessories completed the macaroni outfit; pearlescent buttons adorn Tom's coat and waistcoat. Whereas his father has a working whip, Tom carries an obligatory ivory-topped cane, which he twirls around in peacock-like style. He also holds a large golden embroidered reticule, as later carried by ladies of the court, and a gentleman's sword. **PW**

FOCAL POINTS

1 BICORNE HAT
Tom's hair is topped by a tiny *bicorne* hat; it was a common joke that these could be removed only by the point of a sword, making it hard for the wearer to doff his hat in courtesy. Therefore, being a macaroni also meant losing one's traditional English manners.

3 JABOT AND CRAVAT
Tom is wearing a shirt decorated with ruffles (jabot), the front of which billows up over the opening of his waistcoat. At his neck he wears an elaborate white lace cravat matched with lace cuffs. Macaronis often finished their neckscarves in amplified bows.

2 OUTLANDISH WIG
The greatest sartorial differences between father and son are seen on the head. Tom's powdered wig is impractically high, divided into pompom balls and tied with black ribbon, echoing fashions in aristocratic female hairstyles; hardly a trend to please the father.

4 FOOTWEAR
The footwear of the two men also highlights the differences in their dress and demeanour. Whereas his father wears heavy boots, Tom wears narrow, feminine, gold-buckled shoes. Macaronis would often also wear ornately patterned stockings.

ROCOCO ELEGANCE

Banyan 1770s
MALE DRESSING GOWN

The Prince Regent's banyan (c. 1775).

NAVIGATOR

Named after the Gujarati word for a Hindu merchant, the banyan was a prototype, wide-sleeved men's dressing gown that provided an ideal format to display the lavishly decorated fabrics of the 18th century. In contrast to the fitted formal male silhouette, the banyan was originally a loose-cut, side-fastening robe, inspired by the Japanese kimonos imported to Europe by the Dutch East India Company. The garment reflects the 18th-century taste for oriental exotica, especially in its frequent use of imported Eastern silk and Indian embroidery. This floral, quilted, calico chintz banyan was made for Prince George, later the Prince Regent. Calico chintz came from Calicut in India; the example used here is typical of fabric from the 1770s in its use of red, purple and blue dyes. Although usually worn unfastened, this particular banyan has a built-in waistcoat so that Prince George could wear it open and tied back, to create the impression of a coat and waistcoat. The garment is cut narrower than many more relaxed examples and has formal silk cord, frogged fastenings. It replicates the Chinese and Indian influences seen in the decoration of the regent's private retreat, the Pavilion at Brighton, with its exterior fantasy of onion-domed architecture and interior furnished in chinoiserie style with botanically accurate oriental flowers. **PW**

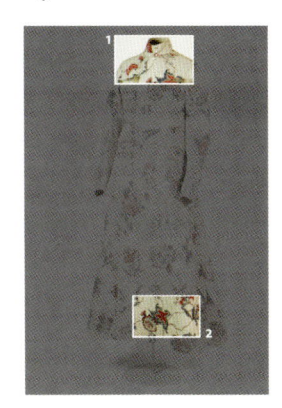

FOCAL POINTS

1 COLLAR AND FASTENINGS
The mandarin collar fastens with self-covered ball buttons. Although the 'T'-shaped, open-fronted robe appeared around 1700, in the 18th century banyans developed standing collars and front fastenings. The distinctive frog fastenings lend an oriental flavour.

2 CHINOISERIE PATTERN
The print of the garment is in a typically British chinoiserie style and the pattern's wide spatial arrangement suggests a copperplate print. This technology used large printing fields, allowing designers to develop rambling branches and asymmetrical foliage.

STATUS SYMBOL

The silk or Indian chintz banyan was an indicator of status and it appears in many male portraits of the 18th century, such as Sir Henry Raeburn's study of John Robison (c. 1798; below), a professor at Edinburgh University. The banyan was deemed appropriate attire for meeting guests at home. As a garment designed for comfort and leisure, it was worn only by society's more affluent members, who could afford the time for relaxation. Moreover, it was an object of 'conspicuous intellectualism', because it combined costly materials with a visual nod to scholarly gowns. The banyan was the perfect garment for a gentleman relaxing at home in his library.

ROCOCO ELEGANCE 115

THE ENGLISH GENTLEMAN

1 *Portrait of Squire Morland with his Gun and Dog* by James Miller (18th century) depicts an English gentleman in clothes appropriate for country pursuits.

2 By c. 1830 the British aristocracy had embraced a new masculine silhouette defined by expert tailoring.

At the end of the 18th century, a definable British style began to emerge that was emulated throughout Europe. It was influenced by the fashions of John Bull, an archetypal Englishman, country squire and landowner depicted in the cartoons of the satirist John Arbuthnot. London tailors such as Meyer, Weston and Schultz placed the importance of cut and fit above the ostentatious embellishment seen at the French court, and manipulated woollen cloth to mould and form the male body.

The traditional pursuits of the countryman, based around sporting activities such as hunting and shooting, required clothes that were practical and serviceable (above). The silks and satins, lace ruffles, silk stockings and powdered wigs were discarded and replaced by a reliance on wool and worsted products tailored to facilitate a rural lifestyle. The woollen coat with brass buttons, waistcoat, buff-coloured riding breeches tucked into boots and a narrow-brimmed, high-crowned hat made a functional country uniform.

KEY EVENTS

1760s	1764–67	1770	1778	1785–92	1795
Caricatures feature John Bull as an archetypal English landowner dressed in a frock coat.	James Hargreaves invents the Spinning Jenny, with which sixteen or more threads can be spun at once.	'Macaronis', precursors of the dandies, steal the limelight with their ostentatious imitations of continental fashion statements, wigs and elaborate ruffles.	Notable upper-class dandy George Bryan 'Beau' Brummell is born in London.	Edmund Cartwright invents the power loom and two wool-combing machines. These inventions are first applied to cotton and later to wool.	The government imposes a tax on hair powder. Only older men, military officers and some conservative professions retain their wigs and powder.

This look was translated into urban sophistication by the skills of the London tailor. Wool, unlike silk, can be stretched and steamed to fit, and a marked feature of male attire during this period was a jacket that emphasized the masculine form through cut alone (below). The indigenous production of wool and the increasing mechanization of the knitting and weaving process meant that the prime product was on hand to be utilized to the full in the tailor's skilful hands. Archetypal dandy 'Beau' Brummell (see p.118) was an exemplary exponent of the tailor's craft. A paradigm of understated good taste, he epitomized the era's ideal and was a new vision of masculinity, with broad shoulders, lean torso and long legs, based on the ideals of Greek statuary.

Brummell popularized personal cleanliness, cleaning his teeth, and shaving and bathing daily. He was also reputedly the first to starch his neck cloth. The early 19th-century neck cloth came in two versions: a folded cravat that passed around the neck and was tied at the front in a variety of ways, or a stiffened reinforced width of fabric called a stock that fitted closely around the neck and hooked behind. From 1810 to 1820 neckcloths became increasingly complex, with descriptive names such as the 'oriental', 'mathematical', 'ballroom' and 'horse collar'. These were worn with a very high shirt collar that reached up to the eyes—the points of which were called 'winkers'—a style that demanded a fixed unbending posture of superiority. Brummell always wore coats of navy blue, but the trend was for differently coloured waistcoats and trousers.

During the evening, boots were replaced with pumps, worn with silk stockings or pantaloons. Influenced by military dress, close-fitting pantaloons were fashioned from fabric cut on the bias, or knitted jersey. They were fastened at the bottom of the leg and back-laced to effect a tighter, higher fit. Their natural buff or cream colour made the lower body appear to be naked, thus emphasizing the sculptural qualities of the male figure. **MF**

1810	1811	1811	1811–16	1818	1819
A variety of more complex neckcloths begins to appear. The time-consuming process of starching and folding becomes part of daily ritual.	The Regency era begins in Britain: the Prince of Wales rules after King George III is deemed unfit.	Carlton House in London hosts a series of extravagant parties, culminating in the Carlton House fete to celebrate the Regency.	Members of the Luddite movement destroy machinery in England's industrial centres: the East Midlands, Lancashire and Yorkshire.	Beau Brummell flees to the Continent to escape his creditors. He is later jailed for debt and dies of syphilis in an asylum.	The Peterloo Massacre occurs in Manchester; the cavalry charges into a large crowd gathered to demand the reform of parliamentary representation.

THE ENGLISH GENTLEMAN

English Dandy Costume 1815
MEN'S DRESS

◈ NAVIGATOR

Presenting a new paradigm for elite manhood, one based on the pursuit of perfection of form seen in Greek statuary, the archetypal dandy during the Regency period (1811–20) eschewed the flounces and furbelows of the previous years to extol the virtues of a body contoured by expert tailoring. The double-breasted coat, cut from wool broadcloth, is moulded to the shoulders and cut high at the waist to draw attention not only to the torso but also the legs, encased in smooth, form-fitting pantaloons. A cross between breeches and trousers, they provide the focal point of the costume. The high-placed seam at the crotch is held in place with braces at the waist and a stirrup of fabric under the foot, defining the fork of the body. Modelled on cavalry garments and therefore suitable for riding, the pantaloons oblige the wearer to 'dress on one side'. The starched white linen neckcloth is encased by the high revers of the coat. It would have been at least a foot wide and therefore had to be manipulated into the correct amount of folds to fit the neck. This was a time-consuming process that might involve many hours of effort and several failures. Decorated with buttons, the jacket is left undone at the top to display the frill of the shirt, and cut square across the body to expose the similarly cut waistcoat beneath. **MF**

◉ FOCAL POINTS

1 COMPLEX NECKWEAR
Starch both protected the linen from grime and stiffened the fabric. The square of linen was folded into a band and wrapped around the neck before being tied at the front. Combined with a very high shirt collar, the style encouraged an upright posture.

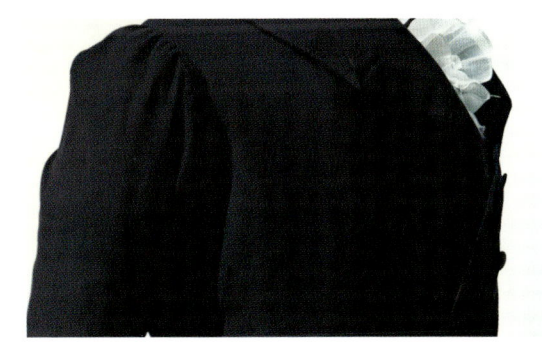

2 NEW TAILORING TECHNIQUES
The introduction of padding between the lining and the outer fabric of the jacket enlarged the chest, while the small armholes, set to the back of the jacket, forced the wearer to hold back his shoulders, thus encouraging a military bearing.

▲ This portrait of Beau Brummell by Robert Dighton (1805) shows Brummell's hair styled *à la Brutus*, unpowdered and curled and swept towards the face in the manner of classical statuary.

THE ENGLISH GENTLEMAN 119

NEOCLASSICAL STYLES

The French Revolution marked a turning point in much of Europe's social and political history. Similarly, fashion changed radically at the end of the 18th century. The formality of the past was rejected, including corsetry, the heaviness and colour of fabrics, and the excessive adornment of the Rococo period (see p.106). Instead, French fashions, which continued to lead Europe, reflected the hope that a new era had been born, emulating the democracy of ancient Greece. Inspired by this ideal, and the archaeological discoveries made at Pompeii, the period's aesthetic was known as neoclassical. The neoclassical style spread into, and took inspiration from, the European states conquered by the French army. Conservative Britain copied this fashion, but English militarism and gentlemanly styles were also in vogue, as all of Europe was at war until Napoleon's final defeat in 1815. However, the new fashion's antecedents were wider than simply French. The Romantic artistic movement was a key influence, which itself had roots in the sentimental pastoral world of French artist Jean-Honoré Fragonard and philosopher Jean-Jacques Rousseau.

Neoclassical fashions from 1780 to 1820 are most associated with the chemise dress (above). Lightweight white muslin or cotton shift dresses first appeared in France in the 1780s, popularized by the queen's circle at the

KEY EVENTS

1789	1789	1792	1793	1794	1795
The storming of the Bastille on 14 July marks the start of the French Revolution.	Marie-Antoinette's dressmaker, Rose Bertin (1747–1813), moves her couture business to London during the French Revolution.	The French Republic is declared on 22 September and the monarchy is abolished.	Louis XVI and Marie-Antoinette are executed. The Reign of Terror begins, during which thousands of 'enemies of the Republic' are executed.	Nicolaus von Heideloff strikes out as an independent publisher with his magazine *The Gallery of Fashion*, a record of fashionable and elegant dress.	The *Incroyables* and *Merveilleuses* (see p.124) cause a stir in Paris with their outrageous outfits and decadent lifestyle.

Hameau de la Reine (The Queen's Hamlet) at Versailles. Numerous portraits by Louise Elisabeth Vigée Le Brun record the rapid uptake of this simple comfortable dress and the wearer's ideological adherence to the pastoral utopia it promoted. Worn without heavy stays, and with some support for the chest, it liberated the female form and displayed only a milky white rounded bosom. However, the chemise dress was deemed unsuitable for formal court occasions, for which the *robe à la française* continued to be worn.

The chemise came to dominate fashion after the Revolution. The Empire-line dress popularized the featherweight muslin cotton that was woven in India and imported to France via England. Attempts to manufacture it in France were made, and Indian fabric was banned during the Napoleonic Wars. However, the fashionable customer bypassed this ban by ordering fabric through the Spanish Netherlands, which continued to import Indian cloth. The chemise dress could be worn as a crossover or round neck, but always with a high waist. Ribbons or Greek key embroidery were tied under the bust, and fur trimming was favoured immediately after Napoleon's defeat of Prussia in 1806. Evening dresses had short sleeves, accessorized with long white gloves (see p.122), whereas day dresses were fashioned with more practical longer sleeves, and in heavier fabrics. Indian cashmere shawls were de rigueur and bolero jackets with military-inspired frogged clasps were also worn for warmth.

Previously, mantua dresses concealed pockets in their drapery, but the cut of the Empire dress did not allow for this. Instead, small drawstring purses or bags began to be carried (right). Known as reticules, *balantines* or *indispensables*, and made of cloth, mesh or knitted yarn, they were the forerunner of the modern handbag. Many reticule designs reflected the continuing interest in exotica, prompted further by the Empress Josephine's Caribbean origins. *Souliers* (low, round-toed pumps) and gladiator sandals replaced the Louis heel, and hair was dressed *à la grecque*, pinned up in a knotted chignon, the face sometimes framed with tiny curls. Jewel or paste tiaras, after the styles of Roman matrons, replaced the extravagant plumes and flowers of *Ancien Régime* hairstyles.

Paris remained the centre of European fashion throughout the Napoleonic era, and the leading couturier was Louis Hippolyte Leroy. Originally a high-class haberdasher and milliner, he learned to sew, popularized the colour pink, invented the puff sleeve and shortened corsetry to give a balcony bust to the low-cut Empire dress. In one year alone, he supplied the Empress Josephine with 985 pairs of gloves, 556 shawls, 520 pairs of pump shoes and 136 dresses. Fashion periodicals and gazettes, such as Pierre la Mésange's *Le Journal des dames et de la mode*, founded in 1797, included colour engravings of the new creations and styles, and carried Parisian fashion into the provinces. In Britain, the Paris-trained printer Nicolaus von Heideloff also saw a gap in the market and began to publish *The Gallery of Fashion* (see p.126). This high-quality illustrated review had a limited and elite subscription. **PW**

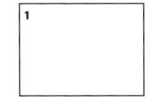

1 *Portrait of Madame Recamier* by Jacques-Louis David (c. 1800) depicts the sitter wearing a white chemise with her hair dressed *à la grecque*. The empty background symbolizes the new beginning created by the Revolution.

2 This silk reticule is embroidered with silk thread and has a string tassel and straps (1790–1800).

1795	1796	1798	1798	1798	1799
The new regime of the Directory begins. Charles Percier and Pierre-François-Léonard Fontaine establish the Directoire style in interior design.	Napoleon Bonaparte marries Josephine de Beauharnais, daughter of a Caribbean planter and widow of a guillotined noble.	Jacques-Louis David paints *Madame Raymond de Verninac* in the neoclassical style.	The French Campaign in Egypt prompts great interest in archaeological finds and designs.	Turbans become popular after the French expedition to Egypt, and simple bonnets replace the picture hats of the 1700s.	After the Coup d'Etat (9–10 November), Napoleon appoints himself the First Consul, thus ending the Directory period.

NEOCLASSICAL STYLES

Muslin Chemise 1790s
WOMEN'S DRESS

French chemise dress
and shawl (c. 1805–10).

NAVIGATOR

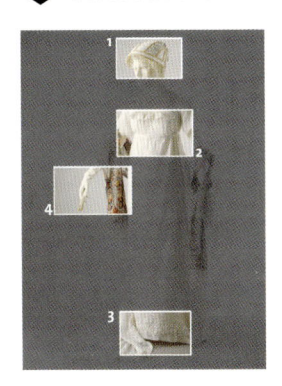

This French muslin robe typifies the evening dress of the neoclassical vogue. The high-waisted columnar style is made up of several layers of transparent cotton muslin and is lined with linen. This gives the garment the necessary weight to achieve its simple vertical lines, and also adds warmth to the otherwise lightweight fabric. Although more modest than the daring chemises worn by the *Merveilleuses*, this costume conforms to their example, and has a delicate lace frill at the low-cut bust. This draws attention to an area of the body that was relatively liberated by the fashion for lighter bra-style stays. Short sleeves also allow a large expanse of the bare arm to be seen.

In comparison to the stiffness of earlier court styles, the informality of early 19th-century fashion and manners is conveyed in the light palette, delicate fabrics and simple uncluttered lines. However, this evening dress is more elaborate than many muslin day dresses, with cotton lace embroidery panels at the front and hem. The additional muslin train, referencing that worn by the Empress Josephine for her coronation, confirms the wearer's status. The design of the classical-style silk and cashmere stole, which has a paisley trim and fringed edging, is echoed in the bonnet. This sits neatly above softly curled hair, dressed *à la grecque*. **PW**

FOCAL POINTS

1 BONNET AND HAIR
The new style of dress is accompanied by a softer, more relaxed hairstyle. Here, natural hair is dressed loosely into Grecian-style curls. A tight bonnet-band decorates and protects the hair. Sometimes feathered headdresses or jewelled diadems were worn.

3 LACE
The lace panels are embroidered in cotton thread over the muslin. They follow a naturalistic design of acorns and vine tendrils, which is an unusual choice among the more popular Greek key designs. It echoes the pastoral vogue of the late 18th century.

2 SOFTENED STYLE
The chemise dress relies on simplicity for effect. No obvious corsetry is visible, although it is likely that a light corset was worn underneath the chemise. Instead, the form is provided by a ribbon sash, the fabric floating over the wearer's torso.

4 GLOVES AND FAN
Evening wear accessories are laden in meaning. White gloves not only protect the skin from dirt but also ensure that the wearer makes no improper physical contact with her dancing partner. The fan is used as a sort of semaphore code for sexual mores.

NEOCLASSICAL STYLES 123

Incroyables and Merveilleuses 1795
OUTLANDISH AND DECADENT DRESS STYLE

L'embarras des Queues, from *Le Bon Genre*, No. 2 (1801).

⚽ **NAVIGATOR**

The *Incroyables* (Incredibles) were a dandyish set of men with royalist sympathies, led by the Vicomte de Barras, one of the members of the Directory; their female counterparts were the *Merveilleuses* (Marvellous women). Prevalent throughout the Directory period (1795–99), both groups adopted affected aristocratic manners and sported outlandish and exaggerated forms of dress. Some wore their hair short at the back *à la victime*, in imitation of the haircut given to those about to be guillotined during the Reign of Terror (1793–94). The men also kept their hair long at the front and spaniel-eared.

This print from the satirical series *Le Bon Genre* shows two *Merveilleuses* being pursued by two *Incroyables*. The exaggerated fashion worn by both sexes is mocked, making them instantly identifiable. The men wear strangely cut jackets that contort their posture, and their stance is deformed further by their deliberately shortened canes. Their chins are hidden by oversized foulard *steenkerke* scarves, which also completely conceal their necks, and refer to death by guillotine. Both men would carry folding lorgnettes (*binocles-ciseaux*) to allow them to peer in affectation at a subject, and the powdered wig is a deliberate reference to the styles of the *Ancien Régime*. The women's low-cut, flowing chemise dresses of sheer white silks, styled after ancient Greek dress, are lengthened into impractical trains that are easily caught by the men's canes. Indeed, the women seem to invite the attack by the *Incroyables*. The two dresses have short sleeves, and are worn with white three-quarter-length gloves. The *Merveilleuses* carry a panoply of accessories—reticules, fans and parasols—and wear flat, pompom *souliers*. **PW**

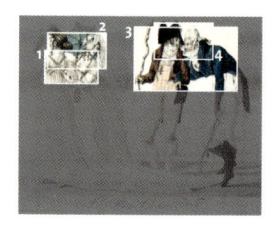

FOCAL POINTS

1 EXPOSED FLESH
The *Merveilleuses*' reputation as breakers of social decency is seen in the extremely low-cut neckline of the woman on the right, whose breasts, already balancing on balcony corsetry, are almost completely exposed. Both women's sexual probity is clearly in question, as they appear to flirt openly with the men.

2 WOMEN'S HAIRSTYLES
The woman on the left-hand side wears her hair in a classic Greek chignon, whereas her companion has a bonnet with a lengthy veil, in imitation of a Roman vestal virgin. Its exaggerated dimensions reflect the ostentatious and extrovert character of many young *Merveilleuses*.

3 DISTORTED SILHOUETTE
The male silhouette is an inelegant form of the Rococo style. The men's postures, like their canes, are distorted, and are deliberately shortened to induce a twisted gait. Both men wear ill-fitting frock coats, oversized scarves and high-waisted unflattering trousers, with baggy, loosely shaped boots.

4 MAN'S WIG
By 1795 many men had abandoned powdered hair or wigs, and adopted natural hair as the style of the 'new' post-Revolutionary world. Here, the outsize wig is a deliberate reference to the aristocratic styles of the *Ancien Régime*. Its wearer intended to satirize both past and future politics and aesthetics.

▲ The clothing of the *Incroyables* was a comic exaggeration of the English aristocratic style, while the *Merveilleuses* referenced Grecian goddesses and adopted the Empire-line chemise dress or tunic.

Afternoon Dress 1800s
WOMEN'S FASHION

Fashion plate by Nicolaus von Heideloff,
from *The Gallery of Fashion* (February 1802).

Each plate of *The Gallery of Fashion* is accompanied by a descriptive text, and the models are often shown engaged in ladylike occupations: driving in town, playing with their children, singing or playing the harp. The illustrations also offer advice on appropriate accessories. Here, the models wear winter afternoon dress. The left-hand design shows that the vertical Empire-line silhouette has gained volume at the bottom and is gathered above the waist with small pin tucks, similar to the *robe à l'anglaise*. This gathering is accentuated by the bolero fitted upper dress, emphasizing the very cinched upper torso.

On the right, the model incorporates a chemise-style dress with a three-quarter-length gilet overcoat, worn with thick stockings, cotton underskirts and boots concealed underneath. A heavy white fabric is used for the underdress, which, like the overcoat, is cut on the Empire line. In comparison to diaphanous muslin, this fabric has a certain stiffness. The three-quarter-length overcoat is similar to a mantua, and functions both as the main dress bodice and as a bottom warmer. It is cut away at the bust to reveal the contrasting underdress. **PW**

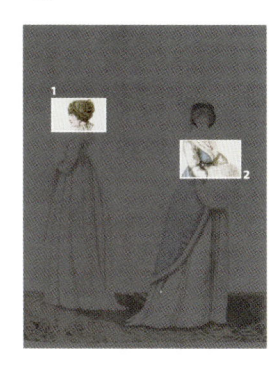

◆ NAVIGATOR

👁 FOCAL POINTS

1 ROMAN-STYLED HAIR
The model on the left wears elaborately coiled and plaited hair in the Roman fashion. This sits above a Renaissance-style ermine collar, accessorized with a small lace ruff. Other hairstyles included the Grecian chignon, often decorated with a feathered toque.

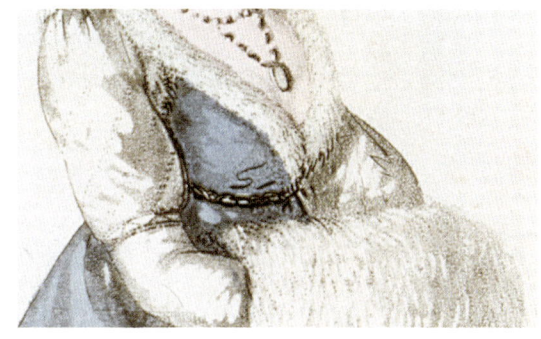

2 ACCESSORIES
The right-hand model wears a simple chained pendant necklace echoing the V-neck overcoat. The collar and edging are trimmed in white ermine, picked up in the outsize snowball muff. The V-neck collar fastens to the underdress, using a brooch and a belt.

THE PRINTED FASHION JOURNAL

Although France and Britain were intermittently at war from 1793 to 1815, fashions crossed the Channel in both directions thanks to the rise of the printed fashion journal. In France *La galerie des modes* began production in 1778 and offered coloured prints (right) of the latest fashions to its readers until 1787. Trained in Paris as an engraver and portrait miniaturist, Stuttgart-born Nicolaus von Heideloff arrived in London to escape the Revolution and quickly realized that the British market had no equivalent publication. In April 1794 von Heideloff launched *The Gallery of Fashion*, a monthly colour journal with two hand-tinted, metallic-embellished prints per issue. It continued to be published until March 1803. Although *The Gallery of Fashion* is an important historical source, it had a very limited British readership because of its very high quality and associated price. At its height, there were approximately 350 British subscribers and 60 overseas; they included the British elite and the first edition was taken by George III's daughters and his second son, the Duke of York.

NEOCLASSICAL STYLES 127

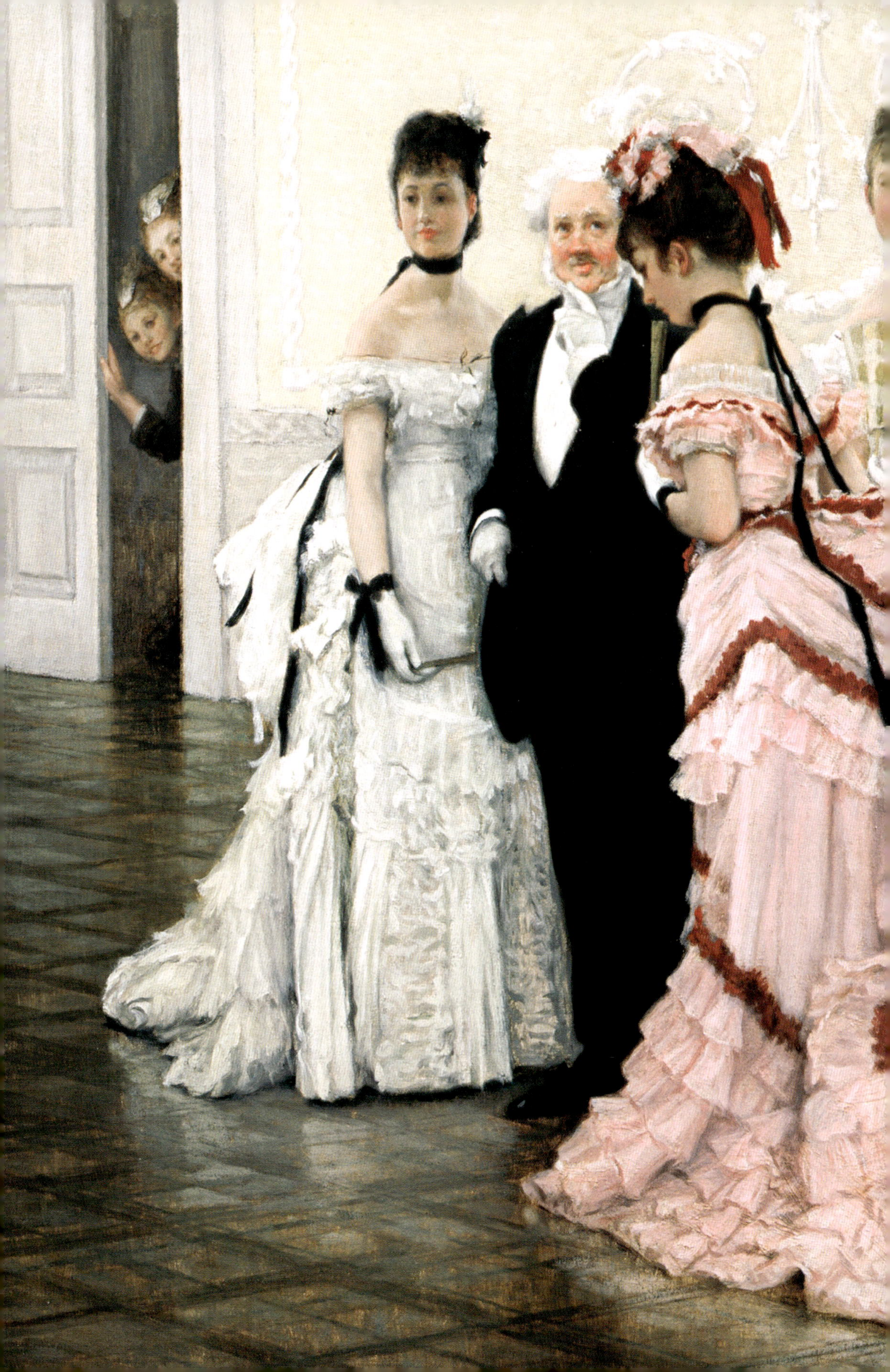

3 | 1800 TO 1899

ROMANTIC DRESS 130

WEST AFRICAN KENTE CLOTHS 134

LATIN AMERICAN DRESS 138

VICTORIAN DRESS 146

THE ART OF ENGLISH TAILORING 154

AFRICAN WAX AND FANCY PRINTS 160

CHINESE DRESS – LATE QING DYNASTY 164

BURMESE DRESS 168

THE BIRTH OF HAUTE COUTURE 172

JAPANESE DRESS – MEIJI PERIOD 180

ARTISTIC AND AESTHETIC DRESS 184

AN AMERICAN ARCHETYPE 190

FASHIONS OF THE BELLE EPOQUE 196

ROMANTIC DRESS

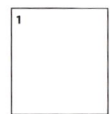

1. Johann Nepomuk Ender's portrait of *Archduchess Sophie* (1830) depicts the wide neckline and ample sleeves that characterized fashion in the Romantic era. The gold-buckled belt and jewelled cuffs emphasize the slim waist and wrists.

2. Small handbags were known as reticules; this example (1810–15) is made from silk-satin, and is decorated with an embroidered floral basket motif and fringe trimming.

The restoration of the French monarchy in 1815 prompted a resurgence of European conservatism. Fashion not only reflected the return of politics to the past, invoking the distant Renaissance period, but also bore direct relation to the interests of the Romantic artistic movement. A mythical Scottish Highlands, popularized in Sir Walter Scott's *Waverley* novels (1814–31), and his founding of the Celtic festival, were particularly inspirational.

The fashions of the Romantic period (c. 1770–1840) provided extremes of differentiation between the genders, with dashing military-inspired costume for men. Women's dresses emphasized female frailty, tiny waists and heavy bosoms. The straight up-and-down style of the Empire skirt was replaced gradually by the A-line, which first appeared in the 1820s, with gored panels allowing for a slightly fuller silhouette. Skirts had become more generous in volume by the 1830s and, during the late Romantic period, layered petticoats were worn to create a bell shape under the panelled skirt. The wearer's bottom

KEY EVENTS

1800s	1803	1820	1820s	1822	1829
The shoelace is introduced. Women begin to wear dainty lace-up boots that emphasize their ankles.	The first of the Napoleonic Wars takes place, following on from the conflict of the French Revolution.	The Prince Regent becomes George IV. Sir Walter Scott founds the Celtic festival in Edinburgh.	The A-line skirt is introduced and hemlines are worn just short enough to show the ankle.	Charles Macintosh invents the waterproof outer garment.	David Wilkie paints George IV's visit to Edinburgh in 1822, showing the king in full Highland dress.

was padded with a small bustle. Skirts of the period are particularly remarkable for their hemline decoration, and the hem itself hovered between the foot and the floor.

The move away from the Empire-line gown saw a return to the natural waistline in 1825 to 1830. Consequently, Romantic-era corset stays had to be longer. Initially they were lightly boned or corded, with rear lacing and a solid ivory or wood busk placed down the front. Later, waists became more waspish, with the return of punitive corsetry. The pointed front bodice of the 1840s was strengthened with whalebone to create the 'basque-fronted' waist. Such underpinning was an essential foundation to female dress, and a measure of female decency. As with Empire gowns, Romantic period dresses were often made in one piece: the bodice was stitched to the skirt, and the garment fastened at the back. Popular fabrics included organza, silk and tartan plaid. The latter was particularly ideal for the carriage dress, a day dress that was designed for outdoor pursuits.

Necklines were rounded, 'V'-shape or bateau. They were invariably worn off the shoulder, with short sleeves for evening wear (see p.132) and long sleeves for day dresses. Indeed, wider shoulders were fashionable from 1830, particularly because they created the impression of an even tinier waist (opposite). Neck ruffles were sometimes worn on day dresses, or ruff frills were added to bateau necklines to further widen the silhouette at the shoulders. This contrast of shoulder width and cinched waist was emphasized by the fashion for voluminous sleeves. The medieval Marie sleeve, which had been worn with the Empire-line dress, had been replaced by the *gigot d'agneau* (leg o' mutton) sleeve by 1830, which was full from shoulder to elbow, then fitted to the wrist. This created a balloon of material on the upper arm, and the upper sleeve was supported by a small pannier tied to the shoulder. Often sleeves were slashed to show a contrasting material underneath, and the fashion was for rich colours.

Exposed shoulders were covered with large lace or linen collars, known as pelerines or bertha collars. Lace or cashmere shawls provided warmth, and Paisley in Scotland became the centre for weaving popular Indian-style shawls. Mantles, paletots and mantelets were cape overcoats of various lengths, frequently cut from the same material as the main dress and accessorized with fur boas and muffs. Other accessories included wide buckled belts that matched the dress fabrics and emphasized the tiny waist. Some buckles had enamel pastings, whereas others were carved or pierced mother-of-pearl. The belt was used to carry reticules (right), lorgnettes and gold watches hanging from a chain. This freed the woman to carry a lace-trimmed parasol. The poke bonnet fitted closely to the head, was tied under the chin and had a high brim. This style accommodated hair *à la chinoise*, a topknot with curls hanging at the side, which was in fashion *c*. 1830. Commonly, hair was parted in the centre, with ringlets around the face, and tied in a knot at the back. **PW**

1830s	1832	1833	1837	1841	1842
The impractical 'imbecile', or *donna Maria*, sleeve is introduced. The off-the-shoulder style makes arm movement difficult.	The Great Reform Act gives greater political representation to British cities, including the textile centres of Manchester and Bradford.	Westminster abolishes the ownership of slaves in the British Empire. This is a direct blow to British cotton producers, but boosts the US market.	William IV dies. He is succeeded by his niece, the eighteen-year-old Princess Victoria.	*The True Principles of Pointed or Christian Architecture* by A. W. N. Pugin is published, popularizing medieval English Gothic art and architecture.	*Vestiarium Scoticum* is published, a text claiming to be an ancient compendium of all Scottish clan tartans.

Evening Gown 1830s
WOMEN'S FASHION

English silk plain-weave (organza)
and silk-satin evening dress (c. 1830).

NAVIGATOR

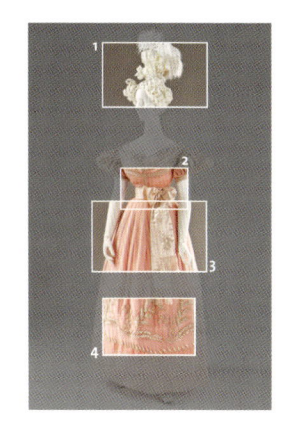

This style of English evening dress was popular among a wealthy clientele in the 1830s and was promoted by magazines such as *The Royal Lady*. The vertical silhouette of the Napoleonic period was replaced by one that was rounder and more feminine. The dress is made from a rose-pink plain-weave organza silk, and a glass pearl bead trim demonstrates the fashion for embellishment of the lower skirts. The rear-fastening dress has a low bateau neckline and is characterized by its short 'puff' style, or *demi-gigot*, pleated sleeves, held tightly with banded hems. These hint at the extravagance of full leg o' mutton sleeves seen on contemporary day dresses. The volume and shape of these sleeves are obtained by the use of truncated sleeve panniers, attached to the dress and shoulder. The bodice is trimmed in overlapping, softly rounded panels, in contrasting oyster and rose silks, meeting in the middle with a vertical anchoring staple, or *agrafe*. The bust is separated by the central staple and is supported by lightweight corsetry. Rather than following the Empire line, the waist has descended to its natural position, and is emphasized by the wide sash, tied in a bow. The skirt is gently gored and rounded, the volume created by stiffened petticoats. The dress would be worn with white stockings and satin slippers, often tied with Scottish 'ghillie' cross-lacing. **PW**

FOCAL POINTS

1 HAIRSTYLE
The hair is worn *à la chinoise*. It is parted down the centre to echo the symmetrical detail of the dress. The front is dressed with tight side curls, and the back raised tightly into a topknot, or stiffened pinned plaits. Further height is added by a bold plumed headdress.

3 GLOVES
Tightly fitting, elbow-length, virginal white gloves are worn with the evening dress. The fabric is heavy, and the style conservative. The gloves allow feminine modesty to be preserved, leaving half the bare arm exposed by the short sleeves.

2 COORDINATED TRIMMING
This rose-pink dress illustrates the fashion for coordinated trimming. A contrasting oyster-colour silk-satin is seen in the wide fringed sash, ribbon bust contrast and foliage-stitched beading. This motif is carried through into the hair accessories and crystal drop earrings.

4 BEADING
The detail on the lower skirt is made from imitation pearl beads. They form a repeating wheat-sheaf pattern, with a base line of interrupted shell shapes. This marks a renewed interest in natural design, after the geometric fashions of the early 19th century.

WEST AFRICAN KENTE CLOTHS

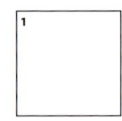

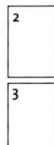

1 King Sakite of East Krobo, Ghana, wears a Kente cloth wrapper in the 1870s. The necklace and sword in the picture were presented to him by Queen Victoria.

2 This handwoven silk kente was made by an Asante weaver in the 19th century. The central panel consists of alternating blocks of warp stripes in yellow, green, red and blue with blocks of weft lozenges and geometric shapes.

3 This handwoven cotton kente shows the oldest dated cloth example of weaving warp sections with weft blocks. The use of plied yarn suggests that it was woven by Ewe weavers.

Kente cloths are among the best-known handwoven textiles from West Africa. They originated in the 18th and 19th centuries on the Gold and Slave Coasts (present-day Ghana and Togo) and historically are woven and sewn by men. Kente cloths comprise narrow strips that are sewn selvedge to selvedge, and they have always reflected changing styles in design, composition and colour. They have been produced in different weaving areas: around Kumasi, the centre of the 18th- and 19th-century powerful Asante confederacy, and in Agotime, Notse, Peki and the coastal area of the Ewe-speaking region. Until the 17th century, bark cloths were commonly worn and cotton textiles made from hand-spun and dyed yarns were luxury items, reserved for the economic and political elites, such as kings (above). Over time, however, they became part of ordinary dress. The conspicuous display of expensive textiles and new designs in kente affirmed the wearer's power, wealth and status when they were used at civic, ceremonial and religious events.

Fashion played an important role in the development of kente. Although written and visual sources are limited, the extensive trade in fabrics and the

KEY EVENTS

Early 19th century	1817	1820	1840	1840–47	1860s
Two pairs of heddles in one strip of cloth are used by Agotime weavers; this soon spreads to other weaving centres.	The British envoy Thomas Bowdich visits Kumasi in the Asante region. The first drawing of a weaver appears.	By this date many European nations have abolished the slave trade, but it continues in many countries until the 1860s. Cloth is an important trade item.	The oldest kente cloth is given to the Basel missionary Andreas Riis by the king of Akropong.	Old kente cloths are collected by departing Danish officials and Basel missionaries.	The first photographs of kente cloths and weavers in the Ewe-speaking region are taken by the missionary Hornberger.

high demand for foreign imports, as well as the variety of patterns in extant local cloth and in 19th-century photographs, indicate that fashion trends in kente were ever-changing. Even in the 17th century, European textile merchants complained about annual changes in taste. Only the manner in which cloth was elegantly draped around the body stayed relatively the same. Men used a large wrapper around the body and over the left shoulder, whereas women wore two wrappers—one around the hips and one around the upper body.

In the 18th century, warp-faced textiles with warp striping were most common in all weaving centres except Agotime. The same warp-stripe pattern could be repeated across the face of the textile, or two or more sequences of strips could be placed next to one another. In Agotime, weavers wove weft-faced textiles with a different type of heddle, allowing for weft-stripe patterning such as the chessboard effect. Textiles became more elaborate as more complicated techniques—such as the creation of motifs with an extra weft or warp, and the use of red cotton and silk unravelled from European cloths exchanged for gold and slaves—opened up new design possibilities (above right; see p.136).

At the wealthy Asante court, weavers were subject to royal patronage and restrictions were in place on what people wore. Unravelled silk and wild silk imported from the north, and the growing incorporation of non-figurative, weft-float motifs were mainly preserved for those in the highest positions. Such restrictions did not exist in the Ewe-speaking region, which—together with the existence of interrelated weaving centres and the large cloth exports to other parts of West Africa—explains the wider variety of cloth woven there over the centuries. Colours have tended to be more subdued and weft-float motifs have been figurative in kente from the Ewe region (see p.136).

At the end of the 18th or in the early 19th century, the main feature of most kente—the alternation of weft and warp elements in one length of fabric—developed in Agotime, where the two pairs of heddles necessary for the process were already in use. This development was soon shared with Asante weavers through direct contact, the extensive trade in textiles and the skill of weavers at copying cloths. The introduction of machine-spun cotton in the 19th century and the replacement of silk by rayon stimulated an increase in weft-float designs framed between weft blocks among Asante and Agotime weavers. Asante weavers developed textiles made with three pairs of heddles and continued creating non-figurative motifs in increasingly bright colours. Ewe weavers had mastered the weaving of two sets of warp by the 18th century and began to use plied and twisted yarns of two or more colours, expanding the design possibilities (right). Coastal weavers in particular developed complicated ways to lay the warp and combine warps and wefts to create any colour shade. The 18th- and 19th-century appreciation for new cloths, designs and colour combinations has only grown in the 20th and 21st centuries. Kente continues to be a fashion that constantly reinvents itself. **MK**

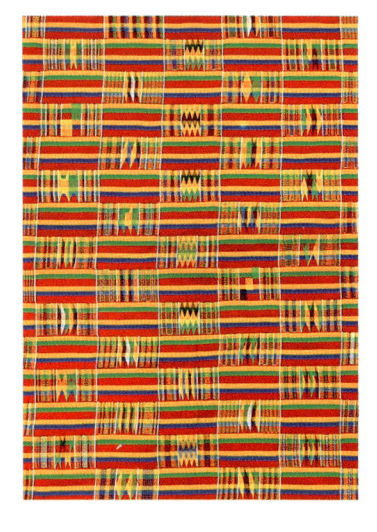

1869	c. 1871	1874	1870s–90s	1888	1920s
With the start of the Asante Wars many people from Krepi, a large part of the Ewe-speaking region, are taken into captivity and sent to Asante.	Queen Victoria presents King Sakite of East Krobo with a necklace and sword.	The Asante Wars end, and the formal British colonization of the Gold Coast and the German colonization of the Ewe-speaking region begins.	Imported machine-spun cotton is used and silk is replaced by rayon, bringing about many new design developments.	The oldest surviving photograph showing two weavers on a Ewe and Asante loom side by side is taken, proving direct contact between the two areas.	Captain R. S. Rattray collects cloth samples during his time working for the British colonial government (see p.137).

Kente Cloth *c.* 1847
WEST AFRICAN WRAPPER

1 CROCODILE MOTIF
The crocodile image can be linked to the saying 'a stump that stays in the river for a hundred years does not become a crocodile'. In Ghana the connection of proverbs to visual imagery is highly valued. Images can be interpreted in various ways, depending on the context.

2 COLOUR RANGE
The colours red, white and blue are used in this kente cloth. Red and white predominate, whereas blue is used sparingly. The plentiful use of red highlights the fabric's expensive nature and would draw attention to the wealth and status of its wearer.

Handwoven kente with figurative weft-float motifs from the Ewe-speaking region in Ghana and Togo (early to mid 19th century).

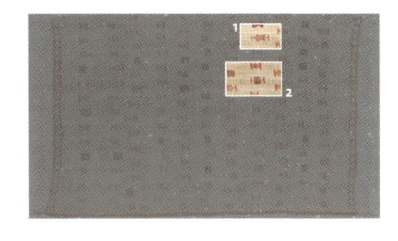

NAVIGATOR

This is one of the oldest extant examples of kente cloth. It is made from hand-spun cotton and consists of twenty-eight strips, all of which feature motifs except one; there are 148 motifs in total. More than twenty of the motifs are figurative and they include a crocodile, snake, frog, comb, drum and sword. The weaving of such figurative weft-float motifs is particular to Ewe weavers and this cloth is one of the most splendid examples from the 19th century. It was most likely woven on commission; textiles that feature the highest-quality, most expensive cloths and most complicated patterns are still mainly produced on commission. By contrast, the less valuable 'market cloth' of the Ewe region was sold to traders who came to Keta in the 19th century. They bought cloth in bulk to sell throughout West Africa. Asante cloth, however, has usually been woven for local use.

The overall design of this kente cloth has been carefully thought through: the pattern of motifs alternates with plain weave areas in both the vertical and horizontal directions. The last strip features no motifs, but being half white and half red creates a clear finish to the textile. Whether spread out or worn around the body as a wrapper, the cloth would have impressed contemporary observers with its dazzling display of weaving skill and innovative creativity.

The cloth was woven before 1847, when it was collected by Edward Carstensen, the last Danish governor of the Gold Coast, before the sale of Danish coastal possessions to Britain. He collected twelve cloths for the newly founded National Museum of Denmark in Copenhagen, the oldest ethnographical museum in the world. **MK**

KENTE SAMPLES

It is a common practice among weavers throughout Ghana and Togo to retain a small piece of the kente cloths that are woven to use as samples to show prospective new customers. This practice goes back to at least the early 20th century, but was probably also common in earlier centuries. Some weavers stitch the samples together as a booklet or as a long string; others put them into a photograph album. These samples (right) form part of a large collection gathered by Captain R. S. Rattray, who was an anthropologist working for the British colonial government in the 1920s.

LATIN AMERICAN DRESS

Independence deeply affected the ways in which people consumed fashion throughout Latin America in the late 18th and early 19th centuries. Urban-based revolutionaries embraced the styles of Paris, as if to align themselves with the ideals of 'liberty, equality and fraternity' espoused by the French Revolution. Creole descendants of Europeans had an inferior social status in colonial society, but with independence many began to advocate a society based on merit rather than inherited privilege. Clothes helped the newly independent countries to distance themselves from Spanish colonialism and forge their own cultural and national identities. After Argentina's revolution in 1810, intellectuals disseminated political ideas under the guise of fashion writing, thus escaping the attention of the authorities. Home-grown fashion magazines, such as Argentina's *La Moda*, inspired by the French *La Mode*, and Uruguay's *El Iniciador*, applauded the democratic ideals of the revolutions in France and the United States. Although expanding British mercantilism and earlier British invasion attempts brought to the fore patriotic sentiments in the River Plate region of Argentina and Uruguay, after independence a form of diplomatic courting developed that continued throughout the 19th century. Under the dictatorship of Juan Manuel de Rosas (1835–52), when all citizens had to wear crimson insignias in support of Federalist rule, men's top hats

KEY EVENTS

1830s	1832	1835	1837	1838	c. 1840s
Post-colonial women of the River Plate region wear an enlarged tortoiseshell hair comb, the *peinetón*, to assert their presence in public.	The Argentine Confederation of Juan Manuel de Rosas adopts a crimson insignia and prohibits the blue and green hues of the opposition.	Venezuelan Manuel Antonio Carreño Muñoz starts writing his *Manual de Urbanidad y Buenas Costumbres* in instalments.	Inspired by the French *La Mode*, intellectuals in Buenos Aires found *La Moda*. Its first issues evade censorship because few associate fashion with politics.	Former contributors to *La Moda* are forced into exile. Those taking up work at *El Iniciador* in Uruguay continue to use fashion writing to critique politics.	The Afro-Peruvian painter Francisco Fierro Palas, known as Pancho Fierro, renders the *tapadas limeñas* in everyday scenes of his native Lima.

138 1800–99

featured red ribbons (opposite). Women's fans also depicted portraits of political figures. Whereas many regions were independent of Spain and Portugal by 1825, the colonies of Cuba and Puerto Rico only gained independence in 1898, after the Spanish–American War. Until then they fashioned identities in dress cautiously.

As 19th-century magazines reveal, the Creole elite altered European styles significantly for practical and symbolic reasons. Fashion writing served as a tool with which to examine and critique post-colonial society. The Uruguayan editors of *La Mariposa* maintained that emerging national customs could serve as 'the expression of people's character and moral condition'. For them, discussions about dress and customs had the potential to transform flawed societies into virtuous ones. 'Our fashions are…nothing more than alterations of European style,' explained an anonymous author in the pages of *La Moda*. 'However, this modification is one that is executed artistically by intelligent men.' Amid the political repression that followed Argentine independence, the emulation of French and US styles implied political alternatives. As Miguel Cané wrote in the pages of *El Iniciador*: 'Our century is a dressmaker because it is a century of creating movement, novelties, progress.'

Europeans used to the ostentatious dress worn at court in their home countries marvelled at the diversity of women's dress in the Americas. In the 1840s Frances 'Fanny' Erskine Inglis, by then known as the Marquise of Calderón de la Barca, described women of Spanish and indigenous heritage who wore finely woven *rebozos* (long, narrow shawls) with loose-fitting, lace-trimmed blouses and colourful, sometimes sequinned skirts. This so-called *china poblana* dress was illustrated by German artist Carl Nebel in 1836 (below) and

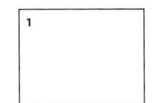

1 Gauchos in a *pulpería* (a store that doubles as a tavern) from a painting by Carlos Morel (1839). They wear clothes suitable for riding—loose, baggy trousers (*bombachas*) and a kind of blanket (*chiripá*) worn looped through the legs and tied at the waist.

2 Women from Puebla, Mexico, in 1836, wearing traditional *china poblana* attire. The name originally referred to the servant dress of a woman from Puebla and is thought to have been named after a legendary Asian woman brought to Mexico as a slave in the 17th century.

1851	1853	1860s	1872	1880s	1898
To reduce dependence on imports, President Carlos Antonio López orders that Paraguayan government ranches grow cotton for military uniforms.	Manuel Antonio Carreño Muñoz publishes the *Manual de Urbanidad y Buenas Costumbres*. It is an instant best-seller.	Foot-treadle sewing machines and the increasing availability of fashion lithographs promote home-made dressmaking in Latin America.	María del Pilar Sinués de Marco starts to edit a transatlantic fashion newspaper, *La Torre de Oro*, which has offices in Seville and Buenos Aires.	With its agricultural exports and massive immigration, Buenos Aires becomes known as the Paris of Latin America.	Cuba and Puerto Rico gain independence following the Spanish–American War.

LATIN AMERICAN DRESS 139

became fashionable to those 19th-century women who aspired to dress boldly. Derived from the Spanish tortoiseshell hair comb, the *peineta*, the *peinetón* (above) emerged and increased in size alongside the quest for independence in Argentina to the point when patriotic slogans could be emblazoned on its ample width. After independence, when women were refused the status of citizenship, men found the public spaces obstructed by women seeking their own independence, wearing enormous *peinetones*.

In Lima, Peru, veiled women known as the *tapadas limeñas* emerged from the Andalusian *cobijada*, brought to the region during the Viceroyalty of Peru. They peered with one eye from behind a long, often dark-coloured and soft shawl (opposite above). This style, which consisted of a *saya* (overskirt) and *manto* (veil), was worn after independence and into the mid 19th century. *Tapadas limeñas* navigated urban spaces ordinarily off limits to women and, with their air of anonymity, represented a mysterious presence.

In other colonies, however, such as the islands of Cuba and Puerto Rico, styles remained particular to their Spanish heritage. In Cuba soldiers fighting for independence wore a *guayabera*—a man's pleated cotton shirt with large pockets. This garment remains a symbol of Cuban national identity and is still worn throughout the Caribbean. In Puerto Rico, although the silhouettes of women's dresses looked like those throughout the Americas, the embroidery and embellishments showed a Spanish influence. After independence in 1898, Puerto Rican women abandoned the use of the mantilla (lace headscarf) but continued to integrate eyelet cutwork along the edges of clothing and the folding fan. Information about the styles of clothes worn during this period lies in the diaries and correspondence of foreign observers, fashion magazines and lithographs, paintings, and other historical documents. For example, in *The Voyage of the Beagle*, naturalist Charles Darwin described the gaucho dress of authoritarian Argentine leader Juan Manuel de Rosas. In Chile, travellers sketched men wearing simple hats and bullfighting jackets, and women wearing flounced skirts, indicating an Andalusian heritage. Paintings of storefronts in Montevideo, Uruguay, show assorted ponchos on display.

Shipping documents indicate that the region became flooded with European goods, which inevitably changed Latin American dress. Even the Andean poncho (see p.144) was manufactured in Manchester or Birmingham. From 'English hats of superior quality' to 'black and buff kid gloves', one report from Argentina revealed that English riding dress had been generally

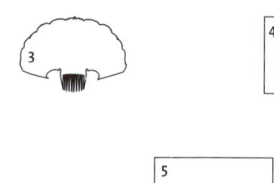

3 This elaborate *peinetón* dates from 1840. It is made from tortoiseshell and bears the silhouette of Juan Manuel de Rosas, governor of Buenos Aires.

4 A photograph of a *tapada limeña* from a 19th-century postcard. This unique style of dress is thought to be Moorish in origin.

5 Colombian mule drivers browsing at a store in 1834 wear the typical rural dress of tunics, ponchos and sombrero hats.

adopted by the ladies of Buenos Aires by 1834. Also available were gentlemen's ready-made frock coats, black vests and fine cloth trousers. In Colombia, a predilection for English and French fashions meant that only rural inhabitants remained associated with iconic traditional dress forms, such as the native *ruana* (poncho) or the *sombrero vueltiao*, a bendable, woven cane hat with laps of Zenú tribal origin (below). The advice columns of fashion magazines were important tools for navigating European trends, with particular patterns described in detail and highlighted with accompanying lithographs.

In the second half of the 19th century, women began to write for fashion magazines. Juana Manuela de Gorriti and Clorinda Matto de Turner, who both established fashion magazines in Buenos Aires, lamented the corseted waists and layers of European dress imposed on women. Dress reform in Venezuela prescribed abandoning the remnants of Spanish dress, and the mantilla, which had religious significance, was discarded. Increasingly, the sewing machine allowed women to choose home-made over store-bought or tailored options.

Everyday dress continued to reflect social and racial inequalities, often designating those of African or indigenous heritage a less fashionable status. Throughout the region many people of colour subverted conventional dress codes by arriving at carnivals and ceremonies in their finest clothes, including aprons, headwraps and ties. In Guatemala, women preserved textile traditions with the use of fibres dyed naturally in a rainbow of hues. *Traje*, or indigenous dress, remained invested with deep cultural and spiritual significance and revealed a great deal about the wearer's social status.

In the early 20th century, foreign investment and British-owned department stores, such as Casa Mappin in Brazil and Harrods in Argentina, offered new ways to buy foreign goods. With the consolidation of nation-states, the region experienced an increase in European immigration, with newcomers dressing for success, like their city-based employers, and forgoing traditional styles. Despite the proliferation of images projecting 'national' types associated with rural culture—from the Argentine gaucho to the Venezuelan *llanero*, and the Mexican *charro* (see p.142)—much of the region began to adopt Western styles. **RR**

Charro Suit 19th century
MEN'S RIDING DRESS

Mexican *charro* (c. 1890).

NAVIGATOR

The *charro* is the Mexican horseman who originally came from the central western states of Jalisco, Michoacán and Guanajuato. Although elements of the costume are Spanish in origin, the *charro* suit acquired its distinctive Mexican identity in the 19th century. The traditionally black suit is decorated elaborately with detailed embroidery and stitching with gold or silver thread. A bolero-style jacket opens to a fabric *moño*, or tied neck scarf, that is also embroidered. Trimmings along the jacket sleeves and trouser legs include intricate stitching and leatherwork. Gold- or silver-plated buttons often display Spanish, indigenous and Mexican national symbols. The suits are embroidered by hand or by machine and feature motifs such as horseshoes, spurs, flowers and eagles. Some suits incorporate an embroidered emblem on the jacket's back; for example, an eagle perched on a flowering cactus with a serpent in its mouth refers to the founding of the Aztec capital at Tenochtitlan (present-day Mexico City) and is a symbol of Mexican national identity. A sombrero and riding boots complete the outfit. Popular representations of the *charro* and its exaggerated aesthetic adopted by mariachi folk bands are seen at Mexican cultural events and have appeared in Hollywood films, such as *¡Viva Zapata!* (1952). Today's *charro* is arguably a Mexican fashion style known throughout the world. **RR**

FOCAL POINTS

1 SOMBRERO
The sombrero hat, which originated in Mexico, has a high pointed crown. This wide-brimmed hat is broad enough to cast a shadow over the wearer's head and shoulders. The hat is also often embroidered.

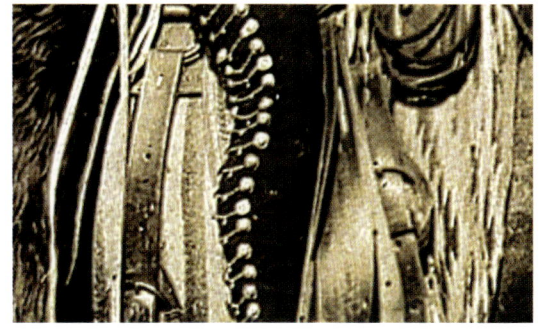

3 TROUSERS
The close-fitting trousers are decorated on the side with double lines of shiny metal buttons, although they can also be embroidered with a suede trim. The buttons are usually made of a metal alloy of silver and nickel known as alpaca but can be made of gold and silver.

2 EMBROIDERED JACKET
The short black wool jacket is meticulously decorated with white embroidery or appliquéd suede trimmings known as *greca*. This work was traditionally undertaken by artisans from certain regions who specialized in making elements of the suit and its accessories.

▲ Members of a mariachi folk band wear the traditional black embellished suits with wide-brimmed sombrero hats and *serape* shawls draped over their shoulders.

LATIN AMERICAN DRESS 143

Poncho 19th century
INDIGENOUS GARMENT

Two gauchos wearing traditional striped ponchos (c. 1890).

NAVIGATOR

In the annals of dress history, the Andean poncho recalls semi-nomadic indigenous origins and frontier culture, yet the power of the garment's form and design still resonates in contemporary fashion. In the 19th century, gauchos of African, indigenous and Spanish heritage, who roamed the River Plate region, utilized this garment as their bed, pillow and card table, as well as using it as a shelter against the elements. Indeed, the poncho might have been an individual's sole possession.

English entrepreneurs quickly realized the significance and utility of this garment for natives and travellers alike. They appropriated the handwoven and embroidered designs and imported prefabricated ponchos from Manchester and Birmingham. As diplomat Sir Woodbine Parish recalled in 1836, the gauchos of the Pampas dressed almost exclusively in English-made ponchos. The garments generally measured 6 feet by 4 feet (1.8 x 1.4 m) and were fashioned with various fibres according to the climates in which they would be worn, from vicuña wool to silk and linen. Highly practical, ponchos were commonly worn with loose-fitting trousers tucked into boots and felt brimmed hats known as *chambergos*. There is also evidence to suggest that indigenous men wore the poncho with a belt. **RR**

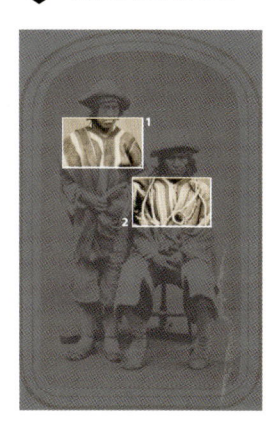

FOCAL POINTS

1 OPENING
The centre opening of the poncho allows it to be pulled on easily over the wearer's head. It rests comfortably on the shoulders and hangs down in loose drapes and folds. There is ample cloth to cover the body and arms without restricting movement.

2 FABRIC
Gaucho ponchos are handwoven in a range of patterns and colours. These ponchos are striped but geometric patterns and other motifs, such as the phoenix, also appear. The garments are worn over shirts, vests and slim-fitting jackets.

◀ A striped Bolivian poncho dating from the early 20th century.

VICTORIAN DRESS

1 An example of the cage crinoline from 1860. The dress was lifted into place over the cage with the aid of long poles and required the assistance of a lady's maid.

2 Dating from 1840, this day dress typifies the drooping silhouette of the Gothic Revival prevalent in France and Britain.

The remarkable exaggeration of the female form in the Victorian era (1837–1901) was exemplified by the crinoline in the middle part of the 19th century; it became ever larger and reached its apotheosis in 1859 before subsiding into the bustle in 1868. Respectable femininity was associated with domesticity and the narrowly defined world of the home. In Coventry Patmore's poem idealizing Victorian womanhood (1854), the woman was described as the 'angel of the house', whose main task—to oversee the upkeep of the home—was firmly rooted in the private sphere. Women's restricted, circumscribed lives contrasted with the many technological advances of the period, industrial expansion and the extension of the British Empire.

Feudal ties and old social hierarchies were replaced by a bourgeois society in which power resided in commerce and entrepreneurship rather than in land ownership or position at court. The emergence of modern capitalism caused shifts in attitudes regarding acceptable forms of masculine and feminine behaviour as men and women were physically segregated in their daily lives: men wore the sombre hues and refined lines of exemplary tailoring, whereas women were almost immobilized by lavishly layered and decorated clothes. In his treatise *The Theory of the Leisure Class* (1899), US economist Thorstein

KEY EVENTS

1830	1837	1840	1846	1848	1849
The first issue of US magazine *Godey's Lady's Book* is published, describing the latest styles.	Queen Victoria ascends the throne in Britain. She reigns until 1901.	The first US silk factory (making thread only) opens in Patterson, New Jersey.	The first lock-stitch sewing machine is patented by US inventor Elias Howe.	Tartan plaid becomes very fashionable when the young Queen Victoria falls in love with the Highlands and buys Balmoral Castle.	Henry Edward Harrod opens Harrod's department store in London. His workforce numbers two shop assistants and an errand boy.

Veblen interpreted the feminine sartorial magnificence of the era as a symbol of the Victorian woman's enforced leisure—the living embodiment of conspicuous consumption, representative of her husband's wealth.

The Gothic Revival, which dominated the arts in France and England in the 1840s, greatly influenced Victorian dress. This resulted in the emergence of a drooping silhouette (right), emphasized by a dropped shoulder line ending in caps over long, tight sleeves, and weighty fabrics. The dress comprised an elongated pointed bodice, usually buttoned down the front, and joined to the skirt by 'gauging', whereby alternate pleats were attached to the bodice. The fullness of the skirt was supported by a petticoat stiffened with horsehair (*crin* in French). In 1856 the first cage crinoline (opposite) appeared, which dispensed with the need for cumbersome petticoats. This was followed by the steel crinoline, first patented by C. Amet in Britain in 1856. The fabric-covered, flexible steel hoops were either constructed as a separate garment, hung by tapes from the waist, or sewn into a petticoat. The silhouette formed two triangles, which emphasized the natural waistline. The width of the dress sleeve dropped from shoulder to wrist, forming a pagoda shape; separate undersleeves in white cotton, embellished with embroidery or lace, were often exposed. The bell-shaped skirt gradually increased in size, emphasized by layers of swags, scallops, ruching and flounces. The Greek key motif was a popular embellishment, and Queen Victoria's love of Scotland encouraged the popularity of colourful tartan and plaid fashion (see p.152).

Many changes of clothes were required to see the Victorian woman through the day. Day dresses included the peignoir, an informal morning dress; the pelisse-robe, also worn indoors in the morning; the redingote, worn for the afternoon promenade; and the highly decorated round dress for afternoon entertaining. Popular fabrics were broadcloth, merino, organdie and tarlatan (transparent muslin). Evenings required a further change and, in contrast to the demure daywear, evening gowns were extremely décolleté and made in luxurious fabrics such as velvet, silk or silk taffeta and *moiré*. Necklines were either off the shoulder or cut into a slight heart shape (known as *en coeur*), and the bertha collar, a gathered cape-like frill usually made of lace, was often attached, covering the top of the arms and breasts.

Victorian outerwear consisted of a hip-length shawl, often in a paisley design (see p.150), or a mantle draped over the skirt, which resulted in a triangular silhouette and completely obscured the waistline. Hair was worn parted in the middle, with coils of plaits or ringlets over the ears, and wide coal-scuttle bonnets blinkered the wearer, whose fashionable complexion needed to be of an interesting pallor. The coal-scuttle bonnet was later replaced by a smaller hat positioned at the front of the head.

1851	1851	1852	1856	Late 1850s	1872
US inventor Isaac Merritt Singer patents an improved model of the sewing machine.	The Great Exhibition is held at the Crystal Palace, designed by Joseph Paxton. Made of glass and steel, the roof reflects the shape of the crinoline.	Le Bon Marché department store opens in Paris, followed by Lord & Taylor in New York.	The English chemist William Perkin develops aniline dyes, which introduce a greater variety of colour to the mass market.	The idea of the paper pattern is conceived by US-born Ellen Curtis Demorest, known as Mme Demorest, and her husband, William.	The English silk manufacturer Thomas Wardle succeeds in printing fast colours on to Indian wild silk and introduces it to the European market.

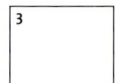

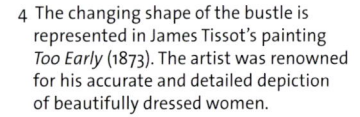

3 An illustration from *Godey's Lady's Book* in 1864 depicts crinoline dresses with gored skirts for day and evening wear.

4 The changing shape of the bustle is represented in James Tissot's painting *Too Early* (1873). The artist was renowned for his accurate and detailed depiction of beautifully dressed women.

As the crinoline increased in size, the skirt was gored to accommodate the width of the hem while still fitting at the waist. A dress cut without a waist seam that emphasized the moulding of the bodice emerged, known as the 'princess line' (see p.178). The style came in a range of variations including the polonaise, a looped overskirt that referenced the fashions of the 17th century. Dresses that continued to be constructed as a separate bodice and skirt included the cuirass bodice (1874), which featured a plastron of different materials worn over a long, tight corset.

By the end of the 1870s, the volume of fabric used in the skirt shifted, which dramatically changed the silhouette. Initially the fullness of the skirt was dropped to the back of the knees and even day dresses featured a long train. Waists became even smaller, emphasized by the external shaping of the bodice to a 'V' and the horizontal draping of the skirt. The bustle moved upwards once more in the mid 1880s, protruding horizontally from the small of the back and kept in place by a device of braided wire. The silhouette became flatter at the front, forming a half crinoline, with the material gathered at the back of the hips ending in a train. By 1868 the crinoline had gone out of fashion and the vast hooped skirts became overskirts, looped up into a bustle at the back (opposite).

In the Victorian era, the steam-powered textile industry developed the first successful power looms for plain weaves, which provided a wide range of fabrics such as taffeta. Japanese sericulture supplied the raw material for this industry, and France was the largest manufacturer of silk and figured silk velvet. Mid-century clothes were too ornate to be produced in large quantities as the details required the handiwork of a skilled dressmaker. However, mechanized production methods were being developed in tailoring and outerwear, which required less fitting. Mass production resulted in the emergence of new production and consumption systems; from 1850 onwards fashionable clothes became available for all but the poorest. Fashion was further democratized by the invention of the sewing machine, first patented in 1846. Machines could be hired on a weekly basis and together with paper patterns, first sold by Ebenezer Butterick in 1863, and dressmaking ideas from magazines, the female consumer could keep up to date with the latest trends. The popular *Godey's Lady's Book* (above), which reached a circulation of 150,000 in the United States in 1860, carried fashion plates and patterns for garments to be made at home.

Greater social freedom for women and an efficient transport system resulted in shopping becoming a leisure activity. With their dazzling displays of consumer goods, the burgeoning number of department stores in the major cities provided a safe place for unchaperoned women to browse while purchasing 'ready-mades'—garments that required no fitting, such as cloaks, shawls, loose-fitting overjackets and branded fashion goods. Haberdashery departments offered lavish trimmings and *passementerie*, enabling the avid consumer to change the details of her costume in line with the latest designs from couturiers such as Charles Frederick Worth (1825–95). Aniline dyes, discovered by the chemist William Perkin in 1856, were man-made from coal and introduced expensive and previously difficult-to-make colours to the mass market. The first one, labelled mauveine, was a purple dye, previously extracted from molluscs; this was followed by magenta, developed by François-Emmanuel Verguin. Other synthetic dyes included Lyons blue and methyl green (1872), and in 1878 a new strong red appeared to rival cochineal.

By the end of the century, at the close of Victoria's reign, bias-cut skirts that fitted smoothly over the hips were replacing horizontal skirt draperies. A high armhole and tight sleeves extended the line of the torso, which was emphasized by the sleeve head gathered to form high peaks. These gathers extended outwards and by 1894 they were padded to enormous proportions, held in place with cushions but still tight around the wrist. Beyond the lavish ostentation of fashionable dress, the tailored suit for women provided a practical alternative. Originally made in weatherproof tweed by tailors such as House of Creed and worn by aristocratic women for sporting activities, these two-piece skirt suits were subsequently made in softer cloth for urban outerwear. This trend reflected the growing emancipation of women and the first steps towards women's suffrage that marked the end of the Victorian era. **MF**

Paisley Shawl c. 1850
OUTERWEAR

Portrait of Fanny Holman Hunt by William Holman Hunt (1866–68).

The paisley shawl was a vital component of outerwear for almost a century, from around 1780 until the 1870s. Woven from the fleece of the pashmina goat, the shawls (from the Persian word *shal*, denoting a class of woven fabric) feature the highly symbolic paisley motif, the exact origins of which remain obscure. Paisley shawls were woven in Kashmir, north-west of India, from the 11th century. They were imported into Britain by the British East India Company at the end of the 17th century. Demand exceeded supply and attempts were made to copy the design on hand looms in both Norwich in 1792 and the Scottish town of Paisley in 1805. Paisley was then a prosperous silk-weaving town, rivalling the better-known Spitalfields of London. Cheaper block-printed versions in wool were produced in large quantities as the woven version of the shawl proved too expensive for any but the wealthiest of the upper classes. Shawls were later replaced by jackets and short capes when the bustle replaced the crinoline in the 1870s. By this time, the town of Paisley was producing such a high proportion of shawls that all shawls were referred to as 'Paisley' shawls. When the Paisley shawl went out of fashion, the pattern continued to be popular and adopted the generic name 'paisley pattern'. The cameo brooch at the neck of the dress was a popular accessory of the Victorian era, with its connotations of classical imagery. Usually the cameo was heavily framed in pinchbeck, a form of brass made to resemble gold. **MF**

NAVIGATOR

FOCAL POINTS

1 DRAPING
This square shawl is worn draped over the shoulders. It is folded in a triangle with the top edge turned over, forming a point at the back. Paisley shawls were manufactured in both squares and rectangles, with the edges left frayed. Large rectangular shawls were folded in half and worn draped around the neck to fall free on either side of the dress and caught with a brooch on the bodice. An essential accessory, paisley shawls were in fashion for almost a century.

2 PATTERN
The characteristic teardrop pattern, here made up of warm red and orange tones with blue and green, is sometimes thought to be the mark made by curling the hand into a fist. Printing with the little finger downwards into the cloth, the comma-shaped cone, known as the *boteh*, or the Paisley pine, is also thought to represent a seed pod and as such is a symbol of life and fertility. The paisley pattern was sometimes referred to as 'Welsh pears'.

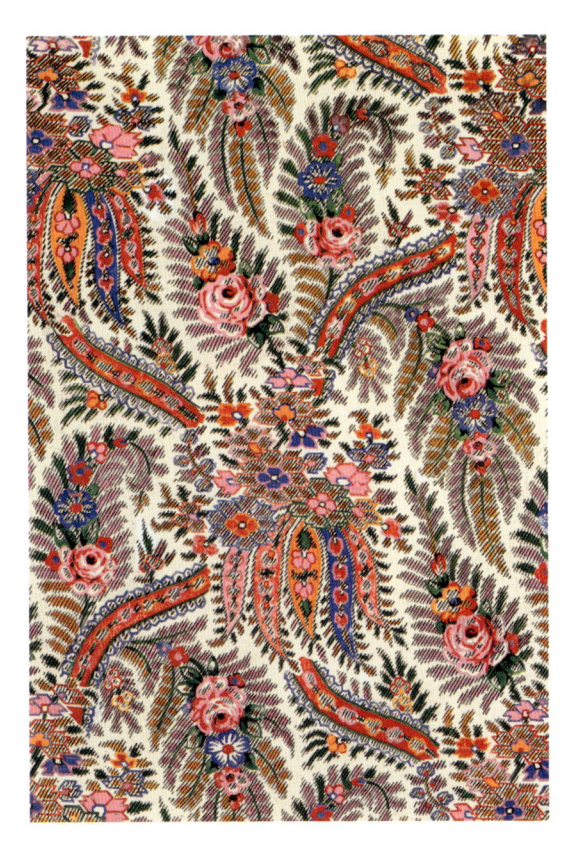

▲ This 19th-century design by George Charles Haité (1855–1924) was created specifically for printed shawl fabric. The delicate floral pattern incorporates the traditional paisley motif.

VICTORIAN DRESS 151

Plaid Day Dress 1857
WOMEN'S DRESS

NAVIGATOR

The bell-shaped skirt of this plaid, silk taffeta day dress is worn over a steel crinoline of flexible steel hoops hung by tapes from the waist. The crinoline is not completely circular, but presents more fullness at the back of the skirt, which is gathered to accommodate the steel hoops. The understructure also includes a whalebone-stiffened and quilted corset, thus providing the triangular silhouette typical of the era. The jacket bodice is close-fitting and heavily darted from the natural waistline, and suppresses the geometric line of the patterned cloth beneath the bust to form a smaller check. The shoulder seam is extended over the sleeve head to form a dropped arm scye from which the sleeves widen outwards; these are split for their full length and brought together with self-fabric ribbon ties. Victorian daywear was decorous, as evidenced by the narrow lace collar attached to the high neckline, which was made from tatting, lace or crochet work to match the deep frilled cuffs of the undersleeves. Tartans and plaids were a popular choice in both Europe and the United States, prompted by Queen Victoria's love of her Scottish home, Balmoral, which was decorated in Scottish baronial style with strong colours and a multiplicity of checked patterns. This costume is made from yarn-dyed silk taffeta, a crisp, smooth fabric that provides the stiffened volume of the skirt. **MF**

FOCAL POINTS

1 BONNET
The bonnet is fitted to the head; it has a small upturned brim at the front and is tied under the chin by long, wide decorative ribbons. Sun bonnets usually featured a curtain sewn at the back, but this example is shaped to protect the wearer's neck.

3 PEPLUM
The jacket bodice features a new style: a short peplum in matching fabric that flares over the hips and is attached to the waist with gathers. The peplum is edged with a box-pleated frill ending in a bow with streamers.

2 SLEEVES
The width of the jacket's sleeve is wider at the wrist, where it forms a pagoda shape and exposes the separate undersleeves known as *engageantes*. These were made from white cotton or linen and were trimmed with lace.

4 FABRIC
Alternating bands of coloured threads are woven with both warp and weft at right angles to each other. At the point where the different colours cross, new colours appear blended from the original ones.

VICTORIAN DRESS 153

THE ART OF ENGLISH TAILORING

On the death of Edward VII on 6 May 1910, the German Chancellor, Prince von Bülow, remarked: 'In the country in which unquestionably the gentlemen dressed best, he was the best-dressed gentleman.' Edward, who was Prince of Wales for fifty-nine years, was a rotund figure—only 5 feet 5 inches (1.65 m) tall and with a 48-inch (122-cm) chest and 48-inch (122-cm) waist at the time of his coronation in 1902—but was enormously influential sartorially. He was still in his teens when he began to make the many foreign trips that were to give him an international profile, and as a playboy prince he had a huge influence on what men wore. Continually photographed, he was a leading exemplar of Savile Row tailoring and helped to establish the street's reputation as the global centre of tailoring excellence.

Originally called Savile Street, the thoroughfare in central London was laid out in the early 1730s by Richard Boyle, third Earl of Burlington, who named it after his wife's family. It quickly became a popular residential area for stylish society, along with its neighbouring roads. Among the first residents were

KEY EVENTS

1830s	1840	1846	1858	1861	1860s
The frock coat, which is related to military styles from the time of the Napoleonic Wars, becomes standard attire.	Most trousers are now made with a button fly front fastening.	Prominent London tailor Henry Poole makes the back door to his premises the main entrance to his business. The address is 36–39 Savile Row.	Henry Poole is appointed court tailor to the French emperor Napoleon III, a client since 1846.	Prince Albert dies and Queen Victoria retreats into mourning, leaving her eldest son, Edward, to live the life of a playboy.	By the early 1860s, what is known as the lounge suit today is made acceptable day dress by Prince Edward.

154 1800–99

doctors, and popular legend suggests that when the tailors began to arrive and set up premises near their fashionable clients the physicians moved out. The first tailor moved in to what is now Savile Row in 1806. By the mid 19th century Savile Row and the surrounding streets, such as Cork, Clifford, Old Burlington, Maddox, Conduit and Sackville, were known for the concentration of cutters and tailors. It has been estimated that London had between 9,000 and 13,000 journeyman tailors organized into trade unions in 1834.

The Industrial Revolution of the late 18th century had produced more varied and cheaper cloth. Wool and worsted cloth could be shaped and stretched under steam and the pressing iron, and by the mid 19th century English tailors had an enviable international reputation for creating clothes with a neatly defined shape. They were also adept at using a tape measure, a device that appeared only in the late 18th century. Taking precise measurements of a client's body allowed cutters to create patterns based on a geometric appreciation of anatomy.

The accepted dress of the early part of the 19th century—the morning suit for daytime and the tailcoat for evening wear (opposite)—had its origins in the English aristocracy's obsession with equestrian sports. Unlike their French counterparts, members of the English nobility of the 18th century did not remain at court all the time, but preferred to spend periods at their country estates, where their principal pastime was hunting on horseback. This activity required the long jackets that were fashionable at the time to be amended. The fronts were cut away to form what came to be known as tailcoats. Another option saw the front of the jacket given a sloping profile, which led to the origin of the morning coat.

The 19th century witnessed an evolution in menswear. The polite uniform and the standard business attire of the Victorian era became the frock coat (right), which was related to Continental military uniforms of the Napoleonic era. It was a lighter-weight alternative to the greatcoat or overcoat and was worn with only a waistcoat and shirt, not a jacket, underneath. Trousers, which had replaced breeches in the early 1800s, could be fashioned in the same cloth or in a contrast pattern. From the 1840s, most trousers were made with a central button fly, which replaced the front-flap openings of the previous pantaloons. Single- or double-breasted (the latter was more formal) frock coats had a distinct emphasis on the waist and in length dropped to around the knee. Typically they had a horizontal waist seam. Frock coats were also considered to be a much smarter option than the paletot, a rather shapeless coat developed in France that simply dropped vertically from the armholes. Indeed, Savile Row experts thought that basic paletots showed no cutting or tailoring skills.

The lounge suit (see p.158) gained favour around 1850 to 1860. The young Prince of Wales, always one to seek practical elegance, was an early

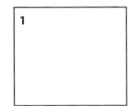

1 Various styles of gentlemen's dress, including, from far left, a frock coat, evening dress and morning suit, from the journal *The Tailor and Cutter: A Trade Journal and Index of Fashion*.

2 This men's waisted frock coat from the 1830s has the typical narrow waist and full skirt that hangs vertically in front. It features an outbreast pocket.

1866	1870s	1871	1876	1886	1901
The tailoring journal *The Tailor and Cutter* is published in London to support the bespoke trade. It continues until 1972.	The Homburg hat becomes popular after Prince Edward brings one back from one of his regular trips to Europe, namely the spa resort Bad Homburg.	Henry Poole makes Western clothes for the first Japanese ambassador to London. *Sebiro* becomes the Japanese word for 'suit'.	Henry Poole dies and his cousin Samuel Cundey takes over the company and begins to reverse its massive debts.	The dinner jacket made for Prince Edward by Poole is worn in the United States and becomes known as the tuxedo.	Queen Victoria dies and her son becomes King Edward VII. His coronation in 1902 is the first to be filmed in the UK.

THE ART OF ENGLISH TAILORING

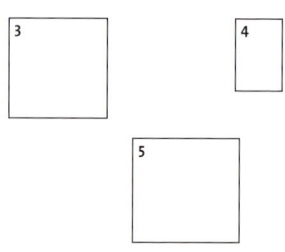

3 Although originally a shooting jacket, the Norfolk jacket was worn for a variety of outdoor pursuits from the 1870s onwards and was frequently paired with matching knickerbockers.

4 In this portrait by photographer Alexander Bassano (c. 1871), Edward, Prince of Wales, wears light-coloured trousers with his morning suit jacket.

5 The shorter dinner jacket (left) was introduced as acceptable evening wear in 1860. From 1886 it was known as a tuxedo in the United States.

champion of this ensemble, which was usually three-piece. Although a stickler for correctness in dress, the prince was eager to simplify the prevailing complicated sartorial codes of the day. At Sandringham, his Norfolk country house, for example, he decreed that it was not necessary for his male guests to change four times a day: a morning suit at first, then hunting clothes for the inevitable horseback ride, followed by a morning suit during the afternoon and finally the formal dress coat for dinner. The prince allowed his companions to wear just two outfits: shooting tweeds for day and evening dress for dinner. The belted single-breasted jacket worn for shooting, known as a Norfolk jacket (above), was loose-fitting and featured two vertical box pleats on the front and one centre back. Endorsed by the prince, the style soon became familiar worldwide.

In 1860 Prince Edward decided to amend the style of evening dress, courtesy of Savile Row's most prominent tailor, Henry Poole. He requested that Poole cut off the tails of his evening suit to create a more comfortable smoking jacket that could be worn for informal gatherings, thereby creating the first modern dinner jacket. According to some sources, after US millionaire James Brown Potter visited Sandringham in 1886, he had the prince's jacket style copied and then wore it at his club in Tuxedo Park, New York. The popularity of the style led to the dinner jacket being called the tuxedo (opposite below) in the United States. As London's foremost tailor, Henry Poole & Co (the origins of which date back to 1806) not only dressed the Prince of Wales but also received a royal warrant from Queen Victoria to make liveries.

The received notion of Victorian times is of sober men with a deep Protestant work ethic dressed in sober fashion, but this is an over-simplification. Certainly 1830 was a watershed, when the death of George IV, who had been Prince Regent from 1811 to 1820, ended the sartorial decadence of the Regency era. However, rather than conservatism *per se*, good taste and a desire to avoid vulgarity were the major influences on men's dress during the Victorian age.

Prince Albert penned a note to the courtiers who attended his son Edward: 'In dress, with scrupulous attention to neatness and good taste, [the Prince of Wales] will never give in to the unfortunately loose and slang style which predominates at the present day. He will borrow nothing from the fashion of the groom or the gamekeeper, and while avoiding the frivolity and foolish vanity of dandyism, will take care that his clothes are of the best quality, well made and suitable to his rank and position...To all these particulars the Prince of Wales must necessarily pay more attention than anyone else. His deportment will be more watched, his dress more criticized.' Albert's comments encapsulated how all Englishmen of breeding viewed matters of dress. However, there was a huge variety in what they could wear, and a journal for the bespoke tailoring trade—*The Tailor and Cutter: A Trade Journal and Index of Fashion*—was launched in 1866 in response to an increased interest in men's fashion.

The Prince of Wales's obsession with dress—he regularly changed outfits up to six times a day—set the trends for the smart set and, by extension, for the middle classes. His stylistic innovations included not only the Norfolk jacket and shorter tails on evening wear, but also the Homburg hat (see p.158)—brought back from Germany—creases at the side rather than the front of trousers (right), the adoption of turn-ups (cuffs) on trousers (to protect the bottoms from muddy ground) and the wearing of tweeds at race meetings. A keen yachtsman, he also popularized the navy blue blazer paired with light-coloured trousers.

If Edward was the best-dressed man, then Savile Row was the place that attracted well-dressed men the world over. Henry Poole, in particular, was the tailor who had unrivalled links to the world's ruling elite. Poole made suits for Japanese imperial princes in 1871; since then the Japanese word for 'suit' has been *sebiro* (or *sabiro*), an approximation of the pronunciation of Savile Row. **EM**

THE ART OF ENGLISH TAILORING

Lounge Suit and Homburg Hat c. 1890
MENSWEAR

Edward, Prince of Wales (c. 1890).

By the time this photograph was taken, Edward, Prince of Wales, was about forty-nine years of age. He had been a playboy prince for more than three decades and would have to wait another ten years to finally succeed his mother, Queen Victoria, to the throne. The suit is most likely one of his holiday outfits, worn to one of the German spas, such as Bad Homburg, or a resort in the south of France. Although the candy-striped cloth would not be acceptable as daywear in London, the style is that of the lounge suit, which the prince had championed from the early 1860s. The jacket has a natural shoulder line and although the trousers taper, they are comfortably wide at the hem above the stack-heeled shoes. The narrow stripes of the jacket elongate his short frame, and the single-breasted front—with all four buttons closed— contributes to the impression of vertical exaggeration. The high closure results in tiny lapels, but still leaves enough space under the chin for a neat detachable collar, shirt and a handsome tie. The modern version of the tie became popular and replaced the cravat or stock around the same time the lounge suit gained acceptance. The silk for the tie may well have been woven in one of the major centres of the English neckwear trade: Spitalfields in east London, Macclesfield in Cheshire or Sudbury in Suffolk. As befits a gentleman of the day, Edward carries a stout walking stick and wears a flower in the buttonhole, which is a relic of when the lapel was closed across the top of the chest. The elegant outfit is completed with a pale Homburg hat, characterized by a dented crown and a shallow, slightly rolled brim. It has a much higher and more tapered crown than the modern version of the Homburg. Although it was to become an example of formal headwear, here the German hat, almost certainly made of felt, still betrays its sporty origins. **EM**

◉ FOCAL POINTS

1 HOMBURG HAT
Edward popularized the Homburg hat during an era when every man wore some kind of headgear, whether a flat cap or a top hat. In its original form it was a hat for leisure time, but the Homburg later became a formal style in a dark colour. Although Edward's Homburg hat has an unbound edge, usually the brim was bound.

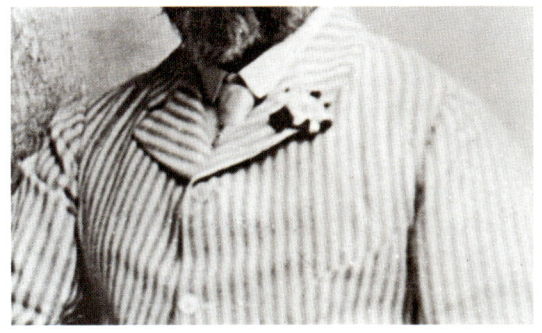

3 SILK TIE
The high-fastening lounge suits adopted in the 1860s made the cravat increasingly redundant as there was not enough room for it. The prince's neckwear, with a neat four-in-hand knot, fills the small space admirably and would not look amiss today. Although not seen here, tie pins were another opportunity to show individuality.

2 'NATURAL' SHOULDER LINE
There is no padding in the 'natural' shoulders of this summer jacket. The arm scyes are beautifully shaped to accommodate Edward's large arms. A fine jacket must fit at the neck and on the shoulders; everything else 'hangs' from here. One of his lasting legacies was to make even formal menswear more comfortable.

4 HEELED SHOES
Edward's shoes may have had an elastic gusset to facilitate a comfortable fit. In common with the fashion of the late 1800s, the heel is 1 ½ to 2 inches (4–5 cm) high, giving the prince a lift. The sole is light and welted in the traditional English manner with a pronounced 'waist' or middle of the shoe.

✦ NAVIGATOR

THE PRINCE'S STYLE

Although Prince Edward championed comfort and practical elegance, he insisted on correctness in dress. He disliked the US sense of fashionable dress, with bright ties and extravagant waistcoats, and dismissed Portuguese nobility as resembling 'waiters in a second-class restaurant'. Game shooting was a passion, whether on his tours or at the royal estates in Norfolk or Scotland. He delighted in the extravagant protective garments of the period, such as the Inverness coat (right), with its protective cape worn over a matching overcoat. It is interesting to consider how heavy this tweed ensemble must have been.

AFRICAN WAX AND FANCY PRINTS

1 In this photograph taken in Ghana c. 1900, the two young women second and third from the right wear African prints, which contrast with those worn by the other women in the group.

2 This vibrantly coloured contemporary wax-print cloth from Ghana features an alternating guineafowl design.

African prints—the generic name for factory-printed textiles produced in Africa, Europe and China for the mainly West African market—are often seen as ubiquitously African. Since the 19th century, most of these prints have been designed and produced outside the continent and then exported to Africa. Nigerian-born artist Yinka Shonibare has used these fabrics to point out that the whole idea of authentic art, and authentic African art, is always ambiguous. A growing awareness of the culturally diverse and complex history of African prints has sparked contemporary debates about their cultural ownership.

The fabrics known as African prints (above) have a variety of names, including Real Dutch Wax, Superwax and Wax Blocks. The most prestigious is the Real Dutch Wax, which figures prominently in contemporary African fashion and is produced by Vlisco, Helmond, the Netherlands. There are two main types of African prints: wax prints (opposite; see p.162), which are made by printing the designs on both faces of the cloth, and fancy prints, which are printed on one side of the fabric. Both types originated in the early 19th century, when European manufacturers found cheaper ways of replicating Indonesian wax batiks. Many of these early imitation prints, often called Java prints, found a ready market in Indonesia and Europe, but some also found their way to West Africa. It is not clear how these prints entered the West African market; some historians suggest that European merchants stopped along the West African coast en route to Asia, whereas others believe that European

KEY EVENTS

1830s	1846	1852	1854	1860s	1861–65
Three cotton mills are established in Haarlem, the Netherlands, under the Nederlandsche Handel-Maatschappij (Dutch Trade Company).	The Van Vlissingen textile company (now Vlisco) is established in Helmond, the Netherlands. It makes imitation Java prints for Indonesia.	The first explicit reference to an imitation Java print textile specifically made for West Africa appears in the Van Vlissingen ledger.	Prévinaire starts production of 'La Javanaise'—an imitation Java wax print.	The market for imitation wax prints decreases in Indonesia.	As a result of the American Civil War, the import of raw cotton to Europe is greatly reduced.

160 1800–99

producers were deliberately diversifying their markets. It is clear that West Africa has a long history of incorporating imported textiles as part of its elite dress.

In the 1860s, as the market for imitation wax prints dwindled in Indonesia, British, Swiss and Dutch companies focused more on the European market. However, the protectionist trade advantages of the Dutch enabled them to continue selling in Indonesia. Haarlem-based company Prévinaire concentrated solely on producing imitation wax prints for the Indonesian market that were much closer to the real Java batiks. In the mid 1850s, J. B. T. Prévinaire had invented the 'La Javanaise', but this print was soon replaced by one made with duplex rollers, which printed hot resin rather than wax on both faces of the cloth. Before dyeing, the cloth was treated mechanically to give it a cracking effect. After the resin paste had been removed, other colours were hand-blocked onto the fabric, and the successive application of colours created a variegated effect. Prévinaire even managed to imitate the distinctive smell of Java batiks.

Indonesians found the prints too expensive for imitations but they proved popular in West Africa, where they were equated with wealth and status, and they spread throughout Central Africa. In the 1890s Prévinaire changed its name to Haarlemse Katoen Maatschappij (HKM), or the Haarlem Cotton Company. In 1893 Scottish trader Ebenezer Brown Fleming began importing wax prints to West Africa and he became the sole agent for HKM in the region. One of the ways in which agents fed back the demands of customers to the manufacturers was through collecting samples of popular locally produced and imported textiles. Early examples from the 20th century demonstrate that Dutch designers drew on Indonesian visual sources, West African proverbs and the Dutch countryside, all in a style that derived from Indonesian batik.

West African tastes and patronage guided the future development of the textiles. Female traders travelled to Europe to place orders direct with the factories and they influenced the design process, giving the prints names that reflected African lived experience and popular wisdom. In turn, European designers explored tastes in different parts of Africa. European companies started to make fancy prints, first with engraved rollers, later with roller screens, partly to provide cheaper imitations of wax prints. The Manchester-based company Arthur Brunnschweiler & Co (now ABC Wax) was the first to produce commemorative fancy prints in 1928. These became especially significant after World War II with decolonization as more textile factories were set up in Africa.

African prints continue to be produced globally but the trade is driven by its African customers. ABC Wax has moved its production to Ghana and maintains only a small design studio in Manchester; Vlisco is now the only European-based producer. Imitation wax prints made in China are increasingly marketed in Africa. African prints are part of elaborate fashion systems throughout the African continent. The question of authenticity is relevant only if it matters to the wearer. **MK**

1874	1893	c. 1894	1894	1895	1908
The British Crown Colony of the Gold Coast is established; the entire Gold Coast (present-day Ghana) is colonized by 1901.	Enterprising Scottish trader Ebenezer Brown Fleming begins importing wax-printed cloths to West Africa.	Prévinaire becomes the Haarlemse Katoen Maatschappij (HKM). It successfully introduces wax prints to the Gold Coast.	Ebenezer Brown Fleming becomes the sole agent for HKM; soon after he forms his own company.	The first dated wax-print cloth is printed by HKM. It shows the 'hand and finger' design.	The Swiss-owned textile company Arthur Brunnschweiler & Co (ABC) is established near Manchester, England.

Sword of Kingship Design 1904
AFRICAN WAX PRINT

Wax resist-dyed cotton textile, made by Julius Holland BV, the Netherlands (2005–06).

The 'sword of kingship' is a classic African wax-print design that has been produced for more than a century. Historically the names of African wax-print designs often refer to popular wisdom and proverbs, or to social relationships and sources of power. They are prestigious textiles with a high social value that derives from the meanings they are given by their African wearers. This is one of the first textile examples in which the main motif was inspired by an actual African object. The design incorporates an Asante ceremonial sword — a potent symbol of power and authority for the Asante people in Ghana — into an Indonesian-style batik design. The original wrought-iron and wood sword (opposite below) is held in the British Museum in London. It was purchased by the museum from William Owen Wolseley, who was part of the Asante expedition to the Gold Coast (present-day Ghana) in 1896, when regalia and many other objects were taken from the Asantehene (ruler) Prempeh I after his defeat by the British.

The earliest known record of the design dates to 1904 in an order book of the Haarlem Cotton Company (now held in Vlisco's archives in the Netherlands) in which it is described as 'sword of kingship'. The history of this textile design is particularly interesting for the way it connects West African and European political and economic history. Over the years, it has been produced in different colour combinations and with minor variations by European, African and Asian wax- and fancy-print producers. The name of the fabric has changed slightly over time and the cloth is known by various names depending on its location. **MK**

NAVIGATOR

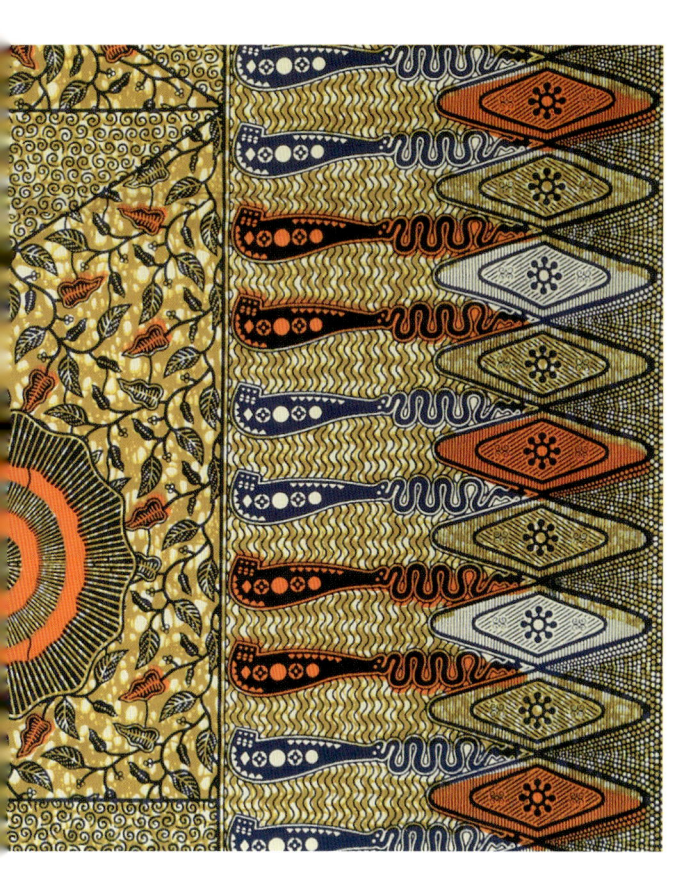

1 FLORAL MOTIF
The fabric includes a blue and orange leaf pattern on a gold wax print. The continuous floral motif has been common in African prints since their first production and it comes directly from Indonesian batik designs. It is sometimes called 'the tree of life'.

2 SWORD MOTIF
The key image of the design, the sword, is clearly repeated in the fabric. It is called 'sword of kingship' or 'chief sword' in Ghana and 'corkscrew' in Nigeria. The Dutch manufacturer Vlisco now markets the fabric as 'chief sword'.

◄ The right end of the sword depicts a tortoise, which becomes the sinuous body of a snake leading to the sword's blade.

AFRICAN WAX AND FANCY PRINTS

CHINESE DRESS – LATE QING DYNASTY

During the first two centuries of the Qing dynasty (1644–1911/12), a strict dress code dominated Chinese court dress. Initially there was resistance from Han Chinese scholars, who refused to serve the Qing and would not shave their foreheads. However, Emperor Kangxi, an enlightened ruler who reigned from 1662 to 1722, soon won over the dissidents, and Manchu-style robes became the standard garment for everyone. The authority of the first few emperors was great and no state officials dared deviate from the dress code.

After the death in 1861 of Emperor Xianfeng, who had ruled since 1850, his only son, Tongzhi, ascended the throne. In reality the country was under the control of the Empress Dowager Cixi, who was a woman of strong will and bold enough to ignore the dress code laid down by past emperors. Before this time, court dress was strictly regulated—based on hierarchy—and there was little

KEY EVENTS

1839–42	1850	1861	1864	c. 1870	c. 1875
The First Opium War is fought between Britain and China over conflicting trade interests.	The riding jacket is adopted by women (see p.166).	Emperor Xianfeng dies and his son, Tonghzi, follows him to the throne; his mother Cixi determines court fashions.	The Qing court gives English officer Charles Gordon a riding jacket and peacock feather for his contribution to defeating the Taiping Rebellion.	Flat gilt-brass buttons made by European firms are used on informal garments made in the imperial workshop.	During Emperor Guangxu's reign, garments become shorter and women's sleeves gradually wider.

room for personal preferences, except with casual wear. It was therefore easier for fashion to develop among the common people. Not considered politically influential, women of the Han race were not obliged by law to wear Manchu-style clothes. Wives and daughters of wealthy merchants wore brocades, damasks and velvets of the most sumptuous designs and colours. Skilled embroiderers created attractive schemes as alternatives to woven patterns and the Han women's clothes were envied by palace ladies inside the Forbidden City.

During her unofficial reign Cixi wore informal dress when she met male ministers to discuss state affairs, itself an unprecedented activity because women had never been allowed to participate in government hitherto. The informal robe made of green gauze from the empress's wardrobe (opposite above) is an example of one of the fashion trends in the 1870s. The main pattern is of 'longevity' characters embroidered in gold and prunus sprigs embroidered in different shades of pink. The sleeves are in three layers, with each layer progressively narrowing towards the wrist and edged with borders and bands of different widths. In addition to the borders in plain black and pale blue, there are three embroidered bands, one with a bird and floral design, one with 'longevity' and prunus that matches the main pattern, and one with lotus and crane. Similar garments include bands of ribbons woven especially on a narrow loom, such as a yellow ribbon with butterfly and floral design, and a golden trim with geometric design. In some cases as many as eighteen trimmings can be found on one garment.

The practice of foot binding in China greatly influenced footwear design. Unlike Han women, Manchu women did not bind their feet; consequently they could wear shoes with high soles. Old photographs of Cixi often show her wearing a type of shoe that was extremely popular and was known as the 'flowerpot shoe' (right). The platforms resemble the shape of a Chinese flowerpot and could be as high as 4 ¾ inches (12 cm). Women believed that walking in these shoes gave them a special gait.

In the last few decades of the 19th century, wealthy men indulged in luxury items such as fur coats and jadeite thumb rings. The thumb ring was originally an accessory used to aid the archer when drawing his bow, but in later times it became a gaudy piece of jewellery. A less extravagant but still splendid accessory for men was the skull cap (opposite below), shaped like half a melon and usually embroidered in colourful threads, tiny seed pearls and coral beads. On the top is a knot formed of red silk cords with long red tassels hanging down. This informal headgear was worn even by emperors and one was found by the bed of Emperor Xianfeng when British troops entered the Summer Palace in October 1860. **MW**

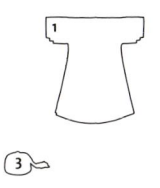

1 Empress Dowager Cixi's informal robe features embroidery that is as exquisite as that on a dragon robe, and no less expensive to produce (1862–74).

2 Flowerpot shoes for women were popular during the Guangxu era (1875–1908). The high platforms greatly hindered the movements of the wearer, but palace ladies seldom had long distances to walk.

3 During the Guangxu period, colourful caps were worn by young men; elderly men wore caps made of black satin.

c. 1880	1900	c. 1904	1908	1911	1912
Fully automated looms are imported from the West. The products, known as 'western' satin or 'western' gauze, are embraced as a novelty.	Cixi supports the Boxer Rebellion, which seeks to drive all foreigners from China.	The army is the first to adopt Western-style uniform, donning a jacket, narrow-legged trousers and a peaked cap.	After the death of Guangxu, two-year-old Puyi is chosen as his successor by Cixi. During his reign, it is popular to tailor false cuffs inside sleeves.	Imperial China comes to an end. Imperial court robes are discarded and members of the new government opt for European suit models.	The practice of foot binding is outlawed by the new Chinese republic but this ban is ignored by many.

CHINESE DRESS — LATE QING DYNASTY

Riding Jacket c. 1875
WOMEN'S GARMENT

1 COLLAR
The jacket has a stand-up collar with an 'L'-shape overlapping closure called the 'pipa style', resembling the shape of a stringed musical instrument of that name. This style was very popular in the late 19th century and continued to be worn after China became a republic.

2 EXPENSIVE FABRIC
The fabric is an apple-green satin damask with a peony and leaf pattern. It has three different borders, of fur, woven satin and lace ribbon. The 'longevity' characters on the fur are formed by beige sables sewn against a brown ground. Only the rich could afford fur.

Pipa-style riding jacket, Palace Museum, Beijing.

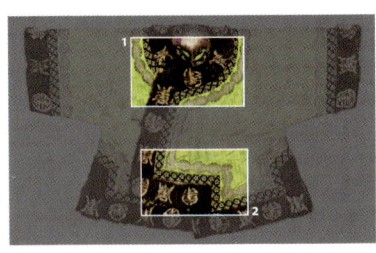

⊕ NAVIGATOR

The *magua* (riding jacket) references the nomadic origin of the Manchu people, who made their living hunting and riding before they gained the throne. Even after moving into the Forbidden City in Beijing, Qing emperors regularly went on hunting trips and visited the provinces. On these occasions the emperor would wear a specially designed travelling robe, with a riding jacket on top.

The riding jacket spread from the court to the common people. In the 1850s women started wearing it as well, even though they were on foot most of the time. A great variety of styles came into existence: no collar or stand-up collar, front closure or overlapping closure, with or without sleeves. The length of the riding jacket falls below the waistline but stops short of the saddle when the wearer is on horseback. The cut of a female *magua* is exactly the same as that of its male counterpart, but it is usually smaller and the fabric more colourful.

The bright yellow colour was normally reserved for the emperor and members of his family, but the riding jacket was an exception. The emperor's personal attendants were allowed to wear bright yellow riding jackets. When a state official, regardless of his rank, did something that particularly pleased the emperor, he would be given a yellow riding jacket as a token of the sovereign's approval. The English officer Charles Gordon, initially China's enemy during the second of the Opium Wars (1856–60) but subsequently employed by China to suppress the Taiping Rebellion, was bestowed a yellow riding jacket plus other imperial gifts when the rebellion was finally defeated in 1864. Not surprisingly the yellow riding jacket quickly became a symbol of prestige and was much coveted by people who moved in high society. **MW**

MEN'S RIDING JACKET

This satin damask and fur riding jacket (right) could be worn on both sides. The dragon roundel motif was mostly worn by members of the imperial family. The colour is known as 'golden yellow', ranking third in importance after bright yellow and apricot yellow, and it was assigned to the emperor's sons. A jacket lined with fur would keep the wearer warm when travelling in winter. However, because fur was an expensive item, people wore fur garments to show off even in the mild southern regions. Demand greatly outstripped supply, and pelts were imported from Siberia and North America, with sable from the former and sea otter skin from the latter being the most prized.

BURMESE DRESS

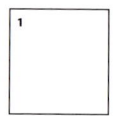

1. In this drawing from 1854, the Burmese king's minister is wearing civil court dress. It includes a long, gold decorated robe over a *paso* and a high domed gold and velvet hat.

2. This Burmese woman's outfit from the 1880s comprises a wraparound skirt, a tailored jacket and a *yinzi* (breast cloth), woven using the *luntaya acheik* tapestry technique.

Dress in 19th-century Burma was an important form of social expression: it defined and displayed an individual's position in society. What people wore was controlled by sumptuary laws that strictly dictated which fabrics, decoration and jewellery each rank in society could wear, with severe punishments meted out to those who disobeyed the rules. In 1853 King Mindon ascended the throne after usurping his brother King Pagan, whose aggressive policies towards the British had contributed to the Second Anglo-Burmese War of 1852. Evidence of court clothing from his reign can be seen in the paintings produced by a court artist during a visit to Calcutta by the Burmese king's minister in 1854. The watercolours show the minister in both court (above) and military dress. On Mindon's death in 1878, political machinations led to Thibaw ascending the throne. The court became particularly conservative during his reign and dress remained similar to that of earlier periods. However, the clothes from this period do show that the Burmese were adept at incorporating existing and foreign ideas into elaborate outfits.

KEY EVENTS

1852	1853	1854–55	1857	1859	1860s
The Second Anglo-Burmese War breaks out and comes to an end eight months later. The British annex the Pegu province and name it Lower Burma.	King Mindon ascends the Burmese throne after leading a palace coup to topple his brother, King Pagan.	King Mindon sends his ambassador Ashin Nanmadaw Payawun Mingyi as envoy to Calcutta on a goodwill mission.	King Mindon relocates the court from Amarapura on the Irrawaddy River to the purpose-built city of Mandalay a few miles to the north.	Thibaw, who would become the last king of the Konbaung dynasty (1752–1885), is born.	The tight-fitting, open-fronted *eingyi* jacket becomes a fashion essential during the Konbaung dynasty.

Basic clothing was much the same across Burmese society. Men wore a *paso* made from a length of cotton cloth, 13 feet (4 m) long by 5 feet (1.5 m) wide. This was wrapped around the waist with the additional material gathered in folds at the front or draped over the shoulder. Sometimes the fabric was pulled between the legs and tied to form trousers. On top of the *paso*, men wore a tight, long-sleeved jacket called an *eingyi*, which usually opened in the centre front. Sashes and waistbands held the clothing closed. Women wore similar garments to men, including a wraparound, sarong-like skirt called a *htamein* (right). On top, women wore a breast cloth and an *eingyi* jacket.

People at court wore the same clothing but in forms that used elaborate decorations, imported textiles and expensive materials — velvet, silk, gold cloth, brocades and satin imported from India and China. Clothing was often heavily decorated with gold brocade, gold- or silver-wrapped yarn and appliquéd designs made of precious metals. The Burmese also produced their own high-quality textiles, in particular the *luntaya acheik*, which features in both the minister's *paso* and the woman's skirt shown. This renowned textile is produced using a technique of interlocking tapestry weaving that may have been taught to the Burmese by Manipuri weavers, who were relocated into central Burma in the 1760s, but the technique also shares similarities with Chinese tapestry weave. The intricate patterns in *luntaya acheik* — horizontal, undulating designs of zigzags, waves, interlocking shapes and floral creepers — are created by weaving 100 to 200 shuttles through a warp of more than 1,000 threads. It takes weavers a day to produce only a few inches.

During court ceremonies the king and queen wore long jackets over silk *paso* and *htamein*. They also wore an elaborate ruffed collar connected to a panel with wing-like projections made of *pazun-zi* (tinsel cloth) and covered in cut glass, pearls, sequins, and gold and silver embroidery. The entire ensemble was very heavy. Generals and some ministers wore military court dress called *myit-do-myi-she* (see p.170). Jewellery was also governed by sumptuary laws; only royalty could wear diamonds, emeralds and rubies. *Salwe* were used to define rank; these chains of gold and silver were worn over the shoulders and across the chest. Only the king was allowed to wear *salwe* with twenty-four chains.

Burmese court dress from 1853 to 1885 drew on historical precedents in determining appropriate clothing for court occasions. Similarities between the outfits worn in the second half of the 19th century and those represented in wall paintings from the 17th and 18th centuries show considerable continuities in the types of robes and headdresses used at court. The representation of *luntaya acheik* patterns and Thai-style headdresses in late 18th-century paintings demonstrates that the Burmese were receptive to new ideas and foreign designs. However, by the mid 19th century the Burmese heavy ruffs and panels with wing-like projections had increased considerably in complexity, thereby reaching a form far beyond those that existed in Thailand. **AGr**

1872	1875	1878	1878	1880s	1885
King Mindon's brother and chief minister, the Kinwunmingyi, travels to Europe and presents jewellery to Queen Victoria and a *salwe* to the Prince of Wales.	King Mindon strives to modernize the kingdom and narrowly avoids annexation by the British.	King Mindon dies and Thibaw becomes king after significant political manipulations and bloodshed within the extended royal family.	Queen Supayalat popularizes the use of jasmine flowers in women's hair.	Aniline (chemical) dyes arrive in Burma, thus expanding the range of colours available to the textile industry.	The Third Anglo-Burmese War ends with the total defeat of the Burmese and King Thibaw's exile to India.

Military Court Costume 1878–85
MEN'S DRESS

This example of military court dress (*myit-do-myi-she*) was taken from the royal palace in Mandalay, Burma, when the British assumed government in 1885. It would have been made for a general or high-ranking military officer to wear at court during the reign of either King Mindon (1853–78) or King Thibaw (1878–85). The ensemble consists of a long, maroon velvet and silk robe and jacket with full-length, tight sleeves. The upper section is composed of white lining fabric, which is covered with a short, sleeveless velvet and silk jacket with a flared front opening and flares along the side vents. Ties at the neck and a sash belt hold the jacket closed. The outfit was worn with a helmet, called a *shwe-pe-kha-mauk*, made of gilded palm leaves or metal, with a central spike. Sumptuary laws regulated the clothing and accessories that each rank of Burmese society could wear and these are illustrated in detailed manuscript drawings from the 19th century. A court chamberlain was responsible for the royal wardrobe and ensured that dress protocol was maintained. Military court dress would have been worn on ceremonial occasions, such as Kadaw Day, an annual event when princes, tributary rulers, ministers, provincial officials and other members of the elite appeared in full ceremonial dress at the Burmese court to renew their allegiance to the king. **AGr**

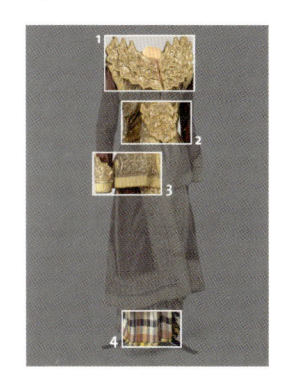

NAVIGATOR

FOCAL POINTS

1 CLOUD COLLAR
This comprises four sections of three scalloped tiers each; three of the sections are stitched together and the fourth is tied onto the others. The collar is made of stiffened *pazun-zi* (tinsel cloth) covered with gold. Such collars also featured in other types of court dress.

3 JACKET
The jacket is made of velvet and silk. It also has wide sections of gold brocade, *zardosi* (applied gold) floral motifs, *yetpya* (braid), sequins and gold-thread embroidery on the cuffs, hem and front of the robe. The neck, shoulders and armholes have the same details.

2 SASH BELT
The decoration in the belt shows the craftsmanship of the costume. Many aspects of an outfit—use of gold, quality of fabric or colour—indicate the wearer's rank. In this case, the general's rank was a high one and the king would have permitted the use of all the elements.

4 PASO
The jacket and robe are worn over a *paso*, a wraparound cloth covering the lower body. This is made of silk and decorated with patterns considered appropriate for men, such as checks, zigzags and interlocking shapes, in *luntaya acheik* tapestry weave.

THE BIRTH OF HAUTE COUTURE

1 Empress Eugénie of France was a leading patron of Charles Worth. Here she is depicted in a white dress with lilac bows, holding flowers and surrounded by her ladies-in-waiting in a painting from 1855 by Franz Xaver Winterhalter.

2 These evening dresses from c. 1887 were owned by the prominent US socialite Caroline Webster Schermerhorn Astor. The quality of Worth's designs were highly valued by society women the world over.

During the mid 19th century, wealth ceased to reside only in the ownership of land and began to be replaced by the 'new' money made from trade, banking and industry. As a result, fashionable dress was no longer confined to the aristocratic upper classes. The subsequent period of burgeoning consumerism and retail expansion created a need for a fashion system, which, until then, had relied almost solely on the skills of the dressmaker. It was British designer Charles Frederick Worth (1825–95) who elevated these humble sewing skills to the heights of 'haute couture'—words originally used to describe high-quality sewing. Through Worth's genius for self-promotion and his astute business sense, the term came to identify bespoke dressmaking techniques and high-end fashion. Worth was the head of the first *maison de couture* and the primary force behind the transformation of an essentially domestic art into an international industry.

Worth was born into a middle-class family of Lincolnshire solicitors in 1825. His unlikely trajectory, from this provincial legal background to becoming head of a couture house, began with an apprenticeship at Swan & Edgar's department store in Piccadilly Circus, London, in 1838. In addition to selling lengths of fabric and trimmings, the shop also offered advice on new styles and trends. A period at Lewis and Allenby, silk mercers to Queen Victoria, followed until 1845 when Worth moved to Paris, a city associated since the late 17th century with luxury silk textiles. In order to familiarize himself with

KEY EVENTS

1858	1860	1865	1868	1870	1870
Charles Worth establishes his dressmaking company.	Worth is appointed court couturier by Empress Eugénie of France.	Elisabeth of Austria is painted by German artist Franz Xaver Winterhalter wearing the quintessential Worth crinoline (see p.176).	The first Chambre Syndicale de la Couture is established as a strictly regulated business.	The Worth salon closes for a year after the collapse of the Second French Empire.	The French legislature establishes the Third Republic. It lasts until the German invasion in 1940 (longer than any government since the Revolution).

172 1800–99

the French language, Worth initially found work in a dry goods store, before taking up a position as assistant draper at Gagelin-Opigez et Cie in rue de Richelieu, where he was to remain for more than ten years, and rose to *premier commis* (chief cutter). Among the innovations he established there was the introduction of ready-made muslin dress samples, from which patrons could choose a style, which he would then match to one of the fabrics carried by the store. At Gagelin's, he met Marie Vernet (1825–98), a *demoiselle de maison* who modelled the clothes, and they married in 1851. After being awarded several gold medals from various international design exhibitions, which garnered him an international reputation and orders from abroad, Worth established his own dressmaking business in 1858, in rue de la Paix, in partnership with Swedish-born Otto Bobergh, who acted as business manager until the partnership dissolved in 1871.

Worth transformed dressmaking—previously a skill almost entirely within the remit of women—from a relatively lowly craft into a business, by creating a role for himself as an arbiter of refined taste. He identified himself as an artist, with an artist's prerogative of total control over the finished garment. Worth's designs came to the attention of the French court through the patronage of Princess Metternich, the wife of the Austrian ambassador to Paris. The Empress Eugénie, wife of Napoleon III, desirous of promoting the French textile industry, happily appropriated the lavish deployment of materials in Worth's designs (opposite). By 1864, the couturier was responsible for dressing the empress for her many formal state occasions, and also supplied her evening gowns for the frequent social gatherings of the Second Empire. Worth dictated not only the fashion of the *haut monde* of Europe, but also served the needs of the newly wealthy elite of North America, such as the Vanderbilts and the Astors, who willingly undertook the long sea voyage to Paris for the time-consuming fittings necessary for a bespoke service. Wearing Worth provided the wives and daughters of these industrial tycoons with social status, and refinement by association. The quality of Worth's dressmaking is exemplified by the silk and metallic thread evening dresses (right) owned by the wife of US real estate heir William Backhouse Astor Jr.

With his reputation as couturier to European royalty in place, Worth was in a position to dictate his own terms. Rather than women describing their requirements to the dressmaker in their homes, Worth expected clients to travel to the couturier's salon. This was an intimate and luxurious arena in which to view the latest designs, modelled by live

1871	1890	1895	1895	1900	1901
The House of Worth employs a staff of 1,200, including seamstresses, embroiderers, models, cutters and *vendeuses*.	The Belle Epoque (Beautiful Era) begins; it is known as the 'Gilded Age' in the United States.	Worth designs the wedding dress of Consuelo Vanderbilt, a US 'dollar duchess', who marries the ninth Duke of Marlborough.	Worth dies on 10 March. *The Times* newspaper describes him as 'the boy from Lincolnshire [who] beat the French in their own acknowledged sphere'.	The House of Worth displays at the Exposition Universelle (World Fair) in Paris, with a set piece depicting a court presentation.	Gaston-Lucien Worth employs Paul Poiret (1879–1944), who remains for two years, attempting to introduce more modern designs.

THE BIRTH OF HAUTE COUTURE 173

3 The fashionable British actress and society beauty Lillie Langtry, photographed c. 1885, was often dressed by Charles Worth.

4 Worth's voluminous dresses used large amounts of Lyons silk. For this late 19th-century reception dress, Worth chose swathes of wine-red silk-satin velvet to drape the fullness of the skirt to sit in the small of the back, where it formed a high bustle.

5 A House of Worth label from 1900. Worth was the first designer to have his label sewn into the garments he created.

mannequins, and overseen by the *vendeuse* (saleswoman). The client would then choose from a series of designs that were subsequently made to measure, and required several fittings for a perfect fit. Further fuelling his propensity for exclusivity, Worth would only take commissions from customers who were presented by a third person of a suitable background. No longer perceived as skilled dressmakers, the couturiers were by this time well-known names, with signature labels (left) identifying their garments, an innovation introduced in the mid 1860s. These were either printed or woven in the petersham tape sewn into the waistband of the dress. All these elements provided the blueprint for the creation of the haute couture system that continues to the present day.

At Worth's instigation, La Chambre Syndicale de la Confection et de la Couture pour Dames et Fillettes was formed in 1868, a type of union that undertook to lobby over issues relating to the administration and manufacture of garments. In 1910, this evolved into the Chambre Syndicale de la Haute Couture Parisienne, which dealt solely with the production of couture. It implemented strict, specific rules for membership. This ensured the ongoing quality and prestige of the institution, and also regulated the sale of designs and reproductions.

The year 1860 marked the apotheosis of Worth's quintessential style: the lavishly embellished crinoline. Dresses were constructed from two pieces: the wide-hooped skirt projecting as much to the front as to the back, and a tightly fitting bodice with very low scyes (armholes) extending to form a rounded shoulder line. The waistline was often emphasized with a 'V'-shape point. Worth experimented with flat-fronted crinolines and gored skirts in the mid 1860s, and continued to use lavish amounts of fabric in his role as promoter of the French textile industry, particularly the once moribund silk mills of Lyons (opposite). From the 1870s, the couturier increasingly deployed more expensive materials, often those more usually associated with interior textiles, such as large-scale floral motifs and *passementerie* (tassels, braids and fringing), designed in conjunction with textile manufacturers, including Tassinari et Chatel and J. Bachelard et Cie. An additional feature was the use of the decorative selvedge of the fabric as part of the design. When a single patterned fabric was used, the motif would be matched at the seams to create greater impact. Family-owned heirloom lace or jewels were often incorporated into the design of a dress.

In the early 1870s, Worth introduced his renowned 'princess line' (see p.178), named after Princess Metternich. The one-piece dress discarded the horizontal waist seam in favour of two parallel seams that passed through the bust point to the hem, thus creating a longer, leaner A-line. Worth displayed all these new lines on mannequins in a series of parties and events that were the precursors of the modern fashion show. The advent of photography, and the increasing popularity of society journalism, disseminated the fashionable finery of the upper classes to their middle-class counterparts, and the House of Worth's model gowns were advertised in *Harper's Bazar* and *The Queen*, as well as in *Gazette du Bon Ton* and *Vogue*. Apart from dressing the royal families of Italy, Spain and Russia, Worth numbered among his clients notable actresses such as Lillie Langtry (opposite above), who was also King Edward VII's mistress. Worth combined his personal attention and the bespoke fitting of individual clients with a formula of standardization, and a concept of using interchangeable pattern pieces, that was characteristic of the emerging ready-to-wear clothing industry. Garments could be ordered with no fittings required, as the customer would supply a well-fitting garment that was then measured. Worth also pioneered the concept of interchangeable skirts and bodices.

There was competition from other skilled dressmakers during Worth's reign as fashion leader, such as Jacques Doucet (1853–1929), who founded his house in 1874. However, Doucet's clients were drawn chiefly from the Parisian demi-monde, who were attracted to the sensuous *fin de siècle* aesthetic of his clothes. It was not until the emergence of the House of Paquin in 1891, towards the end of Worth's life, that his leadership was seriously challenged. Jeanne Paquin (1869–1936) was one of the first women to gain international status in the fashion business. She and her husband, Isidore Rene Jacob dit Paquin, offered a full range of garments that included *tailleurs* (suits) and daywear. Paquin became renowned for her subtle use of colour and the juxtaposition of various materials that went into robes inspired by the sack-back gowns or *robes à la française*, portrayed by 18th-century painter Jean-Antoine Watteau. Highly decorated with a plethora of trimmings, the delicate gowns combined intricate and beautifully executed couture techniques with a lightness more appropriate for the new century.

When Worth died in 1895, the house continued with his sons Gaston-Lucien (1853–1924) and Jean-Philippe (1856–1926) at the helm, both of whom had been working with their father at the house since maturity: Jean-Philippe as a designer, Gaston as a business administrator. They responded to the lighter structures and palette of the Edwardian period, but continued commissioning luxurious textiles, while retaining a conservative clientele. The house underwent a period of retrenchment as a result of World War I, with the subsequent loss of royal patronage, and the devaluation of European currency. Fashion was in transition from the frills of Edwardian frou-frou to the more understated, modern style of the 1920s, at which point Jean-Philippe and Gaston retired from the company. **MF**

Ball Gown 1860s
CHARLES FREDERICK WORTH 1825 – 95

The Empress of Austria by
Franz Xaver Winterhalter (1865).

NAVIGATOR

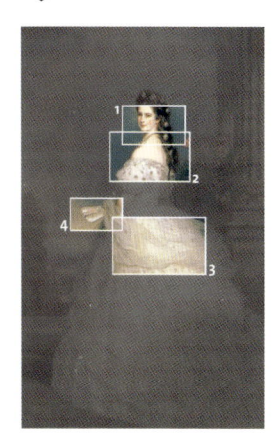

Charles Worth's international reputation for clothing the fashionable and wealthy elite is represented in this court portrait of the wife of Franz Joseph I, Elisabeth of Austria, who was both Empress of Austria and Queen of Hungary. It was painted during the Second Empire—the imperial Bonapartist regime of Napoleon III from 1852 to 1870.

Elisabeth was a noted beauty, who accentuated her extreme slenderness through the practice of tight-lacing. When Winterhalter painted this portrait, Elisabeth's waist span was 18 to 19 inches (45.5 to 48 cm), which emphasizes the enormous volume of the skirt that she is wearing. The crinoline also reached its greatest width during this period. Fashion historian James Laver has drawn a parallel between the excesses of the crinoline and those of the Second Empire itself, which was a time of material prosperity, extravagance and dubious morality. Corsets of the period were fastened up the front with hooks and eyes, but Elisabeth had more rigid, solid-front ones made in Paris out of leather, which were then popular with the fashionable prostitutes known as *grandes cocottes*. She never wore petticoats because they added bulk, and she was often literally sewn into her clothes in order to further highlight her tiny waist. **MF**

FOCAL POINTS

1 BRAIDED HAIR
Elisabeth's lustrous hair is parted at the centre front and then crowned with a twisted braid, which is allowed to fall down the back. Threaded through the hair are diamond-encrusted star-shaped jewels that create an informal tiara.

3 TRANSPARENT FABRIC
A layer of tulle, a sheer fabric otherwise known as illusion or maline, drifts over the bodice and voluminous pleated skirt of the dress, which is embellished with embroidered stars to match the hair ornaments. A further length of tulle is draped around the waist.

2 DÉCOLLETAGE
The white satin dress has a deep off-the-shoulder décolletage that ends in a tulle frill from which the short, puffed sleeves emerge. The empress appears in a sensual pose with naked shoulders and her head turned towards the viewer.

4 HAND FAN
Not simply a cooling device for overheated ballrooms, the hand fan was a decorative accessory deployed in flirtation. In Europe the folding fan became popular after its introduction from East Asia in the 17th century, after which fans became increasingly decorative.

THE BIRTH OF HAUTE COUTURE

Princess Line 1870s
CHARLES FREDERICK WORTH 1825 – 95

Silk velvet afternoon dress with
lace jacket by Charles Worth (1889).

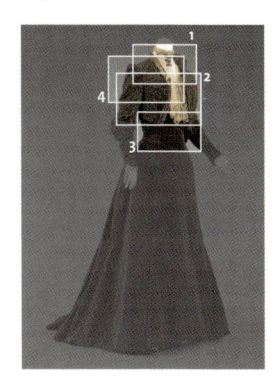

Charles Frederick Worth constantly experimented with two-dimensional pattern pieces in order to alter the proportions and silhouette of three-dimensional form. One of his lasting contributions to the art of pattern cutting was the 'princess line', reputedly named after Princess Metternich, the wife of the Austrian ambassador to Paris. The new line was introduced into the couturier's collections in the early 1870s. It was a departure from the prevailing technique—in which the bodice of the dress was sewn to the skirt with a seam at the waist—which facilitated the wearing of the full-skirted crinoline. By 1868 the crinoline was falling out of favour and skirts were cut into gores, triangular pieces of cloth sewn together vertically to provide volume at the hem while retaining smoothness over the hips. It was a natural step for the gores to be extended to the shoulders in shaped panels, incorporating bust darts, skimming past the waist and resulting in a longer, leaner line. Interior ties held the fabric close around the legs. The bodice was then moulded to fit the lines of the body, an effect similar to that of the tight-fitting *cuirasse* bodice, which was getting longer and by 1878 reached the thighs. The two ideas merged and the whole of the dress was styled in the princess line with shoulder-to-hem panels. The new line rendered skirt supports such as the crinoline obsolete. **MF**

NAVIGATOR

FOCAL POINTS

1 LACE JABOT
A lace jabot (bird's crop) is suspended from the neckline. Originally referring to the ruffles on a man's shirt, at the end of the 19th century the jabot evolved into a decorative fall of lace on a woman's blouse, suspended from or attached to a neckband or collar.

3 LUXURIOUS TEXTILES
Worth's close association with the French textile and trimming producers of Lyons resulted in the prolific use of luxurious materials in his designs. This dress, which is made of moleskin-coloured silk velvet, is matched in colour to the lace jacket.

2 INTEGRAL BOLERO-STYLE JACKET
The bolero-style jacket—cropped to just below the bust to reveal the indented waist—is cut in one with the dress, apart from the front panels, which are allowed to fall free to a point and feature turned-in, notched lapels.

4 COMPLEX SLEEVES
The sleeve head is lightly gathered into the arm scye, forming a raised edge. The volume, however, is seen at the elbow, where the sleeves are ruched to facilitate movement before narrowing towards the wrist, ending in a small curve over the hand.

THE BIRTH OF HAUTE COUTURE 179

JAPANESE DRESS – MEIJI PERIOD

The arrival of US warships in 1853, with their insistence that Japan open itself up to trade, marked the end of more than 200 years of Japan's self-imposed isolation. The political imperatives of the newly opened Japan were complicated and failure to address them effectively or quickly enough risked colonization by the United States or one of the European powers. Political survival required modernization and although there was uncertainty as to what exactly needed to be modernized, early visits to foreign countries and the world fairs convinced Japan that fashion was a crucial element in the modern world. The state then embarked on a self-conscious, elite-led programme to reform Japanese dress.

Independence would be impossible without rapid military reform and modern warfare required the drilling of troops, to which uniforms were essential. Uniforms were key to changing fashion culture during the Meiji period (1868–1912) because universal male conscription was introduced. The key features were divided garments; shirts and trousers; woollen fabric; and, most importantly, clothes that were tailored to the body. A crucial difference between kimono-based clothing and Western garments is that the latter followed the shape of the body rather than wrapping it.

The major fashion change for men during the Meiji period was the adoption of the suit. In 1872 the state legislated that it was to be compulsory dress for the civil service and in 1874 it became standard business attire. Initially, suits

KEY EVENTS

1868	1869	1871	1872	1872	1872	1872
The shogun Yoshinobu resigns, the Tokugawa dynasty ends and imperial rule is restored under Emperor Meiji. The capital relocates to Edo (Tokyo).	Yukichi Fukuzawa's book *Conditions in the West*, which includes detailed descriptions of Western clothes, launches a wave of Westernization.	The Meiji government dismantles the feudal system and forbids private armies. It ends the samurai monopoly on wearing silk and sumptuous colours.	Western dress is prescribed for official ceremonies for civil servants and the emperor himself is photographed in a Western uniform.	The Meiji government founds the Tomioka Silk Factory, which becomes a centre for industrialized silk farming.	Rickshaw drivers are required to wear shirts at all times.

were incompatible with the traditional custom of sitting on *tatami* mats or low stools; however, the government and businesses soon adopted Western-style desks and chairs. The interiors of homes, though, remained traditional, which led to the phenomenon of the 'double life'—the wearing of suits in public but kimonos at home. A well-cut suit created a serious impression in capitalist business, even fostering trust, and with its egalitarian, uniform style it was the suitable mode of dress for modernity—in this Japan was no exception.

Japanese women found it much more difficult to source garments that were appropriate to modernity (see p.182). This was partly because they came to the Western system at a time when women's fashions were at their most impractical, as exemplified by the bustle. There were some valiant early attempts to adopt the bustle, seen at the Rokumeikan (opposite), a casino-like entertainment hall built in Tokyo in 1883 to impress foreigners with perfect Japanese versions of Western fashion, food and dances. Nationalist pressures due to the wars with China (1894) and Russia (1904) also had an indirect effect on dress, compounding the impracticality of women's fashions as militant nationalism caused a general return to the kimono for women (below). It was not until the boom period of the 1920s that women's fashion discovered a female equivalent of the modern male suit.

Although the most visible fashion development in the Meiji period was the engagement with Western clothing, a further change saw all classes adopting clothes previously reserved for the samurai. The development of department stores, along with poster advertising and consumer culture, led the way towards a Japan where everyone could participate in the spectacle of fashion. **TS**

1 A woodblock print from 1888 depicts Japanese couples wearing Victorian fashions at the Rokumeikan in Tokyo.

2 This group portrait of students and teachers in Nagoya in the 1890s illustrates the return to kimono wearing for women. Most of the men continue to wear business suits.

1873	1874	1883	1886	1886	1894
Japan adopts universal male three-year conscription and all men wear Western-style woollen, divided garments.	The Western male suit is prescribed as standard business attire but a divide opens between what is worn in public and in private.	The Rokumeikan opens. It hosts parties and balls for foreign guests, with the Japanese elite adopting Western dress and dance styles.	The Shirokiya is the first traditional silk store to sell Western clothing. It eventually becomes a Western-style department store.	The Association of Merchants and Manufacturers of Western Suits is founded with 123 members.	The first Sino-Japanese War begins, leading to a wave of nationalism and a return to women wearing the kimono.

Sokuhatsu Hairstyles and Western Dress 1880s
WOMEN'S FASHION

Comparison of Beautiful Women in Western Coiffures, colour woodblock print by Toyohara Chikanobu (1887).

With the construction of the Rokumeikan entertainment hall in Tokyo, the wives and daughters of senior government officials and prominent businessmen were able to show off dresses in imitation of European fashion. While the Victorian-style bustle dresses were inaccessible to all but the elite, Japanese women could experiment with modernity by adopting new hairstyles. *Sokuhatsu*—Westernized swept-back hairstyles—became popular, but it was harder to imitate foreign hairstyles than clothes, most likely because of physical differences in hair. They were rendered in combination with traditional Japanese coiffures and resulted in swept-back styles or a turned-up form called *yakaimaki* (literally, *soirée chignon*), which was a hybrid of neither entirely Japanese nor entirely foreign origin. This print by Chikanobu, who was renowned for his exquisite illustrations of both traditional and modern women's fashions, illustrates various dress- and hairstyles. The popular woodcut artists of the time played a significant role in promoting the Meiji government policy of modernization in fashion and hairstyles.

A variety of oils and perfumes for dressing hair had been available in Japan since the Edo period (1603–1868). Companies such as Shiseido and Pola, which emerged from the sophisticated self-grooming culture of the Meiji era, grew into industrial giants by embracing the Japanese desire to look modern. Women stopped shaving their eyebrows and blackening their teeth during this period. Men's hairstyles were also influenced by Western fashions: Emperor Meiji cut off his traditional topknot in 1872, leading many Japanese men to do likewise, and Western haircuts, beards and moustaches soon became the norm. **TS**

⊙ FOCAL POINTS

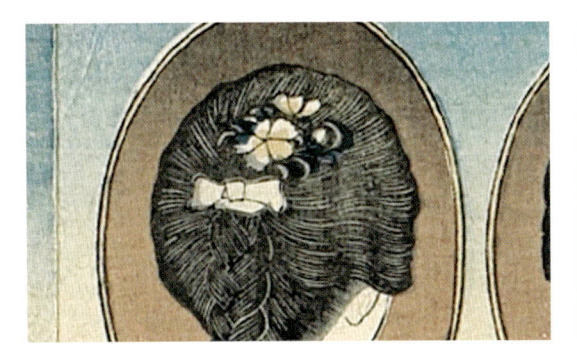

1 FLOWERS
Many new types of flowers began to appear as hair accessories when Japan reopened to the world. New dyes were also introduced and sumptuary laws restricting various clothes and hues to certain classes were abolished. This led to an explosion of colour during the Meiji period.

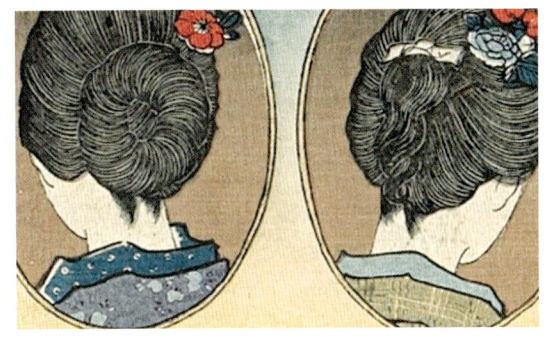

2 EXPOSED NECK
Revealing a woman's bare neck is regarded as a sexually charged act in Japan and these hairstyles induced shocked reactions similar to those that met the introduction of the Western bob in the 1920s. They signalled a desire to be seen as sexually mature and ready to embrace a new, modern way of life.

3 BUSTLE
The bustle was introduced to Japan at the same time as the fashion reached its height in Paris (1887–89), with distorting corsets and the enormous Parisian tail at the back. As these fashions were adopted for political rather than aesthetic or practical reasons, there was no allowance for Japanese taste, lifestyle or body shape.

4 WESTERN DRESS AND HAT
Japanese versions of Western clothing were fairly accurate in their imitation of contemporary European styles. With the arrival of Victorian fashions, men and women also began to wear hats for the first time; the lady on the far left in this print wears a hat decorated with a bird and red flower design.

▲ A young woman having her hair styled *c.* 1885. Although foreign clothes were out of reach for most girls, Western hairstyles were a new trend with which they could experiment.

JAPANESE DRESS – MEIJI PERIOD 183

ARTISTIC AND AESTHETIC DRESS

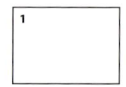

1 Edward Burne-Jones depicts a gown of flame red, devoid of extraneous decoration, in *Laus Veneris* (1873–75).

2 Synonymous with the Aesthetic movement, the peacock-print fabric (1887) by Arthur Silver of the Silver Studio was manufactured for Liberty.

3 In *The Princess from the Land of Porcelain* (1863–65), James Abbott McNeill Whistler depicts dress, textile and interior design influenced by Japanese arts.

The helpless femininity of the 'angel in the house', constrained by ever-expanding voluminous skirts and tight-laced corsets, was challenged in the mid 19th century by proponents of an alternative way of dressing known as 'artistic'. This style was particularly associated with garments of loose, naturalistic draping worn by the models and mistresses of the Pre-Raphaelite painters during the 1860s. Founded in part by Dante Gabriel Rossetti, the English poet, illustrator and painter, the Pre-Raphaelite Brotherhood took its inspiration from those medieval artists who preceded Raphael, and considered the Gothic art and architecture of the Middle Ages to be the high point of civilization, a paradigm of a morally and aesthetically perfect society, engendered by artisanal methods of production. The Pre-Raphaelites promulgated an alternative ideal of feminine beauty epitomized by an abundance of loose, lustrous unbound hair, a pale complexion and a look of soulful ennui or brooding intensity. Their models and muses, among them Jane Morris (see p.186) and Lizzie Siddal, were dressed in the artists' notion of the medieval *bliaut* (robe) with a fitted yet uncorseted bodice, a simple low-scoop neckline and trailing, floor-length sleeves, worn with a skirt gathered onto a high waistband, falling into folds around the feet (above).

Worn in literary and artistic circles, this style of dress became less popular in the 1870s and reappeared as aesthetic dress in the 1880s with the Arts and Crafts Movement. This marriage of crafts, architecture and social reform, which

KEY EVENTS

1870s	1874	1877	1881	1881	1884
Liberty & Co imports fabrics that are popular with the artistic set and feature in paintings by James Abbott McNeill Whistler and George Frederick Watts.	Commissioned by Liberty to design fabrics, William Morris revives the use of vegetable dyes, which are marketed as Liberty Art colours.	English author Eliza Haweis publishes *The Art of Beauty*, decrying contemporary fashion and urging women to adopt historical dress.	The Rational Dress Society is formed, chaired by Viscountess Haberton. It advocates a loose style of clothing that does not deform the body.	The comic opera *Patience; or, Bunthorne's Bride* by Gilbert and Sullivan is first performed in London.	Dr Gustav Jäger exhibits at the London International Health Exhibition. His teachings inspire the creation of the Jaeger clothing brand.

swept through Europe in the late 1890s, was headed in Britain by William Morris, who eschewed the mass-production methods then prevalent to embrace the processes of the medieval artisan. He discarded the overly rich patterning of Victorian weaves and cheap roller-printed textiles and reintroduced weaving by hand looms and block printing. Any embellishment was restricted to folkloric hand embroidery of favourite motifs such as sunflowers—the emblem of the aesthetes—lilies and peacock feathers (right).

The followers of the aesthetic principle wore a restricted palette of neutrals, cream, mustard, russet, old gold, subdued reds and blues, with sage green being particularly identified with the movement and often referred to as 'greenery yallery' (see p.188). Oriental influence came from the display of Japanese applied arts at the International Exhibition in London in 1862, prompted by the opening-up of Japan in 1853. This stimulated an interest in oriental and exotic products, particularly textile and graphic design, and the introduction of kimono-inspired Japonaise gowns as portrayed by the painter James Abbott McNeill Whistler (below right). A young Arthur Lasenby Liberty (1843–1917), then an employee of Farmer and Rogers' Great Shawl Emporium on Regent Street, London, persuaded his employers to open an oriental department and in 1875 opened his own Oriental Emporium, which was one of the first to include the arts of Japan in its design repertoire.

The aesthetic fashions of the day prompted ridicule in the popular press and provided fuel for the pens of caricaturists and playwrights. W. S. Gilbert and Arthur Sullivan's comic opera *Patience; or, Bunthorne's Bride*, satirized the Aesthetic movement and became an instant hit when it was first performed in London in 1881. Irish-born writer and renowned wit Oscar Wilde was invited to lecture across the United States to promote the opera. During his successful year-long lecture tour in 1882, he reportedly sported an extreme version of male aesthete dress, replacing the more conventional frock coat with a purple Hungarian smoking jacket lined with lavender satin, worn with satin knee breeches and black silk stockings. Also popular among male aesthetes were flowing scarves, to replace the cravat, and wide-brimmed felt 'wide-awake' hats, more usually worn by cowboys in the American West.

The 'cult of beauty' permeated every aspect of the aesthete's life and, as marginal dress and the avant-garde became subsumed into conventional dress, the general populace began to avail itself of what had once been a minority taste. As mainstream fashion adopted aspects of aesthetic dress, various historic styles were appropriated: these included *gigot* sleeves with Elizabethan-style slashing and the 18th-century *sacque* dress, which was characterized by a large pleat of fabric falling loosely from the back of the shoulders, seen in the works of the painter Jean-Antoine Watteau and worn by Jane Morris as an alternative to the earlier columnar medieval styles. This was the forerunner of the tea gown, a garment worn for informal occasions. **MF**

1884	1887	1887	1890	1897	1903
Liberty opens a dressmaking department overseen by E. W. Godwin, selling to London's avant-garde.	George du Maurier's cartoons are published in *Punch* magazine; they satirize the Cimabue Brown family, who are wearers of aesthetic dress.	The Arts and Crafts Exhibition Society is founded in London. It arranges exhibitions and lectures to promote the decorative arts.	The Healthy and Artistic Dress Union is formed; the first of three journals, *Aglaia*, is published in July 1893.	The Vienna Secession is created in opposition to the Vienna Academy. It is a forum for radical artists such as Gustav Klimt.	Josef Hoffmann and Koloman Moser open the Wiener Werkstätte; it produces artist-designed furniture and furnishings, with fashion added in 1910.

Pre-Raphaelite Dress 1860s
WOMEN'S DRESS

Portrait of Jane Morris, from an album of photographs taken by John Robert Parsons (1865).

NAVIGATOR

This photograph of William Morris's wife, Jane Morris (née Burden), is one of a series of eighteen portraits taken by John Robert Parsons in the garden of Tudor House, the Chelsea home of Dante Gabriel Rossetti. Jane was Rossetti's mistress and muse, and was portrayed in the work of several members of the Pre-Raphaelite Brotherhood. Rossetti commissioned Parsons to take the photographs but arranged the poses himself.

Jane is captured in typical morose mood and languid pose, wearing an early style of artistic dress. Worn without a body-confining corset and constructed to fall in unpressed pleats from a bound, scooped neckline, the dress is caught at the waist with a matching fabric belt. Jane's silhouette adheres in part to the more tailored and formal gowns that were being worn by her conventional counterparts in that the folds of the heavy silk-satin of the bodice are drawn together to create 'V'-shape folds ending at the waist. At the wrist of the billowing sleeves, a narrow edge of a lace-edged cuff is apparent, which was probably detachable for laundering purposes. At a time when the crinoline was at its zenith, the folds of the skirt, although voluminous, are unsupported by anything other than their own weight. **MF**

FOCAL POINTS

1 UNDRESSED HAIR
Cascades of thick and lustrous hair convey a sexually charged message in an era of Victorian prudery. Hair was a significant feature of the archetypal Pre-Raphaelite woman; Jane wears hers undressed and gathered in a loose knot at the back of the neck.

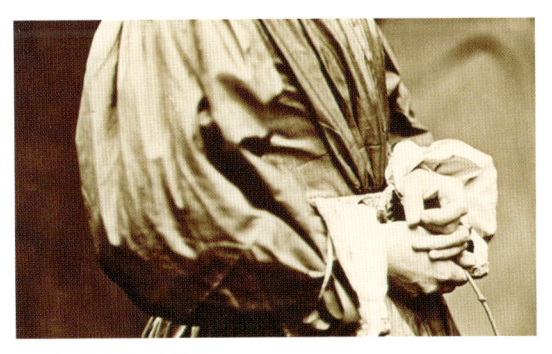

2 VOLUMINOUS SLEEVES
The sleeve head is hand-sewn with gathers into a dropped shoulder seam, thus creating a deep arm scye that supplies width and volume. The fabric billows out, providing freedom of movement, before being caught in at the wrist.

▲ In the painting *Day Dream* (1880) by Dante Gabriel Rossetti, his favourite muse and mistress, Jane Morris, is portrayed wearing a voluminous, unstructured garment of artistic dress.

ARTISTIC AND AESTHETIC DRESS 187

Velvet Gown 1894
LIBERTY

NAVIGATOR

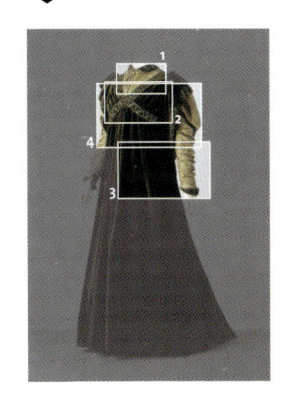

This dark green silk velvet overdress reflects the era's preoccupation with the fashions of the 15th century and the aesthetes' preferred colour palette of 'greenery yallery'. Designed to be worn without corsets, the gown hangs in unpressed pleats from an inverted 'V'-shape bodice. The back of the overdress also has a 'V'-shape neckline, from which the deeply pleated fabric forms a small train. Neoclassical-inspired drapes of fabric fall from the shoulders and are edged in braid, while military-inspired epaulettes exaggerate the shape of each shoulder. The gown is lined with green silk and the boned bodice fastens in the front with hooks and eyes. The back of the skirt is gathered in with tapes at the waist on the underside of the dress.

Worn as a tea gown in the late afternoon, and strictly within the confines of the home, this dress is close in style to Walter Crane's designs for aesthetic dress that featured in *Aglaia*, the journal of the Healthy and Artistic Dress Union. It was made by Liberty's Artistic and Historic Costume Studio under the guidance of E. W. Godwin, the designer who headed the dress department from 1884. An adherent of the Aesthetic movement, he created garments for women inspired by classical, medieval and Renaissance clothing. **MF**

FOCAL POINTS

1 CLOSE-FITTING NECKLINE
The yoke of the undergarment is gathered into a neat series of small pleats at the close-fitting neckline and is open at the centre front. The small turn-back collar in dark green velvet is fitted to a narrow stand.

3 RUCHED SLEEVES
The horizontally ruched sleeves fall from an unpadded *gigot*, or leg o' mutton, sleeve head. These end at the wrists in small, turn-back cuffs that are trimmed in a dark green velvet that matches the overdress.

2 EMPHASIS ON THE BREASTS
The breasts are delineated by the addition of broad braid embroidered with pale green silk-satin stitch and embellished with iridescent beads. The braid holds the soft gathers of the velvet gown in place over the bust.

4 UNDERGARMENT
The main body of the undergarment that is visible beneath the velvet robe is constructed from a fine green and yellow Liberty Hop and Ribbon damask, which lends itself to draping at the neck and ruching at the sleeves.

AN AMERICAN ARCHETYPE

The Gibson Girl represented the sartorial emancipation of the American woman. She was the first American standard of beauty to become recognized globally, disseminated to a mass audience through painting, illustration and photography. The archetype that was created by the artist, illustrator and social commentator Charles Dana Gibson in a series of illustrations from 1890 to 1910 represented the free-spirited, active young American woman at a time when she was the focus of contemporary culture, depicted as a heroine in the works of US novelists Edith Wharton and Henry James, and in the paintings of US artist John Singer Sargent. The simplicity of her fashion and tastes helped consolidate what came to be viewed as 'American' style.

The Gibson Girl personified beauty and independence, and also appeared capable of personal fulfilment. Poised and confident in Gibson's illustrated narratives, she is depicted undergoing all the modern rites of passage: attending college, exchanging lively badinage with men as her equal, and exploring her personal interests and talents. Gibson drew his tall, narrow-waisted ideal woman in black and white sketches in pen and ink (above), portraying her as a multifaceted role model. Serious in her pursuit of physical fitness and engaging with a variety of outdoor pursuits, such as cycling, horse riding, tennis, croquet and sea-bathing, the Gibson Girl also represented the increasing number of US women who were being educated to the same degree as men and were entering the workforce.

The original physical prototype of the Gibson Girl was inspired by Gibson's wife, Irene, one of the four Langhorne sisters, who was born to a once-wealthy

KEY EVENTS

1886	1886	1887–88	1895	1895	1898
Massachusetts-born Charles Dana Gibson sells his first pen-and-ink sketches to John Ames Mitchell's *Life* magazine.	US novelist Henry James publishes *The Bostonians*, which is set against the rise of the feminist movement.	John Singer Sargent visits New York and Boston and undertakes more than twenty portrait commissions, including one of Alice Vanderbilt in 1888.	Gibson marries Irene Langhorne, sister of Nancy Astor, the first woman to serve as a Member of Parliament in the British House of Commons.	The extremely wide *gigot* sleeve, first seen in the 1830s, comes back into fashion.	Gibson illustrates *Rupert of Hentzau*, the sequel to Anthony Hope's Ruritanian romance *The Prisoner of Zenda* (1894).

Virginia family, impoverished by the Civil War. The well-known artist's model Evelyn Nesbit sat for the first drawing of the Gibson Girl, although it was in fact a composite image rather than a portrait of an individual. However, the most widely known model for the character was the Belgian-born stage actress Camille Clifford, the winner of a magazine contest sponsored by the illustrator to find the living embodiment of the 'ideal woman'. Her figure and distinctive coiffure defined the Gibson Girl style.

The prevailing silhouette of the Gibson Girl was the hourglass figure, often constructed from a separate bodice or blouse and skirt rather than a dress (opposite below). It was based on a narrow waist, with a flared, gored, trumpet-shaped skirt that fitted over the hips, and a blouse with sleeves puffed high at the shoulder. By 1895, the size of the sleeves was so extreme that they required pads to keep their shape, and they were known as *gigot*, or leg o' mutton, sleeves. These evolved into the 'bishop sleeve', which was fitted on the arm with fullness at the wrist before being gathered into a cuff. Rows of ruffled ribbon or bands of lace insertion decorated the bodice and extended to the sleeves, drawing the eye outwards, and lace was also used to decorate the high-boned collar. The outer garments were worn over a fashionable, straight-fronted corset that tilted the upper body forwards into a pouter-pigeon monobosom and thrust the hips backwards, thus forming the typical 'S'-shape silhouette of the period (right). The bodice featured small gathers just above the waistline, which added to the pouch effect. Simpler in structure was the combination of shirtwaist and skirt (see p.194), which still endorsed the 'S'-shape silhouette, but pared down the embellishment. This was more suitable for participation in sport, and for work, especially when made from the lighter washable fabrics, including silk chiffon and lightweight cottons such as batiste lawn and voile, which had come into fashion.

The increasing physical activity of women demanded more practical clothing, such as the bifurcated skirt (see p.192), and footwear that was sturdier than the thin-soled slippers previously worn. Shoes with small Cuban or Louis heels were popular, as were front-laced boots. Hair was styled into an elaborate pyramid, pulled up into a loose topknot and padded out at the sides with the use of added hair. Instead of enormous, wide-brimmed hats, decorated with flowers and ostrich feathers, the Gibson Girl chose a straw boater worn at the front of the topknot.

Although the United States' fascination with this paradigm of girlhood came to an end with the onset of World War I, the Gibson Girl's athletic sensibility remained inherent to the aesthetic of US fashion; an American archetype, she formed the bridge between the restrictive dress of the 19th century and the more active clothing of the 20th century, thus representing a modern ideal of progressive femininity. **MF**

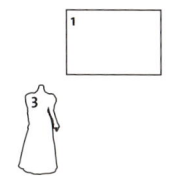

1 The Gibson Girl (1906), as drawn by Charles Dana Gibson for *Life* magazine, embodies a new definition of femininity.

2 Camille Clifford (1900) displays the distinctive 'S'-shape silhouette, which was shown off to great effect by dresses made from the lighter fabrics of the era.

3 This walking dress (c. 1893) is constructed from wool and silk, and designed to emphasize the wearer's tiny waistline.

1900	1900	1900	1901	1901	1905
Socialite Rita Lydig wins a divorce settlement of two million dollars. Her wardrobe is the basis of the Costume Institute at the Metropolitan Museum of Art.	Stage actress Camille Clifford becomes the best-known model for the Gibson Girl illustrations.	Unrestricted marketing sees the Gibson Girl image appear on objects such as table china, bedlinen, screens, fans and even wallpaper.	The Society of Illustrators is founded in New York by artists including Charles Dana Gibson, N. C. Wyeth and Maxfield Parrish.	Press fasteners are introduced in the United States and are used to fasten the blouse or bodice to the skirt.	US chorus girl and artist's model Evelyn Nesbit models for the drawing titled *Women: The Eternal Question* by Charles Dana Gibson.

AN AMERICAN ARCHETYPE 191

Bifurcated Skirt 1890s
SPORTING DRESS

A young woman wears a bifurcated
skirt in St James's Park, London (c. 1897).

NAVIGATOR

Invariably equated with women's desire for social and political emancipation, the wearing of the bifurcated skirt began with the efforts of Amelia Jenks Bloomer in 1851. Her design of baggy, Turkish-style trousers, or pantaloons, gathered at the ankle into a lace frill and worn under a calf-length skirt, dispensed with the need for a crinoline cage. Many feared that the introduction of this garment would erase the differences between the sexes, and women who wore the costume faced initial hostility. The debates over dress reform reintroduced the notion of bifurcation in the 1880s and 1890s, and the word 'bloomers' was sometimes inaccurately used to describe the divided skirt worn by modern women engaging in sporting activities. When worn for the popular sport of cycling, the bloomer-style trousers worn under an overskirt of various lengths deflected the social stigma of 'trousered' women, and before long further types of bifurcation, such as the divided skirt and knickerbockers, began to become fashionable.

The pose of the female cyclist encapsulates the liberation felt at the prospect of the open road. She wears a divided skirt that is cropped to mid calf and part of a tailormade, a matching skirt and jacket fashioned along the lines of men's tailoring. The high, starched collar of the shirtwaist extends above the jacket, which is cinched to emphasize the waist. **MF**

FOCAL POINTS

1 TRILBY-STYLE HAT
A type of fedora, but with a slightly shorter crown, the small-scale trilby is worn angled down at the front and slightly upturned at the back. Perched at the side of the head, it is worn over undressed hair, which is simply tied back.

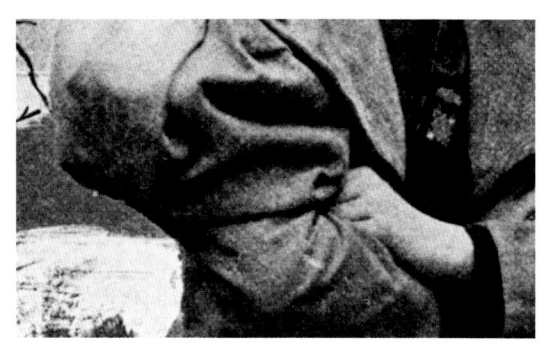

3 EXCESSIVE SLEEVE WIDTH
Cut from a substantial tweed, the tailored jacket features fashionable, voluminous *gigot* (leg o' mutton) sleeves. The fabric is pleated, folded and padded at the shoulder to provide width from where the sleeves taper to a narrow cuff.

2 REVERS
The wide revers of the jacket collar are turned back and secured in place with a row of faux buttons and embroidered buttonholes, which are matched by those that embellish the pockets of the bifurcated skirt.

4 WATERPROOF GAITERS
Beneath the knee-length bifurcated skirt, waterproof canvas-buttoned gaiters, usually worn as part of a military uniform, and known as puttees, are worn to protect the lower legs. These fit over the top of the low-heeled leather boots.

AN AMERICAN ARCHETYPE

Shirtwaist 1890s
READY-TO-WEAR

Golfing Foursome by Walter Granville-Smith (c. 1900).

NAVIGATOR

The simplification of women's clothing at the end of the 19th century resulted in the popularity of the combination of the shirtwaist and skirt, which was widely available as ready-to-wear by 1890. 'Waist' was the term used for the bodice of a dress or a blouse that was fashioned like a man's shirt, with a turnover collar and buttons down the centre-front fastening. The *gigot*, or leg o' mutton, sleeves are less extreme than those seen in more fashionable garments, and end in a businesslike turned-back double cuff. When worn in combination with the tailored jacket, known as a tailormade, the plain, dark skirt and the shirtwaist blouse became the prevailing uniform of the working woman. The shirtwaist was sold as an individual piece or as part of an ensemble, and the mass production of the garment made it available to all, setting in place the foundations of the superiority of the United States in the field of ready-to-wear.

The shirtwaist offered freedom of movement for newly popular leisure activities such as golf. It is worn here without a jacket and tucked inside the gored skirt. Freedom of movement is also represented in the sturdy, lace-up ankle boots and straw boater, worn with naturally dressed hair. By the early 20th century, the utilitarian aspect of the shirtwaist was compromised by lace trimmings and frills, used to embellish the blouse. **MF**

FOCAL POINTS

1 MASCULINE STYLING
The shirtwaist's similarity to men's attire is evident in the neat bow tie at the neckline and the easily laundered white cotton fabric. Men's shirt collars are also sewn on to a stand, which supports the collar and provides height.

2 FLARED AND GORED SKIRT
The skirt is constructed in an unpatterned linen or serge, and is without further embellishment. It is slightly gathered at the back of the belted waistband, which dips slightly towards the front as a result of the corset worn underneath.

THE US TEXTILE INDUSTRY

At the beginning of the 20th century, the majority of shirtwaist blouses were created in Philadelphia and New York, and sold across the country. In Manhattan alone, there were more than 450 textile factories (below), employing some 40,000 workers, many of whom were immigrants. In 1911 there was a devastating fire that led to legislation requiring improved factory safety standards. The Triangle Shirtwaist Factory fire in New York City caused the deaths of 146 garment workers and was the result of management locking the doors to stairwells and exits, a common practice at the time to prevent pilferage and unauthorized breaks. The resultant outcry spurred the growth of the International Ladies' Garment Workers' Union.

FASHIONS OF THE BELLE EPOQUE

1. *The End of Dinner* (1913) by Jules-Alexandre Grün depicts a fashionable social gathering typical of the Belle Epoque period.

2. A woman laces up her corset to give herself a more prominent bust and behind (c. 1890–1900).

3. French comedienne Blanche Toutain wears a hat trimmed with velvet ribbon and a silk rose on the cover of *Le Théâtre* (1906).

The period known as the Belle Epoque (c. 1890–1914) roughly corresponds to the playfully erotic Art Nouveau movement. During the reign of Edward VII, society experienced a transition from the stiff Victorian values of the ageing monarch to what was perceived as an era of decadent moral laxity. Divorce became easier and weekend visits to country houses allowed sexual freedom within marriage. In France the beau monde (above) and demi-monde continued to mingle, and rich men competed for the favours of the greatest courtesans. Such women wore couture dresses, jewelled bodices and parures from esteemed jewellers including Cartier, and their newly acquired power helped to normalize female sexuality.

It was a time of extended European peace, economic growth and scientific advancement. The Entente Cordiale (1904) led British and French consumers to the new salons of designers such as Jacques Doucet (1853–1929), Jeanne Paquin (1869–1936; see p.200), Paul Poiret (1879–1944) and Lucy, Lady Duff-Gordon (1863–1935). The activities of the Franco-British elite—racing at Longchamp, casinos at Deauville, and shooting in Scotland—inspired new leisurewear and sumptuous evening gowns, which were coveted by consumers lower down the social chain. Trains, cars and buses made days out possible for all, and new fashions were adopted for activities beyond the workplace. Among men, the striped blazers of Oxbridge sports clubs and straw boaters were popular.

KEY EVENTS

1889	1893	1895	1895	1895	1898
All eyes are on Paris when the Eiffel Tower opens for the World Fair.	Posters by Henri de Toulouse-Lautrec advertise the cancan dancers at the Moulin Rouge, Paris, a nightspot popular with the Franco-British elite.	The Lumière brothers screen the first moving picture in Paris. The film shows workers leaving a factory in Lyons.	The voluminous *gigot* sleeve is at the height of fashion: the bigger the better.	The pioneer of haute couture, Charles Frederick Worth (1825–95), dies. His designs influence the fashions of the Belle Epoque.	Aubrey Beardsley dies. His illustrations of Oscar Wilde's *Salome* and Alexander Pope's *Rape of the Locke* echo the period's interest in Rococo.

In Art Nouveau, designs were based on the stems rather than the petals of flowers. Fashion imitated art, and the Belle Epoque is characterized by a lengthening of the female silhouette. Dresses began to be fitted sinuously to the body from the ribcage to the hipline, and therefore required different undergarments. Sleeves appeared in many shapes, from the *gigot*, or leg o' mutton, in *c.* 1890 to the handkerchief style seen on tea gowns; other sleeves were more streamlined and accessorized with immaculate long white gloves. Necklines were often worn high to the chin on day dresses, which further elongated the figure, whereas waists were natural or just below the ribcage and lay flat over the hips, with gored A-line skirts falling softly to the floor. Wide, low-brimmed bird-of-paradise or Merry Widow hats, heavily trimmed with silk flowers (below right) or feathered plumes, were pinned to bouffant buns. Lingerie hats, made from meringue-coloured lace, were reserved for the leisured rich. Around 1910 the Queen Mary vertical turban or toque began to be worn to accessorize the columnar silhouette, ideally trimmed with a diamond-studded *aigrette*.

While the High Victorian period was defined by the crinoline and tiny waist, the Belle Epoque was associated with the new 'S'-shape, straight-front, swan-bill or health corset (right). The pursuit of the tightly cinched waist, achievable with the Victorian corset (1860–80), had led to many concerns about women's health. The garment placed extreme pressure on the stomach and was thought to contribute to displaced organs, indigestion, constipation and dizzy spells. Women who 'tight-laced' were condemned as vain, yet at the same time fashion encouraged the practice.

In reaction, a new 'abdominal' corset was developed by Inès Gaches-Sarraute, a *corsetière* who had medical training. This 'S'-shape corset aimed to eliminate medical complications by creating a flat front, with the use of a long wooden busk inserted down the front of the corset. It extended the corset's body down over the hips in order to create a much longer, slender figure rather than an extreme hourglass silhouette. The most expensive versions were trimmed with jewels and had gold suspender clips. The corset began just below the bust, thus forming an enormous monobosom or pouter pigeon chest. Women emulated the matronly mistresses of Edward VII by padding out their bosoms or taking bust-enhancing pills. The fashion for white cotton blouses allowed for embroidery, lace and ribbons to be added to the bib. However, rather than ameliorating women's problems, this corset accentuated them by distorting the musculoskeletal system as hips were displaced backwards, the bottom made more prominent and the bust thrust forward. The 'S'-shape corset's popularity was relatively short-lived because women's desire for a tiny waist persisted.

In the early 20th century the suffragette movement also questioned the imprisonment of women in boned undergarments, and simple bras, lighter

1901	1903	1903	1909	1910	1913
Edward VII becomes king. The choker and high neckline favoured by his wife, the fashion-loving Alexandra of Denmark, are widely copied.	Pierre and Marie Curie share the Nobel Prize for the discovery of radium. Women are now participants in the field of science.	Paul Poiret leaves the House of Worth to found his own *maison de couture* in rue Auber, Paris.	Jacques Doucet buys the Cubist painting *Les Demoiselles d'Avignon* by Pablo Picasso.	Coco Chanel (1883–1971) opens her first milliner's shop in Paris.	Jeanne Paquin becomes the first woman to be awarded the Légion d'honneur in the field of fashion.

FASHIONS OF THE BELLE EPOQUE 197

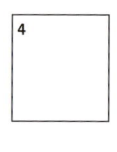

4 This photograph depicting a group of women in 'tea apparel' accompanied Lady Duff-Gordon's column, 'Her Wardrobe', in *Good Housekeeping* magazine (1912).

5 An evening dress made of silk, linen and fur by the House of Doucet (c. 1910) illustrates the changing silhouette. The bosom is still rather heavy, but the extreme flat-stomached silhouette of the 'S'-bend corset has been replaced by a more columnar shape.

6 A painting from 1913 shows a Parisian woman wearing a hobble skirt and tunic, accessorized with a wide-brimmed hat and large plume.

petticoats, suspender belts and even loose bloomers replaced the formal corset. Around 1908 fashion changed direction: taking inspiration from the Empire line, straighter, tighter skirts became increasingly popular. The emphasis on slim legs and hips led to longer-length girdled corsets. Despite the introduction of elastic panels, these 'hobble' skirts (left) reduced mobility for the wearer and long strides were impossible. Designers such as Duff-Gordon and Poiret offered clothes with less corsetry, and draped slit skirts.

The couturiers who popularized the 'S'-bend, Empress and neo-Directoire silhouette balanced fashion and art in their designs. Although London was an important centre for salons, Paris was home to the pre-eminent designers Jacques Doucet, Jeanne Paquin and Paul Poiret. Doucet had inherited from his mother an established milliner's and lace shop in fashionable rue de la Paix. He transformed this into the House of Doucet by targeting the demi-monde rather than aristocrats and plutocrats. Well-known women of the age adored Doucet, including the actress Sarah Bernhardt, the bisexual dancer Liane de Pougy and her rival, the notorious Franco-Spanish courtesan La Belle Otero.

Throughout his life, Doucet combined the role of couturier, artist, patron and bibliophile. His designs drew direct inspiration from the Impressionists, his own collection of glass antiquities and exquisite lingerie. He used pastel colours and diaphanous fabrics, and, following Poiret's example, an Empire line for some of his evening dresses, with layers of lace cascading over one another (opposite). In this example the hips have been gently flattened by longer corsetry, the skirt is relatively narrow and the silk collar diminishes the previous emphasis on the waist. Doucet's creations were accessorized with corsages, ribbon sashes and intricate spiderweb-embroidered evening capes, and the designer was happy to incorporate a client's family lace, so dresses often had elements that were more than 200 years old.

Doucet's contemporary Lucy, Lady Duff-Gordon, was dominant in the British upper-class market, but remained a controversial figure, not least because she and her second husband, Sir Cosmo Duff-Gordon, survived the *Titanic* disaster in 1912 after allegedly having bribed a lifeboat crew. She began sewing in her early twenties to support herself and her child after an early divorce. In 1894 she opened Maison Lucile on London's aristocratic Old Burlington Street, and in 1896 moved to Hanover Square. Maison Lucile traded in London, Paris, Chicago and New York, although Duff-Gordon had a preference for US clients: those 'dollar princesses' who, she explained in 1916, 'have such wonderful intuitions in regard to dress and at once see my point of view'. Her business was built around her own mystique and clever marketing to many sectors of society. When a client bought a Maison Lucile gown, they were buying something of its creator's dramatic personality, and the hope that 'if they wore a certain thing it would make them more attractive to members of the opposite sex'. Duff-Gordon claimed to 'dress the soul rather than merely the physical shell', but also aimed to 'lure women into buying more dresses than they could afford'. Happily, she also believed that she could dress every woman to improve her appearance: her 'personality range' provided the client with an entire outfit, plus accessories specifically tailored to her physique and psyche. She even extended her reach into silk lingerie, perfumes and cosmetics, which she sold from the Rose Room in Paris.

Furthermore, Duff-Gordon is credited with inventing the catwalk show, first hosted at Hanover Square. Invitations to her catwalk shows and the more intimate, dramatically staged 'tea-time' views in her salon attracted various clients among royalty and the nobility, such as Queen Mary, and socialites including Mata Hari and Lillie Langtry, the mistress of Edward VII. Preferred by actresses Mary Pickford and Ellen Terry, Duff-Gordon became a costumier for theatrical productions in London's West End and New York's Broadway, most famously creating the costumes for *The Merry Widow* in 1907. She also influenced the mass market when her diffusion-line designs were published in the Sears-Roebuck catalogue and her fashion columns appeared in *Harper's Bazar* and *Good Housekeeping*. Maison Lucile closed in the 1920s after unsuccessful restructuring, but survives today as Lucile & Co.

Like Doucet, Duff-Gordon also flirted with designs that rejected the corset, and 18th-century pastoral fantasies were highly influential. Her non-boned gowns were loosely fitted to the body and relied on fluid drapery and sophisticated colour combinations such as nude, peach and turquoise. Her lingerie range was easy-fitting, romantic and characterized by layers of floating lace, trimmed with marabou feathers and rosebuds. Bo Peep bows, frills and furbelows accessorized many of the designs. The designer's white-lace afternoon dresses (opposite above) were accessorized with metallic silk bands or a Greek chain motif, referencing the Directory period. Like Poiret, Duff-Gordon also incorporated a heavy dose of orientalism into her gown designs, mixing erotica and elements of the *Arabian Nights*. Turban headdresses with feather plumes topped Empire-cut dresses in shimmering beaded silks. Open mantua coats trimmed with Russian furs were worn over diaphanous gowns, or an overskirt of beaded gauze decorated a silk skirt. Sparkling oriental slippers peeked from beneath hems, while long, knotted necklaces of pearls and metallic beads adorned ample bosoms, or were attached to hairpieces and draped over the gown.

Whereas Doucet dabbled in fashion as an aesthete, Duff-Gordon was an innovative businesswoman who moved between high society and trade. She was a self-inventor, but could also project her client's personality through her clothes. Most importantly, she created the model for later fashion and lifestyle empires such as the houses of Chanel and Dior. **PW**

FASHIONS OF THE BELLE EPOQUE 199

Afternoon Ensemble 1900s
JEANNE PAQUIN 1869 – 1936

Silk and lace afternoon ensemble by Jeanne Paquin (c. 1906).

NAVIGATOR

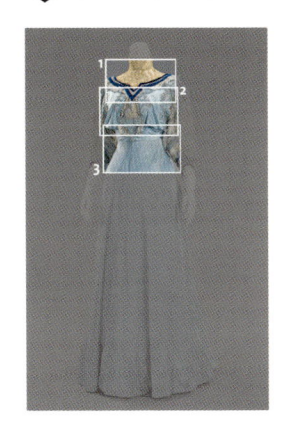

This afternoon dress, bearing the Paquin gold and bronze label, is made from duck-egg blue silk, various styles of lace, brocade embroidery and appliqué, and turquoise pearl button studs. The three-quarter-length sleeves are ruched and cuffed. A royal blue trim outlines the wide neckline, which is cut into a small 'V'-shape at the front. This detail acknowledges the contemporary trend for sailor suits in leisurewear for the upper classes. The dress is typical of Paquin's use of contrasting textures, decoration and colours, and the pastel blue is lightly counterbalanced with the gold trim around the studs and the shimmering lace.

The gown represents the Belle Epoque period's interest in 18th-century splendour; the tailoring recalls the pleats and bustle of the *robe à l'anglaise* (see p.100) and the rear detail of the sack-back gown. The silhouette points to Paquin's mid-career; the waist sits just below the ribcage, dating the dress to before Paul Poiret's reintroduction of the Empire waistline c. 1908. The dress also pre-dates new styles of underwear and is meant to be worn with heavy corsetry. Moreover, the tailoring of the bodice is relatively undefined, providing a monobosom and creating a padded pouter-pigeon chest. Although the neckline is modest, the lace neck panel hints at lingerie. **PW**

FOCAL POINTS

1 CHEMISETTE
The neckline, although not décolleté, is filled with a chemisette, or modesty vest, of heavily textured *guipure* cream lace. This is cut in one with the high collar, and although designed to conceal the upper part of the bosom, it also has intimations of lingerie.

3 SILHOUETTE
The silhouette is created by the heavily boned 'S'-shape corset, which forms a pouter-pigeon profile. The front of the bodice is flat, with the skirt only gaining volume below the hips. The rear of the skirt has a gathered waist and demi-cape.

DESIGNER PROFILE

1869–95
Jeanne Paquin set the business model for modern couture. After an apprenticeship she opened a boutique in rue de la Paix in 1891, in the heart of Parisian haute couture. Like Doucet and Duff-Gordon, she was inspired by the 18th century, and accessorized her silk robes with fur and lace. Paquin was a clever businesswoman and knew how to promote her creations, sending exquisitely dressed models to the Palais Garnier or the races where the beau monde could see the dresses at their best.

1896–1936
Paquin created an international profile with shops in London, New York, Madrid and Buenos Aires. Her designs reflected women's desire for more flexible, wearable clothing. She also designed for the theatre and was the first couturière to receive the Légion d'honneur in 1913.

2 DIFFERENT TEXTURES
The silk is embroidered with raised military-style frogging. The pansy petal appliqué and turquoise studs are juxtaposed with the translucent needlepoint Brussels lace at the neck and the sparkling needleworked *point d'esprit*-style lace overlaying the sleeves.

FASHIONS OF THE BELLE EPOQUE 201

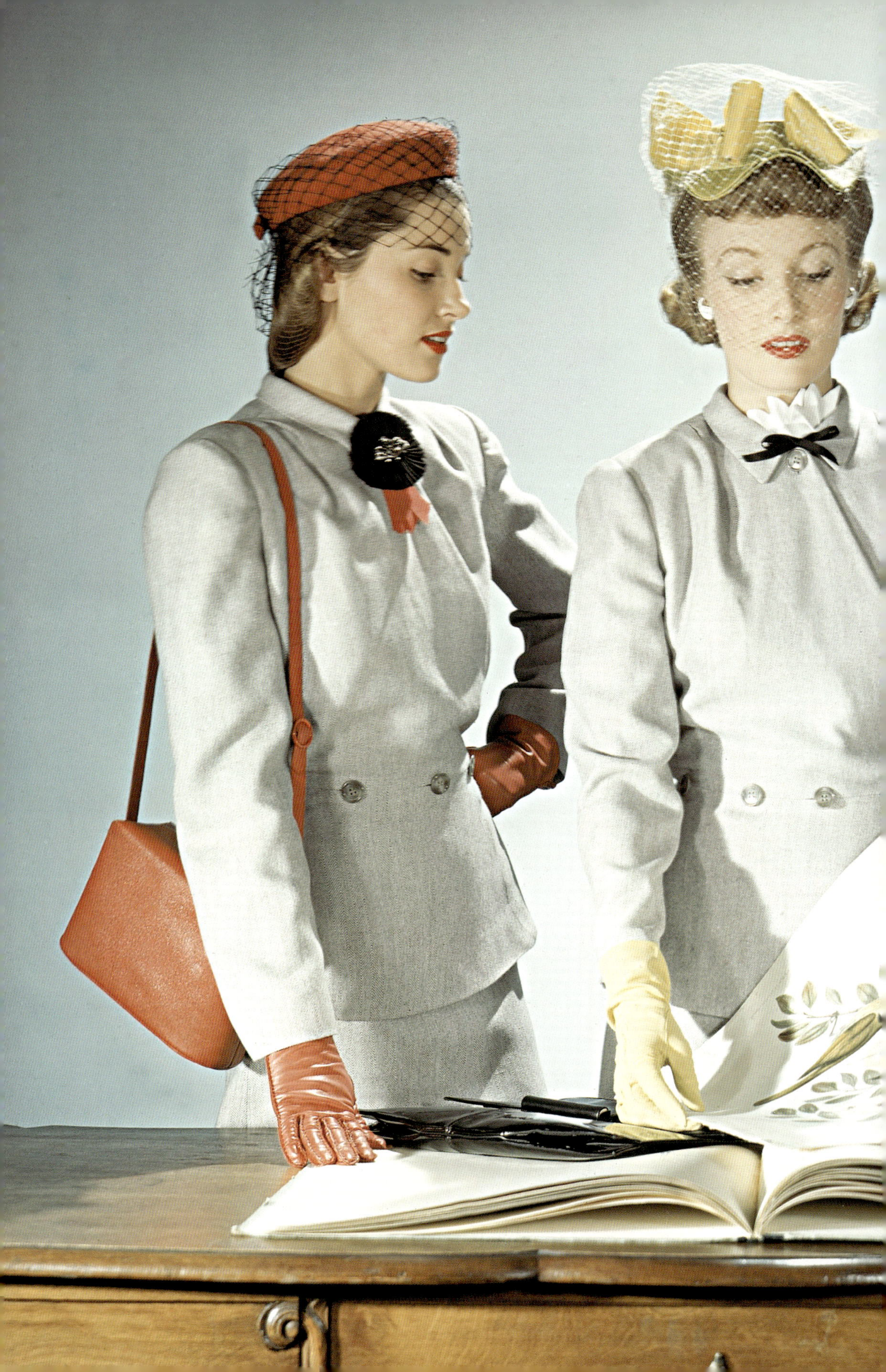

4 | 1900 TO 1945

PRACTICAL DRESSING 204

THE ART OF FASHION ILLUSTRATION 208

EASTERN DECADENCE 214

DEMOCRATIC DRESSING 222

MODERN CHINESE DRESS 228

RUSSIAN CONSTRUCTIVIST DESIGN 232

THE MODERNE 238

EXPERIMENTS IN CUT AND STRUCTURE 246

SPORTSWEAR BY DESIGN 252

DESIGNED KNITWEAR 258

FASHION AND SURREALISM 262

APPROPRIATION OF MALE ATTIRE 266

HOLLYWOOD GLAMOUR 270

AMERICAN READY-TO-WEAR 276

DESIGN IN ADVERSITY 282

AMERICAN HAUTE COUTURE 286

AFRICAN AMERICAN FASHIONS 292

PRACTICAL DRESSING

By the turn of the 20th century, many women in Europe and the United States endorsed the wearing of the simple skirt and shirtwaist blouse in an attempt to adopt a more rational mode of dress. Together with the loose-fitting tailormade (matching jacket and skirt), which had been introduced during the 1860s, these garments epitomized the practical modern woman's wardrobe and were worn without deference to the ostentatious, luxurious fashion of the Parisian ateliers. British tailors Redfern & Sons applied the principles of masculine tailoring to sporting dress for women and designed a more shapely version of the tailormade. These matching jackets and skirts were constructed from sturdy fabrics such as plaid or herringbone tweed; however, the urbanization of the tailormade in the 20th century required lighter fabrics, including serge in winter and linen in summer.

Women were increasingly offered the opportunity to utilize their organizational skills, accrued from running a household, and entered the workplace as secretaries and administrators. The ankle-skimming, shorter, fuller skirt of the tailormade aided ease of movement, making a practical uniform for these new professionals. With greater autonomy and in receipt of a salary or wage, women became much more visible on the city streets as they

KEY EVENTS

1901	1903	1907	1908	1909	1909
The Victorian era comes to an end. Women's fashion enters a new phase with the emphasis on comfort and practicality.	The Women's Social and Political Union is founded at the Pankhurst home in Manchester. It supports militant action to win the vote.	Hemlines are raised to the top of the lace-up ankle boot, which typically has a small Cuban heel.	Eager to embrace physical activities, women participate in various sports at the London Olympics, including archery and tennis.	The American Tailor's Association exhibits the suffragette suit in response to the introduction of the hobble skirt by Paul Poiret (1879–1944).	US-born Harry Gordon Selfridge opens a department store on what was then the unfashionable western end of London's Oxford Street.

moved between the home and the workplace, enjoyed sporting activities and engaged in the new-found pursuit of shopping in department stores. Although many of these shops were established during the Victorian period, it was only with women's greater social freedom, and a more efficient transport system, that shopping became a leisure activity.

At the beginning of the 20th century, the economies of the United States and Europe were transformed by the manufacture and retailing of products brought about by industrial progress and invention. As a result of this mass industrialization, new ways of spending and consuming emerged. Pioneers such as Harry Gordon Selfridge responded to the new status of women by making shopping a pleasurable experience. In Chicago, he introduced fashion shows and musical performances, and when he opened his store in London in 1909, he incorporated a library and writing rooms, and special reception rooms for French, German and US customers. The introduction of in-store restaurants and lavatories meant that women could enjoy lengthier shopping trips.

The invention of the motor car brought about additions to the modern woman's wardrobe. The duster coat was a long, loose-fitting outer garment made from linen in summer and wool or tweed in winter, when it was also often fur lined. Worn to protect the clothes beneath from the dirt and dust of road travel, it was partnered with a motoring hat, enveloped by a transparent silk veil that tied under the chin (opposite). During World War I, in both Britain and the United States, women made a significant contribution to the war effort by driving a variety of vehicles for voluntary organizations. Their uniforms were inspired by the practical tailormade (see p.206).

Greater social freedom required greater physical mobility, and around 1908 the 'S'-shape corset was replaced by a softer, straighter silhouette reminiscent of the Empire style (right). Shorter and less rigid corsets were worn with 'combinations', a conjunction of vest and drawers first mooted in the 1870s and constructed from knitted single jersey, fashioned into shape by the flourishing knitwear industry. These manufacturers were also in the process of pioneering knitted outerwear, and knitted coats and jackets were sometimes worn in place of a tailored jacket. In 1901, Pringle of Scotland introduced a lace edging to the tops of various items of ladies' underwear, including vests, combinations and spencers (short coats), which were initially worn for warmth under dresses. Now embellished with lace, the spencer became an acceptable item of outerwear and a forerunner of the V-neck blouse. Replacing the more customary black lisle stockings were daring flesh-coloured hose, which gave the appearance of bare legs. These developments and innovations represented a significant shift in the move towards practical clothing for the new century, to some extent foreshadowing in their liberalism and utility the eventual emancipation of the female population, both physically and politically, and in which World War I also played its part. **MF**

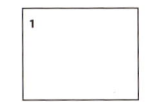

1 This practical style of women's dress (protective overcoat and motoring hat) was introduced as the motor car became increasingly popular (1908).

2 Modern women successfully combine elegance with practicality, from *Le Journal des Demoiselles* (1915).

1910	1910	1912	1913	1914–18	1918
The trade journal *Women's Wear Daily* is founded in the United States by Edmund Wade Fairchild as a supplement to the *Daily Trade Record*.	A knitted coat department is formed by Scottish knitwear manufacturer Pringle of Scotland.	The suffragettes smash the windows of major West End department stores in London in a bid to draw attention to their fight for enfranchisement.	American Mary Phelps Jacob (1891–1970) invents the first boneless bra and sells the patent to lingerie manufacturers Warner Company.	The industrial mobilization of women enhances the war effort.	Women over the age of thirty are enfranchised in Britain.

Motor Corps Uniform 1914–18
WOMEN'S WAR UNIFORM

NAVIGATOR

World War I involved all the major powers, including the United States, which entered the conflict in 1917. The massive relief effort engendered by the war gave women an opportunity to demonstrate and develop their skills. One of the new voluntary organizations to emerge from the war was the Women's Motor Corps of America. After the invention of the motor car, driving became a way for women to participate in the war effort. The uniform of the corps emulated that of the US army, but the well-educated, professional, middle- and upper-class volunteers had bespoke uniforms, and this example was custom made at the upmarket New York department store Franklin Simon and Company, founded in 1902.

The two-piece suit is cut along the lines of the already popular tailormade, but is constructed from army-green wool gaberdine instead of tweed, and features military metal buttons rather than ones made from bone or leather. It is worn over a light olive-green cotton shirt with a high-standing collar and buttoned front pocket. The brown and green tubular, knitted tie completes the facsimile of the male uniform. Four capacious patch pockets on the jacket are matched by two on the button-through, slightly flared, calf-length skirt. The severity of the tailoring is emphasized by the wide leather Sam Browne belt. **MF**

FOCAL POINTS

1 CAP
The cap has a deep crown to accommodate the hair, which would be concealed by the cap or dressed into the nape of the neck. It features a narrow, stiffened, rounded peak and a blue ribbon, to which is pinned the insignia of the corps.

3 SAM BROWNE BELT
The wide leather belt is supported by a similar strap that passes diagonally over the right shoulder, with 'D' rings for attaching accessories. It is named after a British army officer who served in India in the 19th century.

2 COMMODIOUS POCKETS
The upper part of the jacket and the skirt feature the characteristic 'bellows' pocket, customarily seen on military uniforms. The pocket is applied to the outside of the garment and includes an expansion pleat.

4 PROTECTIVE GAITERS
The tan leather gaiters were worn over short boots. They replicate the more usual cloth puttee (derived from the Hindi *patti*), consisting of a long, narrow piece of cloth wound tightly and spirally around the leg, thereby providing support and protection.

PRACTICAL DRESSING 207

THE ART OF FASHION ILLUSTRATION

1 The radically experimental couturier Paul Poiret publicized his work with illustrations by Paul Iribe in an exclusive edition, *Les Robes de Paul Poiret* (1908).

2 The stylization of the figure and flattened form are typical of Georges Lepape in this dramatic cover for the US publication *Vanity Fair* (1919).

Fashion illustration was first recognized as an art form in 1908, when French couturier Paul Poiret (1879–1944) commissioned young printmaker Paul Iribe to illustrate his avant-garde dress designs for a small promotional publication, *Les Robes de Paul Poiret* (above). Previously, illustration had been concerned with the mere representation of clothes, and depicted models frozen in unreal poses against a faux background of neoclassical columns or artificial foliage known as 'spinach'. These images appeared in numerous women's magazines to illustrate the fashions of the day, or in combination with a free dress pattern. Poiret's limited edition was a radical departure from the 19th-century tradition of romantic realism portrayed in French and English magazines such as *La Galerie des Modes* and *The Lady's Magazine*. Characterized by simple silhouettes, fluid lines and bold colour, Iribe's images of Poiret's gowns redefined fashion illustration for the 20th century.

KEY EVENTS

1908	1911	1911	1912	1912	1913
Paul Iribe is commissioned by couturier Paul Poiret to create drawings of his dress designs.	Edna Woolman Chase is appointed managing editor of US *Vogue*. She turns it into the undisputed leader of fashion magazines.	The couturière Jeanne Paquin hires Iribe, Georges Lepape and George Barbier to create a portfolio of her designs, *L'Eventail et la fourrure chez Paquin*.	*La Gazette du Bon Ton* is published; it is a unique collaboration between couturiers, artists and publishers.	Celebrated cover artists George Wolfe Plank and Helen Dryden join the staff at US *Vogue*.	Condé Nast buys men's fashion magazine *Dress* and relaunches it the following year as a society magazine titled *Vanity Fair*.

The movement away from representation and elaborate detailing to this new modernist approach, featuring bold, stylized images, presaged an era in which fashion illustration not only communicated current trends, but also embodied the artistic movements of the day while illustrating the prevailing archetype of female beauty. The most obvious influence on illustration at this time was theatrical rather than pictorial: the appearance in Paris of Sergei Diaghilev's Ballets Russes in 1909, which featured extravagant and bizarre sets and costumes by Léon Bakst (1866–1924). The orientalist spectacle of the ballet influenced all aspects of fashion and interiors, epitomized by the colourful exoticism of Poiret. In 1911, he published his second album of designs, *Les Choses de Paul Poiret*, illustrated by Georges Lepape. Extravagantly mannered and elongated of figure and gesture, the figures were influenced by the work of Amedeo Modigliani and the early bronzes of Henri Matisse. Lepape went on to illustrate numerous covers for *Vogue* and *Vanity Fair* (right) during the 1920s. His bold simplicity and flattened forms described the rangy, elongated silhouette of a new phenomenon, the 'flapper' (see p.239).

As fashionable trends were accelerated by the implementation of speedier and more sophisticated production and distribution processes, fashion magazines became fundamental to the dissemination of style to an ever-increasing audience. The forerunner of the modern fashion magazine, *La Gazette du Bon Ton*, was launched in 1912 by French publisher Lucien Vogel, in collaboration with his brother-in-law Michel de Brunhoff, a future editor of French *Vogue*. Vogel began his career as art director of various publications, before seizing the idea of founding a magazine that not only provided a showcase for the talents of various artists, but also illustrated models from seven couture houses: Poiret, Doucet, Paquin, Chéruit, Redfern, Doeuillet and Worth, with whom the magazine signed exclusive contracts.

Among the group of artists featured in *La Gazette du Bon Ton* were Paul Iribe, Jean Besnard, Bernard Boutet de Monvel, Pierre Brissaud, A. E. Marty, George Barbier, Charles Martin and Georges Lepape. Known satirically as the Beaux Brummells or the 'Knights of the Bracelet', the octet studied together at the Ecole des Beaux-Arts in Paris. Their work characterized a movement that offered a realistic insight into the activities of the leisured classes. Titles included 'The First Flower in the Garden', which illustrated a young child extending a posy to a mother dressed by Doeuillet.

Each edition of *La Gazette du Bon Ton* contained several design sketches (known as *croquis*) and up to ten full-page colour *pochoir* plates that were printed on expensive handmade paper. These were hand-stencilled in a process that was based on a Japanese technique and refined by the French printmaker Jean Saude, whereby layers of colour were built up in gouache paint. *La Gazette du Bon Ton* ran from 1912 to 1914, and again from 1920 to 1925, when it ceased publication. US-born publisher Condé Montrose Nast, whose name first

1915	1916	1919	1920	1921	1925
Erté wins his first major commission with *Harper's Bazar*. He goes on to design more than 200 covers for the magazine.	The British edition of *Vogue* is launched with British-born William Wood acting as proprietor, manager and managing editor.	Paul Iribe moves to New York and is featured in US *Vogue* magazine.	The first copy of French *Vogue* appears on 5 June with Cosette Vogel as editor.	*L'Illustration des Modes*, edited by the Vogel family, is added to the Condé Nast list under the title *Jardin des Modes*.	The Exposition Internationale des Arts Décoratifs et Industriels Modernes opens in Paris and goes on to attract more than 16 million visitors.

THE ART OF FASHION ILLUSTRATION 209

Early November 1920
CONDÉ NAST & CO LTD
LONDON
One Shilling & Six Pence Net

VOGUE

3 The fur toque and voluminous coat are rendered with simplicity of form and sentimentality of subject by Helen Dryden for the cover of the Christmas edition of US *Vogue* (1920).

4 Eduardo Benito's simple composition expresses the speed and urgency of the Jazz Age and the influence of Cubism in a crisply defined advertisement for winter boots (1929).

5 Carl 'Eric' Erickson's first cover for *Vogue* (1930) introduces a softer, more fluid sense of line and form yet retains the chic and elegance of the era.

appeared on the masthead of US *Vogue* as the owner in June 1909, bought a controlling interest in the magazine in the early days of World War I.

A chronicler of fashionable society, Condé Nast pioneered the concept of a limited-circulation magazine that was targeted at an affluent audience, and was a product that was desirable in its own right. His magazines promoted avant-garde movements in art, photography, literature and fashion, in a unique contextualization of culture. The US edition of *Vogue* — which was first published in 1892 — commissioned established US illustrators such as Helen Dryden, who produced many distinctive illustrations for the magazine (above). Her style owed something to the naive romanticism of the children's illustrator Kate Greenaway, and also to George Wolfe Plank, a leading protagonist of a style influenced by illustrators Edmund Dulac, Arthur Rackham and Alphonse Mucha.

When the French edition of *Vogue* was launched in 1920, aspects of modernism in painting, such as Cubism, Expressionism, Futurism and abstraction, that had been in place since before World War I began to be seen in fashion magazines. By the mid 1920s the whimsy of US illustrators Dryden and Plank was supplanted by the work of the 'French school', including Lepape and Spanish-born Eduardo García Benito. The latter graphically represented the spirit of the Jazz Age with his iconic simply drawn figures (opposite above). His sculpted silhouettes, high-arched eyebrows, almond-shaped eyes, small rosebud mouths and flat, head-hugging shingle hairstyle all reflect

210 1900–45

the influence of Romanian sculptor Constantin Brancusi and works such as *Sleeping Muse* (1910), and the primitive art of Pablo Picasso's *Les Demoiselles d'Avignon* (1907). Enraptured by the Hollywood idea of America, both Lepape and Benito designed covers that featured the Manhattan skyline, endless limousines and backless dresses in the pared-down streamlined style typical of Art Deco, which came to the forefront at the Exposition Internationale des Arts Décoratifs et Industriels Modernes (International Exhibition of Modern Industrial and Decorative Arts) in Paris in 1925.

At the start of the 1930s, a new realism emerged with the observational approach to illustration by US-born Carl Erickson, who signed himself 'Eric'. He designed his first cover for *Vogue* in 1930 (below right). An artist foremost, he portrayed the changing fashionable ideal, from stylized flapper to one of a womanly and realistic elegance, with a fluid economy of line. His style was more related to the natural flowing lines of Edgar Degas than the geometric lines of Cubism, an aesthetic that rendered Benito's graphic boldness obsolete. His closest rival was French-born René Bouët-Willaumez. Together they changed the nature of the *Vogue* cover, which, by this time, served the contents of the magazine rather than standing alone as a piece of artwork.

Vogue's rival publication, *Harper's Bazar* (renamed *Harper's Bazaar* in 1929), was founded by Harper & Brothers, and in 1912 was purchased by US newspaper tycoon William Randolph Hearst. In 1915 the magazine signed an exclusive contract with Russian-born fashion illustrator Erté (Romain de Tirtoff; 1892–1990), a collaboration that was to last until 1938. The only designer to illustrate his own creations (see p.212), Erté created the first cover for the magazine in 1915, representing the flagrant exoticism of the period. However, the advent of modernism in the mid 1920s rendered Erté's work inappropriate to the new simplicity and androgyny of the fashions of the era.

Rivalry between the two main fashion magazines of the period, *Vogue* and *Harper's Bazar*, was intensified when pioneer fashion photographer Adolphe de Meyer was poached from *Vogue* by Hearst in 1922, which resulted in a greater emphasis on the use of photography within *Harper's Bazar*'s pages. This was followed by the appointment of another *Vogue* talent, Carmel Snow, who became editor-in-chief of the magazine in 1932. By this time, de Meyer's ethereal studio-centred style, which utilized backlighting and gauze-covered lenses, began to lose its appeal, and he was usurped by the Russian-born, French-based graphic design genius Alexey Brodovitch, appointed by Snow as art director of the magazine in 1934. Throughout his career at *Harper's Bazaar*, Brodovitch revolutionized magazine design, with his innovative use of white space and cinematic organization of layout, often incorporating his signature cropping technique on the figure rather than displaying the whole garment. The shape of the text was manipulated by Brodovitch to reflect the forms within a photograph or an illustration.

Although illustrators were much in demand by the leading journals from the three fashion capitals of New York, Paris and London during the 1930s, illustration began to be challenged by the photographic work of Edward Steichen, Horst P. Horst, George Hoyningen-Huene, Cecil Beaton and Man Ray. Editorial and advertorial content in the magazines diverged: advertisers depended on illustrations to sell their goods, whereas the photographic images appeared on the fashion pages, particularly on the covers of the magazines. The first colour cover photograph for *Vogue* by Edward Steichen appeared in 1932, and by 1936 the publishers concluded that a photographed cover sold more copies than one that was illustrated. From this period onwards, the work of artists and photographers began to be used side by side within the editorial body of the magazine, only shifting in emphasis after 1950, when the use of photography became paramount. **MF**

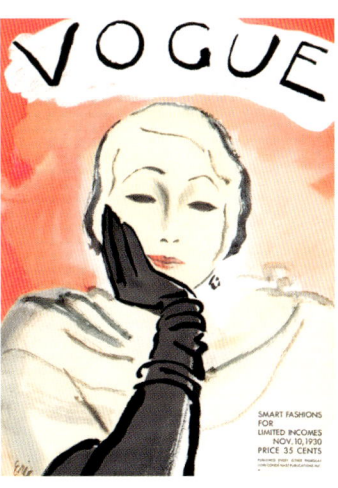

Fashion Illustration for *Harper's Bazar* 1919
ERTÉ 1892 – 1990

New Bridges for the Seven Seas,
by Erté for *Harper's Bazar* (1919).

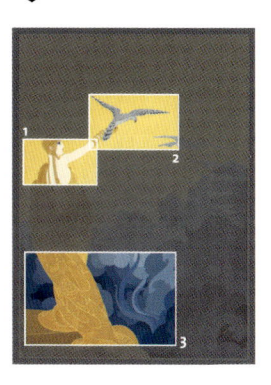

Designer and illustrator Erté was the leading exponent of extravagant theatricality and fashion fantasy in the period between World War I and the second half of the 1920s. His first cover for US fashion magazine *Harper's Bazar* appeared in 1915, and the designer was allowed total autonomy over his subject matter. As a result, he gave full reign to his imagination, creating female archetypes such as the siren, ingénue, Assyrian princess and Egyptian queen. He was the only illustrator at the time to refer to his own designs, which were distinguished by their sensuous exoticism and the accoutrements of excess: fringes, tassels, towering headdresses, metallic embroidery and whole garments composed of strings of pearls or jet beads.

Erté's only restriction in designing the magazine covers was to provide four that related to the various collections: one spring cover, one autumn cover and two devoted to fur and cosmetics. The cover design for the March 1919 issue is titled *New Bridges for the Seven Seas*. Although his contract with *Harper's Bazar* continued until 1938, from 1926 the advent of modernism rendered Erté's designs outmoded in the context of the new simplicity and androgyny of the fashions of the era. His cover designs no longer featured his ideas, but reflected the influence of Cubism and Art Deco. **MF**

NAVIGATOR

FOCAL POINTS

1 COMBINED BODICE AND HAT
The illustration has a futuristic theme, which is also evident in various elements of the dress. Beneath the draping, the gown is engineered into a workman-like bodice, attached to a close-fitting hat in the style of a flying helmet.

3 DRAPED FIGURE
The figure is draped in a bolt of figured fabric around the hips. It extends over one shoulder before cascading to the ground in rich, voluminous folds that are matched in representation by the clouds before the figure.

2 FUTURISTIC BIRDS
The futuristic style of the illustration is reinforced by the representation of birds as aeroplanes, described by Erté as 'great instruments of progress', and by the depiction of the figure swathed in gold 'facing the sunrise of a new world era'.

DESIGNER PROFILE

1892–1922
The illustrator known as Erté (the French pronunciation of his initials, 'R. T.') was born Romain de Tirtoff in 1892 and moved to Paris in 1912 to pursue a career as a designer. From 1913 to 1914 he was apprenticed to couturier Paul Poiret before signing an exclusive contract with US magazine *Harper's Bazar*, for whom he designed more than 200 covers.

1923–90
Erté's theatrical productions included the costumes, sets and programmes for the Ziegfeld Follies in 1923, and in 1925 Louis B. Mayer invited him to Hollywood, where he designed costumes for films including *Ben-Hur: A Tale of Christ* (1925), and for stars Joan Crawford and Norma Shearer. In 1967 Erté's work was reappraised and the designer became instrumental in the Art Deco revival of that era.

EASTERN DECADENCE

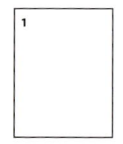

1. Tamara Karsavina stars in the Ballets Russes' production of *The Firebird* by Igor Stravinsky, choreographed by Mikhail Fokine. Designs are by Léon Bakst and Aleksander Golovin (1911).

2. An early watercolour sketch by Léon Bakst for a costume design for *Salomé* depicts the performer mid-flight (1908).

3. This fashion plate depicts the Dione dress designed by Léon Bakst and made by Jeanne Paquin (1913).

In the first decade of the 20th century, Western fashion turned its gaze eastwards and began to absorb a highly orientalist visual language that made its way from dance costumes into the everyday style of ordinary women. Fashions and textiles had long reflected the aesthetic influence of West Asia, parts of Africa, China, Japan, Micronesia and the Indian subcontinent. However, clothing became one of the most visible reflections of the expansion of Western Europe's imperial projects and trade relationships. In the early part of the century, aesthetic and design conventions from various parts of the world were taken up by artists who had a close relationship with the world of fashion, and then by designers themselves. The result was apparent in diverse sites of culture, from mid-range department stores to avant-garde theatre and dance.

KEY EVENTS

1909	1910	1911	1911	1912	1912
The Ballets Russes premieres its first productions in Paris, choreographed by Sergei Diaghilev.	The Ballets Russes launches *Scheherazade*, based on *One Thousand and One Nights*, featuring costumes by Léon Bakst.	Paul Poiret introduces *jupes-culottes* (harem pants) as part of his new 'style sultane'.	Poiret holds his One Thousand and Second Night party, with more than 300 guests dressed in Persian-inspired costume.	US *Vogue* publishes an article on 'harem modes' titled 'Parisian Adaptation of Oriental Fashions'.	Léon Bakst collaborates with couturière Jeanne Paquin on a collection inspired by the Ballets Russes' orientalist productions.

214 1900–45

The person most closely associated with bringing the influence of the so-called 'exotic East' into the world of fashion was Léon Bakst (1866–1924), costume and set designer for the revolutionary dance company Ballets Russes, founded by Sergei Diaghilev. The group that launched the company consisted of Russian artists, originally based in St Petersburg, who had worked together for years as the World of Art group. This organization had been instrumental in promoting the talents of Russian artists to Western audiences and also popularized Western experimental painters in Russia. Bakst fitted well into this group of artists, who were interested in expanding the boundaries of art and challenging the conventional distinction between fine art and craft. Diaghilev, although not trained in dance, became the noted choreographer of the Ballets Russes. He understood that this form represented an important site for the elaboration of new aesthetic philosophies, including the World of Art concept of a single, unified and integrated art form.

The Ballets Russes premiered its first production in Paris in May 1909. From the first performance, the company was sensationally popular—and controversial. The reasons for the company's notoriety ranged from its experiments with atonal music to its sensual and often erotic themes, its unconventional dance styles and the saturating effects of the visual styling (opposite), which were evident in every aspect of the production, including costume and set design. These latter elements were contributed by Bakst, who was brought to the dance company by Diaghilev in 1910. Bakst worked on both sets and costumes, thus creating an integrated overall effect. Unusually, his sketches for costume tended to capture the dancers in motion (above right), adding to the sense of vitality and exuberance associated with his design. The energy of the designs was also reflected in the large bold surface prints— inspired by Russian, Balkan and 'Eastern' design elements—that were his signature. These were enabled by his use of vast expanses of cloth and flat one-dimensional garment structures to showcase the patterns. His work was also notable for its saturation of colour and the general sense of excess, achieved by incorporating Art Nouveau shapes.

The rich costumes that Bakst designed also directly related to the themes of the company's productions; from early on, the Ballets Russes explored Eastern themes and mounted orientalist ballets including *Cleopatra* (1909), *Scheherazade* (1910)—a rewriting of *One Thousand and One Nights*—and *The Blue God* (1912; inspired by Hindu mythology). One of the remarkable contributions of Bakst's design was his integration of diverse themes: he did not use Eastern elements alone or with the aim of representing them purely; rather, he combined elements of West Asian, North African and Indian dress with Russian patterns, ancient Greek lines and contemporary avant-garde visual trends to produce a theatrically decadent style.

The artistic influence of Bakst and the Ballets Russes was not limited to costumes for dance. Bakst's design ethos shared some important characteristics with haute couture design, and Bakst himself designed for couturière Jeanne Paquin (1896–1936; right) and the small design house

1913	1919	1920	1920	1922	1923
Poiret designs costumes for Jacques Richepin's play *Le Minaret*; these include his 'lampshade' tunic.	Brooklyn department store Abraham & Straus hosts a 'Blouse Week' promotion, selling Eastern-inspired blouses.	Stewart Culin becomes contributing editor of *Women's Wear Daily*, influencing content with his knowledge of Eastern fashion.	Jessie Franklin Turner first designs the Mughal Bird dress, which draws on an historic mynah bird pattern.	The influential Colonial Exhibition is held in France, featuring design and clothing from all of France's colonies.	Actress and producer Alla Nazimova releases her film adaptation of Oscar Wilde's *Salomé*, a visually rich production featuring orientalist style.

EASTERN DECADENCE

Trois Quarts in the early 1910s. His work for both reflected the same decadent integrative fusion of elements as his dance costumes. Other Western couturiers experimented with similar fusions, and Spanish designer Mariano Fortuny (1871–1949) conducted extensive research into fabric production and draping techniques from other cultures in order to produce collections of kaftan-like garments and gowns inspired by ancient Greek dress (left; see p.220). Indeed, there was an important confluence between the styles being explored by major designers—again, often inspired by ancient Greece, which seemed to be viewed as exotic and attractive alongside the imagined 'East'— and the uncorseted silhouette on view at the ballet company, which allowed dancers the freedom of movement they required.

French fashion designer Paul Poiret (1879–1944), known as the 'King of Fashion' to his contemporaries, was the most high-profile couturier to engage in the fascination with the East in the first decades of the 20th century. In 1906 he launched his Directoire silhouette, which was inspired by the uncorseted columnar silhouette of the French Revolutionary period, which itself had been modelled after ancient Greek dress. This turn to the Hellenic-influenced sources prefigured and provided a context for Poiret's overall move to oriental designs, which came in the wake of Bakst designing for the Ballets Russes and popularizing such effects through his work there. Poiret responded to the new French vogue for orientalism, triggered by Bakst, by launching 'harem' pants in 1911 and what he called the 'lampshade' tunic in 1913. Both these garments explicitly referenced design elements from West Asia and North Africa and introduced a more dramatic use of colour. In 1913 he also designed the costumes for a play by Jacques Richepin, *Le Minaret*, which was created in the vein of the Ballets Russes' orientalist productions. Poiret's foray into these styles was, like so many similar ventures, deeply affected by fantasy elements and reflects a long-standing preoccupation with a fantastical imagined 'orient' as a counterpoint to the structures of Western society. He is also well-known for reintroducing the turban (below) to fashionable society to accessorize women's clothing. A versatile item of

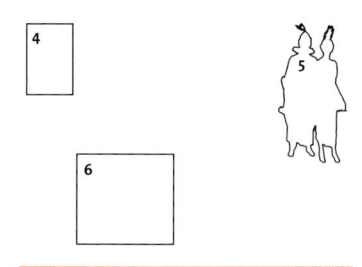

4 French actress and dancer Regine Flory wears a pleated silk gown by Mariano Fortuny, inspired by the drapery of ancient Greek garments (c. 1910).

5 These costumes, embellished with fake pearls, black fur, *aigrette* plumes and gold embroidery, were designed by Paul Poiret and worn at his notorious Eastern-themed party in 1911.

6 A fashion sketch by Erté depicts voluminous harem pants accessorized with a jewelled turban and high plume.

headwear, the turban could be wound into an infinite number of designs and further embellished with jewels or feathers for evening wear.

In 1911 Poiret held his infamous One Thousand and Second Night Party, which is the best example of the use of the supposedly decadent East as a playground for Western desires. Poiret held the lavish event to promote his new designs (right), which drew attention for their rich embellishment and originality, and to build the cachet of his house around the opulence, luxury and fantasy that the party theme foregrounded. He tightly controlled the entire occasion and even sent out detailed instructions to every guest dictating exactly which fancy dress costume they should wear. The party was attended by hundreds of artists, designers, dancers and members of the Parisian elite, all dressed in attire that reflected the aesthetics associated with the Islamic golden age. It is perhaps the best example of the ways in which Eastern-influenced dress and fashion were integrated with an overall aesthetic; Poiret, who also worked in furniture and interiors, designed every element of the evening, not merely the clothing. In this high-society milieu, orientalist fashions became part of a broader lifestyle vision.

It was not only haute couture and avant-garde artistic circles that experimented with the fashions of the East. In the United States, in the late 1910s and early 1920s, there was an intense interest in diverse global fashions, inspired by scholarly research and translated into commercial ventures. Stuart Culin, then curator of the Brooklyn Museum in New York, was a well-travelled anthropologist with eclectic interests in material culture. On his travels, he accumulated an extraordinarily rich collection of clothing and textiles from around the globe, with which he eventually founded the costume collection of the Brooklyn Museum. He and sometime collaborator Morris de Camp Crawford (editor of *Women's Wear Daily* and author of *One World of Fashion*) were instrumental in disseminating the patterns, cuts and other style elements of these garments, and they found their way into the work of many US designers who designed at affordable prices; in this way orientalism in dress found a mass audience in the United States.

Jessie Franklin Turner (1881–1956) designed at the New York department store Bonwit Teller from 1916 to 1922, and continued to design under her own name into the 1940s. Her garments are best known for incorporating motifs and shapes from West and South Asian dress (see p.218). Bonwit Teller and other department stores were, in fact, leaders in the diffusion of Eastern-influenced styles; the mid-range Brooklyn department store Abraham & Straus held a 'Blouse Week' in 1919, during which it exhibited historic tops and tunics from the Brooklyn Museum's collection in display windows, and also sold its own line of blouses inspired by the museum pieces and featuring the silhouettes and styles that were popular that season. Such endeavours confirmed the mass appeal of Eastern fashions, and the way in which oriental motifs and techniques took on new life when animated by commerce.

Fashion's intensified turn to the East was by no means unique. Across the creative arts, numerous artists were researching and experimenting with sources from a variety of cultures. Like the new medium of film, which began to explore similar themes in the 1910s, fashion had an extensive, and spectacularly visible, reach. Clothing and dress—from the affordable to the opulent—assured that the turn to Eastern decadence reached a broad cross section of society and helped to convert the visual language of orientalism into an accessible, legible aesthetic movement. **IP**

Tea Gown c. 1925
JESSIE FRANKLIN TURNER 1881 – 1956

Jessie Franklin Turner's work from the mid 1910s to World War II gained a great deal of attention in its day, and she was recognized as one of a handful of major trend-setting US designers in the interwar period. This brilliant orange tea gown is a fine example of the integration of elements from world dress with contemporary US style. Turner had a working relationship with Stewart Culin of the Brooklyn Museum in New York and Morris de Camp Crawford of *Women's Wear Daily*, who were both experts in costume and fashion from various cultures, and avid collectors. They helped to facilitate her introduction to the diverse costume traditions that influenced her work for decades, and especially in the 1920s when there was a great appetite for orientalist design.

Turner was a dedicated researcher and spent considerable time in the library and nascent costume collection of the Brooklyn Museum, where she first encountered an Uzbek blouse with a bird element design, which she incorporated into the top of this piece and other garments. The Brooklyn Museum collection (now at the Metropolitan Museum of Art in New York) contains three pieces featuring this bird motif. Turner not only designed the pattern but also had the fabric specially manufactured. **IP**

NAVIGATOR

FOCAL POINTS

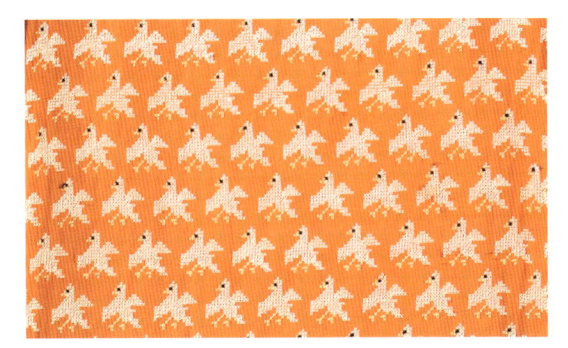

1 BIRD PATTERN
This bird pattern was derived directly from a black-and-white tunic from Bukhara (in Uzbekistan) in the Brooklyn Museum's collection. Turner used this same motif on multiple garments, although in some the birds were closer together than they are here.

2 FABRIC CONTRAST
The line between the plain and patterned fabric on the gown approximates the dropped waists seen on dresses of the later 1920s. It was produced when the fashionable dress line lengthened and became more sinuous.

DESIGNER PROFILE

1881–1921
Jessie Franklin Turner made a remarkable impact on US fashion, but little is known about her life. She grew up in the American Midwest and was employed in a small department store. Her initial area of specialism was lingerie. She moved to the influential department store Bonwit Teller in 1916 and remained there through its years of close collaboration with the Brooklyn Museum, when it was a showcase for globally inspired fashions.

1922–56
Turner designed under her own name while still at Bonwit Teller. She opened her own house in 1922 and orientalist fashions were the cornerstone of her business. From 1922 she took out display advertisements in magazines such as *Vogue*; the marketing stressed craftsmanship and the creation of her own textiles. Designer Elizabeth Hawes (1903–71) praised Turner for not attempting to reproduce Parisian styles. She retired from fashion in 1942.

▲ English dancer Jean Barry reclines in a white crêpe tea gown with grape and leaf decoration at the waist designed by Jessie Franklin Turner c. 1931.

Silk Kaftan *c.* 1930
MARIANO FORTUNY 1871 – 1949

This silk kaftan by Mariano Fortuny is evidence of his deep interest and expertise in textiles, shapes and draping conventions from around the world. He explored kaftan-like garments from diverse cultures throughout his career. This example is a hybrid, its various elements reflecting influences from different parts of the world, including North Africa, China and Japan. The piece is meant to be worn as an evening coat and would have paired well with one of Fortuny's signature gowns, in which the supple lines, columnar shape and saturated colours match the effect of this kaftan. The sheer length of the sleeves and volume of the fabric lend the garment the air of whimsy and excess that attracted the avant-garde artists who first popularized Fortuny's work.

Fortuny was a superb researcher and technician, who translated extensive knowledge of cultural forms of dress into the pieces he produced. Like other designers who experimented with oriental influences, he borrowed from ancient Greek forms. From these he derived his best-known work, the 'Delphos' dress, which featured his patented pleating technique. Pleating was only one of more than twenty techniques that Fortuny patented, all of which involved the resurrection and reproduction of historic global clothing and textile elements. He developed fabric printing systems that took advantage of hand-printing techniques and allowed for the addition of shimmer and other glamorous effects. **IP**

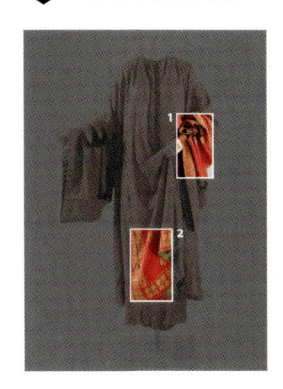

NAVIGATOR

FOCAL POINTS

1 SLEEVES
The sleeves of the kaftan have multiple slashes and the openings are accented with wooden buttons. Fortuny borrows design elements from East Asian kimonos and gowns for a garment that has the overall look and feel of a North African djellaba, thus demonstrating his knowledge of styles from around the world and his ability to seamlessly integrate them in the creation of a new aesthetic. The flowing sleeve adds a theatrical effect to the gown.

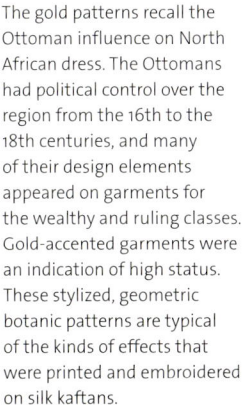

2 PATTERNING
The gold patterns recall the Ottoman influence on North African dress. The Ottomans had political control over the region from the 16th to the 18th centuries, and many of their design elements appeared on garments for the wealthy and ruling classes. Gold-accented garments were an indication of high status. These stylized, geometric botanic patterns are typical of the kinds of effects that were printed and embroidered on silk kaftans.

DESIGNER PROFILE

1871–1900
Mariano Fortuny y Madrazo was born in Granada, Spain, to a family of artists. His family moved to Paris when he was very young, and then to Venice in 1890, where he founded his design workshop. His extensive training in chemistry and physics at university gave him a solid foundation for his later experiments with dyeing, pleating and other techniques, leading to the twenty-two inventions that he patented.

1901–49
Fortuny's contribution to fashion flowed organically from his theatrical work. His knowledge of art history and exposure to Italian masters in Venice informed his designs, and the result was a compelling interweaving of traditions to create timeless clothing. He applied multiple techniques to single pieces of fabric and his work changed little over time in comparison to that of other designers. His trademark tea gown, intended to be worn at home, emphasized the natural lines of the body.

▲ Pleated silk 'Delphos' dresses from the 1930s and 1940s, designed by Fortuny. Inspired by ancient Greek draped clothing, they were made in a variety of styles from c. 1915 and worn without a corset.

EASTERN DECADENCE 221

DEMOCRATIC DRESSING

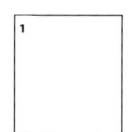

1. Coco Chanel (left) wears her own pioneering knitted three-piece suit and trademark strings of faux pearls; she is accompanied by Lady Abny (1929).

2. Coco Chanel's original jewelled Maltese Cross cuffs were designed by Fulco di Verdura in 1935.

3. A fashion plate from *Art, Gout, Beauté* depicts the easy dressing and simplicity of cut of Jean Patou and Lucien Lelong (1926).

A fashion revolutionary, Gabrielle Bonheur 'Coco' Chanel (1883–1971) designed clothing for the modern emancipated woman. Her easy-to-wear, pared-down aesthetic was perfectly attuned to the needs and desires of women who were actively participating in the new century. In particular, Chanel's pioneering three-piece suit in knitted jersey (above) became a mainstay of every woman's wardrobe. Comprising a cardigan with patch pockets, a skirt and a 'pullover', these suits were constructed from jersey produced on circular knitting machines, developed by the French textile manufacturing company Rodier. In 1916, Chanel transformed the humble fabric into garments that allowed freedom of movement but still acknowledged the shape of the body, thus discarding the corseted silhouette of the Belle Epoque in favour of the streamlined athleticism of the contemporary woman. As mass-production methods became more effective, the three-piece cardigan suit became easy to manufacture and the simple lines were easy to copy, making

KEY EVENTS

1910	1913	1916	1919	1919	1921
Chanel designs and retails an exclusive range of hats from a small shop at 21 rue Cambon, Paris.	Chanel establishes a boutique in Deauville, France, followed by a second in Biarritz in 1915, catering to a wealthy clientele.	An illustration of a chemise dress from Chanel's Biarritz collection features in US *Harper's Bazar*; it is her first appearance in print.	Lucien Lelong establishes the House of Lelong in Paris.	Chanel registers as a couturière and establishes her *maison de couture* at 31 rue Cambon, Paris.	Chanel No. 5 is launched. Blended by Ernest Beaux and based on jasmine, it is the first scent to bear a designer's name.

the ensemble the first democratic high-fashion garment. Such easy-to-wear clothes released women from the ministrations of the lady's maid, in the same way that the Eton bob or newly shingled hairstyles of the period freed women from the time-consuming services of the hairdresser (see p.226).

Chanel's propensity for simplicity in dress and her adoption of utilitarian fabrics can be attributed to the deprivation of her impoverished upbringing. Born to an unwed mother, Chanel was sent to a convent for orphans, before finding employment as a seamstress at eighteen. At the age of twenty-three, she became the mistress of wealthy textile heir Etienne Balsan, who helped her to set up a millinery business. In 1908 Chanel began an affair with one of Balsan's friends, Captain Arthur Edward 'Boy' Capel, and, with his assistance, she opened a shop in the seaside town of Deauville, playground of the French elite. Here, she purveyed her own distinctive personal style of practical, pared-down elegance to an aristocratic clientele more accustomed to buying couture.

In 1923 her relationship with the Duke of Westminster introduced Chanel to the British aristocracy. Their sartorial style fuelled the designer's inclination for transforming male sporting dress into elegant daywear for women, as well as the use of indigenous British fabrics, such as Scottish tweed and woollens in muted shades. She was also inspired by more lowly male attire, including reefer jackets, white shirts and Breton-striped sailor tops. During the 1920s Chanel further simplified the cut of her clothes by basing her silhouette on the chemise, a straight, low-waisted dress that hung from the shoulders. In 1926 Chanel introduced the iconic little black dress (see p.224), a democratic garment that defied class and money in its simplicity and availability. She also popularized the use of costume jewellery and sold versions of her trademark jewelled cuffs (above right) in her own boutiques. Her signature multiple strands of faux pearls worn with gold-coloured chains were copied and made affordable by mass-market manufacturers, and rendered the wearing of real jewels old-fashioned.

An informal way of dressing that emphasized comfort and ease also appealed to the US market. Parisian imports and copies made up the majority of high fashion in the prestigious department stores during the 1920s, and to this were added Chanel's jersey suits and beige tricot dresses. As the French couturiers produced simpler clothing that was adaptable to mass-production methods, the US consumer became increasingly familiar with Continental designers. Successful imports included *trompe l'oeil* sweaters by Elsa Schiaparelli (1890–1973; see p.270) and the sports-influenced clothes offered by Jean Patou (1887–1936) and Lucien Lelong (1889–1958), the latter of whom used the term *kinétique* to describe the ability of his simply cut designs to move with the body (right). With the decline of the French franc and by producing radically simpler clothes, as well as finessing the art of self-promotion, the French couturiers held on to their position as fashion arbiters in the United States for another decade. **MF**

1922	1924	1924	1926	1927	1929
Cosette Vogel is appointed editor of French *Vogue* magazine following its launch in 1920.	As French designers realize the need to appeal to the US market, Jean Patou hires US models for his Parisian fashion shows.	Chanel designs the costumes (hand-knitted bathing costumes, and golf and tennis sweaters) for *Le Train Bleu* by Sergei Diaghilev.	Lucien Lelong opens his salon at 16 rue Matignon, off the Champs-Elysées, Paris.	Chanel collaborates with Duke Fulco di Verdura to launch a House of Chanel jewellery line.	The school of the Chambre Syndicale de la Haute Couture is founded in Paris.

DEMOCRATIC DRESSING 223

Little Black Dress 1926
COCO CHANEL 1883 – 1971

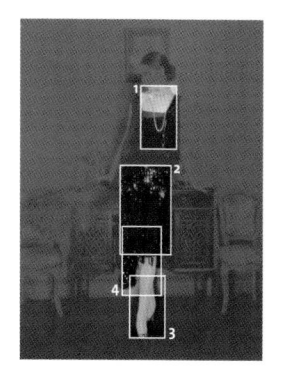

Credited as the originator of the perennial classic 'little black dress', Parisian couturière Coco Chanel designed a quintessential and iconic garment that democratized elegance. Although she had previously introduced black dresses, from as early as 1913, the severe refined cut of the chemise-style dress of the 1920s lent itself to the dramatic geometric patterning of an era in thrall to the motifs of Art Deco. Described by US *Vogue* magazine in October 1926 as 'The Chanel "Ford", the frock that all the world will wear', because its mass appeal rivalled that of the Ford Model T car, the little black dress entered the fashion lexicon as a fail-safe staple that could be worn by all women, whatever their economic class.

Constructed along the parallel lines and dropped waist of the chemise dress, this little black cocktail dress is distinguished from daywear by the luxuriousness of the fabric and decoration. The black crêpe de Chine shift falls just on the knee, and is embellished with deep beaded fringing that forms an asymmetric hemline. The horizontal straight-cut line of the neck is softened by the curved edges of a hip-length bolero, edged with beads. Initially the wearing of black was restricted to mourning, but Chanel made it the smart choice for the newly established early evening 'cocktail hour': a social gathering of private soirées that lasted from 6 p.m. to 8 p.m., enjoyed by the 'flapper', a notoriously free-spirited young woman who supposedly led a hedonistic lifestyle. **MF**

NAVIGATOR

◉ FOCAL POINTS

1 FLATTENED BOSOM
Epitomizing the *garçonne* look of the 1920s, the chemise dress released the wearer from the constraints of the hourglass corset. Although the waistline was no longer emphasized, the long, lean lines of the garment required that the profile of the breasts be suppressed beneath a flattener or bandeau. The flattened bosom also allowed the long multistranded necklaces that were popular accessories at the time to hang straight down the front of the dress.

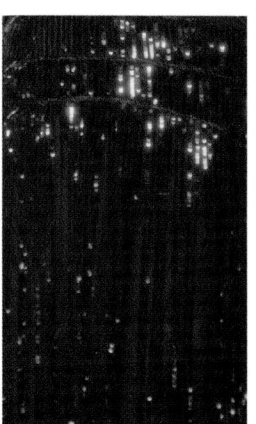

2 EMBELLISHMENT
The simple shape of the chemise dress provides the perfect base for elaborate embellishment that reflects and catches the light, giving the impression of movement. The intricate beadwork would have been executed by hand by workers (*petites mains*) in the atelier. The *petites mains* numbered in their thousands during the 1920s, and serviced the great couture houses of the era, including Patou, Callot Soeurs and Edward Molyneaux.

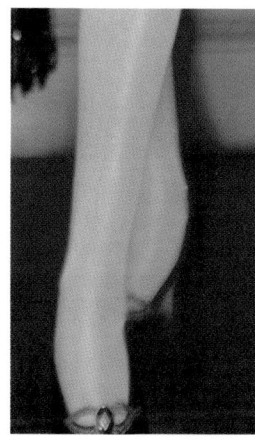

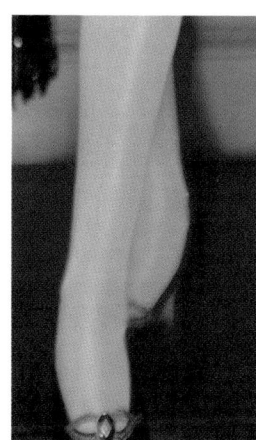

3 'NUDE' LEG
As hemlines rose during the 1920s, the shortened length of the skirt created a need for sheer modern hosiery. Previously knitted on a circular machine and steamed into shape, which meant that with wear they bagged at the knee and ankle, stockings began to be fully fashioned in the 1920s. They were made in two pieces and sewn together, knitted in beige or flesh-toned silk so that the legs appeared naked, apart from the seam up the back of the leg.

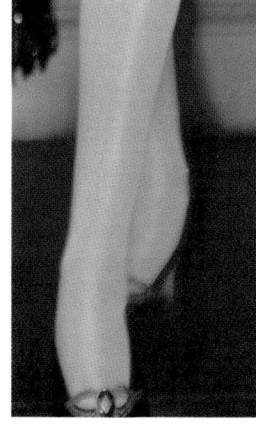

4 ASYMMETRIC HEMLINE
Various devices were deployed to ease the transition from the shorter skirts of the earlier part of the decade to the mid-calf length commonly seen in the 1930s. These include the handkerchief point hem, comprising triangular godets that break up the hemline; a transparent underskirt that is visible from the knee down; and, as employed here by Chanel, an asymmetric hemline that is created by the addition of different lengths of jet bead strings.

DEMOCRATIC DRESSING 225

Bob 1926
FLAPPER HAIRSTYLE

US dancer and actress Louise Brooks (1929).

NAVIGATOR

Identified by her distinctive black helmet of bobbed hair, dancer and silent film star Louise Brooks represented the liberated free spirit of the 1920s and the 'flapper' era. She epitomized the look when she played Lulu in Georg Wilhelm Pabst's film of modern sexual mores, *Pandora's Box* (1929). Given the lengthy and ingrained association of long hair with femininity, the fashion for short hair initially provoked strong reactions—it represented all that society feared about the modern woman.

Bobbed hair had been worn popularly by children at the beginning of the 20th century; it was only with the onset of World War I, and the streamlined fashions of the 1920s, that women discarded the elaborate and time-consuming coiffure of the pre-war years. For those brave enough to have their hair shingled, or cut into an Eton crop—a style that required the back of the neck to be shaved and the hair to be cut above the ears—a visit to the barbershop was necessary. Before long, women were wearing their hair bobbed in a variety of styles, including waved, shingled and fringed. The full-fringed precision bob, neatly dissected by a centre parting and worn by Louise Brooks, introduced short hair into mainstream fashion, and, just like the 'little black dress', it became a fashion classic that has endured to the present day. **MF**

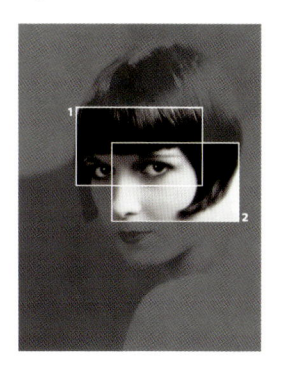

FOCAL POINTS

1 FRINGE
In order to accentuate the eyes, the fringe is precisely cut straight across the forehead to finish above the eyebrows. The sides are cut level with the ears and are left long enough to form 'spit curls', spirals of hair that are dampened and pressed flat to the cheek.

2 PRECISION CUTTING
The bobbed hairstyle was created using expert cutting techniques, rather than styling with tongs or pins, and required the regular attention and expertise of a hairdresser. The hair is tapered into a 'V' shape at the nape of the neck.

CLOCHE HAT
The slender body of the *garçonne* line demanded a neat hairstyle to accommodate the newly fashionable cloche hat ('She had her hair cut' music score cover, 1924; below). Designed by milliner Caroline Reboux in 1908, it became increasingly popular throughout the 1920s. Usually constructed from felted wool, and moulded to the shape of the head, it was the ideal base for embellishment.

MODERN CHINESE DRESS

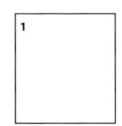

1. A photograph of emperor Yuan Shikai wearing a European-style, belted, heavily ornamented uniform with epaulettes and medals, and a plumed helmet.

2. Calendars, or *yuefenpai,* were influenced by Western advertisements: this one, from 1926, advertises DuPont dyestuff.

3. Advertising posters from the 1930s typically featured a portrait of an attractive woman as the central figure.

What to wear was a big question for all Chinese adults in 1912. The Qing government was blamed for the poor state in which China found itself; therefore much of the population believed that Manchu clothes and the archaic plait should be discarded. The Western nations were seen as worthy of emulation, yet at the same time they were aggressors, harbouring evil intents. When Dr Sun Yat-sen took office as provisional president of the Republic in 1912, he wore a jacket and trousers (later dubbed the 'zhongshan suit'; see p.230). However, in 1911 not everyone had welcomed the Revolution because, to many, the revolutionaries' methods seemed too radical. Some also supported the dethroned Manchu family. So for a while the traditional robe and riding jacket (see p.166) existed side by side with the zhongshan suit.

For Chinese men, cutting off the plait was a relatively easy step to take, although some Manchu men kept their plaits to make a stand. For people with no political affinity—which was equivalent to approximately half of

KEY EVENTS

1912	1912	1915	1919	c. 1920	c. 1925
Dr Sun Yat-sen eschews the Manchu style of dress and wears a zhongshan suit when he takes office as provisional president of China.	The new Republic of China government bans women's foot binding, thus liberating women from social and political repression.	Yuan Shikai declares himself emperor of China but faces widespread opposition and is forced to abolish the monarchy after only eighty-three days.	The appearance of the students at the May Fourth protests indicate changing fashions. Many have cut off their plaits but still wear the traditional robe.	The common fashion for young women is a short jacket with elbow-length sleeves, worn either with a pleated skirt or calf-length trousers.	The *qipao* appears. Initially it is a loose-fitting dress without the revealing slits at the sides.

the population—the West had great appeal because it stood for quality and modernity. The man on the street might be indifferent to whether the head of state was a president or an emperor, but he definitely did not want to be seen as 'backward', and Western-style sunglasses or leather lace-up shoes put him in the 'modern' camp. However, traditional Chinese dress was too deep-rooted to be abandoned overnight, and in the 1920s and 1930s it was not uncommon for men to wear a traditional long robe with an imported trilby hat. This curious mixture of East and West resulted in bizarre scenes. Yuan Shikai, who was in charge of the armed forces, loved European-style military dress (opposite). He declared himself emperor in December 1915, and a ceremony was held at the Altar of Heaven in Beijing. The officials wore pseudo-ceremonial robes with dragon roundels, and a peculiar headgear that looked like a mortarboard; the soldiers' uniform appeared to imitate that of the English Coldstream Guards. Yuan Shikai tried to be seen as both 'Chinese' and 'modern', but failed badly.

The female equivalent to the zhongshan suit was the *qipao*, called the *cheongsam* in the Cantonese-speaking British colony of Hong Kong. Before 1850, women from respectable families wore robes, and because these had slits at the sides, trousers were always worn underneath to cover the legs. The *qipao* was designed to be worn on its own, without trousers. A calendar poster of 1926 (above right) shows a girl wearing an early style with an upright collar, wide, elbow-length sleeves, a fairly loose-fitting cut and no slits. The dress was not particularly radical, but the shoes, dark stockings, wristwatch and fringed hairstyle were 'modern'. The domestic pastime of knitting—indicated by the balls of wool and knitting needles on the rattan stand—suggests that the *qipao*, although a new fashion, was initially a dress worn by women of good social standing. Its association with the seedy entertainment industry came later.

It is not clear who invented the figure-hugging version of the *qipao* with long side slits, but Western-style advertising was quick to exploit the charm of women who wore this alluring dress in the promotion of new products such as cigarettes. A poster from the 1930s (right), from the British Cigarette Company Ltd, advertising the Hatamen brand, is one example. The woman wears heavy make-up, her hair is short and permed, and her pose sensuous. The slogan next to the packet reads, 'He is the best after all.' The ad is persuading women to be adventurous and try new things—with cigarettes or men.

Black-and-white images of Chinese actresses of the period show them wearing similar tight-fitting *qipaos*, but the film-making industry in Shanghai in the 1930s and 1940s was not a reputable one. The *qipao* came to represent 'oriental decadence'—in the West at least—after the release of Hollywood films such as *Shanghai Express* (1932). After 1949, women in Hong Kong and Taiwan wore the *qipao* on occasions when they felt it was necessary to assert their Chinese identity. The *qipao* still features in 21st-century China, although modern reinventions can differ greatly from the original garment. **MW**

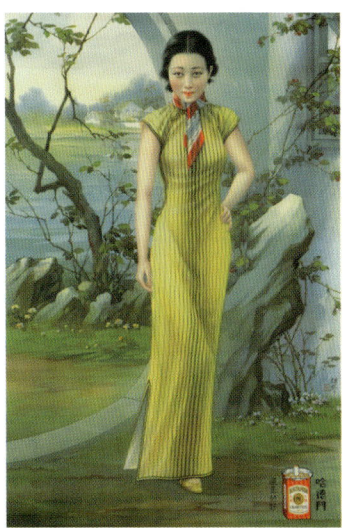

1927	1927	1930	c. 1935	1949	1950
Head of the National Government Chiang Kai-shek marries Soong Mei-ling. She wears a Western-style white bridal dress for the ceremony.	Brassieres are introduced in China from overseas.	China's most fashionable city, Shanghai, hosts the first Miss Shanghai contest. It attracts contestants from reputable backgrounds.	The tight-fitting version of the *qipao* acquires a tarnished reputation as it is the favourite dress of women of disreputable professions.	Chairman Mao Zedong wears a zhongshan suit when he addresses the nation on 1 October, the day the People's Republic of China is founded.	China closes its door to the outside world. Chinese women in Hong Kong and Taiwan continue to wear the *qipao* to show their national identity.

Zhongshan Suit 1920s
MEN'S SUIT

Men's fashion in China in 1912 was rather bewildering. The country had recently become a republic, yet the majority of the male population still braided their hair into a Manchu-style plait. The dragon robe was a thing of the past, but members of the newly formed government did not want to abandon the riding jacket. It would have been inappropriate for China to adopt Western attire wholesale, so the provisional president, Dr Sun Yat-sen, wore an ensemble of jacket and trousers, later known as the 'zhongshan suit'. However, the suit by no means dominated men's fashion after its introduction, and even Dr Sun still wore the traditional robe occasionally. The zhongshan suit was particularly popular among students, and gradually it came to be regarded as synonymous with revolutionary spirit, new ideas and progress.

Later in the century, Chairman Mao Zedong made the zhongshan suit an icon of Communist China. Immediately after 1949, any clothing style that was associated with the capitalist countries was deemed unacceptable, and Chairman Mao always wore the zhongshan suit. During the Cultural Revolution (1966–76), the zhongshan suit became the safest garment to wear, not only for men but for women too. A foreign visitor to China at that time would have thought that the entire nation had only one type of clothing, and in three colours only: blue or grey for the civilian, and green for the military. **MW**

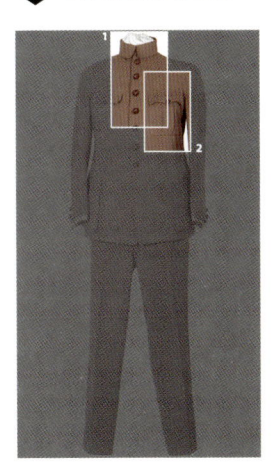

NAVIGATOR

FOCAL POINTS

1 BUTTONED JACKET
The jacket has a high, turned-down collar and is buttoned in the middle from the neck down. For the first time on Chinese garments, buttonholes are used. The zhongshan jacket is hip-length and therefore slightly longer than the traditional riding jacket. The fitting is also much tighter and more tailored to the body. Underneath the jacket, a white shirt would have been worn, although the style of the collar renders a necktie unnecessary.

2 PLEATED POCKETS
The pleated pockets with buttoned flaps are a novel feature and are undoubtedly influenced by Western dress. Before 1900, Chinese garments did not have pockets. Both men and women carried pouches and purses for small articles. For larger items, men used a carrier bag, usually made of textile, which they slung over their shoulders. The version of this suit worn by Chairman Mao in the 1960s and 1970s featured only minor differences in detail.

▲ Dr Sun Yat-sen wears the zhongshan suit for an official portrait in 1912. The cut and tailoring of the suit were in the Western style and truly brought China into the modern era.

MODERN CHINESE DRESS 231

RUSSIAN CONSTRUCTIVIST DESIGN

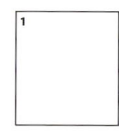

1 These simple costumes for a performance at a book evening were designed by Varvara Stepanova (1924).

2 In this sketch for a geometric fabric, Lyubov Popova eschewed traditional floral prints and created an entirely new style of imperfect dissected geometric shapes and colours in a limited palette, conveying spatial depth on a flat plane (1923–24).

While Art Deco and modernism governed post-war fashion in the democratic West (see p.238), the Revolution of 1917 changed Russia's relationship with European visual style. The Communist Party demanded that Russian visual culture should be home-grown in character, have a clear propaganda value and be of use to the new society that they were building. The Constructivist movement was born in these circumstances, a conjunction of European machine-age Futurism and Communist *proletkult*, a universal culture for the proletariat. The Constructivist Manifesto stated that artists should no longer work apart from society. Lyubov Popova (1889–1924), and Varvara Stepanova (1894–1958) and her husband, Alexander Rodchenko (1891–1956), declared 'war on the easel' and embraced technology. They pursued partnerships with industry and the Communist Party to bring art to the people in architecture, furniture, sculpture, graphic art and fashion (above). This commitment was reciprocated by the state; in the early days

KEY EVENTS

1917	1917–18	1920	1921	1922	1922
Tsar Nicholas abdicates in March. The Bolsheviks overthrow the provisional government and Lenin becomes the leader of Communist Russia.	Russia signs a peace agreement with Germany. Tsar Nicholas and his family are executed and civil war breaks out.	Varvara Stepanova becomes secretary of research to the INKhUK (Institute of Artistic Culture) in Moscow.	The '5x5=25' exhibition is the first to distinguish Constructivist work.	The Soviet Union is founded. Stalin becomes General Secretary of the Communist Party. The Constructivist Manifesto is issued.	Lyubov Popova creates the stage costumes for *The Magnanimous Cuckold* by Fernand Crommelynck.

of the Revolution, design institutes such as the INKhUK (Institute of Artistic Culture) in Moscow were established and Constructivist artists appointed to their boards.

As the aggressive New Economic Policy was implemented in the 1920s (allowing small traders and peasants to sell certain products privately, increasing the flow of capital within the state), it proved impractical to apply Constructivist theory widely throughout industry. The field of textiles and clothing design was an exception, however, and became the most successful partnership between the state and Constructivist artists. Such integration of art and industry was unique to Soviet Russia. Varvara Stepanova and Lyubov Popova were key figures in the Soviet state's attempts to reinvigorate an industry that had previously depended on France for textile samples and threads. Stepanova and Popova were appointed to head the design team of the First State Textile Print Factory in Moscow in 1923 to make textiles that were Russian in character and suitable for everyone in society. Their appointments combined Popova's experience as an internationally travelled and renowned Cubo-Futurist and proponent of 'painterly architectonics', with Stepanova's peasant roots and Russian training in the graphic arts.

In setting up the First State Textile Print Factory, Popova and Stepanova initially faced many difficulties. After many years of warfare, Russian industry and material resources had vastly diminished and only a fraction of the experienced workforce remained. The two women had to create textile designs that reflected their Constructivist ideas, conformed to the state's diktat that any imagery should be clear and comprehensible, and were also technically possible to produce (right). Neither had formally trained in textiles, so they had to educate themselves in the production process in order to integrate art with mass production. It was claimed by the Soviet art critic D. M. Aronovitch that they faced conflicts with the weavers and technical staff, who resented the imposition of 'new' aesthetics and found their designs impractical. The two women hoped to tackle such challenges by participating in the industrial process (weaving and dyeing) and voting over recruitment and the acquisition of designs. They also promoted the factory and their work in the retail trade and in the press.

Whereas other contemporary designers produced crudely Constructivist textiles, Popova and Stepanova's approach was more imaginative. Both women were passionate about fabric design, and felt that its production was a way of arranging 'the material elements of life': textiles and Constructivism were in perfect alliance. Popova wrote that 'no single artistic success gave me such profound satisfaction as the sight of peasants and workers buying pieces of my material'. Although Popova and Stepanova's designs were successful, they were also technically accomplished and they understood that cotton printing was suited to multidirectional small motifs with few compositional layers.

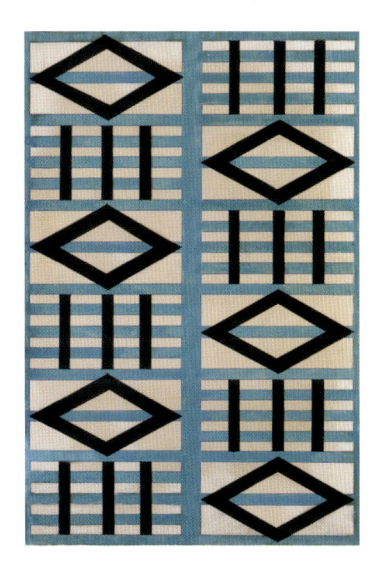

1922	1923	1924	1925	1929	1930
Stepanova designs the costumes for *Death of Tarelkin* (see p.236).	Stepanova and Popova are appointed designers for the First State Textile Print Factory in the former Tsindel works, Moscow.	Popova dies of scarlet fever. A large exhibition of her work opens in Moscow the same year.	Stepanova and Alexander Rodchenko participate in the Paris Expo. Rodchenko's ideal 'Working Men's Club' proposes a universal social space.	Trotsky is exiled from Russia by Stalin. The Constructivists, seen as his ideological supporters, suffer by association.	The first show trial of industrialists is staged by Stalin and his supporters.

3 These designs were made by Popova in 1923 to 1924: a yellow tailleur, a white and pink dress, and a blue and white 'flapper' dress with handkerchief-hemmed sleeves and a dropped waist. All three conform to Constructivist ideology in that their construction is 'transparent' (easy to make and understand).

4 This sketch for a costume design by Vladimir Tatlin (1913) is for the opera *A Life for the Tsar* by Mikhail Glinka.

5 This sports costume design by Varvara Stepanova bears the red star design required for propaganda purposes (1923).

Popova's designs were related to her earlier work within the Suprematist movement, which maintained that the abstract world could be expressed artistically in basic geometric forms. Before abandoning these ideals for Constructivist 'practicality' around 1917, Popova transferred this experiment to architectonic collages, using peasant designs and traditional lace in her sketches for the artisan cooperative Verbovka. Her textile designs continued the dialogue of intersecting spatial planes within a politically appropriate framework. In 1923 her 'Hammer and Sickle' design transformed the politically laden symbol into a delicate motif.

In contrast, Stepanova 'mechanized' her designs by using the limited components of the circle, triangle and square. She used very few colours in unexpected combinations, such as blue, black and white, each textile providing a visually confounding geometric exercise. Like Popova, she stuck rigidly to these principles in her fabric design and rejected 'free, non-objective, Suprematist or Cubo-Futurist-inspired compositions'; 120 of her 150 designs were realized.

Popova and Stepanova were also part of the Constructivist fashion design movement and the debate over *prozodezhda* (production clothing) and *spetsodezhda* (specialist clothing), with Stepanova arguing that 'there is no one single type of clothing, but rather specific clothing for a specific productional function'. Constructivists required garments to be suitable for the wearer's occupation and activity; the challenge was how to use suitable materials economically, encourage mass production, reject Western bourgeois luxury (the commodity fetish) and create an egalitarian, inspiring design. Suggestions included throwaway paper dresses, a revolutionary idea that would provide easy-to-wear, hygienic clothing. Others adapted the traditional peasant *sarafan* (tunic dress) as a universal long-sleeve blouse. Neither of these really proved functional. The couturière Nadezhda Lamanova (1861–1941), who worked by draping textiles directly around the client rather than from paper patterns, initiated a real change by arguing that 'in the clothing business artists must take the initiative and work to produce very simple but pleasing forms of clothing from very simple materials, clothing which will be suitable to the new structure of our working life'. The leading members of the Soviet bourgeoisie, however, embraced the pure Constructivist philosophy somewhat reluctantly, decorating the geometric cuts with lavish pearls and furs.

The versatile artist Vladimir Tatlin (1885–1953), who sought to apply engineering techniques to sculpture, designed an all-purpose suit for men that combined warmth, ease of movement and a simple cut with a spartan use of materials—it became the standard Constructivist dress. In his costume designs Tatlin combined folk motifs and abstract forms (right). Stepanova and Popova were also influenced by their experience as costume and set designers—where clothing could be bold and overtly didactic—when transforming their textiles into garments. Popova's set for Fernand Crommelynck's *The Magnanimous Cuckold* was a constantly moving apparatus of standard white planks in which the speed of movement expressed the strength of emotion. The characters were clothed in crude geometric shapes, which expressed what they represented. In 1922 Stepanova designed the costumes for the play *Death of Tarelkin* (see p.236), using basic geometric shapes in monochrome fabrics.

Both Stepanova and Popova wrote on fashion theory, using the Constructivist art journal *Lef* to explain and disseminate their designs. They insisted that their ideas were aimed at 'the peasant woman from Tula' (an industrialized Moscow suburb), but critics who accused Popova of elitism in her creations claimed that she was in fact designing for the 'lady from Kuznetsky Most' (an area of Moscow where elite couture shops are found).

Popova's fashion designs were animated by the Productivist spirit, described by the Russian Constructivist art scholar Natalia Adaskina as 'democratic [but] a version of proletarian style'. Her dresses were not so much aimed at agricultural or industrial workers but at a more leisured and white-collar worker, with a bohemian spirit. Popova conceived of clothing as a form of Constructivist sculpture: a dress or jacket created a 'spatial form', and the textile was designed to enhance this sculpture. Rather than Art Deco boyishness or linear geometry, Popova's designs emphasized the female curves—cinched waists and exaggerated hips—imagining the female figure as a building frame 'holding and bracing the clothing' at the designer's will. She aimed for the best possible combination of form and fabric, and set printed fabrics off against plainer ones with collars, belts and cuffs (opposite).

In contrast, Stepanova's surviving designs are androgynous and brutally geometric, combining colour with plain geometric shapes. Her red, white and blue athletic outfit patterns of 1923 are a simple assembly of rectangles, circular arcs and a segmented cone. For women this produced a wide-sleeved, loose top and A-line skirt as well as wide-legged shorts; her geometric sports designs bear a simple red star (below right). Together, Popova and Stepanova also designed the *prozodezhda*, a piece of universal clothing for workshops, with only the material and colour as variations.

Constructivist fashion was a rare success in the group's wider project, although after Popova died from scarlet fever in 1924, it started to decline. Stepanova continued to lecture on textile design after her appointment as professor at the Moscow Vkhutemas (Higher Technical Artistic Studios) in 1924, but the sale of Constructivist designs and fabrics became more difficult in an already restricted domestic market. While the New Economic Policy created a certain amount of wealth among profiteers, these potential consumers preferred to acquire the confiscated possessions of the old elite. Despite the Constructivists' political commitment to the Revolution, they had also become identified with Leon Trotsky, who was ousted by Stalin towards the end of the decade. The Constructivists continued to produce propaganda for the Communist Party, but their art was eventually marginalized and condemned as bourgeois. **PW**

Constructivist Garment 1922
VARVARA STEPANOVA 1894 – 1958

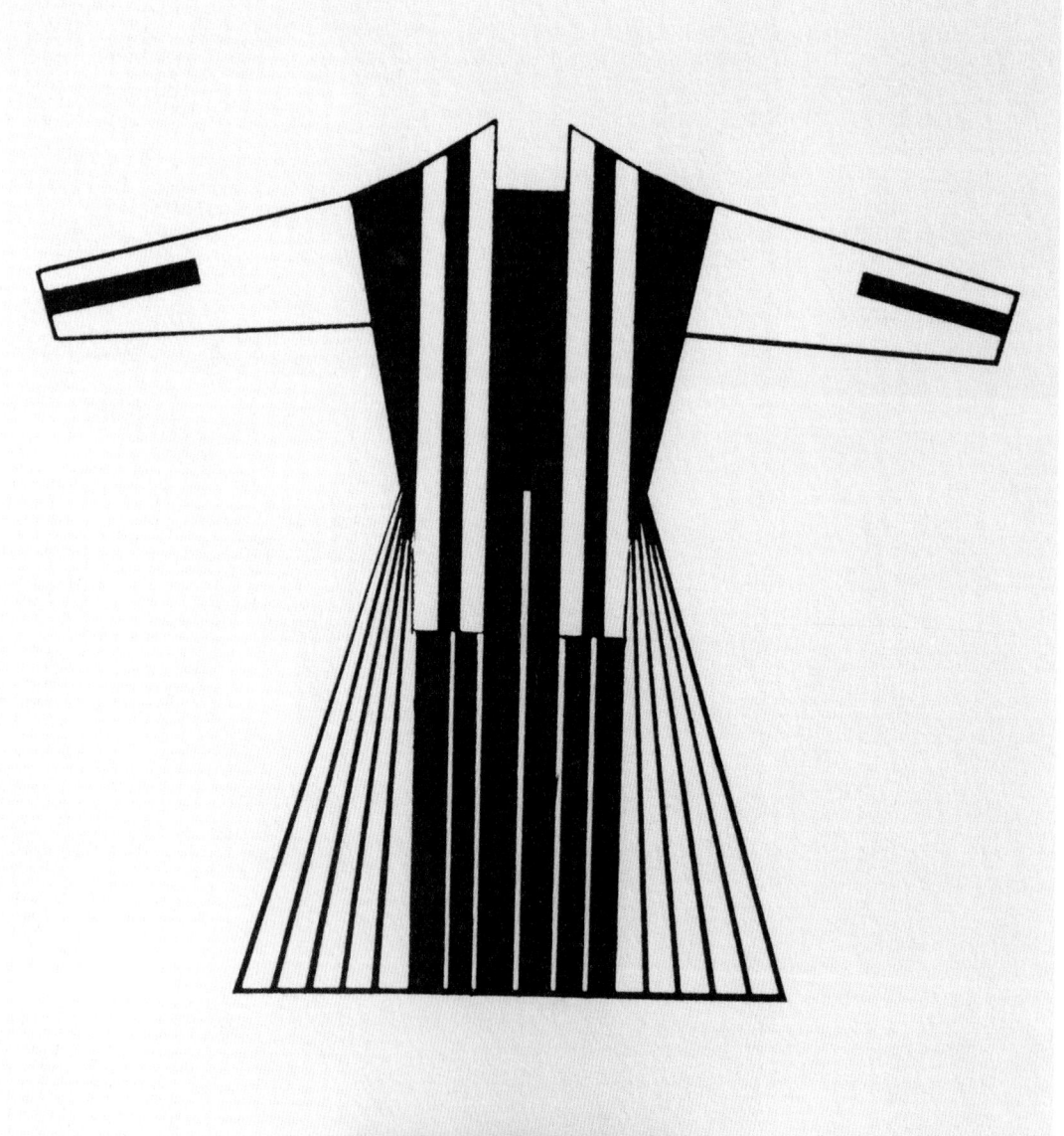

Mavrusha's costume by Varvara Stepanova, sketch for the stage production in 1922 of *Death of Tarelkin*.

This costume for Vsevolod Meyerhold's production of *Death of Tarelkin* in 1922 is one of the garments that Varvara Stepanova created in her role as costume and set designer. The character of Mavrusha, Tarelkin's servant in the play, is a rare female protagonist. In common with the other costumes, Stepanova's design conforms to the Constructivist programme: made from black and white, non-specific fabric, it could be constructed economically. It is strictly geometrical and makes use of her characteristic components of rectangles, triangles and squares. Stepanova's skill as a graphic artist is evident as spatial depth is implied in the weight of the lines or 'pleats'. The vertical lines also reflect the construction of the set, which is composed of a moving apparatus, built using simple, vertically planked furniture. The two-dimensional servant figure is almost invisible against this background, which suggests that she belongs to the state. The costume conforms to the Constructivist idea of *spetsodezhda* in that it is suitable for the character's functional role. It is not in any way decorative; the simple form implies that the woman is integrated into productive Soviet society. Although the design is starkly geometrical on paper, when worn the garment forms a loose tunic that allows for movement and conveys the anonymity of the servant. **PW**

◉ NAVIGATOR

◉ FOCAL POINTS

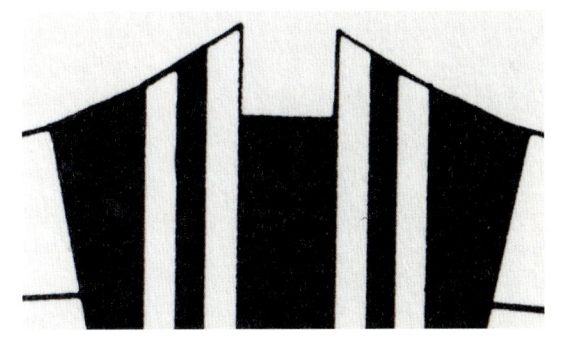

1 TRADITIONAL ROOTS
Based on the traditional peasant dress of the *sarafan*, the tunic has dropped shoulder seams; the contours of the body are implied by surface decoration. This timeless costume could be worn by both sexes, allowing received gender ideas to be tested in the theatre.

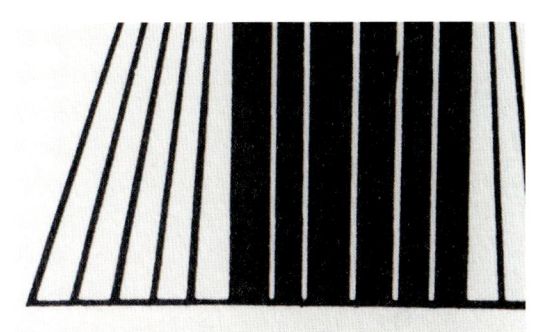

2 GEOMETRIC FORM
Although this two-dimensional composition employs triangles and rectangles, the garment's unusual pleats and folds, implied in the sketch, communicate the clever and devious characteristics associated with the unsophisticated yet wily servant figure.

RUSSIAN THEATRE AND DESIGN

The play *Death of Tarelkin* was written in 1869 by the Russian nobleman Alexander Sukhovo-Kobylin as part of a trilogy tackling the problem of corruption in late Tsarist Russia, prompted by his own involvement in a court case. The subject matter proved irresistible to theatre director Vsevolod Meyerhold, who created a new style of European theatre with highly symbolic productions offering both a critique of the past and a vision of a new age in which men and machine operated together, and individual identity was subordinated to the State. The designs that Stepanova created for the moving stage set for *Death of Tarelkin* (below) demonstrated her commitment to the vision of a mechanized society. Although the costumes for the workers were practical, the stark, top-heavy designs for the male main characters were impractical and unsustainable, like Tsarist Russia itself. Stepanova went on to design fabrics and in her later career concentrated on graphic design and propaganda art.

THE MODERNE

Art Deco originated in Paris, where it was called the 'moderne', and it was showcased at the Exposition Internationale des Arts Décoratifs et Industriels Modernes (International Exhibition of Modern Industrial and Decorative Arts) in 1925. The style dominated decorative design for two decades, peaking in popularity in Europe during the 1920s and continuing in the United States throughout the 1930s. Art Deco emerged as a reaction to the elongated organic forms of Art Nouveau but it also continued to question ideas about natural perception, raised by Cubist and Surrealist abstraction. Decorative elements were drawn from African art, the simplicity of Japanese woodcuts and the objects emerging from Tutankhamun's tomb, which led to a style characterized by trapezoidal, zigzagged, geometric shapes and the bold use of stepped forms and sunray motifs. Alongside Art Deco designs, the exhibition in 1925 showcased modernist design, which was a severe utilitarian

KEY EVENTS

1918	1919	1919	1920s	1921	1921
World War I ends, leading to the dissolution of old European empires and the economic dominance of the United States.	Nancy Astor becomes the first British female MP. British women over the age of thirty are given the vote; this is extended to those over twenty-one in 1928.	Coco Chanel establishes her house of couture at 31 rue Cambon in Paris.	The House of Lanvin is formally founded in Paris, producing *robes de style* for famous clients.	Hollywood silent movie star Rudolph Valentino stars in *The Sheik*. He creates hysteria among female fans, and a vogue for the exotic.	The future King Edward VIII wears a Fair Isle tank top in public, sparking the popularity of the traditional knitting pattern.

vision for the machine age. Extolling the relationship between art, beauty and industry, it was embraced by totalitarian regimes such as the Soviet Union, but was also evident in the designs of architects such as the Swiss-born Le Corbusier.

The Art Deco period followed a major war, which hastened European social, artistic and political change. The huge death toll among young men led to a population imbalance. By day, women took their place in the workforce; by night, female-only couples dominated dance halls, for a lack of male partners. By 1920 British women over the age of thirty and US women had gained the vote for the first time, and these newly enfranchised women took up habits that previously had been confined to men: smoking, driving fast cars and even flying aeroplanes. The age of speed required a streamlined body, and the female silhouette became that of the flat-chested, androgynous 'flapper'. For the first time in the history of fashion, women aspired to be thin.

Furthermore, the active lifestyles of women in the 1920s demanded clothes that allowed freedom of movement. The chemise, a camisole-like, loose-fitting, tubular-shaped dress that skimmed the contours of the body, redefined the female wardrobe (opposite). It was made in jersey or rayon for day and heavily embellished for evening, with bugle beads, appliqué, silver and gold thread, and Cornelli work, or overlaid with lace. The chemise dress brought about immediate changes in dress design, which included the dropping of the natural waistline to the hip in c. 1920, emphasized by a belt or horizontal band worn at hip level. Loosely structured upper bodies had simple round necks or V-necks. Skirts fell straight to the mid calf and, for the greater part of the decade, remained below the knee. Variations included pleated or slit skirts to allow for even easier movement. The garments could be made up in less than an hour from simple patterns, and home sewing boomed.

Hemlines rose above the knee for the first time from 1925 to 1928, and appeared even shorter when they were cut into handkerchief points, scalloped, or composed of tiers of translucent material, lengthened only by beaded fringes. Loosely tailored jackets with belted ties paid lip service to the female silhouette, but dresses were cut for flattened busts and narrow hips, and the French termed this youth-led style *la garçonne*. Identified with young working women or an unchaperoned party-going elite, flappers, as they became known— reputedly for wearing unfastened boots that flapped—came to symbolize a changing female identity representative of the Jazz Age. Such girls rejected the norms of ladylike behaviour and were symptomatic of social changes after World War I. Fringed dresses flying, they danced the Turkey Trot, popularized by Josephine Baker in *La Revue Nègre* in Paris, and the Charleston, a show dance first performed in the *Ziegfeld Follies* in 1923. The daring vogue for bare arms and legs, and dresses cut down to the waist at the back (right), showed off the suntanned limbs garnered from the newly popular pastime of sunbathing. Flappers smoked cigarettes and not only wore make-up, but also applied the

1 Worn with cloche hats and Mary Janes, these chemise dresses are both feminine and practical, perfect for a day at the Ascot races in the 1920s.

2 A new site of erotic interest was the bare back, seen here in George Barbier's illustration *The Judgement of Paris* (1920).

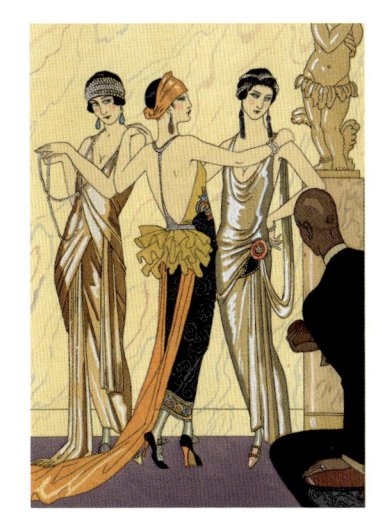

1922	1923	1924	1925	1925	1928
Howard Carter leads the excavation of the tomb of Pharaoh Tutankhamun, provoking a craze for ancient Egyptian styles of ornament.	*Time* magazine is founded, chronicling US social and political change.	Rayon, known in Europe as viscose, is marketed as a man-made alternative to silk.	US-born French dancer, singer and actress Josephine Baker becomes renowned for her 'exotic' dancing wearing a banana skirt.	*The Great Gatsby* by F. Scott Fitzgerald is published. It exemplifies the ethos of the Jazz Age.	Amelia Earhart, noted US aviation pioneer, becomes the first female aviator to cross the Atlantic Ocean.

THE MODERNE 239

fashionable port-wine matt lipstick in public. Lipsticks were kept in miniature jewelled vanity cases, made by jewellers such as Van Cleef & Arpels and Cartier, in silver or gold, enamel, mother-of-pearl, jade and lapis lazuli, with cheap copies constructed from coloured glass stones set into plastic. Vanity cases often had mini lipstick containers that swung on a length of tassel or were fixed to a Bakelite bangle worn on the wrist. As the flapper shimmied around the dance floor, her handbag needed to be lightweight and portable. The popularity of the South American dance the tango lent its name to a purse fitted with finger rings or lengths of cord that could be wrapped around the lower arm. Men's clothes became increasingly informal, and the male partners of the flappers sported wide-legged Oxford bags by day, worn with slim-fitting blazers and a boater (see p.242). The single-breasted lounge suit was adopted for ordinary city wear. Evening wear consisted of the tuxedo, featuring a rolled collar faced in silk or a notched collar in black or midnight blue, worn with a cummerbund instead of a waistcoat from the late 1920s.

Art Deco evening wear for women drew on the simplicity of the classical world and featured floor-length gowns. Ankles were shown, but the new erogenous zones were the back, exposed by loose drapery, and a flat, yet plunging neckline. The deep 'V' back and front bear a direct relation to Cubist geometry. Trails and bustles were added to columnar silhouettes, and lengths of fabric were suspended from shoulders and hip-height rosettes to elongate the form. These were constructed from silk-satin, often used with the shiny side contrasting with the matt side in the same garment. A variation on the tubular silhouette was the 'basque' dress, or *robe de style* (see p.244), worn for smarter day events or as informal evening wear. This combined the decade's tubular bodice with a skirt that began at the natural waist and was gathered into a relaxed bell shape, acknowledging the panniered dresses of the 18th century.

Bands of geometric trimming, such as the popular Greek key pattern, bordered hems or hips. Metallic-toned satins, silks, chiffons and taffetas were embellished with heavy beading (left), which created the impression that the wearer was moving within a shimmering column. With so much of the body exposed and the rest only flimsily covered, fur jackets were favoured by the wealthy. Heavy fur collars featured on side-fastening coats—a single button on one hip or secured with a jewelled clasp—which were also worn as cover-ups.

The changing silhouette, for both day and evening, necessitated different undergarments, and traditional corset sales declined by 66 per cent from 1920 to 1928. Corsets were replaced by a flimsy combination of camisole and knickers, known as camiknickers. Dramatic effects could be achieved with the use of the Symington side lacer, a corset bra with side lacing to flatten the bust, but diehard *garçons manqués* (tomboys) simply bandaged down their breasts. Before long health and beauty clubs began to proliferate, which helped women to achieve a boyish figure through diets, treatments and outdoor exercise. Furthermore, young women no longer needed the services of a dresser or lady's maid, which greatly reduced the numbers of women in domestic employment.

For the first time in fashion history, short hair was favoured by women (see p.226). The chin-level bob and Dutch Boy cut had been worn among Europe's avant-garde before the war, but became fashionable after its conclusion. More scandalous still were those girls who from c. 1926 to 1927 chose to wear the Eton crop, a short back and sides with side parting that was perceived to be dangerously Sapphic. Both hairstyles facilitated wearing the fashionable bell-shaped cloche (opposite above); too much hair and it was impossible to pull this tight felt hat close to the eyebrows and achieve the requisite gamine look. For traditionalists, big garden party hats trimmed with flowers continued to be popular. For evening wear, headbands worn around the forehead held the full-fringed bob in place, trimmed with feather *aigrettes* or rosettes.

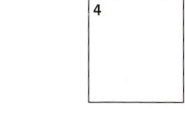

3 The simple shape of the chemise offers a perfect base for beadwork and embroidery. A black satin crêpe dress pictured in *Art, Goût, Beauté* (1925) features embellishment inspired by the geometric motifs of the Art Deco style.

4 The slender silhouette required a small head. This pull-on felt cloche hat from 1927 was moulded to fit the head and worn over cropped hair. It also provided a base for further decoration.

5 The Louis heels of these gold leather evening shoes by Ignazio Pluchino are embellished with a geometric design of diamanté and beads (1925).

The simplicity of the silhouette allowed for excessive accessories. Dramatic costume jewellery, popularized by Coco Chanel (1883–1971), no longer imitated precious gems. Bare arms sported stacked-up bangles, made from malleable, brightly coloured Bakelite or Lucite; rhinestone brooches, clips and necklaces reflected the geometric Cubist-inspired beaded detail on dresses. White pearl, jet or bead necklaces were worn long to the waist, and as the decade progressed, shorter, heavily beaded 'festoon' necklaces were worn, replicating the stepped designs of Art Deco architecture. Scarabs, snakes, sphinxes, pyramids and palm trees all featured in jewellery design, influenced by the preoccupation with the discovery of Tutankhamun's tomb in 1922 and Hollywood biblical epics. Feather boas or fur stoles were draped over bare shoulders, and highly decorated fans were carried. The successful transatlantic crossing by aviation pioneer Amelia Earhart popularized aviator-inspired accessories, including flying jackets, leather helmets and long scarves worn twisted around the neck.

As hemlines rose, shoes became newly visible. Their price also tumbled as mechanized production increased. Throughout the decade, tapered closed-toe Mary Jane shoes were popular, often in black leather with a small, shaped Louis heel, but available in any colour to richer consumers who could choose to jewel or stud their heels (right). These shoes generally featured a strap across the instep or were buttoned at the side, and from 1922 the T-bar became a popular feature. Heeled Oxford brogues were a more practical alternative for daywear and Cuban heels came into fashion from 1930, when the toe shape became rounded or open. At this time a more womanly silhouette emerged, with an increasing importance placed on line and cut. However, the exigencies resulting from the US stock market crash of 1929 included a more serious and conservative approach to fashion. **PW**

Oxford Bags c. 1925
MEN'S TROUSERS

NAVIGATOR

This insouciant photograph taken c. 1925 shows a young man wearing the latest male fashion that was popular in both Britain and the United States: the extremely wide-legged trousers known as Oxford bags. Representative of a new, more casual approach to men's fashion, these trousers reflected a rejection of previous sartorial rules, such as changing one's suit several times a day. In Britain, the garment became associated with the youthful fashions of Oxford University undergraduates, whereas in the United States, the trousers were a statement of pure sporty style. Usually made from a smooth-faced flannel, Oxford bags were known to have a circumference measuring up to 40 inches (100 cm) at the trouser hem, making them inconvenient for physical work but perfect for elegant posing.

Here, the Oxford bags are a pale shade, with a turn-up or cuffed hem, and the leg width, when extended, makes the man's waist appear tiny. In contrast to the voluminous trousers, his upper-body clothes are neatly tailored and are of a college preppy style: he wears a navy blue blazer, sharply accessorized with a tab-collar shirt, flat straw boater and polished brogues that are hidden by his Oxford bags. The aesthetic is of neatness, cleanliness and youth, and he is well groomed. **PW**

FOCAL POINTS

1 LIGHT AND SHADE
In contrast to the dark blazer, the bags are in a light hue of grey or beige, which indicates that they are leisurewear and impractical for work. In the United States, these lighter shades were sold by John Wanamaker of Sears and were the key male fashion item of 1925–26.

2 FLANNEL
These Oxford bags are made from flannel, which has enough weight to give the trousers the correct appearance and 'hang'. Flannel was also used for leisurewear, underlining the garment's association with casual and leisured lifestyles.

THE ORIGINS OF THE STYLE

Like many extreme male youth fashions, Oxford bags were seen by an older generation as a manifestation of effeminacy, atheism and moral decadence. However, they were a symbol of a generation forging its own style, especially in the new cultural climate of the 1920s. British scholar Harold Acton claims to have been their inventor: the wide-leg trousers were part of his Victorian revival look, worn when he was an undergraduate at Christ Church, Oxford. Another possible origin is that college authorities disapproved of their students wearing knickerbockers (below) at lectures, and thus abandoning the formal suit. Students circumvented the prohibition by wearing the enormous 'bag' trousers over their knickerbockers. The bags may also simply be an American exaggeration of a British style, with 'Oxford' inserted into the name for cachet.

THE MODERNE 243

Robe de Style 1926
JEANNE LANVIN 1867–1946

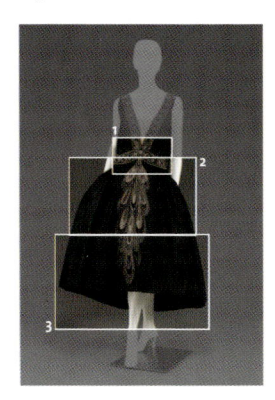

Trimmed in rhinestones and pearls, this midnight black silk *robe de style* represents the meeting of older ideals of femininity, couture craft and the new pared-down aesthetic of Art Deco. The *robe de style* is remarkable for its unique silhouette in comparison to other dresses of the 1920s, when fashion required women to have a thin, androgynous form. Here, a more voluptuous figure can wear the robe without appearing unfashionable. This dress contrasts elements of Art Deco design with an adaptation of the 18th-century pannier. In particular, the sumptuous decoration recalls the dresses of the *Ancien Régime*. As such, it maintains an appeal for those attached to more traditional ideals of femininity and couture.

In form, the dress combines a typically 1920s deep V-neck at front and back, but it is filled with a *chemisette* (modesty panel) of skin-coloured silk. It has a relatively low or dropped waist, although the impression of curves is given by the beaded detailing at the natural waist and the shaping darts that follow the body and form the cloche skirt. The beading, abstract design and metallic hues are typical of the Art Deco period, and reflect a continued interest in oriental exotica and Egyptian treasure. A final feather of beads and pearls descends down the skirt to divide it symmetrically. **PW**

NAVIGATOR

FOCAL POINTS

1 BEADED EMBELLISHMENT
The bodice is edged in a repeated graded peacock feather design, formed of silver demi-bugle beads and clusters of rhinestones, edged in bugle beads and pearls. This level of detail and work for seamstresses recalls *Ancien Régime* court dress.

3 PETAL-SHAPED HEMLINE
The hemline is cut to mid calf when hemlines were at their highest and rested on the knee. The shorter length is hinted at by the indentation at the centre front of the skirt, which forms pannier-like folds.

2 CLOCHE SKIRT
The bell shape of the skirt is created by hoops, boned panniers or stiffened petticoats worn underneath. This contrasts sharply with the typical 'straight up and down' silhouette of the 1920s, and keeps alive some of the details of couture lost in the flapper look.

DESIGNER PROFILE

1867–1925
Jeanne Lanvin trained as a milliner and dressmaker in Paris and Barcelona before opening her own millinery shop in 1889. She married the Italian count Emilio di Pietro in 1896 and had a daughter, Marguerite, who would become her muse and successor. Lanvin developed a children's collection in 1908, and in 1909 joined the Syndicat de la Couture. The House of Lanvin was formally founded in the early 1920s in Paris.

1926–46
Looking to the decorative splendour of the 18th century, Lanvin became known for her exquisite embroidery, delicate trimmings and feminine floral palette. Her favoured dark 'Lanvin blue' was manufactured at her own dye factory. Lanvin was an astute businesswoman and expanded into lifestyle goods. The perfume Arpège was created for her daughter in 1927.

EXPERIMENTS IN CUT AND STRUCTURE

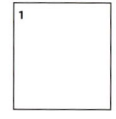

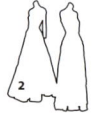

1 The silk crêpe pyjamas and flowing scarf are typical of Madeleine Vionnet's free-flowing forms. Photograph by George Hoyningen-Huene (c. 1931).

2 Vionnet eschews the need for corsetry in favour of draping techniques and wraparound panels in this pair of metal-thread evening gowns (1938).

The move away from the tubular silhouette of the chemise dress of the 1920s to the body-conscious gowns of the 1930s was sudden and dramatic. The change in silhouette was epitomized by Parisian couturière Madeleine Vionnet (1876–1975), whose experimentation in the cut and structure of garments established a new dynamic between fabric and form. Along with Paul Poiret (1879–1944), Vionnet bridged the gap between the previous anonymous workmanship of the couturier's atelier and contemporary couture as an expression of the designer's personality.

Apprenticed to a dressmaker at the age of twelve, Vionnet came to understand the delicate processes inherent in the making of fine lingerie. She honed her skills as a seamstress with a London court dressmaker before returning to Paris in 1901 to work for design house Callot Soeurs. Classical techniques of garment construction were based on the loom width of cloth and involved minimal cutting; Vionnet combined these methods with

KEY EVENTS

1919	1922	1922	1925	1925	1932
Thayaht (Ernesto Michahelles; 1893–1959) begins his collaboration with Vionnet and designs the logo for Maison Vionnet.	Vionnet sets up her company Vionnet et Cie. She is an enlightened employer, providing maternity leave and medical care for her workers.	Vionnet moves her couture house back to Paris and decorates the interior with frescoes of ancient Greek goddesses and contemporary women.	Always innovative, Vionnet introduces seam decoration to invisible seams, embellishing them with floral and star designs.	Madeleine Vionnet Inc. opens on Fifth Avenue, New York, selling ready-to-wear clothing.	Elizabeth Hawes features in a fashion show at Lord & Taylor's store in New York. Her designs are selected as an example of US style.

non-Western techniques, including adapting kimono sleeves to Western dress, thus providing deeper armholes and ease of movement. She discarded the traditional dressmaking practice of fitting together numerous body-shaped pattern pieces, and worked directly onto an articulated half-size mannequin, draping, pinning and cutting the cloth around the form.

In 1907 Vionnet moved to the House of Jacques Doucet (1853–1929). Influenced by the ideals of utopian dress reform that encouraged women to forsake their heavy undergarments, Vionnet designed a collection that required the models to discard their corsets. She was also influenced by the free and natural movements inspired by the classical Greek arts (opposite), promulgated by Isadora Duncan, one of the founders of contemporary dance. Vionnet set up her own fashion house in 1912 in Paris, but closed it almost immediately and moved to Rome when World War I broke out. There she expanded her interest in classical antiquity and experimented with the Greek chiton, an ankle-length garment cut from a single length of cloth (see p.20).

Although Vionnet is generally acknowledged to be the inventor of the 'bias cut'—where material is cut across the grain, rather than along it—the couturière frequently cut the fabric on the straight of the grain (woven fabric has both a warp and a weft, horizontal and vertical threads that cross at right angles to form a straight grain), then turned the pattern pieces so that they draped on the bias. Decorative effects were integral to the construction of the garments, and Vionnet drew heavily on her expertise with lingerie techniques. Bias-cut ties and panels wrapped around the body obviated the need for traditional bust, waist and hip darts, buttons, zips or other fastenings, thus providing a form-fitting yet free-flowing silhouette (right). Halter-necks and deep-draped cowl necklines added to the impression of movement.

Like Vionnet, US designer Elizabeth Hawes (1903–71) favoured the use of integral construction techniques, most famously in the diamond horseshoe dress (see p.248), which skilfully pieced together numerous pattern pieces for a fluid fit. French-born Madame Grès (1903–93), who also derived inspiration from classical antiquities and explored the sculptural possibilities of draped cloth (see p.250), executed many variations of her flowing body-skimming forms. The style continued to evolve over time and eventually incorporated a rigid underbodice—a light but boned corset—to hold the carefully manipulated jersey in place. Grès not only experimented with cut and structure, but also with fabric, such as the circular-knit *djersakasha*, a cashmere jersey. **MF**

1933	1938	1938	1939	1942	1944
Costume designer Gilbert Adrian (1903–59) introduces Parisian couture to the US mass market with his bias-cut backless dress for Jean Harlow.	Elizabeth Hawes publishes *Fashion Is Spinach*, in which she exposes some of the less desirable aspects of the fashion industry.	Claire McCardell (1905–58) designs the innovative 'monastic' dress, a bias-cut garment that is tied at the waist with a rope.	Vionnet closes her fashion house and retires at the outbreak of World War II.	Alix Grès (known as Madame Grès) opens her fashion house in Paris under the name Grès.	Under the German occupation of France, the fiercely patriotic Madame Grès designs an entire collection of red, white and blue garments.

EXPERIMENTS IN CUT AND STRUCTURE

Horseshoe Dress 1936
ELIZABETH HAWES 1903–71

NAVIGATOR

New York couturière Elizabeth Hawes's diamond horseshoe dress epitomizes the designer's favoured technique of incorporating the construction of the dress into its design, rather than applying extraneous decoration to the surface. Like Madeleine Vionnet, Hawes draped and cut her designs on a half-size wooden mannequin before making a full-size pattern.

The elegant body-skimming silhouette and use of sensuous fabric for the evening gown represent the prevailing style of the period, in which arms were left uncovered, and backs were bared to the waist, to reveal tanned skin from the newly popular pastime of sunbathing. The distinctive sculptural effect of the dress is fashioned from ten narrow bias-cut strips, cut from luxurious ivory silk crêpe and chiffon, outlined with rows of gold metallic piping. The pattern pieces radiate precisely equidistant from a high-waisted seam at the front of the dress, thus forming an inverted triangle and elongating the torso. Continuing in a diagonal line, the seams skim over the hips and buttocks and around the fitted torso, outlining the shape of the hips. The deep, narrow 'V'-shape neckline at the back draws the eye downwards to the intricate seaming, which is the focal point of the dress. **MF**

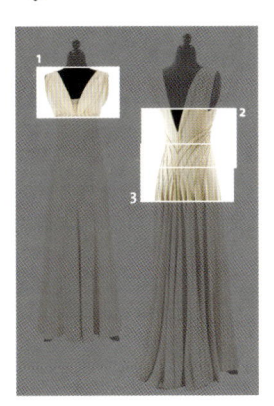

FOCAL POINTS

1 SUBTLE SHAPING OF THE BODICE
The bodice is formed from a single piece of fabric, gently gathered into the high waistline and caught into pleats on the shoulders, creating a bloused effect. The piece of fabric continues into the back bodice, where it is attached at the vertical underarm seam.

2 TEXTILE GEOMETRY
Bias-cut strips of ivory satin that follow the curves of the body come together in flawless alignment. These form a point at the centre back, replicating the line of the low-cut, 'V'-shape back, and the angle of the underarm opening.

3 SENSUOUS HIP LINE
The gradually widening gores, falling from the hips at the back of the dress, cascade to the ground in convoluted folds to form a small extended fishtail train. When the dress design was conceived initially, the fishtail effect was formed by pleats rather than gores.

DESIGNER PROFILE

1903–37
Elizabeth Hawes was brought up in a middle-class family in New Jersey, USA. She founded Hawes-Harden in 1928, with partner Rosemary Harden, as a custom dressmaking house in New York. The following year Harden left the company. In 1932 Hawes was chosen by New York store Lord & Taylor as part of its showcase of US fashion designers. A genius at self-promotion, Hawes took a collection of twenty-five dresses to show in Paris to promote US design in France.

1938–71
Hawes published her exposé of the fashion industry, *Fashion Is Spinach*, in 1938. In 1943 she retired from the fashion world but briefly opened a shop from 1948 to 1949. During the McCarthy era (c. 1950–56), Hawes was openly critical of the US government, which led to her blacklisting.

EXPERIMENTS IN CUT AND STRUCTURE

Evening Dress 1937
MADAME GRÈS 1903–93

NAVIGATOR

Combining cool classicism with sensual glamour, this 'goddess gown' is typical of the sculptural approach of Parisian couturière Madame Grès to the 1930s fashionable outline. The columnar dress, created on the model by the designer rather than from sketches, relies on intricate pleating, gathering and draping techniques for effect. It is resonant of the classical drapery found on Roman and Greek statuary, particularly referencing the chiton worn by both men and women in ancient Greece, and seen in the sculpture *The Charioteer of Delphi* (c. 470 BC; see p.20).

The evening dress is assembled, rather than constructed, using columns of double-width, matt silk jersey, comprising two lengths of fabric sewn together at the selvedges to run continually from the front hem and over the shoulders to the back hem. The peplum is created by folding the drapery over itself and sewing at the waist, a feature derived from the Greek *peplos*, a short skirt section attached to the waist of a dress, blouse or jacket. The edges of the peplum are hand rolled to form a frilled edge, enhancing the lingerie-like aesthetic of the garment. Panels are added to the side seams to increase the volume at the hem, which pools at the floor in a tulip shape. The front of the bodice is deeply décolleté: the bust is contained by the fullness of the gathers originating on the shoulder seam. **MF**

FOCAL POINTS

1 PLEATED BODICE
The back shoulders of the bodice are extended to drape over the front of the bodice at the top of the arm, creating diagonal pleats. This replicates the effect of the pinned chiton, which also features a similar small capped sleeve.

2 UNDULATING HEM
The sculptural qualities of the silhouette are reinforced by the extension of the length and volume of the dress, which falls into carve-like folds at the hem, an effect that is emphasized by the lack of embellishment and the stone-coloured fabric.

▲ In this Grès dress from 1955, silk chiffon is gathered into fine pleats to form the bra-shaped bodice; the fabric is twisted at the centre front and caught with narrow straps that extend to the shoulders.

EXPERIMENTS IN CUT AND STRUCTURE

SPORTSWEAR BY DESIGN

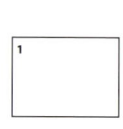

1 Tennis player Suzanne Lenglen wears a sleeveless tennis dress with pleated skirt for ease of movement, accessorized with her trademark bandeau (c. 1920).

2 In this photograph taken in 1929 by George Hoyningen-Huene, the models wear knitted swimsuits by Lelong.

The exhilaration of being at peace, after the nihilism and destruction of World War I, led to a whirl of sporting activity and a period of accelerated consumerism. This combination resulted in an obsession with vigorous pastimes such as polo, sailing, horse-racing and tennis, all of which required an accompanying kit. Sport became accessible to all, from the upper-class passion for skiing to the Women's League of Health and Beauty, which popularized physical fitness and promoted a regime of keep-fit exercise and callisthenics. Sport was emphasized for its health-giving aspect, and the period saw the advent of social clubs devoted to community sports, such as mass bicycle rides. These activities provided women with the opportunity to wear trousers, dungarees or shorts, teamed with masculine shirts, socks and lace-up shoes.

Specially designed sportswear emerged in the 1920s, and the main exponent was French couturier Jean Patou (1887–1936). He freed women from the constraints of heavily layered sportswear and introduced the notion of public 'undress'—in the form of sleeveless dresses worn over bare legs. Together with Coco Chanel (1883–1971), Patou was a leading interpreter of the *garçonne* look, and he therefore made a simple transition from the unstructured, drop-waisted line of the chemise dress to the easy-fitting tennis dress with emphasis on the hips. The couturier was commissioned to design a pleated knee-length skirt and a sleeveless cardigan for sporting heroine Suzanne Lenglen. She represented a new feminine ideal, not only for her athletic prowess on the tennis court, but also for the emancipation of her

KEY EVENTS

1919	1919–26	1924	1925	1925	1927
Jean Patou reopens his couture house in Paris; he goes on to become a leading international couturier.	Suzanne Lenglen reigns as women's tennis champion at Wimbledon and wins thirty-one Championship titles between 1914 and 1926.	Patou opens additional branches of his fashion house at French seaside resorts Biarritz and Deauville, selling ready-made sportswear and accessories.	British tyre and rubber manufacturer Dunlop diversifies and the Dunlop name is applied to sporting footwear and clothing.	Jacques Heim (1899–1967) opens his eponymous couture house in Paris.	US-born Helen Wills, winner of thirty-one Grand Slam tournament titles, adopts the much-copied eye-shade.

dress, cropped hairstyle and wide, coloured bandeau that she wore in place of a hat (opposite), a style that was adopted subsequently by numerous aspirant female tennis players. Patou eventually went on to establish a specialized sportswear department called *le coin des sports* within his couture house.

Tennis fashion for women included knitted sleeveless pullovers with ribbed welts in contrasting colours, the forerunner of the classic tennis and cricket sweater with its striped V-neck. On the golf course, the 'jazz' jumper, as worn by golf fanatic the Duke of Windsor, previously the Prince of Wales, popularized multipatterned polychromatic sweaters for both men and women. The properties of knitted fabric rendered it uniquely suitable for outdoor sporting activities because the flexibility of the fabric facilitated freedom of movement. The fibres in woollen yarn capture the air, thus providing warmth without weight, and allow the skin to breathe. In the 1920s, pliable knitted jersey was used to construct what became known as the classic polo shirt, initially worn by René Lacoste (1904–96; see p.254) for playing tennis.

During the 1930s, the knitted bathing costume (right) played a significant part in pushing the boundaries of what was considered immodest or inappropriate attire for sporting activities. Worn for sunbathing, swimming and water sports, the bathing costume allowed photographers of the day to disseminate images of near nudity legitimately. Elsa Schiaparelli (1890–1973) extended her knitwear repertoire to include bathing costumes that clung to the body, usually emphasized by a play on horizontal or vertical stripes. The low-backed swimsuit also paved the way for more liberating sportswear in other arenas: in 1931, tennis champion Mrs Fearnley-Whittingstall appeared on court without stockings, and a year later, Alice Marble played in white shorts instead of the customary skirt. Other bifurcated styles included wide-legged beach pyjamas (see p.256), playsuits and culottes. Constructed from soft knitted jersey or cotton and linen, these were cut along the same lines as the fluid, body-skimming dresses that were fashionable at the time, with bias-cut panels and an emphasis on decorative features such as buttons, bows and V-neck ties. Halter-necks and low-cut backs left shoulders on show and provided a new area of interest.

An increasing interest in skiing during the 1930s resulted in innovations in skiwear: the long, lean silhouettes and accentuated hip lines of the 1920s gave way to cuffed Norwegian-style trousers, tucked into ski boots, in waterproof fabrics that incorporated Lastex for ease of movement. These were worn with short, boxy jackets with wide shoulders that accommodated the heavy-textured patterned sweaters beneath. Aware of the burgeoning marketing potential for sports goods, opportunist manufacturers developed specific sporting accessories. Superga, an Italian shoe brand founded in 1913, developed white tennis shoes with vulcanized rubber soles in 1925, known as the Classic 2750 model, which went on to be best-sellers and are still sold today. **MF**

1928	1928	1934	1936	1936	1936
Women are allowed to participate in the track and field events at the Olympic Games in Amsterdam.	Jean Patou creates Huile de Chaldée, the first suntan oil, which is relaunched in 1993.	Lastex yarn is introduced to the ankle ribs of ski trousers by French designer Vera Borea. She also introduces the skirted bathing suit.	Elsa Schiaparelli launches her transparent oilskins and tortoiseshell-rimmed ski goggles for high-fashion sport.	The US two-piece shirt and shorts suit is introduced, and it evolves into the 'shorts dress' with buttons up the side.	Jacques Heim establishes sportswear boutiques in the fashionable resorts of Biarritz and Cannes.

Tennis Shirt 1920s
LACOSTE

René Lacoste wears his own shirt design (1920s).

NAVIGATOR

In the 1920s, the French Grand Slam tennis champion René Lacoste decided that the traditional starched, warp-knitted and long-sleeved shirts worn at the time for playing tennis were too restrictive for optimum performance on the court. Consequently, he designed a short-sleeved, loosely knit, piqué cotton (a breathable fabric called *petit piqué*) shirt, with a longer shirt-tail at the back than at the front. Today, this is known as a 'tennis tail', and Lacoste wore it in 1926 for the US Open championship.

The term 'polo shirt', which previously had referred only to the long-sleeved, buttoned-down shirts traditionally used in polo, became the universal name for the Lacoste tennis shirt. However, the original polo shirt was created in 1920 by Lewis Lacey, an Argentine-Irish haberdasher and polo player, and it was embroidered with the logo of a polo player, a design that originated at the Hurlingham Polo Club near Buenos Aires. The identifying crocodile emblem that was embroidered on the breast of René Lacoste's tennis shirt first appeared on the top pocket of the blazer that he wore on the courts, embroidered by his friend Robert George, in homage to the player's reputation in the US press for his aggressive and tenacious style of tennis. Lacoste later placed the crocodile emblem on the left breast of his shirts. **MF**

FOCAL POINTS

1 COLLAR
The unstarched, flat, protruding collar has squared-off ends and a wide spread. It is often worn turned up at the back of the neck to protect the tennis player from the sun, a habit that is known as 'popping the collar'.

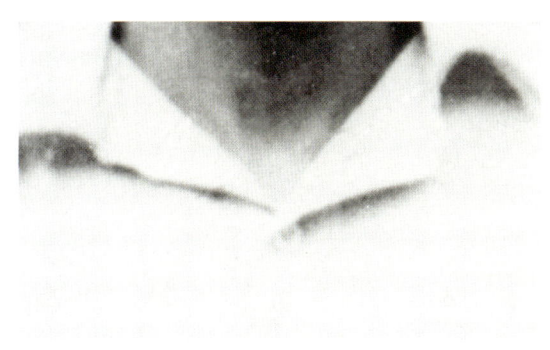

2 PLACKET
The three-buttoned placket is worn partially undone. Constructed from more than one layer of fabric in order to give support and strength to the opening, the two sides of the placket overlap at the base and are reinforced with stitching.

THE LACOSTE EMBLEM
The crocodile logo (below) was one of the first to be made visible on the outside of a garment, and it proved so successful that René Lacoste went on to establish a clothing company with the knitwear manufacturer André Gillier in 1933. From 1953 until the late 1960s, the shirts were exported to the United States to be sold by the clothing store Brooks Brothers. The shirt with the 'croc' proved popular with film stars and celebrities as well as athletes, and it became an essential element of the preppy wardrobe, even getting a mention in Lisa Birnbach's *Official Preppy Handbook* (1980). Soon the company also began to produce other products, including sunglasses and leather goods, usually bearing the trademark miniature crocodile.

SPORTSWEAR BY DESIGN

Beach Pyjamas 1930s
LEISURE DRESS

Day trippers in West Sussex, England, wearing beach pyjamas.

NAVIGATOR

The clothing that had been developed specifically for sport during the 1920s infiltrated mainstream fashion and began to be worn for a variety of leisure pursuits during the following decade. An entirely different wardrobe was required for the recently favoured pastimes of sunbathing and swimming, which included the seaside staple of lounging or beach pyjamas, a trend set by Coco Chanel and her appropriation of sailors' bell-bottomed trousers. As more women pursued diet and exercise regimes, they were able to adopt more unstructured styles, cut from free-flowing fabrics such as knitted jersey for practical daywear and crêpe de Chine for evening lounging pyjamas.

These two outfits in plain single-jersey fabric reverse the colourways: a dark base with light stripes and a light base with dark stripes. More usually worn on its own, the all-in-one is worn here with an undergarment: a mannish-cut white shirt on the left and a fine knitted sweater on the right. The loose-fitting, square-cut cardigan is softly tailored by the cut and sew method, rather than fully fashioned, and is secured with two buttons below a deep 'V' opening that extends into narrow lapels. Patch pockets are sited each side of the centre front. Hair is no longer shingled but worn close to the head. Shoes are flat, or with a small Cuban heel, and slightly pointed. **MF**

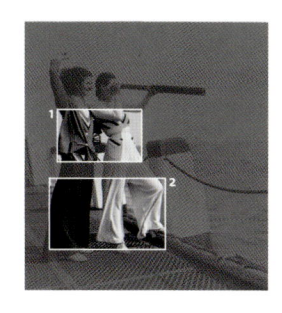

FOCAL POINTS

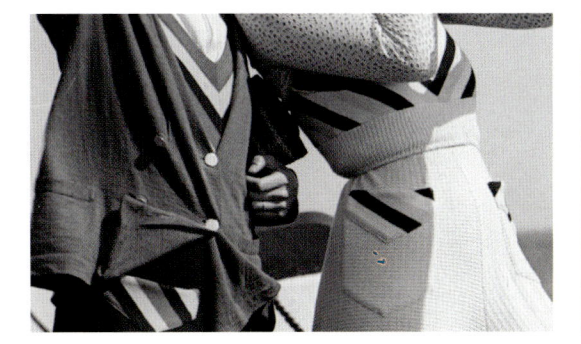

1 ART DECO DETAILING
Influenced by the contemporary trend for Art Deco detailing, the striped fabric of the top is cut to form a chevron at the centre front seam, which is replicated in the decorative flaps of the patch pockets, positioned low on the hips.

2 WIDE-LEGGED TROUSERS
The jersey-knit trousers are cut wide from the hip line and flare out towards the ankle. They are attached at a high waist seam to a halter-neck bodice, giving the impression that they are cut separately, and are dissected by a matching narrow cloth belt.

SUN AND SEA BATHING ON THE CÔTE D'AZUR

Fashionable Europeans promenade along the sea front at Juan-les-Pins in France (c. 1930; right) wearing a variety of beach pyjamas. The figure on the left wears a wide-legged all-in-one with a bib front secured by two crossed straps and a wide-brimmed sun hat pulled down over a short bob. The apple-green beach pyjamas worn by the figure in the centre are cut high in the waist and secured with a tan leather belt. The sleeveless blouse features a deep V-neck and hangs loosely, chemise-style, from the shoulders.

DESIGNED KNITWEAR

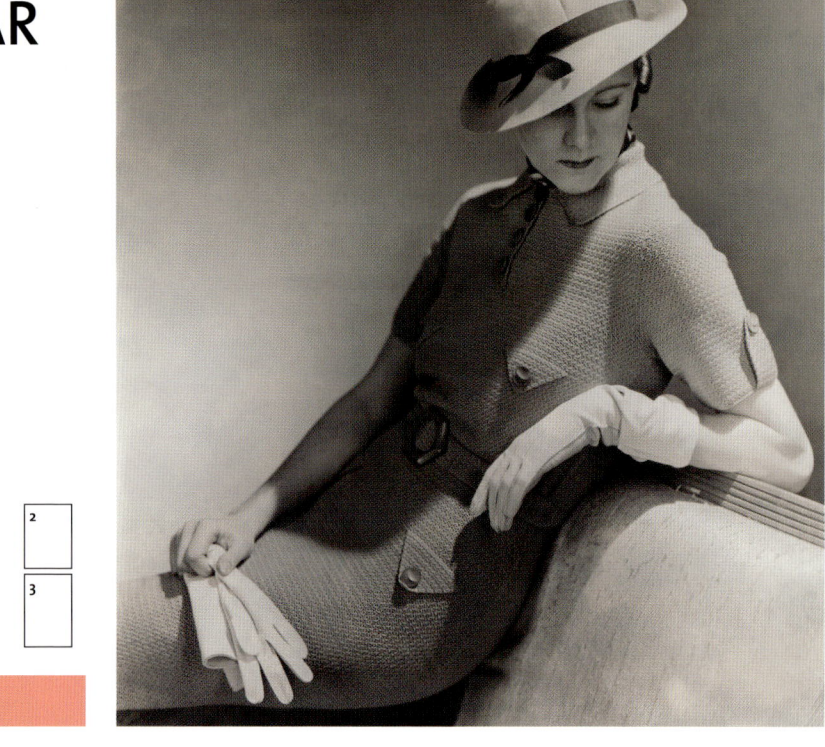

1 This figure-hugging crochet-knit dress, designed by Merle Munn in 1935, brings elegance and femininity to knitwear.

2 The classic Argyle-patterned sweater was popular with golfers during the inter-war years (1925).

3 Scottish manufacturer Braemar advertises its simple knitted twinsets (1930s).

The generic term 'hosiery' initially defined all aspects of knitted garments, from vests and combinations to swimwear. However, in the 1920s and 1930s, manufacturers extended their production of knitted underwear to include outerwear, and the term was replaced by 'knitwear'. Perfectly positioned to fulfil the prevailing modernist ethos of 'form follows function', knitted fabrics—created by the intermeshing of loops of yarn—provided form-fitting garments that also stretched and allowed wearers freedom of movement, thus releasing them from the constraints of high-maintenance clothes. In addition, by varying the number of stitches, garments could be widened or narrowed to accommodate different body shapes, which was ideal for the newly burgeoning mass production process. Furthermore, when Lastex was introduced c. 1925, knitwear fabric was elasticized and therefore retained its shape better. Before long, swimwear manufacturers, such as Jantzen, began to use Lastex in their swimwear collections (see p.260).

As knitwear manufacturers diversified into outerwear, the shape of the garments was no longer dictated by the engineering skills of the framework

KEY EVENTS

1920s	1922	1927	1927	1930s	1930
John Smedley introduces the 'Isis' shirt, with a patented collar design known as the 'Vestee'. It is the forerunner of the polo shirt.	Elsa Schiaparelli (1890–1973) begins her career in knitwear design.	Pringle of Scotland begins to manufacture pure silk stockings called Prinseta.	Ohio Knitting Mills is founded by Harry Stone in Cleveland, manufacturing high-end sweaters for superior labels such as Pendleton.	The British company Jaeger offers fashionable sportswear in knitted jacquard.	Pringle of Scotland claims to be the first British company to use cashmere for outerwear.

258 1900–45

knitter but by the design process. This was particularly true of the twinset (below right), a perennial fashion classic. Originally associated with two British knitwear manufacturers, John Smedley and Pringle of Scotland, the combination of a front-buttoning cardigan worn over a matching round-neck, short-sleeved jumper was initially categorized as sportswear. As the twinset increased in popularity, style variations were introduced: a V-neck replaced the round neckline, a small collar was added to the cardigan and different patterns or stitches were used occasionally. Whatever the variation, the basic premise remained the same: the two garments matched in colour, texture and yarn. When worn with a string of pearls and a tweed skirt, the twinset came to represent a way of life, one that upheld middle-class values and also represented refined good taste.

During the inter-war years Scottish manufacturers were renowned in Europe and the United States for the quality of their production and yarn. However, other European manufacturers, particularly in Italy, understood that knitwear was subject to the same fashionable demands as woven outerwear. This prompted Pringle of Scotland to employ a designer (the first British company to do so), Austrian-born Otto Weisz. Pringle also introduced the intarsia design (known as the Argyle pattern) to knitwear, which became a wardrobe staple for men's leisurewear (right) and was particularly popular on the golf course.

The skills of the pattern cutter, explored by the high-end designers of the era, infiltrated knitwear design. Manufacturers began to develop 'cut and sew' garments rather than shaped garment pieces, and applied the same pattern-making and manufacturing techniques to knitted cloth as they did to woven material. Waist-hugging sweater dresses in fine merino wool had cleverly concealed darts and seams integrated into ruching, cowl necklines and draped bodices. Hips were defined with shaped seaming, and belts became all-important. The prevailing Art Deco style provided inspiration in terms of polychrome stripes and zigzags. As in mainstream fashion, there was an obsession with detail and trimmings (opposite), particularly buttons and buckles. These were shaped using injection moulding in one of the new plastics, such as Bakelite, and were often sculpted into Art Deco motifs, such as the fan or sunray. Necklines extended into bows or long ties, and the padded shoulders of the era were copied by gathering the sleeve head into the bodice.

Hand-knitting flourished as a consequence of the Wall Street crash of 1929 and the subsequent economic depression. A resurgence in handcrafts after the cult of mechanization of the previous decade was evident in the plethora of personalized knitwear. Crocheted flowers, French knots, satin stitch and lazy daisy stitch—together with fringing, pompoms and fur trimmings—decorated not only sweaters but also knitted hats and handbags. The more functional style of 1930s daywear did not extend to evening attire, which was influenced by the glamour of Hollywood (see p.270). The use of 'lace' frames with mechanized patterning and the Raschel warp-knitting machine provided lighter-weight sweaters that were also suitable for evening wear. **MF**

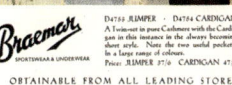

1931	1934	1940s	1940s	1941	1947
Pringle of Scotland takes out a patent for 'Slimfit' underwear, with Lastex incorporated into the rib waist.	Otto Weisz is appointed by Pringle of Scotland as the first dedicated knitwear designer of the industry.	The Hadley company, one of the leading US knitwear manufacturers, produces cashmere and camel-hair sweaters.	Swimwear manufacturer Catalina sponsors the Miss America beauty contest. The entrants wear ready-to-wear Catalina swimsuits.	Swimwear manufacturer Jantzen Inc. expands its business by adding sweaters and sportswear to its collections.	British company Pringle of Scotland is the best-selling brand in the United States.

DESIGNED KNITWEAR 259

Sculpted Elasticized Swimwear 1930s
JANTZEN

Jantzen advertisement (1930s). The logo was designed by Frank and Florenz Clark.

NAVIGATOR

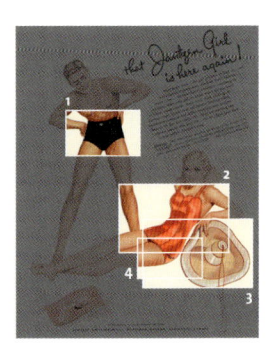

The trio of great US swimwear companies Jantzen, Catalina and Cole all have their provenance in the knitwear industry. Indeed, a number of US manufacturers were quick to exploit the market for machine-knitted bathing costumes and eventually diversified into active sportswear, thus creating a flourishing West Coast fashion industry. During the inter-war period, in the United States and Europe, both men and women became increasingly preoccupied with health and sport. Jantzen skilfully harnessed this interest in physical fitness to fashion trends and associated its products with aspirational lifestyle choices. The knitwear manufacturer applied its fashioning skills to the production of form-fitting swimwear, but these garments had the disadvantage that they became waterlogged and lost their shape when wet. Unsuccessful attempts were made to include elastic in the knitting process but it was only with the introduction of a newly invented yarn, Lastex—woven, satin-finish, elastic and silk material developed by the United States Rubber Company—that the fabric had the firmer, more resistant texture necessary to support and define the body. The designs mutated in response to the changing fashions of the day, and in the late 1940s the suit became strapless. **MF**

👁 FOCAL POINTS

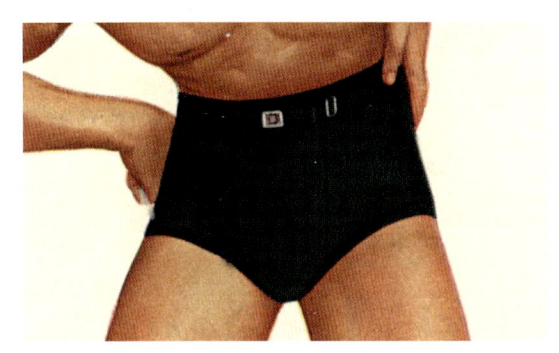

1 MEN'S SWIMMING TRUNKS
Cut reassuringly like outerwear, the high-waisted swimming trunks replicate the line of contemporary trousers and feature an integral belt threaded through loops, thus differentiating the garment from underwear. The trunks are cut straight across the top of the thighs.

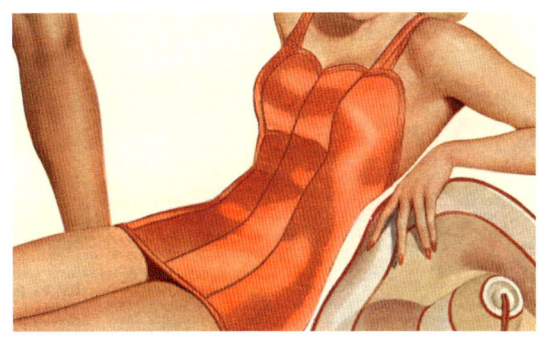

2 WOMEN'S SWIMSUIT
The swimsuit is cut along similar lines to those of a corset. The parallel seams form a princess line that continues into the shoulder straps, which are attached at the waist of the plunging back. The straight edge at the hem of the bathing suit conceals the integral knickers underneath.

3 SOMBRERO
The sun hat features the very wide brim and high conical crown that are typical of the Mexican sombrero, a term derived from the Spanish word *sombra*, meaning 'shade'. Constructed from two tones of straw with a contrasting trim, the hat was a popular and functional accessory for the beach.

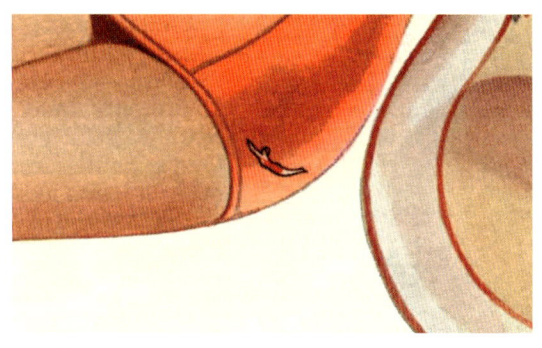

4 LOGO
The Jantzen logo is one of the oldest fashion brand icons and first appeared in advertisements for the company in the 1920s when the insignia of the Diving Girl was embroidered or sewn onto Jantzen swimsuits from 1923. The tag line, 'The Suit That Changed Bathing to Swimming', appeared in the same year.

THE JANTZEN STORY

The Portland Knitting Company was founded in 1910 in Portland, Oregon, by C. Roy and John A. Zehntbauer and Carl Jantzen. The company consisted of a few knitting machines above a small retail store, producing hosiery and sweaters. In 1915 Jantzen designed the company's first commercial bathing costume, comprising long shorts attached to a sleeveless skirted top in vibrant colours with stripes. The name of the company was changed to Jantzen Knitting Mills in 1918, and in 1940 it became Jantzen Inc. In 1938 Jantzen established separate men's and women's divisions, and went on to win six Woolknit awards for men's sweater designs between 1965 and 1980 (below). The sportswear lines were discontinued in 1997 and today the company concentrates solely on swimwear.

DESIGNED KNITWEAR

FASHION AND SURREALISM

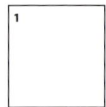

1 The iconic silk organza 'lobster' gown by Elsa Schiaparelli features a handpainted lobster and parsley sprig design by Salvador Dalí. Photographed by André Durst (1937).

2 This 1940s black suede telephone handbag by Anne Marie of France is embellished with gold trimmings and has a clip fastening.

Founded by French writer and poet André Breton, Surrealism was an exercise in displacement, subverting the ordinary by placing it within a new, often unsettling context. The conjunction of avant-garde fashion with the absurdity of Surrealism in the late 1920s provided a much-needed antidote to the worthy functionalism of the modernist movement. The leading exponent was Italian-born designer Elsa Schiaparelli (1890–1973), who made her reputation with the use of *trompe l'oeil* in knitted garments. Schiaparelli insisted that, for her, fashion design was not a profession but simply a different means of artistic expression; she did not sew and barely sketched. Parisian couturier Christian Dior (1905–57) accused her of creating couture that catered only for painters and poets. As Paris was the epicentre of the artistic avant-garde, the two worlds of fashion and the visual arts inevitably collided.

The designer launched her first collection from her boutique in rue de la Paix, Paris in 1929. From here Schiaparelli produced a collection of hand-knitted sweaters, coats, skirts, bathing suits and crocheted berets. Some sweaters

KEY EVENTS

1924	1926	1929	1929	1930	1935
André Breton writes his first Surrealist Manifesto, in which he defines the movement as pure psychic automatism.	A new group of Surrealist artists, including René Magritte, forms in Brussels before moving to Paris in 1927.	Surrealist painter Giorgio de Chirico designs costumes for *Le Bal* by Ballets Russes, using fragments of classical architecture as design motifs.	Salvador Dalí curates important professional exhibitions and officially joins the Surrealist group in the Montparnasse quarter of Paris.	Elsa Schiaparelli employs more than 2,000 people in her twenty-six workrooms in rue Cambon, Paris.	Schiaparelli designs silk and cotton fabrics printed with her own press clippings for the opening of her new boutique, nicknamed 'Schiap Shop'.

utilized the new elastic woollen fabric kasha, which clung provocatively to the body; others were produced in a special double-layered stitch created by two Armenian refugees working in Paris. The *trompe l'oeil* effects included such diverse images as faux bows (see p.264), scarves, neckties and belts, sailors' tattoos, and a white skeleton on a black background. As the Surrealists succeeded the Dadaists, Schiaparelli collaborated with the former's best-known exponent Salvador Dalí, a painter of exquisitely executed dreamscapes of hypnogogic imagery and deliquescent watches in desert landscapes. Garments included a white evening dress adorned with a lobster print painted by Dalí onto the skirt (opposite), and a skirt suit with pockets that simulated a chest of drawers. Schiaparelli also designed accessories and made handbags in the form of commonplace objects such as the piano and telephone. For her Pagan collection in 1938 she created an insect necklace, which gives the illusion of bugs crawling around the wearer's neck.

Schiaparelli was singularly well placed to exploit her artistic connections—her friends included Marcel Duchamp, Francis Picabia, Alfred Stieglitz and Man Ray—a situation that rendered her unique among other designers of the period. Those outside her sphere of influence contented themselves with details: in 1936 fashion house Rochas designed belt buckles in the form of miniature candelabras, crystal chandeliers and kid jewel cases spilling pearl rings and chains. Accessory designers were more fearless. Parisian milliner Louise Bourbon created a beret in 1938 that evoked a curly endive salad, and novelty bags gained favour as designers experimented with shape, form and materials to produce objects of wit and whimsy for an intellectual elite. Chief among these was Anne Marie of France who produced handbags that combined provocative and subversive design with innovative fastenings, such as a mandolin-shaped bag presented in a box decorated with an opera programme, and the black suede telephone bag (right). By the end of the decade, mass-produced Surrealist-inspired handbags proliferated, particularly those featuring a clock face, almost certainly inspired by Dalí.

In 1935 Schiaparelli opened one of the first couture boutiques, Pour Le Sport, selling ready-to-wear knitwear and sportswear. The designer had great international commercial success with a tiny knitted cap; the 'mad-cap' could be pulled into a variety of shapes and, like the bow-front sweater, was copied in its thousands. An iconoclastic designer, Schiaparelli incorporated her own idiosyncratic approach to fashion with experiments in textured fabric, working with Charles Colocombet, a French textile manufacturer. She fashioned bizarre ornamental buttons into hand mirrors or candlesticks, and hats were decorated with clusters of grapes and dive-bombing birds. In 1937 Dalí sketched designs for a shoe hat that Schiaparelli featured in her autumn/winter collection. The hat, shaped like a woman's high-heeled shoe, had the heel standing straight up and the toe tilted over the wearer's forehead. **MF**

1936	1936	1936	1936	1936	1938
Surrealist artist Eileen Agar turns heads with her 'Ceremonial Hat for Eating Bouillabaisse', constructed with bark, coral, a large fish bone and a jigsaw piece.	Editor-in-chief of *Harper's Bazaar* Carmel Snow (a former editor at *Vogue*) appoints Diana Vreeland as fashion editor.	US *Vogue* features an article titled 'Surrealism or the Purple Cow'. It is illustrated by Cecil Beaton's portrait of Salvador Dalí.	Dalí designs a window display for New York store Bonwit Teller; his *Aphrodisiac Dinner Jacket* is hung with shot glasses of crème de menthe.	Three Dalí paintings, one of which is owned by Schiaparelli, feature figures in ripped, skintight clothing suggesting tears and flayed flesh.	Schiaparelli invents the Lite-On handbag in collaboration with Dalí. Two internal light bulbs backlight a mirror, with a compartment for lipstick.

Trompe l'oeil Sweater 1927
ELSA SCHIAPARELLI 1890 – 1973

NAVIGATOR

Elsa Schiaparelli's first excursion into commercial design was an immediate success. She wrote in her autobiography, *A Shocking Life* (1954), that when she first wore her iconic *trompe l'oeil* bow sweater to a lunch at the Paris Ritz, she 'created a furore...All the women wanted one, immediately.' The idea for the sweater originated when Schiaparelli became intrigued by the hand-knitted sweater of a friend. Schiaparelli discovered that its firmer texture was the result of a technique deploying a three-needle, stretch-resistant process, which produced a tweed-like effect. The technique was the work of Armenian immigrants Aroosiag Mikaelian and her brother, who produced a range of knitted goods for the French wholesale trade. Although Schiaparelli herself did not know how to knit, she drew a rough sketch for the couple of a sweater with a large butterfly bow at the neckline, and added a matching *trompe l'oeil* collar and turn-back cuffs to the squared-off boxy shape of the sweater. As Schiaparelli sold more garments, other Armenian women in Paris who were familiar with this method were called upon to increase production levels. It is from these knitters that the knit technique is now known as 'Armenian'.

The first order for forty sweaters with matching skirts was completed in two weeks, and the fashion editor of *Vogue* magazine described the sweater as a 'masterpiece'. Orders from US sportswear wholesaler William H. Davidow Sons Co. followed, and by 1928 the design was so ubiquitous that knitting instructions appeared in the popular US magazine *Ladies' Home Journal* without attributing the source. **MF**

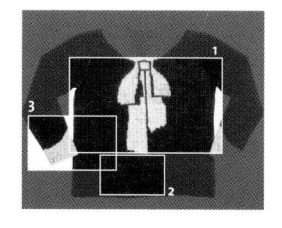

👁 FOCAL POINTS

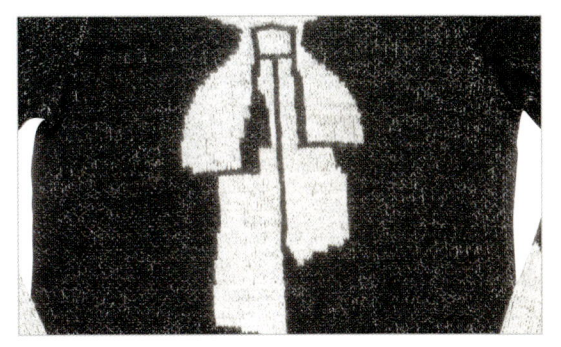

1 FAUX BOW
The faux bow is one of Schiaparelli's most frequently copied designs. The pictorial capacity of hand-knitted intarsia is defined by the stitch density of the fabric. Schiaparelli makes a virtue of the necessary coarseness of her stitch grid to evoke an Art Deco stratification.

2 WHITE-FLECKED BACKGROUND
The single-colour background is flecked with white to create a tweed-like effect. This is achieved by carrying the white yarn across the back of the black yarn and catching it behind every third or fourth stitch as it is knitted. Schiaparelli experimented with several versions of this sweater before she achieved the desired result.

3 ILLUSORY CUFFS
The illusion of a cuffed sleeve is effected by the use of *trompe l'oeil*. The term *trompe l'oeil* literally means 'trick the eye' and it was coined during the Baroque period to describe perspectival illusions in painting, such as the domed ceiling painted by Andrea Pozzo in 1703 in the Jesuit church in Vienna.

▲ Schiaparelli extended the new knitwear technique to encompass bathing costumes. This bathing suit top from 1927 features a fish motif and would have been worn with fitted flannel trunks.

🕒 DESIGNER PROFILE

1890–1922
Elsa Schiaparelli was born at the Palazzo Corsini in Rome to aristocratic intellectual parents. Her mother, Maria-Luisa, was a Neapolitan aristocrat and her father, Celestino Schiaparelli, a renowned scholar and curator of medieval manuscripts. From 1919 to 1922 Schiaparelli lived in New York and worked as a scriptwriter and translator; while there she met the artists Marcel Duchamp and Man Ray.

1923–44
Returning to Paris, the designer launched her first collection from her boutique in rue de la Paix in 1929. In 1937 Schiaparelli launched her scent Shocking, named for the signature bright fuchsia pink of the couture house and with a bottle design based on the enviable torso of Hollywood film star Mae West. This perfume was followed by Sleeping (1938), Snuff for Men (1939), Le Roi Soleil (1946), Zut (1948), Succès Fou (1953), Si (1957) and S (1961). She won the Neiman Marcus Award for Distinguished Service in the Field of Fashion in 1940. During World War II, Schiaparelli left Paris and lived in New York between 1941 and 1944.

1945–73
In 1945 she reopened her fashion house in Paris. Future couturiers Hubert de Givenchy (b.1927) and Pierre Cardin (b.1922) trained as her assistants. In 1954 Schiaparelli closed her French fashion house and returned to New York to concentrate on designing costume jewellery.

FASHION AND SURREALISM 265

APPROPRIATION OF MALE ATTIRE

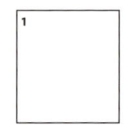

1 Playing with transgendered styles of clothing, Marlene Dietrich is mesmerizing in a tailored tuxedo and top hat (c. 1935).

2 Tailored slacks are worn with a turtleneck sweater and suede jacket for an elegant informal look (1946).

3 Katharine Hepburn wears her trademark slacks and brogues at a rehearsal for *The Millionairess* (1952).

As an advocate of rational dressing, Amelia Bloomer had sought social acceptance for a version of trousers for women at the end of the 19th century; however, they only achieved widespread tolerance in the 1920s, when couturière Coco Chanel (1883–1971) introduced beach pyjamas into her collections (see p.256). Wide-legged trousers were also worn for informal occasions in the evening; known as lounge wear, they were constructed from soft, fluid fabrics that draped around the body, thus highlighting feminine curves. These garments were far removed in both intention and effect from the male-style suits worn by film star Marlene Dietrich in the 1930s.

Contemporary opinion unequivocally perceived the trouser suit as the dress of the sexually ambiguous. The iconic actress Dietrich was notorious for her ability to project her personal style, which included wearing a monocle—a powerful symbol of masculinity. She and her husband, Rudolf Sieber, were part

KEY EVENTS

1920s	1924	1924	1930	1930	1932
Marlene Dietrich continues to work on stage and in film, both in Berlin and Vienna, attracting attention for her individual style.	As the trench coat increases in popularity, Burberry introduces its signature checked lining.	Travis Banton becomes the chief designer at Paramount. He collaborates with Josef von Sternberg to create a visual style known as 'Hollywood baroque'.	Josef von Sternberg directs the widely acclaimed film *Der Blaue Engel* (*The Blue Angel*) in both German and English.	Dietrich is contracted to Paramount Pictures, which seeks to market the actress as Germany's answer to MGM's Swedish star Greta Garbo.	Dietrich stars in *Blonde Venus* with Cary Grant and performs one of her songs dressed in a white tuxedo.

266 1900–45

of the 'divine decadence' of Berlin in the Weimar Republic, which was not only renowned for avant-gardism in the arts, but also for the diversity of its sexual underworld. Dietrich had already appeared in several films before she caught the eye of director Josef von Sternberg in 1929. Captivated by her allure, he cast her as the manipulative, hard-hearted nightclub singer Lola Lola in *Der Blaue Engel* (*The Blue Angel*; 1930). In the film, Dietrich, wearing a top hat and black stockings alongside a tailored tuxedo and wing-tipped collar (opposite), uses the wiles of the seductress to gain the kind of power that is traditionally associated with masculinity. She reprised the role of Lola Lola in many of her films that followed, and took with her to Hollywood the Weimar culture of sexual ambiguity that recognized transvestism as an acceptable code of behaviour. Flying under the colours of male attire, Dietrich also maintained the demeanour of assertion, tempering her undoubted female characteristics with detachment: the antithesis of the female stereotype of the submissive blonde.

The actress's appropriation of masculine dress (see p.268) included accessories such as hat, necktie, brogues and cigar, a classic cinematic prop that represented manhood. Such was Dietrich's status that certain accoutrements of masculinity worn by her—tuxedo trouser suit, trench coat, flat brogues and trilby—became fashion classics, although some not until several decades later. Yves Saint Laurent introduced the tuxedo into mainstream women's fashion in the 1960s with 'Le Smoking' (see p.384), followed by the popularization of the trench coat, which had several incarnations at the height of fashion, and reached its apotheosis under the creative hand of Christopher Bailey at Burberry in the 21st century. Not only did Dietrich wear trousers on screen, she also wore them in publicity shots and in her private life, thus creating a trend for women's 'slacks', which nevertheless remained acceptable only as informal wear. A practical garment worn for outdoor activities, slacks were softly tailored wide-legged cuffed trousers (above right) in sturdy fabrics such as lightweight tweed, moleskin and corduroy. The waist-high rise was finished with a waistband and belt loops. Unpressed pleats featured each side of the centre zipped fastening, and roomy vertical pockets set into the side seams allowed for sundry requirements for the task in hand. Worn informally with a soft cotton blouse or simply styled sweater, slacks became an inherent part of the modern women's wardrobe, confirmed with the onset of World War II, when practical clothing became a priority.

Film star Katharine Hepburn (right) was also a fan of trousers and flat brogues. Ginette Spanier, *directrice* of couture house Balmain, recalls how the actress 'changed straight back from our beautiful embroidered gown into her slacks to be photographed', after being fitted for her part in the West End play *The Millionairess* (1952). Although Hepburn was known for resisting patriarchal norms, both in life and in her films, her choice of garments was perceived as evidence of her athleticism rather than transgression, leading the way for other like-minded women to temper notions of femininity with masculine dress. **MF**

1933	1933	1936	1938	1939	1941
Katharine Hepburn appears in the RKO film *Christopher Strong* as a strong-spirited aviatrix.	Dietrich is photographed in Paris wearing a masculine suit.	The first single-solution cold-wave perm is developed by Professor Speakman to effect the softly tousled waves espoused by Dietrich.	The DuPont company begins producing commercial nylon and by 1939 is producing knitted hosiery, later given the name 'Nylons'.	An article in *Vogue* advises: 'Your wardrobe is not complete without a pair or two of the superbly tailored slacks of 1939.'	Dietrich wears a trench coat in the film *Manpower*. Usually worn for shooting on the moors, the coat is styled by Dietrich with a knotted belt.

APPROPRIATION OF MALE ATTIRE 267

Marlene Dietrich in Man's Suit 1933
TRANSGENDERED DRESS

NAVIGATOR

Wearing the perfect facsimile of a man's tailored suit, film star Marlene Dietrich embodied the glamour inherent in cross-dressing. There were subtle differences, however, between the traditionally tailored male suit and the one worn by Dietrich, which was cleverly constructed to exploit the femininity of the woman beneath. In contrast to the conventional inverted triangular silhouette of the male suit, with broad shoulders and narrow hips, the one-button fastening of the jacket is placed exactly on the waist, before being cut away over the hips and opening up over the bust. This imposes an almost hourglass shape, which is further emphasized by the upward-pointing revers of the collar. The wide-cut trousers are high-waisted to fit neatly under the jacket fastening, and feature a fly front and turn-ups (cuffs). Masculine accoutrements include a starched white shirt, worn with a necktie, and a crisp white handkerchief. The severity of the outfit is confirmed by the austere beret, which conceals the hair and is worn on the side of the head. Dietrich was attired in a similar outfit, worn beneath a heavy, masculine-inspired ankle-length overcoat, during a visit to Paris in 1933. On her arrival she was reputedly warned by the police that she was liable to prosecution, referring to an ordinance dating from 1800, when female to male cross-dressing was explicitly forbidden. **MF**

FOCAL POINTS

1 BERET
Initially a symbol of rebellion, the beret was known as a liberty cap or *bonnet rouge*. Its antecedent was the conical Phrygian cap. Appropriated by the sans-culottes of Revolutionary France, the beret came to represent the archetypal disaffected Parisian bohemian.

2 NECKTIE
Considered a phallic symbol—directing the eye to the crotch when worn by men—the necktie is a descendant of the cravat. Dietrich wears her tie fastened in a wide symmetrical knot, which later became known as a Windsor knot, after the Duke of Windsor.

3 POCKET HANDKERCHIEF
Dietrich sports a white linen handkerchief in the suit pocket, a popular style at the time. Male suit jackets are made with a left breast pocket, specifically to hold a handkerchief or 'pocket square'. Rather than an item of utility, it is deployed for its decorative qualities.

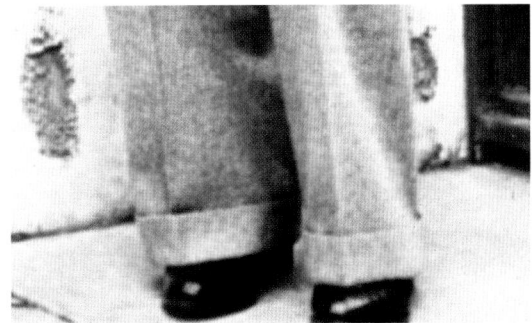

4 TROUSER TURN-UPS
The bespoke tailoring convention of adding cuffs, or turn-ups, to the hem of men's trousers, when they are pleated at the waist, reinforces the cross-gender styling of the suit. The cuff adds weight to the wide trouser leg and protects the cloth from damage.

APPROPRIATION OF MALE ATTIRE

HOLLYWOOD GLAMOUR

1. Jean Harlow's dress in *Dinner at Eight* (1933), designed by Adrian, introduced the 'goddess gown' to the US market.

2. Mae West exudes full-on Hollywood glamour in an extravagant costume designed by Elsa Schiaparelli for *Every Day's a Holiday* (1937).

3. Actor Clark Gable wears a single-breasted three-piece drape suit in 1932. Both the jacket and trousers have a fuller cut for a more comfortable fit.

Hollywood images of desirability and sexual attractiveness have frequently influenced women's fashion, and never more so than during the golden age of the 1930s, when a Depression-hit United States sought escapism at the cinema. Film stars such as Carole Lombard and Mae West, the original blonde bombshells, became fashion leaders, dressed in shimmering white satin gowns set against the glittering mirrored surfaces of Art Deco backdrops. Although Parisian couture was the driving force behind this seductive silhouette, Hollywood costumier Adrian (1903–59) recontextualized the restraint and clarity of the classical idiom of designers such as Madeleine Vionnet (1876–1975) for a wider audience.

Head of costume at Metro-Goldwyn-Mayer (MGM), Adrian popularized Vionnet's bias cut in films such as *Dinner at Eight* (1933), in which Jean Harlow smouldered in a bias-cut backless halter-neck dress, worn with a white ostrich cape and diamonds (above). Previously, Paris had dictated high-end cutting-edge fashion; however, Hollywood now played its part in bringing French couture to the masses and influencing mass taste. Adrian also designed the

KEY EVENTS

1928	1930	1932	1932	1933	1934
Adrian becomes head costume designer for Cecil B. DeMille's film studio before moving to MGM, where he designs costumes for more than 200 films.	Hollywood's Paramount Pictures experiment briefly with two-colour Technicolor.	The ascendancy of Hollywood over Paris as a generator of trends is confirmed by the phenomenon of the Letty Lynton dress (see p.272).	Clark Gable appears alongside Claudette Colbert in Frank Capra's romantic comedy *It Happened One Night*.	Adrian's bias-cut backless dress for Jean Harlow introduces Parisian couture to the US mass market.	The National Legion of Decency is established, dedicated to identifying and combating objectionable content in motion pictures.

270 1900–45

full-length white evening dress worn by Joan Crawford in *Letty Lynton* (1932; see p.272), which proved commercially successful in the United States and Europe.

Film editing often cut away from garment details for the sake of continuity, and costumiers such as Adrian designed dresses with film publicity stills in mind; these featured in the ever proliferating movie magazines such as *Picture Play* and *Modern Movies*. Moreover, fashion photographs in *Vogue* began to resemble film stills, with fantasy props and complex lighting schemes, thus disseminating the look to a greater audience. The US ready-to-wear industry was quick to respond, and mass-produced copies of the garments promoted through feature films were readily available. Advertising agent Bernard Waldman sold star-endorsed styles through his Modern Merchandising Bureau and chain of Cinema Fashion Stores, of which there were 400 by 1937. Sketches or photographs of garments to be worn by various actresses were sent to the bureau from the film studio well in advance of the film's release. These were then produced, along with publicity for the retailers. The garments were exaggerated for the screen and the copies were not manufactured with the extreme styling or the luxurious materials of the originals. For example, the bias-cut evening gown was replicated in the newly invented fabric rayon, previously confined to lingerie and nightwear, which was considered an adequate substitute and had properties similar to those of silk.

An admirer of Parisian couture, Adrian persuaded the head of MGM Studios, Samuel Goldwyn, to lure Coco Chanel (1883–1971) to Hollywood with an offer of one million dollars to design for his stable of stars. However, Chanel's distinctive personal vision and the subtlety of cut did not translate well onto the screen, and the collaboration ended in 1931. Elsa Schiaparelli (1890–1973) sustained a more successful relationship, and her innate sense of theatre resulted in the designer working on more than thirty Hollywood films. She designed the costumes for Marlene Dietrich and Mae West (above right) in *Every Day's a Holiday* (1937), and even based the shape of her perfume bottle Shocking on the embonpoint of the glamorous West. Dietrich was also dressed by Travis Banton (1894–1958), the chief designer at rival studios Paramount Pictures. Considered one of the most important Hollywood costume designers of the 1930s, Banton colluded with director Josef von Sternberg to create costumes set against a background of exotic locations. Trained in the techniques of couture, he lavished on Dietrich the camp excesses of theatrical display, from enormous fur collars to a plethora of veils, luxurious textures, lace stockings and feathers.

Screen idols such as Gary Cooper and Clark Gable (right) epitomized male Hollywood glamour. The American drape suit (see p.274) provided the paradigm of the athletic 'V'-shape masculine ideal: broad of shoulder and narrow of hip. Cut with fullness across the chest and tapered to the waist before flaring slightly, this revolutionary silhouette set the style for the following two decades. **MF**

1934	1935	1936	1937	1938	1941
Claudette Colbert stars in *Cleopatra*, directed by Cecil B. DeMille with costumes by Travis Banton. It popularizes the vogue for Egyptian-inspired fashions.	Adrian designs the costumes for Jean Harlow in the film *China Seas*.	Head costumier at Paramount Pictures Travis Banton designs bias-cut beaded evening gowns for Carole Lombard in *My Man Godfrey*.	Elsa Schiaparelli introduces her first scent, titled Shocking; the shape of the bottle is modelled after the figure of Mae West.	The new wood-fibre-based fabric rayon is introduced by DuPont as a substitute for silk. It is one of many new fabrics.	Adrian sets up a thriving fashion house in Los Angeles after leaving MGM; it produces bespoke and ready-to-wear clothing for the US mass market.

Letty Lynton Dress 1932
ADRIAN 1903 — 59

Joan Crawford stars as New York socialite Letty Lynton (1932).

NAVIGATOR

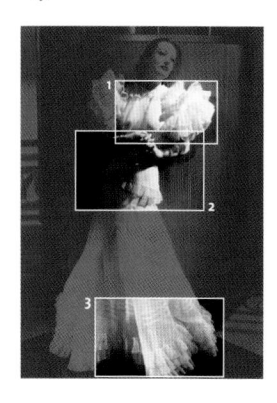

The befrilled long white evening dress worn by Joan Crawford in Clarence Brown's melodrama *Letty Lynton* (1932) inspired a plethora of mass-market copies—known as 'butterfly sleeve' dresses—and was evidence of the increasing dominance of Hollywood style over Parisian couture. Designed by Adrian, head of costume at Metro-Goldwyn-Mayer, the dress was replicated both on film and by designers throughout the 1930s. Constructed from layers of mousseline-de-soi, the ankle-length dress was a fashion phenomenon and also influenced European styles: the popularity of the gown swept through Paris not only after the dress had appeared in the film, but also after it had been retailed extensively in New York.

Within a relatively restrained slimline silhouette of narrow hips and wide shoulders, which was typical of the era, the dress is an effervescent riot of pin-tucked frills at the waist, hem and sleeves. There is no attempt to sexualize the dress with emphasis on the bosom; the bodice remains plain and unadorned, allowing for the full impact of the circular balls of flouncy frills on each shoulder. The ingénue nature of the dress is emphasized by the high neckline, ending in a neat Peter Pan collar that is also edged in frills and fastened with a small brooch. **MF**

FOCAL POINTS

1 MULTILAYERED SLEEVES
The many sunray frills that make up the exaggerated sleeves have a picot edging. Extending from shoulder to elbow, the sleeves form the focal point of the dress and inspired many variations in both day and evening wear.

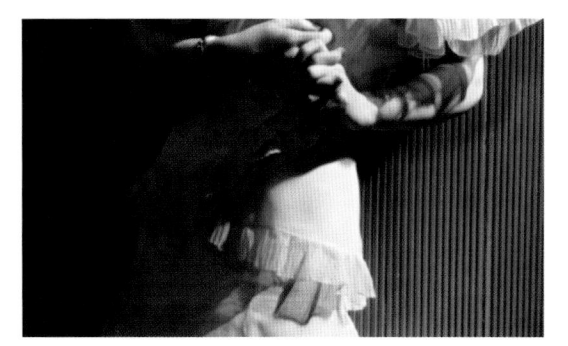

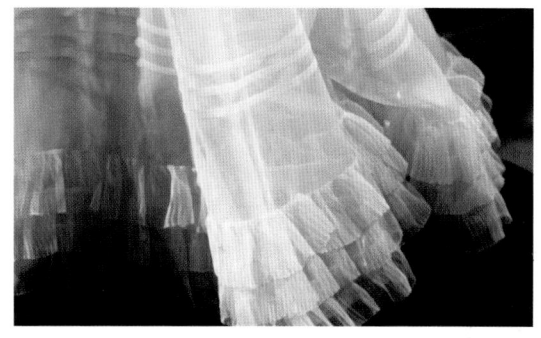

3 FRILLED HEM
Three tiers of finely pleated frills supply additional fullness to the ankle-length gored skirt. These frills decorate the hem below three horizontal rows of appliquéd silk-satin ribbon and echo the frill on the peplum.

2 EMPHASIS ON THE WAIST
A transparent peplum falls to the hips and is shaped to curve upwards into the waistband. The rounded ends are edged in a pin-tucked frill that extends into a rosette at the centre of the self-fabric belt.

DESIGNER PROFILE

1903–29
US-born Adrian Adolph Greenberg, known as Adrian, attended the New York School for Fine and Applied Arts, transferring to its Paris campus in 1922. He became head costume designer for Cecil B. DeMille's independent studio, and in 1928 moved with him to MGM, where he designed for more than 200 films.

1930–59
During the 1930s and 1940s Adrian worked with stars including Greta Garbo, Norma Shearer, Jean Harlow and Katharine Hepburn, although it was with Joan Crawford that he had his most enduring connection. He was behind her signature outfits with large shoulder pads, which later spawned a fashion trend. Adrian left MGM in 1941 to set up his own independent fashion house, although he still worked closely with Hollywood stars.

American Drape Suit 1930s
MEN'S SUIT

Douglas Fairbanks Jr wears a Glenurquhart plaid drape suit.

NAVIGATOR

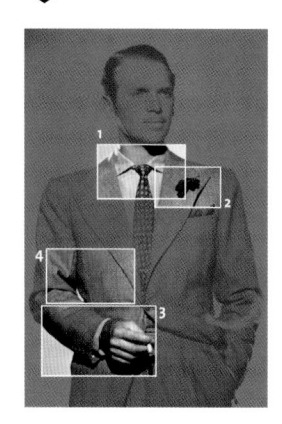

The drape suit introduced a relaxed fit to men's attire, replacing the last vestige of military influence on men's clothing design. The US version, worn here by film star Douglas Fairbanks Jr, is identified by the vertical creases, or breaks, at the front of the jacket, from the sleeve head to the armpit, which create a noticeable and elegant drape. Tailored for the film star by London's Savile Row tailors Anderson & Sheppard, the suit is constructed from a Glenurquhart plaid, meticulously matched at the seams.

The upper sleeves allow for a broad range of motion, but the armholes, cut high and small, hold the coat in place, keeping its collar from separating from the wearer's neck when the arms are raised. The jacket has a low buttoning point, which emphasizes the tapered waist and exaggerates the bulk in the chest and shoulders, as do the extended and upward-slanting revers of the collar. The cutaway collar of the silk shirt allows for a Windsor knot in the foulard tie. A three-pointed handkerchief is tucked into the diagonally placed breast pocket of the jacket. Trousers are cut very full and pegged to the hem, usually with double pleats and a zipper fly. Worn by film stars such as Fred Astaire, Robert Mitchum and Clark Gable at the height of their careers, the American drape suit was often called the Hollywood drape suit. **MF**

FOCAL POINTS

1 DOUBLE WINDSOR KNOT
Worn with the spread collar, the Double Windsor knot—well balanced in left and right bulk to form a wide triangular knot—gives the tie a symmetrical formality. The paisley foulard design would be considered more nonchalant tied in a Half-Windsor.

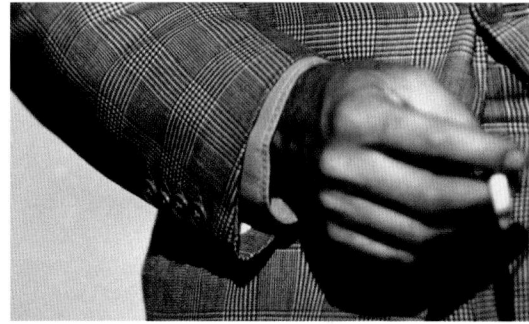

3 SURGEON'S CUFF
Sleeves with 'surgeon's cuffs' have four opening buttons and a vent. As a feature of the tapered drape suit sleeve, this style of cuff was a convention that signalled bespoke tailoring rather than a practical detail that allowed the sleeve to be rolled back.

2 BUTTONHOLE
Boutonnières were in evidence from the mid 19th century. Here a classic clove-red carnation with a bulbous calyx embellishes the wide peaked revers. The bloom is pushed through the buttonhole to secure the flourish of natural colour in place.

4 FABRIC
Nicknamed the Prince of Wales check when adopted by Edward VII before he was crowned, Glenurquhart plaid was designated by the Earl of Seafield as his estate tweed in the 1840s. The original Glenurquhart was black and white.

AMERICAN READY-TO-WEAR

1. Formalized with red, yellow and turf-brown accessories, these grey suits by Claire McCardell are clearly influenced by the designer's trademark popover dress (c. 1943).

2. The original linen popover dress by Claire McCardell was introduced in 1942 for stylish modern wartime women who were obliged to do their own housework.

The concept of ready-to-wear fashion first emerged in the United States in the late 1920s and early 1930s. Previously, fashionable women had patronized the Parisian couturiers, who provided a bespoke service for a wealthy clientele. A version of couture was also available at US department stores such as Ohrbach's and Bergdorf Goodman: they legitimately copied what was on the couture catwalk by buying both the rights to reproduce the garments and a calico toile from the designers that could then be copied stitch for stitch. Women who were unable to spare the time for extensive fittings or the money for the painstaking perfection of this level of couture commissioned local seamstresses to create the garments, or made their clothes themselves.

A more affordable, accessible, fashionable alternative began to materialize in the form of ready-to-wear clothes. The manufacturers of the New York fashion industry, located around Seventh Avenue, honed their technical and financial prowess to improve the design of moderately priced apparel. Among them was entrepreneur Hattie Carnegie (1886–1956), pioneer of the head-to-toe retailing experience, who became aware of the potential for fashionable,

KEY EVENTS

1928	1929	1934	1937	1937	1939
Visionary entrepreneur and retailer Hattie Carnegie launches her first ready-to-wear line, aimed at the high-end market.	The Wall Street Crash signals the beginning of the ten-year Great Depression that affects all Western industrialized countries.	In response to the Depression, Hattie Carnegie establishes her ready-to-wear Spectator Sports line to be sold alongside her bespoke clothes.	Claire McCardell establishes her reputation with the 'monastic' dress, a smock-like garment without darts, secured at the waist with a belt.	Bonnie Cashin becomes the head designer at Adler & Adler, New York, manufacturers of coats and suits.	Paris loses its influence: Madeleine Vionnet (1876–1975) retires and the House of Chanel closes.

276 1900–45

lower-priced garments and produced her first ready-to-wear clothing in 1928. During the Great Depression she offered a more affordable Spectator Sports line, alongside her luxury brand, which proved extremely successful and included ready-to-wear dresses and suits that could be ordered by post or telephone. Her trademark Carnegie suit (see p.280) was an exemplary exercise in the use of proportion that flattered the female silhouette and eschewed the severity of European wartime tailoring.

With the onset of World War II and the German occupation of Paris in 1940, US manufacturers—specifically the International Ladies' Garment Workers' Union—set out to make New York City the clothing capital of the world. This organization was supported by the creative talents of native designers, among them Clare Potter (1903–99), one of the first US designers to become widely known. She commented in Beryl Williams's book *Fashion Is Our Business* (1948): 'The Paris influence used to be too persuasive, I think. It affected everybody and they all turned out clothes that showed its mark. I don't think we should ever let that happen again. American designers know what sort of clothes American women want to wear and they can make them, too.' In contrast to the padded and structurally rigid clothes with built-in corsetry espoused by Dior's New Look in 1947 (see p.302), US designers such as Potter, Jo Copeland (1900–82) and Claire McCardell (1905–58) designed clothes that followed the natural line of the body and were appropriate for the lives of modern women, who were increasingly preoccupied with work in addition to running the home.

Claire McCardell, the designer who is most closely associated with American ready-to-wear style, redefined the look of modern dressing by bringing the functionality of leisurewear (known as sportswear in the United States) into high fashion. Her professional career began with sketching Paris fashions for the US mass market but she eventually translated these into US designs, 'making them a little more casual, a little less self-conscious, and a little more American'. Problem-solving was the defining characteristic of her ethos: she designed sundresses and sunsuits, the one-piece 'diaper' suit from one length of fabric, and playsuits for maximum comfort; she crafted long-sleeved evening dresses in wool during wartime (when heating costs were high) and jersey leotards for dancers (for ease of movement). In 1942, at the request of *Harper's Bazaar*, she created her most popular design: the 'popover' dress (right), with attached oven mitt, for the 'servant-less household'. Worn to protect the clothes beneath, this wraparound utility dress was made from linen or denim and laundered easily. Versions of the dress appeared in all of McCardell's later collections, designed in a range of different fabrics and as suits (opposite) for more formal occasions.

In 1942 the American War Production Board imposed limits on certain textiles, and luxury fabrics such as silk and wool were redirected to the war effort. Thus McCardell elevated 'humble' fabrics such as jersey, cotton,

1941	1941	1941	1942	1950	1951
McCardell, Cashin and Vera Maxwell (1901–95) are invited by Mayor LaGuardia of New York to design the women's civilian defence uniform.	Capitalizing on his influential designs for MGM, costumier Adrian opens a fashion house producing a large ready-to-wear range.	Swimwear manufacturer Jantzen Inc. adds sweaters and leisurewear to its basic line.	Claire McCardell designs the popover dress. Manufactured by Townley Frocks, the garment is classed as a 'utility garment' and sells in its thousands.	Bonnie Cashin receives the unprecedented honour of earning both the Neiman Marcus Award and the Coty American Fashion Critics' Award.	Cashin establishes Bonnie Cashin Design Inc. Working with multiple manufacturers, she designs a range at different price points.

AMERICAN READY-TO-WEAR 277

3 This striking broad-shouldered, slim-waisted look introduced by Adrian in 1944 became known as the V-line.

4 Bonnie Cashin's tweed poncho, accompanied by short spats, was designed as a travel garment in 1943 and recalls men's evening wear.

gingham, chambray and denim, and patterns such as stripes, checks and plaids, to high-fashion status. Attracted by the comfort and ease of men's clothes, McCardell incorporated roomy pockets into her designs, which made handbags unnecessary. She also appropriated the dropped shirt-sleeve shoulder, soft trouser pleats and the rows of top-stitching found on blue jeans, which at the time were worn only as workwear. The concept of 'separates' was born—a capsule wardrobe of practical pieces that could be put together in a variety of ways depending on the weather and the occasion—and the shirtwaist dress, tailored blouse, dirndl skirt, sweater set, easy-wrap pinafore and high-waisted trousers all became US classics. McCardell's ready-to-wear designs were based on simple geometric shapes, and their silhouettes were defined by ties, wraps and drape, or the elasticity of knitted jersey, rather than by shaped pattern pieces that would involve hours of fitting.

This very definable essentially American look, epitomized by McCardell's pioneering designs, soon gained momentum and was consolidated by the leading exponent of US sportswear, Bonnie Cashin (1907–2000), who provided modern uncomplicated designs. Obsessed with the relationship between use and form, Cashin looked beyond Western tailoring and utilized forms of non-Western dress such as the tunic, kimono and poncho (opposite). Approaching dress as a form of industrial design, she favoured luxurious, organic materials that she could sculpt into shape, such as leather, suede, mohair, wool jersey and cashmere, as well as 'non-fashion' materials including upholstery fabrics.

Initially Cashin worked as a costume designer in Hollywood, but she was encouraged by Carmel Snow—influential fashion editor of *Harper's Bazaar*—to apply her skills to the design of ready-to-wear clothing, and in 1937 took up a post as designer to prestigious New York coat and suit manufacturers

Adler & Adler. However, frustrated with the wartime restrictions on clothing design, Cashin returned to California and signed a six-year contract with 20th Century Fox, where she designed costumes for the female characters of more than sixty films. Making use of the resources of the studio's costume department for films such as *Laura* (1944), *A Tree Grows in Brooklyn* (1945) and *Anna and the King of Siam* (1946), Cashin also experimented with designs for off-film clothes and created custom versions for the leading actresses. In 1949 she returned to Adler & Adler in New York, where she produced an award-winning ready-to-wear collection in 1950. However, she soon felt stifled by the manufacturer's desire to control her creativity and formed her own company, Bonnie Cashin Design Inc., in 1951. The designer's innovative concept of layered dressing—a flexible capsule wardrobe of coordinating garments to be worn together or separately—was popular throughout the 1950s, and garments were constructed in easy-care fabrics, such as knitted jersey and natural fibres, tweed, wool, cotton, denim or chambray.

Throughout its growth, the New York ready-to-wear industry faced competition from other regions in the United States. In 1941 California presented its own catwalk shows, 'Fashion Futures', run by the Los Angeles and San Francisco Fashion Groups, which showcased the work of seventy-five designers, including Irene Lentz (1900–62) and Adrian (1903–59), both of whom worked in the Hollywood film industry. Adrian was renowned for dressing Hollywood heroines such as Joan Crawford and Barbara Stanwyck in clothes that made a feature of mitred stripes constructed from textile designer Pola Stout's inventive striped cloth. Adrian's designs included striking suits, which went on to become enormously influential in the fashion industry. As a result he left his post as chief designer at Metro-Goldwyn-Mayer in 1941 to open his eponymous ready-to-wear outlet in Los Angeles. There he showed both ready-to-wear and custom-made clothes, including pioneering designs such as the V-line suit (opposite). Other California manufacturers included the swimwear and knitwear company Jantzen, and Koret, which offered a more relaxed alternative to Adrian's sharp tailoring. Based in San Francisco, Koret provided ready-to-wear 'mix and match' separates that appealed to the new demographic of the teenager: interchangeable components of informal items such as shorts, Capri pants, midriff-bearing tops, all-in-one playsuits and dirndl skirts in madras cotton, calico and knitted jersey.

At the end of World War II, Sally Kirkland of *Life* magazine—reputed to be the most influential woman in the fashion business at the time—led the move to resurrect the French and Italian fashion industries. European consumers were in thrall to the dictates of couturiers such as Christian Dior (1905–57), Cristóbal Balenciaga (1895–1972) and Hubert de Givenchy (b.1927), but in the US market, home-grown luxury ready-to-wear began to take the place of haute couture. Luminaries of this industry such as Norman Norell (1900–72), renowned for the restrained simplicity of his clothes, and Paris-born, US-based Pauline Trigère (1909–2002), the purveyor of the princess cut, set the standard for accessible quality clothing constructed to fit a range of body types. These early pioneers of a distinctive US style were succeeded by a new generation of designers including James Galanos (b.1924) and Roy Halston Frowick (1932–90). Rigorously eschewing embellishment, Halston designed easy-to-wear evening pyjamas, kaftans and halter-neck, bias-cut evening dresses that made him the obvious heir to McCardell's informal, stylish aesthetic and later provided a bridge to the future exponents of US style such as Donna Karan (b.1948) and Calvin Klein (b.1942). **MF**

Carnegie Suit 1943
HATTIE CARNEGIE 1886–1956

NAVIGATOR

An exercise in sophisticated urban tailoring for the working woman, the Carnegie suit—usually an ensemble with dressmaker details in luxury fabrics—traditionally opened the designer's seasonal showings. Beryl Williams reported in *Fashion Is Our Business* (1948) that '[Carnegie] likes suits, and makes them up for every hour of the day and evening. She likes to orchestrate a costume, believing that a well-groomed woman should be as perfectly coordinated as a well-turned-out piece of music'.

Immaculate in execution, this suit evidences the hallmarks of the wartime figure—in the squared-off padded shoulders and the long-line silhouette—but without the prevailing austerity that was evident in the tailoring in Britain. The designer's signature 'Carnegie blue' is partnered with maroon; the cuffs match the buttons on the jacket and the V-neck high-buttoned waistcoat underneath. The single-breasted waistcoat recalls the male three-piece suit and obviates the need for a feminine blouse, thus reinforcing the notion of businesslike tailoring. It is colour-matched to the cuffs to give the appearance of long sleeves. The two-button fastening on the jacket is centred on the waist, which is defined with a seam. The bracelet-length cuffs allow for the long gloves, ruched to fit, and the tan shoulder bag adds a note of practicality. **MF**

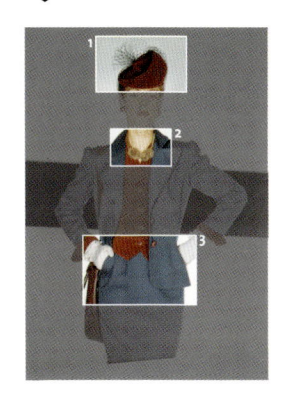

FOCAL POINTS

1 HAT
The upward movement of the revers that extend towards the shoulder line is beautifully calibrated with the upward swirl of the elegant maroon felt hat, to which a fine dot- and cross-net veil is attached.

2 COSTUME JEWELLERY
Costume jewellery played a significant role in the glamorous working woman's wardrobe. Here a necklace in matt gold, known as Russian gold plating, fills the neckline of the waistcoat and is worn with matching button earrings.

3 DIRNDL SKIRT
The skirt of the single-breasted jacket flares over the hips to accommodate the gently shaped dirndl skirt. Vertical pockets are set into the waistband, concealed in the outer of the two unpressed pleats, which provide ease of movement.

DESIGNER PROFILE

1886–1933
From a small millinery shop established in 1909, Hattie Carnegie (born Henrietta Kanengeiser in Vienna) built a clothing empire and became a household name. In 1918 she opened a custom dressmaking salon and began selling her own label. In 1928 she added ready-to-wear, employing designers including Norman Norell and Claire McCardell.

1934–56
Carnegie was one of the first fashion entrepreneurs to recognize the importance of a second, less expensive line, and began to manufacture such garments from 1934. At her salon, customers could accessorize day and evening ensembles with furs, hats and handbags, and try out her cosmetic and chocolate lines. Carnegie was awarded the Coty American Fashion Critics' Award in 1948. She died in 1956, but the business continued until 1976.

AMERICAN READY-TO-WEAR 281

DESIGN IN ADVERSITY

1. These three utility dresses designed by Norman Hartnell in 1943 all comply with the British government restrictions on garment cut and decoration.

2. The utility siren suit, an all-in-one garment with zipped front and large slouch pockets, was worn over nightwear in the event of a bombing raid (1939).

3. US designer Muriel King created practical fashion for the factory floor (1942).

W orld War II had a far-reaching impact on the fashion industry and the subsequent distribution of ideas and modes of manufacture. Paris, isolated by the German occupation of the city, was no longer in a position to dictate fashion trends. Some couture houses closed their doors, but more than ninety, including Lanvin and Balenciaga, still presented small collections; these continued the pre-war trend for full-skirted femininity without the necessity for rationing. Both Britain and the United States were now reliant on domestic talent. In Britain this resulted in the promulgation of a home-grown style that came to be regarded as traditionally British, including well-cut tailored suits and classic knitwear by London couturiers Norman Hartnell (1901–79) and Charles Creed (1909–66). In the United States the war provided an opportunity to formalize the already flourishing ready-to-wear industry that manufactured the sportswear of quintessential designers Claire McCardell (1905–58), Clare Potter (1903–99) and Muriel King (1900–77).

KEY EVENTS

1935	1940	1940	1941	1941	1941
Nylon is first produced by Wallace Carothers at DuPont's research facility.	The German army invades Paris and most couture houses close for the duration of the war.	Lucien Lelong (1889–1958) persuades the Nazis not to move the Paris fashion industry to Berlin.	Japan cuts off its supply of silk to the United States.	The rationing system, which includes clothing, is implemented in Britain.	The implementation of the National Service Act (No. 2) conscripts unmarried women between the ages of twenty and thirty.

The austerity of World War II replaced the desire for innovation in fashion with the need for practical clothing. The majority of women of marriageable age in Europe and the United States were conscripted into war work, and military uniform was a familiar sight on the streets. Even civilian daywear replicated the severity of cut and functional features of the clothes worn by the armed services. In 1942 the British Board of Trade issued a Civilian Clothing Order to save material and labour and increase production. Foremost London-based couturiers of the day, including Norman Hartnell, Hardy Amies (1909–2003), Edward Molyneux (1891–1974) and Digby Morton (1906–83; see p.284), lent their expertise to the project and advised on the design of a collection of four basic lines including a coat, suit, dress (opposite) and blouse, from which thirty-two individual lines were selected for manufacture. More than a hundred British manufacturers placed orders for the patterns and prototypes, which resulted in improved manufacturing and production standards as well as democratizing the notion of good design. In the United States the American War Production Board also imposed restrictions regulating various aspects of clothing manufacture, although they were not as severe as those in Britain.

The wartime women's suit, or costume as it was called, comprised a neatly tailored single-breasted jacket fitted to the waist that stopped just short of the hips and buttoned high to the neck. The skirt was slightly flared and short enough to enable the wearer to ride a bicycle, falling below the knee and cut no wider than 80 inches (203 cm), with a pleat at the back for ease of movement. Any decorative trimmings, top-stitching or pleats were forbidden, flap pockets replaced patch pockets, and no more than three buttons were allowed on a jacket. The manufacture of metal zips was severely restricted in the United States and Europe, resulting in button fastenings. Fabric dyes were also re-routed to the war effort; civilian garments came in subfusc colours such as air-force blue and army tan. In addition to the formal tailored suit, other practical garments, such as the utility siren suit (above right), were introduced. For the first time it was acceptable for women to wear male tailored slacks in daily life; these aided mobility and removed the need for stockings.

As austerity increased so did ingenuity. Posters urged US women to 'Remember Pearl Harbor and Purl Harder' to produce knitted socks and blankets for the forces. In response to the British government edict in 1943 to 'make do and mend', advertisements in magazines and propaganda cinema clips promoted the idea of recycling textiles. Designers on both sides of the Atlantic responded to the challenge by reworking mundane materials. Shoe designers utilized plaited raffia and cork to construct platform and wedge heels with a newly fashionable open toe, although these were banned on the factory floor. Hair was constrained under a turban (right) during the day, but off-duty the severe tailored silhouette was offset by elaborate hats constructed from spotted net, veiling and feathers, with a snood at the back to hold the hair in place. **MF**

1942	1942	1943	1943	1944	1949
The Incorporated Society of London Fashion Designers is founded to promote and support the interests of London couturiers.	The American War Production Board imposes the L85 laws regulating various aspects of clothing manufacture.	Muriel King creates a collection of clothes called Flying Fortress Fashions for female factory workers at Boeing and other West Coast aerospace firms.	Adrian (1903–59) influences the design of the victory suit, the US version of Britain's utility suit.	The first French couture collections are presented since the beginning of the war, with American GIs invited to the shows.	The rationing of clothing in Britain is brought to an end.

DESIGN IN ADVERSITY

Wartime Tailoring 1940s
DIGBY MORTON 1906–83

Fashion Is Indestructible by Cecil Beaton (1941).

NAVIGATOR

Locating fashion firmly in the landscape of urban, war-damaged London, photographer Cecil Beaton captures the dichotomy of the well-dressed woman at a time of conflict. Combining his role as photographer, recording images from the home front for the Ministry of Information during World War II, with his commissions for British *Vogue* magazine, Beaton places the model at London's bomb-damaged Middle Temple.

The indefatigability of the human spirit in the face of death and destruction is represented by the upright stance of the model, who turns to face the wreckage of the building rather than staring into the camera. The woman's Digby Morton suit offers a businesslike approach to fashion at a time when utility and practicality were the order of the British government. Morton transforms his signature classic tweed suit, on which he had founded his reputation in the previous decade, into a fashionable garment through the careful placing of seams, preferring to eliminate extraneous detail rather than decorate. This was an aesthetic that lent itself to wartime restrictions and a need for sobriety. To be well dressed in the face of adversity was a recognized morale booster and almost a civic duty, hence the carefully dressed pageboy style under the neat forward-tilting hat, and the matching gloves and flat-heeled shoes. **MF**

FOCAL POINTS

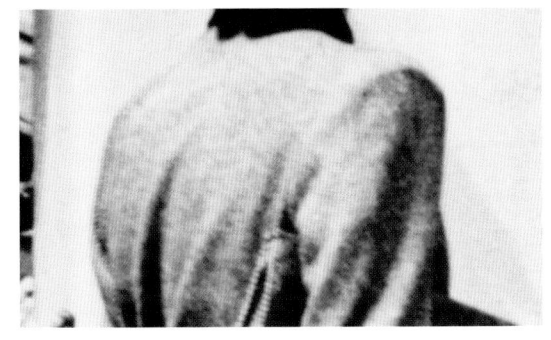

1 SQUARED-OFF SHOULDER
The turn of the model's shoulders as she halts to gaze at the bomb-damaged building replicates the masculine silhouette of the upturned triangle. This effect is increased by the light padding of the sleeves of the jacket that fall from the edge of the shoulder.

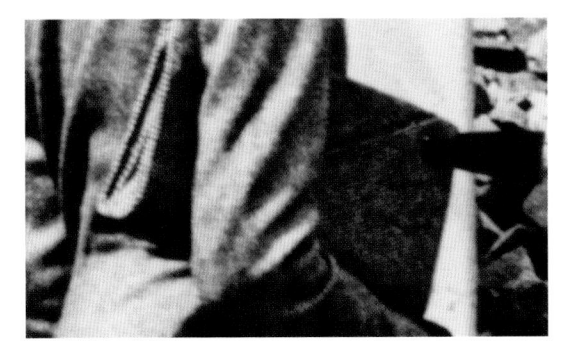

3 INDENTED WAIST
The angular lines of the suit are feminized by the indentation at the fitted waist, which is formed by subtle darting and seaming. This creates ease of movement across the back in contrast to the taut fit of the jacket on the hips.

2 FUNCTIONAL ACCESSORY
The woman carries an unadorned businesslike fold-over clutch bag, tucked under one arm, which leaves her hands free but is large enough to contain the important papers of her daily work. By law, she should also have been carrying a gas mask.

DESIGNER PROFILE

1906–32
Dublin-born designer Henry Digby Morton studied at the Metropolitan School of Art and Architecture before moving to London in 1928, where he worked as a sketch artist for Jay's fashion store before founding the tailoring firm Lachasse.

1933–83
In 1933 Digby Morton established his eponymous house, thus confirming his reputation for tailoring. Together with several other British couturiers, Morton formed the Incorporated Society of London Fashion Designers in 1942, and in 1947 he established an export branch of the Digby Morton business, which enabled him to market his clothes to the United States. In 1957 the couture house closed, and from 1958 to 1973 Morton worked for Reldan-Digby Morton, which produced classic sportswear.

AMERICAN HAUTE COUTURE

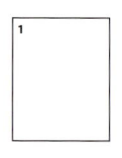

1. Horst P. Horst's iconic photograph for the September 1939 issue of *Vogue* features the back-laced corset designed by Detolle for Mainbocher.

2. Charles James's voluminous four-leaf clover ball gown (1953)—made from silk-satin, silk lace and copper silk shantung—weighed some 15 pounds (5.5 kg).

While US female designers were developing an idiomatic style of ready-to-wear clothes for women's expanding corporate and social worlds, with the emphasis on function and versatility, US male designers such as Mainbocher (1891–1976), Charles James (1906–78) and James Galanos (b.1924; see p.290) concentrated on luxurious, spectacular haute couture. Both Mainbocher and James introduced rigid understructures to their ball gowns, which featured the corseted waist and defined bosom that offered an abrupt shift in silhouette from the more relaxed and sport-influenced garments of the era. Their designs were adopted by New York society women, including the influential paradigms of style Babe Paley and C. Z. Guest.

KEY EVENTS

1937	1939	1940	1941–45	1943	1946
Charles James has his first showing in Paris; it includes garments that feature vintage silk ribbons from the firm Colcombet.	The corset that shaped Mainbocher's last Parisian collection is immortalized by one of Horst P. Horst's best-known photographs.	James moves to New York and opens Charles James, Inc. at 64 East 57th Street.	*Vogue*'s subscriptions surge during World War II under the editorship of noted critic and former *Vanity Fair* editor Frank Crowninshield.	The American Fashion Critics' Awards are first announced by the cosmetics and perfume company Coty, Inc. to promote and celebrate US fashion.	'Théâtre de la Mode' (Theatre of Fashion), a touring exhibit of miniature fashion mannequins by top Paris fashion designers, visits New York.

Mainbocher founded his couture house in 1929 and established himself as a dressmaker throughout the 1930s; in 1937 he was commissioned to design the wedding outfit for Wallis Simpson on her marriage to the former King Edward VIII (see p.288). He began to collaborate with the Warner Brothers Corset Company after the introduction of his Mainbocher corset (opposite) in his final Parisian collection of 1939. This wasp-waisted silhouette presaged the return to the 19th-century crinoline shape that was to re-emerge after World War II, promulgated by Christian Dior (1905–57) and his New Look. In 1940 Mainbocher left occupied Paris to move back to the United States and open what was considered to be the most prestigious and expensive couture house in New York. Throughout the war he consolidated his reputation for discreet luxury, deploying sumptuous materials for casual garments. The inherent theatricality of his designs was harnessed for his many commissions for Broadway shows including *Blithe Spirit* (1941) and *Call Me Madam* (1950).

English-born Charles James had a similarly theatrical approach to fashion. He had no formal design training and began his fashion career making and designing hats. James established his first couture house in the 1930s in London, where he developed all the signature design elements that he continued to rework throughout his career, producing key pieces such as the Corselette or Sylphide evening dress (1937), the body-hugging Sirene evening dress with pleated front panel (1938) and a raised pouf-fronted gown (1939). In 1940 James relocated to New York and, after designing a collection for cosmetics mogul Elizabeth Arden between 1943 and 1945, opened his atelier at 699 Madison Avenue in 1945. With an unorthodox approach based on mathematical concepts that pushed the boundaries of conventional fashion, James was celebrated for the spectacularly engineered evening wear that he produced between 1947 and 1954. His aesthetic incorporated rigid under-structures, often modelled on Victorian prototypes, in weighty materials and lustrous textures such as heavy faille and velvet.

The garment for which James is best known is the four-leaf clover gown (right), first produced in 1953. The bodice, made from ivory duchesse satin, has a rigid infrastructure of buckram, horsehair and covered wire, designed to support the vast overskirt. The skirt is engineered to rest on the hips and distribute its great weight. During the 1950s James developed ready-to-wear lines, but found it difficult to confine his talents within mass-market limitations. His solution was to sell original models to Lord & Taylor and Saks Fifth Avenue for them to create patterns from which to make copies. **MF**

1948	1950	1951	1951	1952	1953
Millicent Huddleston Rogers, a Standard Oil heiress, organizes an exhibition of Charles James's work at the Brooklyn Museum, New York.	James wins the first of his two Coty awards, for his 'great mystery of colour and artistry of draping'.	James works with mannequin manufacturer Cavanaugh Form Company to produce a papier-mâché dress form.	James Galanos launches his own label; it is followed a year later by his New York debut.	Charles James designs collections of separates for Seventh Avenue manufacturer Samuel Winston, retailed by Lord & Taylor.	James makes the four-leaf clover gown for Austine Hearst for the Eisenhower inaugural ball. It is not ready in time so she wears it for Queen Elizabeth's ball.

AMERICAN HAUTE COUTURE

Wedding Dress of the Duchess of Windsor 1937
MAINBOCHER 1891–1976

Wedding portrait of the Duke and
Duchess of Windsor by Cecil Beaton (1937).

Twice-married Wallis Warfield Simpson was renowned for her hard-edged chic, unchanging raven's-wing hairstyle and the motto: 'It's impossible to be too rich or too thin.' When she became engaged to the former King Edward VIII—the couple were later to be known as the Duke and Duchess of Windsor—she chose Mainbocher to design her outfit. A US-born couturier, who was based in Paris at the time of the wedding, he specialized in simple, conservative, elegant and extremely expensive fashions, and designed a dress that combined decorum with simplicity.

The long column of the dress has a bias-cut skirt and it is worn with a matching jacket cropped at the waist. The fullness of the bodice adds shape to Wallis's slender form and is gathered gently into the high neckline. The narrow set-in sleeves are slightly padded and gathered into the shoulder. Edna Woolman Chase, then editor of US *Vogue*, did not approve. She wrote in her autobiography *Always in Vogue* (1954): 'The Duchess has many exquisite gowns in her wardrobe but, candidly, for such an occasion as her wedding to a former English king, I think she and Mainbocher might have done better. The gown is a perfectly straight, full-length, skimpy affair of pale grey-blue crêpe...with a tight little uneventful jacket, and dull it is to look at.' Mainbocher also designed Wallis's trousseau. **MF**

NAVIGATOR

FOCAL POINTS

1 STANDING COLLAR
The collar of the dress is cut into two crescent shapes, tapering towards the centre front and the shoulder seam. The gathers at the neckline are draped from either side of the bodice, thus creating an almost halter-shaped silhouette.

3 BESPOKE JEWELS
Wallis wears a diamond charm bracelet with nine crosses, each with an inscription of a significant event in the couple's lives. She disliked her hands and had matching gloves especially made to accommodate her wedding ring.

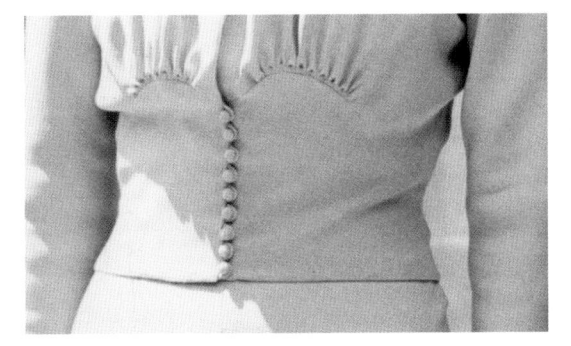

2 JACKET DETAILING
The heart-shaped midriff section of the bride's jacket is brought together at the centre front with a vertical row of close-set covered buttons and rouleaux loops. The hem of the jacket sits neatly just below the waist.

DESIGNER PROFILE

1891–1939
Born in Chicago, Main Rousseau Bocher (Mainbocher) spent his early years in the United States but remained in Paris after his demobilization from the US army in 1918. He joined French *Vogue* in 1923, after working for *Harper's Bazar* as a sketcher, and was appointed editor-in-chief in 1927 before deciding that he would rather design than select clothes. In 1929 he opened a couture salon on avenue George V, Paris.

1940–76
In 1940 Mainbocher moved to New York and opened his salon on 6 East 57th Street, where he produced his first US-designed collection of haute couture. He moved to the KLM Building on Fifth Avenue in 1961 and continued working until 1971. At the age of eighty-one, he closed the doors of his fashion house and died in Munich five years later.

AMERICAN HAUTE COUTURE

Striped Evening Dress 1955
JAMES GALANOS b. 1924

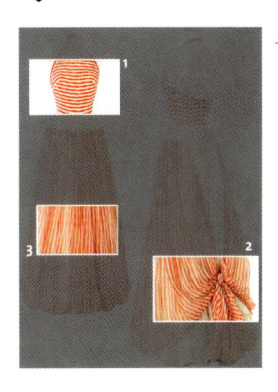

P oised between pre-war US couturiers such as Mainbocher and Norman Norell (1900–72), and the later modernism of Roy Halston Frowick (1932–90) and Geoffrey Beene (1927–2004), James Galanos established a career in the 1950s that continued for several decades. Promulgator of structured and decorative evening wear at a time when French couture was dominant, Galanos was renowned for the meticulous craftsmanship and hand work that emerged from his Southern Californian workshop, on a par with the French couturier's atelier. His initial reputation was made on his dextrous use of silk chiffon, evident here in the red-and-white-striped evening dress.

The irregularity of the wavy stripes, the bare-backed halter-neck redolent of the bathing costume and the tie at the hem all lend the dress an air of nautical informality in spite of the adherence to the hourglass silhouette that was prevalent at the time. Cut to beneath the shoulder blades to expose the back, the line continues around the front to form a narrow halter-neck, fastening at the nape and aligned to the centre-back zip. Silk chiffon is gathered into a seam on the natural waist, falling in loose folds to the hem, and resulting in yards of hand-rolled edges. Superimposed on the surface of the dress is an overskirt that finishes halfway between the side seams and the centre back. **MF**

NAVIGATOR

FOCAL POINTS

1 BODICE
Perfectly aligned side seams feature on the bodice of the dress, which is formed from horizontally striped silk crêpe. The lines of the stripes are distorted at an angle where the bust dart has been inserted.

3 PRINTED STRIPES
The overskirt fabric is printed in the same equidistant narrow wavy stripes as the silk crêpe of the bodice. The gossamer transparency of the chiffon reveals the stripes underneath, creating a subtle chequered effect.

DESIGNER PROFILE

1924–50
Philadelphia-born James Galanos studied at the Traphagen School of Fashion, New York, from 1942 to 1943. He began his career as a general assistant to Hattie Carnegie in New York from 1944 to 1945 and briefly worked as a sketch artist for Jean Louis at Columbia Pictures in Hollywood. Having moved to Paris in 1946, he worked as an apprentice designer to the couture house Robert Piguet, leaving in 1948 to return to New York.

1951–PRESENT
Galanos launched the label Galanos Originals in 1951 and showed in New York the following year. He became particularly well known for his exquisite silk chiffon dresses. Galanos won many awards, including the Coty American Fashion Critics' Award in 1954 and 1956, and the Coty American Hall of Fame Award in 1959. He retired in the late 1990s.

2 NAUTICAL THEME
The edges of the silk chiffon overskirt are gathered together at mid calf and tied in a knot, thus replicating a displaced middy collar. The term 'middy' derives from 'midshipman', a student at a naval academy, and is used to describe a sailor collar.

AFRICAN AMERICAN FASHIONS

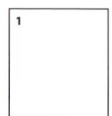

1 A couple dressed in customary swing dance styles. The girl's dress is made from a stretchy fabric to allow ease of movement.

2 A young black woman dressed in a slim-fitting skirt suit wears the obligatory hat, gloves and fur stole to complete the outfit.

Looking back at the United States' recent history, it is clear that the 1940s was an important decade of transformation for minority groups and the disenfranchised. The outbreak and culmination of World War II impacted on the lives of African American citizens in unprecedented ways, paving the way for racial integration, the Civil Rights Movement, and, on the whole, a closer consideration of US citizenship and its true meaning. Much-anticipated change was in the air and as such a manifestation of music, street fashion, style and attitude collided, creating a template for what is now recognized as urban culture.

As the 20th century progressed, demographic shifts occurred within the United States that saw the migration of many black Americans from the rural Southern states to industrial Northern cities. This movement heralded a cultural revolution as music forms born of the black Southern experience—primarily jazz and the blues—became the basis for the big band and swing

KEY EVENTS

1940	1941	1942	1943	1943	1943
Seventy-five years after the end of slavery Hattie McDaniel becomes the first African American to win an Oscar for *Gone With the Wind*.	Jazz singer Billie Holiday's 'God Bless the Child' is ranked third in Britain's top songs of the year.	Langston Hughes's poem 'The Negro Speaks of Rivers' is set to music. The proceeds finance the publication of music by African American composers.	US newspapers carry reports of 'zoot suit riots' between white US servicemen and Latinos, although other minorities are also involved.	Jazz trumpeter Dizzy Gillespie joins the Earl Hines band, which is credited with developing the jazz form bebop.	US jazz singer Cab Calloway raises the profile of the zoot suit by wearing one in the 20th Century Fox musical hit *Stormy Weather*.

292 1900–45

styles that dominated US popular music in the 1940s. The ghetto-ized nature of US society meant that city neighbourhoods were often organized along racial and ethnic lines, and predominately black areas such as the Harlem district of New York saw an outpouring of black sounds, black dance forms and black fashions. However, the single object that defined the African American urban experience during the 1940s was the zoot suit (see p.294). 'Zoot' is a reduplication of the word 'suit' and its etymology lay in the rhyming slang that was a feature of Harlem life in the early years of the 20th century, when 'zoot' was a term of approval used to describe anything 'cool'.

Jitterbug, like the later 20th-century term 'hip hop', became a catch-all phrase to describe non-choreographed dance moves matched to a specific look, style and behaviour that marked out this nascent black urban culture. Similarly born from the swing era, the lindy hop brought excitement to dance floors all around the United States, with performers at Harlem's integrated Savoy Ballroom delighting a crowd that included white spectators who watched the acrobatic abilities of the skilled lindy hoppers in awe. During wartime rationing, the outfit of choice for a female lindy hopper would have been a pared-down rayon or synthetic jersey dress in a slim, streamlined silhouette (opposite); rayon was popular because it did not crease and contained a silklike quality that enabled day-to-evening dressing. A bolero or fitted jacket was a fashionable addition to any swing dancer's wardrobe, creating multiple looks.

This 'make do and mend' attitude did not extend to post-war fashions for women, who started to look to Paris, specifically Dior's New Look, for inspiration in dressing (right). A fashion designer who particularly appreciated this new aesthetic was Anne Cole Lowe (1898–1981), hailed as the first black designer to be part of the fashion establishment. Known for her couture-style clothing offered at a fraction of usual Paris couture prices, Lowe built an illustrious client list that included the Vanderbilts and the Roosevelts. The Alabama-born designer grew up among luxurious gowns as her mother and grandmother made ball gowns for Southern belles. Attending fashion school in New York brought its challenges, with the director mocking the idea of her attendance; however, Cole persisted and Jacqueline Bouvier opted to wear one of her designs on the day of her marriage to John F. Kennedy.

Another black designer of the era who made fashion history was Zelda Wynn Valdes (1905–2001), who was not only the first black designer to open her own shop, but also the first black owner of a business on Broadway. Hailing from Pennsylvania, she developed her love of fashion from studying her grandmother's work as a seamstress and working in her uncle's tailoring shop. She is well known for dressing both black and white stars, including Josephine Baker, Ella Fitzgerald and Mae West, in jaw-dropping, figure-hugging gowns. Valdes also created the original costumes for the Playboy Bunnies and was appointed head costume designer for the Dance Theater of Harlem. **RA/WH**

1945	1946	1946	1947	1948	1948
Ella Fitzgerald records 'Flying Home', which the *New York Times* later declares one of the most influential vocal jazz records of the 1940s.	African American fashion designer Anne Cole Lowe designs the dress worn by film star Olivia de Havilland at the Academy Awards.	Black workers at the Piedmont Leaf tobacco plant in North Carolina go on strike, leading to the emergence of the Civil Rights Movement.	Louis Armstrong debuts with his All Stars Band in Hollywood.	African American fashion designer Zelda Wynn Valdes opens her first shop, Chez Zelda, on Broadway, New York.	African American artist Norman Lewis paints *Jazz Musicians*, which marks a move away from formal painting towards abstraction.

Zoot Suit 1940s
MEN'S SUIT

Two teenagers dressed
in zoot suits (1943).

NAVIGATOR

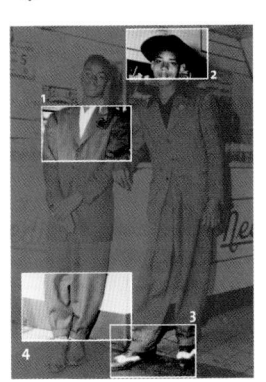

The zoot suit is a fascinating subcultural element that predicted the rise and influence of urban street styles. Although varying in stylistic details, the basic template remained fixed: extremely baggy, and tapering at the waist and trouser cuff. Excessive use of cloth was essential. The zoot suit gave a sense of pride and presence to the wearer while challenging the mores and assumptions of the majority, who saw zoot style as antisocial, conspicuously defiant, and associated with delinquency and criminality. The United States' entry into the war galvanized public opinion against 'zoots' when clothes rationing was introduced; those wearing zoot suits were castigated for being unpatriotic. Moreover, the sight of young black men dressed in garish suits bred resentment. US society in the 1940s was deeply divided along racial lines, with an expectation that blacks should be docile, servile and respectful of whites. This led to an explosion of violence in 1943, in what the newspapers termed the 'zoot suit riots': caught by white vigilante gangs, 'zoots' were not only savagely beaten but often stripped of their suits and left bloodied in the streets. Malcolm Little, who would go on to reinvent himself as the political radical Malcolm X, was a youthful 'zoot', whose early life as a petty criminal and street hustler typified the suit's ne'er-do-well associations. **RA/WH**

FOCAL POINTS

1 LONG JACKET
The broad-shouldered jacket tapers in a low-slung style to mid-thigh level. Single-breasted with three buttons, the jacket also features padded shoulders. Zoot suits were often made from an exaggerated pinstripe or loud check.

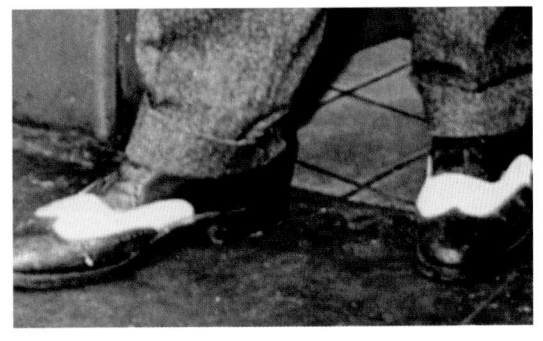

3 OXFORD BROGUES
Oxford brogues, with decorative perforated toe caps, were worn in the popular contrasting black-and-white two-tone style. Accessories, such as key fobs, were always worn in an overt, showy manner and constituted an important feature of the overall look.

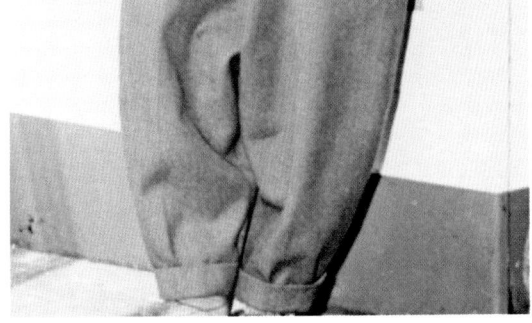

2 WIDE-BRIMMED HAT
Worn tipped back from the forehead, the formal, black felt, wide-brimmed hat makes a clear statement, announcing the wearer's presence and referencing the style of gangsters from the Prohibition era of the 1920s.

4 BAGGY TROUSERS
Excessively baggy and voluminous in the leg, the trousers incorporate an extremely high waistline. Held in place with suspenders (braces), the trousers are cut very wide at the top, with a pleated front, and taper at the cuff.

AFRICAN AMERICAN FASHIONS 295

179

5 | 1946 TO 1989

THE GOLDEN AGE OF HAUTE COUTURE 298

COLLEGE AND PREPPY STYLES 308

YOUTHFUL FEMININITY 314

THE HOLLYWOOD IDEAL 320

DAYTIME DECORUM 326

POST-WAR ITALIAN STYLE 334

POST-WAR WORKWEAR 340

MODERN SIMPLICITY 344

TEXTILES OF EASTERN NEPAL 350

THE RETAIL REVOLUTION 354

THE BRITISH MENSWEAR REVOLUTION 364

AFROCENTRIC FASHION 370

FUTURISTIC FASHION 376

THE NEW PRÊT-À-PORTER 382

HIPPIE DELUXE 386

THE STYLISH STITCH 394

ONE-STOP DRESSING 398

MODERN JAPANESE DESIGN 402

GLAM ROCK AND DISCO STYLES 406

MARKETING A LIFESTYLE 412

THE PUNK REVOLUTION 416

FASHION VALKYRIES 420

SECOND-SKIN CLOTHES 424

RADICAL DESIGN 430

DRESSING FOR SUCCESS 436

THE DESIGNER DECADE 442

HIP-HOP CULTURE AND STREET STYLE 446

THE REGENERATION OF COUTURE 450

UNDERWEAR AS OUTERWEAR 460

THE GOLDEN AGE OF HAUTE COUTURE

1 House models wear Christian Dior's spring/summer 1957 collection in *Time* magazine. Photographed by Loomis Dean.

2 Photographed by Willy Maywald, the 'Bar' dress and jacket was the best-seller from Dior's Corolle collection (1947).

3 This sculpted suit by Cristóbal Balenciaga features signature bracelet-length sleeves (1952).

Haute couture is the apotheosis of fashion. It was implemented in Paris in 1858 by British-born dressmaker Charles Frederick Worth (1825–95), and the city remained the undisputed leader of fashion until World War II, when the occupation by German troops threatened its survival. However, returning prosperity was nurtured in the ruins of Europe's cities by the rebirth of the fashion and textile industries. When Christian Dior (1905–57) launched his couture collection in Paris in 1947 he acknowledged the optimism of the era with his New Look (see p.302), which, despite the elitist overtones of haute couture, entered the common psyche as an icon of a better future.

Dior possessed an aesthetic that was resonant with 19th-century influences (above), including the use of structured fabrics, such as duchesse satin and jacquard wools, and a predilection for the corseted female body. He wrote: 'I designed clothes for flower-like women, with rounded shoulders, full feminine

KEY EVENTS

1946	1947	1948	1948	1949	1951
Christian Dior establishes his fashion house in Paris and presents his first collection the following year.	Dior is the first Frenchman to win the Neiman Marcus Award for Distinguished Service in the Field of Fashion.	Jacques Fath is accompanied by his wife on a promotional tour of the United States, after which sales at his Paris salon quadruple.	The first fashion faculty at London's Royal College of Art opens. It is headed by Professor Madge Garland.	Wartime clothing rations are lifted in Britain.	The Festival of Britain is launched. It is a government-sponsored celebration of the best of British design, art and industry.

busts and handspan waists above enormous spreading skirts. An ethereal appearance is only achieved by elaborate workmanship.' This workmanship was undertaken in the couturier's atelier, which was divided into dressmaking, a traditionally female activity, and tailoring, usually undertaken by men. These were supplemented by the artisans of the ateliers: embroiderers, *plumassiers*, furriers, and specialists in *passementerie* (decorative trimming) and leatherwork.

The couture garment was developed either from sketches or from draping the cloth on the body or mannequin. A couturier was allowed to employ *modélistes* to help with the design but could not buy designs from outside the house. The designer then chose the cloth from various swatches presented by the textile manufacturers, together with trimmings, such as buckles and buttons, which then became exclusive to them. The design would be given to the *première d'atelier* who was in charge of the workroom where the *petites mains* (seamstresses) worked around small tables. The sketch was developed into a calico toile and fitted on an in-house model before being made up in the chosen material. The salon was run by the *vendeuse* (saleswoman) who developed a relationship with the client and negotiated the fitting schedule.

Strict new regulations for membership of the Chambre Syndicale de la Haute Couture (defined as 'the regulating commission that determines which fashion houses are eligible to be true haute couture houses') were implemented in 1945. These required that the designer maintain appropriate premises in Paris, with a suitable ambience to show the biannual collections, and provide private space for fittings, as well as enough room for a studio and workrooms. The collections had to comprise at least seventy-five made-to-measure original designs, each requiring a minimum of three fittings. Although private clients fuelled the prestige of haute couture, commercial buyers, who purchased either a toile for reproduction or a garment to be retailed elsewhere, took precedence at the shows, with North American buyers first, followed by European buyers and lastly private clients. These showings were conducted in the greatest secrecy, with no press access allowed for three weeks.

From the establishment of his couture house in 1946 to his sudden death in 1957, Dior remained the leading protagonist of mid-century haute couture. His New Look was one of fashion's defining moments and consolidated the influence of Paris and the haute couture system. The 'Bar', a dress and jacket, was one of the best-selling items of the ground-breaking collection (above right). The mid-calf black wool skirt featured deep knife pleats, and was partnered with a pale shantung jacket fitted to the waist. The rounded shoulder line, cinched-in waist and convex sculpted skirt of the jacket, worn over the padding on the hips, epitomized the new femininity.

Cristóbal Balenciaga (1895–1972) also reigned supreme at the zenith of haute couture (right). Starting in a small atelier in San Sebastián, Spain, before going on to open his Parisian couture house in 1937, Balenciaga had no interest

1952	1953	1953	1954	1957	1959–60
Hardy Amies becomes the first London couturier to show a collection in New York.	Norman Hartnell designs the dress for the coronation of Elizabeth II.	Pierre Balmain expands into the US market under the brand name Jolie Madame.	Dior develops the A-line, a term that enters the fashion lexicon to describe a narrow-shouldered silhouette that flares out towards the hem.	Elizabeth II wears a Hartnell gown called the 'Flowers of the Fields of France' for her state visit to Paris.	Hardy Amies serves as chairman of the Incorporated Society of London Fashion Designers, founded in 1942 to promote British couture.

THE GOLDEN AGE OF HAUTE COUTURE 299

in influencing current trends or developing a ready-to-wear line, preferring to focus the purity of his vision on the bespoke. He explored innovative cutting techniques that centred on the position of the sleeve, and mastered the art of cutting it in one with the yoke while retaining freedom of movement for the wearer. In opposition to Dior, whose silhouette was predicated on an infrastructure that exploited the breasts and hips, Balenciaga focused on the woman's shoulders and pelvis for a resolutely modern approach to couture (see p.306). The theatricality of Balenciaga's clothes was leavened by an austere architectural quality: collars were cut to stand away from the neck, sleeves were shortened to bracelet length and heavily textured fabrics were moulded to skim the body, resulting in a serene simple line with minimal unobtrusive seaming that formed an elegant carapace. During the 1950s he created a new silhouette, broadening the shoulders and relinquishing any emphasis on the waist, ultimately producing the influential chemise, or sack dress, in 1958.

Together with Dior and Balenciaga, Pierre Balmain (1914–82) formed the post-war nexus of the revived French couture industry. Prior to opening his own house, Balmain was apprenticed to couturier Edward Molyneux (1891–1974) in Paris for five years before working alongside Dior at the couture house of Lucien Lelong between 1939 and 1944. He opened Maison Balmain in 1945. During the 1950s Balmain designed simple, elegant clothes, specializing in slimline dress and jacket combinations, and draped and pleated evening wear in decorative, printed and embellished embroidered fabrics (left). These were popular with European royalty and Hollywood stars such as Ava Gardner and Katharine Hepburn. Balmain is also credited with the popularization of the stole as an accessory for both day and evening, and often included fur trims on his day garments. Equally significant in the revival of post-war couture was French-born Jacques Fath (1912–54), but his untimely death resulted in the closure of his house and a lessening of the impact of his brief successful reign as one of the major influences of the period. He established his couture house in rue de la Boétie, Paris, showing a first collection of twenty garments. After a brief period in the French army he moved his house to avenue Pierre 1er de Serbie in 1937. Fath was a master of self-publicity and an astute businessman: in 1948 he signed a contract with US wholesale manufacturer Joseph Halpert to design several collections a year to be marketed in major department stores throughout the United States. In 1953 he also introduced Université, a ready-to-wear line, sponsored by textile manufacturers Jean Provost, using the sophisticated mass-production methods developed pre-war in the United States. Renowned for their glamorous style, his garments followed the lines of the body with flaring drapery (right), which was particularly evident in the costumes he designed for ballerina Moira Shearer in the popular film *The Red Shoes* (1948).

Couturier Jean Dessès (1904–70) offered a more sculptural aesthetic, exploring the draping and pleating of his Greek heritage with precisely positioned twists, swags and folds in silk chiffon evening dresses (opposite below). Although he designed for a small couture house in Paris in the 1920s, and opened his own house in 1937, it was not until the post-war years and the 1950s that his work gained recognition. He also produced a ready-to-wear line, Jean Dessès Diffusion, in 1949, but by 1965 had closed his couture operation.

London's couture industry was established after World War I, although the designers were known as court dressmakers rather than couturiers. Their clients were the upper classes who required appropriate clothing for the social round of the London season, such as the presentation of debutantes at court and society weddings. The Incorporated Society of London Fashion Designers, established in 1942, was based on the Paris haute couture system but state sponsorship of luxury trades that had existed in Paris since the late 17th century did not apply to British couturiers. Their tradition was rooted in the tailoring skills of Savile Row. Couturiers such as Victor Stiebel (1907–76), Charles Creed (1906–66) and Digby Morton (1906–83) were all renowned for the quality of their tailored tweeds. Both Hardy Amies (1909–2003; see p.304), who opened his house in 1946, and Norman Hartnell (1901–79) achieved recognition for their role as designers for Elizabeth, queen consort of George VI, and later her daughter Elizabeth II. The state visit by the king and queen consort to France in the early summer of 1938 provided Norman Hartnell with the opportunity to showcase his designs in Paris. At the request of the king, Hartnell designed a collection of dresses inspired by the painting by Franz Xaver Winterhalter of Empress Elisabeth of Austria, wearing her spangled tulle crinoline dress. The death of the queen consort's mother, three weeks before the visit, resulted in all the gowns being remade in white, a royal prerogative for mourning. The all-white dresses, composed of Valenciennes lace, silk, satin, velvet, taffeta, tulle and chiffon, became the hallmark of both the queen consort and the couturier, the culmination of which was the design for Princess Elizabeth's dress when she married Prince Philip of Greece in 1947, followed six years later by her coronation robes. The lavish embellishment of these and other formal gowns was produced in-house, rather than outsourced to an atelier.

During the 1950s the demand for haute couture began to decline. Together with couturiers including Jean Dessès and Robert Piguet (1901–53), Jacques Fath founded Les Couturiers associés—a precursor to the creation of prêt-à-porter—and began selling directly to French department stores. The House of Dior continued after the death of Christian Dior thanks to a prior commitment to products manufactured under franchise and the previous formation of independent companies that had to be upheld. The young Yves Saint Laurent (1936–2008) took Dior's place as design head of the house in 1958 marking the arrival of a more contemporary and iconoclastic generation of couturiers, among them Hubert de Givenchy (b.1927) and Pierre Cardin (b.1922). **MF**

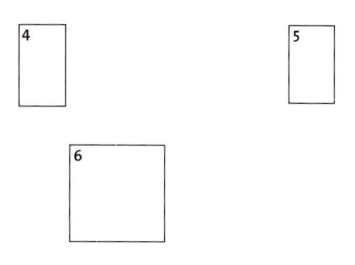

4 This printed silk cocktail gown by Balmain has a shirred bodice and balloon-shaped skirt (1957).

5 A fashion illustration from 1952 shows a dress with a crossover, draped bodice designed by Jacques Fath.

6 Photographed by Norman Parkinson, Jean Dessès's romantic evening dress combines three shades of one hue, twisted together in fluid pleats and gathers (1950).

New Look 1947
CHRISTIAN DIOR 1905–57

Renée, 'The New Look of Dior', Place de la Concorde, Paris, August 1947,
photograph by Richard Avedon © The Richard Avedon Foundation.

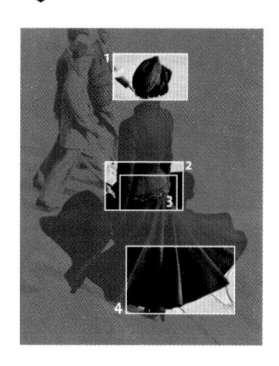

Christian Dior's radical Corolle line, so-called after the botanical term denoting open petals, heralded a new era of luxuriousness when it was unveiled in February 1947. The collection celebrated the return of the hourglass figure, in contrast to the masculine silhouette of uniform-inspired clothes. It was instantly dubbed the 'New Look' by Carmel Snow, editor of US *Harper's Bazaar* magazine, which published a series of sketches detailing the construction of the garments.

Dior's commitment to the lavish use of textiles—the house was financed by textile manufacturer Marcel Boussac—combined with an adherence to a romantic and nostalgic view of femininity that was resonant of the Belle Epoque resulted in a collection that created a furore in the fashion press and spearheaded the post-war revival of Paris as the centre of international fashion. Enlivening the sculptural qualities of the structured suit, photographer Richard Avedon captures the model, Renée, in fluid movement walking along the Place de la Concorde, Paris, to the admiration of male passers-by. The gores of the skirt flare out from the hip to the widening hem, which ends just above the suede court shoes with conical heels. The model carries a black astrakhan muff, a popular accessory of the era that matches the trim of the jacket. **MF**

NAVIGATOR

FOCAL POINTS

1 HAT
A military-inspired hat in fabric matching that of the jacket is positioned at an angle towards the side and back of the head. The model's hair is perfectly coiffed and clears the back of the high-fitting, fur-trimmed collar.

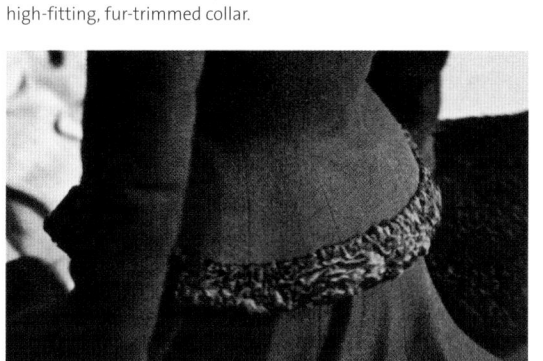

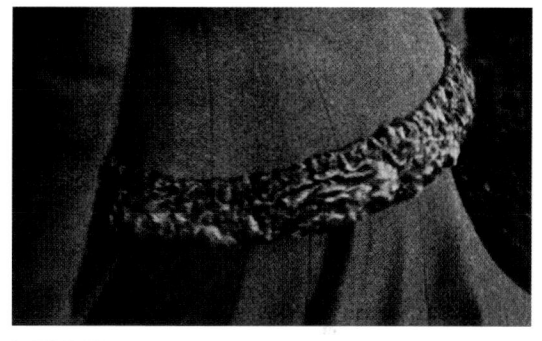

3 FUR TRIM
A narrow band of astrakhan decorates the collar and the hem of the jacket. Astrakhan fur—originally derived from the karakul lamb of Central Asia—has a distinctive tight, whorled, loopy surface with a slight sheen. Black was considered the most desirable colour.

2 HOURGLASS SILHOUETTE
Combining padding over the bust and hips, a judicious mix of seams and darts, and the use of interlining, whalebone and wire to constrict the waist, Dior revisits the popular 19th-century crinoline silhouette.

4 HEMLINE
Worn over stiffened petticoats and with the hemline falling almost to the ankle, the voluminous skirts utilized up to 45 feet (13.5 m) of fabric. The look was denounced by a British MP, Mabel Ridealgh, as 'a stupidly exaggerated use of material'.

Cumberland Tweed Suit 1950
HARDY AMIES 1909 — 2003

NAVIGATOR

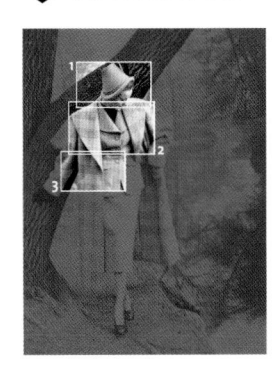

This tweed suit by Hardy Amies acknowledges the tailoring heritage of Savile Row in Mayfair, London, while retaining city sophistication. Renowned for his curvaceous tailoring, Amies created a mid-calf, slim pencil skirt that followed the prevailing hourglass silhouette, although it is slightly easier in shape than its Parisian counterpart. The three-button fastening starts on the waist and ends in a shallow 'V' opening, from which the outsize rounded revers fold over in a softened roll. The large-scale patch pockets are rounded to match and placed close to the centre-front opening, decorated with an ogee-shaped flap sited at the waist.

In contrast to the form-fitting suit, the matching checked coat is cut wide at the shoulders with deep dolman sleeves, cut on the cross of the fabric to juxtapose the horizontal checks of the body of the coat with the diagonal checks of the sleeves. The oversized shawl collar falls to the waist in line with the lower button of the jacket, making it the focal point of the ensemble. The slanted vertical pockets at hip level are without flaps: an element of minimalism that is reflected in the simple wraparound style of the coat. The 1950s was an era that demanded full accessories, and the suit and coat are worn with a hat and matching black leather court shoes and black suede gloves. **MF**

FOCAL POINTS

1 FELT HAT
A felt woollen hat fashioned into the shape of an upturned plant pot perches on the side of the head with a small brim that curves onto the cheek. A jaunty feather is tucked into the hatband, referencing the countryside aspect of the ensemble.

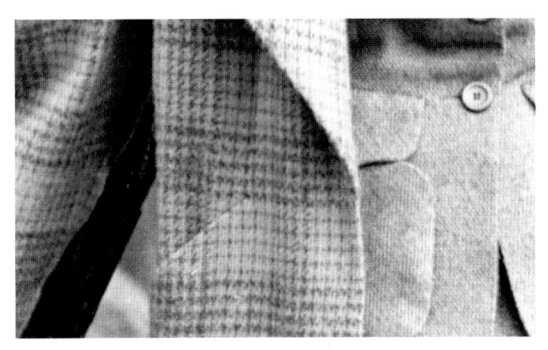

3 TRADITIONAL TWEEDS
The window-pane checks of the coat are matched harmoniously to the smooth-faced tweed of the suit. British couturiers were globally renowned for their use of handwoven and indigenous textiles, particularly those from the north of Scotland.

2 ALL-ENVELOPING COLLAR
Folded back from the waist, the shawl lapel—also called a roll collar or shawl collar—is unnotched and cut in one smooth, continuous curve from the centre front with a small rise at the back of the neck.

DESIGNER PROFILE

1909–44
Born in London, British couturier Hardy Amies secured his first job in fashion in 1934 when he joined the British company Lachasse, for whom he designed bespoke clothes for the British upper classes. After a spell in the army and the Special Operations Executive, he moved to the House of Worth in 1941.

1945–2003
In 1945 Amies set up his own label on Savile Row, and Hardy Amies went on to become the most internationally successful couture house in Britain. In 1952 he was appointed dressmaker to the queen and continued in this role until 1990. His long and successful association with British menswear manufacturers Hepworth's began in the late 1950s and led to a number of licensing agreements throughout the world. Amies retired from fashion in 2001.

THE GOLDEN AGE OF HAUTE COUTURE

Evening Dress with Ruffled Underskirt 1951
CRISTÓBAL BALENCIAGA 1895 – 1972

These evening dresses by Balenciaga were
inspired by paintings by Henri de Toulouse-Lautrec.

Admired for his masterful manipulation of fabric, Cristóbal Balenciaga was particularly well known for using textiles that were sculptural in nature, especially silk gazar. This heavy, stiff silk has a resistant quality and matt texture, and the fabric is used here to create the pink ruffled underskirt of the black silk velvet dress. This garment is sculpted to follow the lines of the body to the knee, where the undulating curves extend outwards into a bell shape, ending just above the calf and supported by the stiffened underskirt. The back of the skirt is cut into a deep curve towards the ankle and ends in a centre-back seam, where the cloth is cut on the cross of the weave. This forms a small fishtail train that billows when the wearer moves.

The pared-down design of these evening dresses is typical of the couturier's evolution from the embellished grandeur of his earlier designs, which were resonant of his Spanish heritage, to an almost monastic aesthetic, with the emphasis on form. Previously, etiquette had decreed that arms should remain covered until 8 p.m., but the popularity of the cocktail party in the 1950s, which generally took place between 6 p.m. and 8 p.m., resulted in a plethora of sleeveless and décolleté garments, frequently worn with a pair of over-the-elbow suede gloves and a matching stole. **MF**

NAVIGATOR

FOCAL POINTS

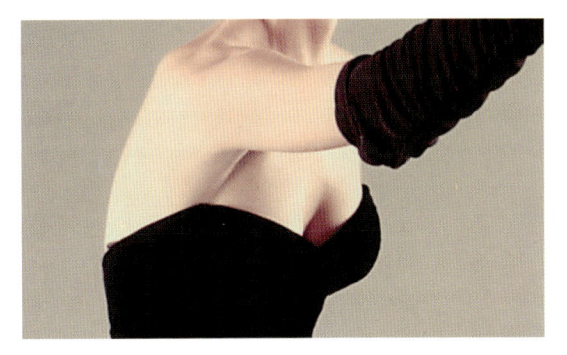

1 CORSETED BODICE
Exposing the shoulders, the bodice of this strapless dress is boned to shape, forming peaks on each side of the breasts that produce a shallow 'V' shape. The line is matched exactly by the top edge of the over-the-elbow gloves.

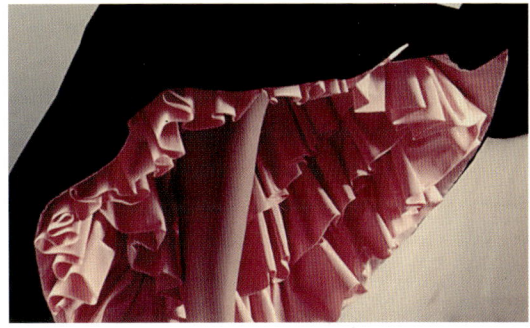

3 CANTILEVERED SKIRT
Balenciaga utilizes the cantilevered skirt to create a sculptural form inspired by the lines and potential for movement inherent in the Spanish flamenco dress. This is evident in the ruffled tiers of silk gazar that make up the underskirt.

2 UNDULATING WAIST SEAM
The waist seam gently undulates to sit in the small of the back and rises slightly at the front to provide a flattering slimmer silhouette on a curvier form. Balenciaga was expert at cutting off a line just before a curve would take the eye into unflattering proportions.

DESIGNER PROFILE

1895–1937
One of the most innovative figures of 20th-century fashion, Cristóbal Balenciaga was born in the Basque village of Getaria, Spain, the son of a talented seamstress. He established the House of Balenciaga in 1937, attracting a sophisticated and dedicated clientele, including royalty and Hollywood stars.

1938–72
Many of Balenciaga's designs were overt allusions to the costumes of the Infanta Maria-Margarita in portraits by Diego Velázquez, and to the toreador's costume, such as the cape and the *borlones* (pompom tassels) of the bolero. By the mid 1950s Balenciaga was established as a revolutionary force in fashion, admired by contemporary designers including Christian Dior. He retired in 1968 and closed his couture houses, but the brand continues.

THE GOLDEN AGE OF HAUTE COUTURE

COLLEGE AND PREPPY STYLES

1. Yale undergraduates wear identikit preppy garb of tartan waistcoats, soft-shouldered sports jackets, 'rep' ties and the obligatory button-down shirts (1950).

2. An Oxbridge university student wears a classic cable-knit cricket jumper (1954).

3. A teenage girl personifies the wholesome preppy look in a plaid skirt, knitted sweater and hairband (1950s).

After World War II, youth subcultures demanded their own unique identity, and for the first time in fashion history young people openly rebelled against wearing the same clothes as their parents. A separate market began to cater specifically for the growing numbers of teenagers who were beginning to define their own distinct image. The 'preppy' style of the period was a carefully constructed look that established an identity for a new generation of style-conscious individuals, retaining their spirit of youth in a manner that lacked the rebellious nature of the rockabilly or the beatnik.

The style took inspiration from the uniforms of the United States' top elite preparatory schools—hence the term 'preppy'—and its foundations can clearly be traced to Britain's most prominent public schools: the pupils of Harrow and Charterhouse, for example, were distinguished by their straw boaters and the house colours that adorned their uniforms. However, there is no mistaking that the preppy look is quintessentially American, a style asserted and celebrated by the young WASPs of the day as a marker of one's national identity and place in US society. It was also known as the 'Ivy look'—after the Ivy League colleges on the East Coast—and the students of single-sex institutions such as Princeton, Harvard, Yale and Dartmouth were famed for sporting ensembles that served as indicators of social, political and economic standing.

KEY EVENTS

Mid to late 1940s	1946	1947	1951	1952	1953
The 'bobbysoxer' look, comprising knee-length skirts and penny loafers, is fashionable with teenage girls (see p.310).	Rationing in the United States ends. Rubber becomes available for shoe soles once again, resulting in renewed tennis shoe production.	The Ivy League tailor Chipp is founded by J. Press alumnus Sidney Winston. The company provides clothing for President Kennedy and his associates.	J. D. Salinger's all-American novel *The Catcher in the Rye* is published, introducing the rebellious prep school protagonist Holden Caulfield.	Lacoste starts to export its ever-popular polo shirts to the United States (see p.254), the embroidered 'croc' logo denoting status and prestige.	Colour television becomes available in the United States, offering viewers a true representation of the colours seen in preppy outfits.

Such an ensemble consisted of a natural shouldered blazer in earthy tones of brown or grey herringbone tweed (opposite), a button-down shirt made of Oxford cloth, a diagonally striped 'rep' tie in tightly woven silk (see p.313) and a pair of flat-fronted trousers in grey flannel or wide ribbed corduroy. Just as important to a true prep was the correct choice of footwear, with loafers and lace-ups in black or brown leather proving highly popular on campus. The Ivy outfitter of choice was the famed heritage menswear company Brooks Brothers, which was founded in 1818 and successfully traded tradition with high-quality bespoke and off-the-peg tailoring. A more casual take on the look included sweaters (right), and specifically Shetland and Fair Isle knits as popularized by Edward, Prince of Wales, in the 1920s. Other favoured items were all-cotton polo shirts with cap sleeves, a narrow collar and two-button placket front; Top-Sider deck shoes (the official shoes of the navy); and the ultimate trophy item of choice: the Letterman sweater (see p.312). The preppy look was also interpreted by young women of the period, who had been granted the freedom to dress more comfortably and practically during the war. As more women began to embrace college life, their way of dressing altered accordingly (below right) and the 'bobbysoxer' look became de rigueur (see p.310).

Sporting the relevant garments from head to toe, however, was only the first step to successful preppy dressing: beyond wearing the correct labels, in the right combinations, detail was paramount with this look and the authentic preppy dresser was well versed in such sartorial matters. Under no circumstances were trousers to be worn with a front-pressed pleat; they had to be flat-fronted at all times and just short enough to flash a little flesh in the form of bare ankles, which meant that socks had no place in the preppy wardrobe. Similarly, jackets always featured a three-button front fastening, two-button cuffs and a hooked back vent. These details, minute as they seemed, were symbolic of the insularity of preppy society and identified for the 'insider' those individuals deemed part of this select group.

As such, the preppy style represented much more than a staunch set of sartorial regulations followed by a cohort of students of the same exclusive institution. These clothes, once conscientiously coordinated, established a 'uniform' for these young people that cemented their sense of identity and belonging, and bonded them in their ideologies. By looking in the mirror and around at their peers, they hoped to establish who they were.

Nostalgia for the preppy look emerged a mere twenty years after its peak in popularity, when television and cinema romanticized the style. The wholesome characters of *Grease* (1978) and *Happy Days* (1974–84) embodied a sentimentality depicted through conventional family values, clean-cut storylines and archetypal costume. Today, the work of Ralph Lauren (b.1939) and Tommy Hilfiger (b.1951) proves the continuing appeal of the preppy look, recognizing and celebrating it as one of the United States' great contributions to global style. **RA**

1953	1954	Mid 1950s	1955	1955	1978
A US *Vogue* feature lists J. Press, Chipp, Sills of Cambridge and Fenn-Feinstein as four of the most prominent Ivy League tailors.	The clothing company Brooks Brothers includes a women's fitting room, indicating the popularity of preppy styles for women as well as men.	Jazz legend and style icon Miles Davis is hailed as an authentic preppy aficionado, influencing the style of other jazz musicians of the period.	Preppy clothing manufacturer Haspel invents a synthetic wash-and-wear seersucker suit that claims to be wrinkle-free.	The film *The Man in the Gray Flannel Suit*, starring Gregory Peck, references the popular suit of the title favoured by many preppy types.	The movie *Grease*, with John Travolta and Olivia Newton-John, makes the wholesome preppy look popular again.

Bobbysoxer 1940s
SKIRT AND SWEATER OUTFIT

1 PETER PAN COLLAR
Attached to the neckline of a high-fastening blouse, the Peter Pan collar has rounded edges and is often cut in white piqué. It was first seen in the costume worn in 1905 by actress Maude Adams, when she played Peter Pan. It is commonly seen in children's wear.

2 CASHMERE SWEATER
Skirts were usually combined with long- or short-sleeved sweaters. Although imported Scottish cashmere was preferred, college girls also wore garments from the largest US cashmere manufacturer, the Dalton and Hadley Knitwear Company of Cleveland.

NAVIGATOR

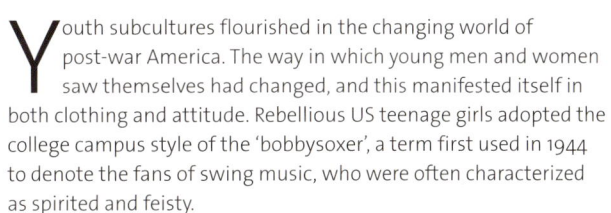

Students at the University of California, Los Angeles campus (1950s).

Youth subcultures flourished in the changing world of post-war America. The way in which young men and women saw themselves had changed, and this manifested itself in both clothing and attitude. Rebellious US teenage girls adopted the college campus style of the 'bobbysoxer', a term first used in 1944 to denote the fans of swing music, who were often characterized as spirited and feisty.

Preferred garments included tight-fitting, turtleneck, short-sleeved jumpers or cardigans in baby-blue and pink angora, worn with blouses that had small, rounded Peter Pan collars, colour-matched to plaid knee-length skirts. Full circular skirts were worn over layers of stiffened petticoats, often edged in ric-rac braid or featuring cut-outs of popular iconography: musical notes, guitars and records of teen heartthrobs Elvis Presley and Jerry Lee Lewis. Particularly popular were images of French-cut poodles, either printed or appliquéd onto the skirt; the poodle supposedly imbued the wearer with Continental sophistication. The circular skirt created and emphasized an hourglass figure.

As an early act of teenage sartorial rebellion, knitted cardigans were worn back to front, with rolled-up denim jeans and saddle shoes. Otherwise, teenagers eschewed the figure-defining sweater for the 'sloppy Joe', an oversized sweater that fell loosely around the body almost to the knees, with a rolled collar, hem and cuffs, often taken from a father's or boyfriend's wardrobe, together with his checked shirt. **MF/RA**

3 SKIRT
The red wool skirt is cut in the style of a Scottish kilt, with sewn-down, broad knife pleats forming a smooth-fitting yoke to the hip, before falling into open pleats to just below the knee. Pleated and circular skirts were particularly popular at the time.

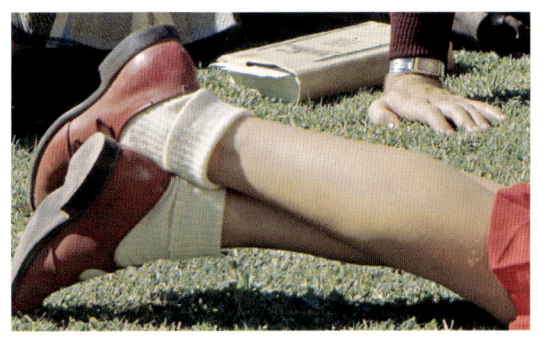

4 PENNY LOAFER
Worn with ankle socks, the penny loafer was originally made by US bootmaker G. H. Bass in 1934, under the name 'Weejuns'. Prep-school students took to inserting a penny into the diamond-shaped slit, hence the origin of the name 'penny loafer'.

Ivy League Style 1940s
COLLEGE LOOK

Ivy League students on campus, photographed by Teruyoshi Hayashida (1960s).

🔘 NAVIGATOR

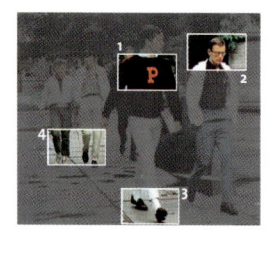

Although the Ivy League style was known and loved for its precision and attention to detail, the Ivy dresser was also celebrated for his innate ability to look simultaneously casual and carefree. This knowing nonchalance was facilitated by the ascendancy of athletic programmes at the Ivies, and the social status bestowed on these athletes encouraged sports clothing to be worn on and off the playing field. Most of the collegians were also almost certainly from what the economist and writer Thorstein Veblen called the 'leisure class'—wealthy families with a natural affinity for leisurely pursuits, such as golfing and tennis, requiring attire that could be worn for both sporting and social occasions. A particular item of clothing that epitomized the relaxed nature of the Ivy look was the award-letter sweater, also known as the Varsity or Letterman sweater. It was ultimately an emblem of achievement and superiority as it was awarded only to the most illustrious players, thereby creating a hierarchy within the team and granting the honoured athletes minor celebrity status. Another garment of iconic status to fill collegiate wardrobes was US army chinos, which emerged as a symbol of victory after World War II, making the transition from military associations to civilian life. This staple of Ivy apparel was perfectly offset by the ever-popular lightweight, waist-length Harrington jacket, a checked shirt—ordinarily worn with the tails trailing behind—and a trusty pair of loafers or tennis shoes. **RA**

👁 FOCAL POINTS

1 AWARD-LETTER 'P' SWEATER
Declaring to everyone on campus the wearer's status as most valuable player, the black Princeton award-letter sweater is unmistakable, emblazoned here with an orange felt 'P'. The girlfriends of the chosen athletes would often borrow these sweaters and experience the enormous prestige they granted.

2 CREW CUT
Otherwise known as a 'Harvard Clip', 'Princeton' or simply 'Ivy League', this particular type of haircut was defined as long enough for the hair to be parted on one side yet still extremely short at the back and on the sides. The crew cut was adopted by the US army in World War II and later became popular in civilian life.

3 LOAFER
The unparalleled popularity of the leather loafer could be seen on any East Coast campus, with the Bass 'Weejuns' monopolizing the market. The shoe was named after the traditional Norwegian fisherman's slipper, which ironically was based on the Native American moccasin. Alden and Winthorp were also popular brands.

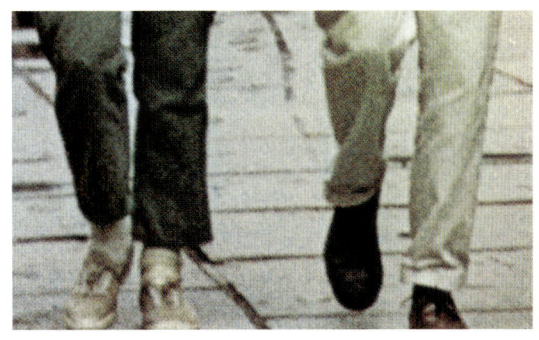

4 CHINOS
All-cotton, standard-issue US army chinos were produced in beige and khaki. They proved highly popular with the preps wanting to exude a casual and cool image, and, as with all prep-style trousers, the cuff was cut or turned up at a precise 1 ¾ inches (4.4 cm).

▲ Inspired by the neckwear of British army regiments, Brooks Brothers sparked the 'rep' tie trend by reversing the stripes of the design, creating an all-American accessory (swatches from c. 1956).

COLLEGE AND PREPPY STYLES

YOUTHFUL FEMININITY

1 Elizabeth Taylor wears a tulle sweetheart-line gown designed by Edith Head for *A Place in the Sun* (1951).

2 Grace Kelly stars in Alfred Hitchcock's thriller *Dial M for Murder* (1954). Her dress was designed by Moss Mabry.

In Europe the Corolle line, first shown in 1947 and dubbed the 'New Look' by the fashion press (see p.302), introduced the wasp waist and crinoline to contemporary fashion after the tailored suits and practical clothing worn during World War II. In the United States, influential Hollywood costumier Helen Rose (1904–85) made the House of Dior's New Look her own when she introduced the 'sweetheart line'—a dress with a heart-shaped bodice, nipped-in waist and billowing skirt. This was first seen worn by Elizabeth Taylor in the film *Father of the Bride* (1950), in which the sweetheart line signified Taylor's metamorphosis from check-shirted 'bobbysoxer' (see p.310), wearing college campus-style plaid skirts and pedal pushers, to young woman. The following year, Taylor appeared in the role of a debutante in *A Place in the Sun* (1951), a film costumed by Rose's great rival, Edith Head (1897–1981). Head designed two gowns, both strapless, with boned bodices. The first dress in white satin was used for publicity stills, but it was a gown of white tulle over pale green satin, with a heart-shaped bodice (above), that brought Head's talent to the attention of the general public.

KEY EVENTS

1947	1949	1950	1950	1951	1951
Walter Plunkett (1902–82) and Irene Sharaff (1910–93) become costume supervisors for all MGM musicals.	The Academy Award for Best Costume Design is established. It has two film categories, for black and white and colour.	Elizabeth Taylor appears in *Father of the Bride*, wearing costumes designed by Helen Rose.	Elizabeth Taylor marries her first husband, Conrad Hilton, wearing a gown designed by Helen Rose.	Edith Head wins an Academy Award for Best Costume Design in Black and White for *A Place in the Sun*.	Moss Mabry is appointed costume design supervisor at Warner Brothers.

Unlike in Europe, where almost every Dior collection introduced a new silhouette, in the United States the sweetheart line became an enduring fashion staple. The belted waist and bell-shaped skirts were preferred by the middle-market consumer to the etiolated silhouette of Dior's Sinueuse line, or the body-skimming lines of the sheath and shift dress that followed. The sweetheart line not only dominated the style of evening gowns, but was also made in lighter fabrics for spring and summer daytime dresses. These provided a non-threatening, feminine prettiness that emphasized the youthfulness of the wearer, which made the style eminently suitable for the teenager's prom night (see p.316), a rite of passage that marked a young girl's transition from childhood to sexual maturity. The sweetheart line was also used to emphasize the wholesome attributes of 'the girl next door'. Teenage idols, such as actress and singer Connie Stevens and a youthful Doris Day, wore the prom-style cotton day dress to signify unthreatening covert sexuality. So disarming was the style that the full skirt and wasp-waisted dress were also deployed by advertisers to promote mass-market, middle-class accoutrements. The 1950s housewife posed in her sweetheart dress to demonstrate the latest gadget or to open a packet of cake mix, a far cry from the glamorous version worn by Elizabeth Taylor in *A Place in the Sun*.

The sweetheart line was not a fashion-led garment, but was worn to describe cinematic archetypes, such as the girl next door or screen goddess. Edith Head at Paramount Pictures was the first woman to lead a design department, and she won more Academy Awards and nominations than any other artist in Hollywood history. Head believed that her role as a costume designer for film was to define the character and to drive forward the narrative. The white tulle dress worn by Taylor in *A Place in the Sun* emphasized both the star's ingénue quality and her burgeoning sexuality. Head was aware of the danger inherent in portraying or initiating fashionable trends because of the risk of the costumes appearing out of date once the film was released. However, the dress designed by Head for Taylor was well received by the fashion press, and it also disseminated the style to a wider audience and was subsequently copied extensively by manufacturers, leading to the affirmation that Head was not only a Hollywood costumier, but also a national taste-maker. In 1954 Grace Kelly wore a white tulle dress designed by Moss Mabry (b.1918), with a similar sweetheart line (right), in Alfred Hitchcock's *Dial M for Murder*.

The shapely silhouette, which epitomized the full-on femininity of the 1950s, remained a favourite for bridal gowns, as exemplified in Helen Rose's design for Grace Kelly on her marriage in 1956 to Prince Rainier of Monaco, whom she had met while filming *To Catch a Thief* (1955). Combined with impeccable grooming and exquisite accessories, such as the iconic Hermès Kelly bag (see p.318) named after the star, the sweetheart line came to be inextricably associated with sophisticated elegance. **MF**

1952	1953	Mid 1950s	1956	1958	1959
Helen Rose wins an Academy Award for Best Costume Design in Black and White for *The Bad and the Beautiful*.	The Costume Designers Guild is formed in Hollywood to promote the research, artistry and technical expertise of costume design.	The classic Hermès travel bag becomes known as the 'Kelly' bag after Grace Kelly, who appeared with the bag on the cover of *Life* magazine.	Grace Kelly marries Prince Rainier of Monaco wearing a lace dress designed by Helen Rose.	Helen Rose designs the costumes for Elizabeth Taylor in *Cat on a Hot Tin Roof*.	Orry George Kelly (1897–1964) wins an Academy Award for Best Costume Design in Black and White for *Some Like It Hot*.

YOUTHFUL FEMININITY 315

Prom Dress 1950s
TEENAGE DRESS

NAVIGATOR

It was only with the new-found prosperity and burgeoning number of teenagers in the 1950s that the school prom came to assume such social significance. Consequently the design of the prom dress for the formal high-school dance became all-important. In the 1950s the full-skirted sweetheart line, with heart-shaped bodice and wasp waist, became the favoured fashion. Debutantes would have been familiar with the sweetheart dress from fashion magazines, such as *Harper's Bazaar* and *Vogue*, but it was only with the influence of Hollywood films that the style was introduced to the mass market. The prom dress defined the desirability of the suburban middle-class teenage girl, and every high-school girl took time to consider her choices, courting opinion from friends over the decision. In this photograph, three girls are grouped around a dressing table mirror; one holds up the matching strappy sandals against the dress, which the girl in the middle holds against her body to gauge the effect. The bodice of the dress is a darker colour, outlining the typical sweetheart neckline and extending into thin, decorative straps. In other versions, the strapless bodice of the sweetheart line might be softened with the addition of wide ruched straps or cap sleeves. The dress was traditionally worn with a corsage, given to the girls by their dates, and pinned to the waistline of the dress. **MF**

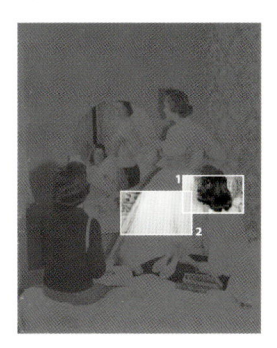

FOCAL POINTS

1 PAGEBOY BOBS
All the girls have pageboy-style bobs, turned under at the back of the neck. Smooth hair was considered the feminine ideal; washed and set once a week, it would be put into pin curls overnight and brushed out in the morning.

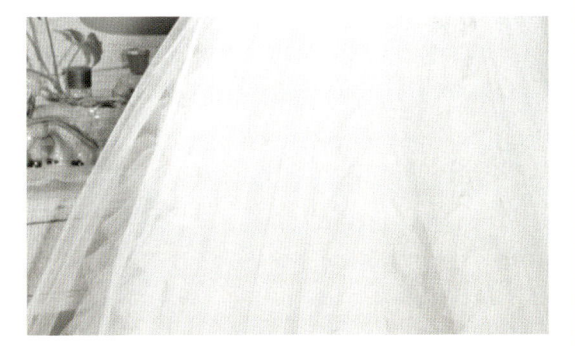

2 CONTEMPORARY CRINOLINE
The mid-calf or ballerina-length full skirt is made up of layers of tiny frills, and supported with inbuilt tiered and starched petticoats. These were constructed from nylon, taffeta or net, and stiffened with starch or sugar water.

THE HISTORY OF THE PROM

Although today perceived as a rite of passage to adulthood, the teenage prom was initially a gathering of debutantes who promenaded at the beginning of a ball or other formal event in the 19th century. The first reference to a prom comes from the journal of a student at Amherst College, Massachusetts, in 1894, and describes his invitation and attendance at an early prom at Smith College. Middle-class parents instituted formal dances that were strictly chaperoned, in the hope of inculcating the same poise and composure in their offspring. The event became associated with college graduation, particularly in the elite colleges of the East Coast. By 1900 high-school proms were relatively simple: students would come in their Sunday best but would not purchase new clothes for the event. From the 1920s, US youth experienced more freedom with the arrival of the car and other luxury items. The prom became an annual event, at which seniors arrived in formal evening clothes and danced (below).

YOUTHFUL FEMININITY

Kelly Bag 1950s
HERMÈS

The Kelly bag has remained essentially unchanged in its design; this example is from the 1960s.

NAVIGATOR

The classic Hermès travel bag, known as the *sac haut à courroies* (tall bag with straps), first appeared in 1930. However, it was not until film star Grace Kelly was photographed carrying a black crocodile version of the bag in the 1950s that it became known as the 'Kelly' bag in her honour, and was a much sought-after accessory. Each bag is handmade from start to finish over a period of eighteen hours and the task is undertaken by a single craftsperson, whose name is embossed inside the bag, together with the date. This practice is not only useful in the event that the bag needs to be returned for repairs, but it also serves as a validity mark to check whether or not the bag is one of many fakes.

The skins for each bag are selected according to personal requirements and arrive at the atelier in hand-cut pieces. The lining, which is made from goatskin, is constructed first, and the base of the bag is then hand-stitched to the front and the back. Each bag necessitates more than 2,600 stitches, all of which require that the skin is first perforated with an awl, a traditional artisan's tool. The grain and density of the leather dictate the size of the stitch. The bag is then ironed to get rid of the crinkles in the calfskin, and the final stage is to stamp the 'Hermès Paris' name on each bag. **MF**

👁 FOCAL POINTS

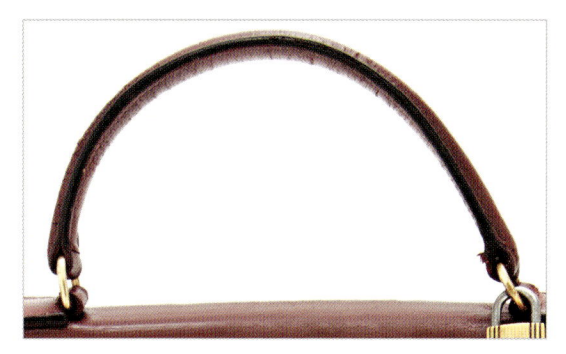

1 HANDLE
Constructed from five pieces of leather, the handle is shaped by hand across the craftsperson's thigh using a special knife. This means that the handle on each Kelly bag is very slightly different. The bevelled edges of the leather are then smoothed away with sandpaper and dyed to match the bag.

2 FRONT FLAP
The shallow front flap is secured with a narrow strip of leather that pierces the pleated sides of the bag before fastening at the centre front, held in place with two unobtrusive gilt horizontal bars. The rectangular minimal clasp on the locking belt can be secured with a tiny padlock.

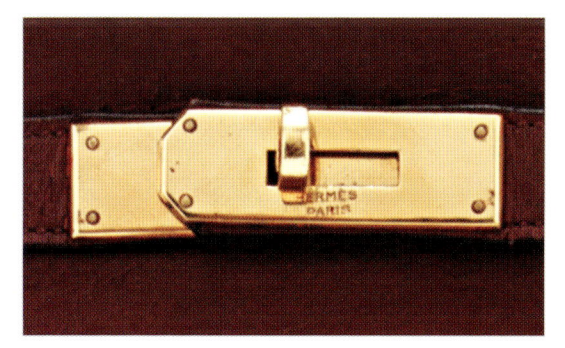

3 HARDWARE
The hardware of the bag is subtle and understated. The metal plate is applied using a time-consuming method called pearling, which involves nailing the plate in place and then smoothing down the cut-off nails to resemble pearls. Four matching gilt metal feet are riveted to the base of the bag.

4 STITCHING
A double saddle stitch, unique to Hermès, is used to construct the bag. This involves a process of two needles working waxed linen threads in tensile opposition. The technique ensures that the bag will not unravel, should a stitch break. Hot wax is used to seal this part of the bag to protect it from moisture.

▲ Grace Kelly is pictured with her future husband, Prince Rainier of Monaco, at the announcement of their engagement in 1956. She carries the bag that was named after her.

YOUTHFUL FEMININITY 319

THE HOLLYWOOD IDEAL

1 Marilyn Monroe wears a gold lamé dress with sunray pleats designed by William Travilla for *Gentlemen Prefer Blondes* (1953). Judged too revealing by the censors, the dress is seen only briefly in the film.

2 Jane Russell smoulders on the set of *The Revolt of Mamie Stover* (1956). Travilla's glamorous costume designs for the film emphasized Russell's curvaceous figure.

3 Jayne Mansfield was one of the best-known 'sweater girls'. The term was coined to describe sex symbols of the big screen who wore tight sweaters with pointed bras.

Far removed from the restrained elegance of the prevailing feminine ideal of the 1950s, the garments seen on the Hollywood screen took the hourglass figure to extremes, exemplifying undiluted sexuality (above). From the cantilevered cleavage of the bra specially designed by director Howard Hughes for Jane Russell in *The Outlaw* (1943), but which she never wore as it was too uncomfortable, to Hollywood's ongoing love affair with the skintight sweater, begun by Lana Turner in Mervyn LeRoy's *They Won't Forget* (1937) and continued by Jayne Mansfield throughout the 1950s (opposite below), an exaggerated embonpoint became the defining look of the post-war years. As cleavage was generally only allowed on-screen in historical dramas, the all-enveloping sweater was one way of defining the breasts without revealing them. It was a silhouette that required many underpinnings. Bras were rigidly constructed with the cups reinforced with circular rows of stitching to form an upward-pointing cone shape (see p.322). Frederick's of Hollywood, which

KEY EVENTS

1946	1947	1949	1949	1952	1953
The Outlaw (1943), starring Jane Russell, whose breasts are prominently displayed in the film, finally goes on general release in the United States.	A green-and-white polka-dot bikini by US sportswear designer Carolyn Schnurer (1908–98) is featured in the US edition of *Harper's Bazaar*.	Marilyn Monroe is photographed nude against a background of red velvet by Tom Kelley. The images are used for a calendar.	Revolutionary lingerie designer Frederick Mellinger opens his original flagship store on Hollywood Boulevard in California.	Aspiring actress Brigitte Bardot models for Lempereur, a French manufacturer of ready-to-wear.	The Academy Awards are televised for the first time, giving stars the opportunity to showcase their designer outfits to the nation.

was established in 1946 by ex-GI Frederick Mellinger, claimed in its slogan: 'We not only dress Hollywood legends, we create them.' The company invented the first push-up bra called 'The Rising Star'. In David Chierichetti's biography of Hollywood costumier Edith Head (1897–1981), Head's assistant Sheila O'Brien summed up a star's desirability: 'If a girl had a 40-inch bust she could be a star at RKO; a 38, a supporting player. Less than 36—not even an extra.'

Both day dresses and evening wear drew attention to the breasts with variations in cut and embellishment to the neckline, such as scalloped edges, and strapless, halter-neck or off-the-shoulder designs (right). The adoption of heavy and ornate necklaces by jewellery makers such as Joseff of Hollywood further emphasized the chest area. Costume jewellery reached the height of popularity in this decade as base metals became available again after World War II.

Waists were cinched in by a girdle, the contemporary version of the corset. From ideas developed by French designer Marcel Rochas (1902–55) in 1942, Christian Dior (1905–57) created the waspie, an essential element of the hourglass figure, which suppressed the waist and resulted in more rounded breasts and hips. With the two-way elasticity provided by the incorporation of Lastex and Lycra into foundation wear, the girdle provided body shaping with comfort. It was an item eschewed by screen goddess Marilyn Monroe, who preferred to go without undergarments entirely and was sometimes sewn into her clothes. Described by some as a UK size 12–14 (her actual size is unclear), the actress subscribed to the waist–hip ratio considered to correlate to the perception of female desirability. In Billy Wilder's screwball comedy *Some Like It Hot* (1959), Monroe wore a near-nude, skintight, lingerie-inspired evening dress for her rendition of 'I Wanna Be Loved by You', for which the designer Orry-Kelly (the professional name of Orry George Kelly; 1897–1964) won an Oscar. The archetypal blonde bombshell reputedly sewed buttons into the bust points of her garments to create the impression of aroused nipples. Swathed in pink duchesse satin with a stand-alone bodice worn with matching over-the-elbow gloves, Monroe provided a paradigm of on-screen sexuality in *Gentlemen Prefer Blondes* (1953) with her performance of 'Diamonds Are a Girl's Best Friend'. The dress was designed by William Jack Travilla (1920–90), then head of costume at 20th Century Fox, who later set up his own high-end fashion salon, Travilla Inc., in Los Angeles. Travilla worked with Monroe on eight of her films.

The figure-defining boned and stiffened bodice of evening and cocktail wear was also translated into one-piece swimwear. These garments were often cut into bloomers or incorporated a short skirt to cover the hips, resulting in the appearance of abbreviated dresses. Although the first bikini was simply constructed from triangular pieces of fabric strung together, popularized by French film actress Brigitte Bardot in Roger Vadim's controversial film *...And God Created Woman* (*Et Dieu...créa la femme*), other versions were constructed like lingerie with underwiring or boned cups for maximum uplift (see p.324). **MF**

1953	1955	1955	1956	1959	1959
The first edition of men's magazine *Playboy* appears. Founded by Hugh Hefner in Chicago, it features photographs of nude women.	British blonde bombshell Diana Dors poses in a mink bikini on a gondola at the Venice Film Festival.	*The Seven Year Itch* is released. Its costumes include the iconic pleated ivory cocktail dress worn by Marilyn Monroe and designed by William Trevilla.	Hollywood sex symbol Jayne Mansfield appears in the musical comedy *The Girl Can't Help It*.	The Barbie doll, invented by Ruth Handler (co-founder of Mattel), is introduced to the world at the American Toy Fair in New York.	Australian-born Orry-Kelly wins an Oscar for his costume designs for *Some Like It Hot*, starring Marilyn Monroe.

Bullet Bra 1949
UNDERWEAR

I dreamed I went to work in my maidenform* bra

CHANSONETTE* with famous 'circular-spoke' stitching

Notice <u>two</u> patterns of stitching on the cups of this bra? Circles that uplift and support, spokes that discreetly emphasize your curves. This fine detailing shapes your figure <u>naturally</u>—keeps the bra shapely, even after machine-washing. The triangular cut-out between the cups gives you extra "breathing room" as the lower elastic insert expands. In white or black: A, B, C cups. **2.00** Other styles: Broadcloth: Cotton, "Dacron"*Polyester 2.50; Lace, 3.50; with all-elastic back, 3.00; Contour, 3.00; Full-length, 3.50. *REG. U.S. PAT. OFF. ©1964 BY **Maidenform, Inc.**, makers of bras, girdles, swimwear, and active sportswear.

US magazine advertisement for Maidenform bras (1950s).

⚙ NAVIGATOR

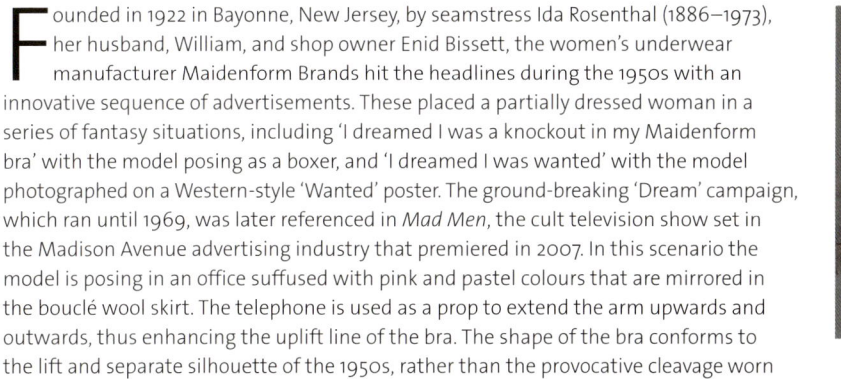

Founded in 1922 in Bayonne, New Jersey, by seamstress Ida Rosenthal (1886–1973), her husband, William, and shop owner Enid Bissett, the women's underwear manufacturer Maidenform Brands hit the headlines during the 1950s with an innovative sequence of advertisements. These placed a partially dressed woman in a series of fantasy situations, including 'I dreamed I was a knockout in my Maidenform bra' with the model posing as a boxer, and 'I dreamed I was wanted' with the model photographed on a Western-style 'Wanted' poster. The ground-breaking 'Dream' campaign, which ran until 1969, was later referenced in *Mad Men*, the cult television show set in the Madison Avenue advertising industry that premiered in 2007. In this scenario the model is posing in an office suffused with pink and pastel colours that are mirrored in the bouclé wool skirt. The telephone is used as a prop to extend the arm upwards and outwards, thus enhancing the uplift line of the bra. The shape of the bra conforms to the lift and separate silhouette of the 1950s, rather than the provocative cleavage worn with a décolleté neckline, and was made to be worn under office-appropriate dresses, sweaters and blouses. Regardless of the exotic locations or costumes depicted in these advertisements of the 1950s, the bra is always shown in a virginal white. **MF**

⊙ FOCAL POINTS

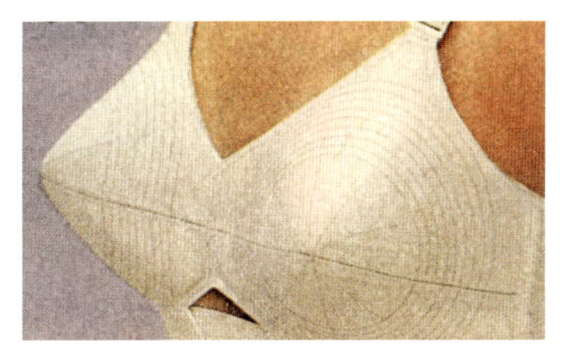

1 CONICAL CONTOURS
Constructed from layers of cotton, the cups of the bra are stitched into concentric circles that move outwards from the bust point and are bisected with a horizontal seam. The bullet bra was probably the most rigidly constructed undergarment since the corset.

2 SUPPORT STRUCTURE
An elasticized insert separates the cups at the centre front, providing freedom of movement and supporting the cups with a stretchy band. Ida Rosenthal was quick to point out that bra construction was a matter of engineering as well as good design.

THE ARCHETYPAL SWEATER GIRL
Marilyn Monroe was portrayed at home for *Life* magazine by staff photographer Alfred Eisenstaedt in 1953, the same year that she starred in three memorable movies: *Niagara*, *How to Marry a Millionaire* and *Gentlemen Prefer Blondes*. The off-duty star—a key exponent of the 'sweater girl' look—looks relaxed yet seductive in a black turtleneck cashmere sweater with pushed-up, bracelet-length sleeves. The garment is fully fashioned; with a set-in sleeve and deep rib at the waist, it clings to the contours of a bullet-shaped bra and enhances Monroe's natural curves.

Bikini 1947
BEACHWEAR

French couturier Jacques Heim (1899–1967) and Swiss engineer Louis Réard are credited with inventing the bikini, which was reputedly named after the nuclear weapon test that took place in 1946 on the Bikini Atoll in the Pacific. The bikini was first seen on the runway, worn by French model Micheline Bernardini in Paris. A green-and-white polka-dot bikini by the US sportswear designer Carolyn Schnurer featured in the US edition of *Harper's Bazaar* in 1947. Although the two-piece swimsuit had previously been accepted as beachwear, this garment had consisted of a structured halter top and substantial bottom half that covered the hips from waist to thigh, revealing only the ribcage. The brevity of the bikini caused outrage, particularly the exposure of the navel, and it was not until the 1960s and a new era of sexual permissiveness that the revolutionary new bathing suit gained widespread acceptance. It is probably now the most popular form of women's beachwear around the world. The bikini initially consisted of two triangles of fabric for the bra top, with strings that tied around the neck and back, and two triangles of fabric for the bottom, connected by strings at the hips, revealing a number of erogenous zones—the back, the upper thigh and the navel—a near-nude look that incensed the Catholic League of Decency. **MF**

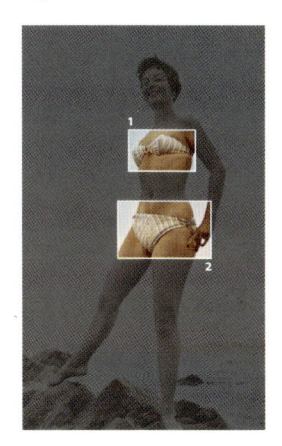

NAVIGATOR

FOCAL POINTS

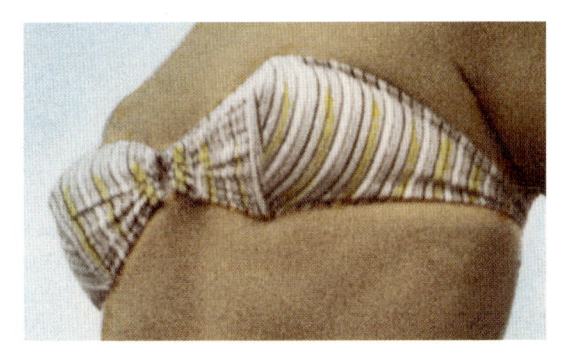

1 BANDEAU TOP
The strapless bikini top is structured in the same way as underwear, and the cleavage enhanced by boned cups that lift and separate the breasts. The striped fabric is aligned on the seam that runs through the bust point.

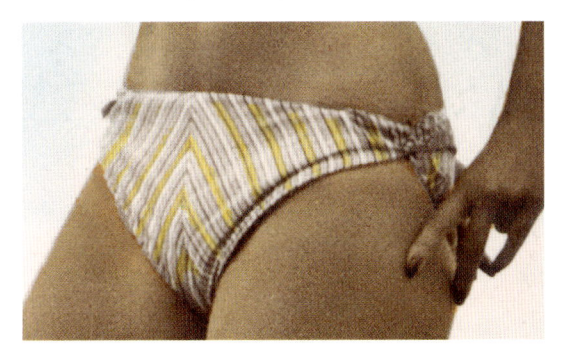

2 HIPSTER BOTTOMS
The bikini's hipster bottoms are cut down to the pubic bone, thus exposing most of the torso. The front and back pieces are joined across the hip bone, and a centre-front seam provides precisely aligned, angled stripes.

THE ULTIMATE BIKINI GIRL

During the 1950s the bikini was worn mainly by pin-up girls and screen sirens such as Brigitte Bardot (below), to whom it is indelibly linked following her appearance in Roger Vadim's film ...*And God Created Woman* in 1956. Although she had appeared in sixteen films, this movie was widely recognized as the vehicle that launched Bardot's career and immediately created her 'sex kitten' persona, not least because of her appearance in a bikini. Bardot symbolized an era of post-war freedom and sexual licence with her 'just got out of bed' blonde hair, bikini and sun-tanned skin, redolent of French Riviera sophistication.

DAYTIME DECORUM

1. Elegant wool separates by designer Greta Plattry epitomize the image of the perfect 1950s housewife (c. 1951).
2. Actress Doris Day wears an embellished fine-knit cardigan and pearl-buttoned blouse (1952).
3. The Revlon 'Fire and Ice' lipstick advertising campaign of 1952 sold Charles Revson's fantasy of the 'Park Avenue whore' to millions of women.

It was a perfect storm of events that resulted in the housewife of the 1950s becoming deified. Targeted by government policies, the fashion industry and advertisers, both she and her home were buffed, groomed and venerated. Liberated from the privations of wartime rationing, her clothing celebrated femininity with strict fashion discipline. A facade of perfection had to be upheld at all costs; to leave the house without a hat was little short of insurrection.

World War II had seen women enter the workforce, but progress for women's liberation stalled post-war with politicians advocating that women should return to their role as home-makers and not deprive homecoming servicemen of employment. The overriding belief in the United States was that social, moral and economic stability was dependent on men returning to their role as head of the household. It was a woman's 'job' to be the perfect housewife.

Fashion played a significant role in this process by restoring the notion of traditional feminine clothing and making the business of dressing

KEY EVENTS

1947	1947	1949	1949	1951	1951
Christian Dior launches the first House of Dior collection, characterized by a new post-war look, embracing full skirts and peplums.	Dior's iconic 'Bar' day suit combines a full skirt with a jacket with sloping shoulders and a fitted wasp waist to create a striking silhouette.	Clothes rationing, which began on 1 June 1941, finally ends in Britain. Austerity measures limit the cut of clothes and the choice available.	Pauline Trigère wins the first of three Coty American Fashion Critics' Awards; the other two are awarded in 1951 and 1959.	Transcontinental television is launched in the United States on 4 September by President Harry Truman, linking the East and West Coasts.	Polyester is introduced to the US public as a magic fibre that needs no ironing; it is cheap, washes well and dries quickly.

complex, with style diktats for every social and domestic function. As in the 19th century, each period of the day required its own style of clothing with rules of appropriate dressing strictly enforced. Women who had made do with rationed clothes, gone without stockings and even donned trousers for practicality were seduced by the exquisite beauty of fashion's first significant post-war statement: the House of Dior's New Look (see p.302). Within one season Christian Dior (1905–57) made every utility wardrobe look déclassé and returned Paris to a position of fashion dominance.

The sublimation of women into such decorative roles could never have been achieved without the aid of television and commercials. Advertisers recognized that while men were earning the money, it was their wives who spent it. Cosmetics firm Revlon's 'Fire and Ice' campaign (below right), launched in 1952, was deemed the most effective advertising campaign ever. In television land, women lived in a bubble of happy contentment: they cooked and cleaned wearing couture with perfect maquillage and not a hair out of place. These paragons sold the fantasy image of the 1950s housewife (opposite) to millions, and Hollywood played its part, too. Stars such as Doris Day (right) exemplified the clean-cut notion of career girl or housewife with her crisp laundered style, which popularized garments such as the narrow-cut suit and beaded cardigan (see p.330).

It was in the interest of the couturiers and designers, many of whom were launching lucrative licensed ranges of make-up and perfume, to reinforce the required standards and keep all women, rich and poor, in thrall to fashion. A plethora of books was published, including Christian Dior's *The Little Dictionary of Fashion: A Guide to Dress Sense for Every Woman* (1954), which states that it is possible for a woman to be elegant without spending very much because simplicity, good taste and grooming are the 'three fundamentals of good dressing', and these do not cost money. US designer Anne Fogarty (1919–80) wrote *The Art of Being a Well-Dressed Wife* (1959) to demystify the process of dressing appropriately for every daily task. She maintained that the business of 'wife dressing' should be run like a military exercise and that it significantly contributed to a happy marriage. Fogarty revelled in every wardrobe detail, from the necessity of owning half a dozen slips to a wardrobe of varying silhouettes.

Pauline Trigère (1909–2002; see p.332), Giuseppe Gustavo 'Jo' Mattli (1907–82), Digby Morton (1906–83) and Charles Creed (1906–66) all designed for sophisticated leisured post-war women. Crisp tailored coats and suits with matching accessories designed by Trigère marked the style of actress Patricia Neal in the film *Breakfast at Tiffany's* (1961). These outfits were firmly rooted in the elaborate and over-accessorized 1950s, in contrast to the modernity of the protagonist of the film, Audrey Hepburn, who was dressed by Givenchy. In the early 1960s, publications such as *A Guide to Elegance* by Genevieve Antoine Dariaux attempted to preserve the status quo and reel in the rebellious teenage consumer, but in truth decorous dressing had had its day. **JE**

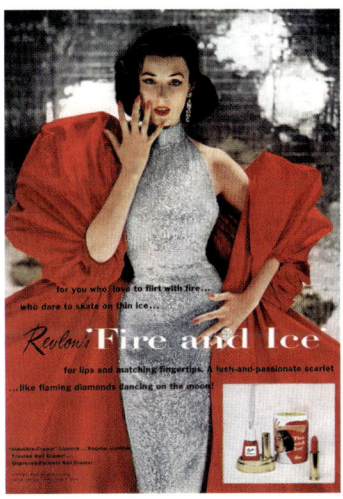

1951	1952	1953	1961	1963	1964
Henry Rosenfeld shows the shirtwaist dress in his spring/summer collection (see p.328); the garment proves popular and forms the core of later collections.	Revlon launches its 'Fire and Ice' campaign, encouraging women to put the war years behind them and pursue a glamorous lifestyle.	Cristóbal Balenciaga (1895–1972) introduces the spherical 'balloon' jacket, which encases its wearer's upper body in a cocoon-like fashion.	Actress Patricia Neal flaunts a sophisticated wardrobe, courtesy of designer Pauline Trigère, in the film *Breakfast at Tiffany's*.	*The Feminine Mystique* by Betty Friedan is published. It highlights women's dissatisfaction with their role as housewives.	Genevieve Antoine Dariaux publishes *A Guide to Elegance*. She states that her mission in life is to transform a plain woman into an elegant one.

American Shirtwaist Dress 1950s
DAYWEAR

Uxbridge Shetland wool shirtwaist dress (c. 1955).

NAVIGATOR

The shirtwaist dress was the ultimate uniform of US women in the 1950s: neat, respectable, crisp, chic and versatile. It evolved from its inception in the 1900s as a shirt and skirt combination into a dress styled to look like a two-piece. The garment was mass produced by Henry Rosenfeld, who offered an affordable range of styles and fabrics to suit all tastes. Elizabeth Hilt designed shirtwaist dresses for Rosenfeld and it was her eye for detail that ensured that her designs were always a cut above those of her competitors: the collars were immaculately tailored and she punctuated every design with other distinctive details to create dresses with universal appeal.

This archetypal shirtwaist dress in lemon-yellow wool has a high-buttoning neckline featuring a deep square collar cut with a slight roll at the back to sit away from the neck. Two seams run up from the waist seam to the bust point, providing a close-fitting bodice. Six box pleats, three in front and three at the back, are sewn down to the top of the hips, from where they flare and open to provide volume and fullness. Vertical pockets are worked into the pleats on either side of the skirt. The tailored shirtwaist dress was considered semi-formal, and required appropriate accessories; this small leopard-print hat is wired to follow the shape of the head. **JE**

FOCAL POINTS

1 MATCHING BELT
A narrow, lemon-coloured, buckled leather belt hides the waist seam and further emphasizes the indented waist. A gilt medallion is pinned just below the belt, a highlight that is replicated in the glass and gilt buttons on the front fastening of the dress.

2 DOLMAN SLEEVE
A popular contemporary feature, the bodice is cut in one with the elbow-length sleeve. This requires an extended seam along the top of the shoulder. A button decorates the outer edge of each sleeve and summer-weight gauntlet gloves in cream complete the outfit.

▲ Designer Henry Rosenfeld and models show various designs from his spring/summer 1951 collection. The Rosenfeld shirtwaist dress by Elizabeth Hilt was key to the label's success.

DAYTIME DECORUM 329

Beaded Cardigan 1950
REGINA KNITWEAR

Photograph by Frances McLaughlin-Gill,
Glamour magazine (November 1950).

NAVIGATOR

The beaded cardigan was a daytime staple for the elegant 1950s woman, sending a subliminal message of sensual feminine softness. This luxurious mint-green cashmere sweater by Regina has a round neckline decorated with beads and additional pearls scattered around the yoke. The groomed hair, pale complexion, sharply defined dark eyes, eyebrows, and dark red lips and nails stand out against the soft, delicate knitwear, contrasting soft femininity with rigid control.

The cardigan also became acceptable wear for the evening, popularized by US couturier Mainbocher (Main Rousseau Boucher, 1890–1976), who produced silk-lined cardigans embellished with appliqué, beadwork or fur collars to be worn with evening sheath dresses or ankle-length skirts. At the lower end of the market, plain sweaters were imported by US manufacturers and subsequently beaded. Many sweaters, especially the highly decorated ones, were made in Hong Kong, which had a considerable knitwear manufacturing base during this period, producing not only cashmere but also lambswool and angora blends in fashionable styles. Decorated cardigans appealed to all generations: teenagers wore them with circle skirts, pedal pushers or jeans, but they were also the respectable face of casual wear for the housewife, and the evening cover-up of choice. **JE**

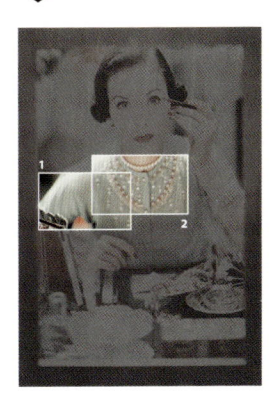

FOCAL POINTS

1 FULLY FASHIONED
The cardigan is knitted rather than cut to shape, with fashion marks above the elbow-length sleeves. Cashmere was the yarn of choice—speaking of wealth and luxury—but wool made the look more accessible.

2 DECORATED YOKE
The rows of beadwork are strung across the neckline like a multistrand pearl necklace. Matching pearl buttons secure the button band of the centre-front fastening. The cardigan is accessorized with a set of coordinating pearl jewellery.

▲ Ensemble with full circular skirt, taffeta blouse and jewel-encrusted knitwear (1950s). The angora cardigan features a high round neckline, three-quarter sleeves and a fitted waistband.

Navy Suit 1954
PAULINE TRIGÈRE 1909 – 2002

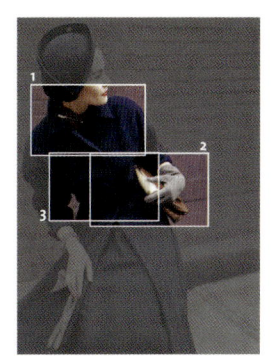

Pauline Trigère's clothes were always elegant, chic and pared down to exemplify key fashion components combined with a flash of understated drama. This matt navy wool coat and crêpe dress ensemble is typical of her conservative ethos. The coat is cut to emphasize the womanly figure, with a small waist, gentle sloping shoulder line and flared skirt, and is designed to reveal the perfectly coordinated and understated dress beneath. The body of the coat is softly constructed, with a turnover collar and dolman sleeves, yet the cut still tightly contains both waist and wrists, which have tiny, turned-back, flared cuffs. Four substantial covered buttons run from waist to throat. The deliberately outsize fastenings do not slip undone by accident, although the top button is designed to be worn open to reveal the throat. The coat skirt is darted at the waist and flares out to sway with movement and reveal the hips and legs.

This is a sophisticated design that, although almost severe in its simplicity, remains unnervingly womanly, contriving to emphasize both the figure and the undulating sweep of the feminine gait. Trigère's hat design provides the perfect foil to her feminine coat. The plain felt sweep cups one side of the head, throwing the carefully groomed hair and immaculately made-up face into sharp relief. **JE**

◉ NAVIGATOR

◉ FOCAL POINTS

1 SILK SCARF
The perfectly tied dark red silk scarf is slashed with a silver pin. A small flash of colour, it barely shows but emphasizes the disciplined approach to grooming that daytime decorum demanded. Every detail was controlled to reinforce an air of elegant respectability.

3 BUTTONS
The fabric-covered button is an integral part of decorous dress. This distinctive detail does not demand attention but blends in, epitomizing good taste. It signifies decency, concealing the fastenings and reinforcing the uptight image of svelte elegance.

2 HANDBAG AND GLOVES
No self-respecting woman in the 1950s left the house without gloves and a handbag. The soft matt grey gloves and cream-and-tan glossy leather clutch are defiantly uncoordinated to create a look that is overwhelmingly confident and assured.

⏱ DESIGNER PROFILE

1909–45
French designer Pauline Trigère moved to the United States at the age of twenty-five and opened her own fashion house in New York in 1942. She is credited with being the first designer to use detachable collars and scarves on dresses and coats, and was known for dramatic reversible capes and the use of fur trim. She was also the first designer to use wool for evening wear.

1946–2002
Trigère began to produce ready-to-wear lines in the late 1940s. Her designs were superbly cut and constructed, and attracted customers such as the Duchess of Windsor. Her mass-produced coat line was affordable yet delivered virtually the same quality of design as couture. She was awarded a Coty American Fashion Critics' Award in 1949, 1951 and 1959, and was the first woman to be elected to the Hall of Fame.

POST-WAR ITALIAN STYLE

Synonymous with stylish living and its associations with the *dolce vita*, Italy became an international centre of fashion after World War II. During this period, known as the *Ricostruzione*, the country underwent industrial reorganization with financial aid from the United States, administered through the Marshall Plan. This attempt to promote post-war trade guaranteed that the textile factories of the north, with their long tradition of artisanship, had access to capital and raw materials, which allowed the small family firms who made up a significant element of the Italian manufacturing sector to continue to expand.

The consolidation of Italy as a source of innovative design continued with the help of the Italian government and its officially sanctioned 'Made in Italy' promotion, making household names of Guccio Gucci (1881–1953), Salvatore Ferragamo (1898–1960) and Emilio Pucci (1914–92). In 1951, in an attempt to distance Italian fashion from the influence of Paris, the first collective fashion show of Italian designers was organized by Giovanni Battista Giorgini and attended by the international press. Such was its success that the show moved to the Sala Bianca in Florence's Palazzo Pitti (above) from 1952. This set the stage for the following decade, during which Florence, and later Milan, became a fashion capital alongside Paris, New York and London.

After World War II, Italy was the destination of choice for a new generation of tourists, who were encouraged to travel by the introduction of the jet plane

KEY EVENTS

1947	1947	1950s	1950	1951	1952
Salvatore Ferragamo is presented with the prestigious Neiman Marcus Award for Distinguished Service in the Field of Fashion.	Emilio Pucci is photographed in Switzerland wearing skiwear of his own design, leading to a commission for *Harper's Bazaar*.	Rome's Cinecittà becomes the filming location for US film productions and the studio most closely associated with Federico Fellini.	Pucci launches his couture house in the exclusive resort of Canzone del Mare on the Isle of Capri.	Giorgini hosts the first Italian fashion show at his villa. He holds it immediately after Paris Fashion Week in order to attract the same buyers.	Italian menswear company Brioni shows its collection on the catwalk for the first time at Palazzo Pitti in Florence.

into passenger service and films such as *Three Coins in the Fountain* (1954), which extolled the romantic adventures to be found in Europe. The jet set shopped at the fashion houses of Rome and Florence, attracted by the casual elegance of 'resort wear' in preference to the more formal constructions found in Paris, whose influence continued to decline after the death of Christian Dior (1905–57). Emilio Pucci excelled at ready-to-wear resort clothes that fulfilled the contemporary demand for ease of fit, vibrant colour and print (right), as well as high-end production values. In 1960 the designer developed 'Emilioform', an elasticized fabric based on a blend of jersey and the synthetic Helauca, which made for a stretchy clinging fit that held its shape. During the 1960s he fashioned the lightweight fabric, featuring kaleidoscopic, polychrome psychedelic prints, into cropped Capri pants and loose shirts worn by influential style setters such as Jackie Kennedy and Marilyn Monroe.

The relationship between film and fashion remained pivotal to the development of the Italian film industry, based in Rome. Accruing publicity from the design of the wedding dress for Hollywood film actress Linda Christian on her marriage to Tyrone Power in 1949, the Fontana sisters (Zoe, 1911–79; Micol, b.1913; and Giovanna, 1915–2004) created luxurious evening wear that attracted the custom of Hollywood film stars and home-grown talents such as Gina Lollobrigida and Sophia Loren. Combining the traditional values of couture with an Italian sensibility, the Fontana sisters went on to design Ava Gardner's costumes for *The Barefoot Contessa* (1954; see p.338).

Italian 'shoemaker to the stars' Salvatore Ferragamo first found success in California, where he designed shoes for Hollywood's luminaries. While there, he studied anatomy at the University of Southern California and went on to incorporate all the technical and ergonomic aspects of shoe production into his bespoke footwear. Ferragamo returned to Italy in 1927 and set up production in Florence, the centre of the Italian luxury leather goods industry. There he created many influential shoe styles, arguably including the invention of the stiletto heel. Named after the slim blade carried by Sicilian gangsters, the stiletto-heeled shoe emphasized the exaggerated femininity of the post-war era: accessorizing the swirling skirts and hourglass figure of the 1950s or adding to the streamlined silhouette of the sheath dress. The insertion of an aluminium spigot into the plastic heel shell added stability and resulted in a heel of unprecedented height and thinness. Ferragamo combined the stiletto heel with a tapered toe, and this design—known as 'winklepicker' after the tools used by diners to pick winkles out of their shells—came to embody post-war Italian style.

Menswear was also influenced by the streamlined tailoring and softer silhouette of the Italian look. The 'Continental cut' of the Rome-based company Brioni (see p.336), which challenged the traditional tailoring of Savile Row in London, appealed to the US male, including film stars Cary Grant and Clark Gable, and also inspired the young 'mods' of swinging London. **MF**

1 Decorated with stucco work and frescoes, the splendid Sala Bianca in Palazzo Pitti, Florence, was a fitting venue for the high fashion of established and emerging Italian designers.

2 Designer Emilio Pucci accompanies his models, who wear a range of colourful Pucci prints and Capri pants (1959).

1960s	1960	1960	1961	1961	1965
Extremely pointed toes, known as 'winklepickers', are added to stiletto-heeled shoes.	The comedy drama *La Dolce Vita*, written and directed by Federico Fellini, disseminates Italian style to an international audience.	Ferragamo dies and his wife, Wanda, and later their six children, take over the company.	The first edition of *Vogue Italia* is published by Condé Nast.	Actress Gina Lollobrigida embodies Italian glamour, starring alongside Rock Hudson in *Come September*, set on the Italian Riviera.	New York ad agency Jack Tinker and Associates hires Emilio Pucci to update the flight attendant uniform for Braniff International Airways.

Continental Suit 1950s
BRIONI

Streamlined afternoon suit by Brioni (1960).

NAVIGATOR

The influential Brioni 'Continental' suit was designed by expert tailor Nazareno Fonticoli, who founded the Brioni Company and label with public relations master Gaetano Savini in Rome in 1945. Its cut was far removed from the wide-shouldered US style that was prevalent in post-war tailoring, or the neo-Edwardian silhouette deployed by the British tailors of Savile Row.

Dubbed the *ordine dorico* (columnar look) by the fashion press, the Brioni suit appealed to both European nobility and the international jet set: it was deemed appropriate for a contemporary, fast-paced lifestyle. Custom made by a team of specialists, the close-fitting and streamlined suit was designed for the modern man—active, debonair and youthful—and introduced both colour and pattern into the male wardrobe. Brioni was the first international menswear company to implement seasonal changes and also staged the first fashion show of men's clothing in Florence in 1952. This was followed in 1954 by a fashion show in New York, thus disseminating Italian style to the US consumer. **MF**

FOCAL POINTS

1 NATURAL SILHOUETTE
The end result of two months' intensive labour and 185 separate operations, the finished suit has an unpadded forward shoulder line. The single-breasted jacket tapers to below the hips with short vents at the sides.

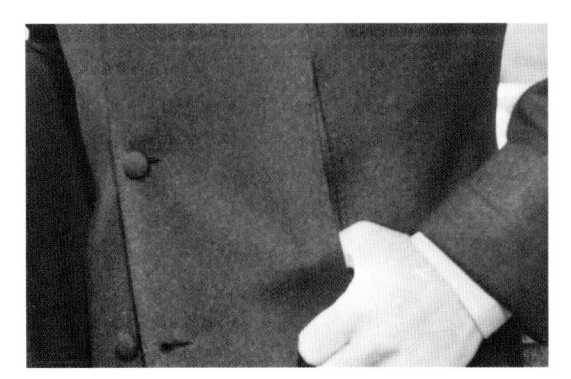

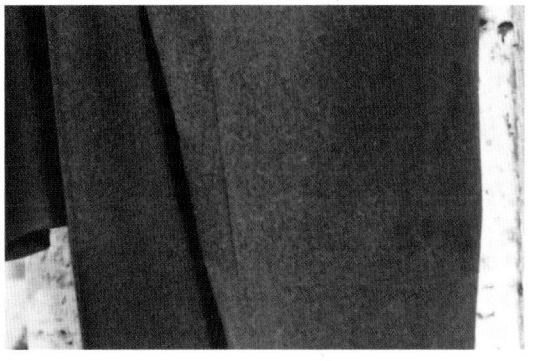

3 TAPERED TROUSERS
Luxurious lightweight fabrics such as silk dupion and noble fibres such as vicuña were used by Brioni and allow for the slim cut of the trousers, which taper at the ankle and measure no more than 17 inches (43 cm) at the hem.

COMPANY PROFILE

1945–89
The Italian fashion house Brioni was founded in 1945 by tailor Nazareno Fonticoli and his business partner Gaetano Savini in Rome's Via Barberini. In 1952 Brioni showed menswear on the catwalk for the first time at Palazzo Pitti in Florence, and in 1954 the company held a fashion show in New York, followed by shows in eight other US cities. US film stars such as Clark Gable and Cary Grant began to buy their suits from Brioni during the 1950s while working at Rome's Cinecittà production studios.

1990–PRESENT
In 1990 Umberto Angeloni was appointed chief executive officer and introduced an expansion plan, which included the introduction of a womenswear line. He also arranged for Brioni, rather than Savile Row, to dress the leading actors in the James Bond movies from 1995.

2 SLIMLINE JACKET
The single-breasted jacket features a three-button closure, with vertical pockets sited either side of the centre-front fastening. The peak lapels are cut narrowly in order to emphasize the slenderness of the silhouette.

POST-WAR ITALIAN STYLE 337

Evening Dress 1954
SORELLE FONTANA

Ava Gardner stars in *The Barefoot Contessa* (1954).

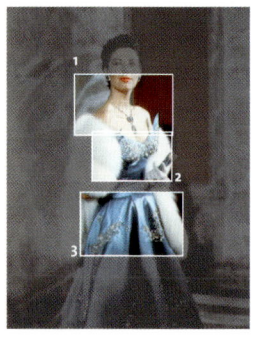

🧭 NAVIGATOR

Combining the traditions of Parisian haute couture with the drama and flamboyance of an Italian aesthetic, the Fontana sisters (Sorelle Fontana) offered Hollywood-style glamour to film stars such as Ava Gardner, Loretta Young and Myrna Loy. For Gardner, they designed the luscious and extravagantly crinolined strapless evening dress, made of sky-blue duchesse satin, that she wore in the Cinderella story of *The Barefoot Contessa*, directed by Joseph L. Mankiewicz; it appears in the scene in which her character, the fictional Spanish sex symbol Maria Vargas, is celebrated as a successful film star for the first time. All the luxurious drama inherent in the Fontana label is utilized to show the heroine's passage from barefoot dancer to acknowledged beauty and screen icon. The dress emphatically adheres to the rigidity of the inner structure, emanating from the form-fitting bodice, which finishes just above the natural line of the waist, with the addition of a faux belt between the bodice and skirt. The bodice extends upwards and outwards to form dramatic winged points almost up to the shoulders, contrasting with the softness of the silver fox stole draped around the arms. **MF**

👁 FOCAL POINTS

1 JEWELLERY
Ava Gardner as Maria Vargas wears matching diamond earrings, ring and necklace. One of the most erotic pieces of jewellery, the necklace leads the eye to the décolletage. Jewellery houses such as Boucheron, Tiffany and Cartier flourished during the 1950s, as costume jewellery was too resonant of recent wartime privations.

2 BODICE
The pronounced form of the bust is delineated by lingerie-style seaming. The cups of the bra top emanate from two parallel darts from the waist and are further emphasized by sequin and rhinestone embellishment that matches the scattered rhinestone scroll motifs appliquéd to the skirt.

3 SKIRT
The folds of the mid-calf-length skirt are reliant on inverted box pleats set into the waistband and fullness in the side seam, further supported by an underskirt of silk tulle tiers that sweep to the ground. Glossy duchesse satin provides the volume and stiffness for the crinoline-style skirt.

▲ A poster for *The Barefoot Contessa* (1954). All of Ava Gardner's costumes in the film were designed by the Fontana sisters.

🕘 DESIGNER PROFILES

1943–50
The three Fontana sisters—Zoe, Micol and Giovanna—from Traversetolo near Parma, Italy, followed in the footsteps of their mother, Amabile Fontana, an accomplished tailor. After completing apprenticeships in Milan, Rome and Paris they opened a workshop called Sorelle Fontana in Rome in 1943. Their international reputation was secured with the design of a spectacular dress for film star Linda Christian when she married Tyrone Power in 1949, which led to an extensive client list that included members of the Italian aristocracy and the international jet set.

1951–59
The sisters participated in the first Italian fashion show held in Florence in 1951. During the 1950s they designed clothes for many of Hollywood's best-known stars, including Grace Kelly and Elizabeth Taylor. They were invited to the White House in Washington, DC, in 1958 as Italy's representatives at the Fashion Around the World conference.

1960–92
Sorelle Fontana introduced a line of ready-to-wear fashion, followed by a line of furs, umbrellas, scarves, costume jewellery and table linen. In 1992 the Fontana label was sold to an Italian financial group.

POST-WAR WORKWEAR

1. James Dean wears Lee jeans in his Oscar-winning role as Jett Rink in *Giant*, directed by George Stevens (1956).

2. A Blue Bell/Wrangler advertisement from the 1950s shows 'authentic Western' denim for men, and for the whole family.

3. Elvis Presley wears a denim jacket and jeans to perform the title song in the film *Jailhouse Rock* (1957).

In the immediate aftermath of World War II, US consumer goods became the touchstone for a modernistic and plentiful future; in some ways US goods, such as motor cars, prepackaged food and clothes, became 'meta' products. For many, the United States represented freedom, opportunity and modernity; it therefore followed that the products of US industry were imbued with similar qualities. The war had helped to spread the message of US consumerism and Hollywood helped to popularize US products. The ubiquity of blue denim has its origins in these processes of cultural communication.

In 1853 Levi Strauss (1829–1902) arrived in California to open a branch of the family's dry goods business and cash in on the West's burgeoning economic development. During the gold rush he manufactured durable workwear for miners, and from these obscure beginnings the US blue denim phenomenon emerged. Within thirty years, Levi's was producing its well-known copper-riveted blue denim work trousers, and by the early years of the 20th century the 'big three' triumvirate of US jeans manufacturers had been established: Levi Strauss & Co, the H. D. Lee Company (manufacturers of Lee jeans; above) and the Blue Bell Overall Company (later the Wrangler brand; opposite above).

The processes of cultural transformation that turned these garments from specialist workwear into ubiquitous leisurewear were fuelled by Hollywood. Wild West shows had long been a popular form of entertainment and with

KEY EVENTS

1951	1952	1953	1954	1955	1956
Singer Bing Crosby is refused a hotel room in Vancouver because he is wearing blue jeans. At the time these were equated to 'denim overalls'.	The H. D. Lee Company first produces Chetopa Twill, a new hard-wearing denim twill, for use in its workwear ranges.	Marlon Brando stars as Johnny Strabler in *The Wild One*. The character's clothes help to create a template for late 20th-century menswear (see p.342).	A fly zipper fastening is introduced in Levi's classic waist jeans. The H. D. Lee Company enters the US leisurewear market with its Leesures range.	Pin-up James Dean popularizes denim in *Rebel Without a Cause*, wearing Lee 101 Riders jeans, dipped to render them more vibrantly blue on screen.	James Dean's film *Giant* is released posthumously. He sports the trendy Lee Riders zip-fly jeans, which were very popular at the time.

the advent of the US film industry, the 'Wild West' was absorbed into the Hollywood canon. By the 1930s studios were producing a plethora of Westerns featuring popular screen idols who regularly appeared dressed in denim; the cinematic myth of the cowboy furthered the mass appeal of blue jeans. Equally, 'dude ranch' holidays popularized blue denim for the middle classes; families could stay on ranches as paying guests and enjoy aspects of the cowboy lifestyle. The right look was essential to the experience, and holidaymakers increasingly adopted the blue denim workwear associated with cowboys and ranch hands. From the 1930s to the 1950s, when the popularity of dude ranch holidays was at its height, US retail institution the Sears Roebuck catalogue featured large ranges of Western wear aimed at a suburbanite clientele. The essentially modernistic link between mass entertainment, personal leisure and consumer activity helped to build a popular narrative around denim; purchasing a pair of blue jeans conferred the status of an American archetype.

By the 1950s the perceived complacency and prosperity of US middle-class lifestyles—built around convenience, comfort and material wealth—were a cause of concern for many younger US citizens. This questioning of the 'American dream' filtered into such cultural phenomena as Abstract Expressionism, beat poetry and edgy films aimed at a more youthful moviegoer. *The Wild One* (1953), starring Marlon Brando (see p.342), and *Rebel Without a Cause* (1955), starring James Dean—morally ambiguous films in which young 'method' actors mumbled, slouched and shrugged to camera—had a seismic effect on audiences. The clothes chosen by film makers to costume these young actors were central to their appeal: short zippered 'bomber' jackets (so called in reference to the jackets worn by US aviators in the war), T-shirts, heavy-duty work boots and blue denim jeans. This simple ensemble of rugged, hard-wearing and functional garments, primarily associated with the world of work rather than leisure, created a matrix from which much post-war menswear evolved.

Blue denim jeans became an easily recognized signifier of youth, sex and rebellion, and in the popular imagination an item that had once been associated with labour, thrift and economy was now regarded as something deviant and threatening to an older generation. The association of blue jeans with rock 'n' roll music underlined a sense of generational demarcation; not only did Elvis Presley (right) appear on screen and in publicity photographs wearing denim, but also references to blue jeans became a staple in popular lyrics of the 1950s. Girls too could adopt denim jeans without sacrificing their femininity; indeed, the visual contrasts created when the curves of the female form were dressed in heavy workwear simply served to emphasize the wearer's gender. The burgeoning appeal of blue jeans encompassed a broad youthful constituency, from teenage girls to bikers, film stars to street gangs, from the respectable suburbs to inner-city housing projects. Blue denim jeans not only clothed the figure, but also defined the wearer. **WH**

1957	1957	1957	1959	1961	1962
Lee Jeans brings out its Double Knees range, a harder-wearing design aimed at boys and youths.	Elvis Presley appears in two films—*Loving You* and *Jailhouse Rock*—dressed head to toe in blue denim.	Levi's causes outrage with an advertisement that features a pupil wearing denim jeans and the strap line 'Right for School'.	An exhibition of US culture, science and technology is held in Moscow to defuse Cold War tensions; one of the exhibits is a pair of Levi's 501s.	Marilyn Monroe wears blue jeans in the film *The Misfits*, written by Arthur Miller.	Howard Greenfield and Jack Keller's song 'Venus in Blue Jeans', recorded by Jimmy Clanton, reaches number seven in the Billboard charts.

Motorcycle Jacket and Jeans 1953
BIKER STYLE

Marlon Brando in *The Wild One* (1953).

◆ NAVIGATOR

Marlon Brando's character in *The Wild One*, Johnny Strabler, became a menswear archetype: leather jackets, boots, T-shirts and jeans are all staples of the modern masculine look. Brando's jacket can be clearly identified as a Schott Perfecto 'lancer style' leather motorcycle jacket. The Schott Perfecto was designed by Irving Schott in 1928 specifically for the motorcycle market (and named after his favourite cigar), and it has remained in production ever since. Early Schott motorcycle jackets were made from horsehide and were well known for their durability; they were also notoriously difficult to break in. James Dean was rarely seen without his Perfecto, and the jacket surged in popularity after the actor's death in 1955.

The jeans are worn with heavy boots known as 'engineer boots'. This type of footwear was produced by many US firms from the 1940s onwards and was originally designed as protective footwear for the engineering and construction trades. The seven-point peaked service cap was popular with bikers in the days before motorcycle helmets became mandatory. It was also often worn by bus drivers and police officers. It is not clear exactly which brand of hat the actor wore because it was a generic item made by a variety of companies at the time. **WH**

👁 FOCAL POINTS

1 LEATHER JACKET
Brando's Schott Perfecto motorcycle jacket is similar to Schott's One Star model, which has a star on each epaulette, recalling military styles. The stars on this jacket were added by the film's costume department and placed in the middle of the epaulettes.

2 JEANS AND BOOTS
The blue denim jeans have a crumpled, lived-in look that is still popular today and, crucially, are worn with rolled-up cuffs, which show off the heavy-duty black leather boots to full effect. These have a stacked Woodsman heel and Goodyear welted sole.

THE HISTORY OF BLUE JEANS

In the early 1870s Jacob Davis, a Nevada tailor, began producing hard-wearing work trousers, using a cotton 'denim' fabric (the name derives from the cotton twill *Serge de Nîmes*) and copper rivets on the pockets, for his clientele of miners, farm labourers and ranch hands (right). He then approached Levi Strauss (from whom he had purchased denim cloth on occasion) for financial backing, and so began the association of Levi Strauss & Co with blue denim jeans. The jeans were made at home by female employees but as demand surged it became necessary to open a factory in San Francisco. In the late 1880s Levi's added its trademark leather patch to the rear of the waistband, and from the 1890s the company began to produce a version of the popular Levi's 501 style.

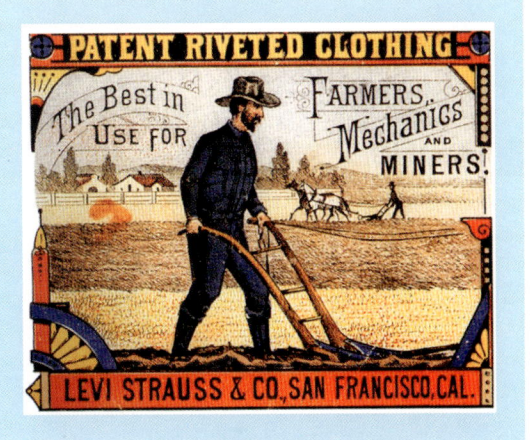

POST-WAR WORKWEAR 343

MODERN SIMPLICITY

1 Film star Audrey Hepburn wears a strapless Givenchy gown as the ingénue model in *Funny Face* (1957).

2 Jackie Kennedy makes a state visit to India (1962). Her signature pearls fill the 'V'-shape neckline of a simple apricot silk dress by Oleg Cassini, which features a single flat bow at the waist.

In post-war Hollywood, glamour was concerned with sensuality rather than sophistication, but this changed when Audrey Hepburn appeared in her first US film, *Roman Holiday*, in 1953. With her performance in Billy Wilder's film *Sabrina* in 1954, which charted her transformation from gauche chauffeur's daughter to sophisticated woman via a series of show-stopping outfits, her status as an enduring style icon was assured. This was followed by *Funny Face* (above) in 1957. Unwilling to rely on Hollywood costumier Edith Head (1897–1981) for her film wardrobe, Hepburn consulted the couturier Hubert de Givenchy (b.1927), which led to the beginning of a long partnership that reached its apotheosis with *Breakfast at Tiffany's* (1961), in which Hepburn wore the archetypal little black dress. Her adoption of Givenchy's chemise line and simple elegance (see p.346) heralded the approach of 1960s minimalism.

Givenchy's streamlined suits in solid blocks of bright colour, caught by a single button or fold of fabric, epitomized clean-cut, unfussy glamour.

KEY EVENTS

1951	1952	1952	1953	1953	1957
Jacqueline Bouvier (later Kennedy Onassis) wins *Vogue* magazine's Prix de Paris junior editorship. Her mother persuades her to turn down the award.	Oleg Cassini opens his fashion house on New York's Seventh Avenue.	Hubert de Givenchy opens his couture house in Paris.	Jacqueline Bouvier marries John F. Kennedy in Newport, Rhode Island.	Roger Vivier designs the shoes worn by Elizabeth II at her coronation ceremony in Westminster Abbey in London.	Givenchy launches his influential knee-length sack or chemise dress. It goes on to be an iconic fashion piece.

1946–89

Although Hepburn incorporated couture into her personal wardrobe, she augmented these pieces with everyday garments, always worn in a way that was unique to her: tightly belted trench coats, Capri pants, fine-knit black turtlenecks, cardigans, ballet slippers and knotted headscarves.

Hepburn's influence extended beyond the cinema audience. The United States' First Lady at the time, Jacqueline Kennedy, admired the star's style and adopted her outsize sunglasses, Givenchy signature boat neckline and body-skimming silhouette. Jackie Kennedy was only thirty-one years old at the time of her husband John F. Kennedy's inauguration in 1961, making her one of the youngest First Ladies in US history. Her lean, androgynous body represented the dawning of a new era of youth and vitality, and her signature bouffant hairstyle added to her height. Givenchy's chemise line provided the silhouette she preferred, with the garment infrastructure cut smaller than the outer garment to form a carapace. This created a current of air between the layers and allowed movement and a mere suggestion of the form underneath. Instantly labelled the 'Jackie look' by the fashion press, the three-quarter-length sleeves and cropped jackets worn over sleeveless A-line dresses were accessorized with white gloves. Her minimal style was emphasized by Givenchy's bright colours, which flattered her year-round tan.

The simplicity of the look extended to formal wear and the First Lady favoured a columnar silhouette in sumptuous textured fabrics, either strapless or with a boat neckline and small cap sleeves. She discarded pattern, furs and jewels, considering them ageing, and replaced fine gems with costume jewellery by designers such as Jean Schlumberger (1907–87). Her much-copied triple-strand pearls (right) were designed by Kenneth Jay Lane (b.1930). Although Christian Dior (1905–57) and Cristóbal Balenciaga (1895–1972) had both featured the pillbox hat previously, it was Roy Halston Frowick (1932–90)—then milliner at Bergdorf Goodman—who reinterpreted it, and Jackie herself who repositioned it to sit on the back of the head. She also favoured the Chanel 2.55 handbag and the bamboo-handled Gucci handbag, which would later become known as the 'Jackie'. Abandoning the pointed toes and stiletto heel then in vogue, Jackie popularized the low-heeled Pilgrim pump (see p.348).

In order to deflect criticism of her spending on European couture, Jackie appointed Oleg Cassini (1913–2006) as her official designer. She used his studio as a cover for the couture that she continued to acquire while collaborating with him on ideas that she or her fashion scouts picked up in Europe. As a former film costume designer Cassini knew the importance of appealing to an audience and included details that could be seen from a distance, such as oversized buttons or a stylized bow. Jackie relished her impact but refused to talk about her look, knowing that this silence would add to her mystique. The Chanel suit that she was wearing when her husband was assassinated in 1963 remains in the collective memory as one of the iconic outfits of the 20th century. **MF**

1957	1961	1961	1961	1961	1962
Stanley Donen's film *Funny Face*, based on the life of fashion photographer Richard Avedon and model Suzy Parker, is released.	John F. Kennedy becomes the thirty-fifth president of the United States.	Oleg Cassini is appointed as the First Lady's exclusive couturier.	The president and his wife make a state visit to France, where Jackie is admired for her fashion sense.	Audrey Hepburn appears as Holly Golightly in *Breakfast at Tiffany's*. Her clothes are designed by Givenchy.	Roy Halston Frowick designs the iconic pillbox hat often worn by Jackie Kennedy.

MODERN SIMPLICITY 345

Pleated Dress *c.* 1955
HUBERT DE GIVENCHY b. 1927

Audrey Hepburn photographed by Norman Parkinson (*c.* 1955).

NAVIGATOR

In complete contrast to the prevailing rigid, corseted style of Christian Dior, the clothes designed by Hubert de Givenchy for his muse, film actress Audrey Hepburn, defined both the fashion ideal and a new paradigm of feminine beauty. Only twenty-five years old when he showed his first collection, Givenchy offered a modern approach to couture, eschewing extraneous decoration and embellishment for purity of line—a philosophy he shared with his mentor, Cristóbal Balenciaga. Designed before the creation of the revolutionary chemise silhouette in 1957, this dress recognizes the natural line of the waist with a seam but is cut with clarity and simplicity. All the interest and volume are restricted to the back of the skirt, which features a series of inverted pleats. The architectural silhouette of the dress is sculpted from a single block of clear colour, which is typical of Givenchy. Hepburn was self-conscious about her bony clavicles so Givenchy devised a neckline that was cut vertically, straight across from shoulder to shoulder and high on the neck. This became a recurring feature of the garments he went on to design for the star over the years. The dress is minimally accessorized with short white kid gloves, with a button fastening on the wrist, and a pearl bracelet. **MF**

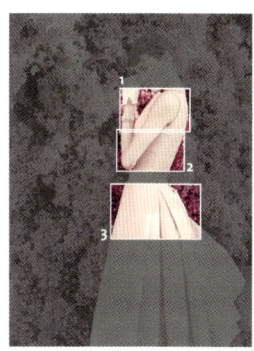

FOCAL POINTS

1 CUTAWAY SHOULDERS
The dress is cut with a high neckline, thus revealing the upper part of the shoulders rather than finishing at the breakpoint of the shoulder and arm. The underarm is cut in a straight horizontal line from the front to the back seam.

3 SKIRT
A series of inverted box pleats is positioned at the small of the back. Secured at the waist seam, they are allowed to fall freely down the back of the skirt to provide ease of movement and volume at the hem.

DESIGNER PROFILE

1927–51
Born in 1927 in Beauvais, Givenchy studied at the Lycée Félix Faure before moving to Paris to attend the Ecole Nationale Supérieure des Beaux-Arts. After a period of working for couturiers Lucien Lelong (1889–1958), Robert Piguet (1898–1953) and Jacques Fath (1912–54), Givenchy started designing separates for Elsa Schiaparelli (1890–1973).

1952–PRESENT
Maison Givenchy was established in 1952 and the first collection proved an immediate success. Givenchy created the clothes worn by Audrey Hepburn in several of her films, including *Sabrina* and *Breakfast at Tiffany's*, and she remained his muse for almost forty years. The company was sold to LVMH in 1988 and Givenchy showed his last couture collection in 1995, after which he retired from the fashion industry.

2 SEAMED BODICE
The bodice of the dress is made up of four equidistant horizontal panels. With the addition of a side seam these incorporate the shaping of the garment. The crisp silk gazar fabric is a delicate shell pink and holds the shape of the skirt.

MODERN SIMPLICITY

Pilgrim Pump 1960s
ROGER VIVIER

NAVIGATOR

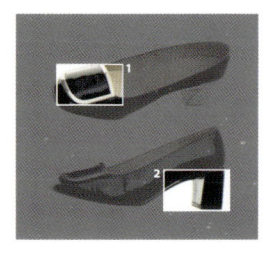

The radical change in silhouette at the beginning of the 1960s demanded an equally dramatic change in the style of footwear as an ever shorter skirt required a flatter shoe. Although inventive French shoe designer Roger Vivier had already been experimenting with a low-heeled, round-toed pump while working for couturier Christian Dior, women were initially reluctant to discard the flattering, leg-lengthening stiletto heel and pointed toe of the previous decade. It was only in the mid 1960s that the new low-heeled shoe in the form of the Pilgrim pump became fashionable, when photographed worn by Jackie Kennedy in the December 1966 edition of *Women's Wear Daily*. The shoe had been designed at the request of Yves Saint Laurent (1936–2008) to complement his Mondrian shift dresses launched in 1965 (see p.360). Vivier had previously created the wedge heel and the contemporary Louis XV or comma heel, but the Pilgrim pump proved to be his most iconic design. It was first constructed from a new type of artificial leather called Corfam, which was developed by DuPont in 1962, but was later manufactured in a range of leathers, particularly coloured patent leather, and with many variations of embellishment. The shoe was further popularized, and endlessly imitated, after French actress Catherine Deneuve wore it in the film *Belle de Jour* (1967). **MF**

▲ Jackie Kennedy steps out in a tailored double-breasted leopard-skin coat, combined with her favourite accessories, the classic Vivier pump and the Chanel 2.55 handbag (1967).

👁 FOCAL POINTS

1 BUCKLE
The square tapered toe features a large silver buckle in a modern interpretation of the Puritan pilgrim shoes of the 17th century. The pump is still in production, and the classic style has remained essentially unchanged and above fashion. The iconic buckle also appears on modern Vivier ballet pumps and accessories.

2 HEEL
The easy-to-wear pump has a sturdy heel of 1 ½ inches (3.5 cm), constructed from a type of japanned (varnished) leather that has been given a high-gloss finish. The low heel is ideal for wearing with short skirts and mini dresses, which creates a look that is more sporty than overtly seductive.

🕐 COMPANY PROFILE

1937–52
The first Vivier shop opened in 1937 in Paris, and Josephine Baker was one of the first clients. Roger Vivier experimented with shoe shapes, including the wedge, and also worked with couturière Elsa Schiaparelli. During World War II he emigrated to the United States and opened a shoe and hat store in New York.

1953–63
Having returned to Europe after the war, Vivier designed a pair of garnet-encrusted shoes for the coronation of Elizabeth II in 1953, and for ten years he worked for Christian Dior, whose New Look put a renewed emphasis on the shoe. He created a number of new heel shapes and has often been credited with the invention of the modern stiletto heel, which he reimagined in 1954 with metal instead of wood.

1964–70
During the 1960s Vivier designed shoes for Yves Saint Laurent, including thigh-high crocodile boots, but the Pilgrim pump, developed to match Saint Laurent's Mondrian dresses, became his best-known creation. He went on to design for Emanuel Ungaro (b.1933), and clients included film stars and international royalty.

1971–98
Throughout the 1970s Vivier worked with a number of eminent designer brands, among them Balmain, Balenciaga, Nina Ricci and Guy Laroche, but Yves Saint Laurent would remain his most important partner. Christian Louboutin (b.1963), who would go on to become a renowned shoe designer in his own right, was apprenticed to Vivier in the 1980s. Vivier died in 1998 but the brand continues today.

MODERN SIMPLICITY

TEXTILES OF EASTERN NEPAL

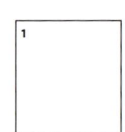

1. Limbu girls on market day (c. 1983). They are wearing gold earrings, nose rings and their one set of best clothes, which includes colourful shawls; these are woven using the Dhaka technique, covering the whole surface in pattern.

2. This black shawl is made from dyed and mercerized cotton. The pattern is described as the 'shoe design' because of the shape of the recurring main motif. Each motif is laid in by hand and judged by eye by the weaver.

The Nepalese national costume for men—the *daura suruwal*—consists of a tunic, waistcoat and trousers, worn with a colourful Dhaka topi hat (see p.352). It has evolved over centuries, but since the days of the Victorian Empire, certain events have established variants and stimulated the manufacture of the distinctive cloths used for the component garments. The *daura suruwal* was widely emulated after Prime Minister Jung Bahadur Rana wore it during a trip to Britain and France in 1850, after which he added a Western tailored jacket to the traditional ensemble. However, the *daura suruwal* was not declared to be national dress, worn at all formal occasions, until the mid 1880s. Between the mid 1950s and the early years of the 21st century this national dress appeared and disappeared in royal portraits on banknotes, reflecting the vacillation between autocratic and democratic government. Patterned Dhaka weaving, used for topi hats, developed in two places in Nepal: in Palpa, west of Kathmandu, and in Tehrathum, in the

KEY EVENTS

Mid 1950s	1955	1960s	1962	1973	1980
Entrepreneur Ganesh Man Maharjan goes to India and returns with the skills to weave *jamdani* cloth.	King Mahendra issues a sumptuary law that designates black Bhadgauni topis official dress for all government workers.	Maturing adolescents are required to be photographed in national costume for their citizenship passes.	Under the Panchayat administration, all office staff have to wear the basic topi, woven in Bhadgaun.	Palpali Dhaka production is at its high point, with 350 workers producing topis for poorer men.	The Khosi Hills Area Rural Development Programme, a British-funded project, fosters entrepreneurial skills among indigenous weavers.

eastern hills of the Himalayas, where hats proved popular with the Rai and Limbu peoples. Palpali Dhaka is held to be an innovation introduced by the entrepreneur Ganesh Man Maharjan, who visited India in the mid 1950s and there mastered the craft of weaving *jamdani* (a handwoven muslin cloth with weft-inserted abstract patterns). *Jamdani* was prized for the intricacy of its structure, and production had been at its height in and around Dhaka (the modern-day capital of Bangladesh) during the 17th century. Creating the fine cotton muslin dotted with motifs was labour intensive: stylized designs of flowers and vases were individually placed by hand as an extra weft effect. The base fabric, on which the motifs were placed, was a fine, undyed cotton, referred to as *mosuli* or *mosulin*. On his return to Nepal, Maharjan started manufacturing these cloths in Palpa, from the mid 1950s onwards. The broad cloth was woven by two women sitting side by side at a shared pedal loom for speedier production, creating a length of fabric from which several topi hats could be constructed.

Palpali weavers were employed in factories all year round, whereas in Tehrathum, Dhaka weavers were subsistent farmers: their farm work came first and the weaving was done only after all household chores had been completed; this was generally in the winter months. The women set up their looms, which were easily transportable and simple to use, in groups outdoors in the sun. Plenty of sunlight made this fine work easier on their eyes; by contrast Palpali weavers had to work in factory buildings with few windows.

The development of Dhaka cloth in the Tehrathum district originated in a similar way to Palpali Dhaka. Situated much closer to the region of Bengal, Tehrathum inevitably engaged in trade: the menfolk would travel to the plains of India and return with gifts, and saris were given as presents to the women of the household at the autumn festivals of Desain and Tihar. The highly prized *jamdani* cloth would be brought into the home and skilled weavers would emulate the complex designs and develop them further. Farms also used to grow and spin their own cotton up until the 1940s, but by the middle of the century the land was required for food crops only.

The design of the Tehrathum Dhaka underwent further transitions: the introduction of dyed, mercerized cotton, with a wider range of colours woven in the weft, led to a diversification of woven Dhaka cloths (right). In the early 1980s dyed yarns were imported from India, and the new vibrantly coloured cotton and acrylic yarns expanded the choice for weaving. From these threads a narrow cloth was created on a loom, which was just the width of a handspan, for a *petty* (a belt wound around the middle). A few inches at the end would be decorated with Dhaka weaving to add a flash of colour. With the introduction of a 24-inch (61-cm) reed (the comb for pushing down the yarn on the loom), a wider warp could be woven, allowing the weavers to produce a cloth to make short, tight-fitting *cholos* (blouses) and flamboyant shawls (opposite). **PH**

1980	1980–85	1986	1990	1990	1990
Dyed yarn is imported from India, widening the colour range. Tehrathum Dhaka is transported from the hills to be sold in Kathmandu.	British textile design consultants work with the weavers to expand their product range and increase their income.	The first Tehrathum Dhaka weaver relocates to Kathmandu.	The Panchayat administration comes to an end with the People's Revolution. It is replaced by an interim government.	National dress, previously a symbol of the monarchy, falls into decline.	Tehrathum Dhaka is taken up by entrepreneurs to develop a fashion range in Kathmandu.

Topi 20th century
MEN'S HAT

Dhaka topi hats worn by Limbu and Rai hill farmers with their version of the *daura suruwal* (c. 1983).

Colourful examples of Dhaka woven cloths have been worn for decades by the men of Tehrathum, the Nepalese 'dandies', in the form of topi hats. Living in the middle hills of the Himalayas in the eastern Koshi zone of Nepal, only the members of the Limbu and Rai ethnic groups choose to wear their topi at the full height of 7 inches (18 cm). Distinguished by the striking colours of their topis, the men appear head and shoulders above the other traders and shoppers at the 'haat bazaar', which is held each Friday. The brimless, fez-shaped hats are woven for the men by their wives and mothers, and are prized gifts at the Desain and Tihar festivals. The handwoven patterns all have an individual touch as they are particular to each family and are passed from mother to daughter, from sister to sister-in-law or among other female weavers in the extended family. In the 1980s the warp colour changed from white to other colours, often blue. Over time, and with daily use, the colours on the topis begin to fade. As the cycle of the farmer's year concludes, the deflated topis are worn until the weavers of the household create new ones. Government officers, on the other hand, have been obliged to wear black Bhadgauni topis since the mid 1950s, the sombre, neat and short shape of the hat identifying their professional status. **PH**

NAVIGATOR

FOCAL POINTS

1 PEAKED SHAPE
The farmers wear their topis at full height. Tehrathum Dhaka topis are constructed from the patterned ends of a length of plain woven cloth, with the weft of the fabric beaten hard to produce a cloth that is dense in structure, enabling the topi to stand up.

2 BOLD COLOURS
The topis are woven in brilliant hues. The fluorescent acrylic yarns appear in orange, green, pink and red on a cotton background in serrated diagonal stripes. The pattern continues across the crown, which is constructed on hand-operated sewing machines.

▲ A woman weaves a traditional Tehrathum Dhaka cloth on a simple loom made of bamboo and carved hardwood. It is a slow and labour-intensive process but provides a way of earning a living.

TEXTILES OF EASTERN NEPAL 353

THE RETAIL REVOLUTION

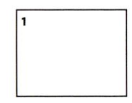

1 Models wear a range of styles at the opening of boutique Just Looking on King's Road, Chelsea, London (1967).

2 A Mary Quant tweed coat with velvet trimmed pocket is teamed with a matching knitted mini dress (1964).

3 John Bates's winter collection of 1966 for the Jean Varon range featured coordinated wool separates.

The opening of London boutiques, such as Mary Quant, Biba, Granny Takes a Trip and Bus Stop, as well as the retail phenomenon of Carnaby Street in London's Soho district, transformed the nature of the shopping experience at a time of massive social upheaval, when the peak of the post-war baby boom in 1947 resulted in unparalleled numbers of teenagers reaching puberty in 1960. Following the aftermath of World War II, Britain experienced a period of affluence, during which the teenager could look forward to an extended adolescence of growing financial independence and diminishing parental control.

The Education Act of 1944, known as the 'Butler Act', expanded opportunities for working-class children to enter further and higher education, and increasing numbers of students enrolled at art colleges, where they enjoyed a curriculum that embraced graphic design, product design, architecture, textiles and fashion design, and learnt to forge new ways of solving new problems. Disaffection arose when these young designers tried to find jobs in industries that were resolutely fixed in the manufacturing and marketing practices of the 1950s. They then decided that in order to fulfil their creative potential it would be necessary to open a retail space to sell their own designs. Although boutiques had previously adjoined the salons of the Parisian

KEY EVENTS

1955	1961	1961	1963	1964	1964
Bazaar, the first fashion boutique, opens on King's Road, Chelsea, London, owned by Mary Quant and Alexander Plunket Greene.	Fashion entrepreneur Vanessa Denza is appointed by retailer Martin Moss to open a boutique, the 21 shop, within the Woollands store in Knightsbridge.	Fashion students Marion Foale and Sally Tuffin find studio premises on Carnaby Street, at the time a rundown back street in Soho, London.	Designer Gerald McCann opens a boutique in Raphael and Leonard's House of Beauty on Upper Grosvenor Street, Mayfair, London.	Fashion journalist Marit Allan heads a column in British *Vogue* titled 'Young Ideas', featuring the new young designers.	The first Biba boutique opens on Abingdon Road, Kensington, London. It is followed in 1968 by the ground-breaking mail order catalogue.

354 1946–89

couturiers, selling less expensive lines and accessories, the independent fashion boutique was essentially a British phenomenon: a product of the entrepreneurial 1960s and one that was predicated on inspired amateurism. These boutiques gave voice, form and location to the youthful desire for fashion as a means of self-expression (opposite).

Prior to the advent of boutiques, shopping for clothes had been a tiresome chore for most teenagers, undertaken in one of the city-centre department stores that sold everything from scarves to saucepans. The boutique changed the shopping experience for ever and transformed it into a social activity. One of the major features of boutique culture was a desire to dismantle the boundaries between work and play, friends and colleagues, and public and private places. The premises were usually sited away from the main shopping areas in the city's back streets, where the rent was cheap, and the boutique owners were not only acquainted with their customers but were also themselves members of the subcultures that were proliferating around this time and thus part of a vast new market. These shared attitudes, values and practices were instrumental factors in the successful development of boutique culture.

The first fashion boutique to achieve national recognition was Bazaar in Markham House, King's Road, London. It was opened by Mary Quant (b.1934) in 1955 at a time when the stoic resignation to the deprivations of wartime Britain was giving way to the first stirrings of desire for colour and life and change. Having trained as a teacher at Goldsmiths College, University of London, where she met her future husband, Alexander Plunket Greene, Quant started her fashion business by adapting paper patterns. She made the day's output of dresses in her bedsitting room, and sold them in the late afternoon to finance the next day's purchase of cloth. Initially her customers were from the same social milieu as herself; the price of a pinafore dress featured in *Vogue* in 1960 was sixteen and a half guineas—at the time almost three weeks' wages for an office girl. The Mary Quant label typified the 'Chelsea Look', a silhouette that allowed freedom of movement and was inspired by children's and dancers' clothing: knee-high socks, pinafore dresses, leotards, gingham and flannel, allied to a style of dress worn by art students, with its roots in the Parisian Left Bank and American 'beats'. Quant played with the proportions of classic fashion garments; scaled-up cardigans and football shirts became dresses. This new look required a new vocabulary to describe the girls dressed by Quant. They were 'dolly birds', wearing 'kooky, kinky gear' (above right). British designer John Bates (b.1938) was part of Mary Quant's early retailing experience, and collaborated with her to create Bazaar's window displays. Like Quant he was one of several designers associated with the invention of the mini (right). Bates set up his Jean Varon label in 1960 and went on to open twenty-four free-standing boutiques around Britain. His Casbah dress (see p.358) won Dress of the Year in 1965 and exemplified his use of innovative materials.

1965	1965	1965	1966	1969	1973
The Society of London Fashion Designers, led by chairman Edward Rayne, promotes British fashion to US buyers on board the cruise ship *QE2*.	Photographer James Wedge and model Pat Booth launch Top Gear and Countdown—two of the most influential boutiques of the era—on King's Road.	British retailer Paul Young opens Paraphernalia on New York's Madison Avenue between 66th and 67th Streets.	Yves Saint Laurent opens the first Rive Gauche boutique in Paris, selling ready-to-wear.	Designer Lee Bender opens Bus Stop in Kensington, London. Painted bright red and gold, it is the first of twelve located in Britain's major cities.	The fourth and final Biba opens in the Art Deco department store Derry & Toms in Kensington. It provides a complete lifestyle shopping experience.

THE RETAIL REVOLUTION 355

London's Royal College of Art, under the auspices of Professor Janey Ironside, was well attuned to the modern desire for young fashion. Sally Tuffin (b.1938) and Marion Foale (b.1939) were both postgraduate students on the fashion course when Quant's husband and business partner, Alexander Plunket Greene, gave a talk on his experience of starting up Bazaar, prompting the girls to rent premises on Carnaby Street, where a similar retail explosion was happening in men's fashion (see p.364). Foale and Tuffin were the first to experiment with cutting trousers for women (left), reducing the numbers of pleats and darts and lowering the waistband to sit on the hips in fabrics such as linen and corduroy. By this time London was attracting international press as the epicentre of a youthful revolution in all aspects of British culture, particularly fashion and music. *Time* magazine (1966) designated London as the 'swinging' city: 'This spring, as never before in modern times, London is switched on. Ancient elegance and new opulence are all tangled up in a dazzling blur of op and pop. The city is alive with birds and beauties, buzzing with mini cats and telly stars, pulsing with half a dozen separate veins of excitement.'

In the early 1960s boutiques were still exclusive in the sense that the clothes were accessible only to a relatively affluent clientele who could journey to London. Biba was the first boutique to enter the popular consciousness and its ever-changing ranges of stylish clothing and accessories (below) revolutionized the way the ordinary girl on the street dressed. The first small shop on Abingdon Road, Kensington, opened by Barbara Hulanicki (b.1936) and her husband, Stephen Fitz-Simon, created a shopping experience in which customers could buy inexpensive fashionable clothes in a striking interior of Art Nouveau fittings and William Morris wallpaper. Whereas Mary Quant had stripped out the front of Markham House to accommodate a wide shop window and had removed iron railings to improve accessibility to Bazaar, the exterior of Biba remained unchanged from the previously dilapidated old chemist's shop.

The boutique concept reached the United States in the mid 1960s, when the work of what *Life* magazine had identified in 1963 as the 'brash new breed of British designers' began to reach the US press. This first response was typical of the conservative nature of the leaders of the US fashion establishment. Influential journalists such as Kathleen Casey, editor of *Glamour* magazine, and Geraldine Stutz, president of the prestigious New York department store Henri Bendel, found it difficult to categorize the avant-garde, the gamine and the kooky, and insisted that the look remain firmly under the aegis of the 'Junior Miss'. This changed when fashion entrepreneur Paul Young, who was responsible for signing up Mary Quant in 1963 to the J. C. Penney label, instigated the New York boutique Paraphernalia. Under the guidance of British buyer Sandy Moss, the boutique sold designs by Foale and Tuffin, Emmanuelle Khanh (b.1937), Sylvia Ayton (b.1937), Zandra Rhodes (b.1940), Ossie Clark (1942–96) and milliner James Wedge (b.1939) to the 'beautiful people', among them style icon Jackie Kennedy Onassis and British model Twiggy (right).

The interior of Paraphernalia was designed by architect Ulrich Franzen as a series of raised dais on which live models gyrated to music and embodied the metallic glitter of the space age. There was no overt selling, the display was confined to live models and the merchandise was unobtrusive. Far more important was the space; innovative tractor seats, later exhibited in the Whitney Museum of American Art, New York, provided the perfect venue for the urban leisure activity of 'hanging out'. Betsey Johnson (b.1942; see p.362) was seen as the home-grown talent who could usurp the British stranglehold on the avant-garde. Her work had been spotted by Paul Young while he was visiting *Mademoiselle* magazine in search of new talent. Johnson was enormously influenced by the boutique Biba, which she had visited while on a trip to London. In her designs Johnson utilized found materials such as plastic and paper, and aluminium foil and vinyl, adding to the transitory nature of the clothes. Fuelled by the impetus of Betsey Johnson's talent, Paraphernalia went on to franchise branches across the United States.

During the 'high' 1960s, boutique culture began to accommodate the hippies' desire for the nostalgic and the extreme. This aesthetic was eagerly embraced by Nigel Weymouth and John Pearse with their unisex boutique, Granny Takes a Trip, in King's Road, London. The style fragmentation of the youth market also resulted in clothes that represented the alternative lifestyle of the counter-culture, including denim jeans, work shirts and ethnic costume purchased on the hippie trail or from the local 'head' shop. Boutique culture had flourished during the entrepreneurial 1960s. However, during the recession-hit 1970s, retail space was too expensive to be used for recreational purposes, and the casual informality of the interiors meant that shoplifting was rife. Furthermore, an increasingly rapacious mass market, eager to exploit the new demographic of teenagers, was quick to copy new ideas that they then retailed through cheaper high-street chains. The replication of not only boutique fashions but also noteworthy garments, such as the Mondrian dress (see p.360) by French couturier Yves Saint Laurent (1936–2008), resulted in a multiplicity of downmarket copies in inferior fabrics. Saint Laurent was quick to appreciate that a wider audience for his work existed, and launched an influential range of boutiques under the name Rive Gauche in 1966, placing the concept of the boutique as a retail experience once again as an addendum to high-end fashion. Those British designers who continued to pursue a career in fashion were now equally eager to enter the international fashion arena and show their clothes in Paris, thus ensuring their participation in the flourishing ready-to-wear industry. **MF**

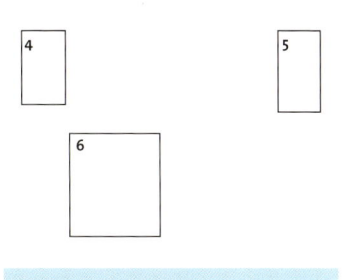

4 Foale and Tuffin's corduroy trouser suit of 1964 quickly became a must-have item for modern women in the 1960s.

5 Twiggy models a white bias-cut dress on sale at Paraphernalia in 1967.

6 A full-length black-and-silver sequin dress with matching headdress and veil from 1969 is characteristic of the glamour and decadence of the Biba label.

Casbah Dress 1965
JOHN BATES b. 1938

British actress, model and style icon Jean Shrimpton wears the Casbah dress, photographed by Brian Duffy for *Vogue* (January 1965).

A symbol of youth, vigour and freedom, the mini emerged amid society's transformation from the dour conservatism of the post-war era to the uncompromising modernism of the 1960s. With a provenance disputed between British designers Mary Quant, John Bates, Barbara Hulanicki of Biba and Parisian couturier André Courrèges (b.1923), the mini's impact was incontrovertible, signifying nothing less than a sexual revolution. Some of the most daring clothes of the era were designed by British-born John Bates under the label Jean Varon. He was the first designer to bare the midriff by raising the waistline and accentuating the line of the hips, using cut-outs, mesh or transparent materials such as plastic to attach the bodice to the skirt, thus redefining the proportions of the dress and raising the hemline.

The Casbah dress, selected by the Fashion Museum in Bath, England, to represent the year 1965, features Bates's signature midriff panel. It retailed at six guineas and was available in the department stores Woollands in London and Darling in Edinburgh. As skirts shortened, posture and attitude changed. The 1960s 'dolly bird' could stride unfettered in her flat boots or Mary Jane shoes, tights replaced stockings and suspenders, and hair was no longer teased into bouffant heights, but cut into head-hugging styles. **MF**

NAVIGATOR

FOCAL POINTS

1 CUTAWAY SLEEVES
The shift-style mini dress has a bodice with sleeves cut away from the line of the shoulder, forming a curved strap with the wide-scooped neckline. Shoulders assumed a new importance in the 1960s and were frequently left exposed.

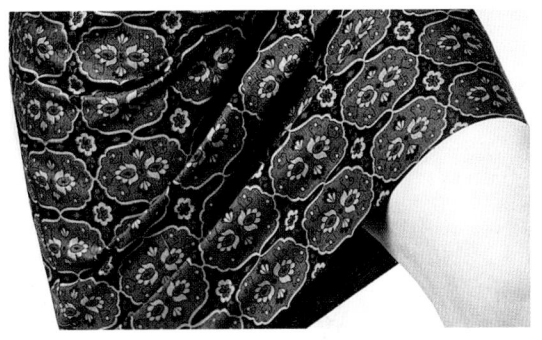

3 A-LINE SKIRT
The A-line skirt widens only slightly towards the hem. The bodice and skirt fabric is a deep terracotta and navy blue synthetic linen by Wallach, which has been printed in a geometric design reminiscent of Moorish tiles.

DESIGNER PROFILE

1938–64
John Bates was born in Ponteland, Northumberland. In 1956 he was apprenticed to Gerard Pipart at the design house of Herbert Sidon on Sloane Street, London, and in 1960 he began designing under the name Jean Varon. Among his best-known designs are the black-and-white and metallic Op art-inspired outfits that he created for British actress Diana Rigg for her role as Emma Peel in the 1960s cult television show *The Avengers*.

1965–PRESENT
Bates's Casbah dress was chosen as the Dress of the Year by the Fashion Writers' Association in 1965. In the 1970s he dressed royalty, such as Princess Margaret, and actresses including Maggie Smith. In 2006 a retrospective of his work was held at the Fashion Museum in Bath, England.

2 EXPOSED MIDRIFF
The dress features Bates's signature focus on the midriff. Here a panel of navy blue mesh, a material usually used for men's string vests, fills the gap between the bodice and the skirt. The panel is close-fitting and accentuates the figure.

THE RETAIL REVOLUTION 359

Mondrian Dress 1965
YVES SAINT LAURENT 1936 – 2008

In 1965 Yves Saint Laurent paid direct homage to the compositional rigour of Piet Mondrian's Neo-Plasticist paintings of the 1930s with a knee-length wool day dress that presented the artist's work to the fashionable elite. The couturier sought to evoke the radically minimized abstractions of primary colour and geometry of the Dutch-born painter on the body-skimming shift dress, which was a development of the 1950s sack dress that bypassed the body's contours to fall straight from the shoulders to the knee.

In paintings such as *Compositional C (III)* (1935), which has a strong visual equivalence to this shift dress, Mondrian chose to constrain his composition to a square format. Here, the emphasis is on the vertical limits of the dress, which is achieved via the solidity of the strong colour block at the shoulder and hem. Saint Laurent's use of Mondrian's bold graphics for couture dresses brokered a cultural bridge for his clientele to the more democratic outburst of Op art and youth-focused fashion, seen on the streets of London and in the boutiques of New York. The Mondrian dress was popularized when it featured on the cover of French *Vogue* in September 1965. Many cheaper copies ensued: some with the design merely printed onto the surface of the dress, and with scant acknowledgement of shape. **MF**

NAVIGATOR

FOCAL POINTS

1 USE OF COLOUR
The palette is limited to three primary colours combined with black and white, creating a strong contrast that reflects Mondrian's style of painting. Influenced by the painter Bart van der Leck, Mondrian developed his distinctive geometric style from 1916 onwards.

3 UNOBTRUSIVE SEAMING
Yves Saint Laurent displays his expertise in garment construction. He pieces together each block of jersey to accommodate the body by imperceptibly hiding the minimal shaping of the shift dress in the grid of seams.

DESIGNER PROFILE

1936–65
Yves Saint Laurent was born in Oran, Algeria. In 1958 he was appointed head designer of the House of Dior, successfully launching the 'trapeze line' with his first collection. After serving in the French army in 1960, he was subsequently declared unfit for service and suffered a nervous breakdown.

1966–2008
Saint Laurent and his partner, the industrialist Pierre Bergé, launched their own fashion house using funds from Atlanta millionaire J. Mack Robinson. In 1966 the first of the company's Rive Gauche stores, selling the innovative prêt-à-porter line, opened in the 6th arrondissement of Paris. Saint Laurent retired in 2002 to live at his homes in Normandy and Morocco, and was awarded the rank of Grand officier de la Légion d'honneur in 2007, a year before he died.

2 THICK BLACK LINES
Respecting the portrait format of the human figure and the stark architecture of the dress, the composition is reconfigured, rather than cropped, and the black delineation between rectangular colour blocks is given heavier proportion than in the painting.

THE RETAIL REVOLUTION 361

Op Art Print Minis 1966
BETSEY JOHNSON b. 1942

⬥ NAVIGATOR

The streamlined mini dresses of the early 1960s provided a perfect canvas for textile designs inspired by Op and Pop art. Although Betsey Johnson drew on both these movements for inspiration, the geometric prints of the three dresses that she designed in 1966 referenced Op art, a term first used by *Time* magazine in 1964 to describe optical illusions in painting that fool the eye. British artist Bridget Riley's first purely optical work, *Movement in Squares*, appeared in 1961 and US dress manufacturer Larry Aldrich was quick to see the commercial potential of the distinctive work. He purchased pieces by both Riley and US abstract painter Richard Anuszkiewicz and commissioned a range of fabrics inspired by his new acquisitions.

Pop art had its roots in the late 1950s, and elevated mundane imagery and everyday objects, such as soup cans, comic books and magazines, to the status of high art, exemplified by the work of Andy Warhol. Johnson included found objects in her designs, such as shower curtain rings and do-it-yourself appliqués on transparent plastic dresses. The printed knit jersey dresses are cut without darts in a simple A-line shape with a just-above-the-knee hemline, longer than the British mini. The prints are in subdued tones; chocolate brown with eau-de-Nil, tartan green with putty, and French navy and beige. **MF**

👁 FOCAL POINTS

1 NARROW SLEEVE HEAD
The full-length sleeves are set into a small arm scye, which fits at the top of the arm rather than at the end of the shoulder. This creates the impression of an elongated torso, an effect that is increased by the narrow cut of the sleeves.

2 GEOMETRIC PATTERNING
Against a backdrop of the vibrant graphics of the Op and Pop art movements, Johnson adopts a simple array of medium-scale, single-screen prints—doughnuts, chevrons and diamonds—that are a commercial expression of modernity.

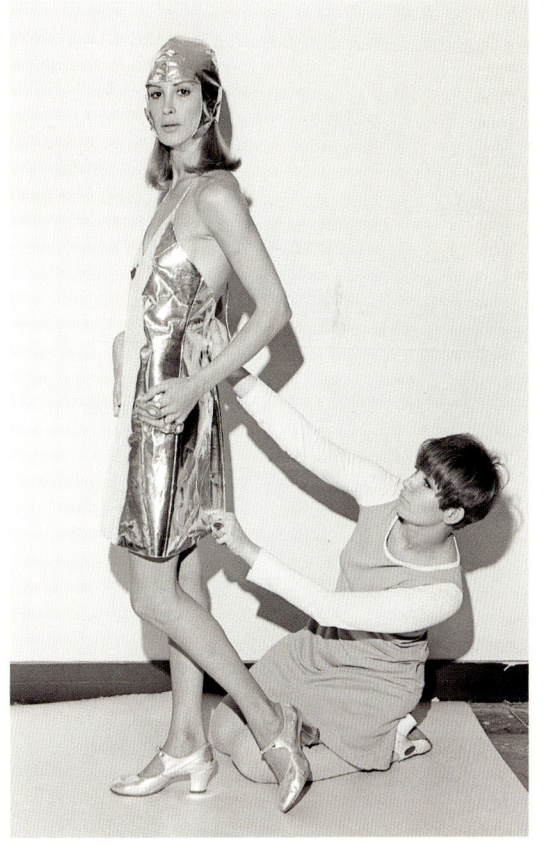

▲ US designer Betsey Johnson (right) favoured unconventional materials, such as metallic foil, seen here in her mirror dress on Spanish model Valma (1966).

THE BRITISH MENSWEAR REVOLUTION

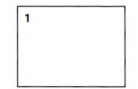

1. Designer John Stephen (centre) poses outside his boutique on Carnaby Street, London (1966).

2. A customer tries on a military jacket outside I Was Lord Kitchener's Valet on Portobello Road, London (1967).

3. Nigel Weymouth, founder of the London boutique Granny Takes a Trip, wears a vintage floral print jacket from his collection.

During the late 1950s the first intimation of London's future status as a 'swinging' city was instigated by Glaswegian-born John Stephen (above) when he opened a one-room boutique, His Clothes, on Beak Street in 1957. After a move around the corner to Carnaby Street, at the time a Soho backwater of shops selling domestic products, Stephen built up an extensive retail empire selling menswear in an atmosphere of lively anarchy. His customers were predominantly mods, who travelled from all over Britain to buy their clothes from his ever-changing stock of short-lived fashions.

Mods were a minority cult, a group of youths whose sartorial preoccupations were expressed in the wearing of a uniform comprising military-issue parkas and Italian-influenced suits. Worn with button-down shirts and a narrow knitted tie, these suits were introduced by Cecil Gee in 1956 and were based on the tailoring of the Brioni label in Rome (see p.336). As Britain's youth culture burgeoned, mod fashion became increasingly flamboyant. Following the line of female fashions, slim-cut shirts were cut close to the body and reduced ease of movement. These vibrantly patterned shirts featured extended collars, worn open or with an exaggerated 'kipper' tie. Hip-huggers (trousers with a low rise and narrow on the hips) were cut to flare out over Chelsea boots, or later were tucked into skinny boots with a heel, bought from the iconic Chelsea Cobbler shop. In addition, the Regency dandy look was evoked by high-standing collars

KEY EVENTS

1957	1964	1965	1965	1966	1966
John Stephen opens his first shop, His Clothes, on London's Beak Street.	Jeff Simons opens The Ivy Shop in Hill Rise, Richmond, London, selling Ivy League clothes.	Traditional London shirt makers Turnbull & Asser employ Michael Fish (b.1940) as designer.	The Dayton Company of Minneapolis introduces the first of the John Stephen boutiques to appear in the United States.	Michael Fish opens his shop, Mr Fish, on Clifford Street, Mayfair, London, selling transparent shirts, flowery hats and vibrant kipper ties.	New York department store Bonwit Teller installs a Pierre Cardin menswear boutique.

on double-breasted jackets in jewel-coloured velvet or ornate brocade, the gap filled with fringed silk scarves or cravats. The success of Stephen's shop precipitated an influx of new menswear boutiques on Carnaby Street, which became an essential destination not only for the mod who wanted to keep up to date with fast-moving trends but also for showbusiness customers, such as Peter Sellers, and the aristocracy, including Lord Snowdon.

By 1967 Carnaby Street had become a tourist venue for overseas visitors who were eager to experience what the press described as 'swinging London'. Consequently the locus of cool moved to King's Road in Chelsea, the site of Bazaar, the first boutique opened by Mary Quant (b.1934). Hung on You, owned by Michael Rainey, opened on King's Road at the end of the 1960s and retailed vintage uniforms alongside the new tailoring, such as pastel-coloured suits with wide lapels, worn with frilled shirts in Liberty tana lawn or see-through voile. British retailer Rupert Lycett Green capitalized on the desire for clothes that combined the sartorial innovations of Carnaby Street with the traditional Savile Row virtues of quality of fabric and make. Together with cutter Eric Joy he launched Blades on Dover Street, Mayfair, in 1963 to serve the needs of the aristocratic customers and pop star celebrities with bespoke suits. London-born Dougie Hayward (1934–2008) also tailored for an international pop celebrity fraternity, including Tony Bennett, Terence Stamp and Michael Caine. Unconcerned with novelty, Hayward provided classic yet modern tailoring featuring a slim-line suit with high vents in the jacket and width at the hem of the trousers. Offering a more extreme tailoring experience to pop stars and their girlfriends was British designer and tailor Tommy Nutter (1943–92; see p.368), who opened Nutters of Savile Row in 1969.

As the 1960s progressed, the modernism of the decade gave way to a period of fashion design retrenchment. A culture that was still reverberating from the sweeping changes in social and sexual mores became nostalgic for the fashions of the past, which for men included playfully subverting historical military uniforms (above right). These were found at such outlets as Ian Fisk's I Was Lord Kitchener's Valet (see p.366) on Portobello Road and the antique markets in Kensington and Chelsea. The look transformed the sharp tailoring of the mods into the fantasy dressing-up box ethos of the hippies. Historical revivalism also included the vogue for the swirling free-flowing forms of Art Nouveau, and textile designs from the era were made up into brightly coloured jackets for men (right), which together with reworked vintage clothes and *fin de siècle* ephemera were sold in boutiques such as Granny Takes a Trip, opened on King's Road in 1967 by Nigel Weymouth, Sheila Cohen and John Pearse.

John Stephen attempted to launch a string of boutiques in the United States. However, the majority of young US males were difficult to divert from the Ivy League collegiate style of button-down shirts worn with a Brooks Brothers 'sack' suit and wing-tip brogues (see p.308). **MF**

1966	1967	1967	1967	1967	1968
Ian Fisk (owner) and John Paul (manager) open the boutique I Was Lord Kitchener's Valet on Portobello Road, Notting Hill, London.	Aristocrat Sir Mark Palmer opens the English Boy agency, featuring long-haired models who redefine the rugged male stereotype.	The release of the Beatles' album *Sgt. Pepper's Lonely Hearts Club Band* confirms the vogue for faux militaria.	The Carnaby Street Traders' Association has the first meeting of the 'Magnificent Seven', appointing John Stephen as secretary.	*Bonnie and Clyde* sets the style for gangster-inspired fashion for men. It is one of the most far-reaching effects on fashion perpetrated by a film.	Tom Gilbey (b.1939) works for John Michael before opening his design consultancy and fashion house on Sackville Street, Mayfair, London.

THE BRITISH MENSWEAR REVOLUTION

Union Jack Jacket 1966
I WAS LORD KITCHENER'S VALET

(Clockwise from left) Keith Moon, John Entwistle, Roger Daltrey and Pete Townshend of The Who (1966).

NAVIGATOR

The appropriation of military uniforms and the adoption of the Union Flag—more popularly known as the Union Jack—as a decorative device were clear indications of the questioning of the post-imperial values that were in place in Britain during the 1960s. Music, art and fashion replaced military might in colonizing other cultures, firmly positioning London as a prime progenitor of contemporary culture. The retail emporium I Was Lord Kitchener's Valet, named after the British field marshal, formerly commander-in-chief of the army in India, enabled young people to subvert the values inherent in the medal-bedecked uniforms of the British army as it sold the garments as fashion items. Likewise, the Union Flag became a useful image in the rebranding of popular culture and was a persuasive emblem of swinging London rather than a traditional symbol of patriotism.

This narrow-fitting single-breasted flag jacket, here worn by Pete Townshend—legendary guitarist and songwriter for English rock band The Who, formed in 1964—has all the hallmarks of mod tailoring. The flag, the design of which dates from the union of Ireland and Great Britain in 1801, is carefully positioned on the jacket to take advantage of its strong graphic lines. **MF**

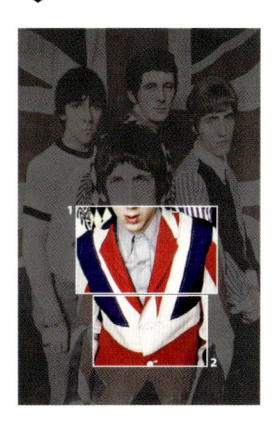

FOCAL POINTS

1 NEAT SHOULDER LINE
The narrowly cut torso is further elongated by the tight arm scye and the high break of the single-breasted fastening, secured with three evenly spaced buttons in white. These match the white top-stitching throughout.

2 FLAG DESIGN
The red cross of St George, patron saint of England, forms the centre of the jacket, broadest at the waist and extending into the narrow revers. The red is superimposed on the white saltire of St Andrew, patron saint of Scotland, which forms the ground colour.

▲ David Bowie wears a distressed Union Jack jacket designed in collaboration with Alexander McQueen (1969–2010). The coat features on the *Earthling* album cover (1997).

Nutter Suit 1969
TOMMY NUTTER 1943 – 92

Ringo Starr features in a magazine
advertisement for Tommy Nutter (1970s).

NAVIGATOR

As a 1960s phenomenon, the designer-tailor was epitomized by the assiduous self-publicist Tommy Nutter. Detached from the reticent tone of his bespoke trade competitors, Nutter embraced the extravagances of earlier epochs, from the flashy debonair urbanity of Fred Astaire to the androgyny of Marlene Dietrich (see p.268) and the reproportioning of physique that is implicit in the zoot suit (see p.294).

Although he dared to revolutionize the external visual impact of tailored garments, Nutter still held firm to the tenets of bespoke manufacture, in which great importance is placed on the hidden infrastructure of horsehair and linen canvas, seam tapes, pads and bridles, set between the lining and the outer fabric. He took the architecture of the classic men's three-piece suit and reformatted it into sartorial kitsch, typically using contrast binding around large-scale lapels, or estate tweeds patchworked with dogtooth checks and bold patch pockets. Although the cut, achieved in collaboration with Edward Sexton, explored radical forms, the make, pitch and fit of the resultant styles behaved impeccably, regardless of the experimental fabric combinations. In 1969 Nutter created suits for three members of the Beatles for the cover of the *Abbey Road* album and was much sought after in the early 1970s by rock stars such as David Bowie and Elton John. **MF**

FOCAL POINTS

1 SQUARED-OFF SHOULDER
Coming to prominence in an era when fashion looked back to the 1930s and 1940s for inspiration, Nutter characteristically padded out the shoulder to form an acute angle, emphasized by a prominent sleeve head.

3 SHAWL COLLAR
The focus of the three-piece suit is the deep rolled shawl collar, which features contrasting binding cut on the cross of the fabric. The collar breaks at the nipped-in waist above the top button fastening of the jacket.

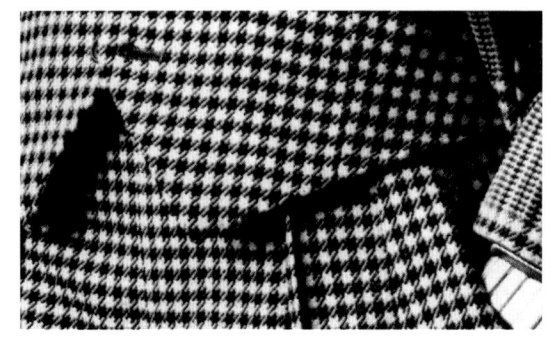

2 REVIVAL OF OXFORD BAGS
The wide-legged dogtooth trousers are cut high in the waist and the centre-front pleats are in alignment with the points of the single-breasted waistcoat above, also in dogtooth. Roomy vertical pockets are set into the side seam.

DESIGNER PROFILE

1943–69
Tommy Nutter studied at the Tailor and Cutter Academy and worked for traditional tailors Donaldson, Williams & Ward. He became inspired by changes in popular culture during the 1960s, and in 1969 opened his own shop in Savile Row, London's bespoke tailoring enclave, as Nutters of Savile Row.

1970–92
Nutter worked with Edward Sexton and was backed financially by English singer Cilla Black and Peter Brown, managing director of the Beatles' company Apple Corps. In the 1970s Nutter's bespoke business was less successful, but he branched out into ready-to-wear clothing, marketed through Austin Reed. Nutter also successfully expanded into East Asia, establishing the Savile Row brand in Japan. In 1989 he created the costumes for the Joker in the film *Batman*.

THE BRITISH MENSWEAR REVOLUTION

AFROCENTRIC FASHION

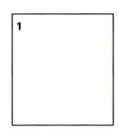

1. *Nuit de Noël* by Malick Sidibé (1963) shows a young Malian couple dancing and wearing French fashions that reflect the post-colonial generation's cosmopolitan sense of style.

2. High-school students in Cape Coast, Ghana, wear skirts made of traditional kente cloth, Africa's best-known textile (c. 1960).

As a continent Africa has a rich, meaningful history of body adornment, textile development and dress practices. It is no wonder, therefore, that, like the West, it embraced the concept of 'contemporary fashion' in the 1960s. Africa's myriad aesthetics had faced centuries of assimilation as traders, invaders and migrants influenced indigenous tastes. The Berbers brought loom-spun textiles, the Venetians brought glass beads, the Dutch brought batik prints and the English brought tailoring skills. Change was nothing new, but as European colonialism drew to an end (Ghana claimed its independence in 1957 under President Kwame Nkrumah and seventeen other countries had followed suit by the end of 1960), fashion became an expression of a renewed sense of cultural identity and ownership of one's sense of self.

Nkrumah urged his people to reject all forms of Western clothing in favour of national dress. However, the young urban elite across Africa was keen to define its own dress sense. Inspired by the resistance music and styles of Fela

KEY EVENTS

1960s	1960	1962	1966	1967	1967
Malick Sidibé takes a series of photographs documenting the youth culture of Mali.	Shade Thomas-Fahm opens the first Afrocentric ready-to-wear boutique in Lagos, Nigeria.	Jackie Kennedy wears a leopard-print coat by Oleg Cassini (1913–2006), sparking a trend for jungle prints also echoed by couture house Christian Dior.	Ghanaian photographer James Barnor shoots young black models in the latest fashions for the Nigerian edition of *Drum* magazine.	Yves Saint Laurent's collection of African dresses sends ripples of adoration through the international fashion world.	Chris Seydou opens a tailoring shop; it is his first step towards becoming one of the first internationally known African designers.

Kuti and Hugh Masekela, and fuelled by university educations abroad, the jet set mixed up pieces by European labels such as Yves Saint Laurent, Pierre Cardin and Balenciaga with more traditional items made by tailors—a designer blouse with a wrapper skirt, for example. Each tailor had his own individual flair, especially in Senegal where the skill was most refined, but it was the textile traders—always women—who held the most sway. They travelled the world collecting desirable cloths and brought them home to eager consumers.

The finest local fabrics, such as Ghanaian kente (right) and Kenyan *kanga*, were also prized, not only for fashion's sake but also traditionally as symbols of wealth, power and status. Nigerian *ase oke*, a Yoruba woven cloth, traditionally came in white, blue, tan and red, but as demand among urbanites grew, new colours, yarns and weave patterns were introduced. Once embroidered, embellished and fitted to the body, these cloths invested the wearer in supreme African style. The concept of African ready-to-wear was introduced to Nigeria by designer Shade Thomas-Fahm (b.1933). She trained in London and opened a line of boutiques in Lagos in the 1960s, offering modern easy versions of traditional Nigerian styles, such as a white cotton *buba* (top) worn with a striped *ase oke iro* (wrapper) and *ipele* (shawl; see p.374).

Post-colonial style in Mali was immortalized by the work of a series of well-known photographers. Following in the footsteps of pioneering studio photographer Seydou Keita, Hamidou Maiga and Soungalo Malé shot their subjects against painted backdrops and posing with their prized possessions, such as a Vespa scooter or a transistor radio—symbols of their upward mobility—whereas Malick Sidibé, aka the Eye of Bamako, headed into the night to photograph young people dancing and expressing themselves (opposite). Boys formed clubs and wore matching suits to show their musical and style allegiances. Girls left their parents' houses wearing grand *pagnes* (wrappers), but took them off when they arrived at the party to reveal mini dresses. They were part of an African youth culture that was hopeful for its future, engaging in a dialogue with international fashion and music trends.

Mali was also the birthplace of ground-breaking designer Chris Seydou (1949–94), who learnt tailoring in the small town of Kali and opened his first tailoring store in Ouagadougou, Burkina Faso, in 1967. Ambition drove him to Paris in the early 1970s, where he worked for several fashion houses and achieved acclaim for his innovative use of *bògòlanfini*. This Malian mud cloth, made by Bamana women, is believed to have ritual powers and is distinguished by its brown and white geometric patterns. Seydou was the first to turn it into a fashion fabric by using it to make Western styles.

An archive of style that reflects Afrocentric fashion can be found in the pages of *Drum* magazine, Africa's first black lifestyle magazine. It was launched in South Africa in 1951 and became a powerful voice against Apartheid. Its reporters were drawn initially to Sophiatown, a racially mixed Johannesburg

1968	1968	1968	1969	1975	1979
J. D. Okhai Ojeikere begins his photographic series of Nigerian women's hair and headwraps.	Yves Saint Laurent invents the safari suit. Franco Rubartelli immortalizes the look by shooting German model Veruschka wearing one in Mali.	The musical *Hair* opens in the West End and Marsha Hunt steals the limelight with her huge Afro. She appears in British *Vogue* the following year.	Ugandan model Princess Elizabeth of Toro becomes the first African to feature on the cover of *Harper's Bazaar*.	Iman is introduced to the fashion world by photographer Peter Beard and goes on to become the world's most successful African model.	Soukous singer Papa Wemba becomes the spiritual leader of Le Sape, the Congolese league of well-dressed gentlemen.

suburb where beatniks cruised the streets. The title expanded its editions to the rest of anglophone Africa throughout the 1960s and chronicled women's Western-influenced fashions, from bell-bottoms to short printed shifts (left).

Europe's sartorial influence in the Congo had a special legacy in the formation of Le Sape (Société des Ambianceurs et Personnes Elégantes; Society of Tastemakers and Elegant People), an elite group of dandies called *sapeurs* who dedicated themselves to high fashion. The movement originated in Kinshasa and Brazzaville in the 1920s, when men defied their meagre circumstances by developing refined tastes in European suits and bourgeois accessories, such as monocles, bow ties and walking sticks. They matched their lavish wardrobes with a gentlemanly code of conduct and morality that marked them out as local celebrities. After Congo's independence in 1960, economic insecurity and the dictatorship of President Mobutu, who as part of his authenticity campaign banned Western fashions altogether in 1971, led many *sapeurs* to flock to Paris. There they became a presence in cafe society and could more easily buy designer labels, or *griffes* as they called them. By donning the fashions of their former oppressors, and pushing the look to its extremes, they were asserting their own rebellious modernity and turning the art of dressing into a kind of religion. The *sapeur* style continues today (see p.552).

Conversely, French fashion showed its first signs of being influenced by Africa in the 1960s, thanks to Yves Saint Laurent (1936–2008). He was born and spent his formative years in Oran, Algeria, and spent much of his later life in Marrakech, Morocco. His landmark spring/summer Africa collection, launched in 1967, featured a series of revealing shift dresses made from raffia and wooden beads (below). US *Harper's Bazaar* described it at the time as 'a fantasy of primitive genius—shells and jungle jewellery clustered to cover the bosom and hips, latticed to bare the midriff'. In 1968 the designer invented the now iconic safari suit, and successive collections featured animal prints as well as his take on North African tunics, kaftans, djellabas and turbans. Yves Saint Laurent was also instrumental in introducing African and black models to the international catwalks in the 1960s and 1970s alongside pro-black fashion houses such as Paco Rabanne, Pierre Cardin, Courrèges, Oscar de la Renta,

Thierry Mugler, Givenchy and Halston, as well as African American designer Stephen Burrows (b.1943). African-born models Rebecca Ayoko, Khadija Adam and Katoucha Niane joined Jamaican Grace Jones and African Americans such as Sandi Bass, Billie Blair, Toukie Smith and Bethann Hardison in the spotlight. Mainstream magazines followed suit, and Ugandan princess Elizabeth of Toro and African Americans Naomi Sims and Donyale Luna became the first black cover girls for *Harper's Bazaar* (1969), *Life* (1969) and *Vogue* (1966), respectively. However, it was Iman who undoubtedly made the biggest impact as a black model. In 1975 she was presented to New York's fashion scene by photographer Peter Beard, who claimed that she was an illiterate tribeswoman whom he had discovered in the Sahara. In reality Iman was born in Somalia, the daughter of a diplomat and a doctor, and had met Beard while studying at the University of Nairobi. The photographer's plan worked, though, because Iman's first modelling assignment was for *Vogue*. She became an Yves Saint Laurent muse and today remains one of the most successful African models of all time. Beard himself was acclaimed for his fashion assignments shot on location in Africa, which became a new wild backdrop for magazines. In response, *Vogue* sent photographer Norman Parkinson to Ethiopia, and Franco Rubartelli photographed German model Veruschka wearing an Yves Saint Laurent safari suit in Mali.

During the 1960s the rise of models of colour was just one outcome of the seismic changes spearheaded by the Civil Rights Movement (1955–68) and its drive for aesthetic self-determination, with its rallying cry 'Black is beautiful'. As Motown artists swept into the charts, Muhammad Ali declared 'I'm so beautiful', and Martin Luther King, Malcolm X and the Black Panthers took on the status quo, fashion and beauty became an expression of African Americans' reassertion of their diaspora status. The rift caused by slavery, paired with the fight for political and social equality, was channelled into the politics of dressing the body as a symbol of racial consciousness. Consequently hairstyles were important. Chemically straightened hair and wigs for women and conks for men were decried as signs of self-hatred and gave way to the loud, proud Afro (right). Black Panthers and student radicals wore their Afros unkempt and paired them with berets, turtleneck sweaters, leather jackets and the West African dashiki, or tunic. Barbers advertised this natural look as 'African style'. In fashion, large rounded pampered Afros became a key trend and Caucasians had their hair permed to achieve the look.

Ironically, in some parts of Africa, Afros were seen as too American and Tanzania's government outlawed the style as an unwelcome import that had become too popular with local women. Meanwhile, Nigerian photographer J. D. Okhai Ojeikere's *Hairstyles* series, which began in 1968 and includes around 1,000 headshots of complicated braided up-dos, celebrated the admirable lengths that African women went to in the name of looking good, but did not include the Afro. Real African styles, such as cornrows, braids and dreadlocks, were adopted in the diaspora in the 1970s, thanks in part to musical stars Stevie Wonder, Nina Simone and Bob Marley.

Britain saw heavy immigration from West Africa and the Caribbean after World War II. Here, fashion was an act of simultaneous self-affirmation and assimilation and helped to define a new cross-cultural identity among successive generations. People fused European fashions with African wear and sported the ubiquitous Afro. The focus was on looking one's best and there was always attention to detail, such as hats ranging from the knitted tam worn by youths who aspired to Rastafarianism, to neat bonnets worn by women going to church. The 1960s and 1970s were exciting decades for Afrocentric fashion, which both reflected and influenced the mainstream. The era's enduring styles and trends continue to have influence today. **HJ**

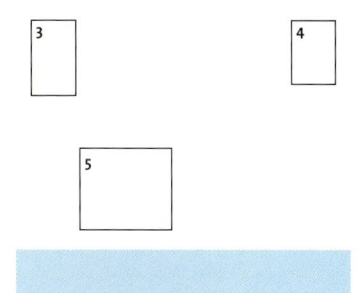

3 This photograph by James Barnor for *Drum* magazine shows the influence of Western styles and prints on African dress in the 1960s.

4 Roanne Nesbitt models an Afro wig adorned with a headdress and matching necklace for *Life* magazine (1968).

5 Yves Saint Laurent's iconic Africa collection features intricate lattice beadwork embellished with shells (1967).

Iro Complete 1960s
SHADE THOMAS-FAHM b. 1933

Mrs Francesca Emmanuel at
Shade Thomas-Fahm's house (1960).

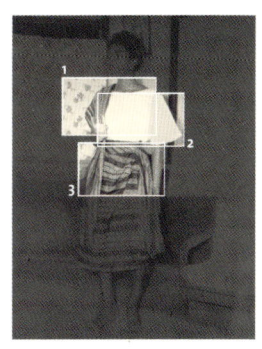

One of Nigerian designer Shade Thomas-Fahm's most popular styles was based on the classic Yoruba *iro* (wrapper) and *buba* (top) worn with a matching *iborun* or *ipele* (shawl). She called it the *iro* complete, or *iro* adaptation. Fahm modernized the look with various styles of blouse and delightful combinations of indigenous textiles. This photograph was taken in 1960 by acclaimed local photographer Mr Ajidagba at one of Fahm's social gatherings. It features the ensemble being modelled by one of the designer's many well-to-do customers in Lagos, Mrs Francesca Emmanuel, the first female permanent secretary of the Federal Republic of Nigeria. The *buba* is constructed from chic white organza, whereas the *iro* and *ipele* are made from a striped *ase oke*, one of the designer's favoured textiles. Meaning 'top cloth' in English, *ase oke* is handwoven by Yoruba men in southwestern Nigeria using a narrow strip loom. It is made of silk and cotton, and the narrow strips are sewn together to make the width required for the garment. Fahm's other best-selling designs and innovations of this period include the pre-tied *gele* (headwrap), the transformation of a man's *agbada* (baggy gown) into a woman's embroidered *boubou* (fitted dress), beachwear based on the *tobi* (pleated skirt) and the *cullote* (one-piece romper). **HJ**

NAVIGATOR

FOCAL POINTS

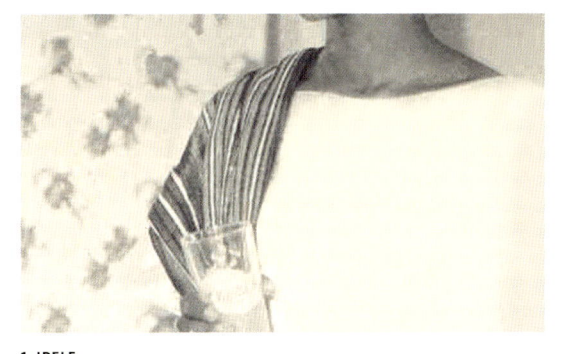

1 IPELE
Mrs Francesca Emmanuel wears an *ipele* draped over one shoulder, but for a full outfit she may also have worn the *iro* complete with a matching *gele*. This look gives a nod to traditional dress yet appears entirely modern.

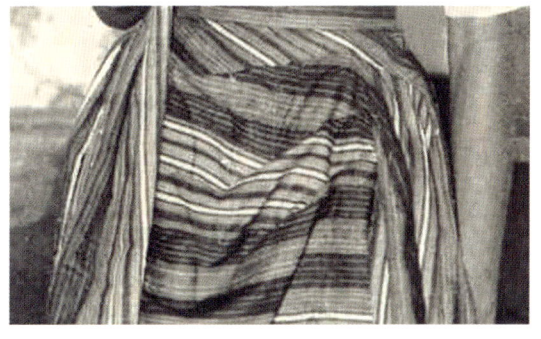

3 IRO
The *iro* is a single piece of fabric wrapped around the lower body. Fahm turned the *iro* into a slip-on skirt with a concealed inside zip. The appearance is the same but the skirt version is much easier to put on and wear.

2 BUBA
The *buba* was introduced into West African fashion by European Christian missionaries who were keen for women to cover their modesty. Fahm kept the *buba*'s authentic wide neckline but designed several sleeve types, including flared, ruffled, gathered and puffed.

DESIGNER PROFILE

1933–60
Shade Thomas-Fahm was born in Lagos. She moved to London to train as a nurse but eventually enrolled at Central Saint Martins College of Arts and Design to study fashion. She also worked as a model and in a fur house. In 1960 she returned to Lagos, where she opened Shade's Boutique, the city's first contemporary African fashion store, which she expanded into a chain alongside Maison Shade, a dress factory.

1961–PRESENT
Fahm's popularity was bred from her pioneering designs, which offered easy-to-wear fashionable versions of traditional styles. Fahm made it her mission to promote Nigerian textiles and won accolades for her ingenious embroidery on neck and hemlines. She showed and sold internationally and also helped to create the Fashion Designers Association of Nigeria.

AFROCENTRIC FASHION 375

FUTURISTIC FASHION

1 Futuristic designs by Pierre Cardin are accessorized with over-the-elbow gloves, wide belts and silver hardware (1968).

2 This dress made of paillettes by Paco Rabanne was constructed using metal cutters, pliers and a blowtorch rather than a sewing machine and thread (c. 1966).

The era of the space age prompted the appearance of a new futuristic style in product design, interiors and fashion: Russia's Yuri Gagarin became the first man in space in 1961 and French couturier André Courrèges (b.1923) launched his mini skirt in the same year. Spare, streamlined designs heralded the beginning of a new decade that offered a future free of sexual, social and fashion constraints.

In Paris a group of designers, including Pierre Cardin (b.1922), Courrèges and Paco Rabanne (b.1934), utilized the latest high-tech synthetic sports fabrics to re-energize ailing French couture with their space-age fashions. The Moon Girl collection launched by Courrèges in 1964 was a modernist all-white and silver collection that featured trousers and matching tunics and thigh-high mini dresses that bypassed the curves of the body and were cut with mathematical precision. Courrèges utilized densely woven fabrics that formed a carapace of cloth, and the rigid constructions could stand up on their own. This mood of an alien warrior was further emphasized by 'astronaut' helmets—bonnets that stood away from the contours of the head—outsize white sunglasses and flat

KEY EVENTS

1961	1961	1962	1962	1964	1964
André Courrèges leaves Balenciaga to launch his own couture house in Paris.	Soviet pilot and cosmonaut Yuri Gagarin orbits the Earth on the first manned space flight.	Cardin launches his pared-down menswear collection from the Place Beauvau, Paris. It introduces the Nehru jacket, which was inspired by his travels.	The first prototype of the monokini appears (see p.378), designed by Rudi Gernreich.	André Courrèges shows his influential Space Age collection.	Emanuel Ungaro starts working with Courrèges. He leaves to set up his own house in 1965.

white patent or kid moon boots, which were cropped at mid calf and featured an open toe, thus heralding the era of kinky boots. This couture version of modernity included double-breasted coats worn over high-necked dresses with cutaway sleeves. Courrèges's signature double-welt seaming added to the resistant quality of the cloth, and contrasting coloured braiding marked out the bold graphic geometry of the silhouette. French designer Emanuel Ungaro (b.1933) worked two seasons with Courrèges (from 1964 to 1965) before establishing his own house with textile artist Sonja Knapp. Ungaro's first collections followed the futuristic lines and abbreviated skirts of Courrèges (see p.380) but in stronger, brighter colours. In protest at the formal nature of the Parisian couture system, Ungaro devoted his first collection to daywear and refused to design evening wear, a couture staple, apart from a satirical gesture in the form of an evening gown decorated with ping-pong balls.

In an attempt to fuse fashion and science, Cardin spearheaded the notion of unisex clothes with his first Space Age, or Cosmo Corps, collection, featuring white knitted all-in-ones worn beneath tabards and tubular dresses. More commercial ranges followed throughout the 1960s comprising mini pinafore dresses and tunics in bright colours with stylized cut-outs, worn with PVC thigh-high boots (opposite). Later the designer combined vinyl and metal for a unisex range of zip-fronted jackets and Op art-inspired, checked gaberdine tabards worn over metallic all-in-one leggings.

An eager exponent of new materials and techniques, Spanish-born Paco Rabanne brought his experience of industrial design to his first 'body jewellery' collection in 1966: ready-to-wear sheaths constructed from squares and discs of rhodoid—a cellulose acetate plastic—attached to the fabric underneath (right). Rabanne eschewed traditional couture techniques, labelling this first collection 'Twelve Unwearable Dresses in Contemporary Materials', and established his reputation as a fashion iconoclast. He pioneered the recycling of materials and experimented with hammered metal, knitted fur, aluminium jersey and fluorescent leather or fibreglass, even producing paper dresses in 1967. Rabanne patented the Giffo process in 1968, in which all the component parts of garments, including buttons and pockets, were moulded in one piece. His iconic chain-mail bag reinvented the mesh bags of the 1920s for the space age.

Courrèges, Cardin, Ungaro and Rabanne were not only radical in their approach towards design, purveying a more expensive version of the youthquake clothes of fashionable London, but they were also instrumental in demystifying and challenging the precepts of haute couture, and thus making it relevant to a new audience. Austrian-American designer Rudi Gernreich (1922–85) was the US counterpoint to Paris's space-age quartet. He experimented with different materials using cut-outs, vinyl and plastic, and also further developed unisex clothing to include kaftans, tunics and the iconic topless bathing suit (see p.378). **MF**

1966	1967	1968	1968	1969	1971
Rabanne's sheath dress is commemorated in *Qui êtes-vous, Polly Magoo?*, William Klein's film satire on the absurdities of the fashion industry.	André Courrèges introduces his Prototype made-to-measure custom line.	Paco Rabanne designs the costumes for Jane Fonda in Roger Vadim's film *Barbarella*.	Pierre Cardin invents an uncrushable fabric of bonded fibres that retains raised geometric forms in complex patterns.	Astronauts Neil Armstrong and Buzz Aldrin land on the Moon and walk on its surface.	Paco Rabanne is recognized as a couturier by his peers and becomes a member of the Chambre Syndicale de la Haute Couture.

Monokini 1964
RUDI GERNREICH 1922 – 85

Gernreich's muse Peggy Moffit provides a paradigm of 1960s avant-garde fashion.

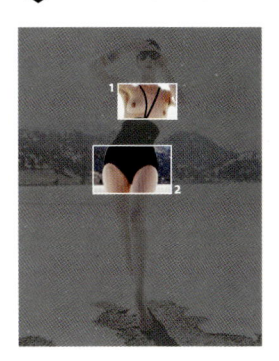

Iconic moments in fashion designate important shifts in attitudes to different areas of the body and mark changing social taboos. California-based designer Rudi Gernreich introduced the monokini—a word coined by the designer—at a point when the conservative 1950s was giving way to the free expression of the 1960s. His experiments with undress culminated in the taboo-breaking topless bathing suit. Gernreich strived to promulgate the notion of unisex clothing and to break down the gender barriers in society. Designed to be worn by both men and women, the earliest prototype of the monokini appeared in 1962 and it went on sale in 1964.

Although modern in its exposure of breasts, the swimsuit appears curiously old-fashioned in the cut of the legs and the high waist. Never particularly intended for actual swimming—it was knitted from water-bearing wool—the black suit extends from the midriff to the upper thigh, with a seam at the centre front. The waistband is neatly turned under and hemmed. The monokini received mixed reviews from the fashion press and was generally reviled by church dignitaries. Despite this reaction, consumers purchased the garment in record numbers, and by the end of the summer season Gernreich had sold 3,000 swimsuits and made a sizeable profit. **MF**

NAVIGATOR

FOCAL POINTS

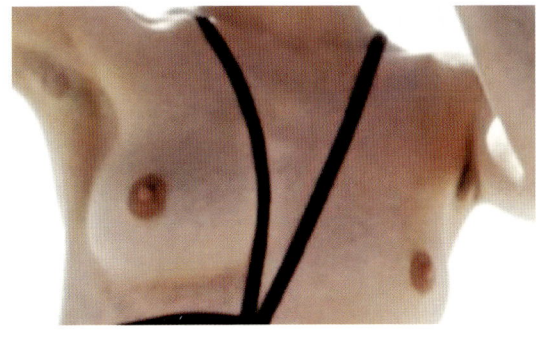

1 HALTER STRAP
A narrow single knitted strap is attached to the centre front of the topless bathing suit and is fastened at the back of the neck. It bypasses the breasts and secures the monokini just above the waistline so that it exposes the breasts.

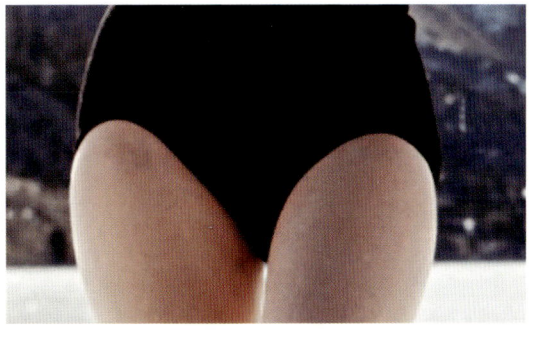

2 LEG LINE
The edges of the leg openings are turned under and hemmed. They are cut straight across the top of the thigh in the style of the maillot, a swimsuit Gernreich popularized in 1952 that eliminated the complicated interior construction of swimwear at the time.

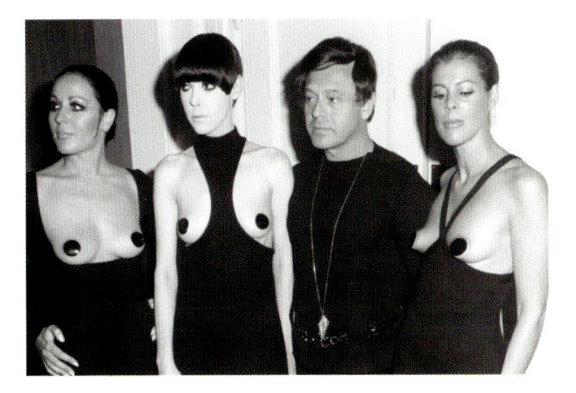

▲ Three models wear full-length, topless knitted jersey evening gowns designed by Rudi Gernreich (c. 1970). Each tube dress features a different top that leaves the breasts fully exposed.

DESIGNER PROFILE

1922–64
Gernreich was born in Vienna, the son of a hosiery manufacturer. After fleeing the Nazis in the late 1930s he settled in Los Angeles. He spent ten years with the Horton Dance Group, using this experience of modern dance as inspiration for liberating the body from the limitations of clothing. In collaboration with the lingerie company Exquisite Form, Gernreich developed the 'no bra' bra in 1964, manufactured in a neutral jersey without padding or boning.

1965–85
Gernreich subsequently branched out into knitted jersey tube dresses and sportswear, opening a showroom on New York's 7th Avenue in the 1960s. He was inducted into the Coty American Fashion Critics' Hall of Fame in 1967 and won the Knitted Textile Association Award in 1975.

FUTURISTIC FASHION

A-line Dress 1967
ANDRÉ COURRÈGES b. 1923

This architecturally sculpted dress by André Courrèges features all the hallmark details consistent with his futuristic approach to fashion design. The A-line dress is constructed from a close-napped woollen double-faced cloth, which is split at the edge, turned in and top-stitched to produce the signature rounded edges of the garment.

The white yoke extends into a placket and is firmly positioned on the front of the tunic dress. This is also top-stitched in place over the black base. Halfway down the arm scye, the placket deviates to cut across the bodice above the bust point, before extending down in a narrow panel to finish at hip level. All the angles of the dress, from the front placket to the wide shallow neckline, are softened into modular curves. This includes the two vertical pockets, which are set in line with the slight flare of the knee-length skirt and trimmed with a pair of smooth white buttons. The proportion of black to white is carefully calibrated: the width of the pocket equals the width of the placket on either side of the chunky plastic zip and matches the depth of the hem. The decorative running stitch in cotton is white on white and is consistent in its depth throughout the garment. **MF**

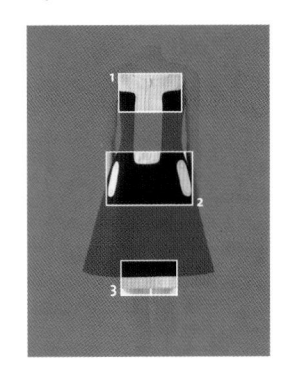

NAVIGATOR

FOCAL POINTS

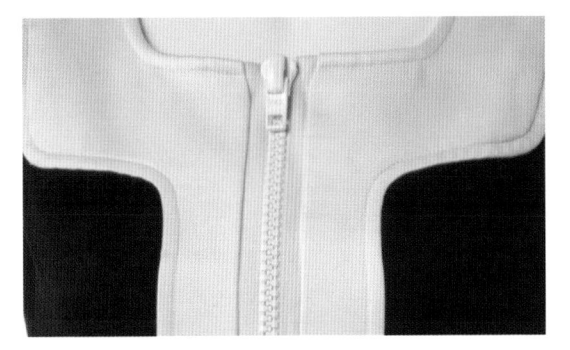

1 PLASTIC ZIP
An industrial-sized, white plastic zip is inserted into the centre front of the placket, extending from neck to hip. The ends are squared off to mirror the shape of the placket. Courrèges's uncluttered aesthetic was much copied by mass-market manufacturers.

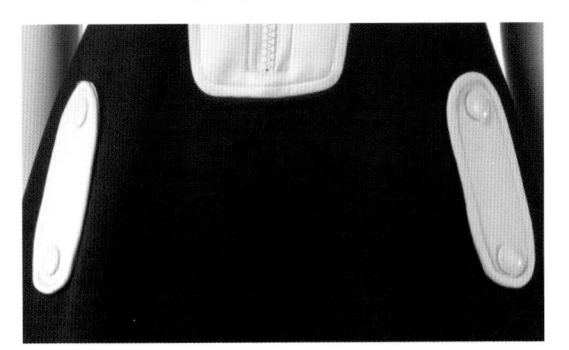

2 CONCEALED POCKETS
The set-in vertical pockets are concealed beneath an ovoid-shaped patch of fabric, which is secured with top-stitching to the surface of the dress. A pair of plain shanked buttons secures each decoration at either end.

3 CONTRAST HEM
The hem is bound in a contrasting fabric to the dress, which emphasizes the brevity of the skirt. A single line of top-stitching generates interest sited below the turn-back, creating a distinctive extension to the skirt.

DESIGNER PROFILE

1923–63
French-born André Courrèges studied to be a civil engineer before he went to Paris to work at Jeanne Lafaurie fashion house at the age of twenty-five. From 1950 he worked under Cristóbal Balenciaga (1895–1972), and left in 1961 to open his *maison de couture*, which he set up with his wife, Coqueline.

1964–PRESENT
Courrèges launched his influential Space Age collection in 1964, which used modern materials such as plastic and metal. After a brief withdrawal following the mass pirating of his designs, he reopened his house and introduced a three-tiered fashion system consisting of Couture Future, Prototype and Hyperbole. Courrèges designed the uniform for the Olympics in 1972, and in 1973 launched a menswear range of sporty separates. He retired in 1996 and was succeeded by his wife.

FUTURISTIC FASHION 381

THE NEW PRÊT-À-PORTER

1 Yves Saint Laurent poses with models in front of his shop, Rive Gauche, in 1969.

2 Heavily influenced by time spent in Africa, Yves Saint Laurent launched his iconic safari suit in 1968.

3 Walter Albini's liberating designs for Etro were featured in *Vogue Italia* in 1971.

When haute couture was initially organized and structured in 1944, there was no French ready-to-wear industry. The new prêt-à-porter emerged during the late 1960s and early 1970s, which was an optimum period for the introduction of fashion-led ready-to-wear because the increasingly sophisticated manufacturing systems that were deployed in the United States were being adopted in Europe. In addition, during the political unrest and youth-led rebellion of the 1960s, haute couture had been deemed irrelevant to modern consumers, whose increasingly fast-paced lives left little time for lengthy fittings and whose social and working lives eschewed the formal dressing offered by couturiers. As trends accelerated and young contemporary designers pioneered the boutique movement, fashion was street-led for the first time, with innovative ideas adopted by designers such as Yves Saint Laurent (1936–2008).

As the immediate successor to Christian Dior (1905–57) in 1958, and having trained at the Chambre Syndicale de la Haute Couture, Yves Saint Laurent founded his own couture house in 1962 in Paris before pioneering ready-to-wear in 1966 with the launch of Rive Gauche (above), a chain of boutiques offering a cheaper line of clothing with overtones of Left Bank bohemianism. These were co-founded with Pierre Bergé (b.1930) and Didier Grumbach (b.1937). Saint Laurent initially showed one of his landmark designs, the tuxedo,

KEY EVENTS

1964	1965	1966	1968	1968	1968
Walter Albini opens his eponymous fashion house in Milan. He begins freelance design for Lanerossi, Basile and other Italian companies.	Walter Albini starts to design for Italian label Krizia alongside Karl Lagerfeld (b.1933).	Yves Saint Laurent launches his ready-to-wear line, Rive Gauche, in Paris. The first customer at the store is actress Catherine Deneuve.	Students protest in Paris throughout May, resulting in a national general strike. Huge crowds gather on the Left Bank during the marches.	Parisian couturier Cristóbal Balenciaga (1895–1972) retires, closing his Madrid, Barcelona and Paris fashion houses in quick succession.	Yves Saint Laurent pioneers his safari look with the trouser suit, thereby revolutionizing what is considered 'appropriate' streetwear for women.

382 1946–89

known as 'Le Smoking', on the haute couture runway in 1966, but after the launch of the Rive Gauche ready-to-wear label he offered a more affordable version of the smoking suit. The trouser suit for women (see p.384) was a design with which he became synonymous, and he featured the safari suit (right) in his spring/summer collection of 1968. Indeed, he designed variations of Le Smoking for all his collections until his retirement in 2002. In 1971 Grumbach and Andrée Putman (b.1925), renowned French interior and product designer, formed the prêt-à-porter collective Créateurs et Industriels, which aimed to bridge the gap between designers and industry. This was followed in 1973 by the first prêt-à-porter fashion week in Paris, featuring designers such as Moroccan-born Jean-Charles de Castelbajac (b.1949), who was known as the 'king of cartoons' for his deployment of cartoon characters on his irreverent knitwear designs. Influential French designer Emmanuelle Khanh (b.1937) was also at the vanguard of prêt-à-porter, alongside Sonia Rykiel (b.1930), Michèle Rosier (b.1930) and fashion house Dorothée Bis.

In Italy the centre for couture, or *alta moda*, was Rome, whereas Florence was the centre for accessories and boutique clothing. Old-style Italian couture was floundering during this period and Walter Albini (1941–83) anticipated the need for a thriving Italian ready-to-wear industry. He was the first designer to initiate a series of innovative reforms that set in motion the move towards a process on a par with French prêt-à-porter. Under his initiative the designers no longer worked anonymously for companies manufacturing unbranded ranges but collaborated instead on collections with specialized companies in different sectors of the industry. After an agreement in 1971 with FTM (Ferrante, Tositti, Monti), the label 'Walter Albini for', followed by the name of the manufacturer, was introduced. Each collection was then sold in its entirety to retailers, resulting in the system of prêt-à-porter that is known today.

In this capacity Albini worked as a freelance designer for various companies such as Krizia, Basile and Etro (below right). Purveying an understated elegance that referenced the liberating designs of Paul Poiret (1879–1944) and the fashions of the 1920s and 1930s, Albini offered a glamorous alternative to the then prevalent fashions of the counter-culture. He was particularly interested in print design and favourite themes for inspiration included ballet, the zodiac and Art Deco. The designer launched his own line, Mister Fox, in 1972. With the rise in manufacturing companies in the north of Italy, Albini, Missoni and Krizia led the fashion designer exodus to Milan in 1972 to present their collections on the runway of the Circolo del Giardino, thus establishing Milan as a fashion capital. In spite of his untimely death at the age of forty-two, Albini had a long-lasting influence on Italian fashion and clothing production, and journalists compared his work with that of Halston in the United States and Yves Saint Laurent in France. He initiated the development of the Italian look that was perpetuated by Giorgio Armani (b.1934) and Gianni Versace (1946–97). **DS**

1971	1971	1972	1973	1975	1975
Yves Saint Laurent provokes a scandal when he is photographed naked by Jeanloup Sieff for the launch of his first men's scent, Homme.	The fashion world mourns the death of Coco Chanel (1883–1971). Main Rousseau Bocher (1890–1976) retires and moves to Europe.	Influenced by Chanel, Albini launches his own line, Mister Fox, founded alongside businessman Luciano Papini.	Albini terminates his agreement with FTM and founds Albini Srl with Luciano Papini. The company produces and distributes the WA label.	Lingerie designer Chantal Thomass (b.1947) launches her eponymous label with Bruce Thomass as licensing and sales director.	Albini presents his first autumn collection for men.

THE NEW PRÊT-À-PORTER 383

Pinstripe Suit 1967
YVES SAINT LAURENT 1936 – 2008

NAVIGATOR

The 1930s-inspired, three-piece pinstripe suit is cut along masculine lines with sharp shoulders emphasized by the angle of the revers and pleat-front trousers worn with a belt. Resonant of the androgynous style of film star Marlene Dietrich in the 1930s (see p.268), the model poses in a typically masculine attitude: one hand hooked in the waistcoat pocket, the other gesturing with a cigarette. The etiolated silhouette is nevertheless sculpted into a feminine shape by the waist darts on the jacket and the form-fitting waistcoat worn underneath.

The tuxedo, an evening version of the suit, was first shown as part of Yves Saint Laurent's haute couture autumn/winter collection in 1966. A series of black-and-white photographs taken for French *Vogue* in 1975 by German-Australian fashion photographer Helmut Newton brought Le Smoking to a wider audience and rendered it one of the most important and influential garments of the 20th century, alongside the 'little black dress' pioneered by Coco Chanel (see p.224). For the next thirty years variations of Le Smoking were included in all the designer's collections. Saint Laurent described the garment as 'continually in fashion, because it is about style, not fashion. Fashions come and go, but style is for ever.' **MF**

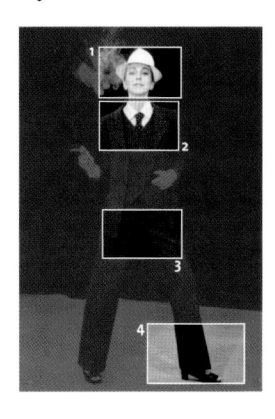

FOCAL POINTS

1 MASCULINE HAT
Characteristic of the male Hollywood screen idols of the 1920s and 1930s is the snap-brimmed white trilby hat, positioned at the back of the head and obscuring the slicked-back cropped hair.

2 ANGULAR SHOULDER LINE
Tailored with the traditional expertise of a man's suit, the squared-off shoulder is emphasized with the use of sleeve head wadding, shaped to form an angle. The high arm scye further narrows the torso.

3 HIGH-WAISTED TROUSERS
Cut from pinstriped cloth—very thin stripes running in parallel and more usually associated with the conservative business suit—the trousers have a deep rise and are cut along the lines of a classic man's trouser, with a fly-front and a single pleat.

4 TROUSER HEM
The boot-cut suit trousers are narrow on the thigh and gradually widen towards the hem. The length is extended to cover the upper part of the low-heeled shoe, thus giving the flattering appearance of a longer leg.

HIPPIE DELUXE

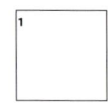

1 Photographed by Patrick Lichfield in 1969, British actress and model Jane Birkin wears an Ossie Clark ensemble with print design by Celia Birtwell.

2 US designer Mary McFadden models her own hand-printed silk designs, inspired by African and oriental fabrics (1973).

3 A characteristic ethnic-inspired print features on a chiffon dress with feathered streamers by Zandra Rhodes (1970).

At the end of the 1960s the youth-led fashions made in futuristic fabrics inspired by the space age were rejected in favour of handcrafted garments and a reverence for natural fibres. The hippies, a youth subculture with its origins in the US beat movement, preferred to wear clothes picked up on their global travels, rather than the mass-produced, machine-made items that were retailing in the Western fashion system. Industrial processes and synthetic products were anathema to the protagonists of the hippie 'back to nature' lifestyle. In the social and political upheavals of 1968, 'flower power' symbolized the force of nature against the power of authority. This adherence to an alternative lifestyle outside conventional society culminated in a desire for free expression in all aspects of culture, from fashion and art to music and the media. All of these were appropriated by the counter-culture and, over time, infiltrated the mainstream.

In fashion the anti-materialist ethos of the hippies resulted in an eclectic sourcing of vernacular dress, in which the construction of the garment is rooted in the simplest way of utilizing all the fabric. Global garments from the hippie trail to India and the Far East, such as Indian prayer shirts decorated with bells, Nehru jackets, gathered ankle-length skirts embellished with fragments of mirror, wrapped trousers, embroidered waistcoats and variations

KEY EVENTS

1964	1966	1967	1968	1968	1969
After graduating from London's Royal College of Art, British designer Zandra Rhodes sets up her first print studio with fellow student Alex MacIntyre.	Thea Porter (1927–2000) sets up an interior design shop in Soho, London, selling floor cushions and French, Italian and Turkish fabrics.	The year 1967 is designated the 'summer of love', a time of liberation from the perceived constraints of white middle-class suburbia.	A series of student protests breaks out in Paris in a number of universities, bringing the country almost to a standstill and involving eleven million workers.	Zandra Rhodes and Sylvia Ayton (b.1937) open The Fulham Road Clothes Shop, selling garments designed by Ayton and printed by Rhodes.	The Woodstock music festival takes place in the United States in August. It becomes a defining moment in music history.

of the 'T'-shape kaftan, appeared in the collections of leading European and US designers including Emilio Pucci (1914–92; see p.388), Zandra Rhodes (b.1940) and Bill Gibb (1943–88).

The accoutrements of Native American dress and decoration, such as fringing and beading, appealed particularly to the US hippie—located chiefly in San Francisco's Haight-Ashbury district—and was a look commercialized by Italian-born American Giorgio di Sant'Angelo (1933–89). Zandra Rhodes also used the beadwork and feathers of Native American dress as inspiration for her print designs, alongside the art and artefacts of other cultures. Renowned primarily for her evening wear, Rhodes maximized the effect of the print (below right), relying on layers, gathers, smocking and shirring to create the silhouette. The clothes were engineered to accommodate the placement of the prints, rather than cut from continuous, repetitive yardage. British design duo Celia Birtwell (b.1941) and Ossie Clark (1942–96) offered a more refined version of the haute-hippie dress, eschewing the simple 'T'-shape silhouette for the fluid sophistication of the bias cut, with colours and patterns inspired by the Ballets Russes costumes and the Art Deco movement (opposite; see p.390).

At this time it was possible for designers to launch themselves by making a small collection and selling it to a single store, and after some initial success Mary McFadden (b.1938) started her own business in 1973. She had worked previously in South Africa, where she joined African *Vogue* in 1965. As a result of her influence, the New York and Paris collections in 1966 and 1967 paid homage to the continent, showing animal-inspired prints and jewellery and safari jackets. McFadden initially designed clothes for herself (right), made to her own specifications from fabrics found on her extensive travels, thus creating an eclectic look that combined designer pieces with ethnic garments. She also created evening gowns in pleated silk using a unique 'Marii' technique, redolent of that used by Mariano Fortuny (1871–1949), which she patented in 1975. She combined this with elements of hand-painting, quilting, beading and embroidery, culling ideas and inspiration from diverse ancient and ethnic cultures. These hippie-deluxe dresses were ideal for her wealthy, well-travelled customers: they were made with satin-backed polyester and did not crease.

The romantic spectacle of Scottish-born designer Bill Gibb's clothes also connected with the mood of fashion during a period in which historical revivalism and the ephemera of other cultures came together (see p.392). Using couture-like details and quality in his fantasy ball gowns, Gibb elevated the street market pickings of the hippie to haute-hippie status. He was drawn to the construction techniques and embellishment of the Renaissance, as well as the visual imagery of other cultures, and mixed floral with geometric prints and patchworked diverse fabrics with abandon. He embellished these fairy-tale dresses with streamers and ribbons, sunray pleats, appliqués, scalloped edges and tasselled *passementerie*. Gibb also applied his aesthetic to daywear. In 1969 he collaborated with US knitwear designer Kaffe Fassett (b.1937) to produce a much-heralded collection that combined an eclectic mix of polychrome checks and tweeds, tartan and Fair Isle knits and Liberty floral prints. **MF**

1969	1970	1971	1973	1975	1976
Rhodes produces her first solo collection, which is featured in US *Vogue*. It includes romantic flowing garments in luxurious fabrics.	While working as a freelance designer for London fashion house Baccarat, Bill Gibb is awarded *Vogue* Designer of the Year.	Celia Birtwell and Ossie Clark cause a media frenzy with their wild catwalk show at the Royal Court in London.	Emilio Pucci presents his Salzburg collection, which includes brightly coloured silk jersey evening gowns that feature print aprons.	Bill Gibb is made a Fellow of the Society of Industrial Artists and Designers, London; the same year he opens his own shop on London's Bond Street.	Mary McFadden operates from the basement of her New York home and becomes established enough to form Mary McFadden Inc.

HIPPIE DELUXE

Psychedelic Print Kaftan 1967
PUCCI

French model Simone D'Aillencourt wears a
Pucci kaftan, Lake Palace, Udaipur, India (1967).

NAVIGATOR

One of the most identifiable print designers of the 20th century, and labelled the 'prince of prints' by the contemporary fashion press, Emilio Pucci designed for the 'beautiful people' and style setters of the time. Drawing inspiration from diverse sources, such as indigenous patterns from exotic countries and the regalia of the Palio bareback horse race in Siena, Pucci produced polychromatic abstract prints in psychedelic swirls of pattern, often bordered by areas of contrasting scale and colour. He embraced the new eclecticism of the burgeoning hippie movement of the late 1960s, and transformed the multipatterned excesses of the counter-culture into high-fashion status. He also engineered the design of the prints to create lightweight, crease-free clothes in dazzling colours, such as 'T'-shape kaftans and loose-fitting djellabas favoured by the US and European haute hippie. Each garment was signed 'Emilio'.

Photographed inside the Lake Palace in Udaipur, India, a favoured destination of the wealthy dilettante in pursuit of enlightenment, model Simone D'Aillencourt wears a transparent silk-printed chiffon kaftan with swirling patterns of fuchsia, red, pistachio, aqua and yellow, partnered with a pair of solid-colour, loose, wide-legged trousers with a narrow embellished hem. The edges of the kaftan are hand-rolled. **MF**

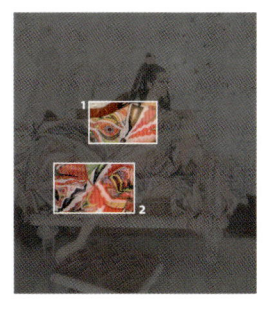

FOCAL POINTS

1 SIMPLE CONSTRUCTION
The sleeves are cut in one with the body of the garment. The deceptively simple construction of the kaftan, together with the slashed neckline, creates the impression of a rectangular piece of cloth simply dropped over the head.

2 ENGINEERED PRINT
Each colour of the print required a separate silk screen with no overlapping or overprinting of colour, resulting in the clarity and definition of the design. The distorting effect of hallucinogenic drugs on perception influenced the designs of the era.

▲ A dramatic photo shoot on the rooftop of the Palazzo Pucci, with the cupola of the Duomo of Florence in the background, captures the diaphanous quality of Pucci's kaftans (1969).

Wandering Daisy Dress 1971
CELIA BIRTWELL b. 1941 OSSIE CLARK 1942 – 96

NAVIGATOR

Celia Birtwell designed prints that were engineered around the fluid sophistication of fashion designer Ossie Clark's pattern cutting, which he deployed with an exquisite sensitivity to the female form. Redolent of the 1930s flowing lines and bias-cut technique exemplified by couturier Madeleine Vionnet (1876–1975), the designs were enhanced by the impact of the refined and complex layering of print by Birtwell.

The coat and matching dress feature the 'wandering daisy' design hand-printed at Ivo Prints in London. The two-colour print—red and black on a cream base fabric—is used for the dress and also on the bodice and lower part of the sleeves. A change of pattern scale is provided by large, solid, stylized flowerheads of graphic clarity printed in a half-drop spot-repeat system. The arm scye is cut high, in order to elongate the torso, with the revers of the collar extending across the full width of the bodice. Chiffon inserts of the single motif design are a feature of the leg o' mutton sleeves, and the lower parts of the long sleeves in the printed crêpe are narrow and fastened with zips at the cuffs. The 'V'-shape neckline has a horizontal modesty band and a high round neck at the back. The dress flares from above waist level: the front has one darted panel and the back four flared panels. The coat is cut into flared panels, two in the front and three in the back. **MF**

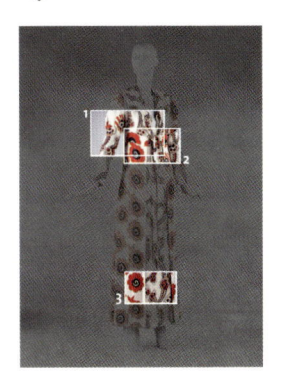

FOCAL POINTS

1 SLEEVES
A juxtaposition of pattern scale is evident on the sleeves, which feature single motifs of graphic clarity with a smaller scale all-over pattern. The sleeves are constructed in two pieces, comprising a puffed sleeve head gathered into a narrow, wrist-length lower sleeve.

2 FLUID TIES
The bodice of the coat incorporates two long ties knotted above the waistline, which extend to knee-length, thus creating a draping effect facilitated by the use of fluid rayon crêpe. The edges are turned under and top-stitched.

3 ART DECO INFLUENCE
Small groups of stylized flowerheads are held together by Art Deco-inspired zigzags with serrated edges. Elsewhere a half-drop spot-repeat design is utilized for both the skirt of the coat and the upper part of the sleeves.

DESIGNER PROFILES

1941–66
Celia Birtwell was born in Salford, Lancashire, England and met fellow Lancastrian fashion designer 'Ossie' Raymond Clark while studying at Salford School of Art. The duo first collaborated in 1966 with a collection for Quorum in London, an exclusive boutique owned by Alice Pollock, selling to international celebrities such as the Rolling Stones, the Beatles, Pattie Boyd, Veruschka and Talitha Getty.

1967–PRESENT
In 1967 Clark presented an iconic first fashion show under the patronage of Alfred Radley, owner of the Radley fashion house, at Chelsea Town Hall for Pathé News, using his celebrity friends as models. In 1969 Birtwell and Clark got married but divorced in 1974. Birtwell revived her fashion career in 2006 with a collection for high-street store Topshop.

HIPPIE DELUXE 391

World Dress 1970s
BILL GIBB 1943 – 88

The world dress by Bill Gibb, photographed by Clive Arrowsmith for *Vogue* (October 1971).

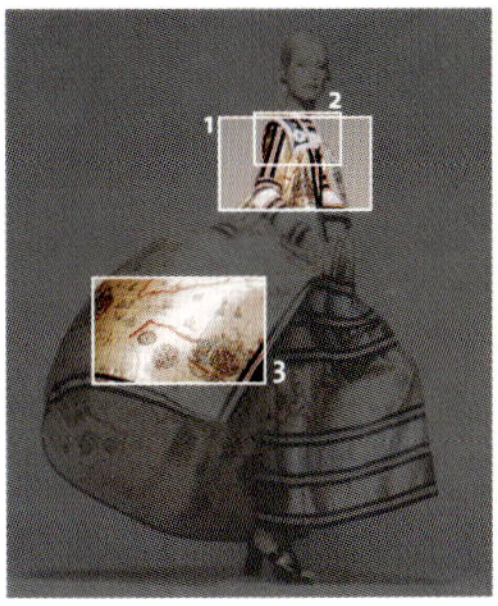

London-based designer Bill Gibb combined the free-flowing eclectic patterning and silhouette of the hippie era with a couture-like approach to garment embellishment and detailing in this champagne satin top, skirt and matching coat designed for the Bill Gibb for Baccarat label. The garments are resonant with Renaissance influences—one of the designer's most frequently used sources—from the stiffened yoke creating a cap sleeve on the coat to the areas of quilting on the bodice and sleeves.

The coat and skirt are both constructed from an all-over print of stripes and a map of the world coloured in silver and gold. The front panels of the ankle-length coat are softly gathered into the abbreviated yoke, which is appliquéd to the body. The black-and-terracotta stripes of varying widths are used both horizontally and vertically. Printed horizontal stripes bisect the billowing skirt, which is gathered onto a waistband; a broader panel of the all-over map print is inserted at knee level. Stripes are used vertically on the sleeves of the coat and are also used to accentuate the hem and centre-front borders. The high-neck tabard-like bodice is lightly quilted throughout, including the long, tight sleeves on which the stitching is diametrically opposed to the horizontal stripes and map grid references of the printed skirt and coat. **MF**

NAVIGATOR

FOCAL POINTS

1 RENAISSANCE-INSPIRED SLEEVES
The stiffened yoke lined with the printed silk extends slightly over the elbow-length sleeves of the coat, thereby creating an arc over the sleeve head that is reminiscent of the design of the Renaissance military jerkin.

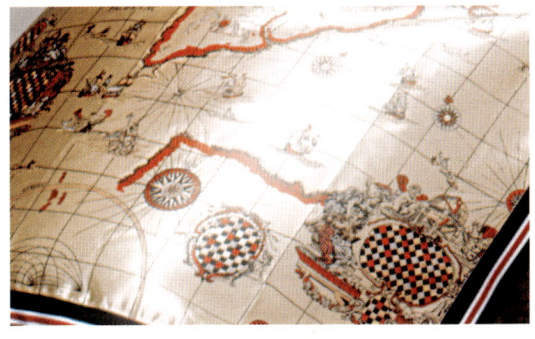

3 ANTIQUE PRINT
Designed by Sally McLachlan and printed by Piero Boboli, the delicate all-over print has an antique quality and includes areas of small-scale chequered patterning in terracotta and black. The billowing nature of the fabric shows off the print to great effect.

DESIGNER PROFILE

1943–72
Born in Fraserburgh, Scotland, Gibb moved to London in 1962 to study at Central Saint Martins College of Arts and Design and the Royal College of Art, after which he founded the boutique Alice Paul. He then worked as a freelance designer for Baccarat from 1969 to 1972, and was awarded *Vogue* Designer of the Year in 1970. In the 1970s his style was influenced by the hippie movement, and he launched Bill Gibb Ltd in 1972.

1973–88
Gibb opened his first independent shop in London in 1975. His complex, polychromatic and hand-loomed patterns of knitwear, inspired by his Scottish origins, and the ethereal romanticism of his evening dresses proved commercially unviable. During the 1980s he designed small capsule collections and created one-off garments for long-term clients.

2 EMBROIDERED YOKE
Within its mitred borders, the yoke of the coat features white appliquéd, flat-petalled roses on a single stem, embroidered by Lillian Delevoryas on a black ground. An established artist, Delevoryas became well known for her appliqué skills in the 1970s.

HIPPIE DELUXE 393

THE STYLISH STITCH

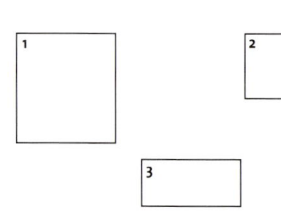

1. A long mohair cardigan is layered over Rykiel's signature striped sweater; the cardigan belt is twisted with a scarf to form a headband (1975).

2. Often likened to an art form, Missoni luxury knitwear is easily identifiable by its combination of rich, vibrant colours (1981).

3. This purple and gold check sweater set by Krizia comprises a V-neck pullover and bolero; it is teamed with an orange wool knit skirt also by Krizia (1979).

Knitwear established its high-fashion status in the 1970s, when it became a vital element in the increasingly important ready-to-wear market. Knitwear designers began to produce collections that offered a total top-to-toe look rather than mere accessories, sweaters, cardigans, gloves and scarves. French-born Sonia Rykiel (b.1930) was one of the first designers to elevate knitwear from its previously frumpy artisanal image to being a high-profile component of contemporary fashion (above). She opened her first boutique in 1968 on Paris's Left Bank, a site synonymous with bohemian style and creativity, and where Yves Saint Laurent offered its luxury prêt-à-porter line Rive Gauche from a shop of the same name. With a signature silhouette created by cutting high in the armholes and close to the body, and narrow sleeves elongating the torso, Rykiel projected a youthful aesthetic that included a distinctive palette of stripes against a backdrop of black. The designer was also at the forefront of deconstruction fashion (see p.498) and utilized

KEY EVENTS

1960s	1965–72	1966	1967	1968	1970
Sonia Rykiel is labelled 'the queen of knitwear' and sells her designs in New York stores such as Henri Bendel and Bloomingdale's.	Laura Biagiotti works in Rome as a freelance designer for Schuberth, Barocco, Cappucci, Heinz Riva, Licitro and others.	The first Missoni collection by Paris-born designer Emmanuelle Khanh (b.1937) is shown in Milan.	Mariuccia Mandelli includes knitwear in her collections, followed by ready-to-wear lines.	Francine Crescent takes the helm at French *Vogue*. She later commissions photographers Guy Bourdin and Helmut Newton.	Missoni opens its first boutique in the United States in the New York department store Bloomingdale's.

394 1946–89

unfinished edges, reverse seams and innovative detailing, such as lock-stitched hems. Moreover, she spearheaded the use of text in knitwear, incorporating rhinestone slogans in evening wear.

Italian company Missoni was one of the earliest to utilize technological innovation to explore the parameters of patterned textiles (right) and the only label to successfully offer the international consumer an entire wardrobe constructed exclusively from knitted fabrics (see p.396). As Rome continued to show only couture labels, Missoni and another leading designer, Mariuccia Mandelli (b.1933) of the Krizia label (below), began to show in Milan, a city that was emerging as one of Europe's fastest-growing fashion capitals and a vigorous centre of ready-to-wear production. Created using the hand-loomed intarsia technique, Mandelli's knitwear designs often featured animals, including sheep, cats, bears, foxes, leopards and tigers; a stylized predatory panther remains the symbol of the label. In 1964 Krizia was awarded the Critica Della Moda Award, and in 1967 Mandelli launched the Krizia Maglia label. Handcrafting her clothes soon proved to be impractical, and garments were manufactured in a factory on the outskirts of Milan.

The original Dorothée boutique opened in Paris in 1958 followed by the ready-to-wear label Dorothée Bis, which promulgated the layered look in knitwear design in the late 1970s. A combination of multitextured and patterned designs, these garments were worn together, creating bulky oversized outer layers in contrast with the slender knitted pieces worn underneath. Disseminating a pared-down Italian style to an international audience, Rome-based designer Laura Biagiotti (b.1943), memorably dubbed the 'queen of cashmere' by *The New York Times*, was credited with moving the luxury yarn—previously confined to classic knitwear pieces such as the twinset—into high fashion; she founded her own label in 1972. In 1974 Biagiotti took over MacPherson Knitwear and began to manufacture sportswear-influenced fashion. **MF**

1970	1972	1972	1972	1973–74	1977
Emmanuelle Khanh establishes her own business but continues to design for Missoni, Krizia and Max Mara.	Laura Biagiotti shows her first collection under her own name.	The Dorothée Bis label offers the mini, midi and maxi in the same collection, with long, narrowly cut knitwear worn over mini dresses and skirts.	Created to promote the best of the Italian fashion industry, the first Pitti Immagine Uomo fair in Florence features men's clothing and accessories.	Italy's systems of manufacture and production are restructured amid political turmoil.	The first Pitti Immagine Filati, a leading trade fair for showing yarns, becomes a reference point for knitwear manufacturers and designers worldwide.

THE STYLISH STITCH 395

Raschel Knit Dress and Hat 1975
MISSONI

At the height of its market saturation in the early to mid 1970s, head-to-toe patterning was the defining look of the inimitable Missoni textile brand. With its combination of technical virtuosity and distinctive use of pattern and extravagant colour, the Italian label became synonymous with positioning knitwear at the forefront of the luxurious ready-to-wear market.

The long tunic sweater is constructed from boldly coloured, simple, weft-knitted stripes matched across the yoke and set-in sleeves. Rayon, rather than silk, is used because it provides a glossier finish and a greater capacity for drape. The tunic is shaped close to the body and is cut from a circular piece of knitted fabric, thus providing a slender silhouette above the voluminous skirt. The flowing drape of the skirt arises from the use of the warp-knitting technique, which produces the zigzag fabric, striped longitudinally but worn transversely. Warp-knitted fabric was utilized to the full by Missoni during the 1970s, when the label produced polychromatic serpentine stripes and lightning bolts of colour in effervescent space-dyed yarns. The designers' interest in the modern art movement of Italian Futurists, such as Giacomo Balla and Umberto Boccioni, influenced the complex geometric patterning of their garments, including their signature flame pattern. **MF**

NAVIGATOR

FOCAL POINTS

1 PULL-ON HAT
The head-hugging knitted hat adds to the attenuated form that represented the silhouette of the era and became a popular accessory in the 1970s. Originally associated with work gear, the beanie hat was previously worn by workers to contain their hair.

2 STRIPED TUNIC
The tunic is created using a technique called weft knitting. It is constructed from horizontal rows of stitches in which a single yarn traverses an entire bank of needles before a different thread produces subsequent groups of rows in different solid colours.

3 VOLUMINOUS SKIRT
The skirt is a lightweight, flexible structure formed from warp knitting, which is a system of textile construction that is a cross between knitting and weaving. A warp of many threads creates vertical chains of loops linked together.

COMPANY PROFILE

1953–68
The Missoni company was founded in 1953 by Ottavio (Tai) Missoni (1921–2013) and his wife, Rosita Jelmini (b.1931), with a small workshop of three knitting machines in the basement of their home in Gallarate, Lombardy, Italy. In 1958 they presented their first collection under the Missoni label in Milan.

1969–PRESENT
In 1969 the Missoni factory opened in Sumirago, Lombardy. During the mid 1970s, the company added furnishing fabrics and household linen to its collections of knitwear, accessories and jewellery. In 1976 the first Missoni boutique was opened in Milan, followed by retail outlets in Paris, Germany, Japan, the Far East and New York. In 1997 the creative directorship was passed to the Missonis' daughter, Angela, while Rosita concentrated on the interiors label.

THE STYLISH STITCH 397

ONE-STOP DRESSING

1. US actress Lauren Hutton encapsulates 1970s lifestyle dressing as she models easy-to-wear separates for Calvin Klein, including a soft-tie blouse, silk jacket and tailored trousers (1974).

2. This trio of silk jersey evening dresses by Halston includes a halter-neck black ruffle dress, a one-shoulder design that is gathered at the hip and a bias-cut green gown with flutter sleeves (c. 1976).

During the 1970s US fashion became less complex as a new modernism emerged, epitomized by the work of Roy Halston Frowick (1932–90) and Calvin Klein (b.1942). Both designers offered an alternative to formal dressing or the difficult-to-wear experiments of the avant-garde. An increasing interest in feminism and a desire for personal autonomy meant that the newly emerging professional working woman required a capsule wardrobe of versatile separates (above), comprising easily interchangeable pieces such as shirts in luxurious fabrics, tailored trousers and knee-length skirts, which could be purchased from a single designer and preferably from under one roof. The desire for high-end ready-to-wear prompted department stores such as Bergdorf Goodman and Saks Fifth Avenue in New York to close down their couture departments and introduce in-house boutiques selling the new designers.

With the increasing popularity of one-stop dressing certain garments became wardrobe staples, such as the one-button single-breasted blazer, worn with either a skirt or trousers and a man-styled shirt. Many consumers resisted the introduction of the midi skirt by designers in favour of trousers, although certain workplaces implemented a dress code that continued to ban

KEY EVENTS

1968	1969	1973	1973	1973	1976
Roy Halston Frowick shows his first eponymous collection in his new showroom in New York City.	In September Calvin Klein's outerwear appears on the cover of US *Vogue*.	Halston sells the 'Halston' name and ready-to-wear and couture businesses to Norton Simon Inc.	Calvin Klein wins the first of three consecutive Coty American Fashion Critics' Awards.	Diane von Furstenberg designs her easy-to-wear wrap dress (see p.400). It features in numerous subsequent collections.	Halston develops a successful perfume, Halston. It has a tear-shaped bottle designed by Elsa Peretti (b.1940).

trousers. These garments were not the palazzo or Capri pants of the previous era but were based on the lines of masculine tailoring, with pleat fronts and vertical pockets incorporated into the side seam. Evening wear also evidenced a new simplicity of style as black-tie dinners and charity balls were replaced by visits to nightclubs such as New York's Studio 54, often frequented by celebrities including Bianca Jagger and Anjelica Huston, dressed by Halston. A proponent of luxurious minimalism and simplicity of cut, referencing the design innovators of the 1950s such as Claire McCardell (1905–58) and Bonnie Cashin (1907–2000), Halston was renowned for his silk kaftans, fluid matt-jersey evening wear (right) and halter-neck jumpsuits. He went on to develop understated, easy-to-wear separates in pliable fabrics such as wool and silk jersey. One-stop dressing included his signature ankle-length cashmere twinsets and his best-selling garment, a version of the shirt dress made from machine-washable ultrasuede, a new man-made fabric from Japan.

During the mid 1970s, US-born Calvin Klein concentrated on outerwear, before successfully gauging the desire of the urban working woman for a professional uniform and offering a more relaxed version of menswear. The designer also expanded his range to include coat dresses, luxe pea coats, silk T-shirts and jumpsuits. His ubiquitous blazer in a restricted palette of white, grey, cream, navy or black was cut close to the body with high narrow arm scyes. In keeping with the increasing informality of the times, Klein eschewed the fashionable 'big occasion' dress and designed restrained, tightly edited collections of signature slip dresses and simple black tubes of jersey for evening wear. To successfully sell a wardrobe of 'timeless' softly tailored separates that differed little from season to season required clever marketing. Klein pioneered the concept of lifestyle dressing and promoted his designs using compelling imagery of urban Manhattanites or languid fun-filled days at the beach. In 1976 Klein showed jeans for the first time on the designer runway, his name embroidered on the back pocket.

Although ready-to-wear separates made up the staple wardrobe of the working woman, the knee-length dress—a button-through shirt dress, pull-on knitted jersey sheath with a drawstring waist or the iconic wrap dress (see p.400) designed by Diane von Furstenberg (b.1946)—appeared in 1973 and became increasingly popular. Exemplifying professional chic, the dress solved the dilemma of day-to-night dressing: it could be worn under a blazer for work and dressed up with jewellery and heels for evening wear. **MF**

1977	1978	1980	1982	1982	1984
Ralph Lauren (b.1939) designs a menswear-inspired wardrobe for Diane Keaton in Woody Allen's film *Annie Hall*.	Calvin Klein launches his first range for men, licensed to French manufacturer Maurice Bidermann.	Calvin Klein launches his jeans line with a commercial featuring Brooke Shields (see p.426); its success propels the brand ahead of competitors.	Photographer Bruce Weber's images of men clad only in Calvin Klein underwear is an homage to the gym-honed body of the era.	Halston signs a multimillion-dollar deal with the J. C. Penney chain of department stores, thus eroding the label's prestige.	Halston leaves the Halston label after disputes with Norton Simon Inc.

ONE-STOP DRESSING 399

Wrap Dress 1973
DIANE VON FURSTENBERG b. 1946

NAVIGATOR

Diane von Furstenberg was inspired by Julie Nixon Eisenhower wearing a wrap top and skirt on television in the early 1970s, and decided to combine the two pieces into one garment: the wrap dress. It was a decision that led to a global fashion empire built on a single style. The designer records her motivation in her autobiography, *A Signature Life* (1998): 'All I had was an instinct that women wanted a fashion option besides hippie clothes, bell bottoms and stiff pant suits that hid their femininity.'

The go-anywhere wrap dress rapidly became a best-seller among working women and celebrities. It featured a V-neck that was formed by tying the wide, wrap sash around the waist, and the bodice was cut to fit closely to the body, with long, narrow, set-in sleeves. The dress could be worn in the evening with high heels and jewellery, or under a blazer for the office. With no zip fastenings, hooks and eyes or buttons, the dress became symbolic of women's sexual liberation. The dress was easy to put on and equally easy to take off. The Diane von Furstenberg Studio produced easy-to-wear cotton and rayon blend knit dresses in the designer's signature wood grain and small-scale geometric prints from 1970 to 1977, introducing snake and leopard prints in 1974. Tops, long dresses and halter-neck dresses were later added to the collection. **MF**

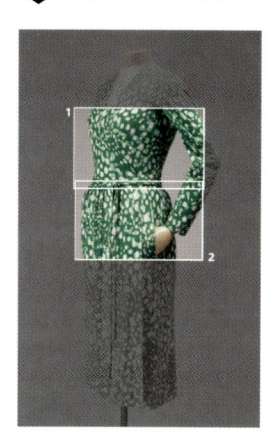

FOCAL POINTS

1 MOULDED BODICE
The knitted jersey fabric of the bodice is close-fitting and moulds to the shape of the body. The narrow waist sash provides both ease and definition, and the tie also enables the wearer to adjust the depth of the décolletage.

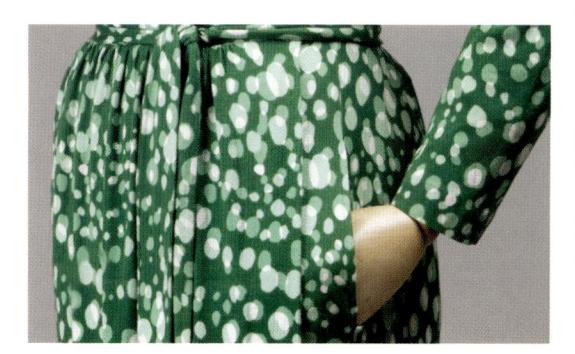

2 FREEDOM OF MOVEMENT
The softly tailored skirt clings to the hips, before flaring out to finish just below the knee, which allows for an unrestricted stride. Vertical pockets are set into the side seams and add to the utility of the garment.

▲ Diane von Furstenberg wears one of her own designs (1973). The slogan 'Feel like a woman, wear a dress!' appeared on every dress tag and became the registered trademark of the company.

ONE-STOP DRESSING 401

MODERN JAPANESE DESIGN

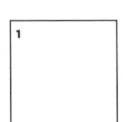

1 This Kenzo ready-to-wear collection featured Chinese floral prints and Peruvian-inspired textiles and knitwear (1984).

2 Yohji Yamamoto combines floral and geometric prints in this ensemble (1985).

From the 1970s onwards a new generation of Japanese fashion designers began to emerge as key players in the international fashion arena. One of the foremost was Kenzo Takada (b.1939; known as Kenzo), who showed his first collection in Paris in 1970 at his boutique Jungle Jap, located in the Galerie Vivienne. His signature juxtaposition of bold, colourful prints mixed with floral intarsia or jacquard knits (above) was prompted by his early days as a student in Paris, when he could only afford to buy his fabrics from flea markets.

Kenzo was the first Japanese designer to be legitimized by Western fashion professionals, and his label continues to be one of the most influential ready-to-wear brands across the globe. In his collections, the designer introduced a new aesthetic to Western fashion, including the tunic-style shirt made from a *yukata* (summer kimono) and a dress made from an obi, or kimono sash. The combination of colours and fabrics, quilting techniques and square shapes that he used all owed their provenance to the Japanese kimono. Kenzo eliminated darts and used bold, straight lines, introducing to the West what was considered unfashionable in Japan at the time. Immediately after his first

KEY EVENTS

1970	1971	1972	1973	1975	1975
Kenzo Takada sets up his first store in Paris and shows his collection to French journalists and editors.	Fashion entrepreneur Joseph Ettedgui introduces the Kenzo label to London.	Yohji Yamamoto forms his own company in Tokyo, having worked as a freelance designer for four years.	Issey Miyake has his first show in Paris alongside European designers Sonia Rykiel (b.1930) and Thierry Mugler (b.1948) to promote prêt-à-porter.	Hanae Mori presents her first collection in Paris and two years later opens her Maison Haute Couture on avenue Montaigne.	Laforet Harajuku, a large-scale fashion complex, is unveiled in Tokyo.

show in 1970, one of his designs in *sashiko*—a traditional Japanese stitching technique—appeared on the cover of influential French fashion magazine *Elle*.

At the beginning of the 1980s, Rei Kawakubo (b.1942)—working under her label Comme des Garçons (see p.404)—and Yohji Yamamoto (b.1943) began to present their collections in Paris alongside the already established Issey Miyake (b.1938). Together these three formed a new school of fashion—the Japanese Avant-Garde—and set the stage for the beginning of a postmodern interpretation of fashion, which eliminated the boundary between the West and the East, fashion and anti-fashion, and modern and anti-modern. Like Kenzo, these designers placed great significance on clothing styles inherited from the past, including Japanese farmers' clothes created and worn through necessity. They adapted dyed textile and quilting techniques from ancient Japan, and presented them to the Western fashion system as high fashion (right).

Comme des Garçons first showed in Paris in 1981, and its uncompromising aesthetic combined subverting the accepted notion of garment construction with a preoccupation with texture and materials. Garments were cut to disguise rather than to reveal the shape of the body, and the label inaugurated black as the signature colour of 1980s avant-garde fashion. Kawakubo's minimalism and austerity epitomized a postmodernist approach to fashion in which any fixed classifications, ideologies and definitions are questioned. By the end of the decade Comme des Garçons had confirmed its status among global fashion brands and a quarter of its 300 retail outlets were located outside of Japan.

Yohji Yamamoto started designing women's clothing in 1970 and two years later established his own line in Tokyo, replacing the Western obsession with fast-moving trends with an ascetic sensibility. From a first catwalk show of womenswear—'Y's for Women'—in Tokyo in 1977, the brand was extended to include a menswear line in 1979 and the diffusion line 'Y's for Men' in 1981, the same year in which Yamamoto showed in Paris for the first time. In the later heat of the DC (Designer Character) brand boom—a phenomenon that introduced more affordable lines by labels such as Comme des Garçons and Issey Miyake—Yamamoto became the only Japanese fashion designer to be appointed a French Chevalier de l'Ordre des Arts et des Lettres. In the field of haute couture Hanae Mori (b.1926) became the only Japanese couturière to be accepted by the prestigious organization the Chambre Syndicale de la Haute Couture when she was elected in 1977. She combined Western dressmaking and draping techniques with Japanese design motifs to create influential couture collections, opera costumes and gowns for royal clients.

The influence of Japanese designers has partially drawn the boundaries of fashion away from Western ideals of the body and conventions of clothing. Furthermore, Western fashion has incorporated non-European influences, traditions and forms into mainstream practices, exemplified by the phenomenal success in 2002 of Y-3, Yamamoto's collaboration with Adidas (see p.532). **YK**

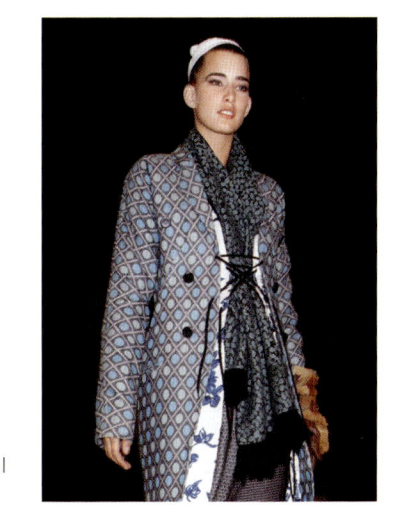

1976	1977	1980	1981	1983	1993
The first Comme des Garçons boutique opens in Tokyo.	Hanae Mori becomes the first Japanese couturière to work in French haute couture.	The DC brand phenomenon begins in Japan, and domestic designer labels become popular.	Yohji Yamamoto and Rei Kawakubo of Comme des Garçons show their first collection in Paris.	Rei Kawakubo wins the first of two Mainichi Design Prizes; the second is awarded in 1987.	The Kenzo label is purchased by the French luxury goods company LVMH.

MODERN JAPANESE DESIGN 403

Asymmetric Ensemble 1983
COMME DES GARÇONS

By the mid 1980s the journalistic tag 'Hiroshima Chic'—as applied to the contemplative austerity of Rei Kawakubo's designs—had been abandoned by the press. The asymmetric beauty of Kawakubo's garments was acknowledged as a refinement of composition; her sculpted aesthetic had the allure of the abstract held in contrast to the physicality of the body. The neutral palette of black, dark grey and white, used continuously by Kawakubo throughout her collections in the mid 1980s, emphasized this sculptural sensitivity. The integration of method and philosophy in her work is dependent on a close dialogue between the designer and her long-term technical collaborators; Kawakubo's garment construction is unconventional and she briefs her team to invent new methods in order to accomplish the nuances of her abstract designs.

In this ensemble, the squared-off top, hood and dropped arm scye, which results in wide, deep sleeves, are resonant of a monastic robe. This is further emphasized by the blousing of the bodice of the dress over the shirred waist, leaving a straight panel at the centre front. The voluminous ankle-length skirt is cut wider at the hips and extends outwards to create two folding pockets. **MF**

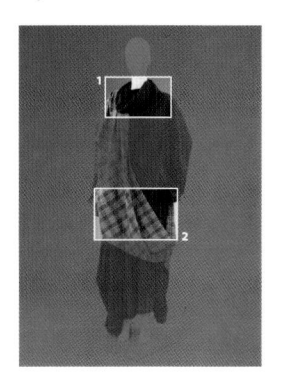

NAVIGATOR

FOCAL POINTS

1 COWL NECK
The large, loose-fitting turnover collar forms a deep cowl neckline and is integrated into the body of the main garment. When worn pulled up over the head, the collar forms an oversized hood that frames the face.

2 DRAPED CLOTH
A length of checked cloth is draped across the body from shoulder to hip, adding to the loose, layered silhouette. The pattern is similar in style to that of Scottish plaid, and the woven checks are mitred at the seam.

DESIGNER PROFILE

1942–75
Rei Kawakubo was born in Tokyo and graduated in fine art from Keio University, one of the most prestigious private universities in Japan. Before founding her label Comme des Garçons (the name alludes to song lyrics by Françoise Hardy) in Tokyo in 1969, she worked in the advertising department of a yarn manufacturer and as an independent fashion stylist. From the beginning she was described by peers as extraordinarily innovative in her designs, creating clothes that challenged industry conventions.

1976–83
In 1976 the designer opened her own shop in Tokyo, which was designed by the artist Takao Kawasaki. The first menswear line, Comme des Garçons Homme, was launched in 1978. It was the idea of fellow designer Yohji Yamamoto to organize his first show together with Kawakubo during the official Paris prêt-à-porter season in 1981, at the Hotel Intercontinental, in order to create a greater impact. Kawakubo opened her first Paris boutique the following year, and in 1983 she diversified into furniture production.

1984–93
In the 1980s and 1990s Kawakubo experimented with techniques of deconstruction, using distressed materials for her garments; in 1992 she designed a series of dresses that looked like paper patterns, surprising and delighting the fashion press. The same year Kawakubo gave protégé Junya Watanabe (b.1961) the opportunity to launch his own line under the Comme des Garçons label. Kawakubo's work was exhibited in 1986 as part of the 'Mode et Photo' (Fashion and Photography) exhibition at the Centre Pompidou in Paris.

1994–PRESENT
Kawakubo's designs were exhibited at the Kyoto Costume Institute in 1993. The brand branched out into fragrances, opening a store in Paris in 2000. A series of pop-up shops was launched in unusual locations across the world in 2004, and in 2008 Kawakubo collaborated with clothing retailer H&M.

GLAM ROCK AND DISCO STYLES

In the 1970s both Britain and the United States produced cultural movements that served as an antidote to the dour economic climate. Britain's answer to economic depression was glam rock—a movement that began in the early 1970s and was defined by theatricality and eccentricity of dress—whereas in the United States the disco movement emerged after 1976.

Although both movements shared the same love of sequins and featured variations of skintight leotards, glam rock was far more flamboyant, epitomized by the stage costumes of British musicians such as Elton John and Marc Bolan (above). The glam rock movement favoured a provocative androgyny, with David Bowie as its poster boy wearing outfits designed by Japanese-born Kansai Yamamoto (b.1944; see p.408). Top-to-toe excess included high platform boots, patterned all-in-ones, dyed mullets, and face and body paint. British shoe designer Terry de Havilland's cartoonishly large platforms were seen on many glam rockers' feet after the opening of his store, Cobblers to the World, in 1972. These flamboyant and bottom-heavy designs were typically fashioned from dyed snakeskin appliquéd with flowers and rainbow stripes, and were worn by men and women alike. Elton John's custom-made pair was

KEY EVENTS

1971	1972	1972	1973	1976	1976
Glam rock band T. Rex's 'Hot Love' rocks the UK charts. Marc Bolan wears a glitter and satin outfit to perform the hit on the TV show *Top of the Pops*.	Fashion label Swanky Modes is set up in Camden Town, London, by Willie Walters, Melanie Herberfield, Judy Dewsbury and Esme Young.	David Bowie introduces his androgynous alter ego to the glam rock scene, depicted in the film *Ziggy Stardust and the Spiders from Mars*.	David Bowie releases his seminal album *Aladdin Sane*. Japanese designer Kansai Yamamoto creates stage costumes for the accompanying tour.	Colour photographs from Mars capture the imagination of a generation. Artists, including David Bowie, are inspired by the idea of space travel.	The disco classic 'Dancing Queen' is released by the internationally successful Swedish pop group ABBA.

embellished with his initials (opposite below). Other London boutiques such as Alkasura on King's Road and Barbara Hulanicki's Biba store spearheaded the glam rock look with an eclectic mix of feather boas, sequinned jackets, elaborate waistcoats and flamboyant capes. The Mr Freedom boutique, owned by Tommy Roberts, opened in 1973 in Covent Garden and offered cartoon-emblazoned T-shirts, satin hot pants, and primary-colour satin bomber jackets and shirts. High-waisted trousers clung to the thighs and flared out over the boots, and were worn with shrunken sweaters featuring space-age motifs.

In the United States, the natural hedonism of the hippie movement gave way to the urban glamour of the disco phenomenon. The throbbing synthetic groove of tracks such as Donna Summer's 'I Feel Love' was the background to a period of fashion reliant on gloss and glitter, seen at New York nightclub Studio 54. Indelibly linked with the hedonistic decadence of the era, the club thrived from 1977 to 1979 and witnessed the excesses of the city's demi-monde. Old and new Hollywood met fashion designers, such as Calvin Klein (b.1942) and Halston (1932–90), and musicians mingled with artists, including Andy Warhol and Jean-Michel Basquiat. A stringent door policy restricted entry to the famous and beautiful, such as Bianca Jagger and Liza Minnelli.

Disco came to be associated with both culture and fashion, and was at its zenith in the late 1970s. The musical inspiration was Latin, funk and soul music, and the inherent sexuality of these genres was reflected in the fashion for figure-hugging garments that skimmed the body as dancers gyrated under strobe lights and mirror balls on the dance floor. Disco lighting reflected the shine from Lurex halter-neck tops, sequinned tube tops and body-hugging Spandex trousers. The fashion crowd favoured the New York club Xenon, which had a reputation for a more extreme interpretation of the disco look and where dancers cavorted in cages wearing only Spandex leotards and body glitter. In 1977 disco was thrust into mainstream culture by the popularity of the movie *Saturday Night Fever*, the high point of the disco boom. The film, with John Travolta in a white three-piece suit (right), disseminated disco style, which was inexpensive and easy to copy by mainstream fashion. Synthetic stretch fabrics in variations of the leotard and body-conscious dresses reliant on Spandex for shape, worn with stiletto-heeled shoes and ankle socks, proliferated.

British label Swanky Modes, consisting of a team of four young designers, promulgated the disco look in Britain with skintight Lycra-based garments featuring raunchy cut-outs, an overtly sexy aesthetic celebrated during the 1970s in images by French photographer Guy Bourdin (see p.410). The popularity of disco and glam rock came to a natural conclusion when a new youth movement rose up in revolt. Disco was replaced by the astringent aesthetics of punk rock. In addition, the sexual freedom and hedonism associated with disco suddenly seemed out of touch, if not dangerous, with the advent of Aids in the early 1980s. **EA**

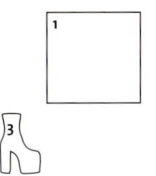

1 Self-styled T. Rex frontman Marc Bolan combined satin, velvet and feathers for 1970s glam rock.

2 John Travolta's white suit and black shirt with pointed collar, designed by Patrizia von Brandenstein in 1977, became an emblem of the disco decade.

3 Elton John's metallic red and silver platform boots were appliquéd with the musician's initials (1970s).

1977	1977	1977	1978	1979	1981
Steve Rubell and Ian Schrager open the seminal disco venue Studio 54 in New York.	Donna Summer, known as the 'queen of disco', releases the iconic disco theme 'I Feel Love' on Casablanca Records.	John Travolta stars in *Saturday Night Fever* as a disaffected youth whose world revolves around disco. The Bee Gees' soundtrack is a global phenomenon.	Peppo Vanini and Howard Stein open Xenon, which becomes the only real competitor for Studio 54 on the nightclub scene.	Guy Bourdin's seductive advertisement for shoe company Charles Jourdan appears in *Vogue* magazine (see p.410).	The idea of free love and the bacchanalian hedonism of the disco era end with the outbreak of Aids.

David Bowie's Ziggy Stardust Costume 1973
KANSAI YAMAMOTO b. 1944

1 THE MULLET
The mullet haircut was a key part of the Ziggy Stardust look. It was cut by Suzy Fussey, who went on to become Bowie's personal hairdresser. The style comprised a short, spiky front, longer sides and a long back 'tail'—all dyed Schwarzkopf red.

2 KNITTING TECHNIQUE
Horizontal rows of knitted black lacework are interspersed between the block colour of the unitard and the panels of diagonal green-and-white stripes that spiral around the body and leg. The garment is cut to shape, rather than fully fashioned.

Bowie performs at the Hammersmith Odeon in London (1973).

NAVIGATOR

This glam rock outfit, worn by David Bowie, was one of many stage costumes from his 'Aladdin Sane/Ziggy Stardust' tour of Britain and the United States (1972–73). It was designed in the vein of kabuki theatre costume by Japanese designer Kansai Yamamoto, who showed his first European collection in London in 1971. The unitard is constructed entirely from knitted yarn, using the innovative punchcard jacquard knitting machines of the era.

Although the knitted material provides stretch, the garment also has a zip placed under the left arm for optimum tautness. The unitard is extremely tight-fitting — especially around the waist and crotch — and serves to emphasize Bowie's emaciated, almost asexual frame. The missing pieces of the garment, exposing the leg to the crotch and the left arm, lend the garment a provocative androgyny appropriate for the character that Bowie had created to embody an 'alien from Mars'. Metallic Lurex thread was introduced throughout to reflect under the stage lighting, and the outfit is accessorized by several doughnut-shaped oversized bangles on the wrists and ankles, made of the same metallic fabric.

Bowie's mullet-style hair is dyed red to match the red of the fabric. His forehead is adorned with a gold circle — the 'Ziggy' logo — and his cheeks are made up with exaggerated blusher, a look that references kabuki stage make-up. The London make-up artist Pierre LaRoche decorated the star's head with a ring of rhinestones for the 'Ziggy' tour, then painted the iconic zigzag lightning bolt on his face for the cover of *Aladdin Sane*, which topped the UK charts in 1973. The outrageous theatricality of the unitard propelled Bowie into the spotlight in both Britain and the United States and caused a slew of imitators in both countries. So popular was the look that US *Rock Scene* magazine published a 'how to' feature titled 'Do It All By Yourself: The David Bowie Look' in its October 1973 issue. **EA**

3 OVERSIZED ACCESSORIES
Four large bangles, two on the left wrist and two on the right leg, provide a visual counterbalance to the asymmetry of the costume. Simply constructed in red and blue matching Lurex yarn, the bangles have overtones of manacles.

DESIGNER PROFILE

1944–70
Born in Yokohama, Japan, Kansai Yamamoto is best known for his costume collaborations with David Bowie. The musician first became aware of Kansai's work when he bought the 'woodlands animal costume' for the Rainbow Concert in 1972 from the designer's London boutique. Kansai initially studied civil engineering and English at Nippon University before going on to study fashion at Bunka College of Fashion in Tokyo.

1971–PRESENT
Following a period working for Junko Koshino (b.1939) and Hisashi Hosono Studio, the designer launched his eponymous label Yamamoto Kansai Company Ltd, Tokyo, in 1971. His first collection debuted in London the same year. His Paris debut took place in 1975 and was followed by the opening of the Kansai Boutique in 1977.

GLAM ROCK AND DISCO STYLES   409

Disco Femme 1979
CHARLES JOURDAN

Advertisement for shoe company Charles Jourdan, photographed by Guy Bourdin for *Vogue* (1979).

Photographer Guy Bourdin created era-defining images that presented women with a potent and sometimes perverse sexuality. This photograph of three semi-comatose women reclining in matching leotards, stilettos and feather boas captures the essence of the 'disco femme'. The three women seem drugged, post-coital and seductive: the epitome of Bourdin's passive, glamorous female trope. The fact that the three garments, shoes and hair are almost identical—except for a minimal variation of colour and strap placement—implies that the women are interchangeable.

This image is typical of Bourdin's approach to representing fashion by challenging taboos. The wearing of the leotard has several layers of meaning and supplies complex sartorial messages: the quintessential 1970s garment is constructed without fastenings and is designed to be put on by pulling up over the body. The one-piece, usually made from a Lycra-mix fabric, is skintight and covers only the torso. Cut high on the thigh, it elongates the legs and with no infrastructure requires the wearer to have a perfectly honed body. The skimpiness of the garment suggests heat, either an exotic tropical location or a hot, sweaty nightclub. Primarily, however, the garment evokes lingerie, and the message of the clothing is essentially sexual. Furthermore, the models are draped with dyed fur stoles, a signifier of luxury, glamour and sex. Designed by French company Charles Jourdan, the sandals are sequinned and strappy, with fine soles and high set-back heels. The series of advertising images that Bourdin created for the shoe brand from 1967 to 1981, of which this is one, was well known for its unconventional and atypical fashion advertisement aesthetics. **EA**

NAVIGATOR

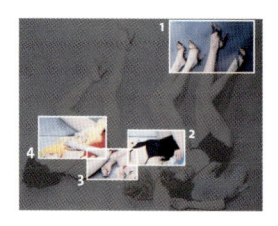

👁 FOCAL POINTS

1 STILETTO SHOES
The Charles Jourdan sandals have narrow straps embellished with sequins. Three different styles and colours are shown, thus allowing each woman a small degree of individuality. All three have the long, thin heel of a stiletto, which serves to arch the foot in a simulacrum of sexual abandonment.

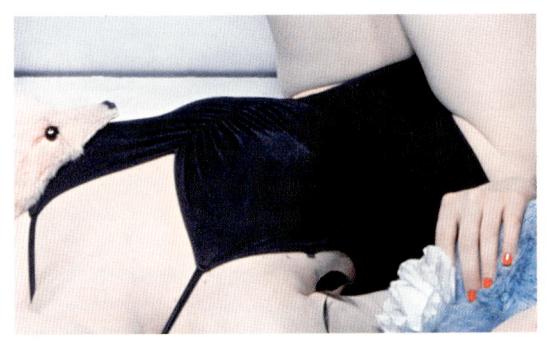

2 LEOTARD
Initially associated with sport, the leotard was inherently practical and allowed for unhindered movement, but over time it began to be worn as nightclub wear. As a close relative of the swimming costume, it is comparatively modest; however, as a garment worn outside the pool, it is highly sexualized.

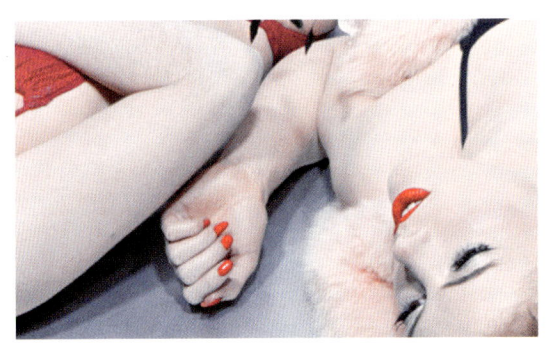

3 MAKE-UP
The models wear bright red lipstick and nail polish, the tone of which is echoed in the left-hand leotard and evokes the screen siren glamour of the 1940s and 1950s. Their eye make-up is minimal and comprises a winged eyeliner style that matches the period reference of the lips.

4 FUR STOLE
The models are draped with luridly dyed fur stoles. Made from soft and light fur, these stoles act as a textural counterpoint to the spiked stilettos and sleek leotards. In this image the stoles are not so much worn as caressed, almost as though they are still-breathing creatures.

🕐 COMPANY PROFILE

1883–1944
Born in 1883, Charles Jourdan trained as a shoemaker, and in 1919 he opened a shoe shop in Romans-sur-Isère, in the Drôme region of France. With the rise of hemlines after the war, Jourdan benefited from an increased focus on shoes. Like his contemporary Coco Chanel (1883–1971), he used only the finest materials to make his shoes and thus quickly gained status in the world of haute couture.

1945–60
After World War II, Charles's three sons—René, Charles and Roland—took over their father's empire. Under the tripartite leadership, Jourdan grew to achieve international recognition as a luxury label. Boutiques opened in major European capitals (the first in Paris in 1957), but also in the United States, making Jourdan the first French shoe brand to be sold there. In 1959, the same year that Jourdan & Sons set up shop in London, a contract was forged, granting them permission to design shoes under the Christian Dior label.

1961–79
In the 1960s and 1970s, Jourdan advanced its avant-garde profile through magazine advertising campaigns, which employed photographer Guy Bourdin's imagery. Despite product diversification in the late 1970s, with the addition of ready-to-wear clothing and fashion accessories lines, the label remained best known for its high heels. After Charles's death in 1976, his youngest son took the lead as head of design.

1980–PRESENT
The 1980s spawned a more conservative Jourdan look. Family control of the company came to an end in 1981; on Roland's retirement, Swiss firm Portland-Cement-Werke took over. In 1997 the firm embraced e-commerce with the launch of its website. Patrick Cox became Jourdan's design director in 2003; the first foreigner to hold the post, he departed after only two years to pursue his own lines. He was replaced by Josephus Thimister. Today the company has eighty boutiques, with almost 90 per cent of its production still based at Romans.

GLAM ROCK AND DISCO STYLES

MARKETING A LIFESTYLE

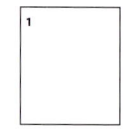

1 Robert Redford wears a three-piece Ralph Lauren suit as Jay Gatsby in *The Great Gatsby* (1974).

2 This Polo Ralph Lauren advertisement from the 1980s features a range of easy-to-wear luxury casuals, suitable for all generations.

3 Eva Wallen models a printed silk crêpe de Chine blouse and gathered burgundy skirt by Calvin Klein (1980).

The branding of products has existed since the age of mass manufacture began in the 19th century, when anonymous commodities were replaced with items universally recognized by their logo. During the 1980s branding emerged as a tangible asset that was vital to a company's success. It was recognized as a promise of consistency, particularly in the luxury goods market where licensing is an option. An exemplar of brand management and a leading early exponent of lifestyle marketing (opposite above) was US-born designer Ralph Lauren (b.1939). His brand drew on the fashions and accoutrements of previous eras—from the polo-playing elite of the British Empire to the pioneers of the American West—and transformed them into highly desirable products. The Ralph Lauren range included clothing and home interiors, and extended to toiletries, eyewear, handbags and accessories. Various entry price points and the covetable Polo logo made the label accessible to a worldwide audience of consumers and affirmed Ralph Lauren's global brand status.

KEY EVENTS

1970	1971	1978	1981	1981	1982
Ralph Lauren receives the Coty Award for menswear and releases his first line of women's suits.	The first stand-alone Ralph Lauren store opens on Rodeo Drive, Beverly Hills, California.	Calvin Klein launches his first menswear range, followed by his first fragrance.	The inauguration of President Reagan marks the return of ostentatious consumption in US society.	The first Polo Ralph Lauren international store opens on London's New Bond Street.	Calvin Klein Underwear is launched and changes the way men's underwear is marketed. A women's range is introduced the following year.

The Polo clothing brand emerged in 1967 from the designer's first tie collection, in which designs were based on the collegiate ties of the US Ivy League and the sports fraternities. In 1971 he added a women's line of male-tailored shirts, which featured a polo-playing horse and rider embroidered on the cuff, followed by 1930s-inspired sweaters, shorts, trousers and trench coats all featuring classic male tailoring details such as French cuffs and fly-front shirts in natural materials including tweed, cashmere and cotton. Traditional luxury sports, such as polo, tennis and golf, inspired his ready-to-wear clothing lines. One of Ralph Lauren's best-known designs is the short-sleeved, piqué fabric cotton tennis shirt—identified by the small embroidered logo on the left breast—which has become known as the 'polo' shirt after the adoption of the style by the Polo Ralph Lauren brand in 1972. This garment continues to sell across the world today and has become a fashion staple.

Ralph Lauren gained international recognition with his depiction of Jazz Age elegance in his designs for Robert Redford as the eponymous hero of *The Great Gatsby* (1974; opposite). Although Theoni V. Aldredge received an Academy Award for her costume designs for the film, it was Ralph Lauren's styling of the film's lead that introduced the label to a wider audience and sparked a fashion trend, further affirmed when influential men's fashion magazine *GQ* featured Redford as Gatsby on the cover. Combining heritage with a contemporary relevance, the aesthetic of US Ivy League classics, such as khaki trousers, double-breasted linen suits, piped blazers and rowing caps, deep-collared shirts, and silk ties in ice-cream coloured pastels, associated the label with upper-class US style, and kick-started the trend for the fashionable 'preppy' look. During the following decade the Prairie collection (see p.414) introduced a more homely rural lifestyle to the fashion world and the Lauren brand also fulfilled consumer requirements for haute-preppy style. Deploying his favourite heritage fabrics—linen, lace and tweeds—in double-breasted, easy-fit blazers and mid-calf dirndl skirts, Ralph Lauren further expanded his label to include evening wear such as floor-length cashmere sweaters in his signature pared-down style.

Increasingly, brands were compelled to offer a total look, rooted in a visible and established brand identity. Fellow designer Calvin Klein (b.1942) promulgated an equally American but more contemporary aesthetic than Lauren (right). Klein's expansion into the global marketplace also included lifestyle products alongside fashion for men, women and children, easily identifiable by the CK logo. However, brand management was not only part of the remit of the high-end ready-to-wear labels. Proffering a more democratic (less expensive) lifestyle brand, US label Gap Inc., first launched by Donald and Doris Fisher in 1969 on San Francisco's Ocean Drive, was transformed from a discount jeans emporium into a global megabrand by chief executive officer Millard Drexler. He introduced an aspirational series of advertisements including 'Who Wore Khakis?', which associated the product with luminaries such as Andy Warhol, Marilyn Monroe and Pablo Picasso, thus positioning the label as one of the most recognized apparel brands in the world. **MF/DS**

1983	1984	1986	1987	1987	1988
Diana Vreeland's retrospective of the work of Yves Saint Laurent (1936–2008) opens at the Metropolitan Museum of Art, New York.	The inauguration of the influential Council of Fashion Designers of America Award takes place. The awards are known as 'the Oscars of fashion'.	The Rhinelander Waldo mansion on Madison Avenue, New York, is transformed into the flagship store for Polo Ralph Lauren.	Gap opens its first store in London. It is also the first Gap store that is located outside the United States.	The second largest stock market crash (known as Black Monday) in United States history precedes another recession.	Anna Wintour replaces Grace Mirabella as editor-in-chief of US *Vogue*.

Prairie Collection 1988
RALPH LAUREN b. 1939

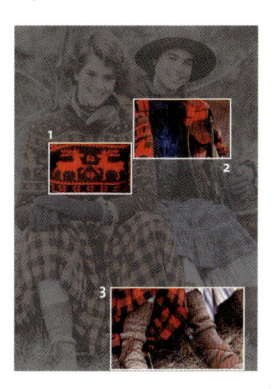

Resonant with rural imagery—seated on a bale of straw, the models have well-scrubbed faces and a healthy outdoor bloom—this advertisement reconstructed a homespun, down-on-the farm feel to appeal to city dwellers who were yearning for a less complex, more leisurely way of life. The Prairie collection featured layers of coordinating colours, and the textures summoned up images of a winter walk on a frosty afternoon.

Voluminous, mid-calf skirts are gathered into the waist and deeply flounced at the hem, and constructed from fine wool challis plaid cloth in primary shades of red and blue with black. These are layered over striped and cream-and-blue flannel petticoats and minutely patterned cream wool tights. The black-and-blue plaid silk blouse has a pie-crust frill around the neck and a frilled placket, finished with a dark blue silk-satin bow. A dark blue herringbone tweed jacket is layered between the blouse and a woollen lumberjack jacket in red-and-black plaid. Chunky hand-knit gloves, a fringed checked scarf and fawn 'game-fleck' socks, so called because of their similarity to the plumage of a partridge, provide extra protection against the elements. The unadorned felted wool hat has a rounded crown and straight flat brim, and is worn pulled down over the ears. **MF/DS**

NAVIGATOR

FOCAL POINTS

1 REINDEER MOTIF
The jumper is constructed in the two-colour patterning typical of Norwegian knitwear. It features a variation of the Selbu star, sometimes called the Norwegian star or snowflake. Other images are floral motifs and initials, or animals including reindeer.

3 SHOES
Worn over the sturdy socks is a pair of soft shoes, based on those worn for Scottish country dancing. Constructed from supple leather, the sole of the shoe is shaped to the foot, with laces criss-crossing over the top and caught into eyelet holes before being tied together.

DESIGNER PROFILE

1939–1974
Born Ralph Reuben Lifshitz in New York in 1939, Ralph Lauren began his retail career as a salesman, selling ties in Brooks Brothers. The Polo Ralph Lauren global fashion empire was founded in 1967 with his first necktie store, which also sold his own designs. Later he moved on to shirts and tailoring, introducing his first womenswear collection in 1971. He also pioneered the concept of lifestyle merchandizing.

1975–PRESENT
Lauren designed costumes for the film *The Great Gatsby* in 1974, which affirmed his reputation for heritage-inspired collections. The Polo Ralph Lauren brand expanded through boutiques, licensing and advertising to become one of the largest global fashion empires, which placed its creator in the Coty Hall of Fame in 1992 with a Lifetime Achievement Award.

2 LUMBERJACK JACKET
In red-and-black double-napped flannel, brushed on both sides for softness, the oversized lumberjack jacket—originally known as the 'logger' shirt when worn by workers harvesting trees—has two practical pockets. The jacket has a zipped centre-front fastening.

MARKETING A LIFESTYLE 415

THE PUNK REVOLUTION

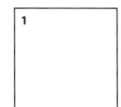

1 Vivienne Westwood's fetish wear is modelled in 1976. The shop Sex used the slogan 'rubberwear for the office'.

2 Jordan poses outside the shopfront at 430 King's Road, London in 1976. She became a walking advertisement for the punk-inspired fashion at Sex.

3 Vivienne Westwood (far right) in one of her tartan bondage suits poses with punk girls on a London street in 1977.

The punk phenomenon erupted in London in 1976. Although many musical influences came from the United States, in particular New York's proto-punk scene, it was in London that all the elements came together to create a blueprint for the movement. This consisted of an explosive mix of simple, loud and aggressive music combined with a startling approach to dress and appearance. Punk espoused a DIY aesthetic whereby the individual was empowered to construct their own identity through music, clothing, attitude and even name changes. Self-expression, experimentation and, above all, outrage were the guiding principles to what became a *bricolage* approach to the reinvention of the self. It is ironic, given the counter-consumerist ethos so ingrained in the philosophy of punk, that it was a clothes shop located on west London's King's Road that initiated the creative pulse of punk.

The shop was Sex and it was owned by Vivienne Westwood (b.1941) and Malcolm McLaren (1946–2010); it was renamed Seditionaries in 1976. McLaren and Westwood's emporium had been through a number of prior guises, before

KEY EVENTS

1971	1972	1973	1974	1975	1976
Malcolm McLaren and Vivienne Westwood open their first London shop Let It Rock at 430 King's Road.	McLaren travels to New York for a clothing trade show, where he meets infamous band the New York Dolls. He considers moving into rock management.	McLaren and Westwood change the name of their shop Let It Rock to Too Fast To Live, Too Young To Die. It is renamed Sex a year later.	McLaren and Westwood create their seminal 'You're Going to Wake Up' T-shirt, a design directly informed by Situationist politics.	McLaren and Westwood are pivotal in the launch of the Sex Pistols. Vivienne's fetish-inspired clothes receive recognition in the fashion press.	Sex is renamed Seditionaries, reflecting its owners' flirtation with anarchism. The Sex Pistols release their first single, 'Anarchy in the UK'.

416 1946–89

Sex appeared in 1974. The shop's mix of heavy-duty fetish wear (opposite) and Nazi chic clothes attracted a vagabond crowd of disaffected teenagers. Chief among this group was a young model and actress called Pamela Rooke who, in keeping with punk's ethos, reinvented herself simply as Jordan (above right). It was from this milieu congregating at Sex that McLaren discovered the band who became the embodiment of punk, the Sex Pistols. McLaren's initial interest in this seemingly unpromising band was that they would act as a promotional vehicle for the King's Road shop, which was referenced in the band's name. For two years, until their collapse in 1978, the Sex Pistols generated a blizzard of headlines and sensational 'news' stories, and as their infamy grew the spotlight fell increasingly on the clothing they wore. From 'anarchy shirts' (see p.418) to 'bondage trousers', 'destroy T-shirts' to 'hangman's jumpers', Westwood, with occasional advice from McLaren, produced a series of garments that redefined notions of fashion and taste.

In contrast to the sharp-suited power dressing of the era, Westwood's designs explored clothes in new and radical ways. The designer's approach to garment production was instinctive (she had limited training in fashion design) and her non-traditional methods gave her designs a distinctly quirky visual edge. Westwood's innovative approaches included cutting the fabric in the round and on the body, rather than on the flat, a process ideally suited to the fluid quality of knitted jersey. The technique was first used with the much-copied ripped T-shirt of 1979, which was based on a traditional shape, but with the opening under the arm, allowing the garment to find its own place on the body. Garments were cut in rectangles with gussets to create a three-dimensional shape; proportions were altered by cutting the top much higher than the waist. Pieces were sometimes adapted from existing items of clothing with deliberately crude manufacturing techniques serving to make a feature of the garment's construction. Hand-printed slogans would sit alongside an array of found objects, all placed in an astonishingly inventive juxtaposition. Westwood, encouraged by McLaren, attempted to imbue her designs with ideas drawn from radical Situationist politics—these clothes were intended to be guerrilla actions aimed at subverting the taste-value systems of the bourgeoisie. In this context of outrage and confrontation, pornographic images were used in T-shirt designs, swastikas appeared alongside portraits of Karl Marx, and overt references to bondage and fetish wear were juxtaposed with ideas drawn directly from military and biker clothing.

Colour was also used to startling effect with a preference for red, black and white, plus fluorescent pinks, Day-Glo yellows and electric blues adding to a sense of an 'all-action' palette. Westwood's use of tartans was equally bold. She produced a range of bondage-inspired garments, including jackets and trousers in a variety of tartans (right), as she linked her modernistic urban themes to Celtic history. **WH**

1977	1978	1978	1979	1980	1981
Elizabeth II's Silver Jubilee gives a focus to the Sex Pistols' music and informs the iconography included in Westwood's designs for Seditionaries.	Westwood produces infamous T-shirts, including 'Prick Up Your Ears', which features a cartoon of a gay punk orgy and text by Joe Orton.	At the end of the Sex Pistols' US tour, Johnny Rotten leaves the band, causing it to break up.	The Sex Pistols' bass player—and McLaren and Westwood's punk muse—Sid Vicious dies from a drugs overdose.	British director Julien Temple's mockumentary film about the Sex Pistols, *The Great Rock 'n' Roll Swindle*, is released.	In a conscious move away from punk, Westwood and McLaren stage the catwalk show 'Pirate'.

THE PUNK REVOLUTION 417

Anarchy Shirt 1976
MALCOLM MCLAREN 1946 – 2010 VIVIENNE WESTWOOD b. 1941

Simon Barker wears an anarchy shirt, photographed by Ray Stevenson for the Sex Pistols' fanzine *Anarchy in the UK* (1976).

The 'anarchy shirt', worn here by early Sex Pistols fan Simon Barker, is one of the most important Sex/Seditionaries designs, epitomizing Malcolm McLaren and Vivienne Westwood's daring, inventive approach to fashion. The shirt was made from a 1960s Wemblex mod shirt; McLaren had acquired a stock of these with the intention of selling them in the shop when it was still called Let It Rock. He took to wearing the unsold shirts until one day Westwood customized one by painting stripes on it. McLaren then further transformed the shirt by adding political images and slogans, turning it into a totally new garment. His aim was to shock with shirts fit for an 'urban guerrilla'. At the time the Sex Pistols were working on the song 'Anarchy in the UK', expressing ideas that had gained currency within the Sex/Seditionaries milieu. Using bleach, McLaren applied anarchic slogans that had appeared on the walls of Paris, also including the emblem and later the names of heroes of the anarchist movement such as the Spanish La Mano Negra (the Black Hand Gang). Each garment was unique (later they were often imitated, and fakes even appeared in museums), dyed red with hand-painted black-and-brown stripes, and a red armband was placed on the sleeve. The anarchy shirt was a provocative collage of contradictory, highly charged symbols including the controversial swastika—it was not so much a garment as a wearable manifesto. **WH**

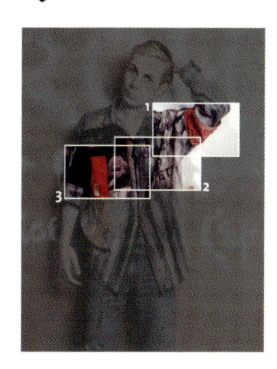

👁 FOCAL POINTS

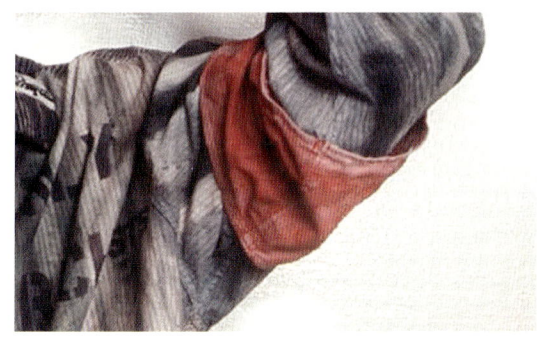

1 ARMBAND
The red armband on the sleeve pays homage to Mao's Red Guards and has the word 'chaos' printed on it. The most controversial element, although not always included on the shirts, was an inverted swastika patch on the right-hand front panel or collar.

3 FRONT PANEL
Dyed oblong silk and muslin patches are sewn onto the right side of the front panel. A printed image of Karl Marx has also been sewn onto the fabric; McLaren acquired these silk patches from a Chinese shop in Soho, London.

2 PRINTED TEXT
The left front panel shows the stencilled slogan 'Only Anarchists Are Pretty'. This and other Situationist graffiti slogans were drawn using a twig dipped in bleach. More words were stencilled onto the sleeves with a stencil set belonging to Westwood and McLaren's son.

⏱ DESIGNER PROFILES

1941–70
Vivienne Swire was born in Derbyshire, England. She briefly studied fashion at Harrow Art College, London, before becoming a primary school teacher. In 1963 she married Derek Westwood and they had a son together. The marriage ended when she met fellow designer Malcolm McLaren; they had a son in 1967.

1971–PRESENT
Westwood and McLaren set up their first venture together in 1971, called Let It Rock, on London's King's Road. They used this address for a series of shops, including their final business together, the pirate-themed World's End. Westwood had her first catwalk show, 'Pirate', in 1981. A major retrospective of her work was held at the Victoria & Albert Museum, London, in 2004. In 2006 Westwood was made a Dame of the British Empire for her services to fashion. McLaren died in 2010.

FASHION VALKYRIES

In the 1970s and early 1980s three designers thrust their way into the public consciousness with a fusion of radical, glamorous retro-chic. French designers Thierry Mugler (b.1948) and Claude Montana (b.1949), and British designer Antony Price (b.1945), theatrically celebrated and exploited women's sexuality. The valkyrie, the warrior princess, the stormtrooper and the sexual dominatrix moved into the realm of high fashion in a curious blend of past, present and future. Sexuality is a commonly used fashion tool; it generates publicity, attracts dissension and sells designs. It can be seductive, misogynistic, gender-bending or empowering—sometimes all of these things. It is an interesting dichotomy that, at the same time as a wave of feminism was gathering strength, fashion images of women became more subjective and sexualized.

Claude Montana explained his vision in an interview with French fashion magazine *Encens* in 2010: 'When I started to create clothes under my own name, all the women were wearing gypsy outfits. High-street fashion revolved

KEY EVENTS

1978	1979	1979	1980	1981	1981
Thierry Mugler opens his first Paris boutique in the Place des Victoires and launches a fashion collection for men the same year.	Antony Price launches his own label and opens shops on London's South Molton Street and King's Road.	Claude Montana founds his own fashion label, which is an immediate success and wins critical acclaim.	Antony Price shows his first collection at London Fashion Week.	Radical feminist Andrea Dworkin publishes *Pornography: Men Possessing Women*. It analyses the damaging effects of pornography on society.	US soap opera *Dynasty* begins showing on television and shoulder pads become so popular that they are mass marketed.

around an ample dress, tiered over a burlesque cascade of petticoats, peasant shirts and other borrowings from Eastern folklore. That was back in 1978 and I had the impression that we were never going to see the end of it...And so my desire was to put some backbone into all of that. To offer a new structure of clothes.' Montana brought the shoulder pad back into fashion along with aggressive, masculine, military-inspired lines (right). Born in Paris to a Catalonian father and German mother, Montana began his career by designing jewellery. One of the first designers to become known for his use of fetish leather, he was a master technician with the second skin, sculpting it into his signature silhouette and utilizing strong, bold colours. His sculptural clothing emphasized a top-heavy silhouette with exaggerated shoulders and oversized collars atop a narrow lower half encased in pencil slim skirts or narrow trousers. Montana also favoured military detailing, epaulettes, masculine collars and tight belts teamed with sadomasochistic studs, chains, buckles and zips.

Thierry Mugler's theatrical, futuristic designs were inspired by the film noir of the 1940s and 1950s, and included various fetish ensembles from the booted and spurred equestrian to the high-heeled dominatrix. He was renowned for his use of leather, constructing entire couture ensembles that included such fetishistic accoutrements as a leather neck corset. Emphasizing a moulded, hand-span waist, he reshaped the body using fabric, seams and artifice to create larger-than-life, cartoon-like superheroes that combined science fiction with Hollywood glamour. An iconic photograph of Mugler's automotive corset dress, taken in 1989 (opposite), sums up the duality of the message. A model lounges back across the bonnet of a car in an unmistakably suggestive pose; her corset emphasizes her sexuality and simultaneously defends it like armour. This look, commandeered by the villainesses of US television soaps in the 1980s and typified by Joan Collins's character in *Dynasty*, was not for shrinking violets. More recently US R&B singer Beyoncé Knowles commissioned Mugler to make her a couture corset for her 'I Am...Sasha Fierce' tour in 2009.

Master tailor Antony Price, who regards himself as responsible for the marriage of fashion and rock music, is unapologetic about his approach, as he explained to *Vogue* in 1994: 'My clothes are men's ideas of what women should wear...Men are looking for the sex robot from Lang's *Metropolis* with the perfect body offering endless fantasy sex. They're obsessed by the size of sexual protuberances—their own as well as women's—and I'm an illusionist. My job is to give them what they want.' A graduate of London's Royal College of Art, Price—who helped to define Roxy Music's retro-chic image for several of their albums, including *For Your Pleasure* (1973; see p.422)—moved from street style to couture. The designer 'built' his frocks for maximum impact with boning and interfacing beneath the silks and taffetas. This overt look was best epitomized by supermodel Marie Helvin in the 1970s and her glamazon Texan contemporary Jerry Hall. **JE**

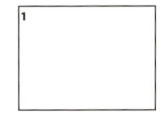

1 Thierry Mugler's automotive corset dress of 1989 was inspired by 1950s Detroit car styling.

2 Extreme shoulders, a nipped-in waist and flaring peplum typify Claude Montana's aggressive tailoring for women in his autumn/winter collection of 1981.

1982
Antony Price designs pastel silk tonic suits for British band Duran Duran's 'Rio' video. It begins a style trend among the New Romantics.

1983
Claude Montana opens his first boutique in Paris.

1989
Antony Price is named Glamour Designer of the Year at the British Fashion Awards.

1991
Montana wins a Golden Thimble Award for his design work for the House of Lanvin. He earns a further award the following year.

1992
Mugler launches his perfume Angel. He also completes his first collection at the request of the Chambre Syndicale de la Haute Couture.

1992
Claude Montana launches a secondary line known as the State of Claude Montana.

FASHION VALKYRIES 421

Roxy Music Cover Leather Dress 1973
ANTONY PRICE b. 1945

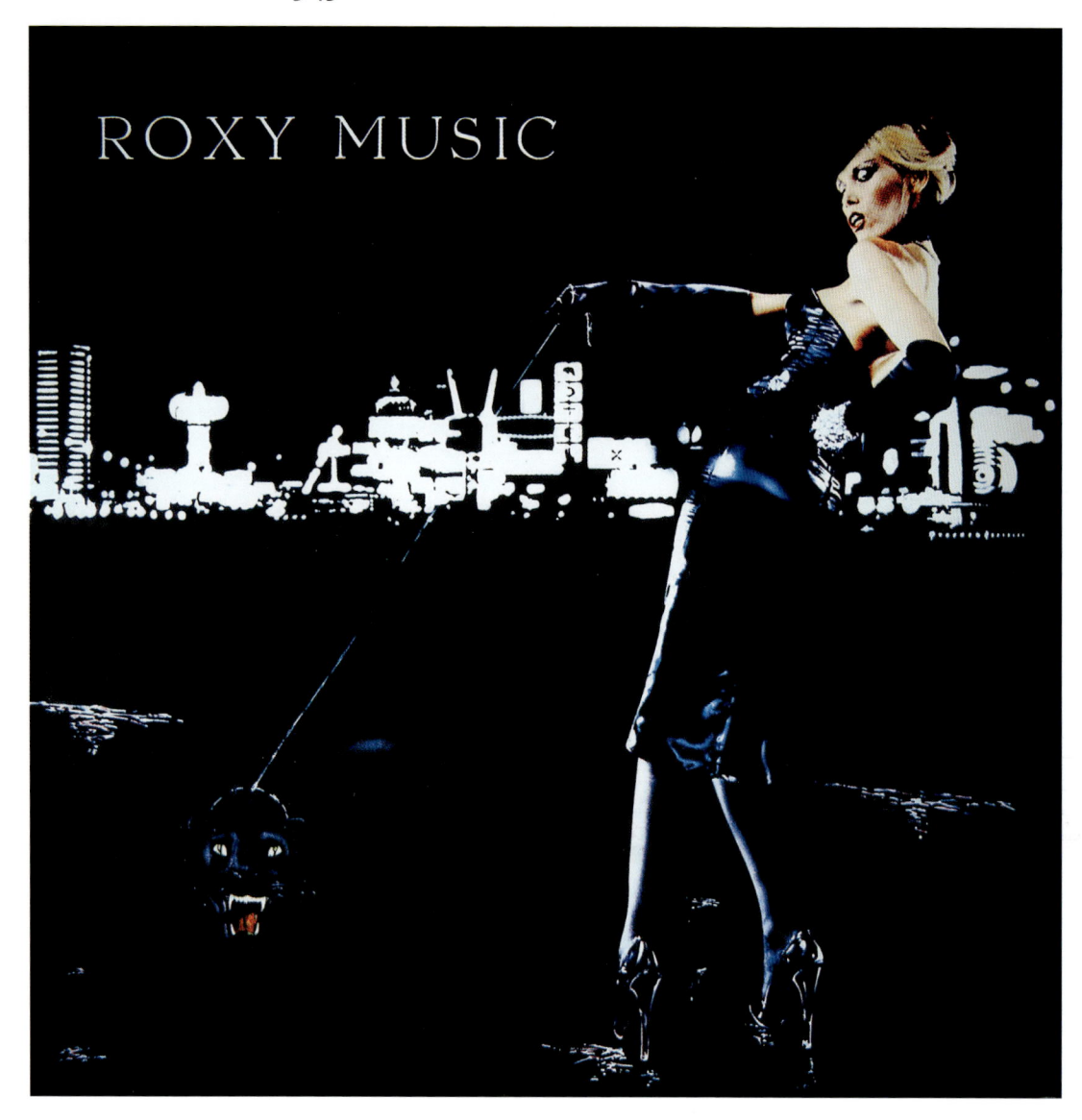

Detail of Roxy Music album *For Your Pleasure*, featuring Amanda Lear.

NAVIGATOR

The panoramic cover of Roxy Music's second album in 1973, *For Your Pleasure*, continued designer Antony Price's collaboration as stylist to the group. The visual tone is set by the nocturnal glamour of a generic, neon-lit city scene, in front of which stands a leather-clad, domineering vamp, who is restraining a snarling panther on a leash. Model and singer Amanda Lear—the stiletto-heeled protagonist—is dressed as a fusion of the opera-gloved sensuality of *Gilda* (1946)—the screen creation of actress Rita Hayworth and costume designer Jean Louis Berthault (1907–97)—and the icily veiled, Teutonic hauteur of Marlene Dietrich. The noirish backdrop of urban playscape created by Price resonates with the alienation and angst of keyboardist Brian Eno's electro-synth innovations and the melancholic, declamatory lyrics of the album. Amanda Lear—at the time briefly lead singer Bryan Ferry's fiancée—poses gleaming in the darkness. Her curved form is taut and glossy; the athletic undulations of her torso are highlighted by the lustre of her leather dress, which forms a continuous sinuous line from breasts to knee, thus creating the classic hourglass shape. With this melange of references, Price established a rich visual code to reinforce the literary, theatrical and musical character of both the album and the band. **JE/MF**

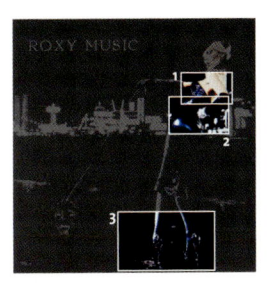

FOCAL POINTS

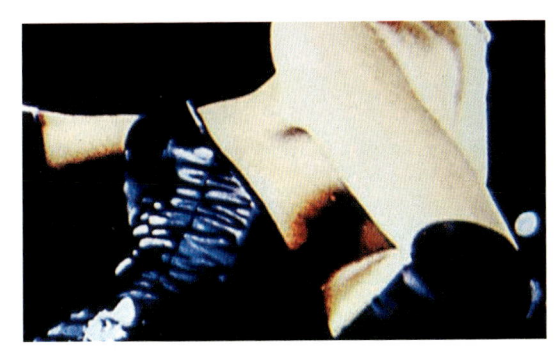

1 BUSTIER BODICE
So rigid in structure that it moves independently of the body, the bustier bodice reveals the upper part of the breasts, which form a horizontal line along Lear's upper arm. The exposed white skin contrasts dramatically with the bodice and elbow-length gloves.

2 JEWELLERY
The Gilda dress that Berthault designed for Hayworth was not Price's sole Hollywood inspiration. The broad, gem-laden bracelet worn over the glove references Marilyn Monroe's ensemble by William Travilla (1920–90) in *Gentlemen Prefer Blondes* (1953).

3 VERTIGINOUS HEELS
Combined with the constricting skintight black leather of the dress, the spiked stiletto heels provide the ultimate in fetish fashion. Constructed from glossy patent leather, the shoes further elongate the length of Lear's legs to Amazonian proportions.

DESIGNER PROFILE

1945–79
Born in England, Price attended Bradford School of Art and the Royal College of Art, London, before working for Stirling Cooper and Plaza Clothing Company in 1972. He began designing under his own name in 1979 and opened a shop on London's King's Road, followed by a flagship store on South Molton Street.

1980–PRESENT
Price collaborated with many musicians; he designed trousers for Mick Jagger, styled all eight Roxy Music albums, including Jerry Hall's mermaid outfit on *Siren*, the back cover of Lou Reed's album *Transformer* and Duran Duran for *Rio*. His influential menswear tailoring has been said to have made the suit 'rock 'n' roll'. Price was awarded the Evening Glamour Award at the British Fashion Awards in 1989. In 2008, 2009 and 2010 he collaborated on collections with Topman.

SECOND-SKIN CLOTHES

1 Azzedine Alaïa presents a collection of sensual body-hugging dresses in muted shades in Paris (1986).

2 Hervé Léger's bandage dress has become a timeless classic that dominates his collections, seen here in 1992.

Although female fashion has pushed the boundaries of decency in clothing throughout history, the emphasis has often been on constriction. During the late 1970s, however, a new generation of second-skin clothing liberated women: it revelled in youth, celebrated vigour and physicality, permitted freedom of movement, and flaunted the body. The term 'second-skin clothes', coined by *Women's Wear Daily* in 1980 to describe the body-conscious designs of Azzedine Alaïa (b.1940), marked the start of a progressive period. The use of elastane in knitted and woven fabrics, the influence of the fitness revolution, and the shift of sportswear into the realm of mainstream fashion combined to create a new style in body-conscious fashion.

US author James Fixx is generally credited with kick-starting the new interest in fitness in 1977 when the success of his publication *The Complete Book of Running* turned jogging into a US obsession. The keep-fit culture, championed by film actress Jane Fonda in her workout videos and by films such as *Fame* (1980) and *Flashdance* (1983), fuelled the impetus for men and women to show off a body toned to perfection by intensive exercise, which in turn popularized second-skin clothing.

Sportswear and dancewear had evolved very little since the 1930s: knitted fabrics were utilized for stretch, but these materials bagged and

KEY EVENTS

1978	1978	1979	1980	1980	1980
The February issue of *Vogue* focuses on summer sportswear as its lead fashion story.	Norma Kamali opens her new store in New York City and launches her OMO (On My Own) line.	Debbie Moore opens Pineapple Dance Studios in London and develops her own line of brightly coloured dancewear, leotards and leggings.	Calvin Klein advertises his range of designer jeans using fifteen-year-old Brooke Shields as a model (see p.426).	Norma Kamali designs her A Fashion at a Price collection featuring sweats.	Azzedine Alaïa launches his first collection. *Women's Wear Daily* dubs him the 'king of cling'.

sagged unattractively. Rubber, which corroded with washing, had been the only material that offered stretch. This changed in 1959 when US chemical manufacturer DuPont developed elastane. DuPont, who named the fibre Lycra (see p.428), began to explore the possible uses for a yarn that could stretch by 600 per cent, yet return to its original shape. Although the initial focus was on developments in underwear, the company recognized the fabric's potential in swimwear and other market sectors, because Lycra could be woven or knitted with other fibres to create an entirely new generation of performance fabrics for the fitness generation.

Calvin Klein (b.1942) was the first designer to fully embrace the cult of body consciousness, although he explored it via cut rather than stretch. He launched his Jeanswear line in 1976 to little success, but when he sculpted his jeans a few years later to reveal more than ever before, emphasizing the crotch and lifting and shaping the buttocks to fit like a second skin, they became a commercial success (see p.426). Another innovative US fashion designer was Norma Kamali (b.1945), who set change in motion by utilizing commonplace fabrics in entirely new ways. Her collection in 1980, made entirely from grey sweatshirt fabric, featured giant padded shoulders, midriff-revealing track pants, ra-ra skirts, hoods and off-the-shoulder tops, which elevated the fabric from its functional sector and provided loose cover-ups that both revealed and concealed the gym-honed body. Kamali's influential collection introduced the concept of active wear into everyday street fashion, and although it was available only in the United States, it inspired mass-market copies.

In high fashion the well-toned body allowed designers such as Azzedine Alaïa and Hervé Léger (b.1957) to create collections of figure-hugging dresses that delineated every curve. Tunisian-born, Paris-based designer Alaïa launched his first collection in 1980: entirely black in colour, it referenced punk and utilized zips and pins. Dubbed the 'king of cling' by *Women's Wear Daily* in 1980, the designer used various bias-cut and stretch fabrics, but it was when he began to use Lycra that he really developed his passion for sculpting the female body. Alaïa's designs were based on the intricate craft of cut, and his work was a web of multi-seaming. The garments were figure-hugging in the best tradition of crafted couture, but they utilized stretch so that they were comfortable and there was no constriction (opposite). The signature Alaïa look began to emerge in 1985 with the iconic side-laced dress, followed in 1987 by long-sleeved scoop-neck dresses accessorized with matching opaque tights and shoes. The original cult bandage dress by Hervé Léger was first launched in 1989 and utilized elasticated bands of fabric wrapped tightly around the body to mould and shape the figure (right). The cut remains so desirable and the impact so significant that the second-skin bandage dress has become the currency of major celebrities, whose carefully honed bodies are a valuable, marketable commodity. **JE**

1981	1981	1982	1989	1994	1995
Time magazine features 'The Fitness Craze with America Shapes Up' as its November cover story.	Olivia Newton-John's single 'Physical' spends ten weeks at No. 1 in the Billboard Hot 100.	Jane Fonda's aerobics video revolutionizes the fitness world and has remained the best-selling home fitness video.	Hervé Léger pioneers the iconic bandage dress design.	Azzedine Alaïa shows a collection of long dresses made from 'houpette', a stretchy new fabric that moulds to the shape of the body.	Azzedine Alaïa makes clothes out of 'Relax', an anti-stress fabric with carbon-dipped fibres that repel electromagnetic waves.

Brooke Shields Jeans Ad 1980
CALVIN KLEIN b. 1942

1 SENSUAL TEXTURE
A generous classically cut silk or satin shirt is worn with revealing jeans: the sensual contrast between the functional all-American denim and the luxe slippery-soft silk highlights Klein's design ethic, combining easy dressing with feel-good fabrics.

2 FORM-FITTING CUT
The sculpting shape of Calvin Klein's jeans was emphasized by the high-rise waistline, which Brooke Shields noted came above her navel. Klein also adjusted the seam that ran between the buttocks to emphasize the shape of the derrière.

NAVIGATOR

It was not only the quality of Calvin Klein's designs, but also the impact of his marketing that led *Time* magazine to declare in 1996 that Klein was one of the twenty-five most influential Americans. The advertising campaign for his jeanswear line had got off to an unspectacular start in 1976, but Klein's ground-breaking series of commercials, directed by Richard Avedon and featuring the fifteen-year-old actress Brooke Shields, changed everything. Shields, tightly encased in her jeans, legs akimbo, enquired: 'You know what comes between me and my Calvins? Nothing.'

The young actress, who had already appeared as a child prostitute in Louis Malle's film *Pretty Baby* (1978), wore a series of casual shirts, grey and rust silk, and gold satin, all teamed with the iconic skintight jeans and finished off with either bare feet or, as in this version, black cowboy boots. Shields posed provocatively, stretching her legs first this way, then that, in order to emphasize the particular cling of the jeans in the most intimate of areas and the seductive properties they bestowed. In another advertisement, Shields declared: 'I've got seven Calvins in my closet, and if they could talk, I'd be ruined.'

The suggestion of underage sexuality in the advertisements provoked a flood of complaints, and they were in fact removed by three leading television networks. Klein himself was unperturbed; the overt sexuality of the promotion had paid off and sales of Calvin Klein jeans reached two million pairs a month and a one-fifth share of the market. In 1982 Klein appeared with Brooke Shields—wearing the infamous jeans once more—on the cover of *People* magazine. 'I always had a clear design philosophy and point of view', the designer told *Women's Wear Daily* in June 2000, 'about being modern, sophisticated, sexy, clean and minimal. They all apply to my design aesthetic.' By 1999 one-third of the company's cash flow was attributed to the sale of Calvin Klein jeans. **JE**

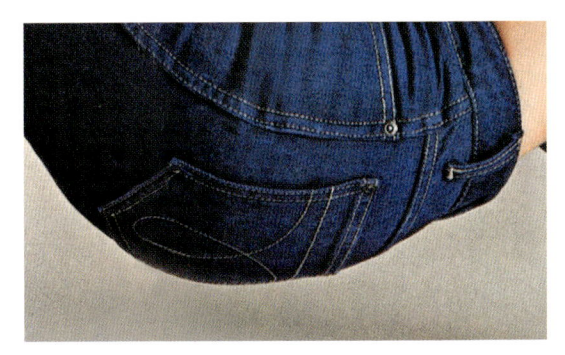

3 BRANDED POCKET
Klein introduced the concept of designer jeans by developing a tight-fitting brand with his signature across the back pocket. His unapologetically erotic jeans advertisements sold sex and created the mood of all his campaigns, from underwear to perfume.

DESIGNER PROFILE

1942–70
Bronx-born Calvin Klein graduated from the Fashion Institute of Technology in 1962. In 1968, with the backing of childhood friend Barry Schwartz, his first collection of women's coats was sold to Bonwit Teller, who placed an order worth US$50,000.

1971–PRESENT
In 1971 Klein added sportswear to his line and in 1973 he received his first Coty American Fashion Critics' Award. Klein's look was always simple and luxurious, and he embraced licensing to expand a range of products: shoes, belts, sunglasses, furs, jeans, underwear and perfume. The men's underwear range grossed US$70 million in its first year alone, and contentious erotic advertisements generated massive income. Despite this success, the brand experienced financial difficulties and in 2002 the company was sold to PVH Corp.

Lycra Aerobics Outfit 1980s
SPORTSWEAR

Christie Brinkley models a long-sleeve unitard (1982).

Glamazon supermodel Christie Brinkley, photographed in a sugar-pink Spandex all-in-one, epitomized the naive early face of second-skin clothes—a world away from the technology-driven, performance-enhancing sportswear of today. While fashion designers utilized Lycra in the 1980s to produce sensual, revealing clothes, the trends from the fledgling sportswear market were heavily influenced by aerobics and dance, and focused on developing user-friendly ranges, with a good fit, in a sugary palette. Brinkley took the prestigious cover on three *Sports Illustrated* swimsuit issues between 1979 and 1981, and wrote an illustrated book on health and beauty that topped the *New York Times* best-seller list. Her success marked the trend towards tall, sublimely built models such as Cindy Crawford, Naomi Campbell and Elle Macpherson. The burgeoning sportswear influence in the late 1970s and early 1980s marked the shift away from formality to sports-influenced designs that were, above all, functional. **JE**

⊙ FOCAL POINTS

1 LEG WARMERS
Gym accessories such as leg warmers, originally worn by ballet dancers to keep working muscles warm, enhanced the fitness message and infiltrated mainstream fashion, appearing as patterned and stripy knits in streetwear.

2 SPRAY-ON SPANDEX
An all-in-one suit with tight-fitting wrist-length sleeves and cut to the ankle provides top-to-toe hold. It was available in a sugary palette of soft tones of baby pink, lavender, powder blue and turquoise in shiny, shimmering finishes.

▲ English model Debbie Moore founded Pineapple Dance Studios in London in 1979. She designed her own brand of dancewear using Lycra in the early 1980s.

⚽ NAVIGATOR

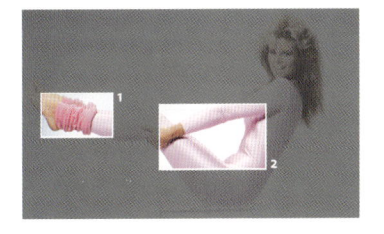

SECOND-SKIN CLOTHES 429

RADICAL DESIGN

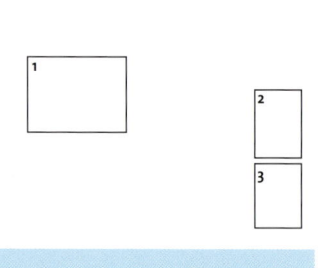

1 The flamboyant New Romantic style of Spandau Ballet made them one of the most fashionable bands of the 1980s.

2 This ensemble from John Galliano's 1989 collection was inspired by styles of the French Revolution.

3 Katharine Hamnett wears a T-shirt with the slogan '58% DON'T WANT PERSHING' to meet Margaret Thatcher at Downing Street, London in 1984.

After the low style of punk in the 1970s, the new decade witnessed a sudden explosion of flamboyant creativity. The New Romantic movement, a subculture, subverted the notion of glamour into an excessive display of pure pastiche, born out of the dressing-up box and reliant on a singular appreciation of other cultures and the history of costume. British designer Vivienne Westwood (b.1941) epitomized this aesthetic in 1981 with her first own-label collection, Pirates, in which she drew inspiration from an eclectic array of sources, including 19th-century tailoring and a Hollywood version of the high-seas buccaneer. This synthesis of cultural ideas spearheaded the antidote to the street style of punk and was a process that ultimately presaged the 'pirating' of ideas that led to the New Romantic movement. In London a generation of art students and their associates flocked to night clubs such as Billy's, Blitz and Hell to indulge in conspicuous narcissism. This high-maintenance in-crowd comprised numerous creatives who emerged as serious contributors not only to the immediate scene, but also to the evolution of popular culture: pop stars Duran Duran, Spandau Ballet (above) and Boy George, style editors Dylan Jones and Iain R. Webb, and fashion designers Stephen Jones (b.1957), Stephen Linnard (b.1959) and Pam Hogg.

The capital resonated with radical ideas and new talent, much of which originated in London's art colleges, particularly Central Saint Martins College of Arts and Design and the Royal College of Art. Moreover, the dynamic London club scene provided a platform for the cross-fertilization of fashion, music

KEY EVENTS

1979	1980	1980	1981	1982	1983
Steve Strange and Rusty Egan launch the Blitz club in London, where the door policy admits only 'the weird and wonderful'.	Style magazine i-D is set up by Terry Jones, a former art editor for Vogue and designer of the Memphis Design Group logo.	The most influential design magazine of the era, The Face, is launched by Nick Logan under the art direction of Neville Brody.	British designer Betty Jackson launches her own design company with her French Israeli-born husband, David Cohen.	New Romantic pop band Culture Club, led by Boy George, releases its first album, Kissing to Be Clever.	Malcolm McLaren (1946–2010) releases his album Duck Rock, featuring the single 'Buffalo Girls'.

and performance art. This attracted established designers such as Jean Paul Gaultier (b.1952) and Issey Miyake (b.1938), both of whom visited the city in search of inspiration. Cross-styling was also adopted by David Bowie, who repositioned himself in the New Romantics genre by styling himself as Pierrot and peopling his 'Ashes to Ashes' video with Blitz Kids dressed in genderless finery. Such post-punk theatricality reinforced the disruption of gender stereotypes by simply transposing elements of traditional dress that are perceived as feminine, such as the use of cosmetics and dyed hair.

Radical upstart design was finally lionized in 1984 with Les Incroyables, the graduate collection of John Galliano (b.1960), which was bought in its entirety by influential retailer Joan Burstein of London store Browns. In his inventive designs Galliano took inspiration from garments worn during the French Revolution (above right). Design duo Bodymap also showed their collection, The Cat in a Hat Takes a Rumble with a Techno Fish, to great acclaim in 1984 (see p.432). It combined woven and stretch materials in a series of separates, and the success of the collection was underpinned by the graphic prints of textile designer Hilde Smith. Printed textiles were also integral to the work of designer Betty Jackson (b.1949), who commissioned British design collective The Cloth for the large-scale prints of her English Rose collection in 1985. The oversized silhouettes of big shirts and ankle-length skirts provided an ideal surface for the dramatic prints.

Designer Katharine Hamnett (b.1947) introduced 'shredded' denim jeans in 1979, prefiguring later trends in washes and dyes, and found inspiration at military surplus stores, such as the renowned Laurence Corner in north London. Easy-to-wear separates in crushed parachute silk, with detailing such as studs, top-stitching and exposed zips, became her trademark. Noted for her commitment to radical politics, the designer also originated the slogan T-shirt in 1983. A year later, she was captured by the global press when she was introduced to the then prime minister, Margaret Thatcher, at a Downing Street dinner party wearing an oversized T-shirt emblazoned with the slogan '58% DON'T WANT PERSHING', in opposition to nuclear armament (right).

The new wave of designers found that fashion industry organizations were keen to capitalize on fresh international media attention with a variety of marketing initiatives. In 1982 Caroline Coates set up Amalgamated Talent, which promoted the work of young, avant-garde, street-style designers on the international market. The British Fashion Council was established in 1983 and the following year staged the first London Fashion Week. The flourishing of British fashion design in this period was driven mainly by the outsider instincts of young media-savvy pioneers, and it has remained the bedrock of the international influence of British design education. Furthermore, the diaspora of innovative designers from the key British colleges continued as a phenomenon and extended its reach over subsequent decades. **MF**

1983	1983	1983	1984	1984	1985
Madonna is styled by fashion designer Maripol (b.1947) in distressed lace, torn leggings and multiple bangles.	The 'New London in New York' fashion show is held in Manhattan's Roxy roller rink, curated by events organizer Susanne Bartsch.	Textile design group The Cloth is formed by Royal College of Art graduates to facilitate the movement between art and design projects (see p.434).	Katharine Hamnett wears an anti-nuclear T-shirt inscribed '58% DON'T WANT PERSHING' to meet British Prime Minister Margaret Thatcher.	British designer Pam Hogg opens her first concession at Hyper Hyper fashion market on London's Kensington High Street.	British designer John Galliano shows his Fallen Angels collection, inspired by the late 18th century and styled by Amanda Grieve.

Knitted Outfits 1984
BODYMAP

British design label Bodymap participated in its first major catwalk show—'The Cat in a Hat Takes a Rumble with a Techno Fish'—in 1984, confirming its position as one of the foremost labels in contemporary British fashion. Using friends, musicians and dancers as well as models, the designers offered performance theatre alongside their fashion collection in an irreverent response to the more formal couture shows. The collection featured a combination of separates in easy-to-wear fabrics, such as knitted jersey and cotton velour, and incorporated black-and-white printed textiles from the Big Mesh collection of British textile designer Hilde Smith. Utilized for the two oversized knee-length sweaters on the right—both with deep, dropped arm scyes—the prints are combined with areas of plain cloth: the sleeves are bisected into plain and patterned, one garment with black, one with white. The deep rolled collars are similarly contrasted, as are the ribbed cuffed hems.

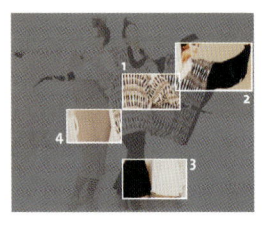

Proportion and scale, as well as the juxtaposition of wide and narrow horizontal and vertical stripes, are playfully engaged throughout the collection; the width of the shoulder extends to the hips before narrowing at the knees and widening once more at the hem. The 'T'-shape tubular dress on the left, in narrow, horizontal black-and-white stripes, is cut long and narrow to mid calf, and features extra-long sleeves cuffed in black to contrast with the white band inserted at the shoulder. Monochrome, horizontally striped socks and pull-on hats are part of the total look produced by the label. In 1984 the clothes were chosen by Brenda Polan of the *Guardian* for the Bath Costume Museum. **MF**

👁 FOCAL POINTS

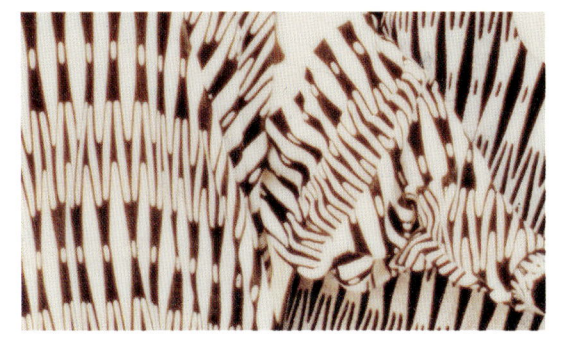

1 MONOCHROME PRINT
The hard-edged patterning of British textile designer Hilde Smith's Big Mesh collection is an essential component of the garments. Printed on a cotton/Lycra mix, the designs form the basis for the oversized sweaters.

3 FLUTED SKIRT
The volume around the ankle-length petal skirts is created from eight panels. The specially commissioned fabric is double-sided waffle viscose and cotton, and was developed in Sweden by Fixtrikafabrika.

2 OVERSIZED 'T'-SHAPE
The displaced shoulder seam creates a batwing effect on the sleeves, which are deep at the arm scye and narrow at the wrist. Constructed with a horizontal seam, the under sleeve is patterned, whereas the top is left plain.

4 CUT-OUTS
Bound in contrasting fabric and much referenced by the mass market, the label's signature circular cut-out on the hip appears elsewhere in the collection on skirts and leggings. The cut-outs brought attention to areas of the body that were seldom exposed.

🕒 COMPANY PROFILE

1982–86
Bodymap was formed in 1982 by Stevie Stewart (b.1958) and David Holah (b.1958), who met while studying fashion at Middlesex College of Art. In 1983 Bodymap won the Martini Award for the Most Innovative Designers of the Year, and in 1984 staged its first major fashion show. The same year the label was chosen to represent Costume of the Year by fashion journalist Brenda Polan, alongside the work of Katharine Hamnett and Betty Jackson. Bodymap was nominated for BBC Designer of the Year in 1986, and the label was invited to take part in the 'Best of British' at the British Embassy in Paris.

1987–91
In 1987 Bodymap won the Bessie Award for its costumes for the Michael Clark Dance Company, a collaboration that continued throughout the 1980s. It also made commissioned pieces for Ballet Rambert and London Festival Ballet. In 1989 Bodymap opened its own retail outlet but its success was short-lived and the label stopped trading in 1991.

▲ The Michael Clark Dance Company performs at Riverside Studios in London in 1984. The dancers' costumes were designed by Bodymap and feature the label's trademark circular cut-outs.

RADICAL DESIGN 433

Textile Prints 1985
THE CLOTH

Print designs by The Cloth, photographed by Corbin O'Grady Studio (1985).

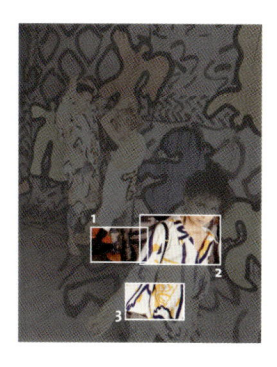

The British design collective The Cloth was known for its expressive, brightly coloured textiles, and the oversized garments popular in the mid 1980s provided an ideal canvas for its prints. In 1985 the group created the backgrounds for the window display of London department store Liberty as a showcase for its Summer Simmitts collection. The print evidenced the influence of such diverse sources as the vibrant cut-outs of painter Henri Matisse and the flat graphic style of US street artist Keith Haring; the latter gained international recognition in the 1980s for his primary colour murals and subway drawings. Deploying fluid mark-making with intense colour, The Cloth eschewed all processes other than the hand drawn and the brushstroke, and used the human form as a source of inspiration, alongside natural and city landscapes, the classical Greek, Roman and Egyptian galleries of the British Museum, and the distressed and eroded surfaces of urban interiors and exteriors. The group worked with a varying intensity of brushstrokes across a wide range of scales, from miniature to large-scale repeat structures that measured up to 6 ½ feet (2 m) long. This resulted in the printed length being cut up and reassembled in order to produce a garment, which further obscured the repeat and abstracted the image even further. **MF**

NAVIGATOR

FOCAL POINTS

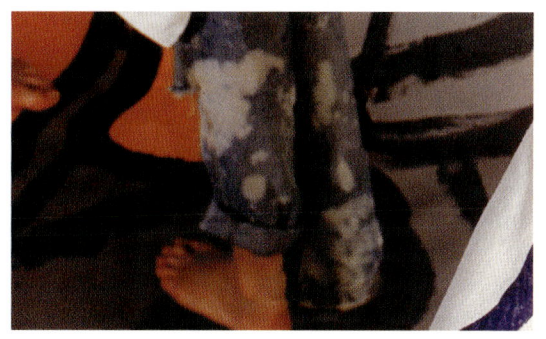

1 DISTRESSED JEANS
Naturally faded and worn jeans are enhanced with rips and tears to provide a deliberately distressed finish. This technique transforms everyday functional jeans into a popular fashion item, here worn rolled up at the hem.

3 BROAD OUTLINES
The dense, broad outlines of the printed, vibrantly coloured figures on the shirt — as well as the backdrop of the store — are resonant of the lively silhouettes that feature in the work of Keith Haring. These are juxtaposed with loose, painterly, free-flowing marks.

DESIGNER PROFILES

1983–85
Graduates of the printed textiles department at London's Royal College of Art, Fraser Taylor (b.1960), Helen Manning, David Band (1959–2011) and Brian Bolger (b.1959) formed their design studio in 1983 to facilitate the movement between art and design projects. These included the design of record sleeves for bands such as Altered Images, Spandau Ballet and Aztec Camera, alongside their own textiles and fashion collections.

1986–87
Clients included Betty Jackson, Bill Blass (1922–2002), Yves Saint Laurent (1936–2008), Calvin Klein (b.1942) and Paul Smith (b.1946). The group disbanded in 1987. Fraser Taylor is now a visiting artist at the Department of Fiber and Material Studies at the School of the Art Institute of Chicago and a interdisciplinary visual artist.

2 CUT
The structure of the traditionally tailored shirt is subverted and obscured by the print. The silhouette of oversized garments that characterized the early 1980s provides a large canvas-like area for the vivid colours of the print.

DRESSING FOR SUCCESS

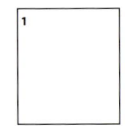

1. A black-and-white skirt suit by Jean-Louis Scherrer (b.1935) from 1983 illustrates the triangular shape popular in the 1980s.

2. Actress Charlotte Rampling shows a softer side to power dressing in a double-breasted pinstripe coat over a striped shirt and skirt by Giorgio Armani.

3. Actors Don Johnson and Philip Michael Thomas wear Hugo Boss in the popular detective series *Miami Vice*.

The 1980s heralded a new feminine ideal. The perfectly honed and groomed glamazon, striding along the catwalk in her stiletto heels, represented the power and sexuality of the contemporary businesswoman. As more women began to enter the boardroom, the self-effacing cardigan and flowing maxi skirt of the previous decade were discarded in favour of sharp-shouldered tailoring. Instructed to wear sombre unassuming clothing by John T. Molloy in *The Women's Dress for Success Book* (1977), the glamazon eschewed the business guru's recommendations for the 'look at me' skirt suit in vivid colours. The squared-off, padded shoulder line of the jacket was balanced at the hips by a flared peplum—a piece of fabric attached to the waist, which had the visual effect of narrowing the waist, often cinched with a wide belt (above). The jacket was worn with a matching mini skirt. Unlike its previous incarnation in the 1960s, which referenced the ingénue element of the look, the 1980s macro

KEY EVENTS

1979	1979	1981	1984	1984	1985
Margaret Thatcher (known as 'The Iron Lady' and an expert power dresser) is elected as Britain's first female prime minister.	Paul Smith opens his first London shop on Covent Garden's Floral Street.	US television soap *Dynasty* begins transmission. The show promotes the fashion for wide shoulders.	Paul Smith signs a licensing agreement with the Japanese trading house Itochu.	US television show *Miami Vice* begins its first season. The programme showcases aspirational menswear from Hugo Boss.	Anna Wintour is appointed editor at British *Vogue*. She targets the new 1980s woman, interested in business but with no time to shop.

436 1946–89

skirt was all about power and freedom. Worn with the spike heel, it represented domination. Big-shouldered blouses featured graphic prints of *trompe l'oeil* effects of chains, swags, bows and ribbons as well as animal prints. Accessories were aspirational. These included the Hermès scarf, the 'gilt and quilt' shoulder bag reworked by Karl Lagerfeld (b.1933) for Chanel, black opaque tights and killer heels by Manolo Blahnik (b.1942).

A more subtle version of workwear was offered by designer Donna Karan (b.1948), who featured a fictional female president of the United States in one of her advertisements. Karan targeted the urban professional woman, and as a designer she catered to the cash-rich, time-poor executive with a capsule wardrobe in black comprising 'seven easy pieces'. Constructed from stretch fabrics, the garments were body-conscious yet forgiving, and included the innovative all-in-one body, wrapped skirts and tubular dresses. Italian designer Giorgio Armani (b.1934) also offered a more relaxed form of power dressing with his pared-down silhouette, neutral palette and luxurious fabrics (see p.438). The softly padded shoulder line of double-breasted long-line jackets in wool crêpe combined ease of movement with boardroom sophistication for both men and women (above right).

The 'young, upwardly mobile professionals'—yuppies—lived and worked in the financial capitals of the world. A burgeoning style press and the advertising industry emphasized the importance of a lifestyle that included not only clothes but also iconic accessories, such as the Gucci loafer (see p.440), Rolex watch and Filofax, which was popularized by British-born designer Paul Smith (b.1946). After the opening of a boutique in his native Nottingham in 1970, Smith opened the first Paul Smith store in London's Covent Garden in 1979. Smith's suits for men became standard wear for the young male executive and aspirant media mogul. His amalgamation of traditional tailoring skills with a witty and subversive eye for detail, together with his quirky use of colour and texture, allowed his customers to be fashion-conscious while still conforming to the dress codes of the city.

German label Hugo Boss provided ready-to-wear suits for the 1980s. Founded in 1923 by Hugo Boss (1885–1948), the company produced work clothes and uniforms before expanding into menswear in 1953. However, it was only with the surge in popularity of the suit in the 1980s that the brand forged an international reputation. Styled by businessmen rather than a single named designer, the suit was made from quality materials and filled the gap between the restrained traditional Savile Row tailoring and the mass-produced suits sold by high-street stores. Usually double-breasted, with pleat-front trousers, the suit reinforced the traditional male shape of upturned triangle with commodious jackets and easy-fitting trousers. The brand engaged in an early example of product placement when it was featured in one of the most stylishly influential US television shows of the decade, *Miami Vice* (right). **MF**

1985	1987	1987	1988	1988	1988
Donna Karan, formerly of Anne Klein, presents her first independent women's clothing collection. It includes her seven essential 'easy' pieces.	Tom Wolfe's novel *The Bonfire of the Vanities* is published. It satirizes the young, aspiring urban professional known as the yuppie.	Liz Tilberis takes over the helm at British *Vogue*. She holds the position until 1992.	Anna Wintour becomes editor-in-chief of US *Vogue*.	Hollywood movie *Working Girl*, starring Melanie Griffith and Sigourney Weaver, epitomizes the aspirations of the working woman.	Donna Karan launches DKNY, a younger and less expensive version of the main line.

DRESSING FOR SUCCESS 437

Deconstructed Suit 1980
GIORGIO ARMANI b. 1934

Richard Gere as Julian Kaye in *American Gigolo* (1980).

NAVIGATOR

Replacing the confining carapace of the traditionally tailored Savile Row suit, Giorgio Armani introduced a notion of fluidity and ease that revolutionized the design of formal menswear. He achieved this more relaxed silhouette by removing the skeleton of stiff interlinings and facings, dispensing with the lining and lowering the buttons of the jacket to emphasize the hips. Armani developed a fresh, modern aesthetic that appealed to men who worked in the creative industries, such as advertising, the media and architecture. The designer also lightened the weight of the suit, replacing tweed and flannel with softer, draped tactile fabrics, such as wool crêpe, which resulted in the same ease of wear as could be found in a knitted cardigan. Discarding the navy pinstripe of the boardroom, Armani created a palette of neutral colours, such as taupe and anthracite, of which greige (between grey and beige) was the most typical. The Italian menswear line achieved global acclaim in 1980 when US actor Richard Gere played a male escort in Paul Schrader's film noir *American Gigolo*. The film provided a useful showcase for Armani's aesthetic of luxurious, soft-tailored and understated glamour. The success of the film led to a long-term collaboration with the cinema: Armani designed costumes for more than a hundred films, including *The Untouchables* in 1987. **MF**

FOCAL POINTS

1 SOFT SHOULDER LINE
Armani's signature soft, moulded shoulder line is formed by extending the shoulder seam beyond the natural line of the body and deepening the arm scye. This provided greater fluidity and ease of movement for the wearer.

2 TORSO
The slim-fitting, darted shirt is in contrast to the loose drape of the jacket. This effect is emphasized by the narrowness of the turndown collar with short collar points and the small knot of the slim, micro-patterned tie.

3 DRAPED JACKET
The single-breasted, brown cashmere wool jacket is long in the skirt and ventless, with a drape on the hips in a glancing reference to the zoot suit of the 1940s. It is open to reveal the mid-rise trousers worn with a narrow leather belt.

DESIGNER PROFILE

1934–74
Giorgio Armani was born in the northern Italian town of Piacenza. After a period studying medicine and completing military service, he worked in retail before joining the Cerruti Group as a designer in the 1960s. In 1973 Armani opened an office in Milan at 37 Corso Venezia after meeting architectural draughtsman Sergio Galeotti, which marked the beginning of a long-term personal and professional relationship.

1975–PRESENT
In 1975 Giorgio Armani SpA was formed. Armani presented his first collection of ready-to-wear in 1976. The brand began to be marketed in the United States in the 1980s. A separate line of ready-to-wear, Emporio Armani, followed in 1989. The Armani Casa home furnishings collection was launched in 2000 and the flagship Armani Hotel Dubai opened in 2010.

Loafer 1980s
GUCCI

Since its introduction in the 1960s, the classic Gucci loafer has been a covetable status symbol for both men and women, worn by the international jet set and the 'beautiful people'. However, it was during the logomania of the 1980s that the moccasin-inspired Gucci loafer became part of Wall Street uniform, when its elegant, visibly expensive image was deemed to be compatible with the lounge or business suit.

This style of low, slip-on shoe originated in northern Europe. In the 1930s a Norwegian manufacturer produced moccasin-style shoes that found a market in the rest of Europe and in the United States, where they became known as 'Weejuns'. In the 1950s, with variants such as the penny loafer and the tasselled loafer, they became a staple of the preppy weekend wardrobe. In Italy a cleaner line evolved, known as the Venetian loafer. The design of the loafer has remained largely unchanged since the 1950s, when Gucci first added a metal strap shaped like an equestrian snaffle bit.

The authentic Gucci loafer is included in the permanent collection of the Costume Institute of the Metropolitan Museum of Art in New York. The original women's loafer—known as the Model 360—was modified to have a stacked leather heel embedded with a narrow gold chain and a matching chain across the front. Fashioned from a range of hand-stained luxury hides at the Gucci atelier outside Florence, the hand-sewn loafers are individually processed by a team of highly skilled artisans. After being sewn together and lasted, the shoes are welted before going through a finishing process that includes polishing, drying and the addition of the signature horsebit. 'Gucci loafer' is now used as a generic term for metal-trimmed slip-ons. Former *Vogue* editor Diana Vreeland installed the Gucci loafer in her 'Man and the Horse' exhibition in 1984 in recognition of the timeless intertwining of moneyed leisure, luxury, equestrian pursuits and high fashion. **MF**

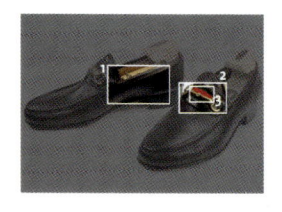

NAVIGATOR

👁 FOCAL POINTS

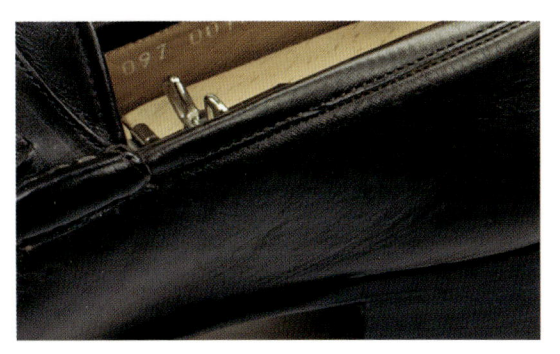

1 SADDLE STITCHING
The softness of the gathered buckskin is reduced to minimal puckering below the saddle-stitched upper rim, which is another example of the equestrian influence on Gucci designs. The step-in leather shoe departs from the loafer stereotype with the addition of a broad, flat heel and the horsebit hardware.

▲ Women's leather pumps by Gucci from the early 1970s. The shoes feature decorative gold chain details both across the front and embedded in the block heel.

2 HORSEBIT SNAFFLE
The gilt snaffle entered the Gucci lexicon in the early 1950s, when many of Gucci's local Italian clients were aristocrats who wanted riding gear. The horsebit was first attached to saddle-stitched handbags. In 1953 it decorated the instep of soft moccasins for men; by 1968 it had become an emblem on women's shoes.

3 RED AND GREEN STRIPE
As a component of the livery that has come to denote the brand identity of Gucci's luxury products, the longitudinal green–red–green webbing stripe originates from the traditional colours of a saddle girth strap. This red-and-green colour combination also references the Italian Tricolore flag.

⏱ COMPANY PROFILE

1921–52
The House of Gucci was founded in Florence in 1921 by Guccio Gucci (1881–1953). Gucci worked in hotels in Paris and London, where he was impressed by the luxurious luggage of guests, particularly at the Savoy Hotel. On his return to Florence in 1921, he established a small workshop that specialized in handcrafted leather saddlery. Together with his sons, he expanded the company to include shops in Rome in 1938 and in Milan in 1951, selling luxury leather goods, silk and knitwear. The bamboo-handled handbag, the first of Gucci's iconic products and still a company mainstay, was introduced in 1947. It became known as the 'Jackie' bag, after First Lady of the United States Jackie Kennedy. The Gucci label became an international status symbol recognized by the signature red-and-green striped webbing derived from the saddle girth.

1953–88
When founder Gucci died in 1953, his sons Aldo, Vasco, Ugo and Rodolfo took over the business, which went from strength to strength. In the 1960s the brand was particularly associated with celebrity chic. The Gucci scarf print Flora was created after a personal request from Princess Grace of Monaco. The Gucci classic loafer with horsebit hardware was acquired for the permanent collection of the Costume Institute of the Metropolitan Museum of Art in New York. In the mid 1960s Gucci adopted the interlocking double-'G' logo and continued to expand abroad with shops in London, Paris and the United States. During the 1970s, Gucci suffered a downturn caused by overbranding and licensing of products.

1989–PRESENT
In 1989 US retail executive Dawn Mello was appointed to reposition the ailing brand. In 1990 she hired US designer Tom Ford (b.1961) to head women's ready-to-wear. He became creative director in 1994 and successfully rebranded the company. Ford left in 2004 and in 2006 Frida Giannini (b.1972), formerly accessories designer, became creative director.

THE DESIGNER DECADE

1 Andie MacDowell wears a pewter-grey, metallic velvet evening dress by Bill Blass in 1983. The one-shouldered style and luxurious fabric reflect the extravagance of the 1980s.

2 Joan Collins accessorizes her big-occasion dress with statement jewellery and immaculate styling.

3 Carolina Herrera wears one of her own designs: a billowing emerald green evening gown and a shimmering, perfectly tailored jacket.

A radical shift in attitudes towards fashion occurred in the 1980s, when society showed itself eager to embrace conspicuous consumption after the recession-hit 1970s—a period in which the growing feminist movement and the 'back to nature' advocates considered fashion inherently frivolous. The youth-led fashions of hippie chic (see p.386) and the punk movement (see p.416) were discarded in favour of over-the-top, grown-up glamour. As Nicholas Coleridge wrote in his book *The Fashion Conspiracy* (1988): 'The decade from 1978 has been decisive for fashion. . . . Designers like Ralph Lauren, Calvin Klein and Giorgio Armani have created from nothing fashion empires on a scale and with a speed that seemed impossible in the mid 1970s. . . . This has produced a compelling new factor in the world economy: designer money.' The strength of the US dollar from 1980 to 1985 resulted in a new demand for haute couture and luxurious ready-to-wear clothing. Designers who had established their careers during the 1950s and 1960s, such as Bill Blass (1922–2002), James Galanos (b.1924), Geoffrey Beene (1927–2004), Arnold Scaasi (b.1930), Oscar de la Renta (b.1932) and Adolfo (b.1933), found their high-style formal look for day and newsworthy glamorous evening wear—such as the metallic velvet dress by Blass (above)—once again in demand.

In 1981 the inauguration of President Ronald Reagan heralded a return to formal entertaining after the unceremonious low-key style of the Carter presidency. Reagan reinstated the traditions of formal charity balls, including

KEY EVENTS

1980	1980	1981	1981	1981	1982
Handbag designer Judith Leiber wins the Neiman Marcus Award for Distinguished Service in the Field of Fashion.	María Carolina Josefina Pacanins y Niño launches the Carolina Herrera label in New York. It offers elegant clothes made from luxurious materials.	Lady Diana Spencer wears a voluminous taffeta crinoline wedding gown when she marries Prince Charles at St Paul's Cathedral, London.	Nancy Reagan wears a white beaded one-shouldered sheath gown of lace over silk satin by James Galanos for her husband's inaugural ball.	Joan Collins joins the cast of *Dynasty* to play Alexis Carrington. Her arrival proves popular.	US designer Geoffrey Beene receives his fifth Coty Special Award citation.

the wearing of white tie and tails, a ceremonial colour guard for state visits and state dinners followed by dancing. Such events provided more opportunities for the aspirant moneyed set to display the lustrous textures and layered embellishment of their big-occasion gowns designed by favoured couturiers.

The lifestyle of the rich and famous as fictionalized in US television soaps, such as *Dallas* (1978–91) and *Dynasty* (1981–89), showcased the work of US designer Nolan Miller (1933–2012). The extravagant creations worn by the cast featured extreme shoulders and statement accessories (above right), thus setting the paradigm for excessive ostentation. The 1980s was a period of pay and display, when the tax reforms and deregulation of the money markets by Reagan and Britain's Prime Minister Margaret Thatcher resulted in a greater amount of disposable income for the upper strata of society. The accessory of choice of this moneyed set was the jewelled minaudière designed by Budapest-born Judith Leiber (b.1921). A combination of high fashion and decadent luxury, the handbag represented the apotheosis of conspicuous consumption in the 1980s: the accessory as collectible for the very rich.

New York's 'shiny set'—the wealthy wives of the United States power brokers—were satirized by novelist Tom Wolfe in his book *The Bonfire of the Vanities* (1987). He described 'women of "a certain age", all of them skin and bones (starved to near perfection). To compensate for the concupiscence missing from their juiceless ribs and atrophied backsides, they turned to the dress designers. This season no puffs, flounces, pleats, ruffles, bibs, bows, batwings, scallops, laces, darts or shirrs on the bias are too extreme. They were the social X-rays.' The most high-profile 'social X-ray' of them all was Nancy Reagan. For daywear the president's wife favoured Adolfo's signature Chanel-inspired knit suits in textured bouclé yarn, worn with a colour-matched silk blouse. While other US designers launched into sportswear, Adolfo continued to provide his customers with printed silk dresses for formal daytime occasions. Adolfo provided many of Nancy's clothes without charge; the resultant publicity increased his sales exponentially, and ensured his inclusion with other favoured designers at state balls and banquets. New York-based designer Carolina Herrera (b.1939; right) offered refined status dressing for the 'ladies who lunch' while Arnold Scaasi produced their luxurious evening wear (see p.444).

For the first time designers mixed socially with their clientele. Oscar de la Renta—whose exuberant feminine clothes were influenced by his roots in the Dominican Republic—dined with the socially prominent clients he dressed. As president of the Council of Fashion Designers of America (CFDA), he raised the profile of the industry with gala events at New York's Metropolitan Museum of Art to celebrate the CFDA's lifetime achievement awards. According to Kitty Kelley, biographer of Nancy Reagan, he welcomed the return of formal entertaining at the White House with the words: 'The Reagans are going to bring back the kind of style the White House should have.' **MF**

1983	1987	1987	1987	1987	1989
The couture house of Chanel is transformed under the creative directorship of Karl Lagerfeld (b.1933); his remit is to attract a new, youthful market.	Christian Lacroix (b.1951) is appointed by Jean-Jacques Picart and Bernard Arnault as head of the twenty-fourth couture house in Paris.	The film *Wall Street* is released. Central character Gordon Gekko espouses that 'Greed is good.'	Tom Wolfe publishes *The Bonfire of the Vanities*, a novel about ambition, racism, class, politics and greed in contemporary New York City.	The world's largest luxury conglomerate is founded, with the merger between Moët Hennessy and Louis Vuitton, forming the LVMH brand.	US retail executive Dawn Mello is appointed to reposition the Gucci brand; she hires Tom Ford as chief ready-to-wear designer.

THE DESIGNER DECADE

Evening Dress 1987
ARNOLD SCAASI b. 1930

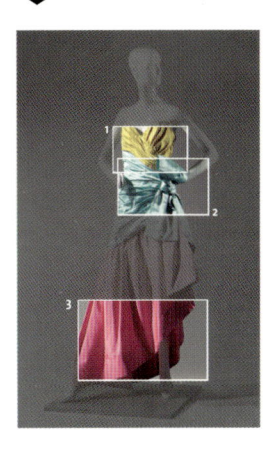

Couturier Arnold Scaasi enjoyed renewed popularity in the 1980s when his opulent formal gowns found favour with New York's 'shiny set'. His designs gratified their desire for ostentatious evening wear and validated their mutual celebrity. Scaasi was renowned for his use of bright colours in surprising combinations that nevertheless were finely calibrated to harmonize in practical expressions of colour theory. In this gown, the gold of the bodice and the fuchsia of the skirt are brought together by the turquoise sash, which overlays both companion colours in the form of an oversized stiffened knot, thus establishing the visual anchor of the form and the focal point of the dress.

The silhouette of the gown references the work of US couturier Charles James (1906–78), with whom Scaasi trained, with its emphasis on the dramatic structure of the garment rather than added decoration or embellishment. Typical of both designers is the attenuated fitted torso swathed in folds of plain weave silk. The gold bodice is pleated and wrapped following a diagonal seam to form a strapless sweetheart neckline that stands away from the breasts—a signature Scaasi feature—colloquially known as a 'crumb-catcher' bodice. Scaasi customarily designed long fitted taffeta or silk-satin edge-to-edge coats faced with a contrasting fabric to be worn with his evening dresses. **MF**

NAVIGATOR

👁 FOCAL POINTS

1 INTENSE COLOUR
Scaasi uses gold with turquoise and fuchsia. These tertiary colours are equidistant on the colour wheel and have the same degree of intensity. They correspond to the distribution values of yellow, cyan and magenta components in print and dyeing output codes.

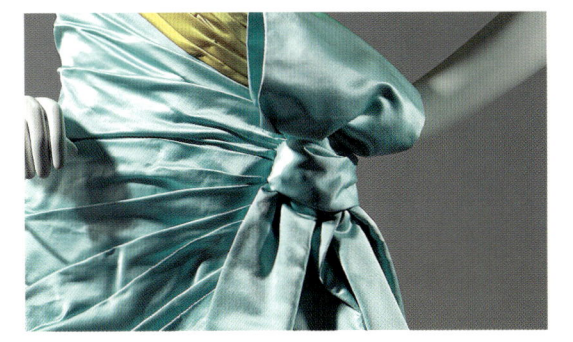

3 ASYMMETRICAL HEMLINE
The asymmetry of the dress continues in the ankle-length fuchsia skirt, which is gathered onto the slanting hipline, raising the hem to above the knee. This pays fleeting reference to the exoticism of Rio de Janeiro's carnival and samba singer-actress Carmen Miranda.

🕒 DESIGNER PROFILE

1930–63
Arnold Scaasi was born in Canada as Arnold Isaacs. He studied at the Cotnoir-Capponi School of Design and completed his education at the Chambre Syndicale de la Haute Couture in Paris. He then had an apprenticeship at the House of Paquin before moving to Charles James where he launched a ready-to-wear line in 1955. In 1958 he won the Coty Award.

1964–PRESENT
Scaasi opened a couture salon in 1964 that specialized in evening wear and cocktail dresses trimmed with feathers, fur, sequins and embroidery. In 1968 he became internationally recognized when Barbra Streisand wore his sheer blouse and trousers to collect her Academy Award for *Funny Girl*. In 1984 he relaunched his ready-to-wear line Scaasi Boutique. He received the Council of Fashion Designers of America Award in 1996.

2 FAUX BOW
The gown's asymmetrical centre panel of turquoise starts under the breasts before being pulled up into an outsize faux knotted bow positioned on the side of the hips. It resembles a flourish of satin ribbon tied around a gift.

HIP-HOP CULTURE AND STREET STYLE

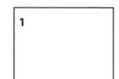

1. East coast rap group EPMD epitomizes hip-hop style in the late 1980s in the cover portrait for its album *Unfinished Business*.

2. This jacket from Vivienne Westwood's Witches collection of 1983 features a print inspired by the graffiti art of Keith Haring.

3. US rap artists Run-DMC accessorize their Adidas tracksuits with extremely heavy gold dookey chains.

Hip hop has always been primarily an expression of the African American experience and it continually engages with social problems facing these urban communities and their aspirations. It is a strong message and one that appeals both to the originating socio-ethnic group and a wider youth culture, as well as to fashion houses. When hip-hop music emerged in the late 1970s and early 1980s, the movement was particularly concerned with black nationalism and empowerment. Performers often wore kente cloth (see p.134)—a traditional Ghanaian fabric—and the Black Nationalist colours of green, red, black and yellow. The movement originated in US cities and is closely linked to gangster culture. Pioneers included the bands NWA and the Wu-Tang Clan, both collectives of artists in which the wearing of a common style signified inclusion in the gang. The first company to specialize in hip-hop couture was established in 1989, when Karl Kani (Carl Williams; b.1968) set up his eponymous label. The Wu-Tang Clan launched its own label, Wu Wear, in 1995.

The political provenance of hip hop led early artists, such as LL Cool J, Public Enemy and Run-DMC (opposite below), to reject high fashion and the traditional aspirational labels, and instead embrace sports clothing and street wear. A typical outfit would include a Kangol bucket hat (above), an Adidas tracksuit and Adidas Superstar or Chuck Taylor Allstar trainers. The Kangol hat, which became an almost obligatory accessory, was a curious addition given that it was from an English company, founded in 1938 and predominantly

KEY EVENTS

1980	1982	1983	1983	1984	1985
Blondie release the single 'Rapture', on which Debbie Harry raps and namechecks Grandmaster Flash, which brings hip hop into the mainstream.	Afrika Bambaataa and Soul Sonic Force produce 'Planet Rock', one of the most sampled tracks in hip-hop history.	Grandmaster Flash releases 'The Message'. Tony Silver's television documentary, *Style Wars*, about graffiti and hip-hop is aired.	The film *Wild Style* is released. It contains various elements of hip-hop culture, including graffiti, breakdancing and MC battles.	Def Jam Records, the genre's most influential rap label, is founded by US producer Rick Rubin and business tycoon Russell Simmons.	US basketball player Michael Jordan begins his endorsement of Nike, which results in hip-hop artists switching from Adidas to Nike.

446 1946–89

known for military millinery. Women, inspired by artists such as Aaliyah, TLC and Salt-N-Pepa, wore similar clothes to men, or tight white vest tops under baggy flannel shirts and jeans, along with large 'door knocker' earrings.

In addition to the artists who made the music, hip-hop culture encompassed other creative communities, most importantly b-boys and graffiti artists, who used the street as an arena for expression. B-boys and girls (breakdancers) needed loose jeans and T-shirts to move without restriction, establishing the street aesthetic of hip hop. As well as this practical reason for baggy clothing, several other factors are cited but it is an urban myth that low-slung jeans were worn without belts to mimic prison clothing. Graffiti and hip-hop culture were also closely entwined. Street art and fashion intersected in the work of designer Stephen Sprouse (1953–2004), who was immersed in the New York art scene in the 1980s and became renowned for his graffiti-inspired prints (see p.448). Other designers, including Vivienne Westwood (b.1941; right), also created garments with distinctive graffiti-type patterns.

While some hip-hop artists continued to address social problems, the culture became more concerned with aspirational imagery as the idea of 'bling' and extravagance came into focus. Wanting to project a successful image, hip-hop artists wore fur coats, sharp suits, alligator-skin shoes and platinum jewellery, largely covered in 'ice' (diamonds) to signify the success of escaping ghetto poverty. Throughout the 1980s, however, the wearing of gold chain jewellery was a key element of the hip-hop look, seen as reflecting the African warrior tradition in which the most powerful men were laden with gold. The heavy gold chains, known as dookey chains, were made up of thick ropes of braided links. To this was added a decorative medallion and increasingly outlandish objects— microphones, car badges and dollar signs—providing further signifiers of gang identity. Another key element was the wearing of 'grillz' (gold dental overlays) to highlight the verbal dexterity of a rap artist. This trend emerged in the 1980s with many artists covering their teeth with plates, sometimes adding precious stones or other decorative features.

The baggy white T-shirt was an important part of the hip-hop look. As long as the garment was pristine and 'box-fresh' it did not matter which brand it was. This neophiliac aesthetic also applied to footwear and underwear (often on show with loose jeans). The conspicuous consumption of clothes, worn once before being discarded, added to the sense of success and affluence. Another vital area of self-expression was the head: by the mid 1980s the high-top fade was the key look (hair shaved at the sides with long top layers styled to stick up; patterns could be shaved into the sides). By the late 1980s the doo-rag— a strip of nylon fabric to keep braided hair in place—was widespread. It was close fitting and wrapped around the front of the head with the ends tied at the back or left loose. **EA**

1985	1985	1988	1988	1989	1995
LL Cool J releases his first album, *Radio*. It marks the moment when old-school hip hop moves into the mainstream and becomes new school.	US designer Stephen Sprouse mixes street culture and pop art in the design of his graffiti coat (see p.448).	Public Enemy release the seminal album *It Takes a Nation of Millions* to wide acclaim.	Stephen Sprouse produces his Signature collection, a collaboration with street artist Keith Haring.	Carl Williams becomes the first black man to launch a hip-hop fashion line with his Karl Kani brand.	Wu Wear is launched by the Wu-Tang Clan; the garments are designed by the group's executive producer, Oli 'Power' Grant.

HIP-HOP CULTURE AND STREET STYLE 447

Graffiti Collection 1984
STEPHEN SPROUSE 1953 – 2004

Graffiti dress from Stephen Sprouse's spring/summer collection of 1984, photographed by Paul Palmero.

NAVIGATOR

The cocoon-like silhouette of this graffiti coat worn here with plain black stilettos is typical of the 1980s but Stephen Sprouse enlivened it by adding his signature graffiti print and pairing it with a hot pink fabric. Sprouse was known for his skill in combining street culture, mixing urban graffiti and tagging with Pop art. His work was influenced by his close relationship with Andy Warhol and the New York art scene, and he lived in the same Bowery apartment block as singer and actress Debbie Harry. Harry was part of the fashion scene, which made her a natural collaborator, and she was often pictured wearing Sprouse's designs.

The plain, form-concealing construction of the coat, with its simple Nehru collar and unobtrusive buttons, serves as an interesting counterpoint to the vibrant and garish design of the graffiti print. The black letters are rendered abstract by the natural movement and the folds of the garment, and the bottom of the coat becomes progressively darker as black thread is interwoven with the pink, creating a dip-dye effect that looks as if the hem of the coat has become dirty over time. This creates an aesthetic in which elements of urban hip-hop culture sit alongside the artisan quality of a high-fashion garment. **EA**

FOCAL POINTS

1 FABRIC
Sprouse was renowned for using very expensive, handwoven and dyed fabric. This coat, made from the highest-quality alpaca and cashmere, would have been woven in Italy with the yarn being dyed to match the designer's exact specifications.

2 GRAFFITI
The hand-painted graffiti writing was one of Sprouse's signature motifs, later revived by Marc Jacobs. Graffiti as a bold means of self-expression becomes provocative when used in high fashion. The coat and leggings together create a striking look.

▲ In 2001 Sprouse collaborated with Marc Jacobs at Louis Vuitton to create a version of the popular 'Speedy' bag, featuring his graffiti print superimposed on the classic 'LV' logo print.

DESIGNER PROFILE

1953–87
Stephen Sprouse was born in Ohio and began his career working for Halston in the 1970s before branching out with his own collection in 1983. He made clothes to the highest standard but production costs far outweighed the profit and his label closed down in 1985.

1988–2004
In 1988 Sprouse put out a new collection based on his collaboration with street artist Keith Haring. Despite great acclaim, the line proved unprofitable and the label had to be closed down once more. Sprouse kept designing throughout the 1990s but did not have much commercial success until 2001, when his long-time fan, designer Marc Jacobs (b.1963), asked him to update the Louis Vuitton luggage line with his signature graffiti print.

THE REGENERATION OF COUTURE

1 Emanuel Ungaro's dramatic autumn/winter 1987 collection of shirred, ruched and ruffled gowns made a huge impact and was widely copied.

2 This Chanel by Karl Lagerfeld ensemble includes a gilt and quilt handbag, faux camellia and gold chain link belt (1985).

During the 1980s the fashionable elite once again invested in European couture, a system that was thriving after the previous era's preoccupation with the promulgation of ready-to-wear. Representing the new glamour, the decade saw the rise of a shy, seemingly self-effacing nursery teacher to the upper echelons of the British royal family: Diana, Princess of Wales, initially publicized British designers, including Bruce Oldfield (b.1950), who dressed London's smart set, and French-born, British-based designer Catherine Walker (1945–2010). For Diana's visit to the White House in 1985, however, it was a full-length midnight-blue velvet dress by Victor Edelstein (b.1945) that cemented her new status as a global fashion icon when she took to the dance floor in the arms of movie star John Travolta, earning her the soubriquet 'Dynasty Di'.

In Paris Emanuel Ungaro (b.1933), one of the pioneers of couture in the 1960s, instigated his revival, and subsequent high profile in the United States, with a seductive collection of occasion wear: tightly wrapped evening gowns with diagonally draped and ruched skirts adorned with frilled and ruffled details (above). These dresses also featured vivid prints in striking colour

KEY EVENTS

1981	1981	1983	1984	1985	1986
The wedding dress of Lady Diana Spencer, designed by David (b.1952) and Elizabeth (b.1953) Emanuel, sets a trend for voluminous taffeta crinolines.	Catherine Walker, private couturier to Diana, Princess of Wales, launches her own label.	The long-established House of Chanel is transformed under the artistic directorship of Karl Lagerfeld; his remit is to attract a new, youthful market.	British designer Bruce Oldfield opens his first shop selling ready-to-wear and couture to an international clientele.	An exhibition at the National Gallery of Modern Art in Rome celebrates sixty years of Fendi.	Jacques Bogart SA acquires couture house Balenciaga and Michel Goma (b.1932) is appointed head designer the following year.

450 1946–89

combinations that were typical of the brash fashions of the decade: turquoise and fuchsia, canary yellow and bottle green, scarlet and purple, lilac and ochre.

Adding momentum to the renaissance of haute couture, in 1983 German-born designer Karl Lagerfeld (b.1933) was appointed as artistic director of the then near-moribund House of Chanel. The designer first refused the position when it was offered by Alain Wertheimer, chairman of the Chanel board, but accepted it when it was understood that he would not be employed as an in-house designer. Initially responsible only for haute couture, with Hervé Léger (b.1957) in charge of ready-to-wear, Lagerfeld soon assumed control of the total output of the house, thereby becoming one of the most prolific and high-profile designers in fashion. He deconstructed the Chanel signature look, specifically the two-piece wool bouclé cardigan suit (see p.454). This comprised a box-shaped edge-to-edge jacket, traditionally braided around the collarless neck and centre front, worn with a knee-length A-line skirt. Lagerfeld transformed its appeal to address a younger, more fashion-aware clientele by introducing 'humble' textiles, such as stretch denim and terrycloth, into the fabrication and by dramatically changing the proportions.

His irreverent approach to fashion included sexing up the original 2.55 gilt and quilt bag, first designed by Coco Chanel (1883–1971) in 1929 and further developed by the designer in 1955. Lagerfeld exaggerated its distinctive features by enlarging the interlocking double 'C's of the logo and repositioning them on the front of the bag. In doing so he created the most coveted status symbol of the decade, and the most easily identified and most counterfeited. Renowned for his emblematic white-powdered ponytail, sunglasses and fashion diktats, Lagerfeld upheld a disciplined personal style of high-collared white shirts and black suits that he translated into his collections, with an emphasis on the monochrome. He continued with the house traditions of the two-piece suit (right) and the *petit noir* (little black dress), injecting irony into the latter by executing his design in fetishistic black vinyl and polyester jersey. Lagerfeld combined the immediacy of ready-to-wear with the luxuriousness of couture and astutely recognized the need to continue the couture traditions of fine workmanship and exclusivity. Under his direction, Chanel re-established haute couture as the zenith of quality, fully exploiting the skills of the ateliers and their artisans. His designs also regenerated couture by referencing street style and club-influenced items, such as black fishnet body stockings, biker-style jackets, PVC jeans, and tweed bra tops and shorts. Energized by models and muses, among them Inès de La Fressange, Lagerfeld engaged many high-profile celebrities to represent the profile of the brand, particularly in the advertising and marketing of the globally renowned Chanel perfumes.

In an overt parody of the new Chanel aesthetic, Italian designer Franco Moschino (1950–94), who also launched his label in 1983, attacked the haute couture system with a series of provocative advertising campaigns in

1987	1987	1988	1988	1989	1989
Christian Lacroix is appointed by Jean-Jacques Picart and Bernard Arnault as head of the twenty-fourth Parisian couture house.	The largest luxury conglomerate in the world, LVMH, is founded, with the merger between Louis Vuitton and Möet Hennessy.	British journalist Liz Tilberis replaces Anna Wintour as editor of British *Vogue*.	Controversial fashion editor Franca Sozzani takes the helm at Italian *Vogue*.	Gianfranco Ferré (1944–2007) is chosen by owner Bernard Arnault to replace Marc Bohan (b.1926) as stylistic director of Christian Dior, Paris.	US retail executive Dawn Mello is appointed to reposition the Gucci brand and hires Tom Ford (b.1961) as chief ready-to-wear designer a year later.

THE REGENERATION OF COUTURE 451

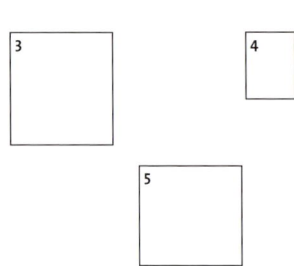

3 This highly embellished gown from Christian Lacroix's extravagant autumn/winter collection of 1989 features a red velvet embroidered corset, with transparent gauze sleeves, and a voluminous grey and pink skirt.

4 Dubbed the 'bad boy of fashion' by the press, Moschino used wit and visual puns to both subvert and exploit 1980s fashion consumerism in this advertising campaign from 1990.

5 This ensemble featured in Moschino's eclectic spring/summer collection of 1991. The tailored two-piece suit is worn with a slogan T-shirt hidden beneath an intricate pearl necklace, and the jacket opening is adorned with dice.

high-end fashion magazines, urging consumers to disregard seasonal trends and bespoke clothing (opposite above). He occasionally offered an outright parody of the Chanel style, as seen in his collection of 1987 that featured blow-up beach toys and plastic flowers (see p.458). Continuing the Surrealist theme adopted by Elsa Schiaparelli (1890–1973) and the tactic of displacement, he constructed a coat in 1989 with a hood and collar formed from teddy bears, and a rayon and Spandex dress with a skirt constructed entirely from black bras. Uninterested in technical innovation and construction, Moschino adopted basic garment forms to promulgate his ideas with wit and verve. Content to decorate the surface of the clothes with visual puns and slogans, in 1991 the designer showed a red trouser suit with the text 'Waist of Money' embroidered around the waistline and slogan T-shirts that read 'Where, When, Why?' (opposite below). This playful collection also featured a jacket embellished with oversized glittery punctuation marks and rainbow-coloured cowboy shirts.

The success of the Chanel relaunch by Lagerfeld inspired many other major brands to revisit their archives and exploit the desire for instantly identifiable status clothing. According to the fashion press, it was the era of 'logomania', when the marque of a brand, used to identify a particular company, became increasingly important and attractive to the consumer. Companies such as Fendi, Christian Dior and Louis Vuitton all offered products and garments that externally featured the repeated use of their logos, which were usually configurations of the brand's initials.

In the 1980s luxury was defined by wearing the right brand. As the decade progressed, branding emerged in the luxury goods market in products that featured visible logos. Consumers eagerly bought into the concept of 'lifestyle marketing', a term used to describe the aspirational nature of the merchandise, and design began to be perceived as a service industry rather than as a creative process. Although haute couture was thriving, it remained a loss leader. However, the spectacle of high fashion provided the publicity for a plethora of money-making and fashion-related products, such as perfumes, cosmetics and signature handbags, the most coveted of which was marketed by Gucci and displayed the monogram of the double-'G' logo.

The world's largest luxury conglomerate was founded in 1987 when Moët Hennessy and Louis Vuitton merged to form the LVMH brand. Their rival for supremacy in the luxury market was the Gucci Group, and the result was a fashion and accessories industry dominated by two conglomerates. Established in Milan in 1906 as a saddlery house, the Gucci company thrived after World War II, when the double-'G' motif became internationally recognized. Overexpansion of licensing agreements during the 1980s, which included clothing and household items, caused a temporary downfall, and internal conflicts within the family-owned company also took their toll. However, with the appointment in 1988 of US retail executive Dawn Mello, many of the licensing deals were rescinded, thus consolidating the prestige of the designer brand.

In 1987 the misplaced optimism in a continuing thriving economy was so great that, on the cusp of a global financial collapse, a new couture house was established by Christian Lacroix (b.1951). He introduced the pouf, or puffball skirt, in 1987 while at the couture house Patou, challenging the prevailing sharp-shouldered power dressing of the boardroom. The fashionable 1980s silhouette underwent an almost overnight change when Lacroix launched his first ground-breaking haute couture collection, also in 1987, which supplanted power dressing with a dramatic range of garments such as crinoline-style skirts and velvet bustier dresses that emphasized the corseted hourglass figure (see p.456). In subsequent collections, Lacroix continued to provide a cornucopia of luxurious textiles, lavish embellishment with Spanish influences and a silhouette resonant of the 18th century (opposite), in what was to prove a short-lived extravaganza before the onset of sober 1990s minimalism. **MF**

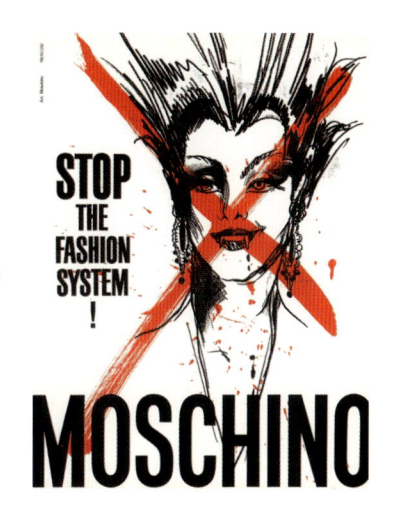

Two-Piece Suit 1980s
KARL LAGERFELD b. 1938 (FOR CHANEL)

Inès de La Fressange models for Chanel.

NAVIGATOR

As model and muse, Inès de La Fressange typified the mannered nonchalance of the regenerated couture house Chanel under the artistic directorship of Karl Lagerfeld. Indeed, de La Fressange embodied the persona and elegant insouciance of Coco Chanel herself. Lagerfeld made reference to Chanel's signature style and parodied the designer's iconic pieces, subverting the archetypal Chanel bouclé two-piece suit by retaining the handwoven edge-to-edge jacket while imposing 1980s tweed. Gilt buttons emblazon each of the sleeve openings, bound in a self-coloured, whipped braid. The same bold detail adorns the horizontal breast pockets each side of the centre front, secured with another pair of buttons.

The bespoke jacket was made by hand by seamstresses, who cut and assembled each component panel before it was sewn together. By festooning the suit jacket with several strands of gilt chains, styled with outsize ropes of pearls, Lagerfeld alluded to the Chanel custom of weighting the jacket and skirt hem of the suit with a metal chain so that the garments fell correctly. The jacket is worn over a plain white starched shirt with a high, turned-back collar. To complete the reiterative pastiche of internal associations, a final flourish lies in the gilded portrait brooches of Lagerfeld and Fressange themselves. **MF**

FOCAL POINTS

1 PILLBOX HAT
In matching tweed, the pillbox hat is perched on the side of the loosely up-swept coiffure. The hat features a pristine white faux camellia—another Chanel hallmark—secured in the centre of a flat black velvet bow.

3 BRANDED ACCESSORIES
Further referencing Chanel's long-standing propensity for faux costume jewellery, Lagerfeld accessorizes the suit with a charm bracelet that is hung with mother-of-pearl medallions, each featuring the Chanel logo.

DESIGNER PROFILE

1938—82
Karl Lagerfeld was born in Hamburg, Germany. He moved to Paris in 1952 and was hired as a design assistant by the couture house Pierre Balmain. From 1958 to 1962 he was art director at the House of Patou before becoming a freelance designer. For the next twenty years he chiefly designed for Chloé, a young, ready-to-wear label offering feminine dresses, but also worked for Italian labels Krizia and Valentino, and on the fur collection for Fendi, where he remains the creative director.

1983—PRESENT
Lagerfeld signed many collections, including his own eponymous lines, and engaged with brands in the wider market. In 1983 he became the artistic director of Chanel, a title he still holds, which is seen as the epitome of his significance in the global fashion industry.

2 SCALED-UP DETAILS
Lagerfeld overloads the classic edge-to-edge collarless jacket with a plethora of outsize pearls as well as gilt buttons at the pockets and cuffs, which run from wrist to elbow. Each button is embossed with the definitive double-'C' Chanel logo.

THE REGENERATION OF COUTURE 455

The First Collection 1987
CHRISTIAN LACROIX b. 1951

The debut collection of Christian Lacroix under his own name garnered global publicity and effusive coverage not seen since the introduction of the ground-breaking New Look by Christian Dior (1905–57) in 1947. Shown at the Hotel Intercontinental in rue du Faubourg Saint-Honoré, Paris, decorated with the signature colours of Lacroix—scarlet, purple, orange and black—and on a stage adorned with bulrushes, the collection was presented to an anticipatory horde of photographers and fashion press. Fashion writer Nicholas Coleridge witnessed the first collection of sixty garments, and recorded his response in *The Fashion Conspiracy* (1988): 'Gasp and the world gasps with you. The models that processed along the catwalk wore clothes with proportions so strange, so topsy-turvy that they defied conventional logic. There were enormous cloche hats pinned with gilded twigs and bulrushes, and skirts made out of pony skin, silver fox and black Persian lamb. There were jackets embroidered with Carmargue motifs and coats made out of red duchesse satin.'

Lacroix drew inspiration from the vernacular details and embellishments of the clothes of southwestern France and Spain juxtaposed with 18th- and early 19th-century influences, fashioning the luxuriously embellished fabrics over hoops and petticoats to form swagged overskirts *à la polonaise*. The dresses utilized all the artisanal virtuosity of the atelier, such as fringing, beading, embroidery and leatherwork, on an eclectic array of garments. **MF**

👁 FOCAL POINTS

1 SILK-SATIN AND MATT VELVET BUSTIER DRESS
Closely ruched around the torso, the rich red duchesse silk-satin extends to form an undulating stiffened hem revealing layers of black tulle petticoats beneath, resonant of the movement of the flamenco dancer. The separate calyx-shaped upper sleeves narrow from elbow to wrist.

2 CRINOLINE-STYLE SILHOUETTE
Vividly theatrical and rich with the riotous colours of Lacroix's birthplace—purple, mimosa, orange, pink and emerald green—the bell-shaped skirt features a centre-front panel of an Impressionistic print. The dolman sleeves are formed in one with the bloused and wrapped bodice.

3 MIX OF CULTURAL REFERENCES
The knee-length, A-line pony-skin skirt is partnered with a tweed jacket tailored along the lines of the 18th-century silhouette, with the emphasis on the waist and a wide collar that extends to the shoulders. The oversized flat-brimmed hat is redolent of the Spanish sombrero.

🕒 DESIGNER PROFILE

1951–86
Born in Arles, France, Christian Lacroix became head designer at the revered House of Patou in 1986. While there he introduced the pouf, bubble or puffball skirt, instantly changing the wide-shouldered tapered silhouette of the 1980s into a more recognizably feminine form. Lacroix's success led fashion entrepreneur Jean-Jacques Picart and businessman Bernard Arnault to create the twenty-fourth couture house in Paris, with Lacroix at the helm. Although enormously influential, the house never made a profit.

1987–PRESENT
The opening of Christian Lacroix's New York store coincided with the stock market crash of 1987, prompting a backlash against overtly luxurious and opulent clothing. The failure of the first Lacroix scent (C'est la vie!), a brand of designer jeans and a ready-to-wear line named Bazaar heralded the descent of the label. In 2005 Bernard Arnault sold the house to the duty-free retailer Falic Group. From 2002 to 2005 Lacroix served as creative director for the Italian fashion house Emilio Pucci, then left to pursue other fashion projects.

THE REGENERATION OF COUTURE 457

Skirt Suit 1987
FRANCO MOSCHINO 1950 – 94

Having launched Moschino Couture in 1983, Franco Moschino was at pains to disrupt the value system and bourgeois affectations of elitist fashion, using Dadaism and Pop art principles as his weapons of choice. Moschino's absorption, as a 1960s fine art student, into the anti-establishment transpositions of artists Marcel Duchamp and Roy Lichtenstein provided a ready vocabulary for ironic dissent.

Karl Lagerfeld's autumn/winter collection of 1986 for Chanel was widely publicized with mannered aristocratic reserve by model Inès de La Fressange in a cornucopia of brand-identity excess—the logo, face, bow and camellia, chains, pearls—and the definitive black-braided white cardigan jacket. In contrast, Moschino's sequel, launched in 1987, presented an irreverent pastiche of the Chanel brand, in which each signifier was granted an alter ego: the off-white camellia was transformed into a row of outsize gaudy plastic buttons in the shape of rosettes; the elegant two-piece suit appeared as a mismatched ensemble emblazoned with Pop art motifs; and Chanel's sophisticated headwear was reproduced as a pile of children's beach toys. Moschino launched his first diffusion collection, Cheap and Chic, in 1988, the international commercial success of which completed the full circle of irony. **MF**

NAVIGATOR

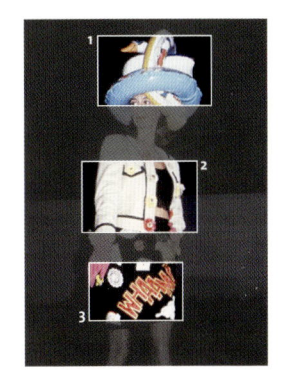

FOCAL POINTS

1 HEADGEAR
The sophisticated boater, bow and camellia blossom of the archetypal Chanel headgear becomes, in the Moschino lexicon, a seaside romp of beach accoutrements. The various plastic inflatables are piled high, almost balancing on the model's head.

3 APPLIQUÉD WRITING
Moschino uses wit and visual puns to subvert the classic lines of the skirt. Mirroring the gilded typography of a chain-letter bracelet, the garment features an appliquéd 'WHAAM!' in the style of the Pop artist Roy Lichtenstein.

DESIGNER PROFILE

1950–83
Born in a small village to the north of Milan, Franco Moschino studied at the Accademia di Belle Arti in 1967. He graduated in 1971, and spent several years collaborating with Gianni Versace (1946–97), working as his illustrator. In 1977 he was appointed designer at Italian company Cadette. He left to launch his own label in 1983, which he showed in Milan.

1984–94
In 1986 the designer produced his first menswear collection, followed in 1988 by the ironically titled Cheap and Chic range, which although less expensive than his main line retailed at the high end of the market. The label continued after the designer's untimely death in 1994 under the aegis of friend and long-time collaborator Rossella Jardini (b.1952), who had been with the label since 1985.

2 SHARP TAILORING
Beneath the Moschino levity lies a traditionally tailored edge-to-edge jacket in cream wool bouclé, neatly trimmed with contrasting black braid on the centre front, patch pockets and bracelet-length sleeves.

UNDERWEAR AS OUTERWEAR

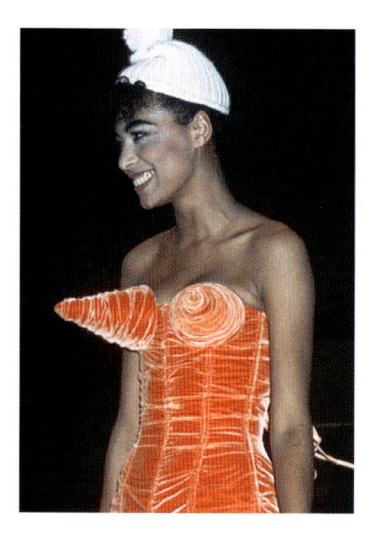

The modern bra was first developed in 1913 by US socialite Mary Phelps Jacob (1891–1970) under the pseudonym Caresse Crosby. Unlike the corset, which was worn to convey a certain social status and sexual probity—and was previously the only means with which to support the breasts—the bra implied modernity and liberated women's torsos from constraint. It was not until the late 20th century, however, that the bra and corset became a visible part of fashion. In reviving and reinterpreting historical corsetry, designers such as Vivienne Westwood (b.1941), Jean Paul Gaultier (b.1952) and Alexander McQueen (1969–2010) transformed an item of constraint and sexualization into an empowering and potent projection of female identity.

British designer Westwood introduced the notion of underwear as outerwear in her Peruvian-inspired Buffalo Girls collection for autumn/winter 1982, which featured a long-line, brown satin bra with a deep back and circular cups that was worn over felted wools and asymmetrical tops. No longer functional or concerned with the traditional values of support and uplift, the bra became an item of decorative clothing that nevertheless broke the rules of what was deemed appropriate. Historically, corsetry strictly controlled the female figure to facilitate a particular silhouette: one that emphasized the

KEY EVENTS

1982	1982	1983	1983	1984	1985
Vivienne Westwood opens her second London shop, Nostalgia of Mud.	Westwood's brown satin bra from her Buffalo Girls collection launches underwear as outerwear beyond the punk/bondage market.	Jean Paul Gaultier launches his Dada collection, which features silhouettes that reference the exaggerated breasts of African fertility symbols.	Gaultier launches a menswear line. His collections include corsets and skirts for men.	Madonna's album *Like a Virgin* catapults her into the public's consciousness as a provocative female artist.	Westwood incorporates an abbreviated crinoline into her Mini-Crini collection.

460 1946–89

waist and helped to construct the vital differentiation between bust and hips, thus producing the hourglass figure traditionally deemed to represent femininity. In 1990 Westwood appropriated the corset's titillating identity by placing a photographic print of 18th-century 'pornographer artist' François Boucher's *Shepherd Watching a Sleeping Shepherdess* on her historically accurate short corsets (opposite above). Although heavily boned, they fastened with a rear zip and ironically the cream side panels were elasticized with Lycra for comfort.

French designer Gaultier revolutionized the corset into a strategic device of empowerment that allowed the wearer autonomy over her own sexuality. His iconic designs for Madonna's 'Blond Ambition' tour in 1990 highlighted the singer's overt sexuality by dressing her in a conical-breasted corset that subverted many ideas of femininity (right). Soft, baby-pink duchesse satin was contrasted with the regimented, closely stitched torso of the 'bullet bra' and its zipped front. Where women's tiny waists were created by the once hidden corset, Madonna's was emphasized by a military-style belt, normally a piece of outerwear. Suspenders were on display, and worn as ornament rather than for practicality. For the same tour, Gaultier juxtaposed the boudoir and the workplace with his design for a tuxedo jacket that was slashed vertically and pierced by Madonna's coned breasts in a new kind of power dressing.

Gaultier reputedly first designed the conical-breasted bra for his teddy bear when he was six years old and it has since become one of his trademark designs. The first runway appearance of the pyramid breast and the rear-lacing corset dress was in Gaultier's Barbès collection for autumn/winter 1984 (opposite below). It was made in tactile, tawny orange velvet, which contrasted dramatically with the rigid conical breasts. The breast cones pointed away diagonally and obtusely from the body rather than compressing the breasts inwards and upwards, as with the cleavage created by traditionally seductive lingerie and historical corsets. The association between sex and corsetry was challenged as the breast was made aggressively conical, prohibiting anyone intruding into the wearer's space. Madonna's corset was clearly related to bras in the 1950s, whereas the tawny orange corset dress was a deliberate choice to suggest something slightly faded yet still venerated.

Following the revival of the corset by Westwood and Gaultier, the integration of the undergarment into contemporary fashion became ubiquitous. French designer Christian Lacroix (b.1951) offered a version of 18th-century historical romanticism with his first collection in 1987, but other designers, such as Belgian-born Olivier Theyskens (b.1977) and Alexander McQueen, promulgated a much darker version with intimations of sadomasochism. McQueen, who combined the garment with fierce tailoring, introduced the corset as fetish into mainstream fashion with his dominatrix corset for the Dante collection (1996) and his Guerrilla corset for the No. 13 collection in 1999 (see p.462). **PW**

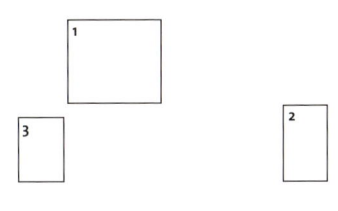

1 Vivienne Westwood revived the corset —printed with a detail of a Boucher painting—for her Portrait collection in 1990.

2 Pop star Madonna wears a conical bra top designed by Jean Paul Gaultier for her 'Blond Ambition' tour in 1990.

3 This faded orange shirred velvet dress from 1984 was inspired by a corset that Jean Paul Gaultier found in his grandmother's wardrobe.

1987	1990	1992	1994	1996	1998
Black Monday results in the stock market crash and the beginning of economic recession in Britain.	Westwood draws inspiration from 18th-century French painting for her Boucher-print corset and Portrait collection.	Male supermodel Tanel Bedrossiantz models a velvet corset dress for Jean Paul Gaultier.	The Wonderbra advertising campaign, featuring model Eva Herzigova, relaunches the brand and resexualizes the bra.	Alexander McQueen's Dante collection eschews the playful qualities of underwear as outerwear to present a much darker aesthetic.	Madonna wears a dress designed by Olivier Theyskens to the Academy Awards; she draws public attention to the work of the young designer.

UNDERWEAR AS OUTERWEAR 461

Guerrilla Corset 1999
ALEXANDER MCQUEEN 1969 – 2010

Ensemble No. 13, consisting of a brown leather corset, cream silk and lace skirt, and prosthetic legs of carved elm wood. Photographed by Sølve Sundsbø.

NAVIGATOR

Alexander McQueen's designs for spring/summer 1999 explored the notion of the noble savage in a collection that featured embroidered *dégradé* hopsack with lace, blanket-stitched suede, raffia-fringed skirts and buckled corsets with draped chiffon. The moulded warrior-princess breastplate draws on the legend of the fearsome Amazonian bows-women.

The corset, which stops short at the hips, reverses the item's traditional function: instead of constraining the breasts, this garment takes the form of breasts themselves, including the line of the nipples and the concavity below the ribs. The glazed leather gives the corset a camouflaged, protective, shell-like hardness, and the diagonal whip-stitching is placed with surgical precision across the body. It recalls the bands of ammunition worn by guerrilla fighters; the thin belt is a potential holster. The wearer's movements are limited by the high collar, which is inspired by the medieval gorget that was worn over armour to protect the throat. Juxtaposing contrasting textures, the moulded corset is partnered with an A-line knee-length skirt composed of asymmetrical layers of lace, stitched in the opposite direction to the bodice, thus creating a focal point on the hip. **PW**

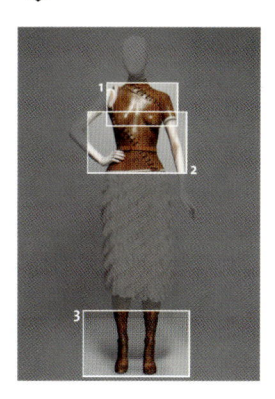

FOCAL POINTS

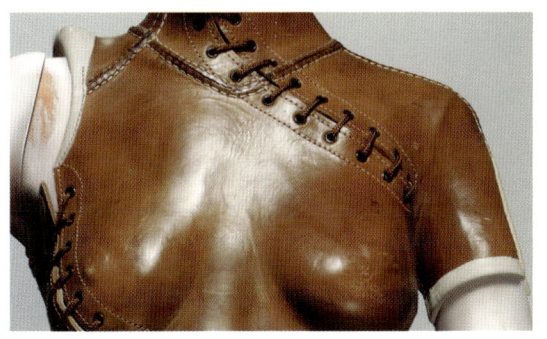

1 TRIMMED SLEEVES
Referring to Amazon legend, the sleeves are asymmetrically cut in order to allow arrows to be drawn more easily from their quivers, and fired without impediment. They are trimmed in neat Grecian style with a contrasting stiff white fabric.

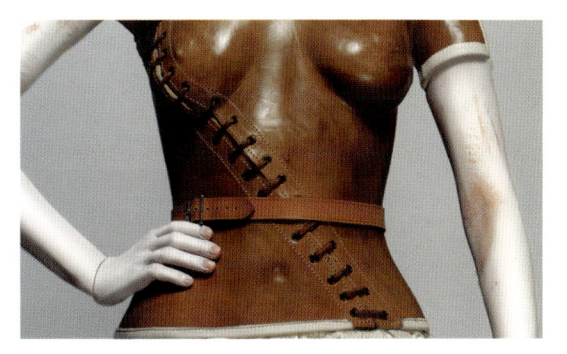

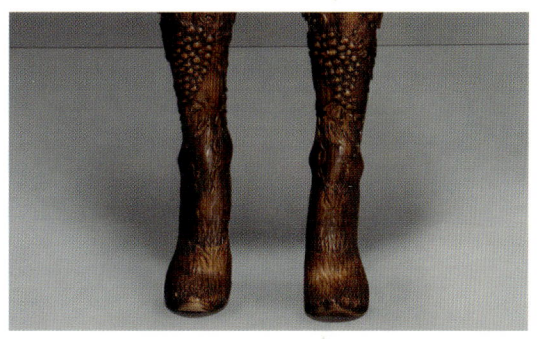

3 WOODEN LEGS
This ensemble, No. 13, was originally modelled by Aimee Mullins, a paralympic athlete, and it includes carved elm prosthetic legs. Their veracity, and the moulded corset, leads viewers to question what is real and what can be projected about bodies.

DESIGNER PROFILE

1969–95
Lee Alexander McQueen was born in London. After leaving school, he was apprenticed to Savile Row tailors Anderson & Sheppard and then Gieves & Hawkes, followed by a period with costumiers Angels and Berman. He was offered a place on the Masters course at Central Saint Martins after applying for a job as a college pattern cutter, and graduated in 1994. His entire graduation collection was purchased by the stylist Isabella Blow.

1996–2010
McQueen was chief designer at Givenchy from 1996 to 2001. In 2000 the Gucci Group took over the majority shareholding of McQueen's own label, retaining the designer as fashion director. McQueen's achievements were recognized by numerous awards, including British Designer of the Year in 1996, 1997, 2001 and 2003.

2 MOULDED CORSET
The moulded form of the corset transforms the woman into a naked shop dummy, itself often used to symbolize women as voiceless sexual objects. In this context, the wide stitches speak of a damaged woman who wears clothes for protection.

UNDERWEAR AS OUTERWEAR

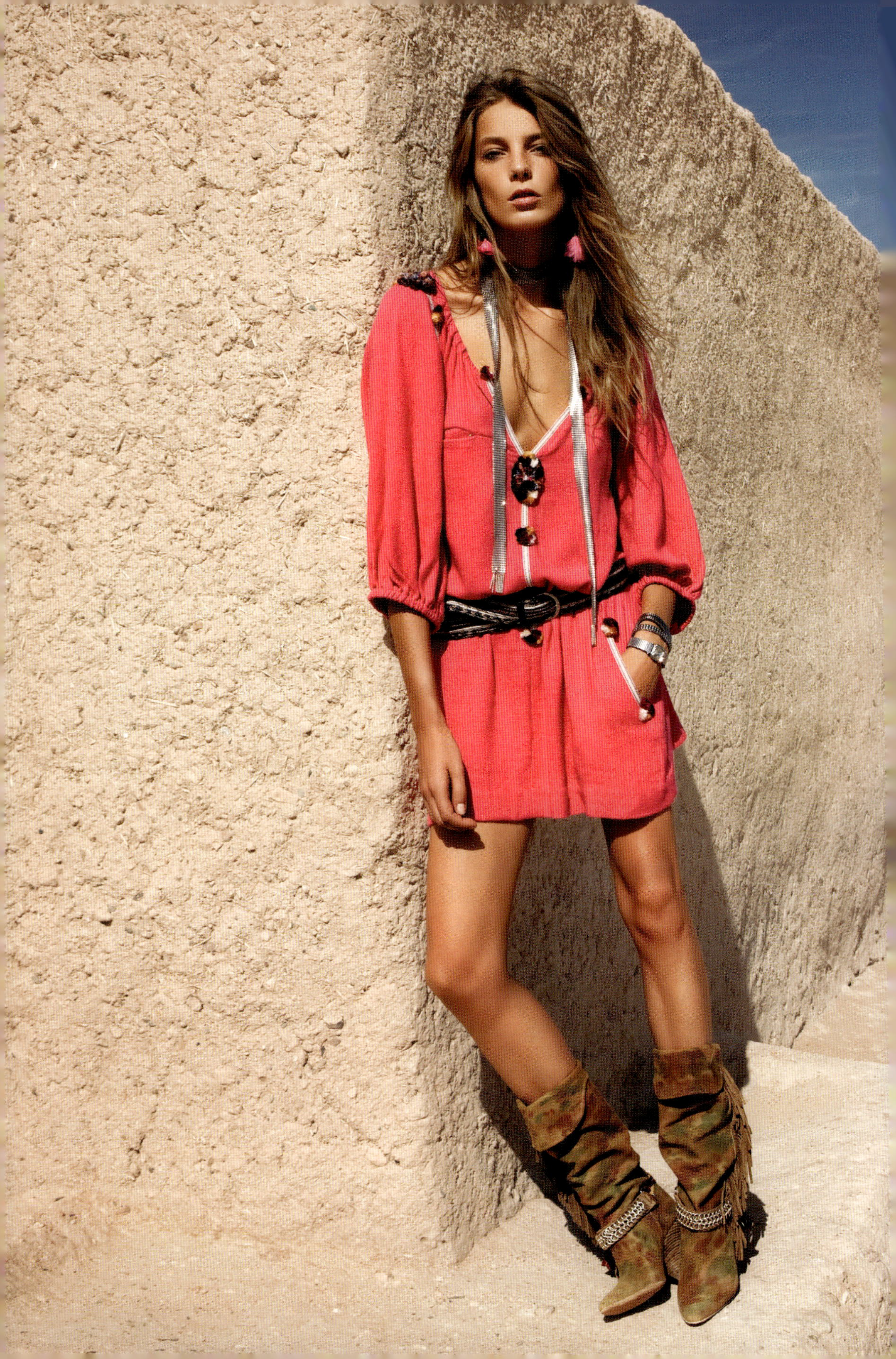

6 | 1990 TO PRESENT

DECADENCE AND EXCESS 466

MINIMALIST LUXURY 474

ANTI-FASHION 482

SUSTAINABLE AND ETHICAL FASHION 486

CRAFT RENAISSANCE 490

DECONSTRUCTION FASHION 498

JAPANESE STREET CULTURE 506

MODERN COUTURE 510

PRINT IN FASHION 518

SPORTSWEAR AND FASHION 528

LUXE READY-TO-WEAR 534

UNDERSTATED AMERICAN STYLE 540

THE RISE OF E-COMMERCE 544

CONTEMPORARY AFROCENTRIC FASHION 548

DECADENCE AND EXCESS

Forthrightly sexual in their aspirations, and with roots in the Italian *dolce vita* of the 1950s, Italian fashion designers Gianni Versace (1946–97), Roberto Cavalli (b.1940) and Dolce & Gabbana (Domenico Dolce, b.1958, and Stefano Gabbana, b.1962) all celebrated the return of high-voltage fashion during the 1990s. Versace's flamboyant prints (above), Cavalli's fascination with animal skins and Dolce & Gabbana's intrinsically Sicilian style, together with the luxurious furs and accessories produced by Fendi (see p.472), all evoked an impression of decadent sensuality. When Versace put supermodels Christy Turlington, Linda Evangelista, Naomi Campbell and Cindy Crawford together on the runway during the 1990s, he epitomized an era of conspicuous consumption allied to hard-core glamour, and turned the models into international celebrities.

Versace showed his first collection of womenswear in 1978 in Milan, which by this time had taken precedence over Rome and Florence as the recognized centre for Italian fashion. His aesthetic combined high art and contemporary culture and his adopted crest was the head of Medusa, which symbolized the decadent glamour and provocative allure inherent in the Versace label. In 1989

KEY EVENTS

1988	1989	1989	1990	1990	1992
Dolce & Gabbana introduces a ready-to-wear line based in Dolce's family-owned atelier in Milan.	Versace opens his couture workshop Atelier Versace for the creation of handmade *alta moda* dresses.	Dolce & Gabbana launches a lingerie and swimwear collection.	Dolce & Gabbana introduces a menswear line.	Roberto Cavalli begins to seriously court the US market, retailing at high-end stores such as Bergdorf Goodman in New York.	Versace provokes controversy with the release of his overtly sexual Bondage collection.

466   1990–PRESENT

he opened the couture workshop Atelier Versace and throughout the next decade pioneered voluptuous evening dresses in dazzling colour combinations for the super-rich. Concentrating on evening wear in the early 1990s, Versace layered an opulent embellishment of beadwork, metal threads, embroidery and appliqué over multicoloured Mannerist-style prints on garments slashed to the waist or cut down to the buttock, often featuring images from popular culture, such as cartoons and Andy Warhol-inspired images of Marilyn Monroe and James Dean (see p.470). His collections were also resplendent with the label's signature gold: gold trench coats and lamé suits, gold fringing and scrolls of gold embroidery, and a gold lace tutu modelled by Christy Turlington (right).

Sex was key to Versace's aesthetic: his bondage collection of autumn/winter 1992 was part of the proliferation of progressively explicit fetish clothing, appropriating the leather straps and stilettos of the female dominatrix. Black leather was a consistent feature of second-skin garments by the designer, who sculpted, quilted, top-stitched and studded it into a series of form-fitting dresses and jackets with exaggerated biker details. He revisited the London punk counter-culture in 1994, and garnered unprecedented global press coverage when British actress Elizabeth Hurley wore the Versace 'safety-pin dress' when she accompanied Hugh Grant to the film premiere of *Four Weddings and a Funeral* (1994). The plunging décolleté and split side seams of the black sheath dress were held in place with gilt and silver kilt pins decorated with a diamanté head of Medusa. A matching jacket for men in white wool had a slashed open seam on the outside of the sleeve, also secured with bejewelled kilt pins. Although Versace had first introduced a menswear range in 1979, it was not until a decade later that his sophisticated exuberant tailoring appealed to rock and pop stars such as Sting, who wore Versace for his marriage to Trudie Styler in 1992.

Throughout Versace's career, vibrantly coloured, large-scale prints of Baroque patterning, the Greek key motif and a lavish use of gold remained the hallmarks of the label for both men and women. The designer constantly deployed a metallic mesh material, which he first patented in 1982, and continued to exploit the sensuality of its lustrous form-clinging and draping qualities. In his final collection for autumn/winter 1997 he featured the material in a double-layered mini bridal gown worn by supermodel Naomi Campbell. Versace's sister and muse, Donatella, who had directed Versus, the more youthful line of the label since 1990, took over the design directorship of the main Versace label after the untimely death of her brother in 1997.

Domenico Dolce, born in Polizzi, Sicily, and Stefano Gabbana, born in Milan, founded their company in Milan in 1982 and showed their first womenswear collection in 1985. Featuring a combination of severe but sexy tailoring, always an essential element of Italian fashion, and a sexually expressive mix of corset- and lingerie-inspired garments, Dolce & Gabbana embodied a nostalgic view

1 Gianni Versace celebrates his collection on the catwalk surrounded by supermodels (1993).

2 Christy Turlington wears a lavishly embellished tweed jacket and delicate lace tutu by Versace (1992).

1993	1994	1994	1997	1998	2000
Karl Lagerfeld causes a stir at Milan Fashion Week by employing strippers to model his black-and-white collection for Fendi.	Elizabeth Hurley receives huge media attention when she wears the 'safety-pin dress' to the premiere of *Four Weddings and a Funeral*.	Dolce & Gabbana launches a diffusion clothing line, prompted by the successful publicity engendered by pop star Madonna.	Versace is murdered in Miami and his sister, Donatella, takes over as head designer.	Roberto Cavalli launches the more youth-orientated Just Cavalli line.	Roberto Cavalli dresses his models head to toe in zebra print for the catwalk debut of his spring/summer collection.

DECADENCE AND EXCESS 467

of southern Italy, epitomized by the heroines of the Italian neo-realist cinema. The incorporation of lace in the form of veils or deep décolleté, figure-hugging dresses and a preponderance of black and white, often accessorized with religious iconography, represented the dichotomy of the label and reflected the design duo's Catholic upbringing. The label's sultry sensuality was inspired by iconic Italian women such as actresses Isabella Rossellini and Monica Bellucci, who both appeared in highly successful advertising campaigns photographed by Steven Meisel and wore the label on the red carpet. Dolce & Gabbana also commissioned German-born photographer and director Ellen von Unwerth to bring her erotic sensibilities to the label. She highlighted the inherent sensuality of the garments by deploying her overtly sexual imagery and languorous poses (above). Dolce & Gabbana achieved further international recognition as a result of their collaboration with iconic pop star Madonna, who commissioned the duo to design a corset and jacket to wear to the launch of her film *Truth or Dare: In Bed with Madonna* in 1990 and subsequently to provide her with 1,500 costumes for her 'Girlie Show World Tour' in 1993. The same key elements of overt sexuality combined with sharp tailoring defined the Dolce & Gabbana range of menswear, first shown in January 1990. Under the supervision of Dolce's father in an atelier of Sicilian craftsmen, the designers produced unstructured suits based on high-buttoning jackets and tight, narrowly cut trousers or leggings in the style of the Italian *briganti* (bandits).

Animal prints, such as tiger, leopard, cheetah and zebra, have long provided inspiration for fashion designers. Whether reduced to abstract form or as an exact replica, the appropriation of spotted and striped animal prints is inextricably linked to the aesthetic of Roberto Cavalli. Early cave paintings show human beings dressed in animal skins, not only as a form of camouflage to deceive the prey, but also in an attempt to take on some of the mythical qualities of the hunted beast. In contemporary fashion, wearing animal skin is interpreted as a desire to convey the same dangerously predatory instincts as those of the big cats. The spotted coat of the female leopard—the female is the fiercest fighter—is perceived to represent the archetypal femme fatale.

Cavalli initially entered the fashion arena with an innovative printing-on-leather procedure, patented in the early 1970s, which won him commissions

3 Ellen von Unwerth utilizes powerful sexual signifiers in this image from *Vogue Italia* (1991): maribou mules, a black silk-satin corset dress by Dolce & Gabbana and vibrant red lips.

4 Eva Herzigova models animal-print excess in Roberto Cavalli's spring/summer collection of 2000.

5 High-end luxury was evident throughout the autumn/winter collection of 2000 by Karl Lagerfeld for Fendi.

from Hermès and Pierre Cardin. During the 1980s he introduced much-copied, high-end, printed and embellished, patchworked denim and leather leisurewear, but it was only when Cavalli concentrated on Baroque and elaborate print designs during the 1990s that the label evolved into an international brand favoured by celebrities. Unlike Milan-based Versace, Cavalli continued to show his seasonal collections in Florence until 1994, which reflected his prevailing predilection for more understated glamour. Cavalli's second wife, Eva, is credited as the inspiration behind the renaissance of the label during this period, which resulted in the signature animal-print gowns appealing to a new generation of celebrity rock and pop stars. In his spring/summer collection of 2000 Cavalli clothed his models in head-to-toe, scaled-down zebra markings (right); the models were corralled in a zebra-printed room and tethered with diamanté collars and leashes.

In addition to animal prints, real fur also promulgated the look of Italian decadence and excess, signifying not only material wealth but also a certain sensuality. Italian designers were unashamedly lavish in their use of fur, regardless of worldwide politicization by the national and international legislation of the Endangered Species Act of 1973 in the United States and the Convention on International Trade in Endangered Species of Wild Flora and Fauna signed in 1973. With the emergence of the animal rights movement People for the Ethical Treatment of Animals in the 1980s, alongside contemporary sensitivities, it became necessary to find a way of interpreting animal skin in fashion that retained the glamour of the original without compromising ethical concerns. Karl Lagerfeld (b.1933), who in 1965 was appointed as creative consultant to the Italian label Fendi, which originally specialized in fur and luxury leather goods, modernized the brand and changed the perception of fur as a conventional status symbol. He exploited and explored novel ways of processing fur and pelts in order to liberate the ways in which the materials are fabricated, enabling them to be printed and dyed (below). This disguises their origins, which results in them being virtually indistinguishable from their faux fur or 'fun fur' counterparts, recognizable only by the garment label. **MF**

Warhol Print Dress 1991
GIANNI VERSACE 1946 – 97

Naomi Campbell models a Versace
evening dress with a Warhol print (1991).

NAVIGATOR

Highlighting a global outburst of conspicuous consumption and brilliantly ornamented seduction, Gianni Versace combined sensuous shapes with references to pop culture in this evening dress worn by supermodel Naomi Campbell. In homage to the vibrantly coloured screen prints of celebrities by US Pop artist Andy Warhol, Versace fashioned an all-over print featuring portraits of Hollywood's most enduring sex goddess, Marilyn Monroe, and screen idol James Dean into a long, body-skimming evening dress. The halter-neck bodice of the dress outlines the circular-stitched cups of the bustier top, which are secured with a matching strap. The appliquéd areas are formed by attaching supplementary pieces of material to wire supports, thereby adding to the three-dimensional appearance of the embellishment.

The collage images are assembled using emerald green, red, cerulean blue, purple and gold, with the registration of each colour slightly off, which leads to an overlap of deliberately mismatched colour. As the print design is one-directional, a number of silk screens would be required to create it. The design also demanded that the scale of the images matched along the seams, which meant that the fabric would be costly to reproduce, yet it is cut with the casualness of a T-shirt. **MF**

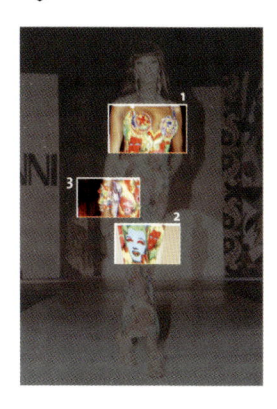

FOCAL POINTS

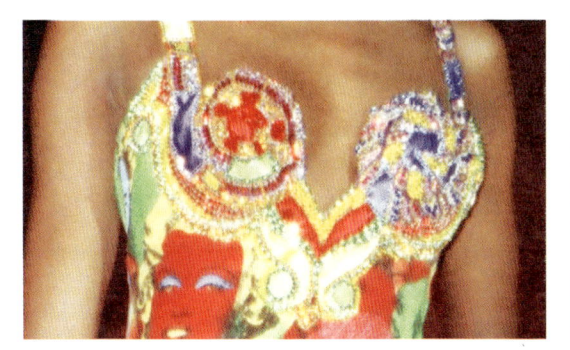

1 BUSTIER TOP
The breasts are lifted and separated with a showgirl-style bustier top that is richly decorated with scrolls of rhinestones and appliquéd with motifs. These form curvilinear patterns around the breasts before plunging into a 'V' shape at the centre front.

3 HIGH-SHINE ACCESSORIES
Attesting to Versace's predilection for exuberant excess, the embellished dress is accessorized with matching polychromatic jewellery, of which gold is the chief component. This extends the glitter and sparkle of the dress to the wrist and earlobes.

DESIGNER PROFILE

1946–88
Gianni Versace was born in Reggio Calabria in Italy. He began his career as a designer in 1972, working for design houses Complice, Genny and Callaghan before starting his own label in 1978. The first Versace boutique opened in Milan's Via della Spiga in 1978, the same year in which he launched the label.

1989–97
In 1989 Versace opened the Atelier Versace, a couture workshop, and throughout the following decade the designer epitomized high-octane glamour with extrovert body-enhancing gowns in his signature Mannerist prints, aimed at the super-rich. Versace launched Versus, a more youthful line, in 1990 under the direction of his sister and muse, Donatella. Following his sudden death in 1997, she assumed creative directorship of the label.

2 ALL-OVER PRINT
Constructed from silk-satin, the dress is cut from a large-scale design with a repeat of 38 by 55 inches (96 x 140 cm), printed by one of Italy's foremost practitioners of the craft of screen printing: Manifattura Ratti.

Baguette Bag 1997
FENDI

Raffia Baguette. The basic design of the bag remains unchanged; this model is from 2010.

NAVIGATOR

The Fendi Baguette was developed by Silvia Venturini Fendi (b.1960), the granddaughter of the Fendi founders, and it became an instant classic when it was launched in 1997. After the consumer excesses of the 1980s, the bag epitomized a return to bohemian values and ethnic detailing that belied its huge price tag. Coveted by the haute hippie and boho set, the bag offered a luxurious and whimsical contrast to the sensible totes and minimalist designs of the era.

The Baguette was the first bag to be subject to seasonal changes, as if it were an item of clothing, and these changes, together with the limited numbers of each collection, ensure that the bag continues to be in demand. It is produced in a plethora of vibrant colours and in more than 1,000 styles in many different materials. These range from the exotic and the expensive, such as mink, reptile skin, pony skin, silk velvet, duchesse satin and feathers, to the more mundane, including tweed, woven raffia and denim. These are often patchworked and appliquéd together with further embellishment in precious metal threads, sequins, crystals and jewels. The price is justified by the artisan production methods and meticulous craftwork, exemplified by the Lisio Baguette. These bags are produced through the Florence-based Fondazione Arte della Seta Lisio. Using traditional hand-weaving techniques on jacquard looms, which can take up to a month to prepare for production, the output is restricted to 2 inches (5 cm) of fabric a day. **MF**

⊙ FOCAL POINTS

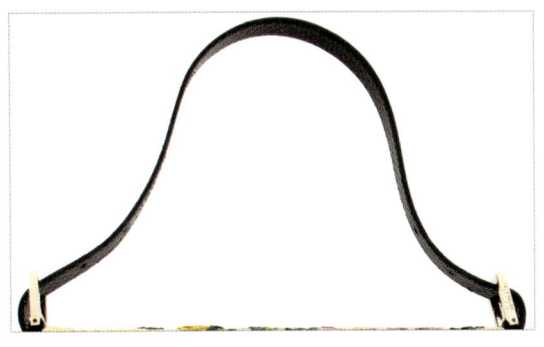

1 SHORT STRAP
The short shoulder strap, secured at each end of the bag, requires the *pochette* to be tucked high under the arm, carried like the baguette from which it takes its name. The Baguette bag is impractically small, and the wearer requires a supplementary bag for anything more than a lipstick and a mobile phone.

2 DECORATION
The raffia base of the Baguette is embellished with black and pastel-coloured grosgrain ribbons, which are appliquéd into floral shapes, lending an otherwise simple design a summery and playful, feminine quality. The flower design extends to the back of the bag.

3 BUCKLE/LOGO
The buckle on the fastening strap is fairly large in proportion to the bag. It is fashioned in the shape of the Fendi logo, which consists of a double 'F' formed by the letters interlocking at opposing angles to create a rectangle. This logo was first introduced in 1965, the same year in which Karl Lagerfeld began to work with the company.

▲ The 'It' bag of the 1990s, the Fendi Baguette, modelled in this magazine advertisement with a signature Fendi fur, invariably displayed the outsize Fendi logo on the buckle.

⊕ COMPANY PROFILE

1918–64
Born in Rome, Adele Casagrande (1897–1978) founded a small leather and fur company in 1918. After her marriage to Edoardo Fendi the couple established a leather and fur workshop on the Via del Plebiscito in Rome in 1925. On his death their five daughters, Paola (b.1931), Anna (b.1933), Franca (b.1935), Carla (b.1937) and Alda (b.1940), shared the management of the company, which was subsequently launched as a fashion label.

1965–99
In 1965 Karl Lagerfeld was hired as creative consultant to oversee the fur collections. In 1977 Fendi launched a full prêt-à-porter collection and expanded into menswear, accessories and home furnishings. Silvia Venturini Fendi became head of leather goods in 1996 and designed the iconic Baguette a year later. In 1999 Fendi assumed partnership with the LVMH conglomerate.

2000–PRESENT
The Baguette proved popular with celebrities and was featured in the US television show *Sex and the City* (1998–2004). A special ten-year anniversary Baguette edition was launched in 2008.

DECADENCE AND EXCESS 473

MINIMALIST LUXURY

1. This Gucci advertising campaign from 1999 projects an image of sleek sophistication, showcasing a simple white coat with a thin bow belt.

2. Helmut Lang's panelled one-piece from his autumn/winter collection of 1999 features silk organza over white cotton and silk jersey, and a futuristic circular collar.

During his tenure as creative director of Italian luxury goods label Gucci, US-born Tom Ford (b.1961), together with his chief executive Domenico de Sole, reflected and shaped the culture of luxury fashion in the 1990s: the brand entered the fashion stratosphere to become the most coveted label of the era (see p.478). Ford pursued a coherent and tightly edited design policy with a visionary approach to marketing and publicity, which provided a paradigm for other brands that were eager to regenerate an ailing label and find a new market share. At Gucci, this strategy included advertising campaigns (above), which were shown alongside editorial coverage of the brand, and the exploitation of a distinctive and easily recognizable logo, the double 'G'.

The 1990s and the decade that followed were defined by the rivalry between two luxury conglomerates and their fight for acquisitions. Gucci's competitor for supremacy in the luxury market was LVMH, the world's largest conglomerate, founded in 1987 with the merger between Louis Vuitton and Moët Hennessy. From the 1990s onwards, the fashion and accessories industry continued to be dominated by these two groups: LVMH, led by Bernard Arnault,

KEY EVENTS

1989	1989	1991	1992	1993	1994
Prada introduces its first ready-to-wear autumn/winter collection at the Palazzo Manusardi in Milan.	Jil Sander AG becomes one of the first fashion houses to go public when it is floated on the Frankfurt Stock Exchange.	Giorgio Armani releases a new affordable clothing line under the label 'A/X Armani Exchange', in a bid to break into the US mass market.	Prada launches its secondary line, Miu Miu, which breathes new life into the brand.	Jil Sander opens a four-floor store in Paris on a site previously occupied by Madeleine Vionnet (1876–1975) and used as her atelier and showroom.	Tom Ford is appointed creative director at Gucci and embarks on his mission to rejuvenate the label.

which included fashion labels Loewe, Céline, Givenchy, Fendi, Pucci and Donna Karan; and the Gucci Group, which had a whole or partial interest in Italian label Bottega Veneta, Yves Saint Laurent, Alexander McQueen, Balenciaga and Stella McCartney. In 1997 Louis Vuitton expanded to include ready-to-wear women's clothing, and US designer Marc Jacobs (b.1963) was appointed to oversee and enliven the brand. His debut collection in 1998 of understated, monochrome, oversized white shirts and knee-length skirts acknowledged the pared-down minimalism of the era, and he restricted the 'LV' monogram to a subtle white on white for a single across-the-body bag.

Another competitor in the luxury market was the Italian house Prada (see p.480), which also engaged in a series of complex business manoeuvres in the late 1990s, buying and selling stakes in Gucci, Fendi, footwear manufacturer Church & Co., Jil Sander and Helmut Lang among others. The obverse of the easily identified product, Prada exemplified stealth wealth with the introduction of the 'Vela' in 1988, a small and lightweight backpack designed by Miuccia Prada (b.1949), granddaughter of the founder of Prada. The discreet triangular logo and utilitarian performance sportswear fabric were in marked contrast to the conspicuous consumption that was prevalent at the time, and the success of the bag led to the addition of a ready-to-wear clothing range. The first collection was an autumn/winter range, which was presented in the Prada headquarters at the Palazzo Manusardi, Milan, in 1989. With an idiosyncratic and intellectual approach to design, Miuccia Prada shunned the extrovert and the excessive in favour of a refinement that was almost a parody of ladylike demureness, with the emphasis on whimsical prints and utilitarian fabrics in complex and subtle colour combinations.

This minimalist aesthetic found its counterpart in the puritan simplicity and fastidious attention to quality and detail of the Jil Sander (see p.476) and Helmut Lang labels, acquired by Prada at the end of the 1990s. From a made-to-measure atelier in 1977 in Vienna, Austrian-born Helmut Lang (b.1956) developed a modernist approach to both menswear and womenswear that pared down an attenuated silhouette with sculptured tailoring produced in monochrome luxury fabrics mixed with edgier synthetics as a counterpoint (right). His essentially urban look included close-fitting layers of contrasting textures, such as clear with opaque, and matt with shiny, in the context of slim-legged tailored suits, with a crossover of fabrics from women to men. In the 1990s the label branched out into eyewear, underwear, denim and fragrances, thus establishing a global retail presence.

By the 21st century heavily branded fashion held little appeal, debased by a flourishing counterfeit trade, in spite of legal redress against copying. With the design direction at Gucci now a collaborative process, rather than the vision of a single designer, the company offered a more diverse product and its marque was once again placed inside rather than outside the garment. **MF**

1995	1997	1999	1999	2001	2001
Helmut Lang introduces underwear into his collection and the following year adds a range of jeans.	Louis Vuitton's newly appointed creative director, Marc Jacobs, produces its first ready-to-wear women's clothing line.	LVMH and Prada buy 51 per cent of the Italian fur and leather company Fendi.	Gucci buys the Yves Saint Laurent brand and the following year takes over the majority shareholding of the Alexander McQueen label.	Stella McCartney (b.1971) launches her own label under the umbrella of the Gucci Group.	LVMH acquires a controlling share of DKI (the conglomerate that includes DKNY, Donna Karan and her popular brand of sportswear and jeans).

MINIMALIST LUXURY

'The Great Plain', *Vogue* 1993
JIL SANDER b. 1943

Christy Turlington and male model, photographed by Ellen von Unwerth for *Vogue* (August 1993).

NAVIGATOR

An uncompromising perfectionist, Jil Sander is one of fashion's most austere purists. During the 1990s the Jil Sander label signified luxurious 'noble' fibres and androgynous minimalism, seen here in an image from the 'The Great Plain' fashion spread, styled by US *Vogue*'s iconoclast and creative director Grace Coddington and photographed by German photographer Ellen von Unwerth. US model Christy Turlington is cast as a Pennsylvanian-Dutch Amish girl, complete with sun-bleached blonde bobbed wig and a face unadorned with make-up. The pose and concept reference the painting *American Gothic* by Grant Wood (1930), which depicts a farming couple standing stoically in front of their Gothic-style home. During the Great Depression, the image came to represent the American pioneer spirit.

The painting's plain design and simple structure clearly inspired the concept behind the photographic shoot, exemplifying the Amish moral imperative to eschew decoration. Turlington's athletic build and square shoulders lend the single-breasted coat a sombre authority. Unseen are Turlington's black lace-up brogues. The male model wears an Amish broad-brimmed felt hat, set squarely on the head, and a single-breasted jacket from French ready-to-wear brand APC, known for its minimalist designs and lack of logo, over a blue denim collarless work shirt. **MF**

FOCAL POINTS

1 SMALL COLLAR
The long uncluttered lines of the voluminous ankle-length coat are emphasized by the small high-standing collar, which is cut in one and turned back to form a narrow rounded faux Peter Pan collar. It is cut to sit closely at the back of the neck. The lack of top-stitching or other tailoring details is consistent with the smooth minimalist outlines of the garment. Large, unshanked buttons, starting under the collar, secure the small overlap of the centre-front fastening.

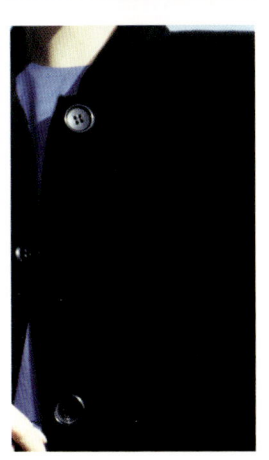

2 COAT
The single-breasted black coat hangs in an uninterrupted line from the shoulders straight to the ankle-grazing hem. The set-in sleeves slightly extend beyond the shoulder line, creating bulk across the width of the garment. The structurally simple coat is worn over a home-sewn, saxe-blue cotton, broad-cloth shirt dress, which was made from a commercially available *Vogue* pattern. It features a neat round neckline and buttons up the back.

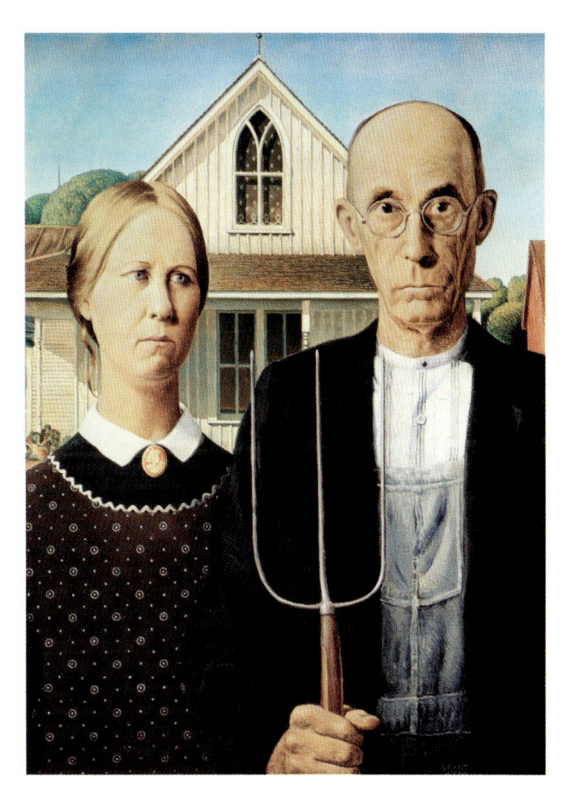

▲ *American Gothic* by Grant Wood (1930) is one of the most enduring images in 20th-century US art, and one of the most parodied. The figures are reputedly modelled on the artist's sister and their dentist, and represent the traditional values of small-town rural life.

MINIMALIST LUXURY 477

White Cut-out Dress 1996
TOM FORD b. 1961 (FOR GUCCI)

NAVIGATOR

US designer Tom Ford defined the pivotal look of the 1990s with a collection of columnar white matt-jersey evening dresses that combine overt sexuality with high fashion. The sensuous lines of the dresses are an homage to US sportswear designer Halston (see p.398) and the liquid jersey evening wear worn by the disco set of Studio 54. Eschewing the obvious sexuality inherent in the plunging décolleté or thigh-high split skirt, Ford emphasizes new erogenous zones, such as the navel and lower hip. These areas are accentuated further by an absence of extraneous detail: there are no fitting darts around the waist or breasts, and no flattering infrastructure to hold in or push out the figure. The dress relies on a perfectly honed body for its shape.

Like the bias-cut dresses of Hollywood in the 1930s, to which Ford's dress also refers, the line of the garment requires a naked body beneath. Furthermore, there is no evidence of construction techniques; the hem and the edges of the sleeves are all invisibly hemmed. Variations of the style include back interest with the wide, shallow scoop of the neckline at the front open to the lower back, caught at the back of the neck with a narrow tie. The unadorned purity of the white dress, apart from the spurious functionality of the 'hardware', renders the figure both untouchable and desirable. **MF**

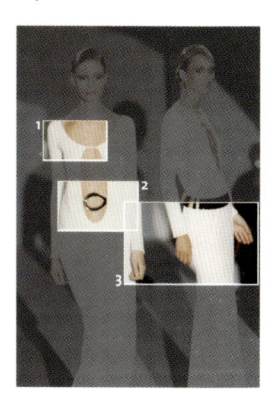

FOCAL POINTS

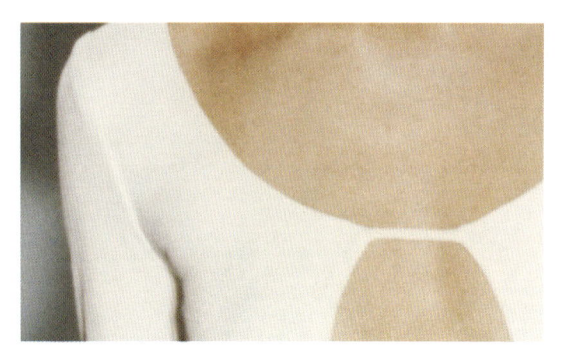

1 SET-IN SLEEVES
The set-in sleeves are cut narrowly to a high arm scye, creating the illusion of a longer, leaner torso. This sensuous silhouette is further emphasized by the narrowness of the tight-fitting, wrist-length sleeves.

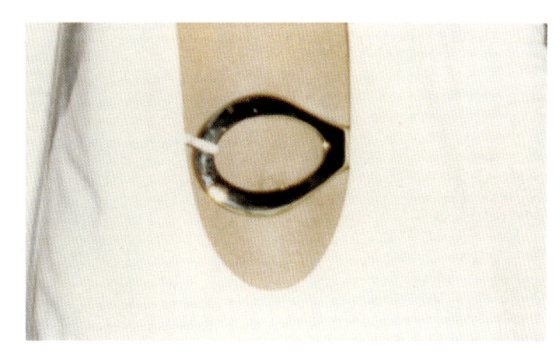

2 GILT HARDWARE
The gilt hardware, a simple buckle shaped to the contours of the body, is the focal point of one of the white evening dresses. It is held in place at the navel by narrow ties that do not distort the sinuous lines of the garment.

3 COLUMNAR SKIRT
Matt jersey is an unforgiving textile and the full-length columnar skirt clings to the outline of the body except when the line is broken by movement, as seen here where the model poses with her weight on one hip.

DESIGNER PROFILE

1961–93
Thomas Carlyle Ford was born in Texas and moved to New York City where he studied architecture at Parsons The New School for Design, spending his final year studying fashion. He worked for US designer Cathy Hardwick's mid-price sportswear company, and in 1988 for Perry Ellis before being appointed as Gucci's chief women's ready-to-wear designer in 1990.

1994–PRESENT
In 1994 Ford was promoted to creative director, and in 1995 his breakthrough collection reinvented Gucci style and resurrected the double-'G' logo as an icon—it now appears on all Gucci products. When Gucci acquired the House of Yves Saint Laurent, Ford was named the creative director. In 2004 Ford showed his last collection for Gucci. He opened his first Tom Ford store in New York in 2006.

Patterned Dress and Coat 1996
PRADA

NAVIGATOR

Miuccia Prada consistently confronts the chic with the outré, and her singularly ironic aesthetic is resolutely at the cutting edge of the evolution of taste. Once copied, the designer moves on to provide another confounding benchmark vision. Her ready-to-wear collection for spring/summer 1996, dubbed the 'bad taste' collection by the fashion press, was staunchly out of step with contemporary fashion.

Exploiting materials and stylistic references that are alien to the luxury market, the collection featured garments such as a nylon zip-up burger-bar worker's uniform and printed textile patterns strongly redolent of Formica, the ubiquitous 1970s plastic laminate. Prada subverted the transient norms of beauty and seductive glamour by playing with perceptions of good and bad taste in an exploration of forms and volumes, rendered in the colours, prints and textiles of the thrift-store warehouse.

This patterned dress and coat ensemble is of the same hues and demonstrates the signature decorum of the Doris Day-era stenographer, and consequently all the hallmarks of Prada. By dissolving the cliché elements of allurement from clothing, the Prada impact elevates garments to the status of objects of carefully chosen interest and, by implication, aims to add intangible intrigue to the persona of the wearer. **MF**

FOCAL POINTS

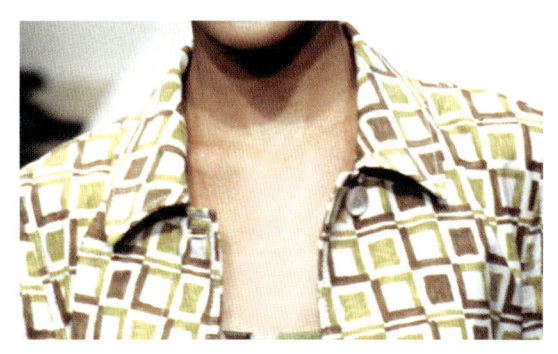

1 SHIRT COLLAR
The simple up-scale shirt collar of the coat breaks from the integrated button overlap, revealing the deep-scoop neckline of the patterned sheath dress worn beneath. The set-in, full-length sleeves are easy fitting.

3 FLORAL DRESS
In contrast to the geometric print of the coat, the dress is constructed from a smooth-surfaced, chinoiserie-inspired, multidirectional, all-over bold floral print. It adds an air of subtle femininity to the ensemble.

2 RETRO PRINT
The coat features a retro-inspired geometric print design of abstract modular squares superimposed in an off-key colour palette of pea green and aubergine on a cream ground. The simplicity of the print affords the coat an edge of refinement.

COMPANY PROFILE

1913–94
From a small store specializing in luxury leather luggage founded by Mario Prada in Milan in 1913, his granddaughter Miuccia turned the company into one of the foremost brands in fashion. A former mime student with a PhD in political science, the designer was initially reluctant to take over the luggage brand that she inherited in 1988, but the first ready-to-wear collection was launched in Milan in 1993.

1995–PRESENT
In 1995 a 'little sister line' was introduced, named after the designer's childhood nickname, 'Miu Miu', followed by Prada Linea Rossa Sport, recognized by the red strap logo. In 2011 the company floated 20 per cent of its business on the Hong Kong stock market, which reflected the fact that the Asian Pacific region is currently the label's biggest market.

ANTI-FASHION

1 Marc Jacobs eschews glamour with his Grunge collection of 1992, featuring fashion inspired by the Seattle music scene.

2 Kirsty Hume models Anna Sui's post-punk bohemian style in 1994.

A new mood of anti-glamour permeated areas of the fashion industry in the early 1990s. Satiated by glossy representations of conspicuous consumption and the diva-like demands of the supermodels, certain designers looked to a new generation of models and to subversive facets of culture. Waif-like British model Kate Moss not only epitomized the antithesis of the runway establishment but also signified a more youthful anarchic style, given voice by the indie-grunge record label Sub Pop and the music of Seattle's Pearl Jam and Nirvana. The simplicity, nihilism and rawness of the music was reflected in grunge fashion; adherents wore thrift-store finds, vintage smock dresses with boyfriend cardigans, baby-doll nightgowns, ripped and faded jeans, plaid flannel shirts layered over T-shirts, beanies and cargo pants. This vernacular style was captured in grittily realistic fashion spreads, featuring Stella Tennant, Kristen McMenamy and Karen Elson, models renowned for their

KEY EVENTS

1989	1990	1990	1991	1991	1992
Marc Jacobs joins Perry Ellis as vice-president of women's design. He wins Women's Designer of the Year.	The US rock band Pearl Jam is formed in Seattle, Washington.	British model Kate Moss is photographed by Corinne Day for the July issue of style magazine *The Face*.	Nirvana releases its second album *Nevermind*, which becomes the first grunge album to go multi-platinum.	Anna Sui launches her first runway show, followed by the opening of her first shop in New York City's SoHo district.	The British magazine *Dazed & Confused* is launched as a sporadically published black-and-white folded poster.

quirkiness rather than for the mature over-groomed voluptuousness of the honed and toned glamazons. They represented aspirational living rather than the darker nihilistic philosophy of what came to be dubbed 'Generation X'.

In Britain, style magazines such as *i-D*, *The Face* and, later, *Dazed & Confused* lionized the protagonists of these cultural undercurrents, experimenting with new graphic styles and subverting the notion of the glossy fashion magazine by using grainy shots, distorted text and handwritten headings. Terry Jones, founder of *i-D*, called these photographs of real people wearing real clothes 'straight-ups', a social documentation of a generation dressing itself. In 1990 Kate Moss was photographed by Corinne Day for *The Face* in a cover shoot titled 'The 3rd Summer of Love'. Two years later the marginal went mainstream, when US designer Calvin Klein (b.1942) endorsed the 'waif' look after featuring Moss in marketing campaigns with Mark Wahlberg, pioneering what came to be described as 'heroin chic'. Moss also appeared on the cover of British *Vogue*, photographed by Corinne Day in 1993 (see p.484), the same year that she created a furore with the controversial advertisements for Calvin Klein's rebranding of his perfume Obsession

The grunge look infiltrated mainstream fashion when New York-born designer Marc Jacobs (b.1963) hit the headlines in 1992 with his groundbreaking collection for US sportswear company Perry Ellis (opposite). The company was renowned for a tasteful aesthetic firmly rooted in preppy-style sportswear, and the grunge collection was a surprise to the consumer and a commercial disaster. The vintage-inspired, flower-strewn, button-through dresses worn over shorts and partnered with combat boots and silk shirts printed to look like flannel were enormously influential, but customers were not prepared to pay for faux shabbiness. However, the collection confirmed Jacobs as a visionary designer and in 1997 he was invited by Yves Carcelle, president of Louis Vuitton, to create the company's first ready-to-wear collection, then perceived as a daring move on a par with the appointment of John Galliano (b.1960) at Givenchy in 1995. US-born designer Anna Sui (b.1964) also picked up on the grunge trend (right). After graduating from Parsons The New School for Design in New York, where she met fashion photographer Steven Meisel, Sui worked for a variety of junior sportswear companies. At the same time she designed clothes that retailed in New York stores such as Bloomingdale's and Macy's before making her name with her version of grunge fashion in 1992.

The anti-fashion moment was short-lived. By the time US president Bill Clinton asserted in 1997 that 'you do not need to glamorize addiction to sell clothes' and accused the fashion industry of making heroin seem 'glamorous, sexy and cool through advertising', a much-fragmented fashion market was already moving on to embrace either the hard-edged glamour of Versace, the easy-to-wear minimalism of contemporary US designers or the theatricality of British designers Galliano and Alexander McQueen (1969–2010). **MF**

1992	1992	1993	1993	1997	1997
Marc Jacobs designs the Grunge spring/summer collection for Perry Ellis.	Grunge is first mentioned in *Women's Wear Daily* on 17 August: 'Three hot looks — rave, hip hop and grunge — have hit the street and stores.'	Marc Jacobs and Robert Duffy launch their own licensing and design company: Marc Jacobs International Company LP.	Kate Moss appears on the front cover of British *Vogue* in June, photographed by Corinne Day (see p.484).	US President Bill Clinton condemns the allusion to 'heroin chic' in fashion advertising.	Luxury goods conglomerate LVMH appoints Marc Jacobs as its creative director for the company's first ready-to-wear range.

'Under Exposure', *Vogue* 1993
LINGERIE

Kate Moss, photographed by
Corinne Day for *Vogue* (June 1993).

Eschewing the artifice inherent in contemporary fashion photography in a shoot for British *Vogue*, Corinne Day depicted the nineteen-year-old Kate Moss in her west London flat, which she shared with her then boyfriend, fashion photographer Mario Sorrenti. Day's first commission for the magazine featured Moss as one of many 'London girls' in a shoot styled by *Vogue* fashion director Kate Phelan. The feature was a tribute to Day's favourite models, which introduced the notion of the model as a real flawed person, rather than merely a mannequin, the antithesis of the Amazonian supermodels. British *Vogue* editor Alexandra Shulman commissioned the notorious 'Under Exposure' feature from Day in 1993. Intended as a lingerie fashion spread, the title of the article was 'What to wear beneath effort-free clothes? Barely-there underwear, naturally.' The editorial spread, styled by Cathy Kasterine, shows Moss posed against a backdrop of casually strewn fairy lights. The images caused a media scandal and Day was accused of promoting heroin chic and anorexia.

Day's fashion shoots were conspicuous for the lack of labels; the photographer preferred to feature vintage or even unbranded goods. She brought a documentary quality to her images with the use of natural light and her choice of mundane venues; locations were equally naturalistic: a shabby bedsitter, a rumpled bed, a dirty carpet. **MF**

NAVIGATOR

FOCAL POINTS

1 VEST AND NECKLACE
Covertly sexy on the waif-like Kate Moss, the pink clinging interlock jersey vest by US-born fashion designer Liza Bruce (b.1955) plunges into a deeply scooped neckline from cutaway narrow straps. A simple innocent gold crucifix from a high-street chain of jewellers is barely visible at the centre of the composition. It is the model's only adornment because she wears little discernible make-up, and her hair is ungroomed, pulled back in a loose ponytail.

2 MASS-MARKET LINGERIE
Kate Moss wears knickers from the popular high-street chain Hennes (now known as H&M), positioned just below the pelvic bone. The see-through animal print chiffon triangle is held in place with a black lace trim. The lingerie was meant to be at the centre of the fashion spread but appears as just one of the elements of the composition, overshadowed by the ambiguous expression of the model and the arrangement of the fairy lights to outline her pose.

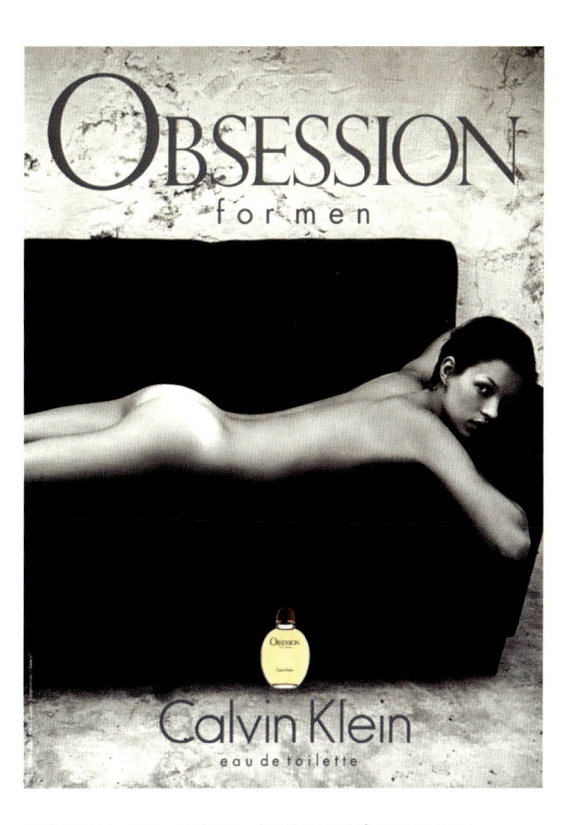

▲ This Calvin Klein perfume advertisement featuring Kate Moss was photographed by Mario Sorrenti (1990s). Sorrenti was part of a group, including Juergen Teller and Ian Rankin, who photographed fashion in an alternative way, using ungroomed models in deliberately down-styled shots.

SUSTAINABLE AND ETHICAL FASHION

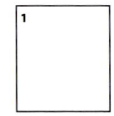

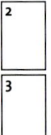

1. Edun shows a draped silk dress with a vibrant tree and zebra print for autumn/winter 2012.

2. The actress Cameron Diaz wears an evening dress made from GOTS-certified (Global Organic Textile Standard) silk by Stella McCartney (2012).

3. This parachute parka by Christopher Raeburn featured in his spring/summer 2013 collection. Every garment bears a 'Remade in England' label.

The success of a fashion label is typically measured against the volume of sales of new products. The obsession with consuming goods has seen a rapid expansion of the 'fast fashion' sector, but this ongoing cycle of buying, wearing and disposing of garments has major implications. Sustainable design—involving the production of garments with minimal harm to the environment and maximized improvements in working conditions—is becoming ever more important. Some designers have been trying to find ways to reduce the negative environmental and ethical impact across the life cycle of a garment. In the early 1990s the industry started to experiment with eco fashion: organic cotton appeared in the mass market but did not fare well with cost-conscious consumers who were fuelling an industry that was producing huge amounts of clothing offshore, with worsening sweatshop conditions. At the same time the market for consumers favouring brands with sound eco

KEY EVENTS

1990	1992	1993	2000	2001	2004
British designer Katharine Hamnett speaks at the United Nations and calls for more eco-responsibility in the fashion industry.	The international fashion retailer Esprit launches its Ecollection line.	The outdoor wear company Patagonia starts to produce fleece garments manufactured from post-consumer waste such as plastic bottles.	Project Alabama is founded by Natalie Chanin and Enrico Marone Cinzano, producing clothes created from sustainable materials.	Stella McCartney launches her fashion label, having previously worked at Chloé. It establishes sustainable fashion as a serious proposition.	The Ethical Fashion Show is launched in Paris, followed by Estethica in London two years later to promote new ethical fashion labels.

credentials, such as Birkenstock, which reuses cork material from the wine industry, continued to grow. Today, an increasing number of brand-conscious consumers are concerned with how clothes are produced.

Mass-market companies such as Marks & Spencer, Patagonia and Nike have responded to these concerns and implemented environmental and ethical strategies. Changing its manufacturing practices, Marks & Spencer has also been re-educating consumers with the 'Look Behind the Label' initiative, providing detailed information on ethically traded products in its displays. Patagonia has been at the forefront of developing a closed-loop, minimal waste system following a mantra of 'reduce, repair, reuse, recycle'. Having produced fleece garments from post-consumer waste from 1993, it began the Common Threads Initiative in 2005, recycling unwanted polyester garments.

Ali Hewson and her husband, U2 lead singer Bono, started their ethical clothing label Edun (opposite) in 2005. It is recognized for its creative design as much as for its mission to improve trade with African countries, such as Uganda and Kenya. All factories undergo biannual audits to ensure that they meet set standards. Creative director Sharon Wauchob describes it as 'more than just a fashion label', viewing the production process as an intrinsic part of the creation. US designer Linda Loudermilk champions organic fibre, and Project Alabama (now Alabama Chanin) produces garments from natural, often recycled fabrics, made by local seamstresses. In Britain, retailer People Tree uses only Fairtrade cotton and has established itself as a fashion-forward brand, also featuring collaborations with designers such as Thakoon Panichgul (b.1974).

Established designer and luxury brands were initially relatively slow to embrace sustainability, but there are exceptions, such as Katharine Hamnett (b.1947) and Stella McCartney (b.1971). McCartney never uses leather or fur, and her collections make use of organic fabric and dyes where possible. In 2012 she launched a range of lingerie made from organic cotton and recycled metal. Her evening dresses (above right) are a popular red-carpet choice with celebrities. British designer Christopher Raeburn (b.1982) is well known for his innovative use of recycled materials, in particular reused camouflage fabric and parkas made from recycled parachutes. He launched his label in 2008, starting with menswear; his first women's collection was shown in 2012, and his parachute parkas have become a staple garment, re-imagined in red for 2013 (right).

London-based Gary Harvey excels at producing couture-inspired garments made from waste materials (see p.488). Known for reconstructing forty-two pairs of Levi's 501s to produce a couture gown, the designer has worked with materials from newspapers to discarded rugby shirts to produce one-off garments that play on the juxtaposition of luxury and the everyday. The Green Carpet Challenge initiated by Livia Firth (see p.488) aims to get big brands more engaged in sustainability and has successfully pushed a number of labels, such as Lanvin, Prada and Valentino, to review their current practices. **AG**

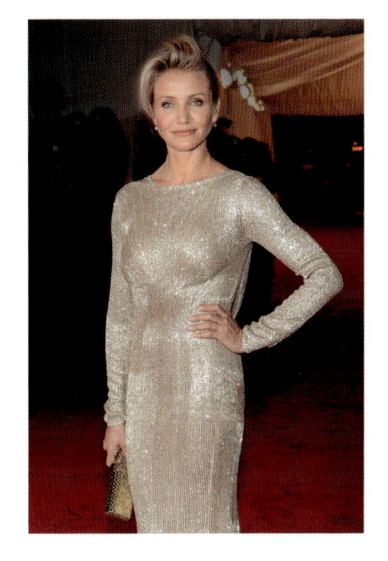

2005	2006	2006	2008	2009	2012
Edun is founded by Ali Hewson and Bono. It aims to position itself as a creative force in fashion while bringing about positive change in Africa.	Marks & Spencer unveils the 'Look Behind the Label' campaign, aiming to raise awareness of environmental issues among customers.	Marks & Spencer announces 'Plan A', detailing the company's environmental and ethical goals over a five-year period.	Christopher Raeburn presents his debut collection, inspired by the challenge of sustainable fashion, featuring reversible recycled garments.	Livia Firth brings eco fashion to red-carpet events for the first time with the Green Carpet Challenge (see p.488).	The Copenhagen Fashion Summit is held to mark the Rio+20 United Nations Sustainable Development conference.

SUSTAINABLE AND ETHICAL FASHION 487

Upcycled Evening Gown 2011
GARY HARVEY

Livia Firth in an upcycled dress at the Academy Awards with her husband, actor Colin Firth (2011).

NAVIGATOR

Livia Firth, film producer and owner of retail store Eco Age, has brought eco fashion to celebrity events such as the Academy Awards, the Venice Film Festival and the Baftas. Since 2009 Firth has regularly worn eco-fashion pieces herself as part of the Green Carpet Challenge, initiated together with British journalist Lucy Siegle. The challenge is designed to raise the profile of eco fashion and has engaged the support of a number of well-known celebrities, including Meryl Streep and Cameron Diaz. Aside from supporting new design talent, Firth has been active in promoting 'green' fashion with established fashion labels, including Gucci and Valentino, which have each produced a garment for the Green Carpet Challenge using recycled or eco-certified materials.

Gary Harvey is known for working with a wide range of unusual waste materials, using the technique of upcycling—adding value to discarded materials through a careful approach to design and decorative details. He produced this upcycled gown for Livia Firth to attend the 83rd Academy Awards event at which her husband, actor Colin Firth, received an Oscar for Best Actor in *The King's Speech* (2010). The material, zips and details were taken from eleven different vintage dresses, which were sourced from charity shops and boutiques across southeast London. The thread for sewing the dress together was the only new material used. Although constructed entirely from recycled materials, the gown was highly appropriate for a red-carpet event. **AG**

FOCAL POINTS

1 CORSET
The dress has a built-in corset, a feature used in many of Harvey's pieces. Constructed from materials recycled from vintage and second-hand dresses, the gown has a romantic appeal, which is emphasized by the use of soft, tonal, neutral hues of colour. The muted colours are inspired by a dress belonging to Firth's grandmother, which had been passed down through the family, and Harvey selected the disused vintage garments for their relevance to the 1930s.

2 JEWELLERY
The dress is accessorized with ethical jewellery by British designer Anna Loucah in collaboration with British jewellery company CRED. Made from Fairtrade and Fairminded gold certified by the Fairtrade Foundation and the Alliance for Responsible Mining, the ring and earrings include traceable aquamarines from a community mine in Zambia, Oro Verde gold from Colombia and diamonds sourced from the Liqhobong Women Miners Cooperative in Lesotho.

▲ The newspaper dress by Gary Harvey, one of the designer's more flamboyant creations from his spring/summer collection of 2008, was made from thirty copies of the *Financial Times*.

SUSTAINABLE AND ETHICAL FASHION

CRAFT RENAISSANCE

1 Sarah Burton's bustier represents the head of a golden owl in an evocation of the goddess Pallas Athena. The illusion of a gilded corn dolly is created by a complex fabrication in metallized threads, galloon braids and bugle beads (2010).

2 Holly Fulton contrasts solid colour with a graphic chequerboard print embellished with crystals, in a seaside theme collection (2012).

3 Olivier Rousteing embellishes a close-fitting white Balmain dress with pearl and crystal embroidery (2012). The intricate patterning recalls the decoration of Fabergé jewelled eggs.

During the 1990s, craft processes began to undergo a global renaissance, driven by the confluence of long-standing craft expertise with the new possibilities of the digital revolution in textile manufacturing, sometimes termed 'haute technology'. The enduring hub of expertise originated in Paris, where craft ateliers operated under the aegis of the Chambre Syndicale de la Haute Couture—an association that reflects the commitment to unbridled luxury that the best of haute couture has demonstrated for more than a hundred years. The haute couture supply chain extended to any niche of manufacturing that afforded exclusive skills and luxury production methods, and its traditions of highly skilled fabrication and embellishment methods have long serviced the habits of conspicuous consumption across the world.

Today advanced technology supports an extraordinarily rich hybridization of techniques, in which the power of digital systems, such as the graphic and

KEY EVENTS

1991	1995	2000	2002	2005	2006
The first digital printer for printing sample patterns directly onto textiles is introduced by Dutch textile manufacturer Stork & Co.	Japanese manufacturer Tajima Inc. develops embroidery machinery with a laser-cutting facility.	Leading knitting-machine manufacturer Shima Seiki ships its 10,000th computer graphic and knitwear design system.	Chanel creates the Paraffection group: it includes Lesage for embroidery, Massaro for shoemaking and Michel for millinery.	Erdem launches his own label; he works from a small studio, where he creates his signature graphic prints in a painstaking series of processes.	Christopher Kane establishes his eponymous label with the support of a New Generation grant from British high-street store Topshop.

490 1990–PRESENT

knitwear design system developed by leading computerized knitting-machine manufacturer Shima Seiki, is harnessed to create complex substrates for the further application of hand-based skills. The principle of taking an elaborate product to a higher level of refinement has led to a resurgence in precious craft expertise. This reverence for craft processes also extends to the prêt-à-porter ranges of designer brands such as Rodarte (see p.492), founded in 2005, whose otherwordly garments are rarely without hand embellishment.

In the 21st century, a number of designers used digital systems to produce textiles that previously would have been impossible to create, and were of such unprecedented complexity that they defined their collections. The digitally engineered exuberance of the prints and embroideries of designers such as Erdem (b.1977; see p.496), Holly Fulton (b.1977) and Mary Katrantzou (b.1983) demonstrated all the refined expertise that would have gained the accolade of a mastercraft in another field. The happy, naive graphics that were printed to the shape of the garment, then further embellished by Fulton, were made additionally playful by the superimposition of solid components (right). The multilayered conceits, realized in fabric and translated into garment form by Sarah Burton (b.1974) for Alexander McQueen, were made more intriguing with natural components. Burton's ability to exploit a surreal vocabulary of sumptuous structures and surfaces—a metallized bodice of faux corn dolly with a skirt of exotic plumes (opposite)—evinced an allegorical impact that would befit a Jacobean masque.

Unabashed in opulence, but less dramatic in imagery, French designer Olivier Rousteing (b.1986), at the couture house of Balmain, took the path of unrestrained surface enrichment to a bejewelled nirvana in his autumn collection of 2012 (below right). Almost outshining his Fabergé inspiration with encrusted pearl embroidery in Baroque formations, he disarmed the impact of formality by offering the heirloom pieces as casual separates rather than as a complete matador's suit of lights. The hand embroidery was at the level of the ceremonial goldwork of court or military regalia, but in the midst of the collection, laser cutting was used to create a leather-perforated filigree, stitched or bonded to contrast leather quilting. The effect had the intensity and delicacy of the work of a silversmith, graphically exact and precisely engineered to the form of the garment, whereas the total was made contemporary and insouciant by the exposed biker-jacket zips.

Similarly, extremist neo-textiles are evidenced in the collections of Scottish designer Christopher Kane (b.1982; see p.494), ranging from coloured liquids encapsulated in gel plastic, bonded on fabrics and edges, to leather that has been comprehensively laser cut into lace. This hunger to find digital and manual fabric-enrichment systems is a market-wide phenomenon. It is a natural expression of the visual saturation of image-driven contemporary culture and Internet commerce, in which the unadorned has become the uninteresting. JA

2007	2007	2008	2009	2010	2011
Rodarte produces a collection inspired by Mexican outworkers; it continues the label's emphasis on hand-worked textiles.	Holly Fulton's postgraduate collection features garments embellished with laser-cut tiles arranged in jewel-like panels.	Erdem presents a luxurious collection of digitally printed floral designs embellished with handmade lace and Swarovski crystals.	Olivier Rousteing joins Balmain after five years at Roberto Cavalli.	Mary Katrantzou collaborates with the Lesage embroidery atelier in Paris to create a collection characterized by *trompe l'oeil* designs.	Shima Seiki exports its 100,000th computerized knitting machine into the overseas market.

CRAFT RENAISSANCE 491

Tulle Dresses 2008
RODARTE

Founders of Rodarte Kate and Laura Mulleavy apply couture-like craftsmanship and a singular vision to their dreamlike and otherworldly, ready-to-wear collections. Their designs are enriched by their experience in the liberal arts and their respective specialisms of art and literature. In the Rodarte autumn collection of 2008 they exercised a potent visual imagination and drew on a complex mix of diverse sources, including both Japan's kabuki traditions and its horror films. The collection was also inspired by the string sculptures of German-born artist Eva Hesse and the traditional ballet costumes depicted by Impressionist painter Edgar Degas.

Dresses of pale tulle are harnessed to the body with twisted ropes of space-dyed chiffon. The fragility of the fabric contrasts with the primitive crudity of the process, giving the appearance of rag dolls with the stuffing coming apart. Barely-there asymmetrical bodices are held in place invisibly by indiscernible back fabric and seem to stand alone. The designers paid great attention to detail and the folds and pleats draped across the bosom are couched with tiny pearls. Filmy textured tutus of layered tulle are caught at the waistline with a drawstring thread that forms a narrow, frayed-edge frill, and the ballerina theme is extended to include tightly drawn-back hair. **MF**

NAVIGATOR

FOCAL POINTS

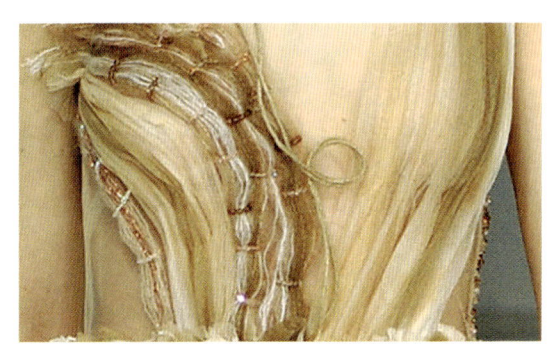

1 WHIP-STITCHED BODICE
Roughly folded and pleated lengths of silk chiffon in various shades of pale tea, apricot and cream curve from the underarm and over the breast to the waist, following the shaping line of the bodice of the dress on the left. These are crudely whip-stitched into place.

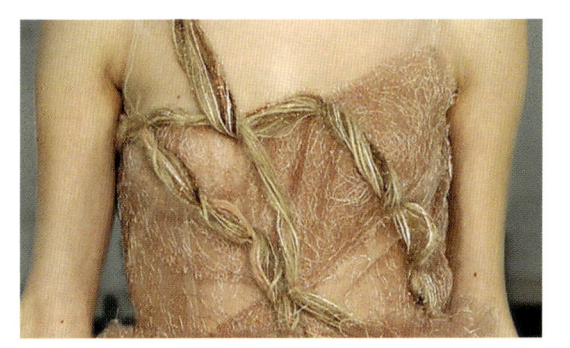

2 BODICE WITH STRAP
The dress on the right has a single asymmetrical strap of coarse twisted fabric, couched with tiny glittering iridescent beads, that gives the appearance of securing the bodice at the centre front, before looping around the body in a seemingly random pattern.

3 DEGAS-INSPIRED TUTU
For the skirt of the dress on the right, layers of fibrous textured fabric burnished with lurex thread are gathered into the waistband to create crisp volume below and a deep upstanding frill above. The edges are left unfinished.

COMPANY PROFILE

2005–07
Having grown up in California and started sketching designs for dresses from an early age, sisters Kate (b.1979) and Laura Mulleavy (b.1980) founded their label in 2005 in Los Angeles. Without any formal training, they studied couture techniques by themselves and put together a first collection of ten hand-finished pieces, which appeared in February 2005 on the cover of *Women's Wear Daily*.

2008–PRESENT
In 2008 the sisters received the Swiss Textiles Award, and became the first women and non-Europeans to achieve this accolade. They designed several of the ballet costumes worn by actress Natalie Portman in the Oscar-winning film *Black Swan* (2010). In 2012 Rodarte collaborated with architect Frank Gehry on the LA Philharmonic's rendition of *Don Giovanni*.

Embroidered Skirt and Knitted Sweater 2012
CHRISTOPHER KANE b. 1982

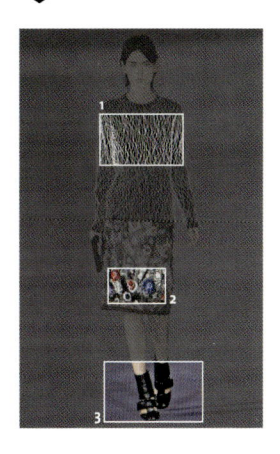

Christopher Kane's autumn collection of 2012 was a cocktail of incongruous ingredients: embroidered and printed leather, plastic floral eruptions, and agitated vertical stripes and geometry, intersected by rotund leather bandings. Beaded into pinstripes, curvy plastic tubes paraded in a flic-flac progression the length of a black cashmere sweater that was fashioned into 'boyfriend' volumes. Kane used the ephemeral quality of plastics in a subtle confrontation with the luxury of classic couture methods and materials to challenge the perverse value system of fashion. Both the pencil skirt and the loose sweater move ponderously from the elaborate superstructure of embroidery.

The complexity of the hand-built fabrics dictates that only essential style lines and minimal detailing are imposed on the garment shapes. The plasticized embroidery canvas of the skirt recalls cross-stitch screens with lacquered frames, creating a dark ground receding under the saturated colours of clematis motifs, bugled with loose beading onto a glossy mesh, reading as perforated leather. The rotund hem binding is echoed in the rectangular border of a billfold clutch that carries a fragment of the embellishment of the skirt. The restraint of gait, from the constriction of the hem, and the bindings and heels of the footwear softly echo Edo culture, from court clothing to quadrate interiors. **JA**

NAVIGATOR

FOCAL POINTS

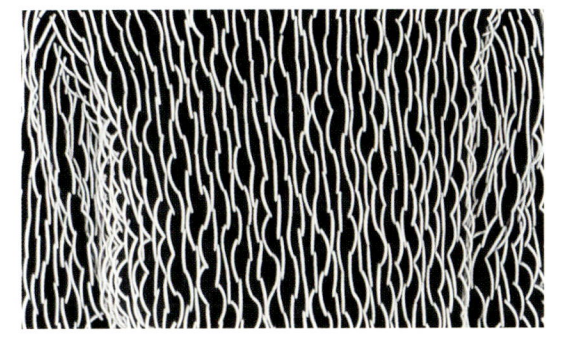

1 SCOTTISH KNITWEAR
Kane's knitwear is produced in the Scottish Borders, a region that is traditionally associated with the manufacture of fully fashioned garments in luxury yarns. The cashmere yarn itself is also sourced in Scotland by Johnsons of Elgin, founded in 1797.

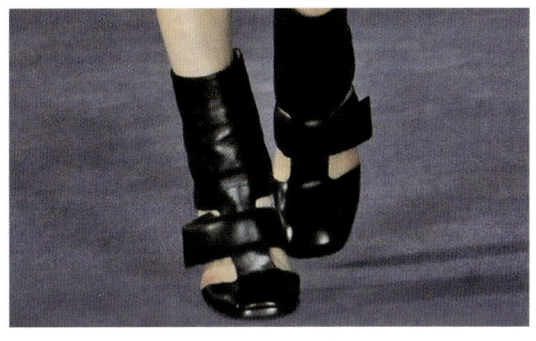

3 HIGH-HEELED BOOTS
High-heeled boots, in padded black kid, are half gladiator sandal and half kick-boxer sparring shoe, encasing the ankle to the lower shin. The glossy geometry recalls Japanese furniture in rotund lacquered bamboo.

DESIGNER PROFILE

1982–2006
Born near Glasgow, Scotland, Christopher Kane has four elder siblings, two of whom are partners in his business. Kane studied fashion design at Central Saint Martins College of Arts and Design in London. In 2006 he secured a window in Harrods department store to show his Masters collection and a contract with Versace to work on the Atelier couture collection.

2007–PRESENT
Having established his own label, Kane launched a body-conscious line in fluorescent bandage dresses that won him Young Designer of the Year at the Scottish Fashion Awards and elevated him to the status of international impact designer, including a diffusion line with Topshop in 2007. The same year he was declared New Designer of the Year at the British Fashion Awards. He won the *Vogue* Fashion Fund prize in 2011.

2 BINCA EMBROIDERY
Needlepoint canvas, sometimes called Binca, provides a perforated grid to give accuracy to traditional embroidery such as Berlin wool work. Kane shuns precision to generate a loose impression of flowers, standing free of the surface in a variety of bugle beads.

Floral Print Dresses 2013
ERDEM

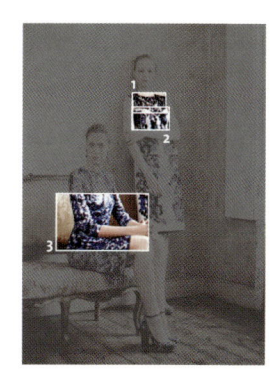

Within the constrained palette of a handful of shades, Erdem conveys a serene femininity that is essentially decorous, without overt fuss. Any subversive gestures are fleeting and demurely implemented: the use of outré neoprene is justified as a fitting substrate because it commands unique sculptural characteristics that naturally maintain a silhouette and carry layered patterning without deformation.

Embellishment follows Erdem's hallmark mantra of Impressionistic floral interpretation. With an all-over print, the three-quarter-sleeved dress has the effect of the tracery of a forest canopy of foliage receding to an open sky of white. The dress holds closely to the contours of the body to the knee, above high-heeled, strapped court shoes in matching fabric print. The easy coordination extends to the three-dimensional re-enactment of the tones and floral forms in tiered earrings, which enjoy clear space above a simple round neckline. In the sleeveless cocktail sheath, there is greater clarity in the plant forms, which are garlanded into a relief cascade of découpé lace and engineered embroidery that runs from the sweetheart yoke line, over the jutting peplum and towards the hem of the pencil skirt. The dark fronds of leaves are applied silhouettes cut from the raschel warp-knit lace of the shoulder and complete a direct coordination of the component fabrics. **JA**

NAVIGATOR

FOCAL POINTS

1 LACE YOKE
The raschel warp-knit lace of the yoke has a long heritage of usage as panel lace in lingerie throughout the post-war period. Contemporary electronic patterning mechanisms now provide a diversity of available designs.

3 DEEPER TONES
Operating within the Claude Monet dogma of building tonality, the tones in the sleeved dress intensify as they progress from background to foreground, passing through cyan to royal, and conclude with the weight of an inky navy at the hem.

COMPANY PROFILE

2004–08
Erdem was established in 2004. Designer Erdem Moralioglu (b.1977) had previously completed work experience with Vivienne Westwood (b.1941), worked for Diane von Furstenberg (b.1946) and studied at the Royal College of Art in London. He won the Fashion Fringe competition in 2005, securing orders with leading fashion retailers such as Harrods, and important celebrity endorsements followed. In 2006 Erdem collaborated with British raincoat manufacturer Mackintosh.

2009–PRESENT
In 2009 Erdem won the Swiss Textiles Award. The same year Erdem collaborated with Cutler and Gross on a range of sunglasses, and with Smythson on luxury stationery. In 2010 Erdem won the inaugural British Fashion Council/ *Vogue* Fashion Fund prize.

2 SWEETHEART NECKLINE
Enjoying a high level of exposure in the prom and red-carpet dress trades, the flattering line of the sweetheart neck is demurely opaque. The embellishment is worked into a mirror image each side of the centre-front seam.

DECONSTRUCTION FASHION

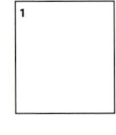

1. In his 'unfinished' see-through blouse from 1995, Martin Margiela deliberately leaves the construction and stitching of the garment visible. In order to focus attention on the actual garments, Margiela often sends models down the catwalk with their faces covered.

2. This dress from Issey Miyake's spring/summer ready-to-wear collection of 1994 is made entirely of pleated material. In turn this is made into a series of 'concertinas', doubling the pleated effect.

Since the 1980s deconstruction fashion has become increasingly common. Deconstruction itself refers to a highly complex and sophisticated critical philosophy associated with the 20th-century French-Algerian philosopher Jacques Derrida. The idea of deconstruction in fashion has resulted from a series of simplifications and misunderstandings of the original philosophy. Many fashion items, techniques and practices—including the styles known as 'deconstruction fashion', 'grunge' and 'destroyed fashion'—have been identified as owing something to deconstruction.

The most important element of deconstruction fashion is to draw attention to the construction of a garment. Traditional and mainstream fashion can be understood as the construction and consumption of complete, finished and conventional clothing. Deconstruction fashion, however, should emphasize the unfinished nature of a garment, the parts of the items of

KEY EVENTS

1993	1994	1995	1995	1996	1996
Issey Miyake launches his first Pleats Please collection. Cut and sewn from one piece of fabric, the garments are fed into a heat press to create pleats.	With an aesthetic labelled 'stealth utility', Vexed Generation is founded in London by Adam Thorpe (b.1969) and Joe Hunter (b.1967).	The Vexed Parka is seen at Vexed Generation's first show. Made from tough nylon, it is padded to protect the wearer.	Hussein Chalayan wins the Absolut Fashion Design award. Singer Björk wears a jacket designed by him on the cover of her third album, *Post*.	Alexander McQueen is named British Designer of the Year for the first time; he wins the title again in 1997, 2001 and 2003.	Belgian designer Ann Demeulemeester launches her first menswear line.

clothing that make up complete garments and the undoing or playful testing of these conventions. Deconstruction fashion aims to display the features that conventionally remain hidden: the darts, tacking stitches, linings and other infrastructure that make the garment possible but are not usually on show. The work of Belgian designer Ann Demeulemeester (b.1959) in the 1990s with tank tops and T-shirts exemplified deconstruction in that it drew the eye to the seams; the garments were twisted almost completely out of shape and their surfaces distressed. The resulting garments looked as though they had been damaged and repaired wrongly or badly, which highlighted the fact that they had been constructed in the first place.

Alexander McQueen (1969–2010) showed some sympathy with this aspect of deconstruction fashion when he was reported as saying that he spent a lot of time learning how to construct garments, because this was necessary to show how they might be deconstructed. Martin Margiela (b.1957) is renowned for this type of deconstruction fashion and frequently displays seams and linings in his designs (opposite). The taking-apart of garments and showing how they are put together can also be seen in the work of Turkish-born, London-based designer Hussein Chalayan (b.1970), such as the Afterwords collection in 2000 (see p.504). Issey Miyake (b.1938) frequently makes use of new fabric technology with elements of deconstruction in his designs and has shown a continuing interest in experiments with pleats (right).

Derrida's writing may also have influenced the use of *bricolage* in fashion—a term often used in the visual arts to refer to a work created from a diverse range of available materials. In an essay about the anthropologist Claude Lévi-Strauss, Derrida claimed that even the man of science, the engineer, was a *bricoleur*. He described the *bricoleur* as a kind of handyman or odd-job man, who used whatever tools, techniques and materials he had, rather than those that tradition would deem to be 'correct'. This idea also relates to recycling because the *bricoleur* will use old or existing items. The use of objects for purposes for which they were not originally intended can be described as recycling or transposition. Margiela's work is sometimes described as *bricolage* or recycling. When he uses socks for sleeves or transposes leather gloves to make a halter waistcoat, he is using whatever he can lay his hands on, rather than going to the trouble of procuring specialist materials and predictable elements.

Decomposition and disintegration are themes that have also been identified as characteristics of deconstruction fashion. Originating from a literal interpretation of Derrida's philosophy, the themes relate to the ways in which designers use the look or appearance of garments as falling apart or decomposing. Derrida said that deconstruction is not a method that can be controlled and applied; it is rather something that happens to ideas, arguments or identities. In fashion this becomes a look that evidences a process, such

1997	1999	1999	1999	2002	2002
Martin Margiela is appointed creative director of women's ready-to-wear at Hermès.	Issey Miyake and Dai Fujiwara's A-POC system (see p.502), made of pre-constructed garments within a single roll of fabric, is launched.	Yohji Yamamoto launches his ground-breaking Wedding collection.	Ann Demeulemeester launches her eponymous shop in Antwerp, Belgium.	Concept boutique 10 Corso Como de Tokyo opens. It is a collaboration between publisher Carla Sozzani and Comme des Garçons.	Hussein Chalayan's Medea dress reveals its construction: the shape of the dress can be changed by closing or opening its zips.

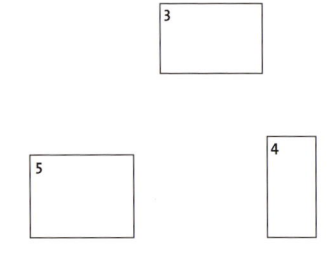

3 The slightly distressed appearance of the wavy pattern in this woven textile by NUNO from 1997 is characteristic of deconstruction fashion. It is produced by the 'rippling' of the reeds in a traditional Japanese loom.

4 Layering different weights and colours of cloth highlights the construction of different parts of this dress from 1998 by Rei Kawakubo for Comme des Garçons. Each element is articulated and picked out in a different shade.

5 Recycled materials and hand-applied patches combine to produce the complex appearance of a dress from the Xuly Bët ready-to-wear spring/summer collection in 1999.

as ageing or corruption, that has caused the garment to unravel or fall to pieces. In 1993, while studying at London's Central Saint Martins College of Art and Design, Hussein Chalayan buried a number of dresses together with iron filings; when they were retrieved for his resulting graduation show, the garments bore all the evidence of decomposition. British designer Shelley Fox (b.1967) uses labour-intensive, pre-industrial techniques such as felting to produce a distressed surface. The process is usually achieved accidentally and is the result of subjecting lambswool to high temperatures and friction, creating a shrunken and solid texture. The designer challenges the precepts of good taste when she degrades the surface of the classic twinset with candle wax, paint or bleach. Similarly, Mali-born Lamine Badian Kouyaté (b.1962) patched, overlocked and embroidered over recycled sweaters for his Xuly Bët line (below). Kouyaté's work is regarded as deconstruction fashion because patching and embroidering over an existing garment is similar to what Derrida described as the 'palimpsest'—a text that has been erased and written over again. Kouyaté's use of recycled sweaters is also a similar process to *bricolage*. The impulse is deconstructive because fashion is not usually thought of as creating something that is being reworked or that has been done before.

The way in which the perfection and repetitive nature of machine-made clothing eventually falls apart and decomposes was first shown in the 'lace' sweater produced by Rei Kawakubo (b.1942) for Comme des Garçons in 1983. It emphasized the imperfections of all garments, but it made a point in particular about handmade items: the garment was not handmade but a hand-crafted look or effect was achieved, according to Kawakubo, by loosening a screw or two on the machine that made the textiles. This resulted in the blurring of the distinction between machine-made, repeatable perfection and the one-off, handmade item, with its inevitable idiosyncrasies. The layers of the dress from the 1998 collection (opposite below) draw attention to how the garment itself was made.

Kawakubo is also known for the aesthetic of *boro boro*, which translates best from the Japanese as 'worn out'. She produces clothing that looks already worn in, and in some cases worn out, by ironing permanent creases into some fabrics and pre-distressing others. Her collaboration with the NUNO Corporation—a global leader in experimental fashion and interior textiles, founded in 1984 by Jun'ichi Arai (b.1932) and Reiko Sudo (b.1953) — has seen the production of highly technical, machine-made textiles that involve weaving tears and holes into felts, or burning away with acid one of the yarns in fabrics made from two yarns to create a destroyed look (above). One of the most significant figures in textile innovation, Jun'ichi Arai, has over the last five decades combined traditional weaving techniques with advanced textile technology, and applied his ingenuity to fabrics for all the major Japanese fashion designers, such as Issey Miyake and Comme des Garçons. Japanese designer Yohji Yamamoto (b.1943) deploys the qualities of various yarns to produce deliberately twisted seams and asymmetrical shapes.

The ploy of playing with and subverting the conventions that govern the production and consumption of fashion is another widespread expression of deconstruction. Derrida repeatedly stated that using the concepts and grammar of language to deconstruct or critique language is unavoidable. This notion also informs deconstruction fashion: designers have no choice but to utilize the existing elements and conventions of fashion in order to subvert them. There are, for example, customs or cultural rules about when and where to display underwear. There are also conventions about the aesthetics of what is worn. High-street fashion demands that shirts have one identically sized collar and evenly spaced buttons, because that is what 'correct' dress requires. Comme des Garçons subverted this notion with the creation of a shirt with two collars and with irregularly spaced and differently sized buttons for its Shirt range in 1988.

The idea of the spectral or the ghostly is an aspect of Derrida's philosophy that has been relatively neglected within fashion deconstruction. Derrida insisted that whatever identity, presence and meaning we experience, it is only meaningful in relation to the idea of radical absence — or death. Margiela's work can be described as 'ghostly' in that his designs are sometimes constructed from older garments, wigs, scarves or gloves that 'haunt' the new pieces. In this sense the condition of the 'living' garment is defined by the 'presence' of the 'dead' ones. Margiela's spring/summer 2008 collection featured skirts and jeans made of shredded denim that were more hole than actual garment. He also transplanted accessories into the clothes themselves, such as a shoulder bag stitched into the armpit of a dress. It could almost be said that all fashion is ultimately deconstructed because all garments are defined by 'the absent' — what has not been used in their design being of as much importance as what has been. **MB**

A-POC 1997
ISSEY MIYAKE b. 1938

A-POC at the exhibition 'Future Beauty: Thirty Years of Japanese Fashion' at the Barbican, London (2011).

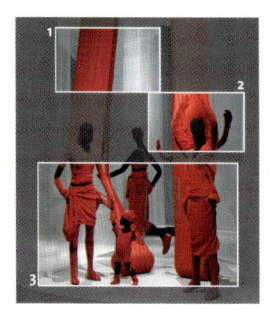

NAVIGATOR

The A-POC concept—an acronym for 'A Piece of Cloth'—was developed in 1997 by Issey Miyake in conjunction with textile engineer Dai Fujiwara (b.1948), although it was initially shown in knitted cotton and linen stripes in 1976. A-POC is a system of dressing created from one piece of cloth, with no waste and a minimum of cutting, much like the kimono. With later developments of the system the bolt of cloth was constructed from a raschel-knit tube: the stocking-like tube is made of double-knit fabric, the yarns of which are linked in a fine mesh of chain stitches. If the fabric is cut, the stretchier fibres in the bottom layer shrink, thus tightening the chain-stitch mesh and preventing the fabric from unravelling. The cloth is inscribed with pattern pieces that do not require stitching when cut out and can be adjusted by the wearer. The date that each A-POC was knitted and the adjustment instructions are attached to the cloth, as is a tiny pair of scissors. The system has undergone various refinements and developments over time: in 1999 the A-POC Eskimo included graphic patterning and padding, whereas the Baguette design of 2000 relinquished pattern pieces and could be cut anywhere in the piece of fabric. This manner of providing garments reintroduces elements of the craft of clothes-making to contemporary fashion production and consumption. The involvement of the consumer in the production of their own garments represents a unique marriage of traditional and non-traditional practices. **MB**

👁 FOCAL POINTS

1 FABRIC
The A-POC garments are cut from one long roll of tubed cloth. The fabric is the product of a complex, computer-driven industrial loom that weaves the shape and pattern of entire garments within the cloth. The customer simply cuts the 'cloth' to suit their own individual size, thus shaping the final garment they wear.

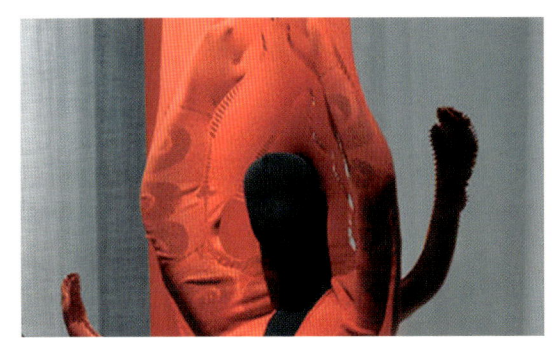

2 TUBE OF CLOTH
The garments are constructed from the tube of cloth and do not require stitching. The process is sophisticated enough that items as complex and different as left-handed and right-handed gloves, as well as relatively simple sleeves, can all be cut from the tube and successfully produced as garments.

3 VERSATILE GARMENTS
The different-sized mannequins demonstrate the versatility of the roll of fabric and the garments that can be constructed from it. Options include a three-quarter dress, with short or long sleeves, leggings and a drawstring bag, or a child's tunic dress with hat, gloves and socks.

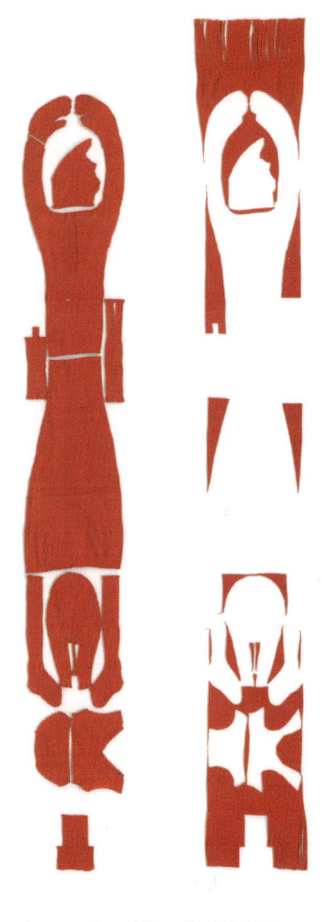

▲ The outlines of garments cut from the A-POC Queen Textile (1997), including a dress, socks, underwear and a hood. This economical system leaves behind very little waste fabric.

🕐 DESIGNER PROFILE

1938–80
Issey Miyake was born in Hiroshima, Japan, and survived the atomic bomb attack in 1945. He studied graphic design in Tokyo and graduated in 1964, later working in New York and Paris. He returned to Tokyo in 1970, where he established the Miyake Design Studio, creating women's fashion and adopting new fabrics such as polyester jersey and the acrylic knit Pewlon. In 1980, inspired by the tailor's dummy, Miyake developed the cast-acrylic torso as a bustier.

1981–PRESENT
In the late 1980s Miyake started experimenting with pleating, which resulted in a new technique (Pleats Please); he also designed costumes for the Frankfurt Ballet. Miyake retired in 1997 and reduced his role within the company to research projects. In 2010 he was awarded Japan's Order of Culture by Emperor Akihito.

DECONSTRUCTION FASHION 503

Afterwords 2000
HUSSEIN CHALAYAN b. 1970

Afterwords autumn/winter ready-to-wear
collection at Sadler's Wells Theatre, London (2000).

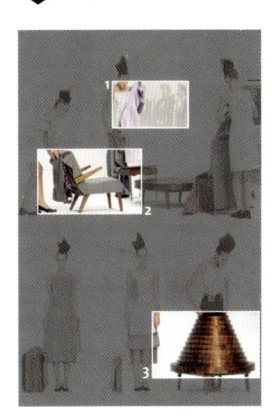

Hussein Chalayan is respected for his intensely cerebral approach to design. His work is embedded with deconstructed and hybridized cultural references that are harnessed to diverse effects, ranging from the aesthetic to the didactic. The Afterwords collection takes inspiration from the plight of refugees who have to flee their homes with no more than what they wear or can carry. Chalayan's own family were displaced following the partition of Cyprus in 1974, when a quarter of a million Turkish and Greek Cypriots were uprooted. The collection is a visual exploration of the instinct to create a locus of residual identity for the displaced. This often lies in the possessions of dress and furniture retained in their flight, which act as a reliquary of their dislocated narrative.

Chalayan presented his collection in a stark interior set at Sadler's Wells Theatre, London, in 2000. The models appeared in garments of evolving complexity. The emblematic drama intensified as fabric loose covers metamorphosed into serenely engineered tunic dresses and the frames of the chairs inverted into suitcases. In a final *coup de théâtre* a model entered wearing a simple petticoat skirt below a ruffled blouse. She withdrew a central circular panel from the table into which she stepped, locating two hidden handles that enabled her to raise the stepped telescopic panels of a wooden A-line skirt. **MB**

NAVIGATOR

FOCAL POINTS

1 TELEVISION SCREEN
The stark stage setting is lightened by the presence of a large plasma television screen on which a group of a cappella singers, in traditional Kosovan costume, are seen singing. The Kosovo War in 1999 resulted in thousands of homeless refugees.

3 TABLE SKIRT
The skirt becomes a table when it is lowered from the model's hips to the ground. Not to be left naked, she wears another skirt beneath, in what some would see as typical deconstructive fashion, negating the purpose of the skirt in the first place.

2 CHAIR SUITCASE
What appears to be an ordinary chair folds up to look like a suitcase. However, it folds to contain nothing but itself. This may be a metaphor for the self-regarding and empty nature of some so-called deconstructive fashion.

DESIGNER PROFILE

1970–97
Hussein Chalayan was born in Cyprus and attended the Turkish Educational College in Nicosia. Following the Cypriot crisis of 1974, the family moved to England in 1978 and settled in London in 1982. Chalayan studied fashion design at Central Saint Martins College of Arts and Design, and graduated in 1993. In 1995 he designed clothes for the cover of Björk's third album, *Post*, and for the resulting tour.

1998–PRESENT
From 1998 to 2001 Chalayan fronted the New York cashmere knit label TSE. He was awarded British Fashion Council Designer of the Year twice, in 1999 and 2000. In 2001 he was appointed fashion director of the British luxury jewellers Asprey, and in 2008 he worked with Swarovski and produced a dress covered with its signature crystals and LED lights.

JAPANESE STREET CULTURE

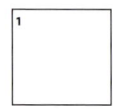

1. Two Ganguro girls with requisite white eye make-up, face stickers, neon accessories and tanned skin pose for a photograph on the streets of Tokyo.

2. This Gothic Lolita outfit is a sweet but provocatively playful adaptation of the Victorian doll aesthetic; it includes a black mini crinoline, demure blouse, alarm-clock handbag and a headpiece placed on a cartoonlike wig.

Japanese street fashion is led primarily by high-school girls who have become extremely influential in controlling style trends. Japanese youth subcultures are also often female-dominant and always geographically defined, as the securing of territory reinforces adolescent identity and a feeling of empowerment. These teenage girls as the agents of fashion change participate in the production and dissemination of street cultures and fashion that emerge from social networks and subcultures. During the mid 1990s this phenomenon was based around the landmark Shibuya 109 building in Tokyo, an eight-floor shopping centre. Originally defined as *kogyaru*, or high-school girl style, it was characterized by pastiche school uniforms in the form of short plaid skirts or pinafore dresses, white socks and demure blouses with Peter Pan collars. Shibuya style has evolved into many subcultures but the main concepts of *ero-kawaii* (erotic and cute) and *kowa-kawaii* (scary and cute) remain.

One of the first fashion subcultures to come out of the Shibuya district was Ganguro (black face), characterized by faces tanned dark by sunbeds or make-up, heavy white eye make-up and bleached hair (above). The style is a rebellious statement against the traditional pale skin and black hair valued by

KEY EVENTS

Early 1990s	Early 1990s	1995	1995	1998	Late 1990s
Ganguro appears as a new style among young women in Japan.	The Japanese girl band Princess Princess influences street fashion; band members wear elaborate costumes.	The fashion brand 6%DOKIDOKI is founded by Sebastian Masuda, marking the beginning of *decora* (use of colour and many accessories).	In Tokyo, Shibuya 109 changes all of its tenants to retailers that sell Shibuya fashion only. Ganguro begins to appear in the Shibuya district.	The Yamamba (mountain witch) style, with heavier and intense make-up, begins to emerge in Shibuya to replace Ganguro.	Gothic Lolita groups begin to appear on a bridge near Harajuku Station in the Shibuya district.

506 1990–PRESENT

Japanese culture and mimics the 'California girl' look. The girls wear bright neon colours, short skirts and high platform shoes in order to appear intimidating, which is an important element of their style. Extreme practitioners of Ganguro style, in which the face is made cartoonishly dark and accompanied by white lips, with sequins stuck to the face and voluminous hair extensions, have more recently become known as Yamamba (or Mamba, or Bamba for short), named after the folklore character of the white-haired crone. These groups are subdivided into smaller groups, depending on their chosen fashion brand: for example, the Egoist boutique in Shibuya is known for its Yamamba styles and for popularizing mini trends such as 'rodeo girl' and 'sexy and boyish'.

For those girls for whom Ganguro style feels too provocative and sexualized, there is the Lolita subculture, based in Tokyo's Harajuku district. This subculture appeared in the 1990s in opposition to Shibuya, and it is one of the most enduring and popular Japanese styles overseas. Although the term 'Lolita' carries a sexual connotation in the West, in reference to Vladimir Nabokov's novel of the same name, members of the Japanese subculture claim the opposite to be true. They portray an innocent and feminine image of a Victorian doll, wearing dresses with frills and lace trimmings, bonnets and sometimes blonde wigs, accessorized with colourful *kawaii* (cute) handbags and umbrellas. Mary Jane shoes and beribboned hair ornaments in ice-cream colours add to the twee image. Lolitas are subdivided into different subgroups and each group has its own stylistic characteristics. Sweet Lolita is a style in pastel colours only (see p.508), while Punk Lolita includes punk elements such as chains and safety pins—a Westernized version of this look was created by Vivienne Westwood (b.1941) for Gwen Stefani's 'Harajuku Girls' tour in 2004. Wa-Lolita is styled with traditional Japanese and kimono elements. Gothic Lolita (right) wears a combination of Lolita and Gothic elements, as the look is a direct descendant of the British 1980s Goth scene, encapsulating Victorian funereal chic with a short version of the bell-shaped crinoline with underpinning frame.

Akihabara and Ikebukuro are districts in Tokyo that attract anime and manga fans, thereby making up another distinct subcultural community. Akihabara used to be known as a shopping area for electronics and computer games, but in 2000 the anime and manga cartoon trends emerged out of these games and Akihabara began to appeal to *otaku* (nerds) and cosplay (costume play) fans. This look is based not only on wearing T-shirts depicting the characters, but also dressing up as the characters themselves, adopting the shapes, silhouettes and proportions of anime characters and wearing fabrics that mimic the plastic qualities of the cartoon figures. These can be customized garments or clothing bought from high-end labels, including Wut Berlin, Jenny Fax and Junya Suzuki, who show their collections at Tokyo Fashion Week. Other labels take the anime aesthetic and reference the extreme shapes and colours without being actual pastiches of the character outfits. **EA/YK**

1999	2000	2001	2002	2004	2010
The Gothic Lolita fashion label Moi-même-moitié is founded by musician and designer Mana.	The anime and manga trend emerges out of computer games, and the Akihabara district in Tokyo begins to attract *otaku* (nerds).	*FRUiTS: Tokyo Street Style*, a photography book by Shoichi Aoki of Japanese youth in Harajuku, is published in Britain.	The photography exhibition 'FRUiTS' opens at the Powerhouse Museum in Sydney, Australia.	US singer Gwen Stefani's 'Harajuku Girls' tour features Punk Lolita elements.	6%DOKIDOKI celebrates its fifteenth anniversary with the Harajuku Fashion Walk, a street fashion event.

Sweet Lolita 1990s
STREET STYLE

1 PARASOLS
Victorian ladies carried parasols to protect their delicate complexions from the sun and, unlike Ganguro, Lolita embraces the pale-skinned traditions of Japanese culture. The parasol also provides more opportunity for embellishment.

2 HEADPIECES
An essential part of the Lolita style is the headpiece, worn here in white or black by all four girls. The stiff bow on a headband sits atop the characteristic fringed pink wig, which accentuates the doll-like image.

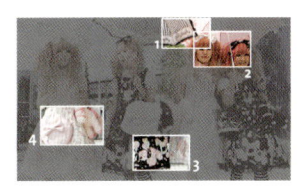

Girls dressed in the Sweet Lolita style pictured outside the Individual Fashion Expo IV, Tokyo (2008).

NAVIGATOR

These four girls, photographed outside the Individual Fashion Expo IV, one of Japan's popular fashion events, are shown wearing variations of the Sweet Lolita style, which is one of the earliest Japanese street styles. Following in the tradition of the demure Japanese geisha, it is a style that is mostly influenced by Victorian young girls' clothing, with an added Japanese 'cute kitsch' twist. The pastel colours, prim necklines and cupcake aesthetic of Sweet Lolita make it one of the most instantly recognizable of the Japanese street-style genres. The key component of the look is the silhouette: clothes invariably comprise a short baby-doll skirt, made fuller by several petticoat layers or a wire frame in a pastiche of a Victorian bell-shaped crinoline. The shortness of the skirt is generally emphasized by thigh-high socks or stockings combined with high heels, although these are usually Mary Janes or Victorian boots rather than stilettos. The use of colour is an integral part of the whole look, and pink is the most important colour in the soft-hued palette, which may also include mauve and mint green. The use of pink is even extended to the hair, and girls usually wear coloured wigs with a prominent fringe. Candy-striped tights, embellished parasols and oversized hair bows all contribute to the look of a life-size Victorian doll. Accessories often make reference to Lewis Carroll's Victorian children's book *Alice's Adventures in Wonderland* (1865). The girls pictured here have deliberately contrived to appear as identically dressed pairs in order to emphasize their group identity and create a cohesive aesthetic. **EA**

3 COLOURS
Soft pastel shades characterize the look; they are chosen for their sweetness and association with childhood innocence, and are combined here with black and white for greater impact. The colour scheme extends to the hair and accessories.

4 HANDBAGS
The handbags match the dresses in tone. Some are decorated with a feminine bow, echoing those on the dresses and headbands; others are horse-shaped, resembling toys and emphasizing the playful, childlike quality of the style.

MODERN COUTURE

A radical shift in the way that couture is perceived occurred at the end of the 20th century, when Bernard Arnault of the powerful LVMH (Louis Vuitton Moët Hennessy) French luxury goods conglomerate invited British designer John Galliano (b.1960) to head the couture house Givenchy in 1995, followed by the prestigious House of Dior in 1996. Harnessing the potency of fresh media exposure to establishment brands, this initiative was a timely response to the market penetration of newer—often US—designer labels that had been brand managed into high visibility and profitability. Once again, haute couture enjoyed contemporary relevance and became a hotbed of ideas, led by a number of young innovative designers who were keen to exploit the skills of the atelier while respecting the heritage of the couture house. Importantly these designers were also at pains to place their own mark on the identity of the label. By the beginning of the new century, haute couture had caught the attention of a younger, edgier clientele and was once again established as the modern epitome of excellence, confirmed with the

KEY EVENTS

1996	1996	1996	1998	2000	2001
Alexander McQueen receives the British Designer of the Year Award, and again in 1997, 2001 and 2003. He receives a CBE in 2003.	LVMH moves John Galliano to Christian Dior, where he remains as creative director until his dismissal in 2011.	Alber Elbaz moves to Paris to head the couture house Guy Laroche.	Elbaz is appointed as head of ready-to-wear at Yves Saint Laurent. Three collections later Elbaz is ousted when the Gucci group takes over the label.	Hedi Slimane introduces his new skinny silhouette and leaves Yves Saint Laurent to accept a role at the helm of Christian Dior's menswear line.	Shaw-Lan Wang, a Chinese publishing magnate, buys a controlling interest in Lanvin, appointing Elbaz as artistic director of the house.

celebration of the sixtieth anniversary of Dior's New Look in 2007, and in 2008, the twenty-fifth anniversary of the arrival of Karl Lagerfeld (b.1933) at Chanel.

Eager to participate in the newly reinforced elevation of couture, other design houses engaged in the dynamics of the growing phenomenon of 'designer mobility'. A designer's career trajectory customarily includes multiple appointments with individual houses and labels. Moroccan-born Alber Elbaz (b.1961) spent several years with US designer Geoffrey Beene (1924–2004) before moving to Paris to head the couture house Guy Laroche (1921–89), followed by a brief period as head of ready-to-wear at Yves Saint Laurent in 1998. Elbaz subsequently assumed his post as artistic director of Lanvin in 2001; since that point he has been one of the most coveted designers of the new millennium. Offering a refined glamour that hinges on the flattery of the female figure with cloth and cut, executed with assuredness and technical bravura, Elbaz is renowned for 'goddess' dresses, lightweight trench coats (now a Lanvin signature garment) and ruffled gowns in opulent fabrics (opposite). The company is small compared to the size of its reputation and influence, and allows Elbaz responsibility for every detail of the label. In 2005 Elbaz appointed Lucas Ossendrijver (b.1970) as head menswear designer (see p.514); he had previously worked with Hedi Slimane (b.1968) at Dior Homme.

One of the most expensive and directional labels in fashion, French fashion house Balmain entered a new era in 2005 under the creative control of Christophe Decarnin (b.1964). He elevated the brand to cult status and Balmain became the most exclusive purveyor of rock-chick style (right), raising the price ceiling on a pair of ripped jeans to US$2,165 in 2009. With a collection that showcased the skinny sleeve and sharp shoulder on military-style jackets and the fringed cowboy boot, Balmain exemplified modern couture for the 21st century.

Creative designers are constantly involved in a serious game of fashion musical chairs. Destabilized by a vector of change—falling sales, burn-out, incompatibility with the heritage style of the house, bad reviews from the fashion press or simply the desire to chase the next big 'prize'—designers move on with relentless regularity. A vacancy at the head of a couture house undoubtedly results in pages of speculation in the fashion press. British designer Sarah Burton (b.1974), long-time assistant of Alexander McQueen (1969–2010), continues the aesthetic of her mentor (see p.516). Similarly Italian design duo Pierpaolo Piccioli (b.1967) and Maria Grazia Chiuri (b.1964) have taken over the helm at revered Italian couture house Valentino (see p.512) and continue its founder's signature elegance. After John Galliano's dismissal from the house of Dior in 2011, the post remained empty for two seasons until Raf Simons (b.1968) was appointed creative director. His disciplined, highly edited, reductive style is in profound contrast to the ebullient fantasy of Galliano, and is considered more appropriate for the modern aesthetic of less-is-more luxury that is prevalent in the second decade of the century. **MF**

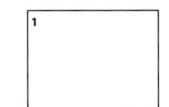

1 The collection of 2012 by Alber Elbaz for Lanvin featured his signature ruffles and fluid drapery.

2 Christophe Decarnin dresses up Balmain's rock-chick look with crystal frogging on the jacket and diamanté-embellished sandals (2009).

2002	2004	2004	2011	2012	2012
Yves Saint Laurent retires. The couture house closes but the brand continues.	After disputes with Gucci's owners, PPR SA, Tom Ford (b.1961) is replaced at Yves Saint Laurent by Stefano Pilati (b.1965).	British designer Julien Macdonald (b.1972) heads the couture house of Givenchy; he is replaced by Italian-born Riccardo Tisci (b.1974) from 2005.	Christophe Decarnin leaves Balmain. French-born Olivier Rousteing (b.1986) is appointed overall creative director in his place.	Nicolas Ghesquière (b.1971) is replaced by New Yorker Alexander Wang (b.1983) after fifteen years at couture house Balenciaga.	Hedi Slimane returns as creative designer at Yves Saint Laurent, changing the name of the brand to Saint Laurent Paris.

Red Dresses 2008
VALENTINO

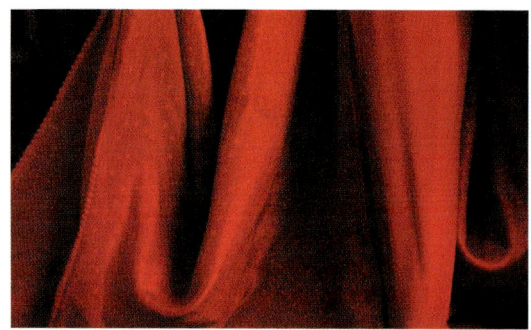

1 TRADEMARK RED
The patented crimson colour (the formula is 100 parts magenta, 100 parts yellow, 10 parts black) was first seen as a cocktail dress in the designer's debut collection of 1959. It remains a consistent element of the Valentino label.

2 SCULPTURED BODICE
Tailoring is represented by the dramatic 'crumb-catcher' bodice, so-called because it is sculpted to extend beyond the line of the breasts. It is filled with one of Valentino's signature bows, in this instance oversized and black.

A film poster for the documentary *Valentino: The Last Emperor*, directed by Matt Tyrnauer (2008).

NAVIGATOR

Taken from the documentary *Valentino: The Last Emperor* (2008), which celebrates forty-five years of the life and work of the internationally renowned Italian designer Valentino, this image resonates with a timeless glamour that is rooted in classic couture and Italian femininity. The models are posed against a spectacular background of Roman antiquities in a variety of red dresses. Shown on the catwalk in Paris in 2007, Valentino's valedictory collection featured thirty models wearing various designs in *rosso Valentino* (Valentino red), his trademark colour from the very beginning of the fashion house. He was one of the last designers to completely handcraft couture—his assistants reportedly never touched a sewing machine—and the gowns exemplify couture attention to detail in luxurious and opulent fabrics.

The designs seen here reference half a century of changing styles, from Valentino's mid-century foray into fashion onwards. All the signature Valentino hallmarks are represented, from the strapless gown featuring a peplum bodice and flat bow at the waist, worn by a model assuming the 'Dior slouch', to the contemporary columnar, full-length strapless sheath dress (far left) with its extended train. The short trapeze-line dress, with its deep double flounce at the hem and integrated cape, acknowledges the youthfulness of the 1960s aesthetic; whereas the sensuous form-fitting evening gown with the horizontally ruched bodice above an ankle-length, two-tiered skirt, with wide, flat bows placed at the neck and hip, evidences the strong-shouldered silhouette of the 1980s. Immaculate tailoring and consideration of proportion and scale are consistently the basis for overt decoration. **MF**

3 ASYMMETRICAL GLAMOUR
The dress on the far right exemplifies Valentino's frou-frou style, with scalloped frills decorating the layers of the skirt, and the half-bustier bodice with a wrap closure ending in a bow at the waist. Valentino is also a leading exponent of one-shouldered glamour.

▲ Former accessory designers for the label Pierpaolo Piccioli and Maria Grazia Chiuri continue the heritage of the Valentino couture house with an extremely feminine spring/summer 2012 collection.

MODERN COUTURE

Two-Piece Suit 2008
LUCAS OSSENDRIJVER b. 1970 (FOR LANVIN)

Head of the menswear division at Lanvin, Lucas Ossendrijver creates a monochrome interplay of luxury layers and proportions in this contemporary version of the two-piece suit. The designer shuffles the pack of familiar menswear touchstones in a celebration of classic elements of the masculine wardrobe, which are then set at odds with the informality of schoolboy dishevelment. The severe palette and rescaled garments evoke a memory of the comic heroes from silent film: the tight jacket characteristically worn by Charlie Chaplin and the oversized sweaters of Jackie Coogan in *The Kid* (1921).

The deliberately undersized jacket, both in width and length, has a soft, unpadded rounded shoulder line and narrow sleeves that emphasize the ingénue quality of the outfit. At the neckline there is a fleeting reappearance of the knit as a slender band of contrast within the close frame of the revered gorge of the jacket. In reference to the gym, the rib-cuffed sweatsuit pants, in sober black, feature a dropped crotch that further elongates the torso, adding to the impression of intentional ungainliness. The composition is finished off with undiluted ingredients of foppish refinement from the morning suit; a shark-skin back collar abuts an opulent boutonnière of burgundy clematis. **MF**

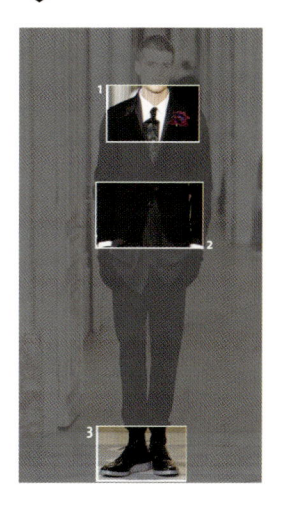

NAVIGATOR

FOCAL POINTS

1 COLLAR AND NECKTIE
Over a pristine white shirt with a cutaway collar on a small stand, the soft-structured broad blade of a patterned necktie is clipped high under a simple four-in-hand schoolboy knot. The crispness of the collar is matched by the cuffs extending beyond the jacket sleeves.

2 SHRUNKEN JACKET
The constricting tailored jacket strains to meet across the torso and only two of the three buttons are fastened. The fullness of a flannel-grey oversized cardigan expansively escapes below the jacket's raised hemline.

3 PLATFORM FOOTWEAR
The superstructure of a black patent evening shoe with front lacing is built on a foundation wedge of contrast rubber that references the trainer sole and utility wear, and discards the notion of traditional footwear to accompany a suit.

DESIGNER PROFILE

1970–95
Lucas Ossendrijver was born in Amersfoort, a small city near Amsterdam, and attended the Fashion Institute in Arnhem. Together with his fellow classmates Viktor Hosting (b.1969) and Rolf Snoeren (b.1969)—later Viktor & Rolf—he formed the collective Le Cri Néerlandais with the intention of creating a new fashion paradigm.

1996–PRESENT
Shortly after moving to Paris in 1996 and a brief spell at womenswear brand Plein Sud, Ossendrijver worked at Kenzo before moving to Munich to take up the position of men's design director for Kostas Murkudis. Less than a year later, he returned to Paris and worked at Dior as assistant to Hedi Slimane. In 2005 Alber Elbaz, the creative director at Lanvin, hired Ossendrijver as the designer for the menswear division.

Ice Queen Dress 2011
SARAH BURTON b. 1974 (FOR ALEXANDER MCQUEEN)

NAVIGATOR

One of the forty-nine era-defining outfits archived at the Fashion Museum in Bath, England, this evening gown from Sarah Burton's autumn/winter collection for Alexander McQueen was chosen by Hamish Bowles, European editor at large at US *Vogue*, as the Dress of the Year. It was first shown at La Conciergerie in Paris, Marie Antoinette's prison, in a memorable show that featured live wolves on the runway.

Exploiting to the full the artisanal expertise of the McQueen workshops, the highly crafted gown combines the severity and *froideur* of the untouchable ice queen of fairy tales with the inherent sensuality of the McQueen signature feature, the laced-up corset. The dress has cross lacing from the waist upwards; the ivory bodice follows the line of the torso to the hips and is cut in a horizontal line beneath the shoulder blades. The severity of the silhouette is emphasized by the metallic silver skull cap, which creates a small, neat head in contrast to the voluminous circumference of the skirt, and dazzling purity of colour. The overall effect is softened by the effervescence of the raw-edged ruffled tulle and embellished surfaces. The Ice Queen and Her Court collection was the second to be designed by Burton after the untimely death of her mentor, Alexander 'Lee' McQueen, in 2010. **MF**

FOCAL POINTS

1 METALLIC CAP
The ethereal quality of the ice queen theme is emphasized by the metallic silver skull cap that conceals the hair. It is seemingly constructed from sections of old-fashioned metal perming rods moulded to fit the shape of the head.

3 TULLE BODICE
The tulle bodice is embellished with embroidered, handcrafted, three-dimensional silk organza feathers. Commonly used for wedding veils, the sheer tulle has a mesh-like structure that provides very fine hexagonal holes as a base for beading and embroidery.

2 NECKLINE
The bodice is cut away to form a halter-neck with a high-standing collar, further embellished with appliquéd feathers to replicate the neck plumage of a bird. The collar is resonant of the high-boned collars of the Edwardian era but also has connotations of bondage.

4 SILK SKIRT
The skirt is constructed from separate panels of silk organza that are looped in deep folds from a seam at the hip, with the edges left soft and frayed in contrast with the crisp, hand-embroidered eagle motifs placed on the surface of the fabric in spot repeat.

PRINT IN FASHION

Throughout the global evolution of textiles there has been a persistent impulse to modify the visual impact of plain fabrics with some degree of variegation—in the form of patterns of colour or imagery—while retaining the homogenous fluidity of the basic cloth. This approach is distinct from the various alternative means of constructing fabrics to produce patterned surfaces: tapestry, embroidery and woven colour effects. These techniques change the nature and behaviour of the plain textile by adding weight and compromising drape and movement. Methods of application of pattern to simple cloth have emerged, subsided and re-emerged throughout the history of craft and manufacture. *Plangi*, *shibori*, ikat and batik are all systems of resist dyeing, in which areas of cloth are occluded from taking the colour of dyestuffs by either the application of wax or pastes or by tying off with thread. For the sake of productivity, systems to mechanize the repetition of the patterns of placement of the resist substances were developed, using variations on the figured stamp, block or stencil. This approach de-skilled and accelerated the output of the artisan.

Innovation in the technology of fabric patterning and printing has been ongoing since the first block or resist methods were created by non-European cultures in China, India, Africa and Japan, and these processes have

KEY EVENTS

1999	2002	2004	2005	2005	2006
London-based, Danish-born Peter Jensen launches his first menswear collection, followed by womenswear in 2000.	Jonathan Saunders completes a Masters degree at Central Saint Martins College of Arts and Design and launches his own label the following year.	As Gucci's creative director of accessories—a specially created post—Frida Giannini (b.1972) reintroduces the Flora print.	British designer Matthew Williamson introduces the trend for 'boho' dressing with the peacock print dress worn by actress Sienna Miller.	The label Basso & Brooke produces an entirely digitally printed collection at London Fashion Week.	Matthew Williamson introduces his first collection for Italian label Pucci.

remained in use for centuries. Derived from the Latin *pater*, the term 'pattern' originally meant 'parent form', and a defining characteristic is repetition using mechanical aids. From these simple origins, contemporary print technology has developed throughout the industrial epoch to the point where near-instant creative results are accessible to all designers, not only those trained in the arcana of print preparation, and not only confined to repetitive patterning.

Fashion designers such as Peter Jensen (b.1969), Peter Pilotto (see p.526), Erdem (b.1977), Jonathan Saunders (b.1977) and Mary Katrantzou (b.1983; see p.524) explore the potent relationship between print and high fashion to marked effect. For these pioneers in the integration of garment form and printed imagery, innovative technology is signally a means to an end. Following the implicit desire to decorate and adorn the human form, contemporary designers discard the notion of print as mere embellishment. By incorporating a complex configuration of printed pattern into the topography of garment components, they are doing nothing less than using it to shape, mould or redefine the form of the body beneath. Originally inspired by the work of such diverse artists as M. C. Escher, Victor Vasarely, Richard Hamilton and Jackson Pollock, Saunders's subject matter, while remaining unequivocally abstract (right), also features much softer interpretations of images, from Art Nouveau-inspired patterning to reworked paisleys and faded photo-montages in bold washes of colour. The same imagery is mediated through both printed and constructed textiles, providing the designer's signature play on textures.

Although designers are eager to harness the convenience of new technology, many prefer to use it in conjunction with screen-printing skills learnt in the art college workshop where most experimentation takes place. Others prefer to limit themselves entirely to the purity of the handcrafted process, such as the forerunners of the 21st-century pattern revival Mark Eley (b.1968) and Wakako Kishimoto (b.1965), who make up design label Eley Kishimoto (opposite, above and below). Foremost exponents of the difficult skill of working an all-over multidirectional print into a garment, the duo created the iconic 'flash' design, which has the longevity of a print classic and the added bonus that it can be applied to all surfaces as well as fashion fabric.

The invention of the screen-printing process was instrumental in providing the market with the first fashion fabrics in bulk. Samuel Simon took out the first patent for a screen-printing process in 1907. This relatively cheap and less laborious method of printing cloth accelerated the speed of response to changing fashion trends and liberated designers from the limitations of expensive block-printing methods or engraved roller machines. Further inventions and patents followed, and by the 1930s screen-printing works were set up throughout Europe and the United States. These innovations democratized print design and revolutionized the textile printing industry, particularly for fashion fabrics.

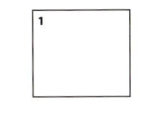

1 London-based label Eley Kishimoto placed print as the main focus of its spring/summer 2010 collection.

2 For 2011 Jonathan Saunders juxtaposed an Escher-type, all-over linear print with an engineered panel of birds and foliage.

3 Eley Kishimoto has utilized traditional craft processes for all its prints from the inception of the label in 1992.

2007	2008	2009	2009	2009	2012
Edinburgh-born Holly Fulton graduates from London's Royal College of Art. She presents her first collection in 2009.	Athens-born Mary Katrantzou shows her first collection at London Fashion Week.	Christopher de Vos and Peter Pilotto launch the Peter Pilotto label.	Dries van Noten is awarded the Chevalier de l'Ordre des Arts et des Lettres by the French Ministry of Culture.	Norwegian-born Peter Dundas (b.1969) shows his first collection for Pucci in the ornate Bracco salon of Milan's 18th-century Palazzo Serbelloni.	The Marni label, founded in 1994 as an offshoot of the Milanese Ciwi fur company, collaborates with Swedish clothing company H&M.

Modern printing practices now enable the designer to integrate print fully into the garment from its inception, rather than simply to accommodate a fixed repetitive pattern into the cut garment components in an arbitrary fragmentation. Digital printing makes it possible to take an image directly from digital camera or computer screen to cloth in a single digital workflow, using unlimited colours, instead of following the time-consuming traditional methods of silk-screening, which requires a separate flat or rotary screen for processing each colour. This colour separation in turn requires each screen and colour to be perfectly 'registered' to produce the accurate composite image, with inking, drying and washing processes between each production length. For this reason the costs of bespoke short runs of screen-printed cloth, often required by a fashion designer in the development stage of creating a collection, are prohibitively expensive.

With digital printing, a pattern can be changed in seconds, be it to rescale, recolour or reconfigure the imagery. It is also a speedy process: fabric lengths can be printed at up to 6,000 square feet (550 sq m) per hour, although high-volume, mass-market, rotary screen-printing can still outstrip this rate. Digital printing can also accommodate a wide range of fabrics, from the sheerest of silks to heavy cottons and velvets, including chiffon, habotai, georgette, poplin, canvas, cotton lawn, fine wool, Lycra and other stretch materials. Different fabrics require different dyestuffs, and different methods of applying ink for maximum effect. These include acid, reactive, disperse sublimation and pigment dyes.

Acid dyes are preferable for silk and wool, but reactives—also known as procion dyes—can work with both cellulosic (cotton, linen and viscose) and protein fibres (wool and silk). Disperse dyes have a great affinity with polyester and can be digitally printed by two methods. Relatively recently it was the normal practice to print disperse inks onto paper and then transfer the dyes by heat sublimation press to the prepared cloth; however, some digital printers now reduce the steps of this process to printing directly to the polyester cloth, which then passes to an in-line drier and rotary heat press unit to complete the chemical bonding of the dyes to fibre. Saturated colours can be used at a fraction of the cost compared with screen methods, and the short-run capability is ideal for the niche market, independent designer. Additionally, all design communications between designer and producer, including transfer of the image from studio to print room, can be expedited electronically, with colour fidelity indexing assuring consistency in output.

An enormous resurgence of interest in print design has seen most major international designers incorporating print into their collections as a way of cementing a visual identity in an era of accelerating visual saturation and literacy. Consuelo Castiglioni (b.1959) for Marni, British designer Matthew Williamson (b.1971), Italian design house Etro (see p.522) and Belgian designer Dries van Noten (b.1958) are all renowned for the symbiotic relationship between garment and print. The Marni label espouses an idiosyncratic and eclectic approach to print, reinterpreting mid-century motifs with graphic pattern hybrids (left). Dries van Noten's powerful compositional sense, abandoned use of colour and evident passion for pattern utilize many varied print techniques, all of which may be incorporated in a single, multilayered garment. Patterns inspired by a heterogeneous cultural mix from global sources and costume archives are combined with embellishments, such as embroidery and beadwork, to create an interrupted surface (opposite below).

Abstract pattern, divorced from representation and rarely attempting the depiction of any form of realism, has the potential to be more demanding on the eye. The fractured motif of an abstract print combines with the cut of the garment to create a complex visual conundrum. The tension lies in the fluidity

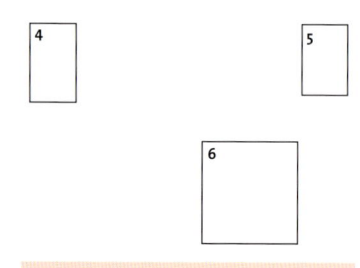

4 Italian design label Marni reinterprets mid-century modern print and colour, combining graphic patterns and textures on simple silhouettes in 2012.

5 Holly Fulton's prints feature futuristic designs inspired by ancient Egyptian and Art Deco motifs, as well as mosaics and 1930s Hollywood glamour.

6 Antwerp-based Dries van Noten sources fashion archives to provide the narrative to his printed textiles, which are then transformed into couture shapes of linear precision for autumn/winter 2012.

of the body animating a graphic style that may be purely geometric and is certainly non-figurative. Abstract patterns are inherently oppositional to the human form, creating an ambiguity that either disguises or enhances the clothed body as the designer fashions an entirely new visual language without associations or precedents. This allows shapes and forms to emerge that have no counterpart in nature, as represented in the work of contemporary Scottish-born fashion designer Holly Fulton (b.1977; right). Art Deco motifs and ancient Egyptian symbols are used as inspiration for futuristic garments with simple silhouettes that combine engineered digital prints with laser cutting, appliqué, beadwork and Perspex embellishment to create *trompe l'oeil* and three-dimensional effects.

Unlike the small independent designer and practitioner, design labels and couture houses buy in print ideas, rather than producing them in-house, either from a high-profile textile designer or from a studio showing at one of the trade fairs, such as Première Vision/Indigo. This is a commercial marketing organization dedicated to promoting the textile industry and hosts up to 800 fashion fabric manufacturers from around the world displaying and selling their work. Print designs are sold from fabric swatches or artwork. The initial artwork may remain the same, whether for screen or digital printing, unless the sheer quantity of hues involved in the design excludes screen-print interpretation. It is only companies such as Hermès that would mobilize endless numbers of screens to produce a single design: its record for one scarf was forty-three colour separations.

Advances in printing now encompass 'smart' dyes such as thermo- and photo-chromic inks that respond to atmospheric conditions by changing colour, plain fabrics that mutate into pattern when wet, and even pigments carrying miniature solar cells capable of harvesting sunlight. Thus print design for fashion enables the body to become uniquely interactive with the outer world. **MF**

Paisley Dress 2006
ETRO

Inspired by a trip to India, 'Gimmo' Etro, the founder of the luxury Italian fashion house Etro, introduced a paisley print collection in 1981 to his home furnishings range, and subsequently to his men's and women's accessory lines. When the company launched its first ready-to-wear collection in 1994, the swirling Indian motif appeared for the first time on Etro garments.

The signature paisley motif is diffused in this ankle-length dress across fluted panels of free-floating chiffon. The polychromatic print of the dress is cleverly engineered to give the impression of a paisley-patterned length of fabric thrown over a plain 'T'-shape bodice, leaving a deep border of aubergine at the base. The skirt of the dress uses the pattern vertically, with the scale of the curled palm-shaped print increasing towards the hem. Colours reference the folkloric nature of the paisley design, both rich and deep, and lightened by areas of apple green. The 1970s hippie-deluxe aesthetic of British designers Bill Gibb (1943–88) and Zandra Rhodes (b.1940) is revisited in the volume of the ethereal printed chiffon at the ankles and the airy sleeves. The maxi dress is toughened up by the introduction of a broad leather belt on the waistline embellished with parallel rows of studs and fastened with a metal buckle. **MF**

NAVIGATOR

FOCAL POINTS

1 FITTED BODICE
The fitted bodice of the dress utilizes the paisley print horizontally, which accentuates the bustline. The design is mirrored on either side of the deep 'V'-shape neckline and a small patterned insert fills the point of the 'V'.

3 FAUX HEMLINE
The printed geometric lines on the skirt create a *trompe l'oeil* handkerchief point hem. The printed area is confined to the main body of the skirt before ending with a deep black border, edged in contrasting stripes.

COMPANY PROFILE

1968–82
Founded by Gerolamo 'Gimmo' Etro in 1968, the original company supplied highly embellished and luxuriant cashmere, silk, linen and cotton cloths to the designers and couturiers of Milan, later branching out into leather goods and home accessories.

1983–PRESENT
The Etro label was made more visible in 1983, when its first dedicated store opened. In 1991, while studying economics at New York University, Ippolito Etro established the company's US business arm. The first ready-to-wear collections appeared on the catwalk in 1994. In classic Italian dynastic mode, the design direction remains in the hands of Etro's children; Veronica, who trained in London at Central Saint Martins College of Arts and Design, designs the women's collection.

2 KIMONO SLEEVES
The transparent aubergine silk-chiffon sleeves are square-set into a straight shoulder seam and hang loosely to finish below the elbow. The deep arm scye is redolent of the ease of cut of the kimono and vernacular dress.

PRINT IN FASHION 523

Trompe l'oeil Dress 2012
MARY KATRANTZOU b. 1983

Mary Katrantzou engineers intricate hyper-real placement prints that feature precious and exquisite *trompe l'oeil* objects, such as Coromandel screens, Fabergé eggs, Qing dynasty china and Meissen porcelain, to form structured silhouettes. In contrast this dress from the autumn/winter 2012 collection features the everyday and the mundane: crayons and pencils—the ephemera of the ordinary office— to create an extraordinary garment in a dizzying mash-up of the real, the surreal and the deceptive hyper-real in an underlying colour of bright chrome yellow.

The skirt of the dress is formed by a swirling log-jam of plastic HB pencils, complete with erasers, fulfilling the irresistible visual pun of the pencil skirt. These real objects are rendered into three-dimensional dress form by the Lesage embroidery atelier in Paris, which has been owned by Chanel since 2002. This collaboration was the first time Lesage had worked with such unorthodox material, and was its first liaison with a London designer. The Lesage atelier had a close commercial relationship with the Surrealist couturière Elsa Schiaparelli (1890–1973) in the 1930s, which set an early precedent for undertaking the realization of the idiosyncratic creative vision of Katrantzou. **MF**

👁 FOCAL POINTS

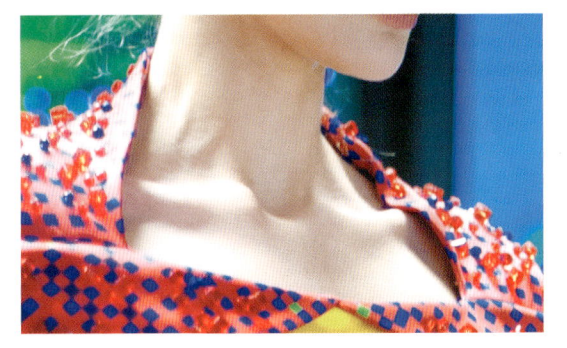

1 SQUARED-OFF NECKLINE
The neckline is formed in one with an exaggerated sleeve head creating an upper bodice, thereby referencing the Elizabethan ruff in rigidity of structure and propensity for lavish embellishment. A printed pattern of bicoloured mosaic is further embellished with intricate beadwork.

2 CORSETED TORSO
The closely fitted bodice of the dress is imprinted with a large bejewelled single rose with double stems, from which a mirror image of shocking-pink carousel horses canters away from the centre front. The horses face two parallel seams, which extend from the waist to the yoke.

3 ORIGAMI SKIRT
Within the Katrantzou strict signature silhouette, the stylish origami effect of the folded-over trims on the skirt hem interrupts the line of the pencil skirt to form a series of dramatic, narrow, circular frills extending outwards from the centre front to provide volume at the sides.

▲ Everyday objects were a recurrent theme in Katrantzou's autumn/winter 2012 collection. This red velvet Rococo-print dress features a *trompe l'oeil* typewriter yoke and keyboard peplum.

🕑 DESIGNER PROFILE

1983–2007
Athens-born Mary Katrantzou left Greece to study architecture in Rhode Island, USA. She changed her course of study to textiles and in 2005 graduated from London's Central Saint Martins College of Art and Design. From 2006 she spent two seasons working with Greek designer Sophia Kokosalaki (b.1972).

2008–PRESENT
Katrantzou's postgraduate collection was themed around *trompe l'oeil*, with innovative digital prints of oversized jewellery inspired by Russian Constructivism (see p.232) and early 1970s movie posters. The designer's first ready-to-wear collection comprised nine dresses and was produced for autumn/winter 2008. In 2012 she collaborated with Longchamp to design two exclusive prints for its Pliage and tote bags and she also designed a ten-piece capsule collection for high-street retailer Topshop.

Waterfall Dress 2013
PETER PILOTTO

NAVIGATOR

With a rich cultural background—Peter Pilotto (b.1977) is half Austrian, half Italian, and Christopher de Vos (b.1980) half Belgian, half Peruvian—the design partners who make up the label Peter Pilotto continue to draw inspiration from many sources. With its visually sumptuous and eclectic juxtaposition of pattern and embellishment, this dress from their spring/summer 2013 collection reflects the duo's trip to the Santa Maria Assunta cathedral in Siena, Italy, and visits to both India and Nepal.

The engineered all-over pattern captures a loose rendition of the Op art impact of the 1960s and 1970s paintings of Bridget Riley abstracted to an optical dazzle with fragments of electric blue. The broad black-and-white stripes with carefully placed, diamond-shaped Art Deco-inspired motifs, enhanced with three-dimensional beadwork, are used to create the curving architectural shapes of the shallow yoke with rounded shoulder line and asymmetrical pencil skirt. The neckline has sporting overtones, with a vest opening where the front bodice crosses over the back bodice at the sleeve head. Combined with this geometric patterning is a delicate pen and brushstroke Baroque flower print in washed-out inky blue and palest green, configured into a deep silk-satin ruffle. This begins at the waist and tapers towards the hem. The same blue provides a *trompe l'oeil* cuff. **MF**

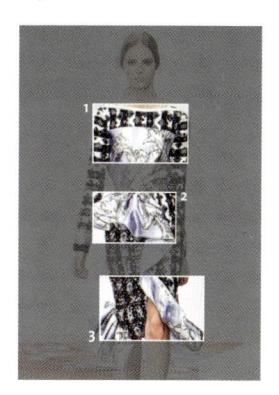

FOCAL POINTS

1 ALL-IN-ONE YOKE
Delineated across the shoulders by white piping, the high-cut yoke seam carries the all-over pattern vertically then horizontally down the full length of the sleeves to the *trompe l'oeil* cuff. The sleeves are then outlined in the same white piping.

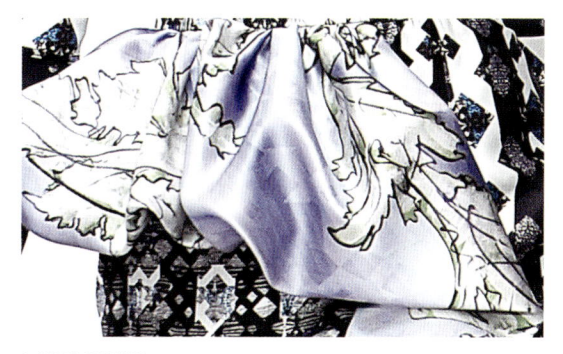

2 HALF-PEPLUM
A narrow self-fabric belt divides the bodice from the skirt. It secures the half-peplum double frill of Baroque-printed silk-satin, which adorns the waist up to the centre front point, from where it is allowed to fall across the body to the hem.

3 WATERFALL RUFFLE
A continuation of the silk-satin waterfall double ruffle forms a deep flounce that is gathered onto the hem of the pencil skirt. It finishes abruptly at a point on the hemline, leaving an asymmetric gap at the front.

COMPANY PROFILE

2000–07
Peter Pilotto and Christopher de Vos met while studying at Antwerp's Royal Academy of Fine Arts, Belgium. Pilotto graduated in 2003, followed by de Vos in 2004.

2008–PRESENT
Pilotto and Vos launched their first joint Peter Pilotto collection in 2009, with support from the British Fashion Council and the Topshop New Generation initiative. In 2008 they were finalists in the second edition of the El Boton Mango Fashion Awards, and in 2009 were awarded the Swarovski Best Emerging Talent Award at the British Fashion Awards and were also finalists in the prestigious Swiss Textiles Award. In 2011 Peter Pilotto won the Fashion Forward Prize, supported by Coutts & Co, and worked on a capsule bag collection with Kipling.

PRINT IN FASHION 527

SPORTSWEAR AND FASHION

Performance sportswear promises to optimize the body's ability to operate at maximum functionality in a wide range of environmental conditions, even to manage extremes of physical hazard. It can also serve to market sportswear-themed clothes for the general public. It influences clothing in general in the form of new materials, and scientific advances in combat clothing and space exploration have in turn helped to expand the repertoire of performance sportswear. Moreover, fashion designers deconstruct the iconography of sportswear mainly for visual impact and also, possibly, to imply participation in sport.

The post-war space race of the 1950s and 1960s spurred on strategic investment in scientific innovation, and brand managers have drawn on connotations of the future ever since, enthusiastically adopting scientific vocabulary for product names, such as Vectran for manufactured fibre. Branded sportswear as fashion emerged fully in the mid 1980s and has shown no signs of abating since; the partnership of Adidas and hip-hop band Run-DMC, whose single 'My Adidas' (1986), about the popular trainers, led to an endorsement deal with the company, is an early example (see p.446).

Sportswear that performs within the context of fashion, rather than at the extremes of physical performance, occupies a middle ground between athletics and high fashion. Interestingly, it has been observed that an elite athlete at his peak has a further, unquantifiable edge in competition when the psychological boost from the feeling of looking good kicks in, and it is no coincidence that high-profile designers are recruited regularly as creative directors by global

KEY EVENTS

2000	2002	2004	2004	2005	2006
Speedo announces the first of its biomimetic swimsuits, which are used in the Olympic Games in Sydney, Australia.	Yohji Yamamoto (b.1943) creates the Y-3 label in collaboration with sportswear giant Adidas, taking sports diffusion to a new level (see p.532).	The inordinate success of the sharkskin suit at the Olympic Games in Athens leads to a ban. The revised Fastskin3 of 2011 is permitted at the Olympics in 2012.	British designer Stella McCartney (b.1971) starts to collaborate with sportswear giant Adidas.	The Adidas 1 trainer with pioneering electronic features is launched, but the model is withdrawn the following year.	Adidas acquires the British sportswear brand Reebok, which was founded in 1895 under the name J. W. Foster and Sons.

sportswear labels to define the visual identity of their branded kit for elite performers, both in action and at leisure. In turn, global fashion designers have diversified into own-brand or co-branded fashion sportswear for the mass market and frequently use sportswear references in their high-end collections.

Performance maximization is implied through the use of superlatives in marketing products as the 'lightest', 'strongest' and 'smartest'. Performance sportswear and sport textiles are often subject to hyperbole in their advertising campaigns, which aim to reinforce scientific validation of technical performance. Big sportswear companies Nike, Adidas and Speedo have fostered a direct relationship with elite performers from the beginning and sustain their rivalry in the use of new technology to this day, competing as fiercely as any of the athletes with whom they work. One of the key examples of a successful partnership between a high-profile designer and a highly technologized sportswear manufacturer is the Adidas and Stella McCartney collaboration on the Team GB athletes' kit for the Olympic and Paralympic Games in 2012 (right). Stella McCartney (b.1971), who launched her own fashion label in 2001, started working with Adidas in 2004, producing critically acclaimed sports performance wear for several athletic disciplines, including running, tennis, swimming, winter sports and cycling. For the Olympic kit she combined sporting innovation with her unique creative touch to provide a range of garments for Olympic and Paralympic athletes, encompassing training gear, performance wear and presentation suits. Adidas provided the textile engineering for optimum performance, including moisture and temperature management, and McCartney worked within this rigorous scientific infrastructure, adding stylistic coherence and fashion brand value.

The close relationship between branded sports garments and athletic performance is evidenced most clearly in the controversy surrounding the swimsuit revolution brought about by Speedo's introduction of fastsuits in 2000; they were made of exceptionally light material and coated with a water-repellent substance. All sportswear brands seek ways to outwit competitors, and mimicry of animal skin, aquatic streamlining and the elimination of drag, as well as scientific 'no-sew' construction, are industry-standard fields of innovation. The Speedo Fastskin (opposite above) was modelled to resemble sharkskin—textured with tiny ridges that push the boundary layer away from the body, reducing drag in the water. By the time the Beijing Olympic Games took place in 2008, it had evolved into the LZR, scooping eighty-three out of ninety-seven Olympic medals and accounting for more than one hundred new world records in just two years. In the United States numerous articles were published on the topic and the fashion press, including *Women's Wear Daily*, reported the phenomenon to a global audience. Eventually, the fastsuit evolved into the shorter Fastskin3 (opposite below).

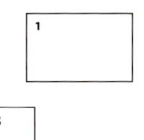

1 Australian swimmer Susie O'Neill wears the Speedo Fastskin swimsuit (2000). Speedo has worked closely with elite swimmers since the 1930s.

2 Heptathlon gold medallist Jessica Ennis wears a training outfit from the Olympic Team GB kit by Stella McCartney (2012).

3 In 2011 the Speedo Fastskin3 was reduced to knee-length from the earlier, ankle-length model, to comply with regulations.

2008	2008	2009	2011	2012	2012
Hussein Chalayan (b.1970) becomes creative director of sportswear company Puma.	Alexander Wang (b.1983) receives the Council of Fashion Designers of America/ *Vogue* Fashion Fund and goes on to design 'luxe athletic' clothes.	The Fédération Internationale de Natation (International Swimming Federation) Congress bans all body-length swimsuits in competition.	Adidas launches the AdiZero 'smart' trainer with integrated Wi-Fi, to be followed by the Hyperdunk basketball trainers.	US designer Vera Wang (b.1949) shows sports-inspired garments in her spring/summer collection.	Stella McCartney presents the official Team GB kit for the Olympic and Paralympic Games in London.

Speedo's competitors Adidas, TYR and Jaked responded to the challenge by introducing further technological advances that seemed to outstrip the LZR, mainly by creating compression suits constructed from polyurethane foils, which scooped twenty-nine world records at the World Championships in 2010. At this point, the Fédération Internationale de Natation (International Swimming Federation; FINA) intervened with a ban on impermeable, high-compression suits that provided 'buoyancy assistance' by extending below the knees and, for men, above the waist. The Olympic Games in 2012 featured FINA-authorized suits, within revised guidelines, by as many as sixty manufacturers.

Futuristic inventions are gradually infiltrating mainstream sportswear and sportswear diffusion lines. There is growing investment in concepts to modify aerodynamic form or prevent tendon damage, and also in knitted apparel, such as the Seamless or Wholegarment, which enhances movement through the absence of constricting seams and reduces lactic acid build-up through compression. Processes of thermal or ultrasound welding of seams are being drawn from extreme sport into a wider arena of utilitarian styling. Complex technical fabrics relating to other spheres, such as geo-textiles or sound insulation, are also transposed into fashion products, including trainers.

The Adidas 1 trainer launched in 2005 pioneered notions of smart electronic interactivity embedded in sports footwear. After some problems with reliability, the trainer was withdrawn in 2006, only to be reincarnated in 2011 as AdiZero with Wi-Fi download capability for track speeds and performance data. Nike responded with the Nike+ trainer, which allows the wearer to communicate training performance data to others, the latest incarnation being the Hyperdunk basketball trainer (left). The form of the lightweight shoe gains stability from strong elastic cords anchored to the uppers. In-built sensors track every step and sync the performance data with the owner's smartphone via a Wi-Fi dongle. Three forms of performance metric are collected—step speed, overall activity and jump height—and the data can be transferred directly to the mobile phone and shared via social networks, which are of increasing importance in the marketing of clothing and sports items, especially with younger customers.

In a different take on the relationship between science, sports and fashion, the sculptor Tom Sachs (b.1966) collaborated with Nike on the upscale NikeCraft, which takes iconic components of NASA equipment and reworks them into unusual accessories and artisan garments: a Mars rover landing airbag is reused as a Vectran sliver in an office trainer, a stylized parka with welded seams has scientific data emblazoned on the lining, and a used automobile airbag becomes a soft nylon tote.

The true scientific content of a new sportswear product is only a small part in the marketing mix. Any positive association that can be established on the foundation of the embedded heritage of the respective label is used in the presentation of new products. Supported by innovative scientific concepts and the use of 'smart' materials, garments are shown as worn by sporting giants or brand ambassadors, and made glamorous by association with leading designer names such as Stella McCartney (opposite above), Yohji Yamamoto (b.1943; see p.532), Giorgio Armani (b.1943), who works with Reebok, the Alexander McQueen 'Black Label' for Puma and Hussein Chalayan (b.1970). Appointed creative director of Puma, Chalayan presented his Inertia collection in 2008, which featured ground-breaking moulded latex garments.

True performance wear will always be required at the Olympic pool, track or velodrome, and needs to be engineered to the highest level with 'clever' materials. Some garments also have to be specially constructed in order to aid the wearer in extreme environmental conditions, such as the gravity-defying wingsuit for base jumpers or phase change materials (PCMs) for mountaineer suits that automatically boost core temperature in extreme cold. At the other end of the spectrum, fashion designers often incorporate sports influences in their collections. With the onset of the 21st-century body-con era, sports-inspired materials and garment construction have transformed fashion and, conversely, serious sportswear items are frequently recast as designer sportswear with a flourish of decorative whimsy.

Sophisticated examples of this latter approach can be seen in the collections of US designer Alexander Wang (b.1983): his take on sportswear is a sleek re-imagining for the urban context, which includes perforated vests, windbreakers and utility track pants. Virtually every season Wang dismantles some aspect of sports iconography, infusing it with greater vigour and attitude by creating unexpected combinations and asserting an alternative view of womenswear and sportswear. In his spring/summer 2012 collection, references were made largely to BMX and Motocross, resulting in a variegated take on aggressive metropolitan street wear, ranging from floral renditions of biker garments to sheer organdie and laser-perforated leather with hazard markings, combined with high-heeled sandals.

Similarly, US designer Vera Wang (b.1949), best known for her stylish bridal gowns, which are hugely popular with film stars and celebrities the world over, has taken inspiration from sports garments in her designs, and high-tech fabrics in particular. These include Nike's Swift Running technology and the geometric layers of the Adidas Techfit/PowerWeb technology, which is used in sports apparel such as running tights to improve body stability and posture by supporting the muscles. In her spring/summer 2012 collection Wang used print circles on ethereal perforated and sculpted chiffon dresses (right); the delicate biomimetic cut-out details of the material evoke the growth patterns of sea urchins. Hoods and drawstring jackets worn with shorts also appeared in the collection, adding a further athletic touch to Wang's signature feminine look. **JA**

4 A variety of sportswear designs from the Adidas by Stella McCartney spring/summer 2009 collection displays McCartney's trademark feminine tailoring mixed with lingerie influences.

5 Vera Wang's spring/summer 2012 collection includes airy broderie anglaise panels in clean white, forming a criss-cross geometry with flimsy layers anchored at the waist.

6 Nike+ Hyperdunk basketball trainers feature sophisticated embedded wireless technology in the form of sensors.

All-purpose Sportswear 2004
Y-3

NAVIGATOR

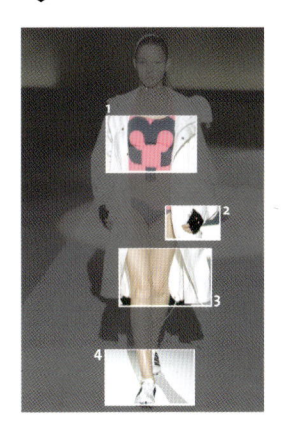

Widely perceived as a designer of intellectual, almost spiritual, inclination, Yohji Yamamoto embraces the distinctly physical in his successful collaboration with sportswear giant Adidas under the Y-3 brand (the 'Y' stands for Yamamoto and the '3' for the copyright-protected three Adidas stripes). In Yamamoto's approach of 'analytical dissection', hallmark sportswear components are realigned and remixed in a witty series of design elements that are largely non-specific in terms of sport discipline but imply athleticism and body awareness.

Here, a voluminous parka, referencing the warm-down kit used in American football, is worn over a fitted graphic crop top and matching bikini bottoms bearing a Y-3 logo that dominates the outfit, combined with black fingerless mitts and white sneakers, all of which are indeterminate in function. The overall palette is tied in with the rest of the collection. Luminous face paint cuts across the brow and cheek; it is approximately the width of a medal ribbon, recalling falling ticker tape or adhesive wound dressings. Embracing playful experimentation within sports apparel, the Y-3 brand also makes use of new fibres, fabrics and methods of construction, incorporating sleek synthetics with inherent novel finishes from ultrasound welding to heat-transfer printing. **JA**

FOCAL POINTS

1 Y-3 LOGO
The pink fitted graphic top and bikini bottoms appear suitable for a range of sports activities including beach volleyball. The large-scale typographic Y-3 logo is stretched across both garments, lending them a cartoonish quality.

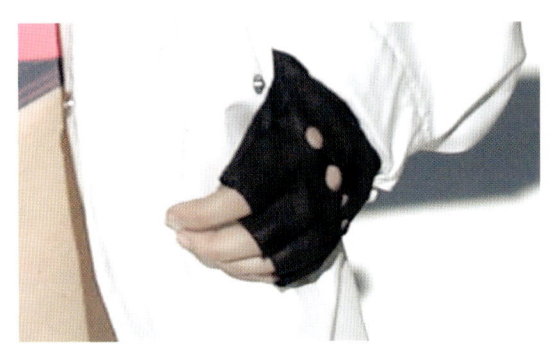

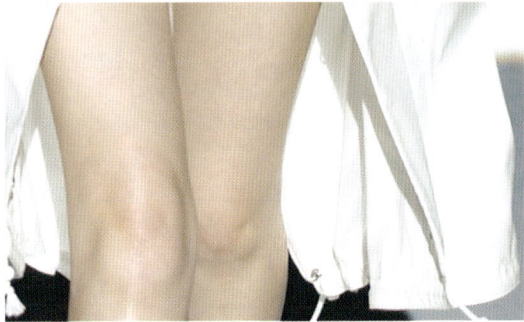

3 VOLUMINOUS PARKA
The knee-length parka envelops the crop top and features parallel Adidas stripes at the back. Worn by the US military during the Korean War in the 1950s, the parka has become a popular utility garment and fashion statement.

2 FINGERLESS MITTS
The black fingerless mitts are non-specific in function but are most closely associated with skateboarding, which has evolved since the 1950s to assume a prominent position in sports. This has brought with it a vogue for related accessories.

4 TRADEMARK STRIPES
The classic white sneakers feature the well-known Adidas triple stripes on the side. These have been an integral part of the brand's identity for decades, having been first introduced in 1949; the company has defended the copyright in the design over many years.

SPORTSWEAR AND FASHION 533

LUXE READY-TO-WEAR

1 This Burberry ad campaign of 2010 epitomizes the renaissance of a heritage brand while retaining modern relevance.

2 Pared-down, oversized tailoring and luxurious textiles, seen in the autumn/winter 2012 collection, are hallmarks of Phoebe Philo for Céline.

3 Victoria Beckham's 'sportier' autumn/winter 2012 collection features polo-shirt collars and cheerleader-style skirts.

The contemporary phenomenon of high-end, ready-to-wear clothing is positioned between haute couture and the wider mass market. The labels that occupy this growing niche offer fashion-led clothes in luxury materials that match haute couture for high-quality production values and price. Luxe ready-to-wear, also known as 'demi couture', is both democratic and accessible, and is often mediated through e-commerce mechanisms, which alleviates the time-consuming process demanded by the bespoke fittings of couture. Although high-end ready-to-wear is far from proletarian in cost, there is an undercurrent of added value residing not only in the designer branding, but also in the artisanal and ethical means of atelier fabrication, which helps to justify the four- and five-figure price tags. Demi couture encompasses all aspects of fashion, from the hippie-deluxe festival wear of Isabel Marant (b.1967; see p.536) to the contemporary red-carpet dressing of Stella McCartney (b.1971; see p.538) and figure-hugging daywear by Victoria Beckham (b.1974). Luxe ready-to-wear labels have become as influential as couture, possibly more so.

Burberry and Burberry Prorsum, arguably the premier British clothing brands, offer their customers instant access to their high-end, ready-to-wear trends (above) via a method of selling by 3-D live streaming, known as 'Runway to Reality'. Chief creative officer of Burberry Christopher Bailey (b.1971)

KEY EVENTS

2000	2001	2001	2001	2004	2004
French designer Isabel Marant launches Etoile, a diffusion line that includes lingerie.	British designer Christopher Bailey is appointed as creative director by chief executive Rose Marie Bravo to design for Burberry.	Phoebe Philo is appointed as creative director of Chloé, fronting the label for five years before resigning in 2006.	See by Chloé, a younger and less expensive line, is introduced to the Chloé label.	Christopher Bailey is awarded an honorary fellowship from London's Royal College of Art.	Victoria Beckham designs a limited-edition line for Rock & Republic, VB Rocks, followed by a line of sunglasses in 2006 and denim label, dvb Style.

launched this approach in 2010, and in 2012 it was deployed across thirty prime international retail sites, including the new Beijing flagship store. During the live streaming, customers can reserve their purchases via direct iPad interaction in-store and online. This immediate feedback supports the commercial logistics of the brand and enables the company to know instantly which items to put into production and which to discard. Bailey is responsible for the company's overall image, including all advertising, corporate art direction, store design and visuals, as well as the design of all Burberry collections and product lines. His success at reinventing Burberry is symptomatic of a transition in consumer mentality. The present Burberry adherent is not necessarily loyal to the fixed identity of the brand, but rather wishes to associate with the creative aesthetic and personality of the designer behind the brand. Alongside Bailey, chief executive officer Angela Ahrendts pioneered the use of webcasts and in-store technology that offers customers the opportunity to browse whole collections on iPad-style screens. Burberry also entered the world of social networking and launched its Art of the Trench website, where photographs can be uploaded and shared.

One of the new generation of women designers at the forefront of contemporary fashion, Phoebe Philo (b.1973) eschews fantasy and drama for clothes where fit and feel are the priorities (above right). Having worked at Chloé for several years, in 2008 she successfully repositioned the French label Céline, and spearheaded a movement towards elegance, practicality and simplicity seen elsewhere in the collections of Hannah MacGibbon (b.1970) at Chloé and those of her replacement in 2011, Clare Waight Keller (b.1971). Keller fuses the attitude and relaxed dressing of the British festival girl with the femininity and ingénue charm of the Parisian *jeune fille*. This mix produces pastel-coloured duffel coats and parkas with lace and silk blouses, a template of tailoring infused with prettiness first provided by Stella McCartney in her years heading the Chloé label. This prêt-à-porter house was founded in 1952 by Gaby Aghion (b.1921) as an alternative to the formality of haute couture and became one of the most covetable labels of the 1980s. Chloé drew in Stella McCartney in 1997 as creative director, and she brought a combination of precise tailoring, feminine prints and vintage style to the luxe ready-to-wear collections; she resigned in 2001 to establish her own eponymous label.

Prime advocate of the marketing conceit of the designer as consumer of their own brand, Victoria Beckham has reportedly proclaimed that everything she makes is something she would wear herself. Her initial aesthetic as a designer was exemplified by body-con styling with minimal adornment, in a tightly edited collection of event gowns, first presented in New York in 2008. The aesthetic has since evolved; the architectural infrastructure of the first red-carpet garments has given way to the use of dense rib jerseys, canvases and quilting techniques that communicate a sportier line (right). **MF**

2004	2008	2009	2009	2010	2011
Stella McCartney forms a partnership with Adidas to produce high-end performance sportswear (see p.529).	British designer Hannah MacGibbon (b.1970) replaces Phoebe Philo at Chloé.	Phoebe Philo is appointed by LVMH as the creative director of French ready-to-wear label Céline.	Bailey is named Designer of the Year at the British Fashion Awards and appointed a Member of the Order of the British Empire (MBE).	Victoria Beckham launches a range of handbags designed in collaboration with accessories designer Katie Hillier.	Victoria Beckham adds a significantly less expensive diffusion line, Victoria by Victoria Beckham, offering a softer, 1960s-inspired A-line silhouette.

LUXE READY-TO-WEAR

Festival Wear 2010
ISABEL MARANT b. 1967

NAVIGATOR

Leader of the Parisian ready-to-wear own-name brands, French designer Isabel Marant epitomizes contemporary, hippie-deluxe festival wear for the fashionable rich. In this photograph by Inez van Lamsweerde and Vinoodh Matadin, featuring Daria Werbowy, the oversized muslin smock in hot pink is cut to fall loosely from the shoulders to end at mid thigh, the fullness caught low on the hips with a sturdy leather and metal belt, providing a contrast in textures. The sleeve head is gathered into a dropped shoulder seam with a deep arm scye; further gathers are caught into a narrow, self-fabric binding cuff sited just above the wrists and left wide to provide freedom of movement.

The garment opens at centre front and is delineated with white binding, matching the narrow white inserts at the shoulder seam. The same binding decorates the vertical pocket, which is set obliquely at hip level, punctuated at each end with a metal disc. The same discs create interest at the sleeve head and four of them decorate the centre front, the larger one placed just below the breasts to hold the opening of the dress together. The hem of the dress is simply turned under and top-stitched. Accessorized with Marant's customary hippie insouciance—tousled hair, brass and silver bracelets and feathered earrings—the look personifies the Marant attitude of youthful cool. **MF**

FOCAL POINTS

1 WIDE-SCOOP NECKLINE
The plainly hemmed, wide-scoop neckline opens at the centre front, from where it is bound on either side with contrasting white trimming to hip level. The neckline is left to fall open, caught just below the breasts with a metal disc.

2 LOW-SLUNG BELT
Adding toughness to the airy muslin smock, the leather belt features a double row of metallic chain mail and a matching buckle. The tail end of the belt is tucked informally rather than fastened, adding to the casual air.

3 SUMMER BOOTS
These highly influential and best-selling suede pirate boots feature a deep turn-back cuff, layers of fringing and a sturdy heel. Several chains are looped around the ankle to match the metallic elements of the belt.

DESIGNER PROFILE

1967–94
Paris-born designer Isabel Marant started selling her home-made creations in the shopping precinct of Les Halles in Paris. In 1987 she enrolled in the Berçot studio and began an apprenticeship at Michel Klein, after which she launched an accessories line. In 1994 Marant debuted her eponymous label and set up her main boutique in an old Parisian artist's studio.

1995–PRESENT
Marant's reputation for effortlessly hip clothes spread from her native France to Europe and the United States with the opening of a store in New York's SoHo district in 2011. Today, the company has ten shops worldwide, including those in Paris, Tokyo, Hong Kong, Beijing, Madrid and Beirut, and retails in more than thirty-five countries. The diffusion line, Etoile, provides a more affordable version of the look.

Patterned Dress 2012
STELLA MCCARTNEY b. 1971

Gwyneth Paltrow wears Stella McCartney in Beijing (2011).

NAVIGATOR

Enjoying official designation as creative designer for Team GB at the Olympic Games in 2012, Stella McCartney incorporated sports influences into thigh-length dresses for her luxe ready-to-wear collection for summer 2012; some of the designs have inserts made of an Aertex-inspired power-mesh sports fabric. However, the underlying inspiration stems from a subtle, asymmetric dissection of the convolute anatomy of late-Baroque stringed instruments. Waisted violas and violoncellos—with their esoteric topology of belly, bouts and purfles, saddle and scroll, neck and tailpiece—evoke a curvy physicality.

Worn here by Gwyneth Paltrow, the body-skimming dress is shaped by the inclusion of waist darts, and the integral lines of the dress, which is constructed predominantly from viscose, curve up and over one breast, creating an outsize, comma-shaped motif that recurs elsewhere in the collection. The printed woven cloth has the fabric structure necessary to anchor the heavy embroidery components throughout the garment. The cutaway halter-neck top also references the sporting provenance of the dress, and the high rounded neckline is unobtrusively bound. A concealed zip at the back is shaped to maintain the emphasis on the natural curves of the body. **MF**

FOCAL POINTS

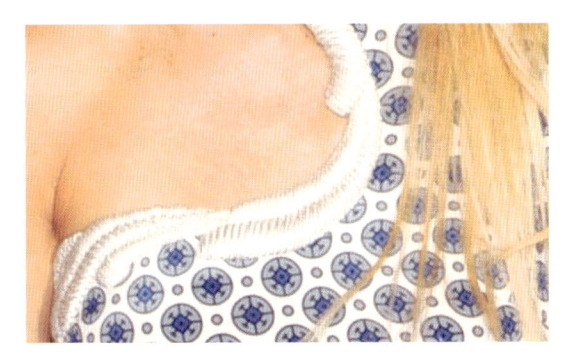

1 THREE-DIMENSIONAL EMBROIDERY
The foulard block repeat print is edged by a large, padded, three-dimensional whorl of Rococo Italian cording embroidered in white satin stitch. The shape recalls that of a paisley swirl or the outline of a Baroque stringed instrument.

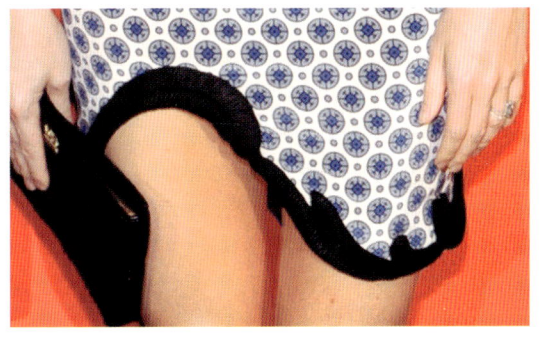

3 ASYMMETRIC HEMLINE
Further stiffened curves are created by weighty swooshes of hyperscale satin-stitch embroidery in black at the mid-thigh hemline. These curve upwards at the centre front to form an inverted 'V' shape.

2 MEDALLION PRINT
McCartney constructed the main fabric of the dress using an ultramarine blue-and-grey print of coin-sized medallions on a white background. Elsewhere in the collection this spot repeat is juxtaposed with mesh fabric and a small-scale paisley print.

DESIGNER PROFILE

1971–2000
London-born Stella McCartney is renowned for her sharp yet feminine tailoring combined with covertly sexy clothes that often resonate with a 1970s sensibility. Her strict adherence to vegetarianism has resulted in all collections being fur- and leather-free. After an internship at Christian Lacroix and working for a Savile Row tailor, McCartney studied at Central Saint Martins College of Arts and Design, where her graduate show was modelled by friends Naomi Campbell and Kate Moss. She was appointed creative director of Chloé in 1997.

2001–PRESENT
McCartney launched her own label in 2001. Accessories and fragrances followed, and in 2007 an organic skincare line was introduced. She started working with Adidas in 2004, and in 2012 she designed the Olympics kit for Team GB.

UNDERSTATED AMERICAN STYLE

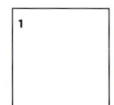

1 Shades of beige and nude are lightened with a flash of leopard print in semi-tailored separates by Thakoon Panichgul for autumn/winter 2012. The easy jacket has a relaxed drop shoulder and gathered tie at the waist.

2 The 3.1 Phillip Lim spring/summer 2012 collection includes soft pastels in a light-as-air unstructured top.

3 Tory Burch's signature tones of yellow and orange are combined in layers of print and knit for 2012. The easy silhouette includes a just-below-the-knee skirt.

The marketing term 'masstige' derives from mass production and prestige and is used to define products that are premium yet attainable: the items are perceived as luxury products but with accessible price points. In fashion this includes the cachet of wearing a designer label without paying the price of high-end ready-to-wear—a concept embraced in particular by a new generation of US contemporary designers. Providing accessible, directional clothing with pieces at affordable prices, labels 3.1 Phillip Lim, Alexander Wang and Theyskens at Theory all offer sport-luxe separates that define urban understated cool with a modern sensibility. Design duo Proenza Schouler, Tory Burch (b.1966) and Thakoon Panichgul (b.1974) add to a uniquely American mix with soft tailoring, preppy overtones and the use of pattern and print. Proenza Schouler reconfigured preppy staples such as the pea coat and the baseball jacket (see p.542), adding overtones of embellishment and embroidery culled from ethnic sources for a laid-back hippie feel. Epitomizing a look defined

KEY EVENTS

2000
US designer Phillip Lim co-founds his first label, Development, which he continues until 2004.

2004
Philadelphia-born Tory Burch launches her fashion label from her uptown Manhattan apartment.

2004
Thai-US designer Thakoon Panichgul produces his first ready-to-wear collection.

2005
The 3.1 Phillip Lim label is launched, expanding into menswear two years later.

2005
The Tory Burch flagship boutique in New York is awarded the Fashion Group International Rising Star Award for best new retail concept.

2007
After only one year of study at Parsons The New School for Design and an internship at *Teen Vogue*, Alexander Wang launches his eponymous label.

540 1990–PRESENT

as MOD (model off duty), the slouchy layers of the Alexander Wang label reinvented leisurewear with variations on the basic T-shirt: oversized with a wide-scooped neckline and dropped armholes or as a racer-backed vest. Wang (b.1983) launched his first full ready-to-wear collection in 2007, shortly followed by a diffusion line, T by Alexander Wang, in 2009. He was appointed creative director of Balenciaga in 2012.

The 3.1 Phillip Lim signature aesthetic of unaffected, streamlined simplicity has been deployed since Phillip Lim (b.1973) and his business partner and former fabric supplier, Wen Zhou, launched the brand in 2005. Minimal without being severe, designs have included cropped trousers in skin-thin leather, luxurious tops (above right) and elongated sleeveless blazers layered over gauzy blouses; the look varies minimally from season to season. The label expanded in 2007 to include menswear, providing well-tailored basics, such as the classic pea coat.

Referencing archetypal pieces, such as blazers, puffa coats, draped day dresses and easy jackets (opposite), with an innovative twist, Thakoon Panichgul produces understated urban fashion with an edge. He often makes use of daring colour combinations and clashing prints, a compelling look that has attracted Michelle Obama as a client. Thakoon produced his first ready-to-wear collection in 2004 and quickly became renowned for his ability to play felicitously with proportion and construction. He is an expert at cross-cultural fusion, combining seemingly clashing elements, such as Indian silk and cowboy styles.

Olivier Theyskens (b.1977) was appointed artistic director of the luxury designer sportswear label Theory in 2011. Previously an exponent of Gothic Grand Guignol (horror theatre) style, he designed the black leather dress for Madonna in her video 'Frozen' (1998) but went on to refine his aesthetic, working at prestigious French couture houses Nina Ricci and Rochas. He used technically advanced fabrics from Japan, such as washed leather for tailored jackets and tight-weave cotton for slouchy cut T-shirts, and designs have included signature floor-skimming, wide-legged trousers and silk blouses.

Transforming a lifestyle into a successful brand, Tory Burch has shown a sureness of touch and an acute awareness of her label's position on the fashion spectrum. Her look is based on her own lifestyle and an understanding of how women want to dress. Burch gained experience while working at Ralph Lauren, Vera Wang and Loewe before perceiving a gap in the market for polished yet subversive prettiness at accessible prices. She launched her clothing line in 2004 and embarked on her first catwalk show in 2012. The label's instantly recognizable palette of yellow-toned orange (right) and olive green is often worked into lively small-scale prints on blouses and drapey knee-length skirts. Her form-fitting knits in jewel colours and belted coats for winter, and drop-waisted A-line dresses and braided jackets for summer, are resonant of the easy-to-wear feminine clothes of Chanel. **MF**

2007	2007	2008	2008	2009	2011
Phillip Lim receives the Council of Fashion Designers of America (CFDA) Swarovski Award for Emerging Talent.	The first stand-alone 3.1 Phillip Lim store opens in New York.	Alexander Wang is the recipient of the CFDA/*Vogue* Fashion Fund.	Tory Burch is awarded CFDA Accessory Designer of the Year. Her Reva ballet flats, with a round medallion made up of her initials, prove a best-seller.	Thakoon Addition, Thakoon Panichgul's second, more affordable line of wearable wardrobe essentials, is launched.	Brussels-born Olivier Theyskens is appointed artistic director at Theory.

Quilted Jacket and Leather Skirt 2012
PROENZA SCHOULER

NAVIGATOR

Interpreting the vernacular costumes from the Himalayan regions of Nepal and Bhutan for the urban rock chick, Proenza Schouler retrieves the concept of clothing as protection; the fabric is layered and quilted in an elaborate remodelling of a contemporary yuppie staple, the baseball jacket. The yoke and sleeve head are in contrasting colours, outlining the breastplate effect of two gold, silk-satin front panels that are quilted in an interlocking wave pattern, which continues horizontally in a separate panel below the waistband, edged in black satin. The large-scale pattern is again used laterally to form a final layer in a vivid orange, incorporating two horizontally placed square pocket flaps bound in black. The sleeves continue the quilt patterning, which is evocative of woven rattan.

Proenza Schouler is an award-winning accessory design brand, and the label's extraordinary leather confections recur in garment form with woven, embossed and punched leather. Detailed finishes are evident here in the glossy leather skirt, which is of the same complex construction that is seen in premium-brand shoes and handbags. Leather thongs ruche the skirt into corrugated vertical pleats with gold and jet leather ribbons, which appear in the eyelets like recessed jewels. **MF**

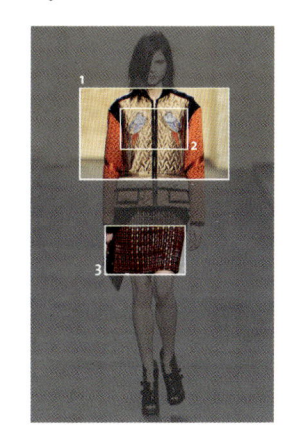

FOCAL POINTS

1 INDIGENOUS DESIGN AND CONTEMPORARY CLASSIC
The close-fitting ribbed neckline and centre-front zip of the classic baseball jacket are combined with the patchwork textures and shape of the *toego*, a short, wide jacket with long sleeves, central to the national costume of Bhutan.

2 ASIAN-INSPIRED EMBROIDERY
Against the geometric lines of the baseball jacket, the front panels are embroidered with twin satin-stitch oriental pheasants in heraldic composition. The plumage is a pale duck-egg blue on a quilted golden background.

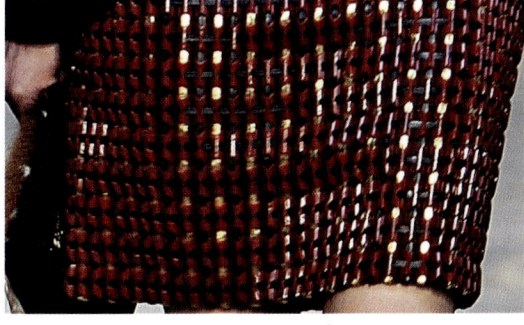

3 PENCIL SKIRT
Cropped to just above the knee, the base leather of the skirt in lacquer red is perforated with a continual offset grid of eyelets with colour-contrasted warp and weft leather thongs inserted through the openings.

DESIGNER PROFILES

1998–2002
Lazaro Hernandez (b.1978) and Jack McCollough (b.1978), the design duo behind the Proenza Schouler label, met as students at Parsons The New School for Design in 1998. While interning at Michael Kors and Marc Jacobs respectively, the designers developed key relationships with factories and suppliers. Consulting work followed while they established their own company. It was launched in 2002, with the brand name made up of their mothers' maiden names.

2003–PRESENT
The Valentino Fashion Group acquired 45 per cent of the label in 2007, allowing the expansion of the business. The same year Proenza Schouler received the CFDA award for womenswear designer, which was followed in 2009 by a further award for accessories designer.

THE RISE OF E-COMMERCE

Electronic commerce (e-commerce) is transforming the way in which people shop. Customers make purchases on the Internet and are alerted to trends via mobile phones and social media. This gives potentially global choices to shoppers both at home and on the move, and it is possible to instantly feed back personal requirements or comments on products. Initially e-commerce suffered from unreliable communications technology and a lack of confidence in the supporting financial and logistical infrastructure. Customers were not comfortable giving credit card information to websites, and digital retailers had not prepared their delivery systems to cope with returns. This has improved as a result of faster broadband, iPhones and other devices.

These developments led to an explosive growth of online shopping. Nowadays people can shop for designer clothes on websites such as Net-a-Porter (above) and also customize styles affordably. Links have been developed to other technologies such as virtual reality, 3-D body scanning, co-design personalization and mass customization manufacturing. Web-based shopping allows retailers to track an individual's shopping habits more efficiently and

KEY EVENTS

2000	2000	2000	2002	2003	2004
Ex-fashion journalist Natalie Massenet founds Net-a-Porter, a website for designer women's clothes in the format of an online fashion magazine.	The dot.com bubble bursts. Internet trading is overestimated due to limited user-friendliness, as well as lack of delivery and returns infrastructure.	Nick Robertson launches ASOS—an acronym for 'As Seen On Screen'—as a 'pure play' (Internet-only) fashion retailer.	The US Internet consumer-to-consumer corporation eBay acquires payment system PayPal for US$1.5 billion.	Amazon.com, which started as an online bookseller in 1995, announces its first yearly profit. It is the world's biggest online retailer.	Computer programmer Mark Zuckerberg starts the social networking website Facebook at Harvard University.

personalize their marketing. Promotional material can be sent via email or text only to those with probable interest, and marketing and advertising can be focused more cost-effectively. Advertisements incorporate 'quick response' codes that can be scanned by mobile phones, giving further web-based information, or linked to immediate discount incentives.

Most retailers have both transactional websites and conventional stores; typically the online stores do more business than the largest 'bricks and mortar' store. The volume of clothing sales achieved online has grown from less than 0.5 per cent of the total in the early 2000s to more than 11 per cent of the market in 2011. The Internet has also given rise to companies that have no stores—so-called 'pure players' such as ASOS (see p.546), which only sells via the Internet.

The drawback of Internet clothes shopping is the absence of a changing room, and the most common reason for returns is 'lack of fit'. However, there are increasingly sophisticated systems for virtual try-on available. It is possible to modify a standard avatar (or 3-D 'e-mannequin') with some user-defined measurements of girth and height. Together with menu choices of face shape, features, colouring and posture, a more realistic 'electronic mirror' can give a better idea of how the customer may look in a garment. 3-D body scanners, such as those at Human Solutions, can capture body shape and take 150 measurements in a few seconds. A body scan of an individual's 3-D shape can then be put onto a smart card. Consequently, a retailer or manufacturer with the appropriate reader can evaluate either which is the best fit in standard sizes or suggest made-to-measure customization. Computerized pattern-cutting systems can also be programmed to make amendments to standard-sized patterns for made-to-measure manufacture.

Style customization or 'DIY design' along with bespoke fit is the ultimate goal of e-commerce, and people can design shoes online with retailers such as Nike (right). Customers select the colours, patterns and materials of their shoe, and personalize it with names or numbers. Customax, based in Amsterdam, offers retailers the facility to provide an interface to link several brands with factory mass customization. For example, a link to Hamburg-based Matteo Dosso offers customers menus of multiple choices of fabric, colour, style features and accessories to personalize the design of ladies' suits.

For consumers who are prepared to pay a little more and forgo the instant gratification of in-store shopping, e-commerce has clear benefits. It also promises styled-to-suit, made-to-measure clothing that has previously been available only to those who could afford haute couture. **AK**

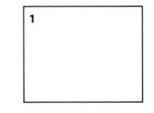

1 Net-a-Porter, the online women's clothing and accessories retailer, offers seasonal collections by more than 350 of the world's leading designers.

2 NikeiD has allowed consumers to customize and design their footwear since 1999. The service is available online and in NikeiD Studios across the globe.

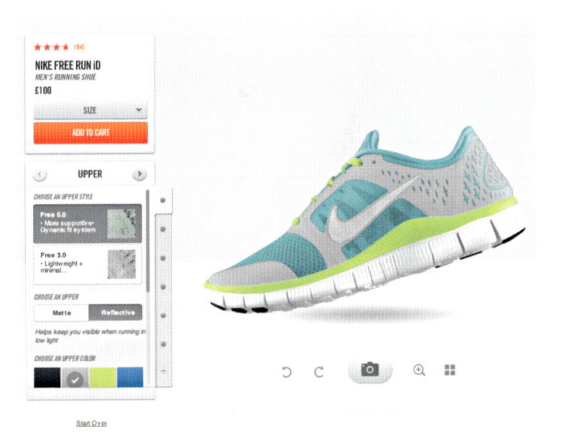

2006	2007	2008	2010	2011	2012
ASOS introduces online catwalk videos of models wearing products available on the website.	Apple Inc. launches its first smartphone—the iPhone.	More than 300 million personal computers are sold globally per year.	Almost all major retailers have developed e-commerce operations, with links to mobile and social media.	The global online retail destination for men's style, Mr Porter, is launched.	Nearly half of UK clothes shoppers go online at least once a month, according to a Cotton Council International survey.

THE RISE OF E-COMMERCE 545

ASOS 2000
FASHION RETAIL WEBSITE

Screenshots from the ASOS website (2012).

NAVIGATOR

One of the best examples of how e-commerce is changing the way fashion is purchased is the e-retailer ASOS. It has no physical stores or traditional mail-order option and operates purely through the Internet. From its start-up in 2000, when it was run by founder Nick Robertson and three colleagues, it has grown to a sales turnover of almost £500 million by 2012. The website has more than four million customers in 160 different countries, with a focus on customers in their twenties.

The business was originally called 'As Seen On Screen' and the aim was to provide so-called 'fast fashion'—selling what looked like replicas of celebrity clothing at affordable prices. The market demand for this already existed because many fashion-forward twenty-somethings took their style inspiration from film and television. Fashion pop culture tends to centre on stars from the worlds of music, sports and entertainment. With headquarters in London and a UK-based logistics centre, ASOS has retained its Internet-only trading formula. The product offering has expanded, however; the site carries not only its own styles, but also includes a portal facility to sell other well-known branded goods. There is even a 'marketplace' where customers can resell their own items, taking advantage of social media such as Facebook. **AK**

FOCAL POINTS

1 MAGAZINE LOOK
The site has a magazine look and feel in terms of fonts and page layout. Editors advise on fashion trends on a daily basis and more than 2,000 new products are offered every week. ASOS launched its own monthly print magazine for Britain in 2007.

2 INTERNATIONALIZATION
International sales increased by 142 per cent during the 2010 financial year. ASOS has launched international 'stores' in the United States, France (above), Germany, Spain, Italy and Australia to cope with the rapidly growing global demand.

3 HIGH-QUALITY VISUALS
Products are displayed in high-quality photographs, with multiple thumbnail images available to show different views and details in close-up. The site also features catwalk video clips showcasing various garments.

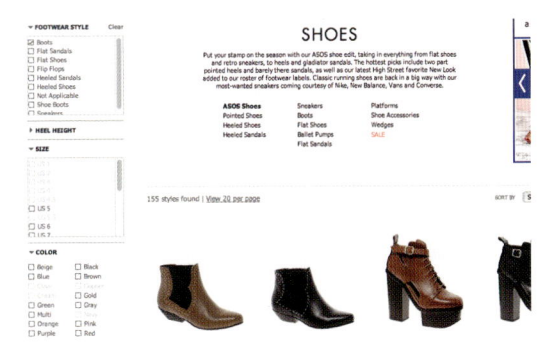

4 USER EXPERIENCE
ASOS has simple global navigation through drop-down menus. Search results can be filtered by style, size, price, colour and brand. The customer is able to see up to 200 items per page at once. Unlike many other online retailers, ASOS offers free delivery.

THE RISE OF E-COMMERCE 547

CONTEMPORARY AFROCENTRIC FASHION

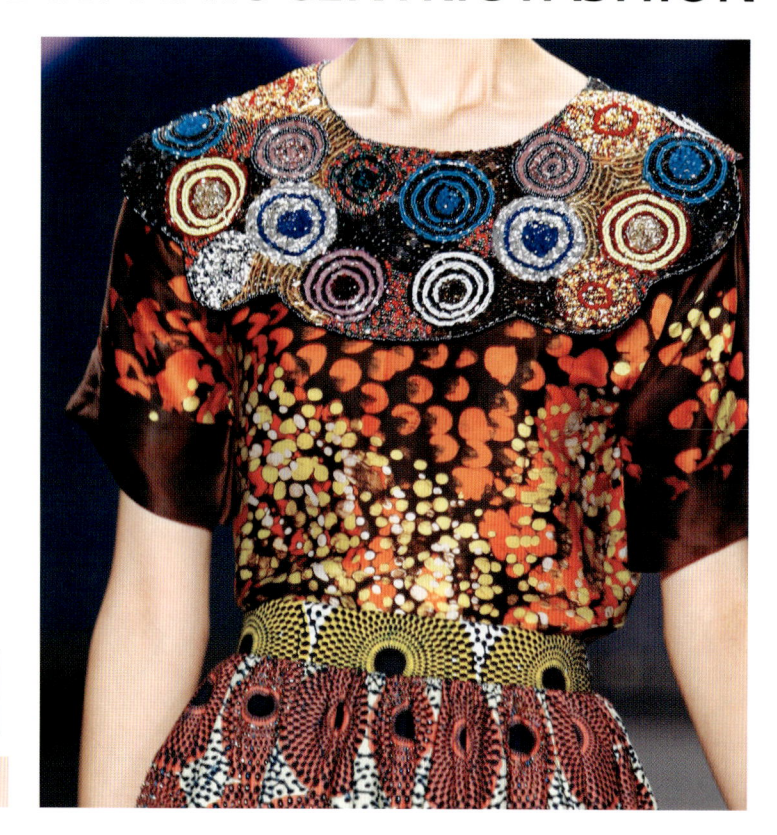

1 The spring/summer 2010 collection by Jewel by Lisa featured garments heavily embellished with beads and sequins and encrusted with jewels to accentuate the African print.

2 Ozwald Boateng combined sartorial elegance with vibrant colour in his flamboyant collection for spring/summer 2011.

A new generation of African-born designers has gained international recognition in the 21st century, both on the strength of their work and as a result of the continent's more broad cultural and economic uplift. This growing creative class has taken advantage of Africa's improved infrastructure, education and good governance in order to contemporize their own rich cultures and traditions, and make desirable collections that are sold all over the world. Their work balances mainstream seasonal trends with an intelligent re-imagining of indigenous fabrics and adornments, thereby creating fashion that feels authentic, ethical and fresh. Designers are also being supported by Africa-focused fashion weeks, media outlets, books and retail environments, as well as social media and e-commerce ventures.

Lagos in Nigeria has become one of the biggest fashion capitals in Africa. Key designer labels include Jewel by Lisa by Lisa Folawiyo (b.1976), known for reinventing wax-printed cotton as a luxury fabric through hand

KEY EVENTS

2004
Duro Olowu launches his label with the Duro dress collection for spring/summer 2004. It establishes him as Nigeria's biggest designer.

2005
Jean Paul Gaultier (b.1952) shows haute couture featuring tortoiseshell shields and a bridal gown consisting of a white leather African mask.

2005
On the strength of his first collection and without having shown on the catwalk, Duro wins New Generation Designer at the British Fashion Awards.

2008
Ghanaian designer Mimi Plange (b.1978) launches her eponymous luxury wear label inspired by African and Victorian fashions.

2008
Big brands Alexander McQueen, Tsumori Chisato, Louis Vuitton, Junya Watanabe and Diane von Furstenberg offer African-influenced collections.

2009
African fashion arrives at New York Fashion Week, courtesy of African lifestyle magazine *Arise*. Grace Jones models for the collective show.

548 1990–PRESENT

embellishments (opposite) and Maki Oh by Amaka Osakwe, who uses *ase oke*, a woven textile, and *adire*, an indigo-dyed fabric printed with meaningful symbols, to create sensual womenswear. Designers based in Johannesburg include Marianne Fassler (b.1949), whose signature is the leopard-print frock, and Gavin Rajah (b.1970), who shines at retro romantic womenswear. KLûK CGDT's opulent gowns cascade with feathers, tulle and ribbons, whereas in menswear, designer Stiaan Louw creates androgynous collections that explore male sexuality and social tribes. Elsewhere in Africa and the diaspora, Paris-based Ivorian Laurence Chauvin Buthaud dedicates her menswear label, Laurenceairline, to helping women learn production skills in Abidjan. Shirts, shorts, pyjamas suits and parkas come in bold West African and bespoke prints. In London, British Ghanaians Ozwald Boateng (b.1967) invigorates Savile Row with his colourful suits (right), and father-and-son menswear duo Joe (b.1956) and Charlie Casely-Hayford have coined the phrase 'Afro punk' for their take on nomadic style.

At the highest level, North African-born designers are making a significant impact: Alber Elbaz (b.1961) celebrated ten years at Lanvin in 2012, Azzedine Alaïa (b.1939), who established his atelier in Paris in 1980, is still revered as the 'king of cling' for his body-conscious dresses, and Max Azria (b.1949) reigns over his BCBG MAXAZRIA global fashion empire. Duro Olowu (b.1966), who was born in Lagos, Nigeria, and is now based in London, is held in the highest esteem as the pioneer of clashing prints (see p.550), a practice that signifies the prestige, power and wealth of the wearer in traditional cultures. Africa's artisanal history and culture have inspired numerous high-end international designers since Yves Saint Laurent's landmark African collection in 1967. Recently Paul Smith (b.1946) based his spring/summer collection 2010 on the dapper, colourful suits worn by the *sapeurs* of the Congo (see p.552), and for spring/summer 2012 Burberry Prorsum incorporated West African-inspired wax prints on wrapped dresses, pencil skirts and peplum jackets encrusted with beads and raffia.

Big brands have also begun to collaborate with African artisans and are basing socially responsible production on the continent. Ethiopian supermodel Liya Kebede uses cotton weavers in Addis Ababa for her casual line LemLem, and ethical fashion label Edun, established by U2 singer Bono and his wife Ali Hewson and part owned by LVMH, is part produced in Africa with profits going to farming communities (see p.487). Other labels that are dedicated to bringing about positive change include Vivienne Westwood, which makes bags in Kenya. *Vogue Italia* editor-in-chief Franca Sozzani is spearheading skills, building and investment in Africa through her role as UN Goodwill Ambassador for Fashion 4 Development and has attracted big brands to her cause. However, there are still many challenges facing African fashion, including a lack of government and fashion institution support, as well as infrastructural weaknesses. Africa is still developing, but progress is rapid and its designers are now going global. **HJ**

2010	2010	2011	2011	2011	2012
The FIFA World Cup puts Africa in the spotlight and on the catwalks, courtesy of Paul Smith, Marc Jacobs and Issey Miyake collections.	Ozwald Boateng celebrates twenty-five years in fashion. At London Fashion Week a record-breaking one hundred models wear his Savile Row suits.	Azzedine Alaïa returns to the Paris catwalk after an eight-year absence to close autumn/winter 2011 Haute Couture Week.	Christopher Bailey (b.1971) reaches for West Africa's most recognized fabric, wax-print cotton, to complete Burberry Prorsum's collection.	*New African Fashion* by Helen Jennings is the first coffee table book to crystallize the burgeoning Afropolitan fashion scene.	Celebrities catch the African fashion bug. Alicia Keys, Kelis, Gwen Stefani, Rihanna and Michelle Obama are seen wearing African designers and prints.

Duro Dress 2004
DURO OLOWU b. 1966

Nigerian designer Duro Olowu announced the arrival of his womenswear label by opening an exclusive boutique on Portobello Road, west London, and filling the rails with his debut collection for spring/summer 2004. The capsule range focused almost entirely on Empire-line dresses, which came in five variations. The design was based on the Yoruba *boubou*, a traditional garment worn by West African women that is roomy, long and often elaborately adorned and embroidered. Also called a kaftan or robe, it is usually worn as a formal, ceremonial outfit and made from gloriously coloured luxury fabrics as a sign of its wearer's high status.

Duro's version was pared down, and much lighter and sexier than its inspiration. 'It was a very effortless and comfortable dress that flowed nicely when you walked and it travelled well. If you were in Paris, London or Lagos, you could have worn that dress, day or night,' says the designer. Both US and British *Vogue* named it their dress of the year, which ignited huge consumer demand and invested the dress with a cult status among those in the know. Olowu's profile subsequently rocketed and he secured stockists worldwide, including Barney's in New York and Maria Luisa in Paris. Olowu's brand has grown ever since and this iconic Duro gown has been much copied but never bettered. **HJ**

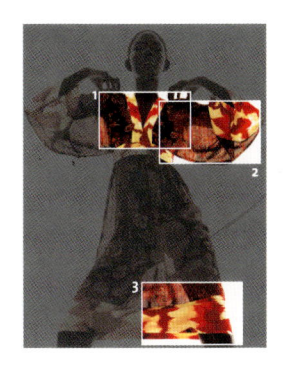

NAVIGATOR

FOCAL POINTS

1 NECKLINE
The neckline is a seductively low 'V' trimmed in silk. The print is reminiscent both of tie-dye and tiger prints, and glows in burnt red and ombré colours that carry on around the high Empire waistband. This shape accentuates the cleavage.

2 GEORGETTE SLEEVES
The body and wide, billowing sleeves of the Duro dress are made from a form-flattering viscose georgette. The print is a perennial paisley in shades of brown, which is classic yet contemporary. Other fabric variations include florals and blocking.

3 SILK HEM
The silk hem of the dress is knee-length and flattering. Although inspired by the *boubou* robe, the dress is also reminiscent of a kimono or a 1970s day dress, and exudes a bohemian and exuberant *joie de vivre*.

DESIGNER PROFILE

1966–2003
Duro Olowu is renowned for his masterful mixing of colourful couture, bespoke and vintage textiles, flattering tailoring and designs inspired by his heritage, the arts and travel. He was born and raised in Lagos, studied law in London and lived in Paris for a year before returning to London, where he met his first wife, shoe designer Elaine Golding. They launched the successful Olowu Golding label in the mid 1990s.

2004–PRESENT
After the marriage ended, Olowu established his eponymous brand in 2004 and became a popular fixture at London Fashion Week for several seasons. He then made the move to New York Fashion Week for autumn/winter 2011. He now has a boutique in St James's, London, and his well-known clientele includes Michelle Obama, Iman and Iris Apfel.

CONTEMPORARY AFROCENTRIC FASHION 551

Contemporary Sapeur 2009
CONGOLESE MEN'S DRESS STYLE

Photograph from *The Gentlemen of Bacongo: The Importance of Being Elegant* by Daniele Tamagni (2009).

This photograph is of the well-known *sapeur* Willy Covary, who lives in Bacongo, a district of Brazzaville in the Republic of the Congo. It is here where some say the *sapeur* movement was first born in 1922, when Congolese political intellectual André Grenard Matsoua returned from Paris dressed as an aristocratic gentleman. The look caught on and *sapeurs* became a celebrated part of the community.

Covary is an electrician by day and a *sapeur* by night and at weekends, when he roams the streets in his finest attire with his contemporaries in tow. His shocking-pink suit makes him stand out from the pack on the downtrodden streets of his native Bacongo. It is matched by his dandy swagger and hand gestures, which show off his white shirt and ruby-red tie, kept in place by the prerequisite tie pin. Members of Le Sape (Société des Ambienceurs et des Personnes Elégantes; Society of Tastemakers and Elegant People) adhere to a lifestyle in which good manners, idiosyncratic gestures and immaculate fashion sense mark them out as sartorial heroes. They are role models and, although poor, are still regarded as the elite, whose stylish presence at important functions is seen to add convivial glamour. Silk ties, pocket squares and Oxford shoes complete a classic *sapeur* look; such items lose their colonial overtones once donned by a *sapeur*. **HJ**

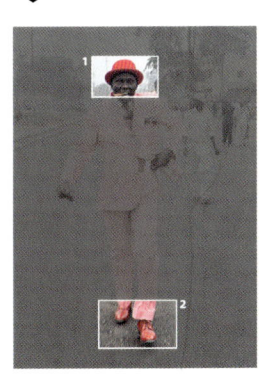

NAVIGATOR

FOCAL POINTS

1 BOWLER HAT
A pristine scarlet-red bowler hat sits on top of Willy Covary's head, and flashes of red recur throughout the outfit, seen in the necktie, handkerchief and shiny shoes. Many *sapeurs* wield cigars, lit or unlit, as one of their many accessories.

2 RED SHOES
Covary's lace-up shoes match his tie and are polished to a rosy glow. Although the exact brands of the outfit he wears are unspecified, they are assuredly designer and expensive. No self-respecting *sapeur* would wear anything less.

▲ Paul Smith reinterpreted Covary's outfit as part of his Afrocentric spring/summer 2010 collection. His female version was the first look to be sent onto the catwalk at his London Fashion Week show.

GLOSSARY

aglet
A protective metal tip at the end of cords, shoelaces or drawstrings, designed to prevent unravelling. Largely functional today, the aglet was an opportunity for decorative extravagance in the 15th and 16th centuries.

appliqué
A method of sewing cut-out pieces of fabric onto a base cloth to create a decorative effect.

arm scye
The fabric edge of a garment onto which a sleeve is sewn.

atelier
French term for a design studio of highly skilled craftspeople, attached to a couture house.

baby-doll
A very short dress or nightdress with a trapeze-line silhouette.

bandage dress
A form-fitting dress made from bands of elasticated cloth sewn tightly together.

bandeau
A fabric headband first worn as decoration and later in sports; also a single piece of cloth designed to cover a woman's breasts.

banyan
A loose, 'T'-shape gown worn by men in the 18th century as a type of informal dressing gown. Also refers to a men's vest or undershirt.

bertha collar
A wide, flat shawl-like collar, worn with a low neckline and large enough to extend over the shoulders.

bias cut
A method of cutting fabric diagonally across the grain at forty-five degrees to the warp and weft of the cloth, giving greater flexibility and stretch.

boutonnière
A decorative flower or posy worn by men in their suit buttonhole.

breechcloth
A form of loincloth that runs between the legs and is secured with a belt.

bricolage
A method of constructing or creating objects or garments from a diverse range of materials at hand.

Capri pants
A type of close-fitting trousers that end at mid calf, worn by women.

Chambre Syndicale de la Haute Couture
French regulatory body that issues a list each year of companies that are entitled to call themselves haute couture houses.

chemise
A simple shirt or tunic made of cotton or linen, worn next to the skin to protect the outer clothes from sweat; also a loose columnar style of dress.

chinoiserie
A decorative style influenced by motifs and techniques seen in Chinese art and design.

chiton
A draped garment made from a single piece of cloth, worn by both men and women in the Classical period.

cloche hat
A close-fitting, bell-shaped women's hat, popular in the 1920s and 1930s.

Cornelli work
A decorative technique in which cotton braid is sewn onto fabric in an abstract wavy pattern.

cote-hardie
A long dress worn by women in the 14th and 15th centuries; one of the first types of dress to be shaped through tailoring. Also a hip-length tunic worn by men.

cravat
A long piece of fabric, sometimes pleated, tied around the neck; the precursor of the modern necktie.

crinoline
A full, bell-shaped stiff skirt with volume created by a frame or layers of petticoats.

crumb-catcher
A band of stiffened fabric that stands away from the bodice of a dress.

Cuban heel
A broad, medium heel usually found on men's shoes; the back edge of the heel tapers away.

cuirass bodice
A form-fitting, hip-length boned corset, popular in the late 19th century.

dagging
A decorative technique applied to a sleeve or hem whereby the edge of the fabric is cut into a pattern, such as waves, scallops or leaves.

décolletage
The part of the female body between the neck and breasts that is left exposed by a low-cut neckline.

déshabillé
The state of being partly undressed. The style was fashionable during the mid 17th century at the Stuart court.

dhoti
A piece of cloth wrapped and knotted to create a garment akin to a skirt; worn by men in the Indian subcontinent.

djellaba
A long, flowing, sleeved gown made of light cotton, sometimes with a hood. Worn in North African countries.

Directoire/Directory
A style movement characterized by neoclassical styles and popular in post-revolutionary France until the beginning of the 19th century.

dirndl
Originally a traditional style of dress for women in Austria, in which the skirt is gathered onto a fitted yoke. Also popular as a skirt in the 1940s, characterized by a horizontal hip seam.

dolman sleeve
Set very low in the arm scye and

tapering at the wrist, this style of sleeve was popular during the late 19th century, creating a sloping silhouette.

doublet
A close-fitting, buttoned, padded jacket almost universally worn by men between the 15th and 17th centuries.

Double Windsor/ Windsor knot
Thought to be named after the Duke of Windsor or his father, George V, this method of tying a necktie produces a full, large knot.

drawloom
A small framed loom usually used in a domestic setting to produce woven cloth.

duchesse satin
A heavy, closely woven satin cloth with a rich lustrous surface.

Empire line
A 19th-century fashion in which the bodice of the dress is gathered under the bust instead of at the waist. The style is named after the period of the Napoleonic Empire.

engageantes
Decorative false sleeves, characterized by ruffles and gathered lace, worn by women in the 18th and 19th centuries.

faille
A type of fine woven fabric with a ribbed texture and slight lustre.

falling collar
A development from the stiff ruff, the falling collar lay flat on the neck and chest, and was worn by both men and women in the early 17th century.

farthingale
An exaggerated hoop underskirt that was worn to maintain the shape of the overskirt; popular at the courts of Europe in the late 15th and early 16th centuries.

fichu
A large neckerchief worn by women in the 18th century to provide a modest covering of the décolletage.

flapper
A term for a young woman of the 1920s known for wearing the controversial short, straight chemise dress and bobbed hairstyle.

foulard tie
A tie made of a lightweight silk, or silk and cotton-mix woven fabric.

frogging
A type of braiding made of knotted threads sewn onto garments to provide surface decoration.

furbelow
A decorative frill, flounce or ruffle often made of the same fabric as the main garment.

gaberdine
A tightly woven, heavy-duty cloth recognizable by a prominent diagonal rib on the surface.

gigot sleeve
French term for **leg o' mutton sleeve**.

godet
A triangular piece of fabric inserted into a seam to provide a flared shape and extra volume.

gores
A dressmaking technique that uses tapered panels to allow the fabric to be fitted more closely to the body before flaring out.

gourmandine bodice
A bodice that was partly loosened in order to reveal the underclothes beneath.

grand habit
An elaborate French court dress with a heavily boned bodice and full hooped skirt, worn in the 18th century.

grosgrain
A close-woven fabric, usually produced as a ribbon with a visible rib.

Half-Windsor
Method of tying a necktie that involves only one loop of the fabric, producing a small, neat knot.

harem pants
Long, loose-fitting trousers gathered at the ankle and Turkish in origin.

heddle
The part of a loom that separates out the threads, allowing the weft to pass through.

hobble skirt
A long, slimline skirt, fashionable in the early 20th century, with an extremely narrow opening around the ankles that made movement difficult.

houppelande
A long robe or gown with flared sleeves and worn as an outer garment in 14th- and 15th-century Europe.

intarsia
A knitting technique used to create patterns with multiple colours that appear to be 'inlaid'.

jabot
An ornamental lace or ruffled fabric bib worn at the neck by men in the 17th and 18th centuries.

justacorps
A long men's jacket with buttons from top to bottom, worn in the late 17th and early 18th centuries. Close-fitting on the body before flaring out.

kaftan
A loose-fitting, ankle-length sleeved robe, often with decorative trimming at the neck and cuffs. Persian in origin.

kirtle
A long one-piece dress worn by women over a smock between the 14th and 16th centuries.

leg o' mutton sleeve
An exaggerated, puffed-out sleeve, tapering at the wrist. Popular in the 1830s, it was named after the joint of meat that it resembled in shape.

Louis heel
A type of high heel said to have been first worn by the French king Louis XIV. The heel is characterized by its concave curve and outward taper at the bottom.

mantle
A type of full-length cloak without a hood, worn by women.

mantua
Originally a loose gown for women; later a more structured overgown worn over stays, a stomacher and a petticoat.

Marie sleeve
Popular in the early 19th century, this version of the leg o' mutton is a full sleeve secured into graduated puffs along the length of the arm.

Mary Janes
A type of court shoe with a round toe and a bar strap, fastened by a buckle across the top of the foot.

mousseline de soie
A fine, stiff fabric made of silk or rayon, with a crisp finish.

obi
Wide belt or sash tied in a decorative manner around the waist, originating in traditional Japanese costume.

pannier
A hooped frame worn on the hips to extend the width of the skirts at the side but not at the back and front.

parure
A set of matching items of jewellery popular in the 17th century.

passementerie
The application of various trimmings, including braiding, tassels and fringing, to decorate a garment.

pedal pushers
A type of close-fitting, calf-length women's trousers popular in the 1950s.

peplum
A decorative feature on skirts, dresses and jackets resembling a short gathered skirt or exaggerated hem to accentuate the waist.

Peter Pan collar
A flat, turned-down collar with rounded edges, usually worn by women.

petticoat breeches
Late 17th-century style of trousers with wide legs resembling a skirt.

picot
An ornamental loop of thread used to decorate the edge of lace, ribbon and crocheted or knitted fabric.

piqué
Method of weaving cotton that produces a stiff, textured fabric similar to cotton twill. It is also known as marcella.

placket
A double layer of fabric at the opening of a garment, such as a polo shirt or trousers, that allows buttons to be sewn on securely.

plastron
A stiff decorative panel on the front of a bodice; popular in 14th-century French court dress.

playsuit
A one-piece garment with short legs originally worn by children but later adopted by adults.

plumassier
Highly skilled artisan who works with feathers and plumes to create decorative accessories.

points
Decorative cone-shaped metal tips placed at the end of ribbons or laces to stop them unravelling.

princess line
An A-line silhouette created by long, curved vertical seams that run the length of the garment. Invented by couturier Charles Worth.

pouter-pigeon/monobosom
Named after a breed of pigeon with an oversized chest, this term refers to a silhouette popular in the 1900s with the upper front half of the body padded with corsetry to balance out the heavy bustle at the back.

prêt-à-porter
French term meaning 'ready-to-wear' or 'off the peg', denoting garments bought as they are rather than custom made for clients.

rabat
A type of backless waistcoat worn by members of the clergy.

raglan sleeve
A sleeve that extends in one piece to the neckline of the garment.

raschel knit
Method of warp knitting that creates a loose, lacelike fabric with openwork patterning.

redingote
A utilitarian coat originally worn for horse riding; evolved into a fashionable, tailored garment in the 19th century.

resort wear
Refers to clothing designed to be worn by affluent clients travelling in warmer climates during the winter. Also known as cruisewear.

revers
Any part of a garment that is turned back to show the reverse side, such as a lapel.

resist-dye
Various methods are used to 'resist' or prevent dye from reaching all areas of cloth, thereby creating a pattern.

reticule
A small, netted drawstring purse and precursor to the handbag.

robe de style
An alternative to the simple 1920s chemise dress, this garment was characterized by its full skirts falling from a simple straight bodice.

robe volante
An early 18th-century style of loose-fitting dress characterized by a large expanse of cloth that is gathered into square pleats at the back, which then cascade to the ground.

robe à l'anglaise
A formal dress worn in 18th-century Britain at the same time as France favoured the more informal *robe volante*. It featured a closely fitted bodice and wide skirts with no decorative pleats at the back.

robe à la française
A development from the **robe volante**, but with smaller pleats of fabric falling from the neckline and a more fitted bodice.

robe à la polonaise
Worn in the 18th century, the *robe à la polonaise*, also known as the *robe retroussée*, was characterized by the flounces created by lifting up and pinning sections of the skirts at three or four points.

ruff
A detachable exaggerated collar made of starched folds of lace, worn by the European elite during the 16th century.

sack-back gown
see robe à la française

sack suit
Otherwise known as a lounge suit, the loose-fitting sack suit was the standard garment for men from the mid 19th century and continues to be worn in the 21st century.

saddle shoe
A low-heeled casual shoe characterized by a plain toe and a contrasting saddle-shaped middle section.

sapeur
An extravagantly elegant style of dressing for men, originating in the Congo. It includes strikingly coloured suits and accessories.

self-fabric
A sewing term for an embellishment made from the same material as the rest of the garment.

selvedge
The edge of a piece of fabric that has been woven or knitted in a way that prevents the material from unravelling.

shawl collar
A type of lapel that has a continuous curve, usually found on tuxedo jackets or jumpers.

sheath dress
A simple dress designed to fit closely to the body, using bust and waist darts.

shirtwaist
A blouse or dress designed to mimic the tailoring of a men's shirt.

silk gazar
A type of stiff silk or cotton fabric woven using a high-twist double yarn.

Spandex
A synthetic fibre also known as elastane and valued for its extreme elasticity. It is often used in sportswear.

spats
A protective or decorative accessory worn over a shoe to cover the instep and ankle.

spencer
A short, waist-length coat dating from the late-18th century and named after George John Spencer, 2nd Earl Spencer. In the Regency period it was a popular close-fitting jacket worn by women.

stomacher
A stiff decorative panel worn to fill in the front opening of a gown and to cover the corset.

surcoat
A loose medieval outer garment worn by men and women. Also worn by knights to protect their armour and often emblazoned with the coat of arms of the wearer.

surgeon's cuff
This feature comprises several functioning buttonholes on the sleeve of a suit jacket, derived from a surgeon's need to roll up his sleeves.

tailormade
A woman's two-piece skirt suit first referred to in the Edwardian period.

tie-dye
A dyeing process whereby the cloth is bound with string before dyeing. The string is untied after the garment has dried, revealing an abstract pattern.

tippet
A small fur cape or scarflike wrap worn around the shoulders, with long ends hanging down the front.

toile
A coarse linen cloth used to create mock-up garments before the final, more expensive, fabric is used. The term can refer to the prototype garment or the cloth itself.

toque
A close-fitting hat with a very narrow brim or no brim at all. Also a chef's hat.

trapeze line
A full-skirted garment with an exaggerated A-line shape.

trompe l'oeil
French term literally meaning 'deceives the eye', whereby an object is made to look like another through the use of optical illusion.

tulle
A very fine, delicate lightweight netting often used for ballet costumes or wedding dresses.

tuxedo
A semi-formal evening suit, usually in black, recognizable by the use of grosgrain, satin or silk ribbon both on the lapels and the side seam of the trousers.

vest
In the United States this term usually refers to a waistcoat, whereas in Britain it denotes an undergarment worn under a shirt to protect it from sweat.

virago sleeve
A type of sleeve that was fashionable in the early 17th century, created by tying strips of narrow ribbon at intervals along a full sleeve to create a series of puffs.

warp
The yarn in a piece of woven cloth that lies lengthways and is held in tension by the loom.

weft
The yarn in a piece of woven cloth that is inserted over and under the warp threads.

whisk collar
A 17th-century ornate collar comprising a half circle of starched material that stands away from the neck at a sharp angle.

wrapper
An early version of a dressing gown or housecoat. Also refers to a West African outfit that includes a wrap skirt.

yuzen
A paste-resist method of dyeing silk velvet to imitate brocade; invented in 15th-century Japan.

CONTRIBUTORS

Rio Ali (RA)
is a fashion writer and historian. After attaining a degree in fashion history and theory at Central Saint Martins College of Art and Design, she studied for an MA in critical writing in art and design at the Royal College of Art. She is also archivist for British heritage brands Burberry and Margaret Howell.

Emily Angus (EA)
has an MA in history of design and material culture and is a lecturer in fashion and graphic design theory. She also works as an editor and designer at Yale University Press.

John Angus (JA)
is principal lecturer at the University of Derby, focusing on design and creative technologies for fashion, textile and architectural applications. He has directed undergraduate programmes and participated in research collaborations at Liverpool John Moores University, the Royal College of Art and Central Saint Martins College of Art and Design, and also worked as a design and innovations consultant.

Dr Malcolm Barnard (MB)
is senior lecturer in visual culture at Loughborough University, where he teaches the history and theory of art and design. His background is in philosophy and sociology. He is the author of *Fashion as Communication* (Routledge, 1996), *Art, Design and Visual Culture* (Macmillan, 1998), *Approaches to Understanding Visual Culture* (Palgrave, 2001) and *Graphic Design as Communication* (Routledge, 2005). He also edited *Fashion Theory* (Routledge, 2007).

Isla Campbell (IC)
studied medieval and modern history at the University of Birmingham, followed by an MA in medieval archaeology at the University of York and further historical research at King's College, London. She started her career at the Society for the Protection of Ancient Buildings, and has since worked in social research, including as a research manager at the Heritage Lottery Fund.

Dr Rosemary Crill (RC)
is a senior curator at the Victoria & Albert Museum, Asian department, specializing in Indian textiles and paintings. Her publications include *Indian Ikat Textiles* (V&A, 1998), *Marwar Painting: A History of the Jodhpur Style* (India Book House, 2001), *Chintz: Indian Textiles for the West* (V&A, 2008) and *The Indian Portrait 1560–1860* (with Kapil Jariwala et al; National Portrait Gallery Publications, 2010). She also contributes to many other catalogues and journals, and is currently preparing an exhibition on Indian textiles.

Jane Eastoe (JE)
is a journalist and author. She has worked for the fashion trade press and has written two fashion books: *Fabulous Frocks* (co-authored with Sarah Gristwood; Pavilion, 2008) and *Elizabeth: Reigning in Style* (Pavilion, 2012). She has also produced books linked to BBC television series and worked on numerous books for the National Trust Books list.

Dr Blenda Femenías (BF)
holds a PhD in cultural anthropology and is a lecturer at the Catholic University of America. A specialist in gender, race and ethnicity of Latin America, she has conducted research in the Andes. Her publications include *Gender and the Boundaries of Dress in Contemporary Peru* (University of Texas Press, 2005). She is co-editor (with Margot Schevill) of the *Berg Encyclopedia of World Dress and Fashion: Volume 2—Latin America and the Caribbean* (Berg, 2011).

Marnie Fogg (MF)
is a fashion expert and media consultant on all aspects of the fashion and textile industry. She is the author of eleven books about fashion, including *Boutique: A '60s Cultural Phenomenon* (Mitchell Beazley, 2003), *Print in Fashion* (Batsford, 2006), *Couture Interiors* (Laurence King, 2007) and *Fashion Design Directory* (Thames & Hudson, 2011).

Dr Alexandra Green (AGr)
holds a PhD from the School of Oriental and African Studies, University of London. The focus of her research is Southeast Asian art, particularly Burmese art. Her publications include three edited volumes: *Burma: Art and Archaeology* (Art Media Resources, 2002), *Eclectic Collecting: Art from Burma in the Denison Museum* (University of Hawaii Press, 2008) and *Rethinking Visual Narratives from Asia: Intercultural and Comparative Perspectives* (Hong Kong University Press, 2012).

Amelia Groom (AmG)
is an art writer and teacher. She is currently writing her PhD in art history at the University of Sydney and editing an anthology of texts on the theme of time for the *Documents of Contemporary Art* series published by Whitechapel Gallery and The MIT Press.

Dr Alison Gwilt (AG)
is a fashion design academic and researcher exploring sustainable strategies for fashion and textile design practice. She is the editor of *Shaping Sustainable Fashion* (Earthscan, 2011), *Basics Fashion Design: Sustainable Fashion* (AVA, 2013) and *Fashion Design for Living* (Routledge, 2014). She is reader in fashion and sustainability in the Art and Design Research Centre at Sheffield Hallam University.

Pam Hemmings (PH)
holds a BA and MA in constructed textiles, and is a lecturer in constructed textiles at Brighton University, Derby University and the University of Wales. She also works as a design consultant in Nepal, Tibet and India.

Will Hoon (WH)
is senior lecturer in design history at the University of Northampton. He teaches and writes about design, and has contributed to the quarterly magazine *Eye: The International Review of Graphic Design*.

Helen Jennings (HJ)
studied at King's College, London, and is an award-winning writer and stylist. She is the editor of *Arise* magazine, which celebrates African fashion, music, culture and society, and the author of *New African Fashion* (Prestel, 2011) about contemporary African style and photography. She has contributed to numerous publications including *i-D*, *The Face*, *Time Out*, *Trace*, the *Guardian* and *Grazia*.

Dr Yuniya Kawamura (YK)
holds a PhD from Columbia University and is associate professor of sociology at the Fashion Institute of Technology, State University of New York. She teaches and writes about fashion, in particular Japanese street fashion and subcultures.

Dr Alistair Knox (AK)
has been teaching at Nottingham Trent University since 1995, following more than twenty years in the fashion and textile industry. His research covers a wide range of management and advanced technology issues related to the fashion industry, including projects such as the SizeUK 3-D body-scanning survey and major EU initiatives including E-Tailor and Servive.

Dr Malika Kraamer (MK)
is a researcher in global fashion and African textiles. She completed a PhD at the School of Oriental and African Studies, University of London. As curator of world cultures at Leicester Arts and Museums Services she led the Cultural Olympiad exhibition 'Suits and Saris' on the interaction between British, East African and South Asian Fashion. She has published extensively on dress and textiles from coastal West Africa in a number of journals including *African Art*, *Material Religion* and *Afrique: Archéologie et Arts*.

Eric Musgrave (EM)
has written widely about the fashion industry since 1980. In 1985 he was the launch editor of *For Him Magazine* (now *FHM*), the first of the modern men's style magazines. He was also editor of *Drapers*, the United Kingdom's leading fashion trade magazine, and is the author of a pictorial history of men's tailoring *Sharp Suits* (Pavilion, 2009).

Dr Ilya Parkins (IP)
is assistant professor of gender and women's studies at the University of British Columbia (Okanagan). Her interdisciplinary work focuses on fashion theory, early 20th-century cultural formations and feminist thought. She is the author of *Poiret, Dior and Schiaparelli: Fashion, Femininity and Modernity* (Berg, 2012) and the co-editor of *Cultures of Femininity in Modern Fashion* (UPNE, 2011). She has published in various journals in the areas of feminist and cultural theory.

Dr Regina Root (RR)
is distinguished associate professor of modern languages and literatures at the College of William and Mary (Virginia, USA). She has written and edited several works on fashion and cultural production, including *The Latin American Fashion Reader* (Berg, 2005) and *Couture and Consensus: Fashion and Politics in Postcolonial Argentina* (University of Minnesota Press, 2010). She collaborates regularly with Latin American designers and intellectuals affiliated with Raíz Diseño, a transnational design initiative.

Dr Jennifer Scarce (JS)
is honorary lecturer in Middle Eastern cultures at Duncan of Jordanstone College of Art and Design, University of Dundee, and was formerly senior curator of Middle Eastern collections at the National Museum of Scotland. She has travelled widely in the Middle East, curated many exhibitions and written about the architecture, dress and textiles of these regions. Her publications include books on the dress of Iran and Turkey, and the history of urban dress in Morocco. She has also catalogued the collections of 19th-century Iranian tiles in the Victoria & Albert Museum.

Dr Toby Slade (TS)
is associate professor at the University of Tokyo, researching Asian modernity and the history and theory of fashion. He focuses on Asian responses to modernity seen through objects of the everyday, and the governing dynamics of systems of fashion. He is the author of *Japanese Fashion* (Berg, 2009), which explores fashion and clothing in Japan from the earliest times to today.

Dawne Stubbs (DS)
has worked in the fashion and clothing industry for more than twenty years in roles focused on design and brand creative direction. She has worked with unique heritage brands including John Smedley, Pretty Polly and Barbour.

Dr Laurie Webster (LW)
is an anthropologist and specialist in textiles from the Southwestern United States. She is a visiting scholar in the department of anthropology at the University of Arizona and a research associate at the American Museum of Natural History. Her publications include *Beyond Cloth and Cordage: Archaeological Textile Research in the Americas* (University of Utah Press, 2000) and *Collecting the Weaver's Art: The William Claflin Collection of Southwestern Textiles* (Peabody Museum Collections, Harvard University Press, 2003).

Ming Wilson (MW)
has an MA from the School of Oriental and African Studies, University of London, and is senior curator in the Asian department of the Victoria & Albert Museum. She organized the exhibition 'Imperial Chinese Robes from the Forbidden City' (2010) and edited the accompanying catalogue.

Dr Philippa Woodcock (PW)
specializes in early modern history, chiefly 16th-century French Milan. She has worked on interdisciplinary projects including The Material Renaissance (University of Sussex), The Renaissance Pharmacy (Queen Mary, University of London) and The Parish Church and the Landscape (Oxford Brookes University).

INDEX

Page numbers in **bold** refer to illustrations

à la chinoise 131, **132**, 133
à la Grecque **120**, 121, **122**, 123, **123**
à la platitude 108
à la polonaise 456, **456**, **457**
A-line: dresses 130, 175, 197, 345, **358**, **359**, **362**, 363, **363**, **380–1**, 381; skirt 235, **235**, **456**, **457**, **462**, 463, 505, **505**
A-POC (Issey Miyake) 502, **502–3**
ABC Prints 161
Abraham & Straus 217
Acton, Harold 243
Adam, Khadija 373
Adaskina, Natalia 235
Adidas 403, 446, **447**, 528, 529, 530, 533, **533**; AdiZero 530; 1 trainer 530; and Stella McCartney 529, **530**; Superstar trainers 446; Techfit/PowerWeb technology 531; Y-3 (Yohji Yamamoto) 403, **532–3**, 533
adire 549
Adler & Adler 278–9
Adolfo 442, 443
Adrian (Gilbert Adrian) 270, 270–1, 273, **278**; Letty Lynton dress 271, **272–3**, 273; V-line suit **278**, 279
aesthetic dress 184–9; Liberty dress **188–9**, 189
Africa: African wax and fancy prints **160**, 160–3, **161**, 549; Afrocentric fashion 370–3, 446; Afro hairstyles 373, **373**; Alaïa, Azzedine 549; *ase oke* 371, **374**, 375, **375**; Boateng, Ozwald 549, **549**; *bògòlanfini* 371; *buba* 371, **374**, 375, **375**; Casely-Hayford, Joe and Charlie 549; contemporary Afrocentric fashion 548–53; dashiki 373; Duro dress **550–1**, 551; Elbaz, Alber 549; Fassler, Marianne 549; *iborun* 375; *ipele* 371, **374**, 375, **375**; *iro* 371, **374**, 375, **375**; Jewel by Lisa **548**, 548–9; *kanga* 371; kente cloth **134**, 134–7, **135**, **136–7**, 371, 446; KLûK CGDT 549; LemLem 549; Louw, Stiaan 549; Maki Oh 549; motifs 135, **136**, 137; Olowu, Duro 549, **550–1**, 551; Rajah, Gavin 549; ready-to-wear 371; samples **137**; *sapeurs* 372, 549, **552–3**, 553; Seydou, Chris 371; 'sword of kingship' design 162, **162–3**; Thomas-Fahm, Shade 371; West African textiles 134–7
African American fashion 13, 292–5; Lowe, Anne Cole 293; swing dance outfits **292**, 293; Valdes, Zelda Wynn 293; zoot suit 293, **294–5**, 295, 369
Afro 373, **373**
Afterwords (Hussein Chalayan, 2000) 499, **504–5**, 505
agbada 375
Aghion, Gaby (Chloé) 535
Aglaia 189

aglets 49, 51
agrafes 133
Ahmet I, Ottoman emperor 60, 61, **62–3**, 63
Ahrendts, Angela (Burberry) 535
Akbar, Mughal emperor 64, **65**, 65–6
Akihabara 507
Alabama Chanin 487
Alaïa, Azzedine 456, **424**, 424, 425, 549
Albert, Prince 157
Albini, Walter 383, **383**
Aldredge, Theoni V. 413
Alexander McQueen 475; Ice Queen dress (Sarah Burton) 12, **516–17**, 517
Alkasura 407
Amalgamated Talent 431
American fashion: 3.1 Phillip Lim 540, 541, **541**; Adrian 278, 279; American archetypes 190–1; appropriation of male clothing 266–9; 'bobbysoxer' style 309, **309**, **310–11**, 311, 314; boutique culture 357; Burch, Tory 540, 541, **541**; Carnegie, Hattie 276–7, **280–1**, 281; Carnegie suit (Hattie Carnegie) **280–1**, 281; Cashin, Bonnie 278–9, **279**; chinos 312, **312**, **313**; Copeland, Jo 277; daywear: beaded cardigans 327, **327**, **330**, 331, **331**; film costume design 314, **314**, 315, **315**; Galanos, James 279; Gibson Girl 190, 190–1; Halston 13, 279; Head, Edith 314, **314**; Hepburn, Katharine 267, **267**; Ivy League style 308, 312, **312–13**, 365, 413; James, Charles 287; Jantzen 279; Karan, Donna 13, 279; Kelly bag 315, 318, **318**, **319**; King, Muriel 282; Klein, Calvin 13, 279; Koret 279; Lentz, Irene 279; Letterman sweaters 312, **312**, **313**; Mabry, Moss 315, **315**; McCardell, Claire 13, **276**, 277, 277–8, 282; Native American textiles (Southwest) 22, 22–5, **23**, **24**, **25**; Norell, Norman 279; Panichgul, Thakoon 540, **540**, 541; Paraphernalia 357, **357**; 'popover' dress (Claire McCardell) 277; post-war workwear 340–3; Potter, Clare 277, 282; preppy styles 13, 308–13, 413, 540; Proenza Schouler 540, **542–3**, 543; prom dress 315, **316–17**, 317; quilted jacket and leather skirt (Proenza Schouler) **542–3**, 543; ready-to-wear 195, 276–81, 398; 'rep' ties 308, **309**, **313**; Rose, Helen 314, 315; shirtwaist dress **328**, 329, **329**; slacks 267; suit 268, 269, **269**; 'sweater girls' 320, **321**, 323, **323**; sweetheart line 314, **314–15**, 317; Theyskens at Theory 540, 541; trench coats 267; Trigère, Pauline 279; trouser suit 266, **266**, 267; tuxedo 266, **266**, 267; understated style 540–3; Wang, Alexander 540–1; wasp-waisted dress 314, 315; wide-legged trousers

256, **257**, **257**, 266, **267**, **268**, 269; youthful femininity 314–19 *see also* African American fashion; Hollywood and fashion
American Gigolo (1980) **438**, 439
American Gothic (Grant Wood) 477, **477**
amictus 19, **19**
Amies, Hardy 283, 301, 305; Cumberland tweed suit **304–5**, 305
Anarchy in the UK (fanzine) **418**
'anarchy shirt' **417**, **418–19**, 419
ancient Greece and Rome *see* Greek clothing; Roman clothing
Anderson & Sheppard 273, **274**, 275
androgyny in fashion 12, 211, 213, 235, 239, 345, 369, 385, 406, 409, 477, 549
angarkha 66
Anne Marie of France 263; telephone bag 263, **263**
anti-fashion 482–5; grunge **482**, 482–3; Jacobs, Marc 482, **482**, 483; Klein, Calvin 483; Sui, Anna 483, **483**; 'Under Exposure' **484–5**, 485
Anuszkiewicz, Richard 363
APC 477
Arai, Jun'ichi (NUNO Corporation) **500–1**, 501
Argyle 259, **259**
Armani, Giorgio 383, 437, **437**, 439, 442; deconstructed suit **438–9**, 439
armour 33, 83, **83**, 421, 463
Arnaut, Bernard (LVMH) 474–5, 510
The Arnolfini Marriage (Jan van Eyck) **46–7**
Art Deco 211, 213, 232, 238, 239, 240, 241, 245, **257**, 259, 265, **387**, 391
Art, Goût, Beauté 211
Art Nouveau 196, **197**, 215, 238
The Art of Being a Well-Dressed Wife (Anne Fogarty) 327
artistic dress 184, **187**, 187
ase oke 371, **374**, 375, **375**
ASOS 545, **546–7**, 547
atlas silk 60, 61, **63**
Avedon, Richard 427; Renée, 'The New Look of Dior' **302**, 303, **303**
award-letter sweater 309, 312, **312**, **313**
Ayoko, Rebecca 373
Ayton, Sylvia 357
Azria, Max (BCBG MAXAZRIA) 549

babette 45
Babur, Mughal emperor 65, **65**
baby-doll skirt **508–9**, 509
Bagaaya Nyabongo, Elizabeth, Princess of Toro 373
baggy trousers **294**, 295, **295**
Baguette bag (Fendi) **472–3**, 473
Bailey, Christopher (Burberry) 267, 534–5
Bakst, Léon 209, **214**; Dione dress (with Paquin) **215**, 215–16
balantine 121
Balenciaga (fashion house) 282, 299, 371, 475, 541
Balenciaga, Cristóbal 12, 279, **299**, 299–300, 307, 347, 381; evening

dress with ruffled underskirt **306–7**, 307; sculpted suit **299**
Ballets Russes 209, **214**, 215, 216, 387
Balmain (fashion house) 511
Balmain, Pierre 300; cocktail dress **300** *see also* Maison Balmain
Bamba 507
Band, David (The Cloth) 435
bandage dress 425, **425**
bandhana 67
Banton, Travis 271
banyan **114–15**, 115
Barbès collection (Jean Paul Gaultier, 1984/85) **460**, 461
Barbier, George 209
Bardot, Brigitte 321, 325, **325**
The Barefoot Contessa (1954) **338**, 339
Barker, Simon **418**, 419
bas de robe **88**, 89
baseball jacket 540, **542**, 543, **543**
'basket' petticoat 99
'basque' dress 131, 240
Bass, Sandi 373
bateau neckline 131, **132**, 133
Bates, John 355; Casbah dress 355, **358–9**, 359; separates 355
batiste 95, **95**, 191
Bazaar 354, 355, 356–7, 365
beach pyjamas **256–7**, 257, 266
beaded cardigan 327, **327**, **330–1**, 331
Beard, Peter 373
Beatles, the 369
Beaton, Cecil 211, **284**, 285, **285**
Beckham, Victoria 534, 535, **535**.
Beene, Geoffrey 442, 511
Belle Epoque 196, **196**, 196–201; afternoon dress **198**, 199, **200**, 201, **201**; corset 197, **197**, 198, 201, **201**; Doucet 196, 198, **199**, 201; Fortuny 216, **216**; 'hobble' skirt 11–12, 198, **198**; Lucile 196, 198, **198**, 199, 201; 'Merry Widow' hat 197, **197**; orientalism 199, 209, **214**, 214–17, **215**, **216**, **217**; Paquin 196, 198, 200–1, 201, 215, **215**; Poiret 11–12, 196, 198, 199, 201, 208, **208**, 209, 213; straw boater 196; toque 197; turban headdress 197, 199, **216**, 216–17, **217**
Bellucci, Monica 468
Benito, Eduardo Garcia 210–11, **211**
beret 262, 263, **268**, 269, **269**, 373
Bergdorf Goodman 276, 345, 398
Bergé, Pierre 382
Bernardini, Micheline 325
bertha collar 131, 147
Berthault, Jean Louis **422**, 423
Bertin, Marie-Jeanne 95
Besnard, Jean 209
Biagiotti, Laura 395
Biba 354, **356**, 357, 407
bicorne 112, **113**
bifurcated skirt 191, **192–3**, 193
biker jacket **342–3**, 343, 451, 467
bikini 321, **324–5**, 325
bird's crop jabot **178**, 179
Birkenstock 487
Birkin, Jane **386**
Birtwell, Celia **386**, 387, 391; Wandering Daisy dress **390–1**, 391

'bishop sleeves' 191
Blades 365
Blahnik, Manolo 437
Blair, Billie 373
Blass, Bill 435, 442, **442**
bliaut 184, **184**
Bloomer, Amelia Jenks 193, 266
'bloomers' (bifurcated skirt) **192**, 193, **193**
The Blue Angel (1930) 266, 267
blue denim *see* denim; jeans
Boateng, Ozwald 549, **549**
boaters 191, **194**, 195, 196, 240, **242**, 243
the bob 223, **226–7**, 227, 240, **241**
'bobbysoxer' 309, **309**, 310–11, 311, 314
Bodymap 431, 433; 'The Cat in the Hat ... ' collection (1984) 431, 432, **432–3**; Michael Clark Dance Company costumes 433, **433**
bògòlanfini 371
Bolan, Marc 406, **406**
bolero **142**, 143, **143**, 178, 179, 224, 225, **395**
Bolger, Brian (The Cloth) 435
bombachas 138
bombast stuffing 50
'bomber' jacket 341, 407
Le Bon Genre 124, **124**, **125**
'bondage trousers' 417, **417**
The Bonfire of the Vanities (Tom Wolfe) 443
Bono (Edun) 487, 549
Bonwit Teller 217, 219
boot-cut trousers **384**, 385, **385**
Boss, Hugo 437 *see also* Hugo Boss
Bottega Veneta 475
boubou 375, 551
Boucheron 339
Bouët-Willaumez, René 211
bouffant 109, 197, 345
Bourbon, Louise 263
Bourdin, Guy 407, 410, **410**, **411**
Boutet de Monvel, Bernard 209
boutique culture of the 1960s 354–7, 361, 364, 365
boutonnière **274**, 275
Bowie, David **367**, 369, 406, **408–9**, 409, 431
bowler hat **552**, 553
Boy George 430
Brando, Marlon 341, **342**, 343
bra 460; conical ('bullet bra') 320, **321**, 322–3, 323, **323**, 461, **461**; corset bra 240; 'no bra' bra 379; push-up 321
breechcloth 23, **27**, 29
bricolage 499, 500
Brinkley, Christie 428, **428–9**
Brioni 335, 337; 'Continental look' suit 335, **336–7**, 337, 364
Brissaud, Pierre 209
Britain *see* English fashion; Scotland
British Fashion Council 431
Brodovitch, Alexey 211
brogues 241, **242**, 243, 267, **267**, **294**, 295
Brooklyn Museum, New York 217, 219
Brooks, Louise **226–7**, 227
Brooks Brothers 255, 309, **313**, 365
Browns 431

Bruce, Liza **484**, **485**
Brummell, George 'Beau' 117, **119**
Brunswick jackets 108
buba 371, **374**, 375, **375**
bucket hat **446**, 446–7
'bucket top' boots 79
Buffalo Girls collection (Vivienne Westwood, 1982–83) 460
Burberry and Burberry Prorsum 267, **534**, 534–5, 549
Burch, Tory 540, **541**, **541**
Burma 168–71; court dress 168, **168**, 169, **170–1**, 171; *htamein* 169, **169**; *luntaya acheik* tapestry weaving 169, **169**, 171; *myit-do-myi-she* 169, **170**, 171, **171**; *paso* **168**, 169, 171; sash belt **171**; *yinzi* 169
Burrows, Stephen 373
Burton, Sarah **490**, **511**; Ice Queen dress (for Alexander McQueen) 12, **516–17**, 517
Bus Stop 354
busks 51, 131, 197
bustier 88, **89**, 422, **423**, 453, **456**, **457**, **470**, 471, **471**, 490
bustle 130–1, 146, 148, **149**, 181, **183**
Buthaud, Laurence Chauvin (Laurenceairline) 549
'butterfly sleeve' dress **272–3**, 273
button-down shirt 308, **309**, 364, 365

cage crinoline **11**, 146, **147**
Callot Sœurs 246
camiknickers 240
Campbell, Naomi 428, 466, **467**, **470**
Capri pants 279, 335, **335**, 345
cardigan suit (Coco Chanel) 12, **222**, 222–3, 451
Cardin, Pierre 265, 301, 371, 372, 376, 377, 469; futurist designs **376**, 377; Space Age (Cosmo Corps) collection 377, 381
Caresse Crosby bra 460
Carnaby Street, London 354, 356, 364, 365
Carnegie, Hattie **276–7**, 281; Carnegie suit 277, **280–1**, 281
Cartier 339
Casbah dress (John Bates) 355, **358–9**, 359
Casely-Hayford, Joe and Charlie 549
Cashin, Bonnie 278–9, **279**
Cassini, Oleg 345, **345**
Castelbajac, Jean-Charles de 383
Castiglioni, Consuelo 520
'The Cat in the Hat takes a Rumble with a Techno Fish' collection (Bodymap, 1984) 431, 432, **432–3**
cavalier dress 79
Cavalli, Roberto 466, 468–9, **469**
Cecil Gee suit 364
Céline 475, **535**
chakdar jama 66, **67**
Chalayan, Hussein 499, 500, 505; Afterwords (2000) 499, **504–5**, 505
Chambre Syndicale de la Haute Couture 174, 299, 382, 403, 490
Chanel (fashion house): 'gilt and quilt' bag 437, 451, **451**; by

Lagerfeld 437, 451, **451**, 452, 454, 455, **455**, 459; logo 451, 454, **455**; suit 345, **454–5**, 455; 2/55 handbag 345, **349**, 451
Chanel, Coco (Gabrielle Bonheur Chanel) 12, **222**, 222–3, 241, 252, 257, 455; beach pyjamas 257, 266; cardigan suit 12, **222**, 222–3, 451; cocktail dress **224–5**, 225; costume jewellery 223, 241, 455; cuffs 223, **223**; film costume design 271; 'gilt and quilt' bag 451; little black dress **224–5**, 225, 451; three-piece suit **222**, 222–3
chaperon 43–4, 47
The Charioteer at Delphi **20–1**
Charles I, king of England 78, **78**, 79
Charles II, king of England 90, **90**, 93
Charles Jourdan 410, **410**, 411, **411**
charro 141, **142–3**, 143
chaya-zome dyeing 77
Chelsea boots 364
Chelsea Cobbler 364
'Chelsea Look' 355
chemise dress: Neoclassical period 120, 120–1, **122–3**, 123, 124, **124**, **125**, 127; 1920s 223, **224**, 225, **225**, 238, 239, 252; 1950s 300, 344, 345
chemises 50, **51**, 92, **93**, 93, 95, 97
chemisette **200**, **201**, 244, 245
cheongsam 229, **229**
Chief of a Scottish Clan (Eugène Devéria) **104–5**, 105
Chikanobu, Toyohara: *Comparison of Beautiful Women in Western Coiffures* 182, **182–3**
China: *cheongsam* 229, **229**; dragon motifs 84, **84**, 85, 167, **167**; headdress 34, **35**; longevity motifs 164, **165**, 166; *magua* 166, **167**, 167; modern period 228–31; phoenix motif 84; Qing dynasty (early period) 82–5; Qing dynasty (early period) court dress 82, **82–3**, 84, **84**, **85**; Qing dynasty (late period) 164–7, 228; *qipao* 229, **229**; riding clothes 30, **30**, 166; skull cap **164**, 165; surcoat 34, **34**, **35**; Tang dynasty 30–5; Tang dynasty court dress 32, 32–3, **33**, 34, **34**, **35**; Twelve Symbols 83, **83**; uniforms 228; veils 30, 30–1; Western influences 228, **228**, 229, **229**; 'zhongshan suit' 228, **230**, 231, **231**
china poblana 139, **139**
chinoiserie 107–8, **115**, **115**
chinos 312, **312**, 313
chintz 95, **101**, 107, **114**, **115**, 115
chiripá 138
chiton 19, **20–1**, 21, 247, 251
Chiuri, Maria Grazia 511, **513**
chlamys 19
Chloé **535**
cholo 67, 71, 351
Les Choses de Paul Poiret 209
Christian Dior (fashion house) 298, 301, 361, 452
Chuck Taylor Allstar trainers 446
Church & Co. 475

circular skirt 310, **311**, **311**, 331
Cixi, Qing dowager empress 164, **164**, **165**
Clark, Frank and Florenz 260
Clark, Ossie 357, **386**, 387, 391; Wandering Daisy dress **390–1**, 391
Clifford, Camille 191, **191**
cloche hat 227, **227**, 240, **241**
cloche skirt 244, **245**, **245**
The Cloth printed textiles 431, **434–5**, 435
'cloud collar' 65, **171**
'cloud-head' shoes 31
clutch bag **284**, **285**, 332, **333**
coal-scuttle bonnets 103, 147
Coates, Caroline (Amalgamated Talent) 431
Cobblers 406
codpiece 44, 49, **49**
Cohen, Sheila 365
Colbert, Jean-Baptiste 86, **86**
Coleridge, Nicholas 442, 456; *The Fashion Conspiracy* 442, 456
college styles 308, **309** *see also* preppy styles
Comme des Garçons 13, 403, 405, 500, 501, **501**; asymmetric ensemble **404–5**, 405
Commonwealth period 79, 90
Comparison of Beautiful Women in Western Coiffures (Chikanobu) 182, **182–3**
compère 101
Condé Nast 209–10
Constantinople 58–9, 61
Constructivism 232, 233, 234, 235, 237 *see also* Russian Constructivist design
'Continental look' suit 335, **336–7**, 337, 364
contouche see robe volante
Cooper, Gary 271
Copeland, Jo 277
copotain 50
Corbin O'Grady Studio **434**
Corfam 348
Corolle line (Dior) *see* New Look
corps de robe 88, **89**
corset dress **420**, **421**, **468**
corset: Belle Epoque 197, **197**, 198, 201, 240; English fashion 79, 148, 153, 187; French fashion 90, 95, 98, 99, 120, 121, **123**, **125**, 177, 197; Mainbocher corset 286, 287; Neoclassical period 120, 121, **123**, **125**; 1930s 286, 287; 1950s 286, 287, **306**, **307**; 1990s 460, 461, **462–3**, 463; Victorian period 148, 153, 177, 187, 191, 197 *see also* stays
costume design: ballet 209, **214**, 215, **215**, 216, 433, **433**; theatre and opera 216, **232**, 235, **235**, **236**, 237, **237**, 287 *see also* film costume design
costume jewellery **222**, 223, **223**, 241, **280**, **281**, 321, 345, **454**, **455**
cote-hardie 43, 45
cotte 42, **42**
Courrèges, André 359, 372, 376–7, 381; A-line dress **380–1**, 381; The Moon Girl collection 376–7
court dress: Burma 168, **168**, 169,

INDEX 563

170, 171, **171**; China 32, 32–3, **33**, 34, **34**, **35**, **82**, 82–3, 84, **84**, **85**; France 86, 86–9, **87**, **88**, **89**, 108; Japan **36**, 37, **38**, 39, **39**, 40, **40**, **41**; medieval period 44; Ottoman Empire **58**, 58–63, **60**, **61**, **62**, 63, **63**; Renaissance period 50, 55, **56**, 57, **57**
Courtesans Strolling Beneath Cherry Trees (Utamaro) **76**, **77**
Les Couturiers Associés 301
Covary, Willy **552**, 553, **553**
cowl neck 247, 259, **404**, **405**
craft renaissance 490–7; Burton, Sarah **490**, **491**; embroidered skirt and knitted sweater (Kane) **494–5**, **495**; Erdem 491, **496–7**, **497**; floral print dresses (Erdem) **496–7**, **497**; Fulton, Holly 491, **491**; Kane, Christopher 491, **494–5**, **495**; Katrantzou, Mary 491; Rodarte 490–1, **492–3**, **493**; Rousteing, Olivier 491, **491**; tulle dresses (Rodarte) **492–3**, **493**
cravat 86, **86**, 91, **112**, **113**, 117
Crawford, Cindy 428
Crawford, Joan **272**, 273, 279
Crawford, Morris de Camp 217, 219
CRED jewellery **488**, **489**
Creed, Charles 282, 301, 327
crespine 45
crew cut **312**, **313**
cricket jumper 253, **309**
crinoline-style skirt 453, **456**, **457**
crinoline 11, 146, **146**, 147, 148, **148**, 153, 174, 177, 187, **303**, 314, **316**, **317**
'crumb-catcher' bodice **512**, 513, **513**
Cuban heel 191, 241, 257
Cubism 210, 211, **211**, 213, 233, 234, **238**, 240
cuirasse 148, **178**, 179
Culin, Stewart 217, 219
cullote 375
culottes 253
Customax 545

dagged edging 43, 47
D'Aillencourt, Simone **388**, **389**
Dalí, Salvador **262**, 263
Daltrey, Roger **366**
dandy 117, **118–19**, 119
Dante collection (Alexander McQueen, 1996) 461
Dariaux, Genevieve Antoine: *A Guide to Elegance* 327
dashiki 373
daura suruwal 350
Davis, Jacob 343
Day, Corinne **478**, 479, 483
Day, Doris 315, **327**, **327**
Day Dream (Dante Gabriel Rossetti) **187**
daywear: American shirtwaist dress **328–9**, **329**; beaded cardigan (Regina) **330–1**, **331**; beaded cardigan 327, **327**, **330**, **331**; Creed, Charles 327; Mattli, 'Jo' 327; Morton, Digby 327; navy suit (Trigère) **332–3**, **333**; the perfect housewife look **326**, **326**, 327, 331; Plattry, Greta **326**; Trigère, Pauline 327
Dazed & Confused 483

De Havilland, Terry 406
De la Renta, Oscar 372–3, 442, 443
De Meyer, Adolphe 211
De Vos, Christopher (Peter Pilotto) 527
Dean, James **340**, 341, 343, 467, **470**, **471**, **471**
Death of Tarelkin (Sukhovo-Kobylin) 237; costume design (Stepanova) 235, **236–7**, 237
Decarnin, Christophe 511, **511**
deck shoes 309
décolletage 45, 50, 79, 147, **177**, **250**, 251, **251**, 468
deconstruction fashion 498–505; A-POC (Issey Miyake) 502, **502–3**; Afterwords (Hussein Chalayan) 499, **504–5**, 505; Chalayan, Hussein 499, **500**, **504–5**, 505; Comme des Garçons **500**, **501**, **501**; Demeulemeester, Ann **499**; Fox, Shelley 500; Kawakubo, Rei 500–1, **501**; Kouyaté, Lamine Badian 500, **500**; Margiela, Martin **498**, **499**, 501; McQueen, Alexander 499; Miyake, Issey 499, **499**, 502, **502–3**, 503; NUNO Corporation 500–1, **501**; Rykiel, Sonia 394; Xuly Bët 500, **500**
Deconstructionism 498, 499
Degas, Edgar 493
'Delphos' dresses (Fortuny) 221, **221**
Demeulemeester, Ann 499
demi-gigot sleeves **132**, 133
democratic fashion 222–7; Chanel 222, 222–3, **223**, **224–5**, 225; chemise dress **224**, **225**, **225**; cloche hats **227**, **227**; Lelong 223, **223**; little black dress **224–5**, 225, 451; Patou 223, **223**
Deneuve, Catherine 348
denim 278, 340, 341, 477 *see also* jeans
denim jacket 341
department stores 149, 172, 205, 217, 219, 223, 276, 398
Derrida, Jacques 498, 499, 500, 501
déshabillé 11, **92**, **93**, **93**
designer knitwear: 1930s 258–61; 1970s 394–7; Biagiotti, Laura 395; Braemar **259**; Dorothée Bis 395; elasticated swimwear 260, **260–1**; golfing clothes 259, **259**; Jantzen 258, 260, **260–1**, 261; Krizia 395, **395**; layered knit look **259**, **259**; Mandelli, Mariuccia 395; Missoni 395, **396–7**, 397; Munn, Merle 258; raschel knit dress and hat (Missoni) **396–7**, 397; Rykiel, Sonia 394, 394–5; sweater dress 258, 259; swimwear 258, 260, **260**, 261; twinset 259, **259**
designer sportswear: 1 trainer (Adidas) 530; 1980s 446, 528; Adidas 529, 530, **530**, 533; Alexander McQueen 531; all-in-one beach wear 257, **257**; Armani, Giorgio 531; bathing costumes 253, **253**; beach pyjamas 253, **256–7**, 257; Chalayan, Hussein 531; Fastskin (Speedo) **528**, **529**; Inertia collection (Chalayan for Puma) 531; Jaked 530; Lacoste, René 253; McCartney, Stella 529, **529**, **530**; Nike 530, 530–1; Nike+ Hyperdunk (Nike) **530**, 530–1; NikeCraft 531; Olympic 2012 Team GB kit (Stella McCartney) 529, **529**, 539; Patou 12, **12**, 252, 252–3; Sachs, Tom 531; Speedo **528**, 529; swimwear **12**, 253, **253**; tennis clothes 252, 252–3, **254–5**, 255; tennis shirt (Lacoste) 253, **254–5**, 255; TYR 530; Wang, Alexander 531; Wang, Vera 531, **531**; wide-legged trousers **256**, 257, **257**; Y-3 (Yohji Yamamoto for Adidas) **532–3**, 533; Yamamoto, Yohji 531, **532–3**, 533
Dessès, Jean 301; evening dress **300**
'destroy T-shirts' 417
Detolle 286
Devéria, Eugène: *Chief of a Scottish Clan* **104**, 105, **105**
dhoti 64
Diaghilev, Sergei 209, 215
Diana, Princess of Wales 450
Diaz, Cameron **487**, 489
Dietrich, Marlene 12, 266–7, **267**, **268–9**, 269, 271, 369, 385, 423
Dinner at Eight (1933) 270, **270**
Dior, Christian 262, 279, 287, 298–9, 300, 327, 335, 348; Corolle line 303; New Look 277, 287, 293, 298, 299, **302**, 303, **303**, 314, 327, 349; 'The Bar' dress and jacket 299, **299**; Summer Collection (1957) **298** *see also* Christian Dior
dirk **104**, 105
dirndl skirt **280**, **281**
disco fashion *see* glam rock and disco fashion
djerakasha 247
Doeuillet 209
Dolce, Domenico 466, **467** *see also* Dolce & Gabbana
Dolce & Gabbana 466, 467–8, **468**; costumes for Madonna 468
'dolly birds' 355, 359
dolman sleeve 12, **304**, **305**, **328**, **329**
Donna Karan label 475
doo-rags 447
dookey chains 447, **447**
double sleeves 31, **54**, **55**, **56**, **57**
doublet 43, 44, 47, 49, **52**, 53, **53**, 78
Doucet, Jacques 175, 196, 198, 201; evening dress 198, **199** *see also* House of Doucet
dragon robe 82, 84, **84–5**
drape suit 271, **271**, **274–5**, 275
dressing gowns 95, 97, **114–15**, 115
Drexler, Millard (Gap) 413
dropped arm scyes **152**, 153, **404**, **405**, 432, **432**, **433**
Drum magazine 371–2, **372**
Dryden, Helen 210, **210**
Duff-Gordon, Lady Lucy 199 *see also* Lucile
Duffy, Brian **358**
Duncan, Isadora 247

Duran Duran 430
duster coats 205
dyes and dyeing 520; *adire* **549**; aniline dyes 149; *chaya-zome* technique 77; Japan 37, 75, **75**, 77, **183**; modern techniques 520, 521; pre-Columbian textiles **26**, 27; resist technique 25, 75, **75**, 77, **162–3**, 518; Russian Constructivism 233; Victorian period 149; World War II 283; *yuzen* technique 75, **75** *see also* tie-dyeing

e-commerce and fashion 544–7; ASOS 545, **546–7**, 547; Customax 545; Matteo Dosso 545; Net-a-Porter 544, **544**; Nike iD Studios 544, **545**
Eco Age 549
eco fashion *see* sustainable and ethical fashion
Edelstein, Victor 450
Edo period, Japan 74–7
Edun **486**, **487**, 549
Edward, Prince of Wales (later Edward VII, king of England) 154, **155–6**, 157, **157**, **158–9**, 159, 175
Edwardian period 175, 196 *see also* Belle Epoque
Egoist, Shibuya 507
eingyi 169
Eisenstaedt, Alfred **323**
Elbaz, Alber **510**, 511, 549
Eley, Mark (Eley Kishimoto) 519
Eley Kishimoto **518**, 519
Elisabeth, empress of Austria **172–3**, 173
Elizabeth Arden 287
Elle 403
Elson, Karen 482–3
'Emilioform' 335
Emmanuel, Mrs Francesca **374**, 375, **375**
Empire line 121, 125, **125**, **126**, 127, 130, 131, 198, 201, 205
The Empress of Austria (Winterhalter) **176–7**, 301
en Coeur 147
en pouf 108
engageantes **99**, **106**, **107**, **110**, 111, **153**
'engineer boots' **342**, **343**, 343
English fashion: bias cut 117, 149; Blades 365; blazer 157; button-down shirt 364; Cecil Gee suit 364; Charles I and the Commonwealth 78–81; Chelsea boots 364; chemises 92, 93, 93; dandy 117, 118, 119, **119**; dinner jacket 156, **157**; English tailoring 154–9; frock coat 155, **155**; gentleman's dress 116–19; high-standing collar 364; hipster trousers 364; 'kipper' ties 364; lounge suit 155–6, 158, **158–9**; masks 80, **80**, 81, **81**; menswear revolution (1960s) 364; Mod fashions 364; morning suit **154**, 155, 156; muffs 79, 80, **80**, 81; neck cloths 117, **118**, 119, **119**; nightgowns **92–3**, 93;

Norfolk jacket 156, **156,** 157; Nutter, Tommy 365, **368–9,** 369; pantaloons 117, **118,** 119, **119;** parka 364; Restoration period 90–3; riding clothing 119, 155; sportswear 116, **116,** 149, 156, **156,** 159, 204; suit 154, **155–6;** tailcoat **154,** 155; tailored clothing 116, 117, **117, 119;** tippets 81; 'undress' (*déshabillé*) **92–3,** 93; uniforms 365, **365,** 367; winter wear 80, **80–1,** 81
English Rose collection (Betty Jackson, 1985) 431
entari **58,** 59
Entwistle, John **366**
epaulettes 85, **85, 188,** 189, **228,** **342, 343,** 421
EPMD **446**
Erdem 491, 497, 519; floral print dresses **496–7,** 497
Erickson, Carl 'Eric' 211, **211**
Erté (Romain de Tirtoff) 211, **212–13,** 213
ethical fashion 469, 548, 549 *see also* sustainable and ethical fashion
Eton bob *see* bob
Etro **383,** 383, 520, 523; paisley dress **522–3,** 523
Etro, Gerolamo 'Gimmo' 523
Eugénie, French empress **172,** 173
Evangelista, Linda 466, **467**
Evelyn, John 91
experiments in cut and structure 246–51; bias cut 247, **248, 249, 249,** 270, **270,** 271, **288, 289;** evening dress (Madame Grès) **250–1,** 251; Grecian style clothing 247, **250,** 251, **251;** Hawes, Elizabeth 247, **248–9, 249;** horseshoe dress (Hawes) **248–9,** 249; Madame Grès 247, **250–1,** 251; Poiret 246; pyjamas 246; Vionnet 246, **246–7,** 247
Exposition Internationale des Art Décoratifs et Industriels Modernes (1925) 211, 238–9
Eyck, Jan van: *The Arnolfini Marriage* **46–7**

The Face 483
Fair Isle sweater 309, 387
Fairbanks, Douglas, Jr. **274,** 275
Fairtrade textiles and materials 487, **489**
fans 140; French fashion **108,** 109, **122, 123,** 177; Latin American 139; Neoclassical period **122, 123;** Rococo period 108, 109
farthingale 51, **54–5,** 55, 57
The Fashion Conspiracy (Nicholas Coleridge) 442, 456
'Fashion Futures' catwalk shows 279
fashion illustration 11, 208–13; Benito **211;** Dryden **210;** Erickson **211;** Erté **212–13;** Iribe 208, **208;** Lepape **209**
Fashion is Indestructible (Cecil Beaton) **284,** 285, **285**
Fashion is Spinach (Elizabeth Hawes) 9, 249
'fashion valkyries' **420,** 420–3,

421; Roxy Music cover (Antony Price) **422–3,** 423
Fassett, Kaffe 387
Fassler, Marianne 549
Fastskin and Fastskin3 (Speedo) **528,** 529
Fath, Jacques 300–1; evening dress **301**
felting 44, 50, 227, 415, 500, **501**
Fendi 452, 466, 475; Baguette bag **472–3,** 473; and Lagerfeld 469, **469,** 473, **473;** logo **473**
Fendi, Silvia Venturini 472
Ferragamo, Salvatore 334, **335**
festival wear 534, 535, **536–7,** 537
fetish wear 416, **417,** 421, 461, 467
fibulae 8, **19**
fichu 94, 95, **101**
film influence on fashion 229, 270–1, 335, 339, 341, **341,** 345, 348
film costume design 213; Adrian **270,** 270–1, **271, 272–3,** 273, 279; Armani, Giorgio **438,** 439, **439;** Cashin, Bonnie 278, 279; Head, Edith **314, 314,** 315; Italian design 338, **338, 339;** Lauren, Ralph **412,** 413, 415; Mabry, Moss 315, **315;** Orry-Kelly 321; Travilla, William **320,** 321, **321**
First State Textile Print Factory, Moscow 233
Firth, Livia 487, **488,** 489
'flapper' 209, 225, 227, 239–40
'flowerpot shoes' **165,** 165
Foale, Marion 356 *see also* Foale and Tuffin
Foale and Tuffin 356, **357;** corduroy trouser suit **356**
Fogarty, Anne 327
Folawiyo, Lisa *see* Jewel by Lisa
Fonda, Jane 424
Fontana sisters (Zoe, Micol and Giovanna) 335, 338, **339;** evening dress for *The Barefoot Contessa* 338, **338–9**
fontange 86, **87,** 91
Fonticoli, Nazareno (Brioni) 337
For Your Pleasure (Roxy Music, 1973) 421, **422–3,** 423
Ford, Tom 441, 474, 479; cut-out dress (for Gucci) **478–9,** 479
Fortuny, Mariano 216, **216,** 221, 387; 'Delphos' dresses 221, **221;** silk kaftan **220–1,** 221
four-in-hand knot **158,** 159, **159**
Fox, Shelley 500
Frederick's of Hollywood 320–1
French fashion: *batiste* 95, **95;** birth of modern fashion 94–101; bustier 88, **89;** Castelbajac, Jean-Charles de 383; corsets **95,** 98, 99, **99;** Créateurs et Industriels 383; Dorothée Bis 383, 395; dressing gowns 95, 97; *engageantes* **99,** 106, 107; fichu 94, 95, **101;** *fontange* 86, **87;** French court dress 9, 11, 86–9; Grand Habit 87, **88–9,** 89; headdress 86, 87; jabot 86, **86;** *jupe* 88, 89; *justacorps* 86, 87; Khanh, Emmanuelle 383; masks **89;** *manteau* 87, **87,** 98, 99, 106; pannier 11, **95,** 97, **99,** 99, 101;

pantaloons 86, 87; prêt-à-porter 300, 301, 359, 382–3; Rive Gauche 383; *robe à la française* 97, **98–9,** 99, 106, **110, 111;** *robe à l'anglaise* **94,** 95, **100–1,** 101; *robe volante* 95, **96–7,** 97; Rosier, Michèle 383; Rykiel, Sonia 383, 394; Saint Laurent 383
Fressanges, Inès de la 451, **454,** 455, 459
frog fastening 108, **114,** 115, **115**
FTM (Ferrante, Tositti, Monti) 383
Fujiwara, Dai: A-POC (with Issey Miyake) 502, **502–3**
Fulton, Holly **491,** 521, **521**
'funnel' boots 79
Funny Face (1957) **344,** 344
Fussey, Suzy **408**
Futurism 210, **212,** 213, **213,** 233, 234
futuristic fashion 376–81, 421; A-line dress (André Courrèges) **380–1,** 381; Cardin, Pierre 376, **376,** 377; Courrèges, André 376, **377, 380–1,** 381; Gernreich, Rudi 13, 377, **378,** 379, **379;** kinky boots 377; monokini (Rudi Gernreich) 377, **378–9,** 379; Moon Girl collection (André Courrèges) 376–7; paillette dress (Paco Rabanne) **377;** PVC boots 376, **377;** Rabanne, Paco 376, **377;** Space Age collection (Pierre Cardin) 377, 381; tabard 377; Ungaro, Emanuel 377

Gabbana, Stefano 466, **467** *see also* Dolce & Gabbana
Gable, Clark 271, **271,** 275, 335
Gaches-Sarraute, Inès 197
Gagelin-Opigez et Cie 173
Galanos, James 279, 291, 442; striped evening dress **290–1,** 291
La Galerie des Modes 127, 208
The Gallery of Fashion 121, **126,** 127
Galliano, John **431,** 483, 510, **511;** Les Incroyables collection (1984) 431
galligaskins 50
Ganguro **506,** 506–7
Gap 413
garçonne **225, 226,** 227, **227,** 239, 252
Gardner, Ava 300, 335, 338, **338,** 339
Garthwaite, Anna Maria 107, **107**
gaucho **138,** 140, 145, **145**
'gauging' **147,** 147
Gaultier, Jean Paul 13, 431, 460, **461;** Barbès collection (1984–85) **460,** 461; conical bras 461, **461**
gauntlet 50, **328,** 329
La Gazette du Bon Ton 175, 209
geisha costume **76–7**
gele 375, **375**
Genji Monogatari (*The Tale of Genji*) (Lady Murasaki Shikibu) 36, **36–7**
The Gentlemen of Bacongo (Daniele Tamagni) 552
Gentlemen Prefer Blondes (1953) **320,** 321, 323, **423**
George, Prince Regent (later George IV, king of England) 107–8, 156

Gere, Richard **438,** 439
Gernreich, Rudi 13, 377, 379, **379;** monokini 377, **378–9,** 379; 'no bra' bra 379
ghaghra 67, 71
Gibb, Bill 387, 393, 523; World dress **392–3,** 393
Gibson, Charles Dana: Gibson Girl **190,** 190–1
Giffo process (Paco Rabanne) 377
gigot d'agneau 131, 133, **185, 189, 190,** 191, **192, 193, 194, 195,** 197
Gilda (1946) **423,** 423
gilets and gilet overcoat 8, **126,** 127
'gilt and quilt' bag (Karl Lagerfeld for Chanel) **437,** 451, **451**
Giorgini, Giovanni Battista 334
gipon 43
Givenchy (fashion house) 327, 475, 483
Givenchy, Hubert de 265, 279, 301, **344,** 344–5, 347; pleated dress **346–7,** 347
glam rock and disco fashion 406–11; 'bomber' jacket 407; Bowie, David 406, **408–9,** 409; Lurex 407, **408–9,** 409; Lycra 407, 410; mullet 406, **408–9;** platform boots **406,** 406–7; Spandex 407; unitards **408–9,** 409; Yamamoto, Kansai 406, **408–9,** 409; Ziggy Stardust (Kansai Yamamoto) **408–9,** 409
Glamour **330,** 357
Glenurquhart plaid **274,** 275, **275**
Godey's Lady's Book 148, **148**
goffering 50, **50,** 57
golfing clothes 259, **259**
Golovin, Aleksander 214
Good Housekeeping **198,** 199
gored skirt 148, 174, **178,** 179, **190,** 191, **194, 195, 197,** 302, **303,** 303
gorget 44, **462, 463,** 463
Gothic revival 147, **147**
GOTS-certified (Global Organic Textile Standard) textiles **487**
GQ 413
graffiti and fashion 447, **447, 449;** Graffiti collection (Stephen Sprouse) **448–9,** 449
Granny Takes a Trip 354, 357, 365, **365**
Grant, Cary 335, 337
The Great Gatsby (1974) **412,** 413, 415
greca 143
Greek clothing: Classical period 18, 19, 20–1; chiton 19, **20, 21,** 21; draped clothing 8, **21;** tunic **18,** 18–19; *xystis* **20, 21,** 21; modern period 8, 215, 216, **216,** 221, **221,** 247, **250,** 251, **251**
Green Carpet Challenge 487, 489
'greenery yallery' **185,** 189
Grès, Madame 8, 247, 251; evening dress **250–1,** 251
Grumbach, Didier 382, 383
grunge **482,** 482–3, **483,** 498
guayabera 140
Gucci 13, 441, 453, 474, 475, 489; cut-out dress (by Tom Ford) **478–9,** 479;

INDEX 565

'Jackie' handbag 345, 441; loafers 437, **440–1**, 441; logo 474, 479
Gucci, Guccio 334, 441
A Guide to Elegance (Geneviève Antoine Dariaux) 327
Guy Laroche 511

hair, artificial 32, **35** *see also* wigs
hair powder 111, **112, 113, 125**
Hairstyles (Ojeikere) 373
hakama **37, 41**
Hall, Jerry 421
Halston (Roy Halston Frowick) 13, **13**, 279, 345, 373, 398, 399, 407; evening wear 398, **399**
halter-neck **20, 21, 21**, 253, 270, **270, 320, 321, 378, 379, 399, 407, 470, 471, 516, 517**
Hamnett, Katharine 431; slogan T-shirt 431, **431**
handkerchief sleeves 197, **234**
'hangman jumper' 417
Hardison, Bethann 373
'harem' pants 216, **216**
Haring, Keith 435, **435, 447**, 449
Harper's Bazaar (from 1929) 211, 277, 289, 303, 317, 325, 372, 373
Harper's Bazar 175, 199, 211, **212–13**, 213
Harrington jacket 312
Harry, Debbie 449
Hartnell, Norman 282, **282**, 283, 301
'Harvard Clip' **312, 313**
Harvey, Gary **14**, 489, **489**; newspaper dress 487, **489**; upcycled evening gown **488–9**, 489
haute couture: 1980s regeneration 442, 450–9; American haute couture 286–91; Amies, Hardy 301, **304–5**, 305; Balenciaga **299**, 299–300, **306**, **307**; Balmain 300, **300**; birth of haute couture 9, 172–9; Burton, Sarah 511, 515, **516–17**, 517; Chanel (by Lagerfeld) 437, 451, **451**, 452, 454, 455, **455**, 459; Christian Dior 452; Creed, Charles 301; Cumberland tweed suit (Amies) **304–5**, 305; Decarnin, Christophe 511, **511**; Dessès 301; Dior 277, 287, 293, 298, **298**, 299, **299**, 301; Doucet 175; Edelstein, Victor 450; Elbaz, Alber for Lanvin **510**, 511; evening dresses (Balenciaga) **306–7**, 307; evening wear 287, **287, 290**, 291, **291**; Fath 300–1, **301**; Fendi 452; Galanos, James 286; golden age 298–308; Gucci 13, 453; Hartnell, Norman 301; House of Worth **174**, 175; Ice Queen dress (Burton for Alexander McQueen) 12, **516–17**, 517; James, Charles 286, 287, **287**; Lacroix, Christian 452, 453, **456–7**, 457, 461; Lagerfeld, Karl (for Chanel) 437, 451, **451**, 452, 454, 455, **455**, 459; Louis Vuitton 452; Mainbocher 286, **286**, 287, **288**, 289, **289**; modern haute couture 510–17; Morton, Digby 301; Moschino,

Franco 451–2, **453, 458**, 459, **459**; New Look 277, 287, 293, 298, 299, **299, 302–3**, 303, 314, 327, 349; Oldfield, Bruce 450; Ossendrijver, Lucas 511, 513, **514–15**; Paquin 175; Piguet, Robert 301; red dresses (Valentino) **512–13**, 513; Saint Laurent 301; Simons, Raf 511; Stiebel, Victor 301; two-piece suit (Ossendrijver for Lanvin) **514–15**, 515; Ungaro, Emanuel 442, **450, 450–1**; Valentino 511, **512–13**, 513; Walker, Catherine 450; wedding dress for Wallis Simpson 287, **288–9**, 289; Worth 149, **172, 172–5, 173, 174, 175, 176–9**, 298
Hawes, Elizabeth 219, 247, 249; diamond horseshoe dress 247, **248–9**, 249; *Fashion is Spinach* 9, 249
Haworth, Rita **422**, 423
Hayward, Dougie 365
Head, Edith 314, **314**, 315, 321, 344
health corset 197, **197**
Heian period, Japan 36–41
Heim, Jacques 325
Helmut Lang 475
Helvin, Marie 421
hennin 45, **45**
Henry VIII, king of England **48**, 48–9
Hepburn, Audrey 327, 344, **344**, 345, **346**, 347
Hepburn, Katharine 267, **267**, 300
Hermès 469; bags 315, 318, **318, 319**; scarves 437
Hernandez, Lazaro *see* Proenza Schouler
Herrera, Carolina 443, **443**
Herzigova, Eva **469**
Hewson, Ali (Edun) 487, 549
Highland dress 102–5, **103, 104, 105**
Hilfiger, Tommy 309
Hilt, Elizabeth 329, **329**
himation 19
hip-hop and street style fashion 425, 431, 446–9, 451; 'bling' 447, **447**; bucket hat **446**, 446–7; doo-rags 447; dookey chains 447, **447**; graffiti 447, **447**, 449; Graffiti collection (Stephen Sprouse) **448–9**, 449; high-top fade 447; Sprouse, Stephen 447, **448–9**, 449; tracksuit 446, 447; trainers 447; Westwood, Vivienne 447, **447**; Witches collection (Vivienne Westwood) 447
hippie fashion 13, 386–93, 407, 534, **536–7**, 537, 540; Birtwell, Celia **386**, 387, **390–1**, 391; Clark, Ossie **386**, 387, **390–1**, 391; Gibb, Bill 387, **392–3**, 393, 523; Indian clothing 386–7, **388**, 389, **389**; kaftans 386–7, **388–9**, 389; McFadden, Mary 387, **387**; psychedelic print kaftan (Pucci) **388–9**, 389; Pucci, Emilio 387, **388–9**, 389; Rhodes, Zandra 387, **387**; Wandering Daisy dress (Celia Birtwell and Ossie Clark) **390–1**, 391; World Dress (Bill Gibb) **392–3**, 393

'Hiroshima Chic' 405
His Clothes 364, **364**
'hobble' skirt 11–12, 198, **198**
Hobsbawm, Eric: *The Age of Extremes* 14
Hogg, Pam 430
Holbein, Hans (the Younger): *Portrait of Charles de Solier* **52–3**, 53
Hollar, Wenceslaus: *Winter* 79, 80, **80–1**
Hollywood and fashion: Adrian 270, **270–1, 272–3**, 273, 279; Banton, Travis 271; bikinis 321, **324–5**, 325; Chanel 271; conical ('bullet') bras 320, **321, 322–3**, 323; drape suit 271, **271, 274–5**, 275; halter-necks **320**, 321; Hollywood glamour 12, 270–5; Hollywood ideal 320–5; Letty Lynton dress (Adrian) 271, **272–3**, 273; Schiaparelli 271, **271** *see also* film influence on fashion
'Hollywood drape suit' 271, **271, 274–5**, 275
Holman Hunt, William: *Portrait of Fanny Holman Hunt* **150–1**
Homburg 157, 158, **158–9**
hoof-shaped cuff **85**
horsebit snaffle 440, **440, 441**
Horst, Horst P. 211, 286
hose 43, 44, 47, 50, **104, 105**
hosiery 258 *see also* hose
houppelande 43, **44, 46, 47, 47**
House of Dior *see* Christian Dior
House of Doucet 198, **199**, 247
House of Paquin 175
House of Worth 175; label **174**, 175
Hoyningen-Huene, George 211
htamein 169, **169**
huadian 32
hufu 33
Hugo Boss 437, **437**
Hulanicki, Barbara (Biba) 356, 359, 407
Humayun, Mughal emperor **64**, 65
Hume, Kirsty **483**
Hung on You 365
hunting clothes 67, **68**, 69, **69**, 116
Hurley, Elizabeth 467
Hutton, Lauren **398**

i-D 483
I Was Lord Kitchener's Valet 365, **366–7**, 367
iborun 375
Ice Queen dress (Sarah Burton for Alexander McQueen) 12, **516–17**, 517
ikat textiles 67
Iman 373
Inca tapestry tunic **28–9**, 29
El Inciador 138, 139
Incroyables 124, **124–5**
Les Incroyables collection (John Galliano,1984) 431
India: *chakdar jama* 66, **67**; draped clothing 64–5, 67, **71**; hunting coats 67, **68–9**, 69; *jama* 66, **67**; Mughal Empire 64–73; *pallu* 67, **71**; sari 64, 67, **70**, 71, **71**; tailored clothing 64–5, **66**, 67; turbans 64, **64**, 65, **65, 67**, 67

indispensables 121
Industrial Revolution 155
instarsia 258, **259**
International Ladies' Garment Workers' Union 195, 277
Inverness coat 159, **159**
ipele 371, **374**, 375, **375**
Iribe, Paul 208, **208**, 209
iro 371, **374–5**, 375
irome no kasane 37–9, 40, **40, 41**
Isabel of France (Rodrigo de Villandrando) **56–7**, 57
Italian fashion: Baguette bag (Fendi) **472–3**, 473; bondage collection (Versace, 1992) 467; Brioni 335, **336–7**, 337, 364; Capri pants **335**; Cavalli, Roberto 466, 468–9; 'Continental look' suit (Brioni) 335, **336–7**, 364; corset dress **468**; decadence and excess 466–73; Dolce & Gabbana 466, **467–8**, **468**; evening dress (Fontana sisters) **338–9**, 339; Fendi 466, **472–3**, 473; Ferragamo 334, **335**; Fontana sisters 335, 338, **338–9**, 339; Gucci 334; post-war period 334–9; Pucci, Emilio 334, 335, **335**; Pucci prints **335**; ready-to-wear 335, **335**, 383, **383**; stiletto heels 335; Versace, Gianni 466, **466–7**, **467, 470–1, 471**; Warhol print dress (Versace) **470–1**, 471
Ivy League style 308, 312, **312–13**, 365, 413

jabot 86, **86, 112, 113, 178, 179**
'Jackie' handbag (Gucci) 345, 441
the 'Jackie look' 345, **345**
Jackson, Betty 431, 435; English Rose collection (1985) 431
Jacob, Mary Phelps 460
Jacobs, Marc 449, **449**, 475, **482**, 483; Grunge collection (1992) **482**, 483
Jahangir, Mughal emperor 66, 67, **67**
Jaked 530
jama 66, **67**
jamdani 351
James, Charles 286, 287, 445; Corselette evening dress 287; four-leaf clover dress 287, **287**; pouf-fronted gown 287; Sirene evening dress 287; Sylphide evening dress 287
jansenistes 99
Jantzen 258, 260, 261, 279; elasticized swimwear 260, **260–1**; logo **260**, 261
Japan: Akihabara style 507; bustle 181, **183**; Comme des Garçons 403, **404**, 405, **405**; court dress 36, **37, 38**, 39, **39**, 40, **40, 41**; Edo period 74–7; Ganguro 506, **506–7**; Geisha costume **76–7**, 77; Gothic Lolita **507**; *hakama* **37, 41**; headdress 183; Heian period 36–41; *juni-hitoe* (layered) dress 40, **40, 41**; Kamakura period 39, **41**; Kawakubo, Rei 13, 403, **404**, 405, **405**; Kenzo **402**, 402–3;

kimono 11, 74, 75, **75**, **76**, 77, **77**, 181, **181**; Lolita style 507; Meiji period 180–3; Miyake, Issey 13, 403; modern design 402–5; Punk Lolita 507; Shibuya style 506; *sokuhatsu* 182, **182–3**; street culture 506–9; suit 180–1, **181**; Sweet Lolita 507, **508–9**, **509**; Western dress 180, 180–1, 182, **182–3**; *yakaimaki* 182; Yamamoto, Yohji 13, 403, **403**, 405
Japanese Avant-Garde 403
Japonaise 185, **185**
Jazz Age 210, **211**, 239
'jazz' jumper 253
Jean Varon (John Bates) 355, **355**, 359
jeans: Calvin Klein 399, 413, 425, **426–7**, **427**; distressed 431, **434**, **435**; as leisurewear 340, **340**, **341**, **342–3**, 343, 357
Jeanswear (Calvin Klein) 425, **426–7**, **427**
Jensen, Peter 519
jerkin 44, 49
Jewel by Lisa **548**, 548–9
Jil Sander 475
John, Elton 369, **406**, 406–7
Johnson, Betsey 357, 363; mirror dress **363**; Op art print mini dresses **362–3**, 363
Jones, Dylan 430
Jones, Grace 373
Jones, Stephen 430
Jones, Terry 483
Jordan (Pamela Rooke) 417, **417**
Joseff of Hollywood 321
Jourdan, Charles 411 *see also* Charles Jourdan
Le Journal des dames et de la mode 121
Le Journal des Demoiselles **205**
Joy, Eric 365
Jungle Jap 402
juni-hitoe 40, **40**, **41**
jupe **88**, 89
Just Looking **354**
justacorps **86**, 87

kadife silk 61
kaftans: Hippie fashion 386–7, **388–9**, 389; orientalism 220–1, 221; Ottoman Empire **58**, 59–60, 61, **61**, **62**, 63, **63**
Kamakura period, Japan 39, **41**
Kamali, Norma 425
kameez 65
Kammu, Heian emperor 36
Kane, Christopher 491, 495; embroidered skirt and knitted sweater **494–5**, 495
kanga 371
Kangol **446**, 446–7
Kangxi, Qing emperor 164
Kani, Karl 446 *see also* Karl Kani
Karan, Donna 13, 279, 437 *see also* Donna Karan
Karl Kani 446
kasha 263
Katrantzou, Mary 491, 519, 524, **525**; *trompe l'oeil* dress 524, **524–5**
Kawakubo, Rei 13, 403, 405, 500–1, **501**; asymmetric ensemble **404–5**, 405 *see also* Comme des Garçons
Kebede, Liya 549
Keita, Seydou 371
Keller, Clare Waight 535
Kelly, Grace 315, **315**, 318, **319**
Kelly bag (Hermès) 315, 318, **318–19**
kemha silk 59, 61, 61
Kennedy, Jackie (née Bouvier) 293, 335, 345, **345**, 348, **349**, 357
kente cloth, West African **134**, 134–7, **135**, **136–7**, 371, 417, 446
Kenzo (Kenzo Takada) 402, **402**, 402–3
Kerouaille, Louise de (Duchess of Portsmouth) **92–3**, 93
kettledrum breeches 50, **50**
Khanh, Emmanuelle 357, 383
kickback jacket 97
kilts **22**, 23, **102**, 103, 105
kimono sleeves 247, **522**, **523**
kimono **10**, 11, 37, 74, 75, **75**, **76**, 77, **77**, 181, **181**, 278
King, Muriel 282, **283**
King's Road, London **354**, 355, 365, **417**
kinky boots 355, 377
'kipper' ties 364
Kirkland, Sally 279
kirtle 44, **47**, 51
Kishimoto, Wakako (Eley Kishimoto) 519
Klein, Calvin 13, 279, 398, 399, 413, 425, 427, 435, 442, 483; Jeanswear 425, **426–7**, **427**; separates **398**, 399, 413
KLùK CGDT 549
Knapp, Sonja 377
knickerbockers 243, **243**
knitwear 205; all-in-one 377 *see also* unitard; bathing costumes 253, **253**, 263; ties **206**, 207, 364 *see also* designer knitwear
Kojun, Empress **41**
Koret 279
kosode 37
Kouyaté, Lamine Badian 500, **500**
Krizia 383, 395
kurta 65
Kuti, Fela 370–1

Lacoste, René 253, **254**, 255; emblem 255, **255**; tennis shirt 253, **254–5**, 255
Lacroix, Christian **452**, 453, 457, 461; first collection (1987) 456, **456–7**, 461
Ladies' Home Journal 264
The Lady's Magazine 208
Lagerfeld, Karl 451, 452, 455; and Chanel 437, 451, **451**, 452, **454**, 455, **455**, 459; and Fendi 469, **469**, 473, **473**; 'gilt and quilt' bags (Chanel) 437, **451**; two-piece suit (Chanel) **454–5**, 455
Lamanova, Nadezhda 234–5
lampas silk 97
'lampshade' tunic 216, **217**
Lane, Kenneth Jay 345
Lang, Helmut 475, **475** *see also* Helmut Lang
Langtry, Lillie **174**, 175
Lanvin 282, 487, 511, 549; two-piece suit (Ossendrijver) **514–15**, 515

Lanvin, Jeanne 245; *robe de style* **244**, 245, **245**
Laroche, Guy 511
LaRoche, Pierre 409
Lastex 258, 260, 321
Latin American dress 138–45; *bombachas* **138**; *charro* 141, **142**, 143, **143**; *china poblana* 139, **139**; *chiripá* **138**; gaucho dress **138**, 140, 145, **145**; *manto* 140, **141**; *moño* **142**, 143; neck cloth **142**, 143; *peinetón* 140, **140**; poncho 140, **141**, **144**, **145**; *ruana* 141, **141**; *saya* 140, **141**; *serape* **143**; shawls 139, 140, **141**, **143**; sombrero 141, **141**; *tapada limeña* 140, **141**; tunic **141**; veils 140, **141**
Lauren, Ralph 13, 309, 412–13, 415, 442; *The Great Gatsby* costume design **412**, 413, 415; Polo Ralph Lauren 412, 413, **413**, 415; Prairie collection 413, **414–15**, 415
Laurenceairline 549
layered (*juni-hitoe*) dress (Japanese Heian period) 40, **40–1**
layered sleeves **272**, 273, **273**
Lear, Amanda **422**, 423
Lee (H.D. Lee Company) 340, **340**
leg o'mutton sleeves 131, 133, 185, **189**, **190**, 191, **192**, **193**, **194**, 195, 197
leg warmers **428**, 429
Leger, Hervé 425; bandage dress 425, **425**
leggings 377, **433**, **448**, 449, 468, **503**
Leiber, Judith 443
leisurewear **243**, 259, 469, 541 *see also* jeans; sportswear
Lelong, Lucien 223, **223**, 253, 300
Lely, Sir Peter: *Louise de Kerouaille* **92–3**, 93
LemLem 549
Lenglen, Suzanne **252**, 252–3
Lentz, Irene 279
leotard 277, **406**, 407, 410, **410**, **411** *see also* unitard
Lepape, Georges **209**, **209**, 210, 211
Lesage 524
Letterman sweater 309, 312, **312**, **313**
Letty Lynton (1932) 271, **272**, 273
Levi's (Levi Strauss & Co.) 340, 343, **343**
Liberty 185, **185**, 189; velvet gown **188–9**, 189
Lichfield, Patrick **386**
Life magazine **190**, 279, 323, 357, 373, **373**
lifestyle marketing 412–15, 442, 443, 452–3; Gap 413; Klein, Calvin 413, **413**, 427; Lauren, Ralph 13, 412–13, **414**, 415; Prairie collection (Lauren) 413, **414–15**, 415
Lim, Phillip 541 *see also* 3.1 Phillip Lim label
lingerie: Belle Epoque 199, **200**, 201, **201**; 1930s 246; 1990s **484**, 485, **485**
Linnard, Stephen 430
liripipe 43, **43**

little black dress **224–5**, **225**, 451
The Little Dictionary of Fashion (Christian Dior) 327
loafer 309, 312, **312**, **313**, 440; Gucci 437, **440–1**, **441**
Loewe 475
logos 255, **255**, **260**, **261**, 412, 413, 452–3
Lokman, Seyyid: *Portrait of Ahmet* **62–3**
Lolita style 507; Gothic Lolita **507**; Punk Lolita 507; Sweet Lolita 507, **508–9**, **509**
Lollobrigida, Gina 335
Lombard, Carole 270
London Fashion Week 431
'loo mask' 80, **80**, **81**
Loren, Sophia 335
lorgnette 124, 131
Louboutin, Christian 349
Loucah, Anna **489**
Loudermilk, Linda 487
Louis heel **81**, 107, 108, 121, **241**, **241**
Louis Vuitton 13, 449, 452, 453, 475, 483; logo 475; 'Speedy' bag **449** *see also* LVMH
Louis XIV, king of France 86, **86**, 90, 107
Louis XV, king of France 97, 107
Louis XV heel 348
Louise de Kerouaille (Lely) **92–3**, 93
lounge suit 155–6, 158, **158–9**, 240
lounge wear 257, 266
Louw, Stiaan 549
Lowe, Anne Cole 293
Lucile (Lady Duff-Gordon) 196, 198, **198**, 199, 201
lumberjack jacket **414**, 415
Luna, Donyale 373
lungi 66
luntaya acheik 169, **169**, 171
Lurex 407, **408–9**
LVMH 453, 474–5, 510, 549
Lycett Green, Rupert 365
Lycra 321, 407, 410, 424, 425, **428**, **428–9**
Lyons silk 174, **175**

Mabry, Moss 315, **315**
macaroni **112–13**, 113
MacDowell, Andie **442**
MacGibbon, Hannah 535
machine-knitting 259, 260, 409, 490–1
Macpherson, Elle 428
MacPherson Knitwear 395
Mademoiselle 357
Madonna 461, **461**, 468, 541
magua 166, **167**, **167**
Maidenform **322–3**, 323
Maiga, Hamidou 371
Mainbocher (Main Rousseau Bocher) 286, **287**, 331; corset **286**, 287; wedding dress for Wallis Simpson 287, **288–9**, 289
Maison Balmain 300 *see also* Balmain
Maison Lucile 199 *see also* Lucile
Maki Oh 549
Malcolm X (Malcolm Little) 295, 373
Malé, Soungalo 371
Maltese Cross cuff (Fulco di Verdura for Chanel) **223**

INDEX 567

Mamba 507
Mandelli, Mariuccia 395
mandilion 50
mang robe 84
Manifattura Ratti **471**
Manning, Helen (The Cloth) 435
Mansfield, Jayne 320, **321**
manteau 87, **87**, 91, **98**, 99, 106
mantelet 131
Mantero Seta **14**
mantilla 140
mantle 103, 131, 147
manto 140, **141**
mantua coat **126**, **127**, 199
mantua 91, 93, 106, 108, 121
Mao Zedong 231
Marant, Isabel 534, 537; festival wear **536–7**, 537
marchandes de modes 87, 94, **94**
Margiela, Martin 498, **499**, 501
Maria Teresa, queen of France **88**, 89, **89**, 109
mariachi folk bands 143, **143**
Marie-Antoinette, queen of France **95**, 111
Marie sleeves 131
'Marii' technique 387
Marks & Spencer 487
Marni 520, **520**
Martin, Charles 209
Marty, A. E. 209
Mary Jane shoes **238**, 241, 359, 507, 509
Masekela, Hugh 371
masks 80, **80**, 81, **81**, 88, 89
mass production 148, 199, 205, 223
'masstige' 540
Matisse, Henri 435
Matteo Dosso 545
Mattli, Giuseppe Gustavo 'Jo' 327
mauveine 149
McCardell, Claire 13, 277–8, 281, **282**; 'popover' dress **277**, **277**; ready-to-wear **276**, 277
McCartney, Stella 487, **487**, 529, 534, 535, 539; for Adidas 529, **530**; Olympic 2012 Team GB kit 529, **529**, 539; patterned dress **538–9**, 539 *see also* Stella McCartney
McCollough, Jack *see* Proenza Schouler
McFadden, Mary 387, **387**; 'Marii' technique 387
McLachlan, Sally **393**
McLaren, Malcolm 416, 417, 419; 'anarchy shirt' **417**, **418–19**, 419
McLaughlin-Gill, Frances **330**
McMenamy, Kristen 482–3
McQueen, Alexander **367**, 460, **461**, 463, 483, 499, 517; Dante collection (1996) **461**; Guerrilla corset **462–3**, 463; No. 13 collection (1999) 461, 463 *see also* Alexander McQueen
medieval period 8–9, 42–7; chaperon 43–4, **47**; cornes **45**; cotte 42, **42**; hennin 45, **45**; houppelande 43, **44**, **46–7**, 47; kirtle 42, **47**; liripipe 43, **43**; *poulaines* 43, **43**; surcoats **44**, 45; veils 45, **45**
Meiji period, Japan 11, 180–3
Meisel, Steven 468, **483**
Mello, Dawn (Gucci) 441, 453

mendeville 50
Las Meninas (Diego Velázquez) **54**, **55**, **55**
Le Mercure Galant 87
Merry Widow hats 197, **197**
Merveilleuses 123, 124, **124–5**
Miami Vice 437, **437**
Michael Clark Dance Company **433**, **433**
Mignard, Pierre: *Queen Maria Teresa and her son* **88–9**
Miller, Nolan 443
minaudière 443
Mindon, king of Burma 168, **171**
mini dress 349, 355, 362, 363, 363, 371, 376, 377
mini skirt 348, **349**, **358**, 359, **359**, 376
minimalism **13**, 344, 399, 403, 453, 474–81, 483; cut-out dress (Gucci by Tom Ford) **478–9**, 479; Ford, Tom (for Gucci) 474, **478–9**, 479; 'The Great Plain' (Jil Sander) **476–7**; Jacobs, Marc 475; Lang, Helmut 475; Louis Vuitton 475; LVMH 474–5; Prada **480**, **481**, **481**; Sander, Jil **476–7**, 477
Missoni 383, 395, **395**, 397; raschel knit dress and hat **396–7**, 397
Mister Fox 383
Miu Miu (Prada) 14, 481
Miyake, Issey 13, 403, 431, 499, **499**, 503; A-POC 502, **502–3**
La Moda 138, 139
La Mode 138
Modern Merchandising Bureau 271
modern simplicity 344–9; chemise dress 344, 345; cropped jackets 345; Givenchy **344**, 344–5; Halston 345; 'Jackie' handbags 345; Pilgrim pump (Roger Vivier) 345, 348, **348–9**; pillbox hat 345; pleated skirt **346**, **347**, **347**; Vivier, Roger 345, 348, **348–9**, 349
the moderne 238–45; blazer 240, **242**, 243, **243**; boater 240, **242**, 243; bob 240, **241**; chemise dress **238**, 239, **239**; cloche hat 240, **241**; 'flapper' 239–40; Lanvin, Jeanne 245; Oxford bags 240, **242**, 243, **243**; Oxford brogues 241, **242**, **243**; Pluchino, Ignazio **241**; *robe de style* (Lanvin) **244–5**, 245 *see also* Art Deco
modernist design 210, 232, 238–9, 258, 376, 377, 398
Mods 364
Moët Hennessy 453 *see also* LVMH
Molyneux, Edward 283, 300
Mondrian, Piet 361
Mondrian dress (Saint Laurent) 348, **349**, 357, **360–1**, 361
monokini (Rudi Gernreich) 377, **378–9**, 379
Monroe, Marilyn 320, 321, **323**, 335, **422**, 467, **470**, **471**, **471**
Montana, Claude 420–1, **421**
Moon, Keith **366**
Moon Girl collection (André Courrèges) 376–7
Moore, Debbie **429**
Moralioglu, Erdem 497 *see also* Erdem

morning suit **154**, 155, 156, 515
Morris, Jane 184, 185, **186–7**, 187
Morris, William 185, 187
Morton, Digby 283, 285, 301, 327; Wartime Tailoring **284–5**, 285
Moschino, Franco 451–2, **453**, 459; Cheap and Chic (1988) 459; skirt suit **458–9**, 459
Moss, Kate **478**, **479**, **479**, 482, 483
Moss, Sandy 357
motorcycle jacket 13, **342–3**, 343 *see also* biker jacket
motoring clothing **204**, 205, **206–7**, 207
Mr Freedom 407
muff 79, 80, **80**, **81**, **127**, **131**
Mughal hunting coat 68–9
Mugler, Thierry 373, 420, 421; corset dress **420**, 421
Mulleavy, Kate and Laura (Rodarte) 493 *see also* Rodarte
mullet 406, **408**
Mullins, Aimée **463**
Munn, Merle 258
Murasaki Shikibu, Lady 36–7, **37**, **38**, **40**, **41**
myit-do-myi-she military court costume 169, **170–1**, 171

Native American dress: early period 22–5, **23**; tie-dyed blankets 22, **24**, 25, **25**; tunic 23, **25**
Neal, Patricia 327
neck cloth 117, **118**, 119, **119**, 142, 143
necktie *see* ties
neo-textiles 491, 495
Neoclassical period 120–31; afternoon dress **126**, 127, **127**; fans **122**, **123**; gloves **122**, **123**, 124, **124**; hairstyles 120, **121**, **122**, **123**, **123**, **124**, 126, **127**; *Incroyables* and *Merveilleuses* 123, 124, **124–5**; muff **127**; reticule 121, **121**
Nepal: textiles of Eastern Nepal 350–3; Dhaka **350**, 350–1, **352**, 353; shawls **350**, 351, **351**; 'shoe design' pattern **351**; Tehrathum Dhaka 350–1, 353, **353**; topi 350–1, **352**, 353, **353**
Nesbitt, Roanne **373**
Net-a-Porter 544, **544**
New Bridges for the Seven Seas (Erté) **212–13**, 213
New Look (Dior) 277, 287, 293, 298, 299, **302–3**, 303, 314, 327, 349; 'The Bar' dress and jacket 299, **299**
New Romantic movement **430**, 430–1, **431**
newspaper dress (Gary Harvey) 487, **489**
Newton, Helmut 385
Niane, Katoucha **373**
Nike 487, 529, 530; Nike+ Hyperdunk **530**, 530–1; NikeCraft (Sachs) **531**; Nike iD Studios 545, **545**; Swift Running technology 531
Nina Ricci 541
1920s fashion: blazer 240, **242**, 243, **243**; boater 240, **242**, 243; bob 240, **241**; Chanel 222, **222–3**, **223**, **224–5**, 225; chemise

dress **224**, 225, **225**, **238**, 239; cloche hat 227, **227**, 240, **241**; costume design 232, 235, 236, 237, **237**; *Death of Tarelkin* costume design (Stepanova) 235, **236–7**, 237; fabric design 233, 233–4; 'flapper' 239–40; 'flapper' dress (Popova) **234**; Lacoste, René 253, **254**, **254–5**, 255; Lanvin, Jeanne **244–5**, 245; Lelong 223, **223**; 253; little black dress **224–5**, 225, 451; Oxford bags 240, **242**, 243, **243**; Oxford brogues 241, **242**, **243**; Patou 12, **12**, 223, **223**, 252, 252–3; Pluchino, Ignazio **241**; Popova 232, **233–4**, **234**, **235**; *robe de style* (Lanvin) **244–5**, 245; Russian Constructivist design 232–7; Schiaparelli, Elsa 12, 223, 262–3, 264, **264–5**, 265; sports costume (Stepanova) 235, **235**; Stepanova 232, **232**, **233**, 234, 235, **235**, **236–7**, 237; swimwear 12, **253**, 253; tailleur (Popova) **234**; tennis clothes 252, 252–3, **254–5**, 255; tennis shirt (Lacoste) 253, **254–5**, 255; tunic 234, **236**, **237**, 237
1930s fashion: Adrian 270, 270–1, **272–3**, 273, 279; all-in-one beach wear **257**, 257; Banton, Travis 271; bathing costumes 253, **253**; beach pyjamas 253, **256–7**, 257; bias cut 247, **248**, **249**, 249, 270, **270**, 271, **288**, **289**; Braemar 271; Chanel 271; designer knitwear 258–61; drape suit 271, **271**, **274–5**, 275; elasticized swimwear 260, **260–1**; evening dress (Madame Grès) **250–1**, 251; experiments in cut and structure 246–51; golfing clothes 259, **259**; Grecian style clothing 247, **250**, 251, **251**; Hawes, Elizabeth 219, 247, **248–9**, 249; Hollywood glamour 12, 270–5; horseshoe dress (Elizabeth Hawes) **248–9**, 249; Jantzen 258, 260, **260–1**, 261; Letty Lynton dress (Adrian) 271, **272–3**, 273; Madame Grès 8, 247, **250**, 251, **251**; Munn, Merle 258; Poiret, Paul 246; pyjamas **246**; Schiaparelli, Elsa 262, 271, **271**; surrealism and fashion 262–5; sweater dress 258, **259**; swimwear 258, 260, **260**, 261, **261**; twinset 259, **259**; Vionnet 246, **246–7**, 247; wide-legged trousers **256**, 257, **257**
1940s fashion: Adrian 278, **279**; American fashion 277, 282, 283, 293; American ready-to-wear 195, 276–81, 398; Amies, Hardy 283; Bar dress and jacket 299, **299**; bikini 321, **324–5**, 325; 'bobbysoxer' style 309, **310–11**, 311, 314; Carnegie, Hattie 276–7, **280**, 281, **281**; Carnegie suit (Hattie Carnegie) **280–1**, 281; Cashin, Bonnie 278–9, **279**; conical

('bullet') bra 320, **321, 322–3**, 323; Copeland, Jo 277; Dior 277, 287, 293, 298, 299, **299, 302, 303, 303, 314**; English fashion 282, **282**, 283; French fashion 277, 279, 282; Galanos, James 279; Halston 13, 279; Hartnell, Norman 282, **282**, 283; Ivy League style 308, 312, **312–13**, 365, 413; James, Charles 287; Jantzen 279; Karan, Donna 13, 279; King, Muriel 282, **283**; Klein, Calvin 13, 279; Koret 279; Lentz, Irene 279; McCardell, Claire 13, **276, 277**, 277–8, 282; Molyneux, Edward 283; Morton, Digby 283, **284–5**, 285; New Look 277, 287, 293, 298, 299, **299, 302**, 303, **303**, 314, 327, 349; Norell, Norman 279; 'popover' dress (Claire McCardell) **277**; Potter, Clare 277, 282; separates 278, 279, **398, 398**, 399; siren suit 283, **283**; slacks 283; suit (female) 283, **283, 284–5**, 285; Trigère, Pauline 279; turban 283; utility clothing 282, 283, **283, 284–5**, 285; World War II 277, 282–5; zoot suit 293, **294–5**, 295, 369

1950s fashion: American shirtwaist dress **328–9**, 329; American youthful femininity 314–**19**; Amies, Hardy 301, **304–5**, 305; Balenciaga **299**, 299–300, **306–7**, 307; Balmain 300, **300**; beaded cardigan 327, **327, 330–1**; Brioni 335, **336–7, 337**, 364; Capri pants 335, **335**, 345; chemise dress 344, 345; 'Continental look' suit (Brioni) 335, **336–7, 337**, 364; Creed, Charles 301, 327; cropped jacket 345; Cumberland tweed suit (Amies) **304–5**, 305; daywear 326–**3**; Dessès **300**, 301; Dior **298**, 301; evening dresses (Balenciaga) **306–7**, 307; evening dress (Fontana sisters) **338–9**, 339; Fath, Jacques 300–1, **301**; Ferragamo, Salvatore 334, 335; film costume design 314, **314**, 315, **315**; Fontana sisters 335, 338, **338–9**, 339; Givenchy **344**, 344–5; Gucci 334; Halston 345; Hartnell, Norman 301; Head, Edith 314, **314**, 315; Italian postwar fashion 334–9; Kelly bag (Hermès) 315, 318, **318–19**; Mabry, Moss 315, **315**; Mattli, 'Jo' 327; modern simplicity 344–9; Morton, Digby 301, 327; navy suit (Pauline Trigère) **332–3**, 333; the perfect housewife look 326, **326**, 327, 331; Piguet, Robert 301; Plattry, Greta **326**; pleated skirt **346**, 347, **347**; prom dress 315, **316–17**, 317; Pucci 334, 335, **335**; ready-to-wear fashion 335, **335**; Regina knitwear **330–1**, 331; Rose, Helen 314, 315; Saint Laurent, Yves 301; Stiebel, Victor 301; stiletto heel 335;

sweetheart line 314, **314**–15, 317; Trigère, Pauline 327, **332–3**, 333; wasp-waisted dress 314, 315; 'winklepicker' shoes 335

1960s fashion: Afrocentric fashion 372, 373, **383**; A-line dress (André Courrèges) **380–1**, 381; Ayton, Sylvia 357; Bates, John 355, **355, 358–9**, 359; Bazaar 354, 355, **356–7**, 365; Biba 354, 356, **356**, 357; Birtwell, Celia 386, **387**; Blades 365; Bus Stop 354; Cardin, Pierre 376, **376**, 377; Casbah dress (John Bates) 355, **358–9**, 359; Cassini, Oleg 345; Cecil Gee suit 364; Chanel suit 345;   Chelsea boots 364; Clark, Ossie 357, **386**, 387, 391; Courrèges 376–7, **380–1**, 381; Foale and Tuffin 356, **356**, 357; futuristic fashion 376–81; Gernreich, Rudi 13, 377, **378–9**, 379; Granny Takes a Trip 354, 357, 365; Hippie fashion 386–7; hipster trousers 364; His Clothes 364, **364**; Hung on You 365; I Was Lord Kitchener's Valet 365, **366**, 367, **367**; 'Jackie' handbags 345, 349; Johnson, Betsey 357, **362–3**, 363; Just Looking 354; kaftans 386–7, **388–9**, 389; Khanh, Emmanuelle 357; kinky boots 377; 'kipper' tie 364; McFadden, Mary 387, **387**; menswear revolution 364–9; mini dress 355, **362**, **363**, 363; mini skirt **358**, 359, **359**; mirror dress 363; Mod fashions 364; Mondrian dress (Yves Saint Laurent) 348, 349, 357, **360–1**, 361; monokini (Rudi Gernreich) 377, **378–9**, 379; Moon Girl collection (André Courrèges) 376–7; Nutter, Tommy 365, **368–9**, 369; Op art print mini dresses (Betsey Johnson) **362–3**, 363; paillette dress (Paco Rabanne) 377, **377**, **382–3**, **384–5**, 385 psychedelic print kaftan (Pucci) **388–9**, 389; Pucci 387, **388–9**, 389; PVC boots **376**, 377; Quant, Mary 354, 355, **356–7**, 361; Rabanne, Paco 376, **377**; retail revolution 354–7, 361; Rhodes, Zandra 357; Rive Gauche 357, 359, **382**, 383; Saint Laurent, Yves 348, 349, 357, **360–1**, 361, 372, **372**, **382**, 382–3, **384–5**, 385; Space Age collection (Pierre Cardin) 377, 381; tabard 377; Ungaro, Emanuel 377; **388–9**; uniforms 365, **365**, 367; Vivier, Roger 345, 348, **348–9**, 349; Wedge, James 357

1970s fashion: Albini, Walter 383, **383**; 'anarchy shirt' 417, **418**, 419, **419**; Biagiotti, Laura 395; Birtwell, Celia 387, **390**, 391,

391; 'bomber' jackets 407; 'bondage trousers' (Vivienne Westwood) 417, **417**; Bowie, David 406, **408–9**, 409; Castelbajac, Jean-Charles de 383; Cavalli, Roberto 468–9; Clark, Ossie 387, **390**, 391, **391**; Créateurs et Industriels 383; designer knitwear 394–7; 'destroy T-shirts' 417; Dorothée Bis 383, 395; evening wear (Halston) 399, **399**; 'fashion valkyries' 420–3, 421, **421**; fetish wear (Vivienne Westwood) **416**, 417; French prêt-à-porter 300, 301, 359, 382–3; Gibb, Bill 387, **392**, **393**, **393**; glam rock and disco fashion 406–11; Halston 13, **13**, 398, 399, **399**, 407; 'hangman jumper' 417; Hippie fashion 390–3; kaftan 386–7, 399; Khanh, Emmanuelle 383; Klein, Calvin 13, 398, **398**, 407; Krizia 395, **395**; layered look 395; leotard 406, 407, 410, **410**, **411**; Lurex 407, **408–9**, 409; Lycra 407, 410, **424**, 425; Mandelli, Mariuccia 395; McFadden, Mary 387, **387**; Missoni 395, **396–7**, 397; mullet 406, **408**; one-stop dressing 398–401; platform boots 406, 406–7; punk rock fashion 407, 416–419; raschel knit dress and hat (Missoni) **396–7**, 397; Rhodes, Zandra 387, **387**; Rive Gauche 383; Rosier, Michèle 383; Roxy Music cover (Antony Price) **422–3**, 423; Rykiel, Sonia 383, 394, 394–5; Saint Laurent 383; separates **398**, 398–9; sexuality and fashion 420, 422–3; Spandex 407; unitard 408–9, **409**; Von Furstenberg, Diane 399, **400–1**, 401; Wandering Daisy dress (Celia Birtwell and Ossie Clark) 390–1, 391, Westwood, Vivienne 416, 417, **417**; World Dress (Bill Gibb) **392–3**, 393; wrap dress (Diane von Furstenberg) 399, **400–1**, 401; Yamamoto, Kansai 406, **408–9**, 409; Ziggy Stardust (Kansai Yamamoto) **408–9**, 409

1980s fashion: Adolfo 442, 443; Alaïa, Azzedine 424, **424**, 425, 549; Armani, Giorgio 437, **437**, **438**, 439, **439**, 442; bandage dress 425, **425**; Beene, Geoffrey 442; Blahnik, Manolo 452; Blass, Bill 442, **442**; 'bling' 447, **447**; Bodymap 431, 432, **432–3**, 433; bucket hat 446, 446–7; Buffalo Girls collection (Vivienne Westwood) 460; 'The Cat in the Hat ...' collection (Bodymap) 431, 432, **432–3**; Chanel (by Lagerfeld) 437, 451, **451**, 452, **454, 455, 455**, 459; Christian Dior 452; The Cloth 431, **434–5**, 435; Comme des Garçons 403, **404**, 405, **405**; deconstructed suit

(Armani) **438–9**, 439; de la Renta, Oscar 442, 443; designer fashion 442–5; doo-rags 447; dookey chains 447, **447**; Edelstein, Victor 450; English Rose collection (Betty Jackson) 431; evening dress (Arnold Scaasi) **444–5**, 445, **445**; 'fashion valkyries' 420, 420–1, **421**; Fendi 452; Galanos, James 442; Galliano, John 431, **431**; Gap 413; Gaultier, Jean Paul **460**, 461; graffiti 447, **447**, 449; Graffiti collection (Stephen Sprouse) **448–9**, 449; Gucci 13, 453; Gucci loafers **440–1**, 441; Hamnett, Katharine 431; Herrera, Carolina 443, **443**; high-top fade 447; hip-hop and street style fashion 425, 431, 446–9, 451; Hogg, Pam 430; Hugo Boss 437, **437**; Les Incroyables collection (John Galliano) **431**; Jackson, Betty 431; Japanese design 402–5; Jeanswear (Calvin Klein) 425, **426–7**, 427; Jones, Stephen 430; Kamali, Norma 425; Karan, Donna 437; Kawakubo, Rei 13, 403, **404**, 405, **405**; Kenzo **402**, 402–3; Klein, Calvin 413, 425, 427, 425, **426–7**, 427, 442; knitted outfits (Bodymap) 432, **432–3**; Lacroix, Christian 452, 453, **456–7**, 457, 461; Lagerfeld, Karl (for Chanel) 437, 451, **451**, 452, **454, 455, 455**, 459; Lauren, Ralph 13, 412–13, **414**, 415, **415**, 442; Leger, Hervé 425, **425**; leggings 448, **425**; Leiber, Judith 443; lifestyle marketing 412–15, 442, 443, 452–3; Linnard, Stephen 430; Louis Vuitton 452; Lycra 407, 410, 424, 425, 428, **428–9**, 429; Miyake, Issey 13, 403, 431; Moschino, Franco 451–2, **453, 458, 459, 459**; New Romantic movement 431, 430–1, **431**; Oldfield, Bruce 450; Pirates collection (Vivienne Westwood) 419, 430; power dressing 436–41, 452, 453; Prairie collection (Ralph Lauren) 413, **414–15**, 415; printed textiles (The Cloth) 431, **434–5**, 435; radical design 13, 430–5; ready-to-wear fashion 445, 451; regeneration of haute couture 450–9; Scaasi, Arnold 442, 443, **444–5**, 445; Scherrer, Jean-Louis **436**; second-skin clothing 421, 424–9, 447; sexuality and fashion 420, 420–1, **421**; slogan T-shirt 431, **431**; Smith, Hilde 431, **432, 432, 433**; Smith, Paul 437; Spandex 428, **428–9**, 429; Sprouse, Stephen 447, **448**, 449, **449**; 'T-shape' tubular dress 432, **432**; underwear as outerwear 13, **460, 460, 461**; Ungaro, Emanuel 442, **450**, 450–1; Walker, Catherine 450; Westwood, Vivienne 430,

INDEX 569

447, **447**; Witches collection (Vivienne Westwood) **447**; Yamamoto, Yohji 13, 403, **403**, 405
1990s fashion: Akihabara style 507; anti-fashion movement 482–5; A-POC (Issey Miyake) 502, **502–3**; Baguette bag (Fendi) **472–3**, 473; bondage collection (Versace) 467; Cavalli, Roberto 466, 468–9; Chalayan, Hussein 500; Comme des Garçons 500, 501, **501**; conical bra 461, **461**; corset dress **468**; corsets 460, **461**; cut-out dress (Gucci by Tom Ford) **478–9**, 479; Dante collection (Alexander McQueen) 461; deconstruction fashion 498–505; Demeulemeester, Ann 499; Dolce & Gabbana 466, 467–8, **468**; Fendi 466, 472, **473**, 473, 475; fetish wear 461, 467; Ford, Tom (for Gucci) 474, **478**, 479, **479**; Ganguro **506**, 506–7; Gaultier, Jean Paul 461, **461**; Gothic Lolita **507**; grunge fashion **482**, 482–3; Gucci (by Tom Ford) 474, 475, **478**, 479, **479**; Guerrilla corset (Alexander McQueen) 461, **462–3**, 463; Italian decadence and excess 466–73; Jacobs, Marc 475, 482, **482**, 483; Japanese street culture 506–9; Kawakubo, Rei 500–1, **501**; Klein, Calvin 483; Kouyaté, Lamine Badian 500, **500**; Lang, Helmut 475; Lolita style 507; Louis Vuitton 475; LVMH 474–5; Margiela, Martin **498**, 499; McQueen, Alexander 461, **462**, 463, **463**, 499; minimalism 474–81, 483; Miyake, Issey 499, **499**, 502, **502–3**; No. 13 collection (Alexander McQueen) 461, 463; NUNO Corporation 500–1, **501**; Portrait collection (Vivienne Westwood) **460**, 461; Prada 475, **480**, 481, **481**; Punk Lolita 507; Sander, Jil 475, **476–7**, 477; Shibuya style 506; Sui, Anna 483, **483**; Sweet Lolita 507, **508–9**, 509; 'The Great Plain' (Jil Sander) **476–7**, 477; 'Under Exposure' fashion **484–5**, 485; underwear as outerwear 460–3; Versace, Gianni **466**, 466–7, **467**, 470–1, 471; Warhol print dress (Versace) **470–1**, 471; Westwood, Vivienne **460**, 461; Xuly Bët 500, **500**
No. 13 collection (Alexander McQueen, 1999) 461, 463
Norell, Norman 279, 281
Norfolk jacket 156, **156**, 157
Nuit de Noël (Malick Sidibé) **370**
NUNO Corporation 500–1, **501**
Nutter, Tommy 365, 369; Nutter suit **368–9**, 369

obi **10**, 77, 402
odhni 67

Offering of the Heart (tapestry) 9
ohaguro 37, **41**
Ojeikere, J. D. Okhai: *Hairstyles* series 373
Oldfield, Bruce 450
Olowu, Duro 549, 551; Duro dress **550–1**, 551
Olympic 2012 Team GB kit (McCartney) 529, **529**, 539
one-stop dressing 398–401; evening wear (Halston) 399, **399**; Halston 13, **13**, 398, 399, **399**; Klein, Calvin 13, 398, **398**, 407; separates **398**, 398–9; Von Furstenberg, Diane 399, **400–1**, 401; wrap dress (Diane von Furstenberg) 399, **400–1**, 401
One Thousand and Second Night Party (1911) 217, **217**
Op art 361, **362**, 363, **363**, 377, 527
organic textiles 486, **487**
orientalism 214, **214**–17, 214–21, **215**, **216**, **217**, 218–21; aesthetic dress 185, **185**; American fashion 217, **218**, 219, **219**; Bakst **214**, **215**, 215–16; Belle Epoque 199, 209, **214**, 214–17, **215**, **216**, **217**; costume design 214, 215, **215**, 216; English fashion 185, **185**, 199; Fortuny 216, **216**, 220, 221, **221**; French fashion 199, 209, **215**, 215–17; Italian fashion 216, **216**, 220, 221, **221**; Paquin 215, **215**; Poiret 216–17, **217**; Turner 217, **218**, 219, **219**
'origami' skirt **524**, 525
Orry-Kelly (Orry George Kelly) 321
Osakwe, Amaka *see* Maki Oh
Ossendrijver, Lucas 511, 513; two-piece suit (for Lanvin) **514–15**, 515
Ottoman Empire 58–63; court dress 58, 58–63, **60**, 61, **62–3**, 63; *entari* 58, 59; kaftan 58, 59–60, 61, **61**, **62**, 63, **63**; turban 61, 63, **63**
Oxford bags 240, **242–3**, 243, **368**, 369
Oxford brogues 241, **242**, 243, 267, **267**, **294**, 295

Pagan collection (Elsa Schiaparelli) 263
pagoda sleeves 147, **152**, 153, **153**
paijama 65, 66
paisley motif **522**, 523, **523**; shawls 131, **150–1**, 151
paisley shawl **150–1**, 151
pallium/palla 18, 19
pallu 67, **71**
Palmero, Paul 448
paltoks 43
Paltrow, Gwyneth **538**, 539
paned sleeves 49, **53**
Panichgul, Thakoon 487, 540, **540**, 541
pannièred skirt 11, 95, **97**, 99, **99**, 101
panniers (sleeves) 131, 133
pantaloon 86, **87**, 117, **118**, 119, **119**
Paquin, Jeanne 175, 196, 198, 201, 215; afternoon dress **200–1**, 201; Dione dress (with Bakst) **215** *see also* House of Paquin
Paraphernalia 357, **357**
parka 364, 487, **532**, 533, **533**

Parkinson, Norman **300**, **346**, 373
Parsons, John Robert: *Jane Morris* (photo) **186–7**, 187
partlet 50, **51**
paso 168, 169, **171**
passementerie 149, 175, 299, 387
Patagonia 487
patka 67
Patou, Jean 12, **12**, 223, **223**, 252, **252–3**
Paul Smith 437 *see also* Smith, Paul
pazun-zi 169, **171**
pea coat 399, 540, 541
Pearse, John 357, 365
peasecod doublet 50
peignoir 147
pelerine 131
pelisse-robe 147
pencil skirt **304**, 305, **496**, 497, 524, **524**, 525, 542, 543
penny loafer **310**, 311
People Tree 487
peplos 19, 251
peplum **152**, 153, **250**, 251, **272**, 273, 421, 436, **496**, 497, **512–13**, 515, 525, 526, 527
Pepys, Samuel 90–1
periwig 91, **91**
Perry Ellis 483
peruque à crinière 91, **91**
pet 97
petal skirt **432**, 433
Peter Pan collar **272**, 273, **273**, 310, **311**, 506
Peter Pilotto 527; Waterfall dress **526–7**, 527
Philip II, king of Spain 50, **50**
3.1 Phillip Lim 540, 541, **541**
Philo, Phoebe (Céline) 535, **535**
Picciolo, Pierpaolo 511, **513**
pie-crust frill **412**, 413, **413**
Piguet, Robert 301
Pilgrim pump (Roger Vivier) 345, 348, **348–9**, 349
pillbox hat 345, **454**, **455**
The Pillow Book (Sei Shonagon) 36, **38–9**
Pilotto, Peter 519, 527 *see also* Peter Pilotto
pinafore dress 355, 377, 506
Pineapple Dance Studios **429**
pinked edging 53, 108
'pipa style' fastening **166**
pinstripe suit (Yves Saint Laurent) 267, 382–3, **384–5**, 385
pirate boots **536**, 537
Pirates collection (Vivienne Westwood, 1981) 419, 430
plaid: men's suit **274**, 275, **275**; Scottish clan dress **102**, 103, **104–5**, 105, 131, 147; skirt **309**; Victorian period **152–3**, 153, 204
Plank, George Wolfe 210
plastron 79, 148
platform footwear: boots **406**, 406–7; platform heels 283; shoes 165, **165**, 514, 515
Plattry, Greta **326**
pleated skirt **176**, 177, **252**, 310, **311**, 346–7, **347**, 375
Pluchino, Ignazio 241
'pocket squares' 268, **269**
Poiret, Paul 383; Belle Epoque

design 11–12, 196, 198, 199, 201, 208, **208**, 209, 213; orientalism 216–17, **217**; 1930s 246
polo shirt 255, 309, 412, 413, **413**
polonaise skirt 108, **109**, 148, 456
Pompadour, Madame de **106**, 107
poncho 140, **141**, 144–5; Cashin, Bonnie 278, **279**
Poole, Henry 156, **157**
Pop art 363, **363**, 449, 458, 459, **459**
Popova, Lyubov 232, **233**, 233–4, 235; 'flapper' dress **234**; tailleur **234**
Portrait of Ahmet (Seyyid Lokman) **62–3**
Portrait of Charles de Solier (Hans Holbein the Younger) **52–3**, 53
Portrait of Fanny Holman Hunt (William Holman Hunt) **150–1**, 151
Portrait of Lady Murasaki Shikibu **40–1**
Potter, Clare 277, 282
pouf (puffball) skirt 453
poulaines 43, **43**
pouter pigeon chest 191, **191**, 197, **200**, 201, **201**
power dressing 436–41, 453; Armani, Giorgio 437, **437**, 438–9, **439**; Blahnik, Manolo 437; deconstructed suit (Armani) **438–9**, 439; Gucci loafer 437, **440–1**, 441; Hugo Boss 437, **437**; Karan, Donna 437; Lagerfeld, Karl 437; Scherrer, Jean-Louis **436**; Smith, Paul 437
practical clothing 204–7; cap **206**, **207**; duster coat 204; French fashion 95, **96**, 97; motoring clothing 204, **205**; shirtwaist 191, **192**, 193, **194–5**, 195, 204; tailormade 204, 205, 207; uniform 205, **206–7**, 207, 228; Victorian period 149, 155, 159, 181, **183**, 191; working clothing 204–5; World War II 283 *see also* motoring clothing; sportswear
Prada **15**, 475, 481, 487; patterned dress and coat **440–1**, 481; 'Vela' backpack 475
Prada, Miuccia 14, 475, 481
Prairie collection (Ralph Lauren) 413, **414–15**, 415
pre-Columbian textiles 26–9; *t'oqapu* 27, **28**, 29, **29**; tunic 26, **27**, **27**, **28**, 29, **29**
Pre-Raphaelite Brotherhood 184, 187, **187**
Première Vision/Indigo trade fairs 521
preppy styles 13, 308–13, 413, 540; blazers **308**, 309; 'bobbysoxer' style 309, **309**, 310–11, 311, 314; chinos 312, **312**, 313; Ivy League style 308, 312, **312–13**, 365, 413; Letterman sweaters 312, **312**, 313; 'rep' ties **308**, 309, 313
Presley, Elvis 311, 341, **341**
Price, Antony 420, 421, 423; Roxy Music cover leather dress **422–3**, 423
Prince of Wales check **274**, 275
Princess line (Charles Worth) 175, **178–9**, 179

Pringle of Scotland 259
print in fashion 518–27; animal prints **329**, 372, 387, 401, 437, 468, 469, **486**, 549; Erdem 519; Jensen, Peter 519; Katrantzou, Mary 519, 524, **524–5**; Olowu, Duro 549, **550–1**, 551; Op art print mini dresses, Johnson, Betsey **362–3**, 363; Peter Pilotto 519, **526–7**, 527; psychedelic print kaftans (Pucci) **388–9**, 389; Saunders, Jonathan 519; screen printing 363, 471, **471**, 519, 520; *trompe l'oeil* dress (Mary Katrantzou) 524, **524–5**; Warhol print dress (Versace) **470–1**, 471; Waterfall dress (Peter Pilotto) **526–7**, 527
prints in fashion: Castiglioni, Consuelo (Marni) 520; digital prints 520; Etro 520, **522–3**, 523; Fulton, Holly 521, **521**; paisley dress (Etro) **522–3**, 523; Van Noten, Dries 520, **521**; Williamson, Matthew 520
Proenza Schouler 540, 543; quilted jacket and leather skirt **542–3**, 543
Project Alabama 487
prom dress 315, **316–17**, 317
prozodiejda 235
Pucci (fashion house) 475
Pucci, Emilio 334, 335, **335**, 387; psychedelic print kaftan **388–9**, 389; Pucci prints 335, **335**
Pueblo Indians 22, 22–5, **25**
Puma 531
punk rock fashion 407, 416–19; 'anarchy shirt' 417, **418**, 419, **419**; 'bondage trousers' 417, **417**; 'bondage trousers' (Vivienne Westwood) **417**; 'destroy T-shirts' 417; fetish wear (Vivienne Westwood) 416, 417; 'hangman jumper' 417; Westwood, Vivienne 416, 417, **417**
Putman, Andrée 383
puttees **193**
pyjamas 246, **257** *see also* beach pyjamas

Qianlong, Qing emperor 83, 84
Qing dynasty, China 82–5, 164–7
qipao 229, **229**
Quant, Mary 355, 356–7, 359, 365; coat and mini dress **355**
Queen Maria Teresa and her son (Pierre Mignard) **88–9**
queue 88, 89
quilting 61, **114**, 115, **115**, 392, 393, **393**, 402, 403, **542**, 543, **543**

Rabanne, Paco 372, 376, 377; Giffo process 377; paillette dress **377**
rabat 91
radical design 13, 430–5; Bodymap 431, 432, **432–3**, 433; 'The Cat in the Hat…' collection (Bodymap) 431, 432, **432–3**; The Cloth 431, **434–5**, 435; English Rose collection (Betty Jackson) 431; Galliano, John 431, **431**; Hamnett, Katharine 431; Hogg, Pam 430;

Les Incroyables collection (John Galliano) 431; Jackson, Betty 431; Jones, Stephen 430; knitted outfits (Bodymap) 432, **432–3**; Linnard, Stephen 431; Miyake, Issey 13, 431; New Romantic movement **430**, 430–1, **431**; Pirates collection (Vivienne Westwood) 419, 430; printed textiles (The Cloth) 431, **434–5**, 435; slogan T-shirt 431, **431**; Smith, Hilde 431, 432, **432**, **433**; 'T-shape' tubular dress 432, **432**; Westwood, Vivienne 430
Raeburn, Christopher: parachute parka 487, **487**
Rainey, Michael 365
Rajah, Gavin 549
Rampling, Charlotte **437**
Rankin, Ian 479
raquette sleeves **96**, 97
raschel **396**, 397, **496**, 497, 502, **502**, **503**
Ray, Man 211
ready-to-wear fashion (prêt-à-porter): African fashion 371; Italian fashion 335, **335**, 383, **383**; luxe 534–9; 1950s 300, 301, 335, **335**; 1970s 383, **383**, 398, 399, 450; 1980s 445, 451; 2010s **534**, 534–9, **535**; shirtwaists **194**, 195, **195**, 204; Victorian period 175, **194**, 195, **195** *see also* American fashion; French fashion
Reagan, Nancy 443
Réard, Louis 325
Reboux, Caroline 227
rebozo 139
recycled textiles 283, 377, 487, **487**, 499
Redfern & Sons 204
Redford, Robert **412**, 413
redingote 94, **95**, 147
Reebok 531
Regina Knitwear 330, **331**, **331**; beaded cardigan **330–1**, 331
Renaissance period 11, 48, **48–58**; codpiece 49, **49**; court dress 50, 55, **56**, **57**; doublet 49, 50, **52**, 53, **53**; farthingale 51, **54**, 55, **55**, 57; partlet 50, **51**; ruffs 11, 50, 51, **51**, **56–7**, 57
Renée **302**, 303
'rep' ties **308**, 309, 313
Restoration period 90–3; chemise 92, **93**, 93; nightgown **92–3**, 93; 'undress' (*déshabillé*) **92–3**, 93
retail revolution (1960s) 354–7, 361; Ayton, Sylvia 357; Bates, John 355, **355**, 358–9, 359; Bazaar 354, 355, 356–7, 365; Biba 354, 356, **356**, 357; Bus Stop 354; Casbah dress (John Bates) 355, 358–9, 359; Clark, Ossie 357; Foale and Tuffin 356, **356**, 357; Granny Takes a Trip 354, 357; Johnson, Betsey 357, **362–3**, 363; Just Looking **354**; Khanh, Emmanuelle 357; mini dress 355, 362, 363, **363**; mini skirt **358**, 359, **359**; mirror dress **363**; Mondrian dress (Yves

Saint Laurent) 348, 349, 357, **360–1**, 361; Op art print mini dress (Betsey Johnson) **362–3**, 363; Quant, Mary 354, 355, **355**, 356–7; Rhodes, Zandra 357; Rive Gauche 357, 359, 382, **382**; Saint Laurent, Yves 357; Wedge, James 357
reticella 50
reticules **112**, 113, 121, **121**, 131, **131**
Revlon 'Fire and Ice' 327, **327**
Revson, Charles (Revlon) 327
Rhodes, Zandra 357, 387, **387**
Riley, Bridget 363, 527
'The Rising Star' bra 321
Rive Gauche 357, 359, 382, **382**
robe à la française 97, **98–9**, 99, 106, **110**, 111, 121
robe à la polonaise 108, **109**
robe à l'anglaise 94, 95, **100–1**, 101, 127
robe battante 97
robe chemise 95, **95**
robe de style 240, **244–5**, 245
robe volante 95, **96–7**, 97, 185
Roberts, Tommy 407
Robertson, Nick (ASOS) 547
robes de chambre 95
Les Robes de Paul Poiret 208, **208**
'robing' 108, **110**, 111
Rochas (fashion house) 263, 541
Rochas, Marcel 321
Rococo period 106–15; bicorne **112**, 113; cravat **112**, 113; dressing gown **114–15**, 115; fans **108**, 109; headdress 109, **110–11**, 111; jabot **112**, 113; Macaroni **112–13**, 113; *robe à la polonaise* 108, **109**; three-piece suit 106, **112**, 113, **113**
Rodarte 490–1, 493; tulle dresses **492–3**, 493
Rodchenko, Alexander 232
Rokumeikan, Tokyo **180**, 181, 182
Roman clothing: Classical period 18, 18–19; toga 18, **19**; tunic 18–19; wrapped clothing 8, **8**, **19**, **19**
Romantic period 130–3; gloves 133; hairstyles 131, **132**, 133; headdress **132**, **133**; reticule 131, **131**
Rose, Helen 314, 315
Rosenfeld, Henry 329, **329**
Rosier, Michèle 383
Rossellini, Isabella 468
Rossetti, Dante Gabriel 184, **187**; *Day Dream* **187**
rosso Valentino **512–13**, 513
Roxy Music 421, **422**, 423
The Royal Lady 133
ruana **141**, 141
Rubartelli, Franco 373
ruff 11, 50, **50**, 51, **56–7**, 57
Run-DMC 446, **447**, 528
Russell, Jane 320, **321**
Russian Constructivist design 232–7; costume design **232**, 235, **235**, **236**, 237, **237**; *Death of Tarelkin* costume design (Varvara Stepanova) 235, **236–7**, 237; fabric design **233**, 233–4, 234; 'flapper' dress (Lyubov Popova) 234; 'Hammer and Sickle' motif 234; Popova, Lyubov 232,

233, 233–4, **234**, 235; sports costume (Varvara Stepanova) 235, **235**; Stepanova, Varvara 232, **232**, 233, 234, 235, **235**, **236–7**, 237; tailleur (Lyubov Popova) **234**; tunics 234, **236**, **237**, 237
Rykiel, Sonia 383, **394–5**; striped sweater **394**, 394

'S'-shape 12, **191**, 191, 197, **197**, 198, 201
sable 47, **53**, 81, 85, 166, 167
sac haut à courroies see Kelly bag
Sachs, Tom 531
sack-back dress 101, 106, 108, 175, 201
sack dress 300, 361
sacque see robe volante
saddle stitching 440, **441**
safari suit 372, **373**, 383
Saint Laurent, Yves 267, 301, 348, 361, 371, 372, 373, **382**, 382–3, 435; Africa collection (1967) 372, **372**; Mondrian dress 348, 349, 357, **360–1**, 361; pinstripe suit 267, 382–3, **384–5**, 385 Rive Gauche 357, 359, 382, **382**, 383; safari suit 372, **373**, 383; trouser suit 383 *see also* Yves Saint Laurent
Saks Fifth Avenue 398
Sam Browne belt **206**, 207, **207**
samurai dress 74, 75, **181**
Sander, Jil: 'The Great Plain', *Vogue* **476–7**, 477 *see also* Jil Sander
Sant'Angelo, Giorgio di 387
sapeurs 372, 549, **552–3**, 553
sarafan 234, **237**
sari 64, 67, **70–1**, 71
sashiko 403
Saturday Night Fever (1977) 407, **407**
Saunders, Jonathan 519, **519**
Savile Row tailoring 154, 155, 156, **157**, **274**, 275, **275**, 305, 337, 369
Savini, Gaetano (Brioni) 337
saya 140, **141**
Scaasi, Arnold 442, 443, 445; evening dress **444–5**, 445
Scherrer, Jean-Louis **436**
Schiaparelli, Elsa 12, 223, 253, 262–3, 264, 265, 452, 524; film costume design 271, **271**; 'lobster' gown **262**, 263; 'madcap' 263; *trompe l'oeil* sweater 223, 262–3, 264, **264–5**, 265
Schott Perfecto leather jacket **342–3**, 343
Scotland: knitwear manufacture 259, **259**; Scottish dress 102–5, 130; **105**; kilt 102, 103, 105; shoulder plaid **102**, 103, **104**, 105; sporran **104**, 105, **105**
Scott, Sir Walter 130
Scottish 'ghillie' cross-lacing 133
screen printing 363, 471, **471**, 519, 520
second-skin clothing 421, 424–9, 467; Alaïa, Azzedine 424, **424**, 425, 549; bandage dress 425, **425**; Kamali, Norma 425; keep-fit fashion 424–5, 428, **428–9**, 429; Klein, Calvin 425, **426–7**, 427; Leger, Hervé 425, **425**;

INDEX 571

Lycra 407, 410, 424, 425, 428, **428–9**; Spandex 428, **428–9**
Selfridge's 205
Selim II, Ottoman emperor 60, **60**, 61
serape 143
seraser 61
serenk 63
Sex 416–17, **417**, 419
Sex Pistols 417, **418**, 419
Sexton, Edward 369
sexuality and fashion: 'fashion valkyries' **420**, 420–3, **421**, **422**, 423, **423**; Hollywood and fashion 270, **270**, 320, **320**, 321, 325; Italian decadence 466–71, **467**, **468**, **469**, **470**, **471**; second-skin clothing 424, 424–7, **425**, 426–7
Seydou, Chris 371
Shah Jahan, Mughal emperor 66, 69, **69**
shalwar 65
Shibuya 506
Shields, Brooke **426–7**, 427
Shima Seiki knitting machines 491
shingled hairstyle *see* bob
shirtwaist dress **328–9**, 329
shirtwaist 191, **192**, 193, **194–5**, 195, 204
shoulder plaid 102, 103, **104–5**, 105
Shrimpton, Jean **358**
shwe-pe-kha-mauk 171
Sidibé, Malick (the Eye of Bamako) 371; *Nuit de Noël* **370**
Siegle, Lucy 489
Silver, Arthur **185**
Simon, Samuel 519
Simons, Raf 511
Simpson, Wallis (Duchess of Windsor) 287, **288**, 289, **289**
Sims, Naomi 373
siren suit 283, **283**
skull cap 164, 165, **516**, **517**
slacks 267, **267**, 283
Slimane, Hedi 511
smart technology 521, 529, 530, 531
Smith, Hilde 431, 432; Big Mesh collection 432, **432**, **433**
Smith, Paul 435, 437, 549; spring/summer collection (2010) 549, **553**
Snow, Carmel 211, 278, 303
sokuhatsu 182, **182–3**
sombrero 141, **141**, 142, 143, **143**, 260, **261**
Sorelle Fontana *see* Fontana sisters
Sorrenti, Mario 479, **479**
South America: pre-Columbian period 26–9; *t'oqapu* 27, **28**, 29, **29**; tunics **26**, 27, **28**, 29, **29**
Sozzani, Franca (*Vogue Italia*) 549
Space Age collection (Pierre Cardin) 377, 381
Spandau Ballet 430, **430**
Spandex 407, 428, **428–9**
Spanier, Ginette (Balmain) 267
Speedo 529; Fastskin and Fastskin3 528, 529
'Speedy' bag (Louis Vuitton) **449**
spencer 205
Spitalfields silk weaving 107, **107**
sporran **104**, 105, **105**
sportswear 191, **192–3**, 193;

American fashion 190, 277, 278; English fashion 116, **116**, 149, 156, **156**, 159, 204; keep-fit fashion 424–5, 428, **428–9**; Russian Constructivism 235, **235**; 1920s 252, **252–3**, **254**, 255, **255**; Victorian period 149, 156, **156**, 159, 190, **192**, **193**, **193**, **194**, 195, **195**, 204 *see also* designer sportswear
Sprouse, Stephen 447, **449**; Graffiti collection **448–9**, 449
'standing water' border **85**
Stanwyck, Barbara 279
Starr, Ringo **368**
stays 121, 123, 131
Steichen, Edward 211
Stella McCartney 475 *see* McCartney, Stella
Stepanova, Varvara 232, **232**, 233, **234**; sports costume 235, **235**
Stephen, John 364, **364**, 365
Stevenson, Ray **418**
Stiebel, Victor 301
stiletto heel 335, 348, **410**, **411**, **422**, **423**, 437, **448**, 449
Strauss, Levi 340, 343
straw boater 191, **194**, 195, 196, 240, **242**, 243
street-style fashion *see* hip-hop and street style fashion
Studio 54 407
Sudo, Reiko (NUNO Corporation) **500–1**, **501**
Sui, Anna 483, **483**
Süleyman I, Ottoman emperor 58, **58**, 59
Sun Yat-sen, Dr 228, 231, **231**
Superga 253
surcoat 34, **34**, **35**, **44**, 45, 83
'surgeon's cuff' sleeve **274**, **275**
surrealism and fashion 12, 238, 262–5, 452, 524; Schiaparelli, Elsa 12, 223, **262**, 262–3, 264, **264–5**, 265
sustainable and ethical fashion 14, 486–9; Edun **486**, 487; Green Carpet Challenge 487, 489; Hamnett, Katharine 487; Harvey, Gary 14, 487, **488–9**, 489; Marks & Spencer 487; McCartney, Stella 487, **487**; newspaper dress (Gary Harvey) 487, **489**; Panichgul, Thakoon 487; parachute parka (Christopher Raeburn) 487, **487**; People Tree 487; Raeburn, Christopher 487; upcycled evening gown (Gary Harvey) **488–9**, 489
swan-bill corsets 197, **197**
Swanky Modes 407
sweater dress **258**, 259
'sweater girls' 320, **321**, 323, **323**
Sweet Lolita 507, **508–9**, 509
sweetheart line **314**, 314–15, 317, **444**, 445, **445**, **496**, 497, **497**
swimwear: elasticized swimwear (Jantzen) 260, **260–1**; knitted **12**, 258, 260, **260**, 261, **261**; 1920s **12**, 253, **253**; 1930s 258, 260, **260**, 261, **261**; 1940s 321,

324, **325**, **325**; 2000s and 2010s 528, **529–30**
swing dance outfits 292, 293
'sword of kingship' wax print 162, **162–3**

T by Alexander Wang 541
'T-shape' tubular dress 432, **432**
T-shirt 341, **342**, 343; 'destroy T-shirts' 417; oversize 447, 541; slogan T-shirt 431, **431**, 452, **453**
tabard 377
The Tailor and Cutter 157
tailored clothing: English fashion: early 20th century 204; 1960s **368**, 369, **369**; 19th century 116, **117**, **117**, **119**; Victorian period 146, 149, 154–9, **158**, **159**; India 64–5, **64**, 66, 67; Italian fashion 335, **336**, **337**, **337**; Victorian period 146, 149, 154–9, **158**, **159**, **193**, 195, 204; World War II **284**, 285, **285**
tailormade 195, 204, 205, 207
Taizong, Tang emperor **32**, 33
Taj-i 'Izzat (Crown of Glory) turban 64, **65**
The Tale of Genji (Lady Murasaki Shikbu) **36**, 36, **37**
Tamagni, Daniele: *The Gentlemen of Bacongo* **552**
Tang dynasty, China 30–5
Tang women's court dress 34, **34–5**
tapada limeña 140, **141**
tapestry and tapestry weaving: Burma 169, **169**, **171**; French fashion 86; *luntaya acheik* technique 169, **169**, **171**; Native American 23; pre-Columbian textiles **26**, 27
tartan 102, **102–5**, **103**, **105**, 131, **152**, **153**, **153**, **417**, **417**
Tatlin, Vladimir 235
Taylor, Elizabeth 314, **314**, 315
Taylor, Fraser (The Cloth) 435
tea gown **199**, **212**, **213**
tebenna 19
Tehrathum Dhaka 350–1, **352–3**, 353
Teller, Juergen **479**
Tennant, Stella 482–3
tennis clothes 252, **252–3**; shirt (Lacoste) **253**, **254–5**, 255
textile industry 74, **74**, 86, 148, 173, 174, 195, **195**, 233, 521
Thakoon *see* Panichgul, Thakoon
'The Great Plain', *Vogue* (Jil Sander) **476–7**, 477
Theyskens, Olivier 461, 541 *see also* Theyskens at Theory
Theyskens at Theory 540, **541**
Thibaw, king of Burma 168, **171**
Thomas, Philip Michael **437**
Thomas-Fahm, Shade 371, 375; *gele* 375, **375**; *iro* complete **374–5**, 375
tie-dye shoulder blanket **22**, 24–5, 25
tie-dyeing **22**, **23**, **24**, **25**, **27**, 67, 518
Tiffany 339
toga 18, 19
top hat **11**, 138, 159, **266**, 267

Top-Sider deck shoes 309
topi 350–1, **352–3**, 353
Topkapi Palace, Constantinople 58–9, 61
t'oqapu 27, **28**, 29, **29**
toque 197
Townshend, Pete **366**, 367, **367**
trapeze-line dress 361, **512**, 513
Travilla, William Jack 320, **321**, **321**, **423**
Travolta, John **407**
trench coat 267, 345, 467, 511
Trigère, Pauline 279, 327, 333; navy suit **332–3**, 333
trilby **192**, **193**, 267, **384**, **385**
Trois Quarts 215–16
trompe l'oeil cuffs **526**, **527**, 527
trouser suit 266, **266**, 267, 283, **283**, 356, **356**, 383
Tuffin, Sally 356 *see also* Foale and Tuffin
turban ornament 67, **67**
turban and turban headdress: Belle Epoque 197, 199, 216, 216–17, **217**; India 64, **64**, **65**, **65**, 67, **67**; medieval period 43, **43**; Ottoman Empire 61, 63, **63**; *Taj-i 'Izzat* 64, **65**; World War II 283
turf 53
Turlington, Christy 466, 467, **476**, **477**
turn-ups (cuffs) 157, 267, **268**, 269, **294**, **295**
Turner, Jessie Franklin 217, 219; tea gown **218–19**, 219
Turner, Lana 320
turtleneck sweater **267**, 311, **323**, **323**, 345, 373
tutu skirt 467, **467**, **492**, **493**
tuxedo 156, **157**, 240, **266**, 267, 385
Twiggy **357**, 357
twinset 259, **259**, 395, 399, 500
2000s fashion: Adidas 529, **530**, **530**, 533; Afterwords collection (Hussein Chalayan) 499, **504–5**, 505; Cavalli, Roberto 469, **469**; Chalayan, Hussein 499, **504–5**, 505, 531; craft renaissance 490–1; Decarnin, Christophe 511, **511**; Edun **486**, 487; Elbaz, Alber 510, **511**; Etro 520, **522–3**, 523; Fastskin (Speedo) **528**; Fendi (by Lagerfeld) 469, **469**; Fox, Shelley 500; Green Carpet Challenge 487, 489; Hamnett, Katharine 487; Harvey, Gary 14, 487, **488–9**, 489; Inertia collection (Hussein Chalayan for Puma) 531; Lagerfeld (for Fendi) 469, **469**; Margiela, Martin 501; Marks & Spencer 487; McCartney, Stella 487, **487**; McCartney, Stella (for Adidas) 529, **530**; modern haute couture 510–17; newspaper dress (Gary Harvey) 487, **489**; Ossendrijver, Lucas 511, 513; paisley dress (Etro) **522–3**, 523; Panichgul, Thakoon 487; parachute parka (Christopher Raeburn) 487, **487**; Raeburn, Christopher 487, **487**; 513; Rodarte 490–1,

492–3, 493; Speedo **528**, 529; sustainable and ethical fashion 14, 486–9; tulle dresses (Rodarte) **492–3**, 493; two-piece suit (Ossendrijver for Lanvin) **514–15**, 515; upcycled evening gown (Gary Harvey) **488–9**, 489; Valentino 511, **512–13**, 513; Y-3 (Yohji Yamamoto for Adidas) **532–3**, 533; Yamamoto, Yohji 403, 531, **532–3**, 533
2010s fashion: Adidas 530; AdiZero (Adidas) 530; Alaïa, Azzedine 549; Alexander McQueen 531; Armani, Giorgio 531; ASOS 545, **546–7**, 547; Beckham, Victoria 534, 535, **535**; Boateng, Ozwald 549, **549**; Burberry **534**, 534–5; Burch, Tory 540, 541, **541**; Burton, Sarah 490, 491, 511, **516–17**, 517; Casely-Hayford, Joe and Charlie 549; craft renaissance 490–1; Duro dress **550–1**, 551; e-commerce and fashion 544–7; Elbaz, Alber 549; Eley Kishimoto 518; embroidered skirt and knitted sweater (Christopher Kane) **494–5**, 495; Erdem 491, **496–7**, 497; Fassler, Marianne 549; Fastskin3 (Speedo) **528**, 529; festival wear (Isabel Marant) **536–7**, 537; 497; Fulton, Holly 491, **491**, 521, **521**; hippie fashion 534, **536–7**, 537, 540; Ice Queen dress (Sarah Burton for Alexander McQueen) 12, **516–17**, 517; Jaked 530; Jewel by Lisa **548**, 548–9; Kane, Christopher 491, **494–5**, 495; Katrantzou, Mary 491, 519, 524, **524–5**; Keller, Clare Waight 535; KLûK CGDT 549; LemLem 549; Louw, Stiaan 549; luxe ready-to-wear fashion 534–9; MacGibbon, Hannah 535; Maki Oh 549; Marant, Isabel 534, **536–7**, 537; Matteo Dosso 545; McCartney, Stella 529, **529**, 534, **538–9**, 539; Net-a-Porter 544, **544**; Nike **530**, 530–1; NikeCraft (Sachs) 531; Nike+ Hyperdunk (Nike) **530**, 530–1; Nike iD Studios 544, **545**; Olowu, Duro 549, **550–1**, 551; Olympic 2012 Team GB kit (Stella McCartney) **529**, 539; Panichgul, Thakoon 540, **540**, 541; patterned dress (Stella McCartney) **538–9**, 539; Peter Pilotto label **526–7**, 527; Phillip Lim 540, 541, **541**; Philo, Phoebe (for Céline) 535, **535**; Pilotto, Peter 519, 527; Proenza Schouler 540, **542–3**, 543; quilted jacket and leather skirt (Proenza Schouler) **542–3**, 543; Rajah, Gavin 549; Rousteing, Olivier 491, **491**; Sachs, Tom 531; *sapeur* 549, **552–3**, 553; Saunders, Jonathan 519, **519**; Simons, Raf 511; Speedo **528**, 529; Theyskens at Theory 540, 541; *trompe l'oeil* dress

(Mary Katrantzou) 524, **524–5**; understated American fashion 540–3; Van Noten, Dries 520, **521**; Wang, Alexander 531, 540–1; Wang, Vera 531, **531**; Waterfall dress (Peter Pilotto) **526–7**, 527

'Under Exposure', *Vogue* **484–5**, 485
underskirt 98, 99, **101**, 127, 306, 307, **307**
undersleeves 47, 51, 57, 147, 152, 153
underwear and undergarments: as outerwear 460, 460–3, **461**, **462–3**; Restoration period 92, 93, **93**; 1950s 320, 321, **322**, 323, **323**; Victorian period 189 *see also* bra; chemise; corsets; lingerie; stays
'undress' (*déshabillé*) **92–3**, 93
Ungaro, Emanuel 377, **450**
uniforms: modern China (male) 228; 1960s fashion 365, **365**, 367; World War I (female) 205, **206–7**, 207
Union Jack jacket **366–7**, 367
unisex fashion 13, 33, 377, 379
unitard **408–9**, 409
United States *see* American fashion
upcycled textiles **488–9**, 489
Utamaro, Kitagawa: *Courtesans Strolling Beneath Cherry Trees* 76, **77**

V-line suit (Adrian) **278**, 279
Valdes, Zelda Wynn 293
Valentino 487, 489, 511, 513; red dresses **512–13**, 513; Valentino red (*rosso Valentino*) **512–13**, 513
Valma 363
Van Noten, Dries 520, **521**
Vanity Fair 209, **209**
Varsity sweater 309, 312, **312**, 313
'Vela' backpack (Prada) 475
Velázquez, Diego: *Las Meninas* 54, 55, **55**
Verdura, Fulco di **223**
Versace, Donatella 467, **471**
Versace, Gianni 383, **466**, **467**, 471, 483, 466, 467; bondage collection (1992) 467; Warhol print dress **470–1**, 471
Veruschka 373
Victoria, queen of England **134**, 149, 153, 156, 158
Victorian period 11, 146–54; bifurcated skirt 191, **192**, 193, **193**; bustle 146, 148, **149**; corset 148, 153, 177, 187, 191, 197; crinoline 11, 146, **146**, 147, 148, **148**, 153, 174, 177, 187; *cuirasse* bodice 148, **178**, 179; dinner jacket 156, **157**; frock coat 155, **155**; gored skirt 148, **148**, 174, **178**, 179; Homburg 157, 158, **158**, 159; Inverness coat 159, **159**; Liberty dress **188–9**, 189; lounge suit 155–6, 158, **158**, **159**; morning suit 154, 155, 156; Norfolk jacket 156, **156**, 157; plaid 147, **152**, 153, **153**; tailcoat **154**, 155; tailored clothing 146, 149, 154–9, **158**, **159** *see also* Belle Epoque

Villandrando, Rodrigo de, *Isabel of France* 56, 57, **57**
Vionnet, Madeleine 246, 246–7, **247**, 271, 391
Vivier, Roger 348, 349; Pilgrim pump 345, 348, **348–9**
Vlisco 161, 162, **163**
Vogue: African 387; British 209, 210, **284**, 285, 355, **358**, 373, **392**, 421, 483, **484–5**, 485, 551; French 209, 289, 361, 385; US 210, 211, 225, 264, 271, **286**, 317, 373, **476–7**, 477; *Vogue Italia* 383, 468
Von Brandenstein, Patrizia **407**
Von Furstenberg, Diane 399, **401**, **401**; wrap dress 399, **400–1**, 401
Von Heideloff, Nicholas **126**, 127, **127**
Von Sternberg, Josef 269, 271
Von Unwerth, Ellen 468, **468**, **476**, 477

Waldman, Bernard 271
Walker, Catherine 450
Wang, Alexander 531, 540–1; T by Alexander Wang 541
Warhol, Andy 363, 407, 449, 467, **470**, 471, **471**
Warhol print dress (Versace) **470–1**, 471
Wari Empire, Peru 25, 26, **26**, 27
weaving and woven clothing: ancient Greek and Roman clothing 8, 18, **18**, 21; *ase oke* 371, **374**, 375, **375**, 549; China 30, 34; Dhaka **350**, 350–1, **352**, 353; French fashion 86, **97**, 99, 106; India 67; kente cloth **134**, 134–7, **135**, **136**, **137**, 371, **371**, 446; medieval period 43; Native American 22, 23; Nepal **350**, 350–1; Ottoman Empire 58, 59, **59**; Palpali 351; pre-Columbian textiles 26, 27, **28**, 29, 29; Rococo period 106–7, **107**; Romantic period 131; Russian Constructivism 233; Spitalfields silk 107, **107**; Victorian period 148, 151, **153**; West Africa **134**, 134–7, **135**, **136–7**, 371, **371** *see also* tapestry
Webb, Iain R. 430
Wen Zhou *see* 3.1 Phillip Lim
Wenzong, Tang emperor 31, 34
West, Mae 270, **271**
Westwood, Vivienne 13, 416, **416**, **417**, **417**, 419, 447, 460, 507, 549; 'anarchy shirt' **418–19**, 419; 'bondage trousers' 417, **417**; Buffalo Girls collection (1982–83) 460; 'destroy T-shirts' 417; fetish wear **416**, 417; 'hangman jumper' 417; Pirates collection (1981) 419, 430; Portrait collection (1990) 460, 461; Witches collection (1983–84) 447
Weymouth, Nigel 357, 365, **365**
whalebone 51, 55, 89, 97, **99**, 131, 153
The Who **366**, 367
The Wild One (1953) 341, **342–3**, 343
Williamson, Matthew 520
willow boning 55, 89, 97, **99**
Windsor knot **268**, 269, 275, **275**
'winkers' 117

'winklepicker' shoes 335, 348
Winter (Wenceslaus Hollar) 79, 80, **80–1**
Winterhalter, Franz Xaver **172**; *The Empress of Austria* **176–7**, 301
Witches collection (Westwood, 1983–84) 447
Women's Wear Daily 217, 219, 348, 424, 425, 427
Wood, Grant: *American Gothic* 477, **477**
World War I 207
World War II 277, 282–5; American fashion 277, 282, 283, 293; Amies, Hardy 283; English fashion 282, **282**, 283; French fashion 277, 279, 282; Hartnell, Norman 282, **282**, 283; King, Muriel 282; McCardell, Claire 277–8, 282; Molyneux, Edward 283; Morton, Digby 283, **284–5**, 285; Potter, Clare 282; siren suit 283, **283**; slacks 283; suit (female) 283, **283**, **284–5**, 285; turban 283; utility clothing 282, 283, **283**, **284–5**, 285
Worth, Charles Frederick 149, **172**, 172–9, **174**, 176–9, 298; ball gown **176–7**, 177; evening dress 173, **173**; Princess line 175, **178–9**, 179 *see also* House of Worth
Wrangler (Blue Bell Overall Company) 340, **341**
wrap dress 399, **400–1**, 401
Wu-Tang Clan (Wu Wear) 446

Xianfeng, Qing emperor 164, 165
Xuanzong, Tang emperor 32, 35
Xuly Bët wear 500, **500**
xystis **20**, 21, **21**

Y-3 (Yohji Yamamoto for Adidas) 403, **532–3**, 533
yakaimaki 182
Yamamba 507
Yamamoto, Kansai 406, 409; Ziggy Stardust **408–9**, 409
Yamamoto, Yohji 13, 403, **403**, 405, 501, 531; all-purpose sportswear **532–3**, 533; Y-3 (for Adidas) 403, **532–3**, 533; 'Ys for Men' (1981) 403; 'Ys for Women' (1977) 403
Yang Guifei, Imperial concubine 31, 35
yetpya 171
yinzi 169
Yongzheng, Qing emperor 82
'Ys for Men' (Yohji Yamamoto) 403
'Ys for Women' (Yohji Yamamoto) 403
Yuan Shikai, Chinese emperor **228**, 229
yuzen 75, **75**
Yves Saint Laurent 475, 511

zardosi 171
zari 67, 71
zhongshan suit 228, **230–1**, 231
Zhou Fang 34
Ziggy Stardust (Kansai Yamamoto) **408–9**, 409
zoot suit 293, **294–5**, 295, 369

INDEX 573

PICTURE CREDITS

The publishers would like to thank the museums, galleries, collectors, archives and photographers for their kind permission to reproduce the works featured in this book. Where no dimensions are given, none are available. Every effort has been made to trace all copyright owners but if any have been inadvertently overlooked, the publishers would be pleased to make the necessary arrangements at the first opportunity. (Key: **above** = a; **below** = b; **left** = l; **right** = r)

2 Pierre Vauthey/Sygma/Corbis **8** © The Trustees of the British Museum **9** Musée National du Moyen Age et des Thermes de Cluny, Paris/The Bridgeman Art Library **10–11** Getty Images **12** Condé Nast Archive/Corbis **13** Condé Nast Archive/Corbis **15** Fairchild Photo Service/Condé Nast/Corbis **16–17** Victoria and Albert Museum, London **18** De Agostini/Getty Images **19** Araldo de Luca/Corbis **20–21** De Agostini/Getty Images **22** Smith, Watson, *Kiva Mural Decorations at Awatovi and Kawaika-a: With a Survey of Other Wall Paintings in the Pueblo*. Papers of the Peabody Museum of Archaeology and Ethnology, Harvard University, Volume 37. Copyright 1952 by the President and Fellows of Harvard College. Reprinted courtesy of the Peabody Museum of Archaeology and Ethnology, Harvard University **23** Arizona State Museum, University of Arizona **24–25** Courtesy of the Penn Museum, image # 29-43-183 **25 br** Smith, Watson, *Kiva Mural Decorations at Awatovi and Kawaika-a: With a Survey of Other Wall Paintings in the Pueblo*. Papers of the Peabody Museum of Archaeology and Ethnology, Harvard University, Volume 37. Copyright 1952 by the President and Fellows of Harvard College. Reprinted courtesy of the Peabody Museum of Archaeology and Ethnology, Harvard University **26** © 2013. Image copyright The Metropolitan Museum of Art/Art Resource/Scala, Florence **27** © The Trustees of the British Museum **28–29** © Dumbarton Oaks, Pre-Columbian Collection, Washington, DC **30** Liaoning Province Museum, China **31** Court lady in ceremonial dress, late 7th century earthenware with traces of colour over a white slip, 36.8 cm. Art Gallery of New South Wales, Gift of Mr Sydney Cooper 1962, [Accn # EC27.1962] **32, 33** a UIG via Getty Images **33 b** Victoria and Albert Museum, London **34–35** Liaoning Province Museum, China **35 b** Indianapolis Museum of Art, USA/Gift of Mr and Mrs William R. Spurlock Fund and Gift of the/ Alliance of the Indianapolis Museum of Art/The Bridgeman Art Library **36** Detroit Institute of Arts, USA/The Bridgeman Art Library **37** Private Collection Paris/Gianni Dagli Orti/The Art Archive **38** De Agostini Picture Library/akg-images **39** Tokugawa Reimeikai Foundation, Tokyo, Japan/The Bridgeman Art Library **40–41** The Art Archive/Alamy **41 br** Gamma-Keystone via Getty Images **42** The Gallery Collection/Corbis **43 a** Private Collection/The Bridgeman Art Library **43 b** Gianni Dagli Orti/Corbis **44** The J. Paul Getty Museum, Los Angeles, 91.MS.11.2.verso Coëtivy Master (Henri de Vulcop?), *Philosophy Presenting the Seven Liberal Arts to Boethius*, about 1460–1470. Tempera colours, gold leaf and gold paint on parchment, Leaf: 6 x 17 cm (2 3/8 x 6 11/16 in.) **45 a** De Agostini/Getty Images **45 b** Historical Picture Archive/Corbis **46–47** National Gallery, London/The Bridgeman Art Library **48** Popperfoto/Getty Images **49** Kunsthistorisches Museum, Vienna, Austria/The Bridgeman Art Library **50 a** Giovanni Battista Moroni/Getty Images **51** Corbis **52–53** Staatliche Kunstsammlungen Dresden/The Bridgeman Art Library **54–55** Prado, Madrid, Spain/Giraudon/The Bridgeman Art Library **55 br** Getty Images **56–57** Prado, Madrid, Spain/The Bridgeman Art Library **57 b** Victoria and Albert Museum, London **58** British Library Board. All Rights Reserved/The Bridgeman Art Libra **59** Victoria and Albert Museum, London **60** Topkapi Palace Museum, Istanbul, Turkey/Giraudon/The Bridgeman Art Library **61** Topkapi Saray Museum **62–63** © National Museums Scotland **64** Arthur M. Sackler Gallery, Smithsonian Institution, Washington, D.C.: Purchase - Smithsonian Unrestricted Trust Funds, Smithsonian Collections Acquisition Program, and Dr. Arthur M Sackler, S1986.400 **65, 66, 67 a** Victoria and Albert Museum, London **67 b** © 2013. Museum of Fine Arts, Boston. All rights reserved/Scala, Florence **70–71** Victoria and Albert Museum, London **72–73** © Wallace Collection, London/The Bridgeman Art Library **74** Erich Lessing/akg-images **75** Victoria and Albert Museum, London **76–77** Brooklyn Museum/Corbis **77 br** Victoria and Albert Museum, London **78** The Royal Collection © 2011 Her Majesty Queen Elizabeth II/The Bridgeman Art Library **79 a** His Grace The Duke of Norfolk, Arundel Castle/The Bridgeman Art Library **79 b** Private Collection/The Bridgeman Art Library **80–81** Private Collection/The Bridgeman Art Library **81 br** Thomas Fisher Rare Book Library/University of Toronto Wenceslaus Hollar Digital Collection **82** The Palace Museum, Beijing. Photograph by WangJin **83 a** The Palace Museum, Beijing. Photograph by SunZhiyuan **83 b** The Palace Museum, Beijing. Photograph by HuChui **84–85** The Palace Museum, Beijing. Photograph by FengHui **85 br** The Palace Museum, Beijing. Photograph by HuChui **86** Chateau de Versailles, France/Giraudon/The Bridgeman Art Library **87** © 2013. Image copyright The Metropolitan Museum of Art/Art Resource/Scala, Florence **88–89** Prado, Madrid, Spain/Giraudon/The Bridgeman Art Library **90** Ham House, Surrey/The Stapleton Collection/The Bridgeman Art Library **91** Royal Armouries, Leeds/The Bridgeman Art Library **92–93** The J. Paul Getty Museum, Los Angeles/Peter Lely, *Portrait of Louise de Kerouaille, Duchess of Portsmouth*, c. 1671–1674, oil on canvas. Size: Unframed: 125.1 x 101.6 cm (49 1/4 x 40 in.) Framed [outer dim]: 160 x 124.8 x 5.7 cm (63 x 49 1/8 x 2 1/4 in.) **94 a** Wallace Collection, London/The Bridgeman Art Library **94 b** © 2013. Image copyright The Metropolitan Museum of Art/Art Resource/Scala, Florence **95** akg-images **96–97** Photo Les Arts décoratifs, Paris/Jean Tholance. All Rights Reserved **98–99** © 2013. Digital Image Museum Associates/LACMA/Art Resource NY/Scala, Florence **100–101** © 2013. Image copyright The Metropolitan Museum of Art/Art Resource/Scala, Florence **102** City of Edinburgh Museums and Art Galleries, Scotland/The Bridgeman Art Library **103** The Drambuie Collection, Edinburgh, Scotland/The Bridgeman Art Library **104–105** City of Edinburgh Museums and Art Galleries, Scotland/The Bridgeman Art Library **106** Alte Pinakothek, Munich, Germany/The Bridgeman Art Library **107** Victoria and Albert Museum, London/The Bridgeman Art Library **108** Czartoryski Museum, Cracow, Poland/The Bridgeman Art Library **109 a** Historical Picture Archive/Corbis **109 b** Private Collection/Giraudon/The Bridgeman Art Library **110–111** Getty Images **112–113** British Library Board. All Rights Reserved/The Bridgeman Art Library **114–115** The Royal Pavilion and Museums, Brighton & Hove **115 br** Edinburgh University Library, Scotland/With kind permission of the University of Edinburgh/The Bridgeman Art Library **116** Private Collection/Photo © Christie's Images/The Bridgeman Art Library **117** Victoria and Albert Museum, London **118–119** Collection of The Kyoto Costume Institute, photo by Masayuki Hayashi **119 br** Private Collection/The Bridgeman Art Library **120** The Gallery Collection/Corbis **121, 122–123** Victoria and Albert Museum, London **124–125** Roger-Viollet/Topfoto **125 br** Getty Images **126–127** Private Collection/The Bridgeman Art Library **127 br** Musée de la Mode et du Costume, Paris, France/Archives Charmet/The Bridgeman Art Library **128–129** Heritage Images/Corbis **130** Getty Images **131** Collection of The Kyoto Costume Institute, photo by Masayuki Hayashi **132–133** © 2013. Digital Image Museum Associates/LACMA/Art Resource NY/Scala, Florence **134** Basel Mission Archives/Basel Mission Holdings/QD-30_006_0012 **135 a** © The Trustees of the British Museum **135 b** III 23336, Photo: Peter Horner © Museum der Kulturen Basel. Switzerland **136–137**

© The National Museum of Denmark, Ethnographic Collection **137 br** © The Trustees of the British Museum **138** Museo Nacional de Bellas Artes, Buenos Aires **139** Library of Congress, LC-DIG-ppmsca-13219 **140** Museo Histórico de Buenos Aires "Cornelio de Saavedra", Buenos Aires **141 a** The Library of Nineteenth-Century Photography **141 b** Royal Geographical Society, London/The Bridgeman Art Library **142–143** Bill Manns/The Art Archive **143 br** Underwood & Underwood/Corbis **144–145** Getty Images **145 br** © 2013. Image copyright The Metropolitan Museum of Art/Art Resource/Scala, Florence **146** Getty Images **147** Fashion Museum, Bath and North East Somerset Council/Gift of Miss Ingleby/The Bridgeman Art Library **148** Getty Images **149** Heritage Images/Corbis **150–151** Private Collection/Photo © The Maas Gallery, London/The Bridgeman Art Library **151 br** Victoria and Albert Museum, London **152–153** © 2013. Image copyright The Metropolitan Museum of Art/Art Resource/Scala, Florence **155** Victoria and Albert Museum, London **156** Mary Evans Picture Library/Alamy **157 a** Interfoto/Alamy **157 b** Mary Evans Picture Library/Alamy **158–159** Time & Life Pictures/Getty Images **159 br** Mary Evans Picture Library **160** Basel Mission Archives/Basel Mission Holdings/QD-30.019.0005 **161, 162–163** © The Trustees of the British Museum **164 a** The Palace Museum, Beijing. Photograph by FengHui **164 b** The Palace Museum, Beijing. Photograph by LiFan **165** The Palace Museum, Beijing. Photograph by LiFan **166–167** The Palace Museum, Beijing. Photograph by LiFan **167 b** The Palace Museum, Beijing. Photograph by FengHui **168–169, 170–171** Victoria and Albert Museum, London **172** Chateau de Compiegne, Oise, France/Giraudon/The Bridgeman Art Library **173** © 2013. Image copyright The Metropolitan Museum of Art/Art Resource/Scala, Florence **174** Getty Images **175** Collection of The Kyoto Costume Institute, photo by Takashi Hatakeyama **176–177** Bundesmobiliensammlung, Vienna, Austria/The Bridgeman Art Library **178–179** © 2013. Image copyright The Metropolitan Museum of Art/Art Resource/Scala, Florence **180** © 2013. Photo Scala, Florence/BPK, Bildagentur für Kunst, Kultur und Geschichte, Berlin **181** Kjeld Duits Collection/MeijiShowa.com **182–183** Arthur M. Sackler Gallery, Smithsonian Institution, USA/Gift of Ambassador and Mrs. William Leonhart/The Bridgeman Art Library **183 br** Alinari via Getty Images **184** Laing Art Gallery, Newcastle-upon-Tyne/© Tyne & Wear Archives & Museums/The Bridgeman Art Library **185 a** Victoria and Albert Museum, London **185 b** Freer Gallery of Art, Smithsonian Institution, USA/Gift of Charles Lang Freer/The Bridgeman Art Library **186–187** Victoria and Albert Museum, London/The Stapleton Collection/The Bridgeman Art Library **187 br** Victoria and Albert Museum, London/The Bridgeman Art Library **188–189** Victoria and Albert Museum, London **190 l** © 2013. Image copyright The Metropolitan Museum of Art/Art Resource/Scala, Florence **190 r, 191, 192–193** Getty Images **194–195** American Illustrators Gallery, NYC/www.asapworldwide.com/The Bridgeman Art Library **195 br** ZUMA Wire Service/Alamy **196** Musée des Beaux-Arts, Tourcoing, France/Giraudon/The Bridgeman Art Library **197 a** Bettmann/Corbis **197 b** Getty Images **198 l** Mary Evans Picture Library/Alamy **198 r** Victoria and Albert Museum, London **199, 200–201** © 2013. Image copyright The Metropolitan Museum of Art/Art Resource/Scala, Florence **202–203** Condé Nast Archive/Corbis **204** Bettmann/Corbis **205** amanaimages/Corbis **206–207** © 2013. Image copyright The Metropolitan Museum of Art/Art Resource/Scala, Florence **208** Christel Gerstenberg/Corbis **209** Corbis **210** Advertising Archives **211 a** akg-images **211 b** Erickson/Vogue © Condé Nast **212–213** © Sevenarts Ltd/DACS 2013 **214** ullstein bild/akg-images **215 a** akg-images **215 b** De Agostini Picture Library/The Bridgeman Art Library **216 l** Roger-Viollett/Topfoto **216 r** © Sevenarts Ltd/DACS 2013 **217** Collection of The Kyoto Costume Institute, photo by Takashi Hatakeyama **218–219** © 2013. Image copyright The Metropolitan Museum of Art/Art Resource/Scala, Florence **219 b** Condé Nast Archive/Corbis **220–221** © 2013. Image copyright The Metropolitan Museum of Art/Art Resource/Scala, Florence **221 br, 222** Getty Images **223 a** Verdura **223 b** Bibliotheque des Arts Decoratifs, Paris, France/Archives Charmet/The Bridgeman Art Library **224–225** Condé Nast Archive/Corbis **226–227** John Springer Collection/Corbis **227 br** Private Collection/Archives Charmet/The Bridgeman Art Library **228** Shanghai Museum of Sun Yat-sen's Former Residence **229** Victoria and Albert Museum, London **230–231** Shanghai Museum of Sun Yat-sen's Former Residence **231 br** Getty Images **232** Fine Art Images/Heritage-Images/Topfoto/© Rodchenko & Stepanova Archive, DACS, RAO, 2013 **233, 234, 235 a** © 2013. Photo Scala, Florence **235 b** Fine Art Images/Heritage-Images/Topfoto/© Rodchenko & Stepanova Archive, DACS, RAO, 2013 **236–237** MuseumStock/© Rodchenko & Stepanova Archive, DACS, RAO, 2013 **237 br** © Rodchenko & Stepanova Archive, DACS, RAO, 2013 **238** Getty Images **239** Stapleton Collection/Corbis **240** amanaimages/Corbis **241 a** Getty Images **241 b** Museum of London/The Bridgeman Art Library **242–243** Popperfoto/Getty Images **243 br** Getty Images **244–245** Indianapolis Museum of Art, Gift of Amy Curtiss Davidoff **246** Condé Nast Archive/Corbis **247** © 2013. Image copyright The Metropolitan Museum of Art/Art Resource/Scala, Florence **248–249, 250–251** © 2013. Image copyright The Metropolitan Museum of Art/Art Resource/Scala, Florence **251 br** Gamma-Rapho via Getty Images **252** Corbis **253** Condé Nast Archive/Corbis **254–255** Getty Images **255 br** Lacoste L.12.12 polo shirt, courtesy Lacoste **256–257** William G Vanderson/Getty images **257 br** Private Collection/Archives Charmet/The Bridgeman Art Library **258** Condé Nast Archive/Corbis **259 a** Getty Images **259 b, 260–261** Advertising Archives **262** Andre Durst © Vogue Paris **263** Courtesy Leslie Hindman Auctioneers **264–265** Philadelphia Museum of Art, Pennsylvania, PA, USA/Gift of Mme Elsa Schiaparelli, 1969/The Bridgeman Art Library **265 r** Philadelphia Museum of Art, Pennsylvania, PA, USA/Gift of Mr. and Mrs. Edward L. Jones, Jr., 1996/The Bridgeman Art Library **266** Getty Images **267** Bettmann/Corbis **268–269** SNAP/Rex Features **270** MGM/Harvey White /The Kobal Collection **271 a** Bettmann/Corbis **271 b** Getty Images **272–273** MGM/George Hurrell/ The Kobal Collection **274–275** Sunset Boulevard/Corbis **276** Condé Nast Archive/Corbis **277** © 2013. Image copyright. The Metropolitan Museum of Art/Art Resource/Scala, Florence **279** © 2013. Image copyright The Metropolitan Museum of Art/Art Resource/Scala, Florence **280–281** Condé Nast Archive/Corbis **282** Popperfoto/Getty Images **283 a** Getty Images **283 b** Time & Life Pictures/Getty Images **284–285** Cecil Beaton/Vogue © The Condé Nast Publications Ltd **286** Condé Nast Archive/Corbis **287** © 2013. Image copyright The Metropolitan Museum of Art/Art Resource/Scala, Florence **288–289** Popperfoto/Getty Images **290–291** © 2013. Image copyright The Metropolitan Museum of Art/Art Resource/Scala, Florence **292** Bettmann/Corbis **293** Carnegie Museum of Art, Pittsburgh; Heinz Family Fund. © 2004 Carnegie Museum of Art, Charles "Teenie" Harris Archive **294–295** Bettmann/Corbis **296–297** Condé Nast Archive/Corbis **298** Time & Life Pictures/Getty Images **299 a** Rex Features **299 b** Condé Nast Archive/Corbis **300 l** © Les Editions Jalou, L'Officiel, 1957 **300 r** © Norman Parkinson Ltd/Courtesy Norman Parkinson Archive **301** Getty Images **302–303** Renée, "The New Look of Dior," Place de la Concorde, Paris, August, 1947, photograph by Richard Avedon © The Richard Avedon Foundation **304–305** Hulton-Deutsch Collection/Corbis **306–307, 308** Time & Life Pictures/Getty Images **309 a** Getty Images **309 b** ClassicStock/Topfoto **310–311** Superstock **312–313** Teruyoshi Hayashida, originally published in Japanese in 1965 by Hearst Fujingaho, Tokyo, Japan, and now in Japanese, English, Dutch and Korean **313 br** © The Museum at FIT **314** Paramount/The Kobal Collection **315** Sunset Boulevard/Corbis

PICTURE CREDITS 575

316–317 ClassicStock.com/SuperStock 317 br Retrofile/Getty Images 318–319 Courtesy Leslie Hindman Auctioneers 319 br Time & Life Pictures/Getty Images 320 Photos 12/Alamy 321 a Sunset Boulevard/Corbis 321 b Getty Images 322–323 Advertising Archives 323 br Time & Life Pictures/Getty Images 324–325 Mary Evans Picture Library/Alamy 325 br Bettmann/Corbis 326 Condé Nast Archive/Corbis 327 a Warner Bros/The Kobal Collection 327 b Advertising Archives 328–329 Condé Nast Archive/Corbis 329 br Time & Life Pictures/Getty Images 330–331 Condé Nast Archive/Corbis 331 br Bettmann/Corbis 323–333 Genevieve Naylor/Corbis 334 Fotolocchi Archive 335 David Lees/Corbis 336–337 Topfoto 338–339 Sunset Boulevard/Corbis 339 r Getty Images 340 Everett Collection/Rex Features 341 a Advertising Archives 341 b MGM/The Kobal Collection 342–343 Bettmann/Corbis 343 br Advertising Archives 345 Time & Life Pictures/Getty Images 346–347 © Norman Parkinson Ltd/courtesy Norman Parkinson Archive 348–349 Collection of The Kyoto Costume Institute, photo by Masayuki Hayashi 349 l Condé Nast Archive/Corbis 350–353 Pam Hemmings 354 Mirrorpix 355, 256 l Courtesy of the London College of Fashion and The Woolmark Company 356 r Topfoto 357 Dalmas/Sipa/Rex Features 358–359 Brian Duffy/ Vogue © The Condé Nast Publications Ltd 360–361 Interfoto/Alamy 362–363 Condé Nast Archive/Corbis 363 br Bettmann/Corbis 364 Time & Life Pictures/Getty Images 365 a Rex Features 365 b, 366–367 Colin Jones/Topfoto 367 br Redferns/Getty Images 368–369 Advertising Archives 370 © Malick Sidibé, Courtesy André Magnin, Paris 371 Getty Images 372 l James Barnor, Drum cover girl Erlin Ibreck, London, 1966. Courtesy Autograph ABP. © James Barnor/Autograph ABP 372 r WWD/Condé Nast/Corbis 373 Time & Life Pictures/Getty Images 374–375 Photography by Mr Ajidagba, courtesy of Shade Fahm 376 Time & Life Pictures/Getty Images 377 Condé Nast Archive/Corbis 378–379 Interfoto/Mary Evans Picture Library 379 b Bettmann/Corbis 380–381 Collection of The Kyoto Costume Institute, photo by Takashi Hatakeyama 382 Getty Images 383 a AFP/Getty Images 383 b Courtesy Archivio Alfa Castaldi 384–385 Getty Images 386 Photograph by Lichfield/Vogue © Condé Nast 387 a Condé Nast Archive/Corbis 387 b Ernestine Carter Collection, Fashion Museum, Bath and North East Somerset Council/The Bridgeman Art Library 388–389 Condé Nast Archive/Corbis 389 br Ted Spiegel/Corbis 390–391 Victoria and Albert Museum, London 392–393 Clive Arrowsmith/Vogue © The Condé Nast Publications Ltd 394 Topfoto 395 a Vittoriano Rastelli/Corbis 395 b Condé Nast Archive/Corbis 396–397 Getty Images 398 Condé Nast Archive/Corbis 399 Getty Images 400–401 © 2013. Image copyright The Metropolitan Museum of Art/Art Resource/Scala, Florence 401 br ADC/Rex Features 402 Bettmann/Corbis 403 Pierre Vauthey/Sygma/Corbis 404–405 Victoria and Albert Museum, London 406 l © 2013 Bata Shoe Museum, Toronto, Canada 406 r Dezo Hoffmann/Rex Features 407 Paramount/Holly Bower/The Kobal Collection 408–409 Ilpo Musto/Rex Features 410–411 © Estate of Guy Bourdin. Reproduced by permission of Art + Commerce 412 Steve Schapiro/Corbis 413 a Advertising Archives 413 b Condé Nast Archive/Corbis 414–415 Advertising Archives 416 David Dagley/Rex Features 417 a Sheila Rock/Rex Features 417 b Condé Nast Archive/Corbis 418–419 Ray Stevenson/Rex Features 420 Julio Donoso/Sygma/Corbis 421 Roger Viollet/Getty Images 422–423 Redferns/Getty Images 424 Sipa Press/Rex Features 425 Neville Marriner/Associated Newspapers/Rex Features 426–427 Advertising Archives 428–429 Bettmann/Corbis 429 br Ros Drinkwater/Rex Features 430 Fabio Nosotti/Corbis 431 a AP/Topfoto 431 b PA Photos/Topfoto 432–433 Andy Lane 433 br Brendan Beirne/Rex Features 434–435 The Cloth Summer Simkit 1985 by Corbin O'Grady Studio 436 Getty Images 437 a Condé Nast Archive/Corbis 437 b Moviestore Collection/Rex Features 438–439 Paramount/Everett Collection/Rex Features 440–441 © 2013 Bata Shoe Museum, Toronto, Canada 442 Condé Nast Archive/Corbis 443 a Spelling/ABC/The Kobal Collection 443 b Christopher Little/Corbis 444–445 © 2013. Museum of Fine Arts, Boston. All rights reserved/Scala, Florence 446 Getty Images 447 a © Museum of London 447 b Getty Images 448–449 Photograph by Paul Palmero. Courtesy of The Stephen Sprouse Book by Roger and Mauricio Padilha 449 b Courtesy Leslie Hindman Auctioneers 450 Pierre Vauthey/Sygma/Corbis 451 Getty Images 452 AFP/Getty Images 453 a Advertising Archives 453 b Neville Marriner/Associated Newspapers/Rex Features 456–457 Pierre Vauthey/Sygma/Corbis 458–459 Sipa Press/Rex Features 460 a Catwalking 460 b Sipa Press/Rex Features 461 AP/PA Photos 462–463 Sølve Sundsbø/Art + Commerce 464–465 Daria Werbowy photographed by Inez van Lamsweerde and Vinoodh Matadin for Isabel Marant SS10 466 Sipa Press/Rex Features 467 Michel Arnaud/Corbis 468 Ellen von Unwerth/Art + Commerce 469 a Wood/Rex Features 469 b FirstView 470–471 Getty Images 472–473 Courtesy Leslie Hindman Auctioneers 473 ar, 474 Advertising Archives 475 FirstView 476–477 Ellen von Unwerth/Art + Commerce 477 br Art Institute of Chicago, Illinois, USA/Bridgeman Art Library 478–479 Ken Towner/Associated Newspapers/Rex Features 480–481 FirstView 482 Catwalking 483 Michel Arnaud/Corbis 484–485 Corinne Day/Vogue © The Condé Nast Publications Ltd. 485 br Advertising Archives 486 WWD/Condé Nast/Corbis 487 Getty Images 488–489 FilmMagic/Getty Images 489 br Andrew Gombert/epa/Corbis 490 AFP/Getty Images 491 Wireimage/Getty Images 492–493 Getty Images for IMG 494–495 Gamma-Rapho via Getty Images 496–497 Courtesy Erdem 498 Associated Newspapers/Rex Features 499 Gamma-Rapho via Getty Images 500 Thierry Orban/Sygma/Corbis 501 a Victoria and Albert Museum, London 501 b Ken Towner/Evening Standard/Rex Features 502–503 View Pictures/Rex Features 503 r © 2013. Digital image, The Museum of Modern Art, New York/Scala, Florence 504–505 Catwalking 506 Eriko Sugita/Reuters/Corbis 507 Adrian Britton/Alamy 508–509 Yuriko Nakao/Reuters/Corbis 510 WWD/Condé Nast/Corbis 511 Catwalking 512–513 Courtesy of Lorenzo Agius/Orchard Represents 513 br Getty Images 514–515 FirstView 516–517 Gamma-Rapho via Getty Images 518 a AFP/Getty Images 518 bl Courtesy Eley Kishimoto 519 Gamma-Rapho via Getty Images 520 AFP/Getty Images 521 a Catwalking 521 b WWD/Condé Nast/Corbis 522–523 FirstView 524–525 Morgan O'Donovan 525 ar Catwalking 526–527 FirstView 528 a Paul Miller/epa/Corbis 528 b Getty Images 529 adidas via Getty Images 530 a Wirelmage/Getty images 530 b Nike 531 Getty Images 532–533 Catwalking 534 Advertising Archives 535 a WWD/Condé Nast/Corbis 535 b Catwalking 536–537 Daria Werbowy photographed by Inez van Lamsweerde and Vinoodh Matadin for Isabel Marant SS10 538–539 Getty Images 540 WWD/Condé Nast/Corbis 541 a Rex Features 541 b Catwalking 542–543 Gamma-Rapho via Getty Images 544 Net-a-Porter 545 Nike 546–547 ASOS 548 WWD/Condé Nast/Corbis 549 Getty Images 550–551 Peter Farago 552–553 Daniele Tamagni 553 br FirstView

Quintessence would also like to thank Rio Ali and Paul Gorman for their assistance with selected texts, and Sue Farr for the index.